Western Civilization

BEYOND BOUNDARIES

Sixth Edition   ## VOLUME II: Since 1560

Thomas F. X. Noble
University of Notre Dame

Barry Strauss
Cornell University

Duane J. Osheim
University of Virginia

Kristen B. Neuschel
Duke University

Elinor A. Accampo
University of Southern California

David D. Roberts
University of Georgia

William B. Cohen
Late of Indiana University

WADSWORTH
CENGAGE Learning™

Australia • Brazil • Japan • Korea • Mexico • Singapore • Spain • United Kingdom • United States

WADSWORTH
CENGAGE Learning

Western Civilization: Beyond Boundaries,
Volume II, Sixth Edition
Thomas F. X. Noble, Barry Strauss, Duane J.
Osheim, Kristen B. Neuschel, Elinor A.
Accampo, David D. Roberts, William B. Cohen

Senior Publisher: Suzanne Jeans

Senior Sponsoring Editor: Nancy Blaine

Associate Editor: Adrienne Zicht

Editorial Assistant: Emma Goehring

Senior Media Editor: Lisa Ciccolo

Executive Marketing Manager:
Diane Wenckebach

Marketing Coordinator: Lorreen Pelletier

Marketing Communications Manager:
Christine Dobberpuhl

Senior Content Project Manager: Jane Lee

Senior Art Director: Cate Rickard Barr

Senior Print Buyer: Judy Inouye

Senior Rights Acquisition Account Manager:
Mollika Basu

Production Service: Elm Street Publishing
Services

Text Designer: Henry Rachlin

Senior Photo Editor: Jennifer Meyer Dare

Cover Designer: Harold Burch

Volume II cover image: *Sloane Street, London,*
c. 1908-09 (oil on canvas) by Jacques-Emile
Blanche (1861-1942). © York Museums Trust,
York Art Gallery/The Bridgeman Art Library

Text Credits: Page 751: Excerpts from *A Room
of One's Own* by Virginia Woolf, copyright
1929 by Harcourt, Inc. and renewed 1957 by
Leonard Woolf, reprinted by permission of
the publisher.

Compositor: Integra Software Services Pvt. Ltd.

For product information and technology assistance, contact us at
Cengage Learning, Customer & Sales Support, 1-800-354-9706

For permission to use material from this text or product,
submit all requests online at **www.cengage.com/permissions**.
Further permissions questions can be e-mailed to
permissionrequest@cengage.com.

Library of Congress Control Number: 2009934607

ISBN-13: 978-1-424-06962-0
ISBN-10: 1-424-06962-9

Wadsworth
20 Channel Center Street
Boston, MA 02210
USA

Cengage Learning is a leading provider of customized learning solutions with
office locations around the globe, including Singapore, the United Kingdom,
Australia, Mexico, Brazil, and Japan. Locate your local office at
international.cengage.com/region.

Cengage Learning products are represented in Canada by Nelson Education, Ltd.

For your course and learning solutions, visit **www.cengage.com.**

Purchase any of our products at your local college store or at our preferred
online store **www.ichapters.com.**

Printed in the United States of America
1 2 3 4 5 6 7 13 12 11 10 09

CONTENTS

MAPS

DOCUMENTS

THE VISUAL RECORD

PREFACE

An old adage says that each generation must write history for itself. If the adage is true, then it would also be true that each generation must teach and learn history for itself. The history, of course, does not change, although new discoveries come to light all the time. What does change is us, each succeeding generation of us. What causes us to change, and thus to experience and understand history in ever new ways, are the great developments of our own times. Think of the world-changing events of the last century: two world wars, the Great Depression, the cold war, nuclear weapons, the civil rights movement, the women's movement, the explosion in scientific knowledge, and the media revolutions involving radio and television, the computer, and the Internet. The pace of change has accelerated in our time, but the process of change always affects people's view of their world.

As we launch the sixth edition of this book we are once again acutely aware of the need to address big questions in ways that make sense to teachers and students right now, in the world we live in today. As these words are being written, the news is full of reports from Afghanistan, Iraq, Iran, Darfur, Somalia, and North Korea. The world's economy is in a perilous state. The United States has elected an African American as its president. In such circumstances we might well ask, What is the West; what is Western? Some believe that we are engaged in a "Clash of Civilizations." Is one of these Western Civilization? If so, who or what is its adversary? The West is sometimes understood geographically and sometimes culturally. For most people, the West means western Europe. And yet western Europe itself is the heir of the peoples and cultures of antiquity, including the Sumerians, Egyptians, Persians, Greeks, Romans, Jews, Christians, and Muslims. In fact, Europe is the heir of even earlier civilizations in Asia and Africa. As a cultural phenomenon, "Western" implies many things: freedom and free, participatory political institutions; economic initiative and opportunity; monotheistic religious faiths (Judaism, Christianity, and Islam); rationalism and ordered thought in the social, political, and philosophical realms; an aesthetic sensibility that aspires to a universal sense of beauty. But the West has felt free to evoke tradition as its guiding light and also to innovate brilliantly, to accommodate slavery and freedom simultaneously, and to esteem original thought and persecute people who deviate from the norm. "Western" indeed has meant many things in various places at different times. This book constantly and explicitly attempts to situate its readers in place, time, and tradition.

Another big question is this: What exactly is civilization? No definition can win universal acceptance, but certain elements of a definition are widely accepted. Civilization is the largest unit within which any person might feel comfortable. It is an organizing principle that implies common institutions, economic systems, social structures, and values that extend over both space and time. Cities are crucial; with cities emerge complex social organizations that involve at least a minimal division of labor. Some people work in the fields, some in the home. Soldiers defend the city, and artisans provide its daily goods. Governing institutions have a wide measure of acceptance and have the ability to enforce their will. Civilizations also develop religious ideas and authorities; literatures and laws that may be oral or written; monumental architecture, especially fortifications, palaces, and temples; and arts such as music, painting, and sculpture. Every civilization enfolds many cultures, a term that may be applied to the full range of expressions of a people in a given place and time. So, for example, the cultures of Egypt, Greece, and Rome were distinctive but all fit under the broad umbrella of Western Civilization.

Western Civilization has had an influence on almost every person alive today. The West deserves to be studied because its tale is compelling, but it demands to be studied because its story has been so central to the development of the world in which we live. Many of the world's dominant institutions are Western in their origin and in their contemporary manifestations—most notably parliamentary democracy. Commercial capitalism, a Western construct, is the world's dominant form of economic organization. The Internet, fast food, and hip-hop music are all western in origin but world-wide in reach today.

Until a generation or so ago, Western Civilization was a staple of college and university curricula and was generally studied in isolation. Although it was, and is, important for us to know who we are, it is also important for us to see that we have changed in dramatic ways and that we can no longer understand ourselves in isolation from the world around us. Accordingly, this book repeatedly sets the experience of the West into its global context. This is not a World History book. But it is a book that sees Western Civilization as one significant segment of the world's history.

BASIC APPROACH

Nearly two decades ago the six original authors of *Western Civilization: Beyond Boundaries* set out to create a textbook for a course that would, as a total effort, inform students about essential developments within a tradition that has powerfully, though not always positively, affected everyone in the contemporary world. Although each of us found something to admire in all of the existing textbooks, none of us was fully happy with any of them. We were disappointed with books that claimed "balance" but actually stressed a single kind of history. We regretted that so many texts were uneven in their command of recent scholarship. Although we were convinced of both the inherent interest of Western Civilization and the importance of teaching the subject, we were disconcerted by the celebratory tone of some books, which portrayed the West as resting on its laurels instead of creatively facing its future.

We decided to produce a book that is balanced and coherent; that addresses the full range of subjects that a Western Civilization book needs to address; that provides the student reader with interesting, timely material; that is up-to-date in terms of scholarship and approach; and that is handsome to look at—in short, a book that helps the instructor to teach and the student to learn. We have kept our common vision fresh through frequent meetings, correspondence, critical mutual readings, and expert editorial guidance. The misfortune of the untimely death of one member of our team has brought us the fortune of a new colleague who has inspired and challenged the rest of us in new ways. Because each of us has focused on his or her own area of specialization, we believe that we have attained a rare blend of competence, confidence, and enthusiasm. Moreover, in moving from plans for a first edition to the preparation of a sixth, we have been able to profit from the experience of using the book, the advice and criticism of dozens of colleagues, and the reactions of thousands of students.

Western Civilization is a story. Therefore, we aimed at a strong chronological narrative line. Our experience as teachers tells us that students appreciate this clear but gentle orientation. Our experience tells us, too, that an approach that is broadly chronological will leave instructors plenty of room to adapt our narrative to their preferred organization, or to supplement our narrative with one of their own.

Although we maintain the familiar, large-scale divisions of a Western Civilization book, we also present some innovative adjustments in arrangement. For instance, we incorporate a single chapter on Late Antiquity, the tumultuous and fascinating period from about A.D 300 to 600 that witnessed the transformation of the Roman Empire into three successors: Byzantine, Islamic, and European. One chapter studies those three successors, thereby permitting careful comparisons. But we also assign chapters to some of the greatest issues in Western Civilization, such as the Renaissance, the age of European exploration and conquest, the Scientific Revolution, and the industrial transformation. Our twentieth-century chapters reflect an understanding of the last century formed in its closing years rather than in its middle decades. What is new in our organization represents adjustments grounded in the best scholarship, and what is old represents time-tested approaches.

In fashioning our picture of the West, we took two unusual steps. First, our West is itself bigger than the one found in most textbooks. We treat the Celtic world, Scandinavia, and the Slavic world as integral parts of the story. We look often at the lands that border the West—Anatolia/Turkey, western Asia, North Africa, the Eurasian steppes—in order to show the to-and-fro of peoples, ideas, technologies, and products. Second, we continually situate the West in its global context. Just as we recognize that the West has influenced the rest of the world, we also carefully acknowledge how the rest of the world has influenced the West. We begin this story of mutual interaction with the Greeks and Romans, carry it through the European Middle Ages, focus on it in the age of European exploration and conquest, and analyze it closely in the modern world of industry, diplomacy, empire, immigration, and questions of citizenship and identity.

Another approach that runs like a ribbon throughout this textbook involves balance and integration. Teachers and students, just like the authors of this book, have their particular interests and emphases. In the large and diverse American academy, that is as it should be. But a textbook, if it is to be helpful and useful, should incorporate as many interests and emphases as possible. For a long time, some said, Western Civilization books devoted excessive coverage to high politics—"the public deeds of great men," as an ancient Greek writer defined the historian's subject. Others felt that high culture—all the Aristotles and Mozarts—was included to the exclusion of supposedly lesser figures and ordinary men and women. In the 1970s, books began to emphasize social history. Some applauded this new emphasis even as they debated fiercely over what to include under this heading.

In this book, we attempt to capture the Western tradition in its full contours, to hear the voices of all those who have made durable contributions. But because we cannot say everything about everybody at every moment, we have had to make choices about how and where to array key topics within our narrative. Above all, we have tried to be integrative. For example, when we talk about government and politics, we present the institutional structures through which power was exercised, the people who possessed power as well as the people who did not, the ideological foundations for the use of power, and the material conditions that fostered or hindered the real or the would-be powerful. In other words, instead of treating old-fashioned "high politics" in abstract and descriptive ways, we take an approach that is organic and analytical: How did things work? Our approach to the history of women is another example. A glance at this book's table of contents and then at its index is revealing. The former reveals very few sections devoted explicitly and exclusively to women. The latter shows that women appear constantly in every section of this book. Is there a contradiction here? Not at all. Women and men have not been historical actors in isolation from one another. Yet gender, which is relational, reciprocal, and mutual, is an important variable that has shaped individual and collective experience. Hence we seek to explain why certain political, economic, or social circumstances had differing impacts on men and women, and how such conditions led them to make different choices.

Similarly, when we talk of great ideas, we describe the antecedent ideas from which seemingly new ones were built up, and we ask about the consequences of those ideas. We explore the social positions of the authors of those ideas to see if this helps us explain the ideas themselves or gauge their influence. We try to understand how ideas in one field of human endeavor prove to be influential in other fields. For instance, gender is viewed as connected to and part of the larger fabric of ideas including power, culture, and piety.

We invite the reader to look at our narrative as if it were a mosaic. Taken as a whole, our narrative contains a coherent picture. Viewed more closely, it is made up of countless tiny bits that may have their individual interest but do not even hint at the larger picture of which they are parts. Finally, just as the viewer of a mosaic may find his or her eye drawn especially to one area, feature, color, or style, so too the reader of this book will find some parts more engaging or compelling than others. But it is only because there is, in this book as in a mosaic, a complete picture that the individual sections make sense, command our attention, excite our interest.

One word sums up our approach in this book: "balance." We tell a good story, but we pause often to reflect on that story, to analyze it. We devote substantial coverage to the typical areas of Greece, Rome, Italy, France, Great Britain, and so forth, but we say more about western Europe's frontiers than any other book. We do not try to disguise our Western Civilization book as a World History book, but we take great pains to locate the West within its global context. And we always assume that context means mutuality and reciprocity. We have high politics and big ideas alongside household management and popular culture. We think that part of the fascination of the past lies in its capacity to suggest understandings of the present and possibilities for the future.

Our subtitle, "Beyond Boundaries," is intended to suggest growth, challenge, and opportunity. The West began in Mesopotamia but soon spread to all of western Asia. Gradually the Greeks entered the scene and disseminated their ideas throughout the Mediterranean world. The Romans, always heirs of the Greeks, carried ideas and institutions from Britain to Mesopotamia. As the Roman order collapsed, Rome's imprint was left on a small segment of Europe lying west of the Rhine and south of the Danube. Europeans then crashed through those boundaries to create a culture that extended from Iceland to the Russian steppes. At the dawn of the modern age Europe entered into a complex set of commercial, colonial, military, and political relations with the rest of the globe. Our contemporary world sees Western influences everywhere. No western "boundary" has ever been more than temporary, provisional.

DISTINCTIVE FEATURES

To make this book as accessible as possible to students, we have constantly been aware of its place in a program of teaching and learning. In the preceding paragraphs something has been said about this book's distinctive substantive features and how, we believe, they will contribute to the attainment of a deeper understanding of Western Civilization, as well as of its importance and place in the wider history of the earth's peoples. Teaching and learning also involve pedagogical techniques and innovations. We have attended conscientiously to pedagogical issues from the start, and we have made some significant changes in this edition.

Our chapters have always begun with a vignette that is directly tied to an accompanying picture. These vignettes alert the reader to one or more of the key aspects of the chapter. Thus the readers have encountered a thematic introduction that evokes interest while pointing clearly and in some detail to what follows.

To make our chapter introductions more effective, which means to give students greater confidence as they proceed through the book, we have taken numerous steps. First, as in past editions, we reviewed and revised our opening vignettes to connect text and picture more closely and to use both to invite the reader into the chapter.

Second, the first page of each chapter contains a succinct Outline that immediately and dramatically tells the reader what he or she is going to encounter in the following pages. Third, the chapter introductions conclude with a list of Focus Questions that both echo the introduction and set the reader off on the right path into the following pages. Fourth, as the student begins to read the chapter proper, a Chronology serves as yet another orientation to the material contained in the chapter. Subject-specific chronologies still appear in various parts of the book, but we felt readers would benefit from a chronological guide at the beginning of each chapter.

In this edition, we have repeated each Focus Question at the head of the section to which it pertains. At the end of each major section, we provide a succinct Section Summary. Each chapter concludes with a Chapter Summary that reiterates the Focus Questions and then briefly answers them once again.

As a complement to text coverage, a ready reference, and a potential study guide, all of the Key Terms have been gathered into a Glossary included in the website that accompanies the book. For this edition, we have also placed definitions on the pages where the Key Terms first appear.

In addition to this fundamental attention to chapter themes and contents, we have sought to improve the book's teachability by adding a pronunciation guide. Whenever we use an unfamiliar name or term, we show the reader how to pronounce it. Instead of using the intricate rules of phonetics, we provide commonsense guides to pronunciation in parentheses directly following the word.

This edition is a bit shorter than its predecessors. Relevance, "teachability," and "learnability" were our guides in streamlining our coverage at many points. Virtually every chapter experienced some slimming in the interest of keeping major points and themes front and center.

Having always been conscious of this book's physical appearance, we have this time adopted a dynamic, single-column design to enhance the reader's experience of the book. Attractively laid-out pages, a handsome full-color design, engaging maps, and beautifully reproduced pictures enhance the book's appearance. In keeping with our desire to integrate the components of the book into a coherent whole, we carefully anchor the maps and pictures into the volume. Our maps, always chosen and conceptualized by the authors, have for the sixth edition been completely redesigned to make them fresher, more attractive, and more informative. Map captions have been carefully written, and revised, to make them effective elements of the book's teaching program. The same is true of the pictures: the authors selected them, worked with the book's designers to place them advantageously (and not just decoratively), and wrote all the captions. For this edition, we paid particular attention to reviewing all the captions and to revising many of them. All of the maps are cross-referenced in the text, some of them several times, and the text often refers directly to the pictures.

From the start, every chapter in this book has had boxed documents, one of which treated a "global" theme, as well as a two-page feature entitled "Weighing the Evidence." For this edition, we thought hard about our features and decided to take some decisive steps to make them work better for teachers and students. First, we reduced the number of features to three per chapter. Second, we introduced a uniform structure and format. One feature, entitled "The Global Record," presents a significant document that sets some aspect of Western Civilization within the global perspective. These documents are substantial, are carefully introduced, and conclude with study questions. Another feature is called "The Written Record." This feature contains a significant document relevant to the text materials then under discussion with a careful introduction and study questions. The third feature is called "The Visual Record." This feature represents a reconceptualization of our former "Weighing the Evidence" feature. Most of those features did focus on visual evidence, but now the Visual Record features all do so. As with the Global Record and Written Record features, the Visual Records have helpful questions. Whereas the Weighing the Evidence features always concluded our chapters, now the Visual Records are placed into the chapters at the most appropriate position. For the fifth edition, we cast a careful eye over all the Visual Record features and prepared eight new ones, and for the sixth edition, we have prepared two new ones. Finally, we took two last steps. We deleted the "Looking Ahead" sections because reviewers suggested that this "telegraphing" of what was to come might confuse the student reader as to what he or she has just read. And we moved the "Suggested Readings" to the book's website.

ORGANIZATION AND CONTENT CHANGES

Throughout the book, the authors have made changes to improve the narrative and to incorporate new ways of talking about particular topics. Chapter 1 has been trimmed by cutting the short section "The First Cities" and by eliminating the larger section "Widening Horizons: The Levant and Anatolia, 2500–1150 B.C." The original subsection "War Abroad, Reform at Home, 1786–1075 B.C." has been divided into two separate sections and the material on the Amarna Archives and the Hittites has been moved to the new "War Abroad" section.

Chapter 2 gained a new main section, "Traders Invent the Alphabet: Canaanites and Phoenicians, ca. 1400–450 B.C.," with new subsections on "The Canaanite City-States, ca. 1400–1200 B.C." and "The Phoenicians, ca. 1050–450 B.C." Material on the Phoenicians, formerly found under "Assyrians and Babylonians," has been moved to the new section. These revisions create sharper focus and clearer organization. A new Visual Record feature, "The Siege of Lachish," has been introduced. The entire main section on "Early Greece" has been moved to Chapter 3, once again in the interest of sharpening the focus.

In Chapter 5, two subsections, "The Roman Household" and "Patrons and Clients," have been combined and shortened into one new section entitled "Families and Patronage." The sections on Roman expansion, both in Italy and in the wider Mediterranean, have been recast as follows: The former section on "The Latin League and Beyond" has been replaced by a section entitled "Keeping the Peace," which has been moved to the section "Republican Expansion: The Conquest of Italy, ca. 509–265 B.C." The sections on "Rome Versus Carthage: The Punic Wars, 264–146 B.C." and "Victories in the Hellenistic East, ca. 200–133 B.C." have been combined into one new section, "Punic Wars and the Conquest of the Greek East." The sections on "The Gracchi" and on "Marius and Sulla" have been recast as "Reformers and Revolutionaries." Chapter 6 has a new Written Record feature on "Boudicca's Revolt."

Chapter 8 has been substantially revised. The long and largely introductory section "Catholic Kingdoms in the West" has been deleted. Its material, much abbreviated, has been recast as the opening subsection, "Medieval Europe takes Shape," under the main section "The Rise of the Carolingian Empire." This main section includes revised and trimmed subsections entitled "The Carolingian Dynasty," "Carolingian Government," "The Carolingian Renaissance," and "The Fragmentation of Charlemagne's Empire." The former subsections "Social Patterns" and "The Experiences of Women" have been combined into a new section, "Social Patterns."

In Chapter 12, the section "Renaissance Court and Society" has been revised as "Politics and Renaissance Culture." In Chapter 14, the map "Reform in Germany, 1517–1555" has been replaced by a new map, "The Global Empire of Charles V." Chapter 15 has been significantly reorganized. The material in the subhead "The Failure of the Invincible Armada" has been moved into the section on "The Formation of the United Provinces." Material from the former subhead "Henry IV and the Fragile Peace" has been moved into the section "Decades of Civil War." The main heading "Religious and Political Conflict in Central and Eastern Europe" has been recast as "The Holy Roman Empire and the Thirty Years' War." The subheads in this main section have been revised, shortened, and renamed. The social and cultural sections of this chapter have been revised and reorganized. One old map 15.4 ("Two Empires in Eastern Europe, ca. 1600") has been deleted. In Chapter 16, material on "The Dutch War" has been moved into the section on "The Burdens of War and the Limits of Power." The section on "Competition Around the Baltic" has been tightened.

Chapter 17 has a new subsection, "Women Scientists and Institutional Constraints," and the former section on "Pierre Bayle" has been revised as "Skepticism and the Spread of Scientific Rationality" to signal the central issues more clearly. Similarly, in Chapter 18, the old section "Adam

Smith and David Hume" has been recast as "Economic Thought and the Scottish Enlightenment." Some subsections within the former section on "Monarchy and Constitutional Government" have been eliminated and the whole section reorganized under "Monarch and Parliament in Great Britain." The subheads in the rest of this chapter have been revised, and two main headings "The Widening World of Commerce" and "Economic Expansion and Social Change" have been eliminated with some of their material reorganized and placed in other sections and other material retained under the new main heading "The Widening World of Trade and Production." Finally, this chapter acquires the new main heading "The Widening World of Warfare" that pulls together military history issues. In Chapter 19, several minor subheads have been shortened and combined into other sections, but a new subhead on "Revolution in the Atlantic World" has been added to the section "The Legacy of Revolution for France and the World" and an old section, "The View from Britain," has been deleted. In general, the revisions in Chapters 15 to 19 aim to gather like with like, to streamline the narrative, and to make topics more explicit.

Two important sections in Chapter 20 have been renamed: "Advances in the Cotton Industry" to "Mass Production" and "Iron, Steam, and Factories" to "New Energy Sources and Their Impacts." Several small, fifth-edition subheads have been incorporated into the larger section on "The Spread of Industry to the Continent." The former subhead "The Working Classes and Their Lot" has been renamed "Social Class and Family Structure," which also gained some material from the deleted section "Industrialization and the Family." This chapter acquired a new Visual Record feature, "St. Giles," while material from the former Visual Record "Collective Action" has been creatively reintegrated into the chapter.

Chapters 21 and 22, which deal with the tangled political history of the nineteenth century, received significant attention in this edition. The first major heading in Chapter 21, "The Congress of Vienna," has been reorganized under a heading entitled "Restoration and Reaction." This move permits new subheads, "The Congress of Vienna," "Restored Monarchs in Western Europe," "Eastern Europe," and "Spain and Its Colonies," to carry the political story effectively down to 1830. Then, the former main heading "Restoration, Reform, and Reaction" has been recast as "The Quest for Reform." In other words, the chapter now establishes Europe's restored regimes and then looks inside them to understand their internal political dynamics. Accordingly, the old heading "Western Europe: From Reaction to Liberalism, 1815–1830" has been deleted because its essential material has already been presented. The chapter does receive a new heading entitled "The Revolution of 1830 and the July Monarchy in France," but a number of smaller subheads have been eliminated and their material redistributed. In Chapter 22, the former main heads "Italian Unification, 1859–1870" and "German Unification, 1850–1871" have been combined into one major section, "Forging New States," that itself contains subsections on the main stages in Italian and German unification subordinated to central themes. The main heading on "The Emergence of New Political Forms in the United States and Canada, 1840–1880" has been eliminated, along with its maps. As in earlier chapters, the aim has been to streamline and focus the narratives in these two as well.

In Chapter 23, some headings received new titles, for instance "The Declining Aristocracy" became "The Adapting Aristocracy," while "The Workers' Lot" shifted to "Improving Conditions Among the Workers and the Poor." The former main heading "Social and Political Initiatives" has been deleted with its most important material, particularly "Educational and Cultural Opportunities," redistributed elsewhere. Old Map 23.1, "European Rails, 1850–1880," has been cut.

Chapter 24 has a new title: "Imperialism and Escalating Tensions, 1880–1914." Its first main heading, "The New Imperialism and the Spread of Europe's Population," has been changed to "The New Imperialism and the Spread of Europe's Influence." This change permitted deletion of the subsection on "Overseas Migration and the Spread of European Values." A new subhead on "Unanticipated Consequences: Rebellion and Colonial War" has been added. Former Map 24.3, "European Migrations," has been replaced by a new map on the Ottoman Empire. In Chapter 25, two maps (25.1 and 25.2) have been combined into one new map called "The War in Europe, 1914–1918," and a new map has been added, "The European Peace Settlement and the Peace in the Middle East." In Chapter 26, one main head, "Weimar Germany and the Trials of New Democracies," has been renamed "The Trials of the New Democracies." In Chapter 28, the main heading "The Victory of Nazi Germany, 1939–1941" received a new title, "German Military Successes, 1939–1941." In Chapter 29, the subhead "The Energy Crisis and the Changing Economic Framework" has been moved under the main heading "Prosperity and Democracy in Western Europe." The subhead "New Nations in Asia" has been deleted with its most important information transferred to "The Varieties of Decolonization."

Our attempt to bring the story up to date means that Chapter 30, as always, received considerable attention. This begins with a new opening photo and vignette on the financial crisis, the meeting of the G-20 in London in April 2009. Several subheads received new titles, for example "Origins of the Union" became "Renewing the Union," "War Crimes Tribunals" became "War Crimes Trials," "Unemployment and Economic Challenges in Western Europe" became "Responding to New Economic Challenges," and "Immigration, Assimilation, and the New Right" became "Immigration, Assimilation, and Citizenship." The subhead "The Post-Communist Experiment" has been expanded with new material on Vladimir Putin and the confrontation between Russia and Georgia. One subhead, "Consensus in the Established Democracies" was deleted. The last section, "The West in the Global Age," has been rewritten, especially the subsection "Questioning the Meaning of the West."

ANCILLARIES

Instructor Resources

PowerLecture CD-ROM with ExamView® and JoinIn® This dual platform, all-in-one multimedia resource includes the Instructor's Resource Manual; Test Bank, revised to reflect the new material in the text by Dolores Grapsas of New River Community College (includes key term identification, multiple-choice, short answer, essay, and map questions); Microsoft® PowerPoint® slides of both lecture outlines and images and maps from the text that can be used as offered, or customized by importing personal lecture slides or other material; and *JoinIn®* PowerPoint® slides with clicker content. Also included is ExamView, an easy-to-use assessment and tutorial system that allows instructors to create, deliver, and customize tests in minutes. Instructors can build tests with as many as 250 questions using up to 12 question types, and using ExamView's complete word-processing capabilities, they can enter an unlimited number of new questions or edit existing ones.

HistoryFinder This searchable online database allows instructors to quickly and easily download thousands of assets, including art, photographs, maps, primary sources, and audio/video clips. Each asset downloads directly into a Microsoft® PowerPoint® slide, allowing instructors to easily create exciting PowerPoint presentations for their classrooms.

Instructor's Resource Manual Prepared by Janusz Duzinkiewicz of Purdue University North Central, the Instructor's Resource Manual has been revised to reflect the new material in the text. This manual has many features, including instructional objectives, chapter outlines and summaries, lecture suggestions, suggested debate and research topics, cooperative learning activities, and suggested readings and resources. The Instructor's Resource Manual is available on the instructor's companion site.

WebTutor™ on Blackboard® With WebTutor's text-specific, pre-formatted content and total flexibility, instructors can easily create and manage their own custom course website. WebTutor's course management tool gives instructors the ability to provide virtual office hours, post syllabi, set up threaded discussions, track student progress with the quizzing material, and much more. For students, WebTutor offers real-time access to a full array of study tools, including animations and videos that bring the book's topics to life, plus chapter outlines, summaries, learning objectives, glossary flashcards (with audio), practice quizzes, and weblinks.

WebTutor™ on WebCT® With WebTutor's text-specific, pre-formatted content and total flexibility, instructors can easily create and manage their own custom course website. WebTutor's course management tool gives instructors the ability to provide virtual office hours, post syllabi, set up threaded discussions, track student progress with the quizzing material, and much more. For students, WebTutor offers real-time access to a full array of study tools, including animations and videos that bring the book's topics to life, plus chapter outlines, summaries, learning objectives, glossary flashcards (with audio), practice quizzes, and weblinks.

Student Resources

Book Companion Site A website for students that features a wide assortment of resources, which have been revised to reflect the new material in the text, to help students master the subject matter. The website, prepared by David Paradis of the University of Colorado, Boulder, includes a glossary, flashcards, crossword puzzles, tutorial quizzes, essay questions, weblinks, and suggested readings.

CL eBook This interactive multimedia eBook links out to rich media assets such as video and MP3 chapter summaries. Through this eBook, students can also access self-test quizzes, chapter outlines, focus questions, chronology and matching exercises, essay and critical thinking questions (for which the answers can be emailed to their instructors), primary source documents with critical thinking questions, and interactive (zoomable) maps. The CL eBook is available on ichapters.

Wadsworth Western Civilization Resource Center Wadsworth's Western Civilization Resource Center gives your students access to a "virtual reader" with hundreds of primary sources including speeches, letters, legal documents and transcripts, poems, maps, simulations, timelines, and additional images that bring history to life, along with interactive assignable exercises. A map feature including Google Earth™ coordinates and exercises will aid in student comprehension of geography and use of maps. Students can compare the traditional textbook map with an aerial view of the location today. It's an ideal resource for study, review, and research. In addition to this map feature, the resource center also provides blank maps for student review and testing.

Rand McNally Historical Atlas of Western Civilization, 2e This valuable resource features over 45 maps, including maps that highlight classical Greece and Rome; maps document European civilization during the Renaissance; follow events in Germany, Russia, and Italy as they lead up to World Wars I and II; show the dissolution of Communism in 1989; document language and religion in the western world; and maps that describe the unification and industrialization of Europe.

Document Exercise Workbook Prepared by Donna Van Raaphorst, Cuyahoga Community College. A collection of exercises based around primary sources. This workbook is available in two volumes.

Music of Western Civilization Available free to adopters, and for a small fee to students, this CD contains many of the musical selections highlighted in the text and provides a broad sampling of the important musical pieces of Western civilization.

Exploring the European Past A collection of documents and readings that give students first-hand insight into the period. Each module also includes rich visual sources that help put the documents into context, helping the students to understand the work of the historian.

Writing for College History, 1e Prepared by Robert M. Frakes, Clarion University. This brief handbook for survey courses in American history, Western Civilization/European history, and world civilization guides students through the various types of writing assignments they encounter in a history class. Providing examples of student writing and candid assessments of student work, this text focuses on the rules and conventions of writing for the college history course.

The History Handbook, 1e Prepared by Carol Berkin of Baruch College, City University of New York and Betty Anderson of Boston University. This book teaches students both basic and history-specific study skills such as how to read primary sources, research historical topics, and correctly cite sources. Substantially less expensive than comparable skill-building texts, *The History Handbook* also offers tips for Internet research and evaluating online sources.

Doing History: Research and Writing in the Digital Age, 1e Prepared by Michael J. Galgano, J. Chris Arndt, and Raymond M. Hyser of James Madison University. Whether you're starting down the path as a history major, or simply looking for a straightforward and systematic guide to writing a successful paper, you'll find this text to be an indispensible handbook to historical research. This text's "soup to nuts" approach to researching and writing about history addresses every step of the process, from locating your sources and gathering information, to writing clearly and making proper use of various citation styles to avoid plagiarism. You'll also learn how to make the most of every tool available to you—especially the technology that helps you conduct the process efficiently and effectively.

The Modern Researcher, 6e Prepared by Jacques Barzun and Henry F. Graff of Columbia University. This classic introduction to the techniques of research and the art of expression is used widely in history courses, but is also appropriate for writing and research methods courses in other departments. Barzun and Graff thoroughly cover every aspect of research, from the selection of a topic through the gathering, analysis, writing, revision, and publication of findings presenting the process not as a set of rules but through actual cases that put the subtleties of research in a useful context. Part One covers the principles and methods of research; Part Two covers writing, speaking, and getting one's work published.

Reader Program Cengage Learning publishes a number of readers, some containing exclusively primary sources, others a combination of primary and secondary sources, and some designed to guide students through the process of historical inquiry. Visit Cengage.com/history for a complete list of readers.

Custom Options Nobody knows your students like you, so why not give them a text that is tailor-fit to their needs? Cengage Learning offers custom solutions for your course—whether it's making a small modification to *Western Civilization: Beyond Boundaries* to match your syllabus or combining multiple sources to create something truly unique. You can pick and choose chapters, include your own material, and add additional map exercises along with the *Rand McNally Atlas* to create a text that fits the way you teach. Ensure that your students get the most out of their textbook dollar by giving them exactly what they need. Contact your Cengage Learning representative to explore custom solutions for your course.

ACKNOWLEDGMENTS

The authors have benefited throughout the process of revision from the acute and helpful criticisms of numerous colleagues. We thank in particular: **Stephen Andrews,** Central New Mexico Community College; **Sascha Auerbach,** Virginia Commonwealth University; **Jonathan Bone,** William Paterson University; **Kathleen Carter,** High Point University; **Edmund Clingan,** Queensborough Community College/CUNY; Gary Cox, Gordon College; **Padhraig Higgins,** Mercer County Community College; **John Kemp,** Meadows Community College; **Michael Khodarkovsky,** Loyola University; **William Paquette,** Tidewater Community College; **David Paradis,** University of Colorado, Boulder; **Sandra Pryor,** Old Dominion University; **Ty Reese,** University of North Dakota; **Michael Saler,** University of California, Davis; **Janette VanBorsch,** Midlands Technical College; and **Matthew Zembo,** Hudson Valley Community College.

Each of us has benefited from the close readings and careful criticisms of our coauthors, although we all assume responsibility for our own chapters. Barry Strauss has written Chapters 1–6; Thomas Noble, 7–10; Duane Osheim, 11–14; Kristen Neuschel, 15–19; and David Roberts, 25–30. Originally written by William Cohen, Chapters 20–24 have been substantially revised and updated by Elinor Accampo.

Many colleagues, friends, and family members have helped us develop this work as well. Thomas Noble continues to be grateful for Linda Noble's patience and good humor. Noble's coauthors and many colleagues have over the years been sources of inspiration and information. He also thanks several dozen teaching assistants and more than 4,000 students who have helped him to think through the Western Civilization experience.

Barry Strauss is grateful to colleagues at Cornell and at other universities who offered advice and encouragement and responded to scholarly questions. He would also like to thank the people at Cornell who provided technical assistance and support. Most important have been the support and forbearance of his family. His daughter, Sylvie; his son, Michael; and, above all, his wife, Marcia, have truly been sources of inspiration.

Duane Osheim thanks family and friends who continue to support and comment on the text. He would especially like to thank colleagues at the University of Virginia who have engaged him in a long and fruitful discussion of Western Civilization and its relationship to other cultures. They make clear the mutual interdependence of the cultures of the wider world. He particularly wishes to thank H. C. Erik Midelfort, Arthur Field, Brian Owensby, Joseph C. Miller, Chris Carlsmith, Beth Plummer, and David D'Andrea for information and clarification on a host of topics.

Kristen Neuschel thanks her colleagues at Duke University for sharing their expertise. She is especially grateful to Sy Mauskopf, Bill Reddy, John Richards, Tom Robisheaux, Alex Roland, Barry Gaspar, and Peter Wood. She also thanks her husband and fellow historian, Alan Williams, for his wisdom about Western Civilization and his support throughout the project, and her children, Jesse and Rachel, for their patience and interest over many years.

Elinor Accampo is deeply indebted to the late Bill Cohen whose chapters in the first four editions offered a model of expertise and prose, and she continues to carry on what he originated with pride and respect. She owes special thanks to Kristen Neuschel and Rachel Fuchs for friendship and advice, to her daughter, Erin Hern, for her expert input as a consumer of college textbooks, and, as always, to her husband Robert Hern for his encouragement and enduring support.

David Roberts wishes to thank Sheila Barnett, Vici Payne, and Brenda Luke for their able assistance and Walter Adamson, Timothy Cleaveland, Karl Friday, Michael Kwass, John Morrow, Miranda Pollard, Judith Rohrer, John Short, William Stuek, and Kirk Willis for sharing their expertise in response to questions. He also thanks Beth Roberts for her constant support and interest and her exceedingly critical eye.

The first plans for this book were laid in 1988, and over the course of twenty-one years there has been remarkable stability in the core group of people responsible for its development. The author team lost a member, Bill Cohen, but Elinor Accampo stepped into Bill's place with such skill and grace that it seemed as though she had been with us from the start. Our original sponsoring editor, Jean Woy, moved up the corporate ladder but never missed an author meeting with us. Through five editions we had the pleasure of working with production editor Christina Horn and photo researcher Carole Frohlich. For this edition Jane Lee and Catherine Schnurr filled those roles, and we are grateful for their efforts. Our sponsoring editor for more than a decade, Nancy Blaine, has been a tower of strength. She believes in us, as we believe in her. We have been fortunate in our editors, Elizabeth Welch, Jennifer Sutherland, Julie Swasey, and Adrienne Zicht. All these kind and skillful people have elicited from us authors a level of achievement that fills us at once with pride and humility.

Thomas F. X. Noble

ABOUT THE AUTHORS

Thomas F. X. Noble   After receiving his Ph.D. from Michigan State University, Thomas Noble taught at Albion College, Michigan State University, Texas Tech University, and the University of Virginia. In 1999 he received the University of Virginia's highest award for teaching excellence and in 2008 Notre Dame's Edmund P. Joyce, C.S.C., Award for Excellence in Undergraduate Teaching. In 2001 he became Robert M. Conway Director of the Medieval Institute at the University of Notre Dame and in 2008 chairperson of Notre Dame's history department. He is the author of *The Republic of St. Peter: The Birth of the Papal State, 680–825; Religion, Culture and Society in the Early Middle Ages; Soldiers of Christ: Saints and Saints' Lives from Late Antiquity and the Early Middle Ages; From Roman Provinces to Medieval Kingdoms; Images, Iconoclasm, and the Carolingians;* and *Charlemagne and Louis the Pious: Five Lives.* He was a member of the Institute for Advanced Study in 1994 and the Netherlands Institute for Advanced Study in 1999–2000. He has been awarded fellowships by the National Endowment for the Humanities (twice) and the American Philosophical Society. He was elected a Fellow of the Medieval Academy of America in 2004.

Barry Strauss   Professor of history and Classics at Cornell University, Barry Strauss holds a Ph.D. from Yale. He has been awarded fellowships by the National Endowment for the Humanities, the American School of Classical Studies at Athens, The MacDowell Colony for the Arts, the Korea Foundation, and the Killam Foundation of Canada. He is the recipient of the Clark Award for excellence in teaching from Cornell. He is Chair of Cornell's Department of History, Director of Cornell's Program on Freedom and Free Societies, and Past Director of Cornell's Peace Studies Program. His many publications include *Athens After the Peloponnesian War: Class, Faction, and Policy, 403–386 B.C.; Fathers and Sons in Athens: Ideology and Society in the Era of the Peloponnesian War; The Anatomy of Error: Ancient Military Disasters and Their Lessons for Modern Strategists* (with Josiah Ober); *Hegemonic Rivalry from Thucydides to the Nuclear Age* (co-edited with R. New Lebow); *War and Democracy: A Comparative Study of the Korean War and the Peloponnesian War* (co-edited with David R. McCann); *Rowing Against the Current: On Learning to Scull at Forty; The Battle of Salamis, the Naval Encounter That Saved Greece – and Western Civilization; The Trojan War: A New History;* and *The Spartacus War.* His books have been translated into six languages. His book *The Battle of Salamis* was named one of the best books of 2004 by the Washington Post.

Duane J. Osheim   A Fellow of the American Academy in Rome with a Ph.D. in History from the University of California at Davis, Duane Osheim is professor of history at the University of Virginia. He has held American Council of Learned Societies, American Philosophical Society, National Endowment for the Humanities and Fulbright Fellowships. He is author and editor of *A Tuscan Monastery and Its Social World; An Italian Lordship: The Bishopric of Lucca in the Late Middle Ages; Beyond Florence: The Contours of Medieval and Early Modern Italy;* and *Chronicling History: Chroniclers and Historians in Medieval and Renaissance Italy.*

Kristen B. Neuschel   After receiving her Ph.D. from Brown University, Kristen Neuschel taught at Denison University and Duke University, where she is currently associate professor of history and

Director of the Thompson Writing Program. She is a specialist in early modern French history and is the author of *Word of Honor: Interpreting Noble Culture in Sixteenth-Century France* and articles on French social history and European women's history. She has received grants from the Josiah Charles Trent Memorial Foundation, the National Endowment for the Humanities, and the American Council of Learned Societies. She has also received the Alumni Distinguished Undergraduate Teaching Award, which is awarded annually on the basis of student nominations for excellence in teaching at Duke.

Elinor A. Accampo   Professor of history and gender studies at the University of Southern California, Elinor Accampo completed her Ph.D. at the University of California, Berkeley. Prior to her career at USC, she taught at Colorado College and Denison University. She specializes in modern France and is the author of *Blessed Motherhood; Bitter Fruit: Nelly Roussel and the Politics of Female Pain in Third Republic France;* and *Industrialization, Family, and Class Relations: Saint Chamond, 1815–1914*. She has also published *Gender and the Politics of Social Reform in France* (co-edited with Rachel Fuchs and Mary Lynn Stewart) and articles and book chapters on the history of reproductive rights and birth control movements. She has received fellowships and travel grants from the German Marshall Fund, the Haynes Foundation, the American Council of Learned Societies, and the National Endowment for the Humanities, as well as an award for Innovative Undergraduate Teaching at USC.

David D. Roberts   After receiving his Ph.D. in modern European history at the University of California, Berkeley, David Roberts taught at the Universities of Virginia and Rochester before becoming professor of history at the University of Georgia in 1988. At Rochester he chaired the Humanities Department of the Eastman School of Music, and he chaired the History Department at Georgia from 1993 to 1998. A recipient of Woodrow Wilson and Rockefeller Foundation fellowships, he is the author of *The Syndicalist Tradition and Italian Fascism; Benedetto Croce and the Uses of Historicism; Nothing but History: Reconstruction and Extremity After Metaphysics; The Totalitarian Experiment in Twentieth-Century Europe: Rethinking the Poverty of Great Politics;* and *Historicism and Fascism in Modern* Italy, as well as two books in Italian and numerous articles and reviews. He is currently Albert Berry Saye Professor of History *Emeritus* at the University of Georgia.

Introduction: The West Before 1560

Historians sometimes say that "History begins at Sumer," a region of ancient Mesopotamia located in the south of modern Iraq. For the reader of Volume II of *Western Civilization: Beyond Boundaries*, history begins forty-five hundred years after Sumer, in the last decades of the sixteenth-century European world. Some orientation may therefore be helpful to situate the start of this volume in time and place.

"Western civilization" is the traditional name for the history you will encounter in these pages. Before we go back to Sumer, let us reflect a little on these two words. The "West" is sometimes understood geographically and sometimes culturally. Each understanding is complex. For most people, the "West" means western Europe. And yet western Europe was itself the heir of the peoples and cultures of the Mediterranean world of antiquity. These included Mesopotamians—people such as the Sumerians—and Egyptians, Greeks and Romans, Jews and Christians. Moreover, through exploration, war, and commerce, the "West" gradually imposed its influence on the whole globe. Concerning Europe itself, one view might encompass Rome, Paris, and London whereas another might stretch from Dublin to Moscow.

As a cultural phenomenon, "Western" implies many things: freedom and free, participatory political institutions; economic initiative and opportunity; monotheistic religious faiths (Judaism, Christianity, and Islam); rationalism and ordered thought in the social, political, and philosophical realms; an aesthetic sensibility that aspires to a universal sense of truth and beauty. But the West has felt free both to evoke tradition as its guiding light *and* to innovate brilliantly; to accommodate slavery and freedom simultaneously; to esteem original thought and to persecute people who deviate from the norm. "Western" has different meanings depending on time, place, and circumstance.

What, then, is civilization? No definition has won universal acceptance, but certain elements are seen in almost every civilization. Cities are crucial. Cities require complex social organizations that involve at least a minimal division of labor: Some people work in the fields, some in the home. Soldiers defend the city, and artisans provide its handcrafted goods. Governing institutions have a wide measure of acceptance and the wherewithal to enforce their wills. Cultures grow more complex and exhibit such traits as religious ideas and authorities; a literature and law that may be oral or written; monumental architecture, especially fortifications, palaces, and temples; and arts such as music, painting, and sculpture. Civilization emerged in the West over a long time after about 3500 B.C. It appears that a slowly but steadily increasing population made it imperative to secure a predictable food supply. This need led to agriculture and animal husbandry, the taming of fields and flocks to the needs of a human community. The many processes involved in agriculture led to specialization of labor. The sharper definition of social and economic roles led to the delineation of gender roles. Communities defined certain tasks— government and war, for example—as essentially male, while reserving domestic responsibilities and some religious duties for women. The interests of self-sufficiency became subordinated to the needs of the community.

THE ANCIENT WORLD, CA. 3500–323 B.C

Historians usually begin their accounts of Western civilization with the Sumerians and Egyptians because they were, between about 3500 and 3000 B.C., the first peoples to attain civilization within the orbit of the West.

Western Asia

Sumer lies in *Mesopotamia,* the land "between the rivers" Tigris and Euphrates. After the Sumerians, a succession of peoples in Mesopotamia itself—Akkadians, Babylonians, and Assyrians, for example—and many other peoples in the lands bordering Mesopotamia—Medes and Persians to the east, Hittites to the north, Phoenicians, Canaanites, and Hebrews to the west—also crossed the line that marks the beginnings of civilization.

All of these peoples are interesting and important in their own rights, but they concern the continuing course of Western civilization in one particularly important way: they were the cultural ancestors of the founders of the West, the Greeks and the Romans. The Greeks were a millennium behind them in developing civilization; the Romans were another millennium behind the Greeks. Western Asia (often called "the Middle East") contributed religious ideas, artistic norms, mathematical concepts, ways of reckoning time, and even the alphabet. Ideas, technologies, and practices from western Asia radiated far beyond the Greek and Roman worlds and helped spark the rise of civilization in Europe, where the Neolithic period (the "new stone" age, the time of carefully fashioned stone tools) gave way to civilization more slowly than in the Mediterranean world.

Egypt

The Greek historian Herodotus (480–425 B.C.) called Egypt "the gift of the Nile." Historical Egypt is a fertile strip of land, ranging from 5 to 15 miles wide, that hugs the Nile River along its 750-mile course. Whereas the Tigris and Euphrates flood irregularly, sometimes violently, the Nile usually floods annually and beneficently. Efforts to manage irrigation, grain production, and storage along the course of the river led to an early (just before 3000 B.C.) replacement of local autonomy by a unified monarchy under god-kings called pharaohs.

Under the pharaohs of the period that historians now call the "Old Kingdom" (2695–2160 B.C.), Egypt faced no foreign threats and built up its central institutions. The great monuments of this time, the pyramids—pharaonic tombs—symbolize the power, wealth, and security of Egypt. An invasion brought an end to the Old Kingdom, but the eventual overthrow of the invaders ushered in the Middle Kingdom (1963–1786 B.C.), a time of political innovation—pharaohs had to share power with aristocrats—and cultural stimulation from Mesopotamian sources. The Middle Kingdom yielded in turn to the New Kingdom (1550–1070 B.C.), when Egypt became an imperial state whose reach extended all the way to Mesopotamia. The treasures of Tutankhamon ("King Tut") exemplify the wealth and sophistication of this age. Imperial Egypt was eventually ground down in a series of wars with the Hittites, an Indo-European-speaking people who settled in Anatolia (present-day Turkey).

Small Kingdoms and Great Empires

After the Egyptians and Hittites wore each other out, western Asia experienced a time of smaller, independent states. Phoenicia (roughly today's Lebanon) emerged as a major commercial power. The Phoenicians gathered up goods bought from Asia and Arabia via long-established overland trade routes and exchanged them for products acquired in their colonies all over the Mediterranean. Phoenician commerce thus initiated the cultural unification of the Mediterranean world.

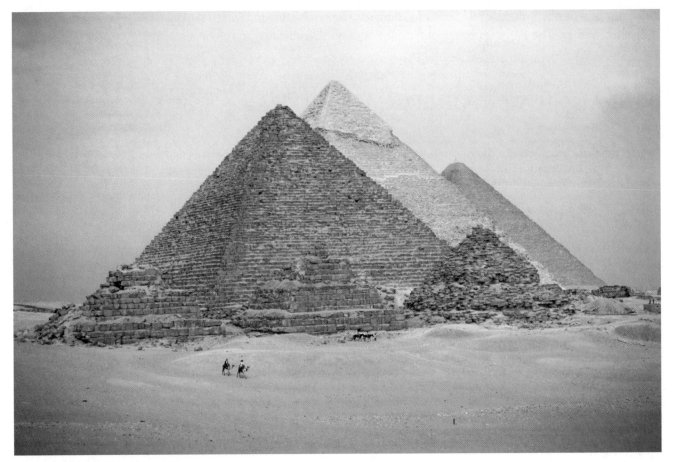

Great Pyramids of Giza Royal funerary monuments of three Egyptian kings of the twenty-sixth century B.C., the pyramids symbolize the power and ambition of the Old Kingdom. The pyramid of King Khufu (or Cheops, rearmost in the photo) is still the largest all-stone building in human history. (Michael Holford)

Another small state of immense importance was the kingdom created by the Hebrews. Oral traditions and much later writings suggest that as early as 2000 B.C. a band of Hebrews under their tribal leader Abraham migrated from Mesopotamia to Palestine, on the eastern shore of the Mediterranean. Neither numerous nor united nor powerful, the Hebrews were often victimized by stronger neighbors. Around 1200 B.C. a group of Hebrews, slaves and workers in Egypt, cast off their bondage and returned to Palestine. This formative experience, remembered as the Exodus ("journey out" in Greek), forged a nation. For a century after 1000 B.C., Kings Saul, David, and Solomon built a state that was a match for its neighbors. Later, fierce rivalries among the Hebrews led to the disintegration of the unified monarchy, and the fragmented Hebrew communities were eventually conquered by powerful enemies.

The unique religious vision of the Hebrews makes them key founders of the Western tradition. The Jewish faith is very much alive today and serves as the basis for two other major religious traditions: Christianity and Islam.

The Hebrew religious vision is revealed to us in the Hebrew Bible, a large collection of writings that Christians call the Old Testament. The Hebrew Bible consists of historical writings on the unfolding relationship of the Hebrews with their God, legal books that lay down rules for personal conduct and social organization, prophetic books that express some of humanity's deepest spiritual insights, and wisdom literature that is full of humane guidance for daily life.

The central truth revealed by these Scriptures is exclusive monotheism. There is only one God. With this God the Hebrews have a covenant, a special pact. As long as the Hebrews do God's will by observing the Law and heeding His prophets, they will enjoy God's blessings and protection.

The period of small states was concluded by the creation, one after another, of ever larger states culminating in the Persian Empire (ca. 550–334 B.C.), which was centered in modern

Iran. The Persians spread ideas and institutions through their vast empire, the largest the world had yet seen. The Persians were finally conquered by the armies of Alexander the Great (r. 336–323 B.C.), from Macedon in the northern Balkans.

This long succession of states and peoples led to the diffusion of many ideas and practices. We have remarked on one example already: the religious vision of the Hebrews. Another is a style of rulership that we call "theocratic." In a "theocracy," rulers are placed in office by, and are answerable only to, a god. In Mesopotamia rulers were generally believed to be the agents of the gods; in Egypt rulers were believed to *be* gods. In Alexander and his successors, notably Roman emperors, theocratic rulership had a long run. Egyptian ideas of a last judgment and of life after death circulated widely. Scientific and mathematical advances are another legacy of the ancient kingdoms and empires. In building huge monuments such as pyramids, in preserving human remains by mummification, in measuring fields, in observing the heavens, people in Mesopotamia and Egypt laid up a huge store of practical information from which later peoples, especially the Greeks, drew enthusiastically.

CLASSICAL ANTIQUITY, CA. 1000 B.C.–A.D. 284

*C*lassical means normative, a standard by which to judge. In the nineteenth century, intellectuals were fond of saying to one another, "You were born in Greece." Such an assertion insisted that many cultural and aesthetic standards still prevalent in their own day had arisen in ancient Greece. So powerful has been the hold of Greece over architecture and sculpture, for example, that some modern movements have been deliberately "anticlassical." The Romans were the great interpreters of Greek culture, but they also added their own distinctive contributions to Western civilization.

Ancient Greece

The Greeks made fundamental—classical—contributions in two areas: political ideas and institutions, and culture. Homer's epic poems, the *Iliad* and the *Odyssey,* probably composed not long after 800 B.C. but the products of a long oral development, open before us the course of Greek political development. The poems purport to tell of Greece in the days of the Trojan Wars. Greek memory fixed those wars in about 1200 B.C., when undoubtedly the Greeks engaged in some nasty commercial squabbles with their neighbors in the Aegean basin. It is grand to imagine, with Homer, that the beauty of Helen of Troy launched a thousand Greek ships. It is unlikely, however, that it is historically accurate to think so.

The *Iliad* and the *Odyssey* profess to describe actual events in the Greek world in the Mycenaean period, so called because Mycenae was the greatest city of that time. Between about 1500 and 1200 B.C., several remarkable cities were built in the Greek lands by peoples who were the ancestors of the Greeks of the classical period. Before the Mycenaeans a remarkable culture had flourished, then faded, on the island of Crete. Historians call this culture "Minoan" after the legendary King Minos. But there is nothing legendary about the spectacular Minoan palaces, whose ruins are still impressive, or about the exquisite artistic remains of Minoan culture. The Minoan and Mycenaean periods played a key role in connecting the Greeks with the realms of western Asia and Egypt. The *Iliad,* after all, is a tale about a Greek expedition to Anatolia.

Homer sings of a world of kings and aristocrats. Huge armies are mustered on his pages; individual warriors are described in minute detail. A common soldier could be flogged for speaking in the presence of his betters. This regal, aristocratic society, whose leaders were *Eupatrids,* "well-fathered men," dominated Greece for centuries.

Slowly the polis, the city-state, the basic Greek political institution, began to emerge. The people of rugged, craggy Greece clustered in small territories; as a result, many independent poleis arose in a land smaller than most American states. Each polis had a central urban zone and an agricultural hinterland. Often the urban zone featured an easily fortified hill: an *acropolis.* The acropolis sheltered people in times of attack and served as a meeting place for the conduct of civic and religious affairs.

Many poleis outstripped the locally available food supplies and looked enviously at their neighbors' provisions. Weaker poleis had to see to their defenses just as stronger ones had

The Parthenon The temple of Athena Parthenos ("the Maiden") on the Athenian Acropolis, the Parthenon was dedicated in 438 B.C. One of the largest and most complex Greek temples, it was built of fine marble. The partially restored ruins symbolize the wealth, power, and greatness of Classical Greece. (William Katz/Photo Researchers)

to beef up their capacity for attack. This competition resulted in the expansion of political and social participation in the public life of the polis. The infantryman, known as the hoplite, gained a role in defending his city and then insisted on a role in its government. Some cities, most notably Athens, moved toward greater and greater participation until *demokratia,* the rule of the people, was achieved. In Athens, all adult male citizens could vote and hold any of the key offices in the city. Sparta, however, became a military juggernaut in which the rights of all were subordinated to the dictates of a small number of the oldest, most conservative citizens. Corinth, where large landowners invested in trade, became a commercial oligarchy. In all cases, expanded or redefined participation belonged only to men. Women were excluded from participation in political life. Yet in Sparta women exercised effective daily control over the private lands allotted to soldiers, and in Athens women played leading roles in public religious celebrations.

As their populations exceeded the available resources of their tiny homelands, many Greek cities exported surplus population to colonies all over the Mediterranean world. As well as defusing Greek tensions, these colonies spread Greek culture far and wide.

While they were creating their basic political institutions between about 750 and 500 B.C., the Greeks also began to reflect systematically on political organization. Indeed, much of our political vocabulary is Greek in origin. Politics, after all, is what people do publicly in a polis.

Although Athens invented democracy, most Greek political thinkers were hostile to democratic ideas. They argued that democracy elevated the rabble over the best citizens and permitted the masses to satisfy their immediate desires, cast aside restraint, and neglect the long-term needs of the community. In one way or another, every Greek political thinker addressed an issue that has been critical in Western political discourse ever since: How can a person reconcile personal interests with the needs of the community?

The second Greek achievement lies in the realm of culture—in art, architecture, literature, science, and philosophy. Generalizations are difficult, but it may be fair to say that the Greeks, or at least the elite among them, set out very early to pursue truth and beauty. The Greeks were not unique in this quest. What sets them apart is the way they defined their objectives.

To a Greek thinker, beauty existed in the balance, order, and harmony that seemed to underlie everything really good. Greek scientific writers looked for a single, unchanging substance behind everything in existence. Failing in this search, they looked for overarching theories capable of explaining everything. Failing in this, they explored the nature of thought and language to see what could be known and communicated. In relative terms, the Greeks added rather few concrete details to the huge fund of Mesopotamian and Egyptian discoveries. What the Greeks contributed was a vast mental framework designed to systematize and explain what is known. In Classical Greece we see the birth of both science and philosophy.

Greek literature is full of memorable characters who present the reader, or the theater audience, with dilemmas of conscience. Oedipus, the main character of *Oedipus the Tyrant* by Sophocles (ca. 495–406 B.C.), whom Shakespeare called "the most tragic of poets," kills his father and marries his mother. He has absolutely no idea that he has done so. Is he nevertheless guilty of a hideous offense? It is to Greek literature that we must turn for insights into the roles of women, for they were excluded from formal, public positions. Antigone, the central character in Sophocles' *Antigone,* is one of the most memorable women in literature. She struggles courageously to reconcile the conflicting demands of political allegiance and family ties. What is justice; what does it mean to be just; is it possible to be just? Can a rule apply to one person alone, or must it apply to everyone? Do rules exist at all? Reading the best of Greek literature today evokes the same feelings it did then: gut-wrenching agony over life choices.

To look at a fine Greek statue or building is, first of all, to admire the astonishing technical skill that went into making it. Second, the viewer is moved by its beauty. Another look will usually prove disconcerting. The object in our gaze is *too* perfectly executed, *too* beautiful. It is like nothing we have ever seen, although it is vaguely like everything we see all the time. It is as if the object is meant less to remind us of things in this world than to provide a glimpse of a better, purer world.

Greek art opens up a vista on the greatest Greek philosophers. Plato (427–348 B.C.) distrusted the senses as guides to truth or reality. He believed that we are all prisoners of the world and of our human limitations. According to Plato, ultimate reality exists not here and now but in a transcendent world. In our world, and in this life, we can gain only hints of what really exists. His greatest pupil was Aristotle (384–322 B.C.), whose mania for classification has been the despair of many a biology student. Aristotle reminds us of the technical artistry of the Greek sculptor. For Aristotle, knowledge was possible in this world. But knowledge was the result of knowing what you wanted to find out, of working immensely hard to discover truth, and of living with the consequences of the truths you found.

Fame and success are not the same. Greek political ideas, institutions, and terminology have been famous for ages, but the Greeks were, finally, unsuccessful at politics. Only during the Persian Wars (490–479 B.C.) were the Greeks able to rally together, and even then they quarreled over strategy and leadership. Individual Greek states were notoriously unstable and violent, and most of the time the poleis of Greece found themselves forced to accept membership in leagues and alliances. Between 431 and 404 B.C., Sparta's Peloponnesian League and the Athenian Empire—an involuntary association of the Greek states that had fought against Persia—convulsed the whole Greek world in the Peloponnesian War.

Philip II of Macedon, an increasingly powerful and well-organized kingdom to the north of Greece, conquered the Greeks in 338 B.C. and bequeathed his prize to his remarkable son, Alexander the Great. After securing the Balkans, Alexander set off on a tour of military conquest unrivaled before his time. He conquered the Persian Empire and much more besides. His conquests ushered in a period that historians call "Hellenistic."

Hellenistic, the customary name for the period following Alexander's death, roughly 323 to 30 B.C., when Greek language and culture dominated the Mediterranean world, means "Greeklike," as opposed to *Hellenic,* "purely Greek," the term applied to the preceding period from about 750 to 323 B.C. Alexander's generals carved his vast empire into many smaller states that survived despite many struggles, until one by one they fell to Rome. Greek leaders and elites mixed with local populations of many traditions to produce a rich, international culture that was everywhere recognizably, but nowhere purely, Greek.

The expanding, fluid nature of Hellenistic culture and states provided unprecedented opportunities for women in commerce and in government. Unlike cities, which reserved offices to men, monarchies had courts in which women could be influential advisers and sometimes actual rulers. Cleopatra of Egypt (r. 51–30 B.C.) is the most famous but by no means the only powerful Hellenistic woman.

The Roman Republic and Empire

The Roman poet Horace (65–8 B.C.) once said that "Captive Greece took her captor captive." His clever epigram is an apt transition from Greek to Roman history. But what did he mean? First, to be sure, the Romans conquered Greece—and many more lands. Second, Greek culture deeply influenced the Romans, who in general were not as original and creative as the Greeks.

The Romans considered their history to have begun with the founding of Rome itself, an event that they dated to what we call 753 B.C. Actually, the historical Romans were in Rome's neighborhood long before that date, and Rome's familiar society and institutions arose long after it.

From 509 B.C., when the Romans believed that their Republic had been instituted, until 27 B.C., when that Republic was definitively transformed into a military monarchy, Rome was remarkably stable. That stability was partly institutional. Rome had several magistrates with differing degrees of power, responsibility, and prestige, and several representative institutions with varying areas of authority. All adult men participated in important but very different ways. In addition, Rome's stability was partly cultural. In society and politics, Rome was hierarchical and deferential in equal measure. Rome accorded responsibility for running the Republic to a small number of men. As in Greece, women in Rome were systematically excluded from public life. Roman literature depicts women as domestic and submissive.

Prominent Romans ruled through office and assembly and also through patronage and private influence. Leading Romans were firmly opposed to innovation. The only good ways were the old ways, they believed. A Roman speech almost always began with an appeal to the "way our ancestors would have done things." Thus, it took a long time for the Roman system to emerge, and it seemed unchanged and unchanging.

Slowly the Romans conquered their neighbors in Italy (509–265 B.C.). Then victory in wars (264–146 B.C.) against Carthage, an old Phoenician colony, gave Rome dominance in the western Mediterranean. Finally, a series of wars against the Hellenistic monarchies (200–31 B.C.) left Rome in control of the whole Mediterranean world. It is easy to appreciate the old saying, "All roads lead to Rome."

Rome's wars came at a high price. Political and social stability was destroyed as personal and imperial ambition became regular weapons in domestic politics. Generals came to count for more than statesmen. Vast wealth, new and unevenly distributed, fractured the old structures of social deference that had long organized Roman society. Great fortunes and shifting social realities also created unprecedented opportunities for women to influence public life through family politics and artistic patronage. The culture of the Hellenistic world, as Horace correctly saw, overwhelmed the earnest Romans, who were less bumpkinish than they pretended but less sophisticated than most of their neighbors.

The Republic collapsed in a century of civil wars. Augustus Caesar (r. 31 B.C.– A.D. 14) created a dramatically changed regime. He inaugurated a two-centurylong period, the *pax Romana* (the Roman peace), that brought the Mediterranean world as close as it has ever come to unity. Peace and prosperity, good government, spectacular building projects, and a process of cultural diffusion now called "Romanization" also characterized the pax Romana.

Augustus took the title *Princeps* ("First Citizen"). The Augustan Principate rested on a few basic notions. Rome's ruler was now an emperor whose power depended on his control of the military. The Roman Empire was now less and

Bust of Julius Caesar A general gifted at war and politics, Caesar was named dictator in 49 B.C. and was assassinated by members of the senate in 44 B.C. This marble sculpture accurately conveys the conqueror's firmness of expression and perhaps his intelligence—but not his looks, since Caesar was bald. (Vatican Museums/ Scala/Art Resource, NY) less an exclusively Roman entity: People from all over Italy and from the provinces shared in the benefits of empire. Augustus and the emperors who succeeded him forged a partnership with local elites everywhere. For instance, the Herods of Judea are villains in the Christian Scriptures, but from the Roman point of view, they were loyal, pliable, competent servants. And they were hardly alone. One of the ways in which such people showed their loyalty to Rome was by adopting the trappings of Roman culture—that is, by Romanizing.

Although the Romans were less innovative than the Greeks, they were by no means uncreative. Roman architecture achieved heights of complexity and sophistication. Roman law remains influential to this day. Cities from England to Mesopotamia still reveal their Roman street plans, and highway systems all over Europe lie atop Roman roads. Roman writers were learned, technically expert, verbally adroit, and at their best they ranged from moving to hilarious. Virgil's *Aeneid,* the story of Aeneas, one of the defeated at Troy and the legendary founder of Rome, presents the archetypal Roman hero: strong, familial, humble, loyal, and, above all else, perseverant.

The third century A.D. brought the Augustan Principate and the classical order to a close. From one end of the Roman Empire to the other, both the forms and the feelings of classical literature vanished. Large-scale building ceased. New religions, perhaps capable of explaining the difficulties of the age, proliferated. One prominent historian speaks of an "age of anxiety." What happened?

First, as the Roman historian Tacitus dryly observed in the first century A.D., "the army made the emperor." And, we might add, unmade him too, with alarming frequency. Civil wars between military commanders competing for the imperial office became endemic. Civil strife undermined the empire's ability to meet military threats along its exposed frontiers. Military and civil unrest contributed to a loosening of the old ties between the imperial government and the provincial elites. The economy was disrupted by political turmoil and was further weakened by uncontrollable inflation. At the end of the third century, Rome's prospects looked grim.

THE WORLD OF LATE ANTIQUITY, 284–CA. 600

The years from about 284 to 600, now usually called Late Antiquity, witnessed changes in the structure of Roman institutions, alterations in the composition and functions of the social and political elite, and the elaboration of a Christian culture and an undivided, universal—that is, catholic— church.

The Transformation of the Roman Empire

To preserve the empire, Diocletian (r. 284–305) and Constantine (r. 306–337) radically expanded the imperial bureaucracy and army. Constantine established a second capital for the empire at Byzantium on the Bosphorus, which he renamed after himself: Constantinople. These reforms were costly in several senses. They necessitated higher taxes and more vigilant tax collecting. Roman officials seemed more intrusive and, quite often, less honest. A larger army solved neither border problems nor political ones. The armies themselves were increasingly recruited from Germanic peoples living along the frontiers. Some of these people were loyal to Rome; others sought to profit from its weakness. Not only the legions but the military leaders in the fourth and fifth centuries were likely to be Germanic. These men were usually loyal and competent, but divided allegiance could be a problem for them in ways unknown to the sturdy Romans of old.

The greatest change in the political landscape of Late Antiquity can be seen on a map. In 300 the western half of the Roman Empire consisted of a number of provinces governed by a hierarchy of Roman officials. In 600 a number of Germanic kingdoms had replaced those provinces. One might suppose that Rome had "fallen," that the ancient world had ended. It is true that after 476 there were no more emperors in the western half of the empire. But a closer look at those supplanting kingdoms reveals some interesting continuities.

The earliest kingdoms were actually founded by Roman-Germanic collaboration, and their kings continued to cultivate close relations with the eastern Roman Empire headquartered at Constantinople. Kings covered themselves with Roman titles, adapted Roman public ceremonies, and acted like imperial magistrates. They issued laws and recorded documents in Latin and maintained, under their own authority, features of Roman local administration. Given that most Germanic kings were the descendants of late antique Roman military officers, it is unlikely that most people detected much difference between Roman and Germanic rule.

Who were these Germanic kings and their followers? The lands beyond the Rhine and Danube, the two rivers that formed Rome's northern frontier, held innumerable peoples with whom the Romans had long, complex relationships. Rome traded with, fought against, allied with, and recruited many Germanic peoples at one time or another. The Germanic peoples were confederations, not ethnic groups. "Frank," the name of one Germanic people, applies not only to persons who were Frankish but also to their relatives by marriage, clients, allies, defeated foes, and hangers-on. Such peoples created kingdoms by violent encounters and by peaceful settlement, by usurpation and by delegation. One might say that the kingdoms were Germanized and militarized versions of formerly Roman provinces. In other words, Rome provided the framework within which its own transformation took place.

The Triumph of Christian Culture

Continuity and change are also evident in the most important cultural transformation of Late Antiquity: the triumph of Christianity. Christianity arose in first-century Palestine among a dedicated band of followers of Jesus of Nazareth. Jesus, a Jewish teacher of great charisma and compassion, preached an uncompromising morality, a need for repentance, and preparation for a coming kingdom of God. Jesus's teachings were intimately connected to venerable strains in Jewish thought and life. His followers believed him to be the Son of God.

From unpromising beginnings among a minority sect of Jews in a small, poor province, Christianity rose by the end of the fourth century to become the dominant religion in the Roman world. Fundamental teachings, the basic message of Jesus as related in the New Testament books of Matthew, Mark, Luke, and John—four accounts of Jesus's life and teachings written a generation or two after his death—were critical to this success. Jesus's teachings were universal, addressed to men and women, people of every land, persons of every status.

Christianity spread initially through towns. In each town, communities of believers installed officials whose customary titles in English are *bishop, priest,* and *deacon.* Bishops—the word means "overseers"—gradually came to have administrative, moral, and intellectual responsibilities in their towns. They controlled the local church and its property, recruited and trained priests and deacons, disciplined heretics (dissenters from official doctrine), and preached. A growing Christian church adapted the administrative geography of the Roman Empire. Bishops from towns and provinces began to meet in councils to decide complex matters of theology and ordinary matters of Christian living.

Christians were at times persecuted, but in 314 Constantine granted Christianity legal equality with all other religions. By 400 the most eminent local personage in almost every town of the empire was the bishop. Bishops came from the same families that had long given Rome its greatest citizens. Following the lead of the bishops was not difficult for local populations. Leading people from the pulpit was easy for men accustomed to authority and respect.

Christians were invited both to change the world around themselves and also to flee that world and its temptations. The church's public institutions represented an effort to respond to the first of these invitations. Another institution, monasticism, responded to the second. All over the Roman world, groups of men and women settled as monks or nuns in communities dedicated to prayer, study, self-denial, and work. Monasticism attracted people from every region, class, and level of education. This powerful spiritual force was one of Late Antiquity's most enduring legacies.

Christianity touched the lives of women in a variety of ways. Church teachings held out two models to women. There was Eve, the eternal temptress, who had tricked Adam and cost humanity the joys of paradise. Then there was Mary, the holy, obedient, and exemplary mother of Jesus. Women were gradually denied clerical positions in the church but gained great prominence in monasticism. Generally, Christian teachings accorded women more respect and dignity than secular laws did.

The bishop of Rome attained special prominence. This status owed something to the doctrine of apostolic succession, according to which all bishops inherited the teaching authority of the apostles, the twelve most prominent original followers of Jesus. In the Roman version of this doctrine, Peter had been the leader of the apostles and Peter's successors, the bishops of

Rome—they began to be called popes in the third century—were the leaders of the church as a whole. Roman prominence is also attributable to the connection between the popes and the city of Rome itself, the capital of the empire to which all roads led. Finally, papal leadership matured during bitter theological struggles in the Christian community. Popes routinely intervened on behalf of, or entertained appeals from, persons they supported. As the popes attained leadership and defined dogmas, they laid the foundations for the Roman Catholic Church.

The quarrels were many but tended to focus on two key issues: the problem of the Trinity and the person of Jesus. The majority of Christian thinkers argued that God was triune, three persons—Father, Son, and Holy Spirit—in one. Christian tradition also maintained that the second person of the Trinity, Jesus Christ, was true God and true man.

Between about 350 and 450, Christian thinkers all over the Mediterranean world addressed themselves to solving such theological problems, to explaining both the Jewish and the Christian Scriptures (which Christians call the Old and the New Testaments), and to defining practical rules for living. We call such thinkers "Church Fathers" and their age "patristic" (from *pater,* the Latin word for "father"). The most famous of the Latin Church Fathers was Augustine (354–430), a North African who became a professor of rhetoric and converted to Christianity as an adult. Augustine's writings chronicled his own spiritual quest and commented on the religious issues of his day.

The Church Fathers are among the most learned, prolific, accomplished, and influential writers in all of history. They were products of the Roman world, but they did not suppose, as Virgil had, that time would last only as long as Rome. For them, the source and goal of human existence was in heaven, not on earth.

MEDIEVAL CIVILIZATIONS, 600–1300

The Roman world left not one but three heirs. The first comprised the Germanic kingdoms that replaced Rome's western provinces. The second was the eastern Roman Empire centered in Constantinople. The third was a surprising development that no one in Late Antiquity could have predicted: the emergence of the Islamic faith and the Muslim empire.

Islam and the Arabs

Islam arose in Arabia, a large, barren land in western Asia deeply influenced by all the currents of ancient culture but never wholly conquered by any ancient people. In 570 Islam's pivotal figure, Muhammad, was born in Mecca, a great commercial city. Tradition holds that when Muhammad was a young man, his spiritual sensibilities were awakened by visits from the archangel Gabriel, who commanded him to "recite" a holy text. That text revolved around one great truth: "There is no God but Allah, and Muhammad is his prophet."

Like many religious leaders, Muhammad gained both followers and foes. Enemies forced Muhammad to flee in 622 to Medina, a city about 200 miles from Mecca. There he gave full force to his religious and social vision. Before he died in 632, Muhammad saw that vision triumph in Mecca and throughout Arabia.

The faith of Muhammad is revealed in the Quran, a collection of Allah's revelations to the prophet. Muhammad's religion demands absolute surrender to Allah: *al-Islam,* "the surrender," whence the name of the faith. Like Judaism, Islam has two central components: faith and community. The faith is simple, direct, uncompromising. There is no God but Allah, the creator and ruler of all. Islam had no creeds, no statements of religious belief, and no hierarchical clergy. The community, the *umma muslima,* was the totality of those who had surrendered to Allah. Class, status, occupation, gender, ethnicity—none of these mattered at all.

After Muhammad's death, his followers rallied to the standard of the caliph, the successor to the prophet and commander of the faithful, and in a century created an empire that extended from France to the frontiers of China. That empire, the caliphate, centering on Arabia plus the ancient lands of Mesopotamia and Egypt, hugged the Mediterranean. Over time Muslim scholars reflected on the Judeo-Christian and the Greco-Roman heritages, and their writings proved influential when western Europeans discovered them in the twelfth and thirteenth centuries. As it expanded, the caliphate also absorbed rich cultural ingredients from Persia, India, Africa, and Asia.

Dome of the Rock   This magnificent mosque in Jerusalem (built in 691–692) is the third-holiest shrine of Islam—after the Kaaba in Mecca and the Prophet's mosque in Medina. Muslims believe that Muhammad ascended to heaven from this spot.   (Tamir Niv, 2009/Used under license from Shutterstock.com)

Internal rivalries and external threats eventually pulled the caliphate apart. Spain broke away first, then a series of small states across North Africa, then Egypt, then parts of Anatolia. Caliphs sat on their jeweled thrones until 1258 while a succession of foreigners dominated the state. Byzantines, Italian merchants, and Turkish mercenaries were among the most prominent of the caliphate's external foes until the Mongols overwhelmed the caliphate in that year in their bid for world domination. A collection of peoples from the frontiers of Mongolia and China, the Mongols turned the Islamic world so that its back was to the Mediterranean and its face to Asia. Until then, the Islamic world had been very much a part of the West. Since that time, neither the Islamic world nor the West has been quite sure about their relationship.

The Byzantine Empire

As the western Roman Empire was being parceled into kingdoms, the eastern half survived almost intact. In the sixth century, the Roman emperor Justinian (r. 527–565), based in Constantinople, regained several of Rome's former western provinces, reformed the imperial administration, issued a major codification of Roman law, and regulated ecclesiastical affairs. In the next two centuries his successors created new military and administrative institutions to address Muslim threats in the east and Slavic threats in the Balkans.

In 726 Emperor Leo III (r. 717–741) issued the first major revision of Roman law since Justinian's. Leo's code, a drastically abbreviated version of Justinian's, provided a simplified, unified body of law for provincial judges in the empire. In religion, the Orthodox tradition of Christianity began clearly to emerge, based on the writings of the Greek Church Fathers, Greek forms of worship and church discipline, and a close partnership between the emperors and the patriarchs of Constantinople, the highest religious officers. For almost a thousand years this eastern incarnation of the Roman Empire, usually called the Byzantine Empire, preserved the Roman legacy.

In 867 a new and highly talented dynasty, the Macedonian, came to the throne in the person of Basil I (r. 867–886). Until 1025, rulers from this family expanded the empire's frontiers, carried out impressive legal and government reforms, and continued a close partnership with the Orthodox Church. This period proved the high point of Byzantine political, military, and diplomatic influence.

The years after 1025 brought short reigns, disputed successions, aristocratic and ecclesiastical factionalism, a bitter feud with the papacy in Rome over theology and worship, and, worst of all, military threats from the Turks. In 1071 the Byzantines suffered a devastating defeat by the Turks at Manzikert in central Anatolia. Appeals to western Europe for assistance brought not mercenaries to recapture Anatolia from the Turks but Crusaders intent on liberating the Holy Land—the Palestine of Jesus—from the Muslims. In 1204 a crusading army conquered Constantinople, and until 1261 a "Latin Empire" held sway in the east. The Byzantines eventually rallied, expelled the Latins, and restored independent rule. Down to the fall of Constantinople to the Turks in 1453, however, Byzantium was a shadow of its former self.

Western Europe

In Late Antiquity the Roman West had been divided among several Germanic kingdoms. Those that did not confront more powerful neighbors, that experienced reasonable religious harmony, and that had room to expand managed to succeed. Thus, the late antique heritage fell to the Franks in Gaul and the Anglo-Saxons in Britain.

By the middle of the eighth century, continental Europe was dominated by a single family whom we call "Carolingian" from *Carolus Magnus,* Charles the Great (or Charlemagne). Charlemagne's dynasty united France, the Low Countries, most of Germany, northern Italy, and northeastern Spain into a single empire that lasted in reality for a few generations—and in memory for a millennium—as "Christendom." In 800 Charlemagne was crowned emperor in Rome by the pope. By force of will the Carolingians imposed standards of worship, education, law, and institutions throughout Christendom. Their success was very uneven, but much of the similarity in the later history of the western European countries derives from their common Carolingian past.

In Britain, Germanic Anglo-Saxons from continental Europe jostled with local Celts, especially in Wales and Scotland. Anglo-Saxon, or English, Britain was moving toward unity, as were Wales and Scotland, until attacks by the Vikings. These seaborne raiders from Scandinavia provoked a crisis of authority in Britain that was resolved to the advantage of the central government only in Scotland. In 1013 and again in 1066, bands of Northmen conquered England. Bands of Vikings called Varangians founded the beginnings of a new state near Kiev in Ukraine. Vikings attacked the Continent too, but so did Muslims in the south and Magyars, the ancestors of the Hungarians, in the east. The Carolingian Empire, already weakened by struggles among Charlemagne's descendants, succumbed to these attacks and crumbled into a number of kingdoms and smaller political entities.

For more than two centuries social and political development was more creative at the local than at the central level. Powerful men (lords) forced lesser men (vassals) into bonds of dependence that we usually refer to as feudalism. Vassals pledged homage (honor), fealty (fidelity), and service; lords promised maintenance and protection. To maintain their vassals, lords sometimes gave them fiefs—estates consisting of farms and peasants.

Between the collapse of the Carolingian Empire around 900 and the renewal of central authority around 1150, Europe experienced effective government only at the local level. In fact, counties, duchies, principalities, and cities displayed an amazing institutional creativity. The population of Europe expanded dramatically, perhaps doubling in two and a half centuries. Trade expanded everywhere. In a sense, Europe grew physically. New states emerged in the Celtic world (Ireland, Scotland, Wales), in Scandinavia (Denmark, Norway, Sweden), and in the Slavic regions (Poland, Bohemia, Serbia, Hungary, Bulgaria, Kievan Rus). The Crusades extended Europe's frontier to Muslim Palestine. People everywhere felled forests, drained marshes, and brought new land into cultivation.

Twelfth- and thirteenth-century Europe was marked by a series of struggles for authority between secular and religious rulers. If, as all seemed to agree, government existed to promote eternal salvation, who was to have final authority: the pope and the ecclesiastical hierarchy or the emperor and other secular rulers? No land in Europe escaped these battles between 1050 and 1300. The Catholic

Church, with its elaborate administration, its sophisticated canon law, and its command of people's spiritual loyalties, won most of the early battles. Then, slowly, secular governments began to define their responsibilities in nonreligious terms and to treat churches as subordinate institutions. By 1300 the church was exhausted from decades of struggles with a variety of rulers, European society had become more secular, and public institutions were growing more effective. The advantageous position the church had enjoyed in, say, 1100 or 1200 had been reversed by 1300.

Central governments gained strength as kings promoted themselves through ceremonies, built up their financial resources, won key military victories, reduced great aristocrats to submission, and allied themselves to rising urban and commercial movements. But Europe was a complex place, and the governments were fragile. England, France, and Spain were headed toward centralization by 1300 but then suffered reverses and differed sharply in their basic institutional structures. Imperial and royal power collapsed in Germany. Italy remained disunited but its many urban communes produced regimes of infinite variety and robust creativity. In 1300 Europe was teeming in its political complexity.

European culture was likewise rich and complex. Latin culture was primarily religious culture, fostered by the church. The church needed educated clergy to carry out its tasks of preaching and teaching. Moreover, religious leaders were conscious of belonging to a rich intellectual tradition that needed to be mastered and transmitted.

Schools and libraries were found in cathedrals, bishops' churches, and monasteries. Monasteries preserved books and learning while serving as witnesses to a holy way of living.

Gothic Interior, Chartres Cathedral Looking down the early-thirteenth-century nave of Chartres Cathedral provides an opportunity to visualize each of the major building components of Gothic architecture: pointed arch, ribbed vault, point support. The desired verticality is evident. (Éditions Gaud)

Many convents of nuns were also intellectual centers and places where women could attain a control over their lives that was denied them in the male world of lords and vassals. Gradually a new kind of religious intellectual establishment, the university, achieved prominence. Though changed in important ways since its twelfth-century origins, the university has never lost its position as the paramount intellectual institution in the West.

Although medicine and law were important courses of study in some places, university teaching and research were focused primarily on the key texts of the Christian tradition. The approach to those texts was increasingly through the logic of the Greek philosopher Aristotle. Scholasticism is the name for this encounter between Greek logic and Christian revelation. Thomas Aquinas (1225–1274), prolific author, immensely learned scholar, and Paris professor, was the greatest of the Scholastics.

A vernacular culture flourished alongside the Latin culture of the Catholic Church. Literature in Welsh and Irish had appeared already in the seventh century; Old English literature, capped by the epic poem *Beowulf,* came only a little later. French literature produced an epic—*The Song of Roland*—around 1100, then romances and adventures. German literature preceded French but took longer to reach a high standard. Italian emerged last but was the first to produce a true masterpiece, Dante's *Divine Comedy* of the early fourteenth century. More and more literatures appeared, especially in Scandinavian and Slavic lands. In addition to imaginative literature, law-books, ordinary legal documents, and commercial texts were written in languages other than Latin.

Architecture produced two stunning leaps forward. In Romanesque (after 1050) and Gothic (after 1150) cathedrals, all existing forms were recombined in buoyant new styles that have lost none of their power to move and inspire. Romanesque façades saw the reappearance of large-scale sculpture, lost since antiquity, and freestanding sculpture reappeared. Gothic stained glass was one of medieval Europe's crowning achievements.

Medieval Europe remained a challenging place for women. Public power was generally reserved for men in a society that prized military qualities. Except in convents, church offices were confined to men, as were student and teaching positions in schools and universities. Nevertheless, on Europe's many expanding frontiers, where old conventions were observed less strictly, women had opportunities for social and political power. Bustling, innovative cities accorded women a wide range of occupations. Some women, such as the gifted theologian Hildegard of Bingen (1098–1179), made distinguished contributions to Latin literature, and a number of women, such as Marie de France (active ca. 1170), became prominent as vernacular authors. Women played key roles in the many new religious movements of the Middle Ages. The thirteenth-century Beguines made up the first religious movement created by and only for women in the history of Christianity.

FROM MEDIEVAL TO RENAISSANCE EUROPE, 1300–1500

The biblical Book of Revelation depicts Four Horsemen of the Apocalypse: war, slaughter, famine, and death. Those grim riders trod hard on fourteenth-century Europe.

Crisis and Recovery

Old hostilities dragged France and England into the conflict now known as the "Hundred Years' War" (1337–1453), which, before it ended, drained the talent and treasure of many parts of Europe. This conflict was only one of the age's struggles. Trade wars rocked the Baltic and North Seas, religious and ethnic battles flared in the Holy Roman Empire (as the German Empire came to be called), Christian-Muslim struggles continued in Spain, peasants rebelled in France and England, and workers staged revolts in Flanders and Italy. Violence seemed to be the norm.

To all this slaughter must be added economic dislocation. Several problems combined to produce economic and social crisis. Population began leveling off in the thirteenth century. The weather turned foul. And in 1348 Europe was visited by an outbreak of bubonic plague that carried off perhaps one-third of the population and worked its cruelest ravages on the cities that were Europe's most creative, productive areas. The epidemic of 1348–1349 was only the first of many recurrences of the plague.

A sense of despair fell over a Christian society convinced that God was punishing it. But for what? Moralists complained about dissolute living, and ecclesiastical powers worried about heresy. Jews sometimes became scapegoats as people sought to blame others for their own misfortunes.

The church could not salve Europe's wounds because it too was going through deep struggles. By the end of the thirteenth century the papacy seemed focused more on political power than on spiritual leadership. From 1305 to 1378 the popes resided not in Rome but in Avignon, in the south of what is now France. They had settled there temporarily to settle some outstanding controversies with the French monarchy but scandalized people all over Europe by staying for three-quarters of a century. When the popes tried to return to Rome, the college of cardinals, the aristocrats of the church, split into factions. From 1378 to 1417 the Catholic Church suffered the Great Schism, as two or more men claimed to be the legitimate pope. The schism was healed and the pope restored to Rome only after a council proclaimed a new vision of church government: "conciliarism" maintained that the church was not a monarchy under the pope but a collegial body of all bishops. Churchmen argued for years over the implications of this pronouncement.

After surmounting these trials, western Europe began to recover in the fifteenth and early sixteenth centuries. France emerged from its long war with England with a greatly strengthened royal government that could raise armies, collect taxes, and control nobles. England suffered through a civil war after the Hundred Years' War but then, after 1485, began a long, steady process of political consolidation under the Tudor dynasty. Major compromises in 1356 provided the Holy Roman Empire with a formula not for unity but at least for stability. The Spanish monarchies grew stronger by the year. In Italy a profusion of independent cities deferred, by choice or by force, to Florence, Milan, or Venice.

The Renaissance

The years from 1300 to about 1550 were both constructive and destructive in the political and material realms but were boundlessly creative in the cultural realms. This was the Renaissance (from a French word meaning "rebirth"). Its pioneers were Italians, who believed that they were calling back to life the spirit, the ideals, of classical Greece and Rome. They sought out works of classical literature and combed through them for models of style and for long-lost gems of practical wisdom and guidance. Though by no means irreligious, Renaissance writers were more concerned with the ancient world, and their own world, than they were the next. We call them "humanists" because of their interest in the humane disciplines. The "study of humanity" (*studia humanitatis*) that was central to the Renaissance was grounded in the seven so-called liberal arts—grammar, rhetoric, logic, arithmetic, astronomy, geometry, and music—that had formed the core of Western education since antiquity. The "arts" were the skills or methods used by the "liberal"—literally, the free—in the conduct of their affairs in society. Armed with the liberal arts, the humanists sought beauty and harmony; they cultivated elegance in the spoken and written word. Their achievements in literature, art, and architecture represent for many the dawn of a new age.

"They," however, were mostly men. A great historian has asked whether women had a Renaissance at all. Some women humanists have come to light, and the importance of vernacular writers such as Christine de Pizan (1364–1430) and Marguerite de Navarre (1492– 1549) has long been acknowledged. But women's daily lives do not seem to have changed much during the Renaissance.

The Renaissance was disseminated from Italy—first by northerners who had studied in the south and then, after 1454, by printing, which made books and ideas more accessible than ever before. In northern Europe, Renaissance scholars turned to the sources of the Christian tradition—to the Scriptures and the Church Fathers—with the same zeal and scholarship that the Italians had applied to classical sources. Such study led some figures to harsh criticism of the institutional, intellectual, and moral failings of the late medieval Catholic Church.

The Pietà Michelangelo sculpted three versions of Mary holding the crucified Jesus. This late, unfinished work reveals Michelangelo's desire to show the suffering of Christ. (Scala/Art Resource, NY)

GLOBALIZATION, RELIGIOUS REFORMATION, POLITICAL TRANSFORMATION, 1500–1560

As the Renaissance was wending its way through European space and consciousness, other momentous changes began to appear. Spanish and Portuguese explorers and conquerors had begun building vast overseas empires in North and South America and in the Indian Ocean basin. The whole globe was being brought within the orbit of Western civilization. The European world was riven by religious differences that reflected old political and cultural divisions and generated new tensions. The late medieval state system was marked by ever larger empires and ever more intricate, and fickle, alliances.

Europe and the Wider World

A glance at a map of the world today will show that Europe is not especially well placed for global domination. It is smaller than other continents, its population is modest, and its material resources are unexceptional. One of the important questions in world history is why it was Europeans, of all peoples, who succeeded in exploring and exploiting the rest of the world.

Europeans long had had contacts with non-Europeans. From ancient times, trade routes running across Africa and Asia had brought the products of the whole world to Europe's markets. Occasional bursts of crusading ferocity or missionary zeal carried Europeans beyond their own frontiers. Travelers, such as the renowned Italian Marco Polo (1254–1324), were sometimes drawn by an irresistible urge to know what lay beyond the horizon. Nevertheless, most Europeans traveled little and knew almost nothing about the world.

In the fifteenth century an accumulation of factors changed forever Europe's place on earth. Travel literature aroused some people's curiosity. Real and imagined threats from the Turks fanned the remaining embers of crusading and missionary zeal. Above all, the Italian stranglehold on Mediterranean trade encouraged other nations to seek alternative commercial routes. New technologies for sailing and navigation made possible long voyages beyond the security of familiar coastlines. Better maps and charts and improved ship and sail designs— some of the latter borrowed from the non-European world—gave Europeans distinct advantages. The consolidation of powerful states such as Spain and, a century later, France and England put financial resources at the disposal of brave and ambitious seamen.

From modest explorations of the West African coast sponsored by the Portuguese royal family, European involvement with the rest of the world expanded to the creation of vast empires. By 1560 the Spanish had conquered southwestern North America, Central America, and South America, except for Brazil, which fell to Portugal. The Portuguese had established military and commercial bases in the Indian Ocean and the South China Sea. The Dutch would eventually contest Portuguese control of the seas and islands lying to the south of China, as well as land colonists in southern Africa and North America. Yet the Dutch presence in North America would pale into insignificance before the territorial acquisitions of France and England.

Did Europeans bring real benefits to the rest of the world, or were they merely cruel exploiters? How did the non-Western world influence the West? People continue to argue over these questions. What cannot be denied is that during the 1500s, Western civilization assumed a role in world history that it had never held before.

A Mystical Reformer Saint Teresa of Avila came from a converso family. She believed that renewal within the Christian church would come through mysticism, prayer, and a return to traditional religious practices. She founded a reformed Carmelite order of nuns to further religious renewal in Spain. (Institut Amatller d'Art Hispanic)

Religious Divisions

For hundreds of years after Charlemagne (r. 768–814), many people held up the ideal of Europe as "Christendom." Christianity was seen as a badge of citizenship in a world where the purpose of governments—indeed of organized societies—was to assist people in their quest for eternal salvation.

A truly Christian political order that transcended national boundaries never existed in the Middle Ages, but a fundamentally Christian society certainly did. The beliefs of ordinary people were not their own affair. Deviation from official beliefs brought swift punishment. "Correct" belief was nurtured, imposed, and reinforced in countless ways. Most schools were run by the church to promote religious learning and culture. The major turning points of life—birth, baptism, marriage, death—were attended by religious ceremonies. Celebrations, from royal feasts to humble village revels, were held on saints' days. Christianity, and churchmen, were literally and figuratively inescapable.

In the sixteenth century western Europe's religious life was sundered in unprecedented ways by a series of developments that are usually called the Protestant Reformation. The reformers shared fundamental beliefs. The first was that everything necessary for salvation had been revealed by God in the Bible; thus, the teachings of the Catholic Church were as nothing compared to the word of God. The second was that salvation resulted from faith in God and from God's grace;

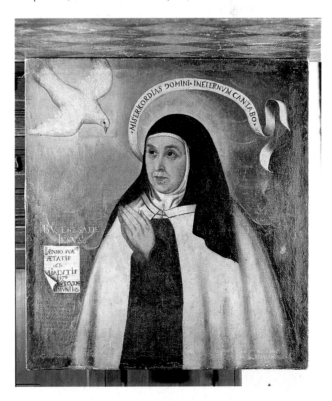

thus, good works and upright behavior were no guarantees of salvation. The name *Protestant* was coined in 1529 and has become a common designation for many groups of people who both dissented from the Catholic Church and embraced devout views of their own.

Protestant reformers such as the German Martin Luther (1483-1546) and the French-born John Calvin (1509-1564) sought to restore Christianity to the form they believed it had possessed in the first centuries of its existence. Royal reformers such as Henry VIII of England (r. 1509-1547) decreed the reform of the church in their lands. Fiery radicals wished to cast down the existing order of society in the name of a purified religion, and humble pietists sought to withdraw from all social and political entanglements. The Catholic Church corrected many of the abuses that had offended its critics but reaffirmed its basic teachings at the Council of Trent (1545-1563). There was no longer a possibility of attaining or enforcing a single pattern of belief. The Roman Catholic Church and Catholic rulers had permanently lost their control of England and Scotland, Scandinavia, the Netherlands, Switzerland, and northern Germany.

Many of the political and diplomatic controversies of the sixteenth century were related to religious issues. The English crown vastly strengthened itself by promoting religious reform, while bitter religious quarrels threatened more than once to destroy the French monarchy. Spain set itself up as the guardian of Catholic orthodoxy but usually lacked the power to impose its will in matters of religion. Since the Holy Roman emperors were Catholic, and most northern German rulers were Protestant, religious divisions worsened old antagonisms and generated new ones.

The Protestant Reformation did not dramatically alter the roles of women in European society or in the Christian churches. From the beginning, ambivalence marked women's participation in the Christian religion. On the one hand, the teachings of Jesus proclaimed the essential equality of women and men and opened heaven equally to both. On the other hand, both Protestant and Catholic Churches denied official and educational roles to women. The reformers were not social revolutionaries. They said, for example, that a housewife was as pleasing to God as a nun, but they refused to suppose that a woman could be a minister. And the Protestants' closing of convents denied some women the intellectual and administrative opportunities long available in those houses.

States and Empires

Europe's state system was dominated by two multi-ethnic empires. Through marriage alliances, the Habsburg family, originally from Switzerland, had established extensive claims: to Spain and its overseas empire, to parts of Italy and much of Austria, to the crown of the Holy Roman Empire, to Burgundy, and to the Netherlands. The Habsburg dominions literally surrounded France. The chief dynamic in western Europe was continuing rivalry between the Habsburgs and the Valois rulers of France. At the opposite end of Europe, the empire of the Muslim Ottoman Turks reached from central Asia to the gates of Vienna.

Other states in Europe sought a place alongside the greater ones. Scandinavia was dominated by Sweden, whose rulers continually entered the complicated politics of northern Germany. Those complications, and Sweden's opportunities, were directly tied to the fluctuating influence of the Holy Roman emperors. Prussia, a small Baltic state founded by German knights and adventurers, was hemmed in by other German states, Sweden, Lithuania, and, on occasion, Russia. In the fifteenth century, the Russians threw off the yoke of the Mongols and began expanding to the east, without ever losing sight of their western frontier with Germanic and Slavic Europe or their southern frontier with the Turks. The Turks threatened, or at least contemporaries perceived them to threaten, the Holy Roman Empire in the northern Balkans, Russia in the Black Sea region, and Italian merchants all over the Mediterranean. The traders of Venice and Genoa, in particular, were anxious about their old commercial superiority after the Portuguese and the Spanish opened vast new economic opportunities as a result of their commercial exploitation of the Americas, Africa, and the Indian Ocean basin.

In the fourteenth century the Florentine man of letters Francesco Petrarch (1304-1374) and his contemporaries, the earliest humanists, explicitly stated their feeling that they were unlike the people and times that had just preceded them and were instead similar to the ancient Romans. Petrarch and the others created the traditional tripartite division of Western history into ancient, modern, and the part in the middle—the so-called Middle Ages, or Dark Ages.

Scholars today do not think Petrarch was right either in his dismissal of the medieval period as the "Dark Ages" or in his claim that he and his contemporaries resembled the Romans. His argument reveals more about how people thought in his period than about the realities of the past. Modern historians do not see sharp breaks between historical periods. Historians now talk about continuity and change operating in tandem. Nevertheless, the old three-part division persists because it represents the major way in which we in the West have reflected on our history and because broad chronological divisions accommodate academic programs of study. In this volume, you will explore the possibilities and paradoxes, triumphs and tragedies of the modern phase of Western civilization.

THOMAS F. X. NOBLE

15

CHAPTER OUTLINE

Imperial Spain and the Limits of Royal Power

Religious and Political Conflict in France and England

The Holy Roman Empire and the Thirty Years' War

Economic Change and Social Tensions

Writing, Drama, and Art in an Age of Upheaval

The Saint Bartholomew's Day Massacre   (The Art Archive/Musée des Beaux Arts Lausanne/Gianni Dagli Orti/Picture Desk)

Europe in the Age of Religious Wars, 1560–1648

Three well-dressed gentlemen stand over a mutilated body; one of them holds up the severed head. Elsewhere, sword-wielding men engage in indiscriminate slaughter, even of babies. Corpses are piled up in the background. This painting memorializes the grisly events of August 24, 1572. A band of Catholic noblemen, accompanied by the personal guard of the king of France, had hunted down a hundred Protestant nobles, asleep in their lodgings in and around the royal palace, and murdered them in cold blood. The king and his counselors had planned the murders as a preemptive strike because they feared that other Protestant nobles were gathering an army outside Paris. But the calculated attack became a massacre when ordinary Parisians, overwhelmingly Catholic and believing they were acting in the king's name, turned on their neighbors. About three thousand Protestants were slain in Paris over the next three days.

This massacre came to be called the Saint Bartholomew's Day Massacre for the Catholic saint on whose feast day it fell. Though horrible in its scope, the slaughter was not unusual in the deadly combination of religious and political antagonisms it reflected. Religious conflicts were, by definition, intractable political conflicts, since virtually every religious group felt that all others were heretics who could not be tolerated and must be eliminated. Rulers of all faiths looked to divine authority and religious institutions to uphold their power.

In the decades after 1560, existing political tensions led to instability and violence, especially when newly reinforced by religious differences. Royal governments continued to consolidate authority, but resistance to royal power by provinces, nobles, or towns accustomed to independence now might have a religious sanction. Warfare over these issues had consumed the Holy Roman Empire in the first half of the sixteenth century. The conflict now spilled over into France and the Netherlands and threatened to erupt in England. In the early seventeenth century, the Holy Roman Empire once again was wracked by a war simultaneously religious and political in origin. Regardless of its roots, warfare itself had become more destructive than ever before thanks to innovations in military technology and campaign tactics. Tensions everywhere were also worsened by economic changes, especially soaring prices and unemployment. The political and religious struggles of the era took place against a background of increasing want, and economic distress was often expressed in both political and religious terms.

FOCUS QUESTIONS

- What circumstances permitted Spain's ambitious policies and to what degree were they successful?

- What conditions led to civil war in France? How did religious and political conflict develop differently in England?

- Why did war erupt again within the Holy Roman Empire and what was the significance of the conflict?

- What caused the economic stresses of these decades and how did ordinary people cope with them?

- In what ways do the literature and art of this period reflect the political, social, and religious conflicts of the age?

This icon will direct you to additional materials on the website: www .cengage.com/history/ noble/westciv6e.

See our interactive eBook for map and primary source activities.

A period of tension, even extraordinary violence, in political and social life, the era of the late sixteenth and early seventeenth centuries was also distinguished by great creativity in some areas of cultural and intellectual life. The plays of Shakespeare, for example, mirrored the passions, but also reflected on the dilemmas of the day and helped to analyze Europeans' circumstances with a new degree of sophistication.

IMPERIAL SPAIN AND THE LIMITS OF ROYAL POWER

What circumstances permitted Spain's ambitious policies and to what degree were they successful?

Philip II King of Spain (r. 1556–1598), son of Charles V who ruled Spain at the height of its influence.

To contemporary observers, no political fact of the late sixteenth century was more obvious than the ascendancy of Spain. **Philip II** (r. 1556–1598) ruled Spanish conquests in the New World, as well as wealthy territories in Europe, including the Netherlands and parts of Italy. Yet imperial Spain did not escape the political, social, and religious turmoil of the era. Explosive combinations of religious dissent and political disaffection led to revolt against Spain in the Netherlands. This conflict revealed the endemic tensions of sixteenth-century political life: nobles, towns, and provinces trying to safeguard remnants of medieval autonomy against efforts at greater centralization—with the added complications of economic strain and religious division. The revolt also demonstrated the material limits of royal power, since even with treasure from American conquests pouring in, Philip could, at times, barely afford to keep armies in the field. As American silver dwindled in the seventeenth century, Philip's successors faced severe financial and political strains, even in their Spanish domains.

The Revolt of the Netherlands

Philip's power stemmed in part from the far-flung territories he inherited from his father, the Habsburg king of Spain and Holy Roman emperor Charles V: Spain, the Low Countries (the Netherlands), the duchy of Milan, the kingdom of Naples, the conquered lands in the Americas, and the Philippine Islands in Asia. (Control of Charles's Austrian lands had passed to his brother, Ferdinand, Philip's uncle; see **MAP 15.1**.) Treasure fleets bearing silver from the New World began to reach Spain regularly during Philip's reign. Spain was now the engine powering a trading economy unlike any that had existed in Europe before. To supply its colonies, Spain needed timber and other shipbuilding materials from the hinterlands of the Baltic Sea. Grain from the Baltic fed the urban populations of Spain (where wool was the principal cash crop) and the Netherlands, while the Netherlands, in turn, was a source of finished goods, such as cloth. The major exchange point for all of these goods was the city of Antwerp in the Netherlands, the leading trading center of all of Europe by 1550.

The Netherlands were the jewel among Philip's European possessions. These seventeen provinces (constituting mostly the modern nations of Belgium and the Netherlands) had been centers of trade and manufacture since the twelfth century. In the fourteenth and fifteenth centuries, they had enjoyed political importance and a period of cultural innovation under the control of the dukes of Burgundy. Like his father, Philip was, technically, the ruler of each province separately—that is, he was count of Flanders, duke of Brabant, and so forth. (See **MAP 15.2**.) By Philip's reign, a sort of federal system of government had evolved to accommodate the various centers of power. Each province had an assembly (Estates) in which representatives of leading nobility and towns authorized taxation, but each also acknowledged a central administration in Brussels that represented Philip. Heading the council of state in Brussels was a governor-general, Philip's half sister, Margaret of Parma.

BACKGROUND TO THE REVOLT Philip's clumsy efforts to adjust this distribution of power in his favor pushed his subjects in the Netherlands into revolt. Born and raised in Spain, Philip had little real familiarity with the densely populated, linguistically diverse Netherlands, and he never visited there after 1559. Early in his reign, tensions in the Netherlands arose over taxation and Spanish insistence on maintaining tight control. Bad harvests and disruptions of trade, caused by wars in the Baltic region in the 1560s, depressed the Netherlands' economy and made it difficult for the provinces to pay the taxes Spain demanded. When the Peace of Cateau-Cambrésis (kahtoe kam-bray-SEE) of 1559 brought an end to the long struggle between the Habsburgs and the Valois (val-WAH) kings of France, the people of the Netherlands had reason to hope for lower taxes and reduced levels of Spanish control, yet neither was forthcoming. Indeed, Philip named to the council of state in Brussels officials who were Spaniards themselves or had close ties to the Spanish court, bypassing local nobles who had fought for Philip and his father before 1559.

Philip only added to the discontent by unleashing an invigorated repression of heresy. Unlike his father, Philip directed the hunt for heretics, not just at lower-class dissenters, but also at well-to-do Calvinists—followers of the French Protestant religious reformer John Calvin—whose numbers were considerable. Punishment for heresy now included confiscation of family property along with execution of the individual. By 1565, town councils in the Netherlands routinely refused to enforce Philip's religious policies, believing that their prosperity—as well as their personal security—depended on restraint in the prosecution of heresy. Leading nobles also stopped enforcing the policies on their estates.

Encouraged by greater tolerance, Protestants began to hold open-air meetings and attract new converts in many towns. In a series of actions called the "iconoclastic fury," Calvinist townsfolk around the provinces stripped Catholic churches of the relics and statues they believed idolatrous. At the same time, reflecting the economic strain of these years, some townsfolk rioted to protest the price of bread. One prominent nobleman warned Philip, "All trade has come to a standstill, so that there are 100,000 men begging for their bread who used to earn it…which is [important] since poverty can force people to do things which otherwise they would never think of doing."[1]

CHRONOLOGY

1556–1598	Reign of Philip II
1558–1603	Reign of Elizabeth I
1559	Act of Supremacy (England)
1562–1598	Religious wars in France
1565	Netherlands city councils and nobility ignore Philip II's law against heresy
1566	Calvinist "iconoclastic fury" begins in the Netherlands
1567	Duke of Alba arrives in the Netherlands
1571	Defeat of Turkish navy at Lepanto
1576	Sack of Antwerp
1579	Union of Utrecht
1588	Defeat of Spanish Armada
1589–1610	Reign of Henry IV
1598	Edict of Nantes (France)
1609	Truce between Spain and the Netherlands declared
1618–1648	Thirty Years' War
1620	Catholic victory at Battle of White Mountain
1621	Truce between Spain and the Netherlands expires; war between Spain and the Netherlands begins
1629	Peace of Alais
1631	Swedes under Gustav Adolf defeat imperial forces
1635	Peace of Prague
1640–1653	"Long Parliament" in session in England
1648	Peace of Westphalia

THE PROVINCES REVOLT

In early 1567, armed Calvinist insurgents seized two towns in the southern Netherlands in hopes of stirring a general revolt that would secure freedom of worship. Margaret of Parma quelled the uprisings by rallying city governments and loyal nobles, now fearful for their own property and power. But by then, far away in Spain, a decision had been made to send in the Spanish duke of Alba with an army of ten thousand men.

When Alba arrived in August 1567, he repeated every mistake of Spanish policy that had triggered rebellion in the first place. He billeted troops in friendly cities, established new courts to try rebels, arrested thousands of people, executed about a thousand rebels (including Catholics as well as prominent Protestants), and imposed heavy taxes to support his army.

Margaret of Parma resigned in disgust and left the Netherlands. Protestants from rebellious towns escaped into exile, where they were joined by nobles who had been declared traitors for resisting Alba's policies. The most important of these was William of Nassau (NAS-saw), prince of Orange (1533–1584), whose lands outside the Netherlands, in France and the Holy Roman Empire, lay beyond Spanish reach and so could be used to finance continued warfare against Spain. A significant community with military capability began to grow in exile.

In 1572, ships of exiled Calvinist privateers, known as the "Sea Beggars," began preying on Spanish shipping and coastal fortresses from bases in the northern provinces. These provinces,

🌐 **MAP 15.1—The Spanish Habsburgs and Europe, ca. 1556**

Philip II's control of territories in northern Italy permitted the overland access of Spanish troops to the Netherlands and heightened the Spanish threat to France. Lands bordering the western Mediterranean made the sea a natural sphere of Spanish influence as well. Habsburg lands in central Europe were controlled after 1556 by Charles V's brother Ferdinand and his descendants.

increasingly Calvinist, became the center of opposition to the Spanish, who concentrated their efforts against rebellion in the wealthier southern provinces. Occasionally, the French and English lent aid to the rebels.

The war in the Netherlands was a showcase for the new and costly technology of warfare in this period. Many towns were (or came to be, as a consequence of the revolt) equipped with "bastions," newly designed walled defenses that could resist artillery fire; such cities could not be taken by storm. Where bastions had been built, military campaigns consisted of grueling sieges, skirmishes in surrounding areas for control of supplies, and occasional pitched battles between besiegers and forces attempting to break the siege. Vast numbers of men were required, both for effective besieging forces and for garrisoning the many fortresses that controlled the countryside and defended access to major towns.

In an attempt to supply the Netherlands with veteran troops and materiel from Spain and Spanish territories in Italy, the Spanish developed the "Spanish Road," an innovative string of supply depots where provisions could be gathered in advance of troops marching to the Netherlands (see **MAP 15.1**). Maintaining its large armies, however, taxed Spain's resources

The City of Antwerp   Antwerp, in the southern Netherlands, was the point of sale for Portuguese spices brought around Africa from India; the selling and transshipping center for Baltic goods, including timber, fur, and grain; and the source for manufactured goods such as cloth.   (Musées royaux des Beaux-Arts de Belgique)

to the breaking point. Even with American silver at hand, Philip could, at times, barely afford to keep armies in the field. Inevitably, large numbers of troops also exhausted the country-side, and both soldiers and civilians suffered great privations. On occasion, Spanish troops reacted violently to difficult conditions and to delayed pay (American treasure dwindled badly between 1572 and 1578). In 1576, they sacked the hitherto loyal city of Antwerp and massacred about eight thousand people. Bitterly remembered as the "Spanish Fury," the massacre prompted leaders in the southern provinces to raise their own armies to protect themselves against the Spanish. Late in 1576, they concluded an alliance with William of Orange and the northern rebels.

The alliance between northern and southern provinces did not last. The provinces were increasingly divided by religion, and their differences were skillfully exploited by Philip's new commander, Margaret of Parma's son Alexander Farnese (far-NAY-zee), duke of Parma. With silver from America filling the king's coffers again, Parma wooed the Catholic elites of the southern provinces back into loyalty to Philip, in return for promises to respect their provincial liberties and safeguard their property from troops.

FORMATION OF THE UNITED PROVINCES

In 1579, the northern provinces united in a defensive alliance, the Union of Utrecht (OO-trekt), against the increasingly unified south. Parma's forces could not push beyond the natural barrier of rivers that bisect the Low Countries (see **MAP 15.2**), particularly as Spain diverted money to conflicts with England in 1588 and France after 1589. In 1609, a truce was finally concluded between Spain and the northern provinces. This truce did not formally recognize the "United Provinces" as an independent entity, though in fact they were. The modern

North Sea

MAP 15.2—The Netherlands, 1559–1609
The seventeen provinces of the Netherlands were strikingly diverse politically, economically, and culturally.

0   50   100 Km.

0   50   100 Mi.

United Provinces as of 1609

Spanish Netherlands

— Truce line, 1609

— Boundary of the Holy Roman Empire

United Provinces The seven northern provinces of the Low Countries that successfully revolted against Spanish rule in the late sixteenth century and became the modern nation of the Netherlands.

Armada Massive fleet of Spanish warships sent against England by Philip II but defeated by the English navy and bad weather in 1588. The tactics used by the English helped set the future course of naval warfare.

nations of Belgium (the southern Spanish provinces) and the Netherlands are the distant result of this truce.

The independent **United Provinces** (usually called, simply, the Netherlands) was a fragile state, an accident of warfare at first. But commercial prosperity began to emerge as its greatest strength. Much of the economic activity of Antwerp had shifted north to Amsterdam in the province of Holland because of fighting in the south and a naval blockade of Antwerp by rebel ships. Philip's policies had created a new enemy nation and had enriched it at his expense.

In addition, the revolt of the Netherlands lured Spain into wider war, particularly against England. Spain and England had a common foe in France and common economic interests, and Philip had married Mary Tudor, the Catholic queen of England (r. 1553–1558). Even after Mary's death and the accession of her Protestant half sister, Queen Elizabeth (r. 1558–1603), Spanish-English relations remained cordial. Relations started to sour, however, when Elizabeth began tolerating the use of English ports by the rebel Sea Beggars and authorizing attacks by English privateers on Spanish treasure fleets. In response, Spain supported Catholic resistance to Elizabeth within England, including plots to replace her on the throne with her Catholic cousin, Mary, Queen of Scots. Greater Spanish success in the Netherlands, raids by the Spanish and English on each other's shipping, and Elizabeth's execution of Mary in 1587 prompted Philip to order an invasion of England. A fleet (*armada*) of Spanish warships sailed in 1588.

"The enterprise of England," as the plan was called in Spain, represented an astounding logistical effort. The **Armada** was supposed to clear the English Channel of English ships in order to permit an invading force—troops under Parma in the Netherlands—to cross on barges. The sheer number of ships required —about 130—meant that some, inevitably, were slower supply ships, or vessels designed for the more protected waters of the Mediterranean. The English also had the advantage in arms, since they had better long-range artillery and better-trained gunners. Spain's Armada was defeated by the English and by bad weather that dispersed much of the fleet. The invasion failed and fewer than half of the 130-ship Armada ever made it back to Spain.

Successes at Home and Around the Mediterranean

Despite his overseas empire and his preoccupation with the Netherlands, many of Philip's interests still centered on the Mediterranean. In his kingdoms of Spain and their Mediterranean sphere of interest, Philip made his power felt more effectively, though not without effort.

Philip's father, Charles V, had tried to secure the western Mediterranean against the Ottoman Turks and their client states along the African coast, but it was under Philip that the Turkish challenge in the western Mediterranean receded. The Spanish allied temporarily with the papacy and Venice—both were concerned with Turkish naval power in the Mediterranean—and their combined navies inflicted a massive defeat on the Turkish navy at Lepanto, off the coast of Greece, in October 1571 (see **MAP 15.1**). The Turks remained the leading power in the eastern Mediterranean,

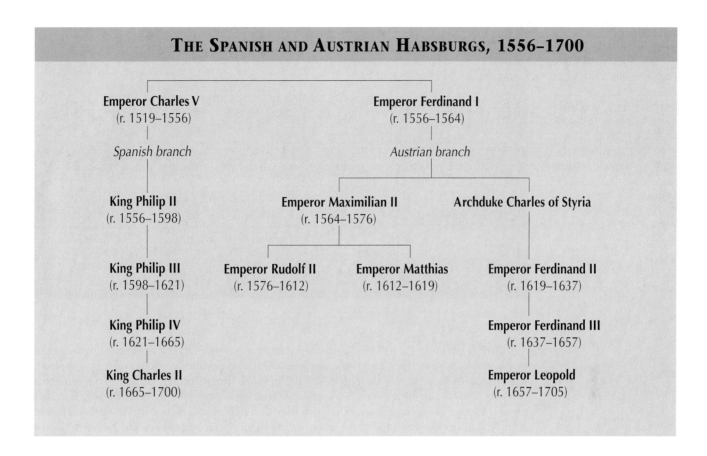

THE SPANISH AND AUSTRIAN HABSBURGS, 1556–1700

Emperor Charles V
(r. 1519–1556)

Spanish branch

Emperor Ferdinand I
(r. 1556–1564)

Austrian branch

King Philip II
(r. 1556–1598)

Emperor Maximilian II
(r. 1564–1576)

Archduke Charles of Styria

King Philip III
(r. 1598–1621)

Emperor Rudolf II
(r. 1576–1612)

Emperor Matthias
(r. 1612–1619)

Emperor Ferdinand II
(r. 1619–1637)

King Philip IV
(r. 1621–1665)

Emperor Ferdinand III
(r. 1637–1657)

King Charles II
(r. 1665–1700)

Emperor Leopold
(r. 1657–1705)

but their ability to threaten Spain and Spanish possessions in the West was over.

To Philip and his advisers, the Turks represented a potential internal threat as well, since it was feared that they might incite rebellion among his Muslim subjects. These were the nominally Christian descendants of the Muslims of Granada, who had been conquered by the Spanish in 1492. Called moriscos, they had been forced to convert to Christianity in 1504 or be expelled from Spain. Yet, no serious effort had been made to teach them Christian beliefs in their own language (Arabic), and they had not been assimilated into Spanish society. Philip inaugurated a new wave of persecution and provoked a massive rebellion by the moriscos that began on Christmas Day in 1568. The revolt took two years to suppress. After it was crushed, the moriscos of Granada were forcibly exiled and dispersed farther north in Spain.

Philip II in 1583 Dressed in the austere black in fashion at the Spanish court, Philip holds a rosary and wears the Order of the Golden Fleece, an order of knighthood, around his neck. Though conscientious to a fault, Philip was a rigid, unimaginative man ill-suited to meet the challenges he faced. (Philip II of Spain (1527–98) 1565 (oil on canvas), Anguissola, Sofonisba (c. 1532–1625)/Prado, Madrid, Spain /The Bridgeman Art Library)

The Battle of Lepanto On October 7, 1571, vessels of the Holy League (Spain, Venice, and the papacy) defeated the Ottoman fleet off the coast of Greece. Lepanto was the last great battle between galleys—the oared warships that had dominated Mediterranean waters since ancient times. (Courtesy, National Maritime Museum)

Philip's power in each of his Spanish kingdoms was limited by the traditional privileges of towns, nobility, and clergy. In Aragon, for example, he could raise revenues only by appealing to local assemblies, the Cortes (core-TEZ). Philip made inroads into Aragonese independence by the end of his reign, however, because noble feuds and peasant rebellions during the 1580s provided an excuse to send in veteran troops from the Netherlands campaigns to establish firmer control. Philip was successful, in the long run, in Aragon, as he had not been in the Netherlands, because he used adequate force but tempered it afterward with constitutional changes that were cleverly moderate. He cemented the peace by appearing in Aragon in person, in the words of a contemporary, "like a rainbow at the end of a storm."[2]

In Castile, the arid kingdom in the center of the Iberian Peninsula, the king was able to levy taxes more easily, but only because of concessions that gave nobles undisputed authority over their peasants. Philip established his permanent capital, Madrid, and his principal residence, the Escorial, there. The Spanish Empire became more and more Castilian as the reign progressed, with royal advisers and counselors increasingly drawn only from the Castilian elite. Yet, the rural economy of Castile was stunted by the dual oppression of landholders and royal tax collectors.

Philip also invaded and annexed Portugal in 1580, temporarily unifying the Iberian Peninsula. The annexation was ensured by force but had been preceded by careful negotiation to guarantee that Philip's claim to the throne—through his mother—would find some support within the country. When Philip died in 1598, he was old and ill, a man for whom daily life had become a painful burden. His Armada had been crushed; the Netherlands had slipped through his fingers. Yet, he had been more successful, by his own standards, in other regions that he ruled.

Spain in Decline, 1600–1648

Spain steadily lost ground economically and strategically after the turn of the century. Imports of silver declined. The American mines were exhausted, and the natives forced to work in them were decimated by European diseases and brutal treatment. Spain's economic health was also threatened by the very success of its colonies: Local industries in the Americas began to produce goods formerly obtained from Spain. Also, Spanish colonists could now buy, from English, French, and Dutch traders, many of the goods they needed. Often, these competitors' goods were cheaper than Spanish ones. Spanish productivity was low and prices were high because of the inflationary effects of the influx of American silver.

Spain renewed hostilities with the United Provinces in 1621, after the truce of 1609 had expired. Philip IV (r. 1621–1665) also aided his Habsburg cousins in the Thirty Years' War in the Holy Roman Empire (see page 428). Squeezed for troops and revenue for these commitments, other Spanish territories revolted. The uprisings reflected both economic distress and unresolved issues of regional autonomy. Castile bore the brunt of the financial support of the state. When Philip IV's chief minister tried to distribute the burdens more equitably among the various regions of Spain, rebellions broke out in Catalonia and Portugal.

In Catalonia, a province of the kingdom of Aragon, Spain resumed control only in 1652, after years of fighting and promises to respect Catalan liberties. In Portugal, a war of independence began in 1640, launched by a popular revolt against Spanish policies. The Spanish government tried to restore order with troops under the command of a leading Portuguese prince, John, duke of Braganza. The duke, however, was the nearest living relative to the last king of Portugal, and he seized this opportunity to claim the crown of Portugal for himself. Although war dragged on until 1668, the Portuguese, under John IV (r. 1640–1656), succeeded in winning independence from Spain. In 1647, upheaval would shake Spain's Italian possessions of Sicily and Naples. By mid-century, Spain had lost its position as the preeminent state in Europe.

SECTION SUMMARY

- Spain was the most powerful state in Europe in the second half of the sixteenth century because it controlled territory in Italy and in the Netherlands, as well as colonies in the Americas.

- The prosperous Netherlands revolted against Spanish control for political, economic, and religious reasons.

- The invention of new kinds of fortifications increased the cost and destructiveness of the war.

- The northern provinces within the Netherlands, called the United Provinces, won independence from Spanish control by 1609.

- Spain attempted, but failed, to invade England with the Armada.

- The Spanish state weakened economically and politically in the seventeenth century as its income from colonies declined.

RELIGIOUS AND POLITICAL CONFLICT IN FRANCE AND ENGLAND

What conditions led to civil war in France? How did religious and political conflict develop differently in England?

In the second half of the sixteenth century, France was convulsed by civil war that had both religious and political causes. A fragile peace was achieved by 1598, but the kingdom was still divided by religion and by military and political challenges to royal authority. England, in contrast, was spared political and religious upheaval in the second half of the century, in part because of the talents and long life of its ruler, Elizabeth I. But in the seventeenth century, religious dissent and political opposition combined to dramatically threaten royal power.

The French Religious Wars, 1562–1598

Civil war wracked France from 1562 until 1598. As in the Netherlands, the conflicts in France had religious and political origins and international consequences. The French monarch, like Philip, was unable to monopolize military power. In 1559, the king of France, Henry II (r. 1547–1559), had concluded the Peace of Cateau-Cambrésis with Philip II, ending the Habsburg-Valois Wars, but died in July of that year from wounds suffered at a tournament held to celebrate the new treaty. His death was a political disaster. Great noble families vied for influence over his young sons, Francis II (r. 1559–1560) and Charles IX (r. 1560–1574). The queen mother, Catherine de' Medici (day MAY-di-chi) (1519–1589), worked carefully and intelligently to balance the nobles' interests. But it proved impossible to keep the conflicts among the great courtiers from boiling over into civil war.

In France, as elsewhere, noble conflict invariably had a violent component. Noblemen carried swords and daggers and were accompanied by armed entourages. Provincial land holdings, together with the royal offices they enjoyed, afforded enough resources to support private warfare, and the nobles assumed the right to wage it.

In addition, religious tension was rising throughout France. Public preaching by and secret meetings of Protestants (known as **Huguenots** in France) were causing unrest in towns. At court,

BACKGROUND TO CIVIL WAR

Huguenots French Protestants, followers of the teachings of John Calvin.

Le Maſsacre fait a Vaſsy le premier iour de Mars. 1562.

A. La grange ou l'on preſchoit ou eſtoyent enuiron 1200 perſonnes.
B. Monſieur de Guiſe qui commandoit.
C. Le Miniſtre dedans la Chaire priant Dieu.
D. Le Miniſtre ſe cuydant ſauuer eſt bleſſé en pluſieurs lieux

& euſt eſté tué ſi l'eſpee ne fuſt rompue en deux.
E. Le Cardinal de Guyſe appuyé ſur l; cimentiere de la paroiſſe.
F. Le toict que les gens du preſche rompent pour eux ſauuer.
G. Pluſieurs qui ſe iettans ſur la muraille de la ville ſe ſauuent

aux champs.
H. Pluſieurs qui ſe cuydans ſauuer ſur le toict ſont harque, bouſés.
I. Le tronc des poures arraché,
k. Les trompettes qui ſonnerent par deux diuerſes fois,

Massacre at Vassy This contemporary engraving by two Protestant artists depicts the Duke of Guise (*center left*) and his men coldly butchering Huguenot worshipers at Vassy. In a Catholic version of the event, the Protestants were killed by gunfire after pelting Guise's men with rocks when they tried to disperse the worshipers. (HIP/Art Resource, NY)

members of leading noble families—including the Bourbons, princes of royal blood—had converted to Protestantism and worshiped openly in their rooms in the palace. In 1561, Catherine convened a national religious council to reconcile the two faiths. When it failed, she chose provisional religious toleration as the only practical course and issued a limited edict of toleration of Huguenots (HEW-guh-nots) in the name of the king in January 1562.

The edict solved nothing. Ignoring its restrictions, Protestants armed themselves, while townspeople of both faiths insulted and attacked one another at worship sites and religious festivals. In March 1562, the armed retainers of a Catholic duke killed a few dozen Protestants gathered in worship at Vassy (vah-SEE), near one of the duke's estates. The killing, bringing the military power of the nobility to bear on the broader problem of religious division, sparked the first of six civil wars.

DECADES OF CIVIL WAR In some ways, the initial conflict in 1562 was decisive. The Protestant army lost the principal pitched battle of the war in December. This defeat reduced the appeal of the Protestant movement to nobles. The limited rights granted by the peace edict in 1563 made it difficult for Protestants in towns—where the vast majority of them lived—to worship. But if the Huguenots were not powerful enough to win, neither were they weak enough to be decisively beaten.

The turning point most obvious to contemporaries came a decade later. The Protestant faction, still represented at court by the Bourbon princes and their allies, pressed the king for war against Spain to aid Protestant rebels in the Netherlands. Opposed to another war against Spain and alarmed by rumors of Huguenot armies massing outside Paris, Charles IX (r. 1560–1574) and his mother authorized royal guards to murder the Protestant leaders on August 24, 1572—Saint Bartholomew's Day. These murders touched off a massacre of Protestants throughout Paris and, once news from Paris had spread, throughout the kingdom.

The Saint Bartholomew's Day Massacre revealed the degree to which religious differences had strained the fabric of community life. Neighbor murdered neighbor in an effort to rid the community of heretical pollution; bodies of the dead were mutilated. Gathered in the south of France, the remaining Huguenot forces vowed "never [to] trust those who have so often and so treacherously broken faith and the public peace."[3] Huguenot writers published tracts arguing that royal power was by nature limited and that rebellion was justified against tyrants who overstepped their legitimate authority.

Many Catholics also renounced reconciliation. Some noblemen formed a Catholic league to fight in place of the weakened monarchy. Charles's successor, his brother Henry III (r. 1574–1589), was forced to cooperate with first one of the warring parties and then another. In December 1588, he resorted to murdering two leaders of the ultra-Catholic faction; in turn, he was murdered by a priest in early 1589.

The new king was the Bourbon prince Henry of Navarre, who became Henry IV (r. 1589–1610). He was a Protestant, and he had to fight for his throne. He faced Catholic armies now subsidized by Philip II of Spain, an extremist Catholic city government in Paris, and subjects who were tired of war but mainly Catholic. Given these obstacles, the politically astute Henry agreed to convert to Catholicism.

After his conversion in 1593, many of Henry's subjects believed that only rallying to the monarchy could save France from chaos. In any case, nobles were increasingly inclined to cooperate with the Crown. Service to a successful king was honorable and a source of patronage; Henry was personally esteemed because he was a talented general and brave, gregarious, and charming. The nobility forced the citizens of Paris and other cities to accept Henry's authority. The civil war period thus proved to be an important phase in the accommodation of the nobility to the power of the state.

In April 1598, Henry granted toleration for the Huguenot minority in a royal edict proclaimed in the city of Nantes (NAHNT). The **Edict of Nantes** was primarily a repetition of provisions from the most generous edicts that had ended the various civil wars. Nobles were allowed to practice the Protestant faith on their estates; townspeople were granted more limited rights to worship in selected towns in each region. Protestants were also guaranteed rights of self-defense—specifically, the right to maintain garrisons in about two hundred towns. About half of these garrisons would be paid for by the Crown.

Edict of Nantes 1598 edict of Henry IV, granting France's Protestants (Huguenots) the right to practice their faith and maintain defensive garrisons.

The problem was that the Edict of Nantes, like any royal edict, could be revoked by the king at any time. Moreover, the provision allowing Protestants to keep garrisoned towns reflected concessions to Protestant aristocrats, who could support their followers by paid garrison duty. It also reflected the assumption that living peacefully amid religious diversity might prove to be impossible. Thus, although Henry IV ended the French religious wars, he had not solved the problem of religious and political division within France.

The Consolidation of Royal Authority in France, 1598–1643

During Henry IV's reign, France began to recover from the long years of civil war. Population and productivity began to grow; the Crown increased royal revenue by nibbling away at traditional local self-government and control of taxation.

Yet, Henry's regime was stable only in comparison with the preceding years of civil war. The power of the great nobility had not been definitively broken. Also, the king had agreed to a measure, known as the *paulette* (named for the functionary who first administered it), that allowed royal officeholders to own their offices and to pass on those offices to their heirs in return for the payment of an annual fee. The paulette was primarily a device to raise revenue after decades of civil war, but it also helped cement the loyalty of royal bureaucrats at a critical time, particularly that of the royal judges of the supreme law court, the Parlement of Paris, who had recently agreed to register the Edict of Nantes only under duress. However, the paulette made royal officeholders largely immune from royal control, since their posts were now in effect property, like the landed property of the traditional nobility.

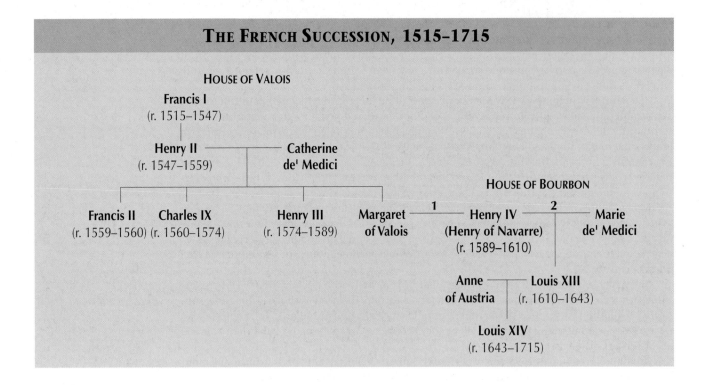

THE FRENCH SUCCESSION, 1515–1715

HOUSE OF VALOIS

Francis I
(r. 1515–1547)

Henry II ———— Catherine
(r. 1547–1559)   de' Medici

HOUSE OF BOURBON

Francis II   Charles IX   Henry III   Margaret ——1—— Henry IV ——2—— Marie
(r. 1559–1560) (r. 1560–1574)   (r. 1574–1589) of Valois   (Henry of Navarre)   de' Medici
                                                                 (r. 1589–1610)

Anne ———— Louis XIII
of Austria   (r. 1610–1643)

Louis XIV
(r. 1643–1715)

In 1610, a fanatical Catholic assassinated Henry IV. Henry's death brought his 9-year-old son, Louis XIII (r. 1610–1643), to the throne with Louis's mother, Marie de' Medici, initially serving as regent. Within four years, Louis faced a major rebellion by his Huguenot subjects in southwestern France. Huguenots felt that Louis's policies, including his recent marriage to a Spanish princess, meant that royal support for toleration was wavering. The war persisted, on and off, for eight years, as the French royal troops, like the Spanish in the Netherlands, had difficulty breaching the defenses of even small fortress towns held by the Protestants. The main Huguenot stronghold was the well-fortified port city of La Rochelle, which had grown wealthy from European and overseas trade. Not until the king took the city, after a siege lasting more than a year, did the Protestants accept a peace on royal terms.

The Peace of Alais (ah-LAY) (1629) reaffirmed the policy of religious toleration but rescinded the Protestants' military and political privileges. It was a political triumph for the Crown because it deprived French Protestants of the means for further rebellion, while reinforcing their dependence on the Crown for religious toleration. Most of the remaining great noble leaders began to convert to Catholicism.

The Peace of Alais was also a personal triumph for the king's leading minister, who crafted the treaty and had directed the bloody siege that made it possible. Armand-Jean du Plessis (1585–1642), Cardinal Richelieu (RISH-el-yiuh), came from a provincial noble family and rose in the service of the queen mother. He was admired and feared for his skill in the political game of seeking and bestowing patronage—a crucial skill in an age when elites received offices and honors through carefully cultivated relationships at court. He and the king—whose sensitive temperament Richelieu handled adeptly—formed a lasting partnership that had a decisive impact, not only on French policy, but also on the entire shape of the French state.

Richelieu favored an aggressive foreign policy to counter what he believed still to be the greatest external threat to the French crown: the Spanish Habsburgs. After war resumed between the Netherlands and Spain in 1621 (see page 428), Richelieu attacked Spanish possessions in Italy, superintended large-scale fighting against Spain in the Netherlands itself, and subsidized Swedish and German Protestant armies fighting the Habsburgs in Germany.

Richelieu's policies were opposed by many French people, who saw taxes double, then triple, in just a few years. Many courtiers and provincial elites favored keeping the peace with Spain, a fellow Catholic state, and objected to alliances with German Protestants. They were also alarmed by the revolts that accompanied the peasants' distress. Their own status was also directly threatened by Richelieu's monopoly of royal patronage and by his creation of new offices, which undermined their power. In 1632, for example, Richelieu created the office of *intendant*. Intendants had wide powers for defense and administration in the provinces that overrode the established bureaucracy.

By 1640, Richelieu's ambitious foreign policy seemed to be bearing fruit. The French had won territory along their northern and eastern borders by their successes against Habsburg forces. But when Richelieu and Louis XIII died within five months of each other, in December 1642 and May 1643, Louis XIII was succeeded by his 5-year-old son, and the warrior-nobility, as well as royal bureaucrats, would waste little time before challenging the Crown's new authority.

Precarious Stability in England: The Reign of Elizabeth I, 1558–1603

England experienced no civil wars during the second half of the sixteenth century, but religious dissent challenged the stability of the monarchy. In **Elizabeth I** (r. 1558-1603), England—in stark contrast to France—possessed an able and long-lived ruler. Elizabeth was well educated in the humanistic tradition and was already an adroit politician at the age of 25, when she acceded to the throne at the death of her Catholic half sister, Mary Tudor (r. 1553-1558).

Elizabeth faced the urgent problem of effecting a religious settlement. Her father, Henry VIII (r. 1509-1547), had broken away from the Catholic Church for political reasons but had retained many Catholic doctrines and practices. A Calvinist-inspired Protestantism had been prescribed for the Church of England by the advisers of Henry's successor, Elizabeth's young half brother, Edward VI (r. 1547- 1553). True Catholicism, such as her half sister Mary had tried to reimpose, was out of the question. The Roman church had never recognized Henry VIII's self-made divorce from Mary's mother and thus regarded Elizabeth as a bastard with no right to the throne.

Elizabeth reimposed royal control over the church and made limited concessions to accommodate the beliefs of a wide range of her subjects. In 1559, Parliament passed a new Act of Supremacy, which restored the monarch as head of the Church of England. Elizabeth dealt with opposition to the act by arresting bishops and lords whose votes would have blocked its passage by Parliament. The official prayer book, in use in Edward's day, was revised to include elements of both traditional and radical Protestant interpretations of Communion. But church liturgy, clerical vestments, and, above all, the hierarchical structure of the clergy closely resembled Catholic practices. The Act of Uniformity, also passed in 1559, required all worship to be conducted according to the new prayer book. Although uniformity was required in worship, Elizabeth was careful, in her words, not to "shine beacons into her subjects' souls."

Catholicism continued to be practiced, especially by otherwise loyal nobility and gentry in the north of England, who worshiped privately on their estates. But priests returning from exile beginning in the 1570s, most newly imbued with the proselytizing zeal of the Counter-Reformation (the Catholic response to the Protestant Reformation), practiced it more visibly and were zealously prosecuted for their boldness. In the last twenty years of Elizabeth's reign, approximately 180 Catholics were executed for treason, two-thirds of them priests. (By 1585, being a Catholic priest in itself was a crime.)

In the long run, the greater threat to the English crown came from the most radical Protestants in the realm, known (by their enemies initially) as **Puritans**. Puritanism was a broad movement for reform of church practice along familiar Protestant lines: an emphasis on Bible reading, preaching, and private scrutiny of conscience; a de-emphasis on institutional ritual and clerical authority. Most Puritans had accepted Elizabeth's religious compromise because they had no choice, but grew increasingly alienated by her insistence on clerical authority and her refusal to change any elements of the original religious settlement. A significant Presbyterian underground movement began to form among them. Presbyterians wanted to dismantle the episcopacy—the hierarchy of priests and bishops—and to govern the church instead with councils, called "presbyteries," that included lay members of the congregation. Laws were passed late in the queen's reign to enable the Crown to prosecute

Elizabeth I Able and long-lived ruler who firmly established Protestantism in England and defended the nation against the Spanish Armada, but who bequeathed financial, religious, and political problems to her successors.

Puritans Radical Protestants in late-sixteenth- and seventeenth-century England who became a majority in Parliament during the reign of Charles I and led opposition to the king.

more easily, and even to force into exile, anyone who attended "nonconformist" (non-Anglican) services.

The greatest challenge Elizabeth faced from Puritans came in Parliament, where they were well represented by many literate gentry. Parliament met only when called by the monarch. In theory, members could merely voice opinions and complaints; they could not initiate legislation and prescribe policy. However, only Parliament could vote taxes. Further, since it had in effect helped constitute royal authority by means of the two Acts of Supremacy, Parliament's merely advisory role had been expanded by the monarchy itself. During Elizabeth's reign, Puritans capitalized on Parliament's enlarged scope, using meetings to press for further religious reform. In 1586, they went so far as to introduce bills calling for an end to the episcopacy and the Anglican prayer book. Elizabeth had to resort to imprisoning one Puritan leader to end debate on the issue and on Parliament's right to address it.

Also during Elizabeth's reign, efforts at English expansion in the New World began, in the form of unsuccessful attempts at colonization and successful raids on Spanish possessions. However, the main focus of her foreign policy remained Europe itself. Elizabeth, like all her forebears, felt her interests tightly linked to the independence of the Netherlands, whose towns were a major outlet for English wool. Philip II's aggressive policy in the Netherlands increasingly alarmed her, especially in view of France's weakness. She began to send small sums of money to the rebels and allowed their ships access to southern English ports, from which they could raid Spanish-held towns on the Netherlands' coast. In 1585, in the wake of the duke of Parma's successes against the rebellions, she committed troops to help the rebels.

Her decision was a reaction, not only to the threat of a single continental power dominating the Netherlands, but also to the threat of Catholicism. From 1579 to 1583, the Spanish had helped the Irish fight English domination and were involved in several plots to replace Elizabeth with her Catholic cousin, Mary, Queen of Scots. These threats occurred as the return of Catholic exiles to England peaked. The victory over the Spanish Armada in 1588 was quite rightly celebrated, for it ended any Catholic threat to Elizabeth's rule.

The success against the Armada has tended to overshadow other aspects of Elizabeth's foreign policy, particularly with regard to Ireland. Since the twelfth century, an Anglo-Irish state, dominated by transplanted English families, had been loosely supervised from England, but most of

Elizabeth I: The Armada Portrait Both serene and resolute, Elizabeth is flanked by "before" and "after" glimpses of the Spanish fleet; her hand rests on the globe in a gesture of dominion that also memorializes the circumnavigation of the globe by her famous captain, Sir Francis Drake, some years before. (Elizabeth I, Armada Portrait, c. 1588 (oil on panel), Gower, George (1540–96) (attr. to)/ Woburn Abbey, Bedfordshire, UK/The Bridgeman Art Library)

Ireland remained under the control of Gaelic chieftains. Just as Charles V and Philip II attempted to tighten their governing mechanisms in the Netherlands, so did Henry VIII's minister, Thomas Cromwell, streamline control of outlying areas such as Wales and Anglo-Ireland. Cromwell proposed that the whole of Ireland be brought under English control, partly by the established mechanism of feudal ties: The Irish chieftains were to pay homage as vassals to the king of England.

Under Elizabeth, this legalistic approach gave way to virtual conquest. Elizabeth's governor, Sir Henry Sidney, appointed in 1565, inaugurated a policy whereby Gaelic lords, by means of various technicalities, could be entirely dispossessed of their lands. Any Englishman capable of raising a private force could help enforce these dispossessions and settle his conquered lands as he saw fit. This policy provoked stiff Irish resistance, which was viewed as rebellion and provided the rationale for further military action, more confiscations of lands, and more new English settlers. Eventually the Irish, with Spanish assistance, mounted a major rebellion, consciously Catholic and aimed against the "heretic" queen. The rebellion gave the English an excuse for brutal suppression and massive transfers of lands to English control. The political domination of the Irish was complete with the defeat, in 1601, of the Gaelic chieftain Hugh O'Neill, lord of Tyrone, who had controlled most of the northern quarter of the island. Although the English were unable to impose Protestantism on the conquered Irish, to Elizabeth and her English subjects, the conquests in Ireland seemed as significant as the victory over the Spanish Armada.

The English enjoyed relative peace at home during Elizabeth's reign. However, her reign ended on a note of strain. The foreign involvements, particularly in Ireland, had been very expensive. Taxation granted by Parliament more than doubled during her reign, and local taxes further burdened the people. Price inflation related to government spending, social problems caused by returned unemployed soldiers, and a series of bad harvests heightened popular resentment against taxation. Despite her achievements, therefore, Elizabeth passed two problems on to her successors: unresolved religious tensions and financial instability. Elizabeth's successors would also find in Parliament an increasing focus of opposition to their policies.

Rising Tensions in England, 1603–1642

In 1603, Queen Elizabeth died, and James VI of Scotland, the Protestant son of Mary, Queen of Scots, ascended to the English throne as James I (r. 1603–1625). Tensions between Anglicans and Puritans were briefly quieted under James because of a plot, in 1605, by Catholic dissenters. The Gunpowder Plot, as it was called, was a conspiracy to blow up the palace housing both king and Parliament at Westminster. Protestants of all stripes again focused on their common enemy, Catholics—though only temporarily.

JAMES I

Financial problems were James's most pressing concern. Court life became more elaborate and an increasing drain on the monarchy's resources. James's extravagance was partly to blame, but so were pressures for patronage from courtiers. To the debts left from the Irish conflicts and wars with Spain, James added new expenses to defend the claims of his daughter and her husband, a German prince, to rule Bohemia (see page 427).

To raise revenue without Parliament's consent, James relied on sources of income that the Crown had enjoyed since medieval times: customs duties, wardship (the right to manage and liberally borrow from the estates of minor nobles), and the sale of monopolies, which conveyed the right to be sole agent for a particular kind of goods. James's increase of the number of monopolies for sale was widely resented. Merchants objected to the arbitrary restriction of production and trade; common people found that they could no longer afford certain ordinary goods, such as soap, under monopoly prices. Criticism of the court escalated, particularly by the nobility, as James indulged in extreme favoritism of certain courtiers. He even created a new noble title—baronet—which he sold to socially ambitious commoners.

When James summoned Parliament to ask for funds in 1621, Parliament used the occasion to protest court corruption and the king's financial measures. The members revived the medieval procedure of impeachment and removed two royal ministers from office. In 1624, still faced with expensive commitments to Protestants abroad, James again called Parliament, which voted new taxes but also openly debated the wisdom of the king's foreign policy.

CHARLES I

Tensions between Crown and Parliament increased under James's son, Charles I (r. 1625–1649). Charles's foreign policy caused both financial strain and political opposition. Charles declared war on Spain and supported the Huguenot rebels in France. Many merchants opposed this

Criticism of Monopolies   Holders of royally granted monopolies were bitterly resented by English consumers and tradespeople alike, as this contemporary print reveals. The greedy beast pictured here controls even ordinary commodities such as pins, soap, and butter.   (Courtesy of the Trustees of the British Museum)

aggressive foreign policy because it disrupted trade. In 1626, Parliament was dissolved without granting any monies, in order to stifle its objections to his policies. Instead, Charles levied a forced loan and imprisoned gentry who refused to lend money to the government.

Above all, Charles's religious policies caused controversy. Charles was personally inclined toward "high church" practices: an emphasis on ceremony and sacrament reminiscent of Catholic ritual. He also was a believer in Arminianism, a school of thought that rejected the Calvinist notion that God's grace cannot be earned, and hence emphasized the importance of the sacraments and the authority of the clergy. Charles's views put him on a collision course with gentry and aristocrats who leaned toward Puritanism.

Charles's views were supported by William Laud (1573–1645), archbishop of Canterbury from 1633, and thus leader of the Church of England. He tried to impose changes in worship, spread Arminian ideas, and censor opposing views. He also challenged the redistribution of church property, which had occurred in the Reformation of the sixteenth century, and thereby alienated the gentry on economic as well as religious grounds.

Charles's style of rule worsened religious, political, and economic tensions. Cold and intensely private, he lacked the charm and the political skills to disarm his opponents. His court was ruled by formal protocol, and access to the king was highly restricted—a serious problem in an age when proximity to the monarch was a guarantee of political power.

Revenue and religion dominated debate in the Parliament of 1628–1629, which Charles had called, once again, to get funds for his foreign wars. Parliament presented the king with a document called the Petition of Right, which protested his financial policies, as well as arbitrary imprisonment. (Seventeen members of Parliament had been imprisoned for refusing loans to the Crown.) Though couched conservatively as a restatement of customary practice, the petition, in fact, claimed a tradition of expanded parliamentary participation in government. Charles dissolved Parliament in March 1629, having decided that the money he might extract was not worth the risk.

For eleven years, Charles ruled without Parliament. When he was forced to summon it again in 1640, the kingdom was in crisis. Royal finances were in desperate straits, even though Charles had pressed collection of revenues far beyond traditional bounds.

1640: THE KINGDOM IN CRISIS

The immediate crisis and the reason for Charles's desperate need for money was a rebellion in Scotland. Like Philip II in the Netherlands, Charles tried to rule in Scotland through a small council of men who did not represent local elites. Worse, he also tried to force his "high church" practices on the Scots. The Scottish church had been more dramatically reshaped during the Reformation and now was largely Presbyterian in structure. The result of Charles's policies was riots and rebellion. Unable to suppress the revolt in a first campaign in 1639, Charles was forced to summon Parliament for funds to raise a more effective army.

But the Parliament that assembled in the spring of 1640 provided no help. Instead, members questioned the war with the Scots and other royal policies. Charles's political skills were far too limited for him to reestablish a workable relationship with Parliament under the circumstances. Charles dissolved this body, which is now known as the "Short Parliament," after just three weeks. Even more stinging than Charles's dissolution of the Parliament was the lack of respect he had shown the members: A number of them were harassed or arrested. Mistrust, fomented by the eleven years in which Charles had ruled without Parliament, thus increased.

Another humiliating defeat at the hands of the Scots, later in 1640, made summoning another Parliament imperative. Members of the "Long Parliament" (it sat from 1640 to 1653) took full advantage of the king's predicament. Charles was forced to agree not to dissolve or adjourn Parliament without the members' consent and to summon Parliament at least every three years. Parliament abolished many of the traditional revenues he had abused and impeached and removed from office his leading ministers, including Archbishop Laud. The royal commander deemed responsible for the Scottish fiasco, Thomas Wentworth, earl of Strafford, was executed without trial in May 1641.

The execution of Strafford shocked many aristocrats in the House of Lords (the upper house of Parliament), as well as some moderate members of the House of Commons. Meanwhile, Parliament began debating the perennially thorny religious question. A bare majority of members favored abolition of Anglican bishops as a first step in thoroughgoing religious reform. Working people in London, kept updated on the issues by the regular publication of parliamentary debates, demonstrated in support of that move. Moderate members of Parliament, in contrast, favored checking the king's power, but not upsetting the Elizabethan religious compromise.

An event that unified public and parliamentary opinion at a crucial time—a revolt against English rule in Ireland in October 1641—temporarily eclipsed these divisions over religious policy but did not diminish suspicion of the king. Fearing that Charles would use Irish soldiers against his English subjects, Parliament demanded that it control the army to put down the rebellion. In November, the Puritan majority introduced a document known as the "Grand Remonstrance," an appeal to the people and a long catalog of parliamentary grievances against the king. It passed by a narrow margin, further inflaming public opinion in London against Charles. The king's remaining support in Parliament eroded in January 1642, when he tried to arrest five members on charges of treason. The five escaped, and the stage was set for wider violence. The king withdrew from London, unsure he could defend himself there, and began to raise an army. In mid-1642, the kingdom stood at the brink of civil war.

SECTION SUMMARY

- France suffered through more than thirty years of civil war after 1562, caused by religious conflict, weak rulers, and powerful nobility.

- The French religious wars ended in the 1590s, when war-weary elites rallied behind the talented king Henry IV; Henry decreed religious toleration in the Edict of Nantes.

- After Henry, religious and political conflict broke out again, but the king's minister, Cardinal Richelieu, successfully reinforced royal authority.

- Elizabeth I of England weathered religious and political tensions at home and challenges from abroad during her long reign.

- James I and Charles I struggled with limited financial resources, unpopular policies, and religious division.

- Parliamentary resistance to Charles's authority and policies led England to a political crisis in 1640.

THE HOLY ROMAN EMPIRE AND THE THIRTY YEARS' WAR

Why did war erupt again within the Holy Roman Empire and what was the significance of the conflict?

The Holy Roman Empire enjoyed a period of comparative quiet after the Peace of Augsburg halted religious and political wars in 1555. The 1555 agreement had permitted rulers of the various states within the empire to impose either Catholicism or Lutheranism in their lands. By the early seventeenth century, however, fresh causes of instability brought about renewed fighting. One factor was the rise of Calvinism, for which no provision had been necessary in 1555. Also destabilizing was the attempt by the Austrian Habsburgs to reverse the successes of Protestantism, both in their own lands and in the empire at large, and to solidify their control of their own diverse territories. The result was a devastating conflict known as the **Thirty Years' War** (1618–1648).

Like conflicts elsewhere in Europe, the Thirty Years' War reflected religious tensions, regionalism versus centralizing forces, and dynastic and strategic rivalries between rulers. As a result of the war, the empire was eclipsed as a political unit by the regional powers that composed it.

Thirty Years' War Destructive war (1618–1648) involving most European countries but fought in Germany, resulting from religious tensions, regionalism versus centralizing forces, and dynastic and strategic rivalries between rulers.

Fragile Peace in the Holy Roman Empire, 1556–1618

The Austrian Habsburgs ruled over a diverse group of territories in the Holy Roman Empire, as well as northwestern Hungary. On his abdication in 1556, Emperor Charles V granted the Habsburg lands in the Holy Roman Empire to his brother, Ferdinand (see the chart on page 415), who was duly crowned emperor when Charles died in 1558.

🌐 **MAP 15.3—Europe During the Thirty Years' War, 1618–1648**

The Thirty Years' War was fought largely within the borders of the Holy Roman Empire. It was the result of conflicts within the empire as well as the meddling of neighbors for their own strategic advantages.

Though largely contiguous, Ferdinand's territories comprised independent duchies and kingdoms. In addition to the Habsburgs' ancestral lands (separate territories more or less equivalent to modern Austria in extent), Ferdinand also ruled the non-German lands of Bohemia (the core of the modern Czech Republic) and Hungary (see **MAP 15.3**). Both kingdoms bestowed their crowns by election and had chosen Ferdinand, the first Habsburg to rule them, in separate elections in the 1520s and 1530s. Most of Hungary was now under Ottoman control, but the kingdom of Bohemia, with its rich capital, Prague, was a wealthy center of population and culture.

Unlike the Netherlands, each of these linguistically and culturally diverse lands was still governed by its own distinct institutions. Moreover, unlike their Spanish cousins, the Austrian Habsburgs made no attempt to impose religious uniformity in the late sixteenth century. Ferdinand was Catholic but tolerant of reform efforts within the church. Both he and his son, Maximilian II (r. 1564–1576), believed that an eventual reunion of the Catholic and Protestant faiths might be possible. During his reign, Maximilian worked to keep religious peace in the empire as a whole and granted limited rights of worship to Protestant subjects in the Habsburgs' own lands. Catholicism and many varieties of Protestantism flourished side by side in Maximilian's domains, particularly in Hungary and, especially, Bohemia, which had experienced a religious reform movement under Jan Hus in the fifteenth century.

Maximilian's son, Rudolf II (r. 1576–1612), shared the religious style of his father and grandfather. He patronized education and the arts and sponsored the work of scientists. Yet, Rudolf was a weak leader politically and was challenged by his brother and ambitious cousins for control both of Habsburg lands and of the empire itself. Meanwhile, the resurgence of Catholicism in the wake of the Council of Trent (1545–1563) had begun to shift the religious balance. Members of the Jesuit order arrived in Habsburg lands in the reign of Maximilian. Tough-minded and well trained, they established Catholic schools and became confessors and preachers to the upper classes. Self-confident Catholicism emerged as a potent form of cultural identity among the German-speaking ruling classes, and thus, as a religious impetus to further political consolidation of all the Habsburg territories.

Resurgent Catholicism spread in the empire as a whole, too, and many Catholic princes believed they might now eliminate Protestantism, as their ancestors had failed to do. Like the English under Elizabeth, Habsburg subjects and peoples in the empire had enjoyed a period of calm in political and religious matters. Now, as in England, the stage was set for conflict of both kinds.

The Thirty Years' War, 1618–1648

The Thirty Years' War was touched off in 1618 by a revolt against Habsburg rule in the kingdom of Bohemia. Rudolf II had made Bohemia's bustling capital, Prague, his imperial capital. Its powerful Protestant community had wrested formal recognition of its right to worship from Rudolf and his younger brother, Matthias (r. 1612–1619).

Matthias was quickly succeeded by his cousin Ferdinand II (r. 1619–1637), who did not honor these agreements. Educated by the Jesuits, Ferdinand sincerely believed that reimposing Catholicism was his Christian duty; he once stated that he would "sooner beg than rule over heretics."[4] He would not tolerate the political independence of nobles and towns in Bohemia or the religious pluralism that independence defended. As Philip II had done in the Netherlands, Ferdinand appointed a council to govern in his name, which enforced unpopular policies, such as denying the right to build Protestant churches and barring non-Catholics from serving in government.

On May 23, 1618, delegates to a Protestant assembly that had unsuccessfully petitioned Ferdinand to honor his predecessors' earlier guarantees marched to the palace in Prague where his officials met. After a confrontation over their demands, the delegates "tried" the officials on the spot for treason and, literally, threw them out of the palace window. The incident became known as the "Defenestration of Prague" (from the Latin *fenestra*, or "window"). (The officials survived because they fell into a pile of garbage in the moat.) The rebels set up their own government.

This upstart Bohemian government officially deposed Ferdinand and elected a new Bohemian king in 1619: Frederick, the Protestant elector of the Palatinate. His election had implications for the Holy Roman Empire as a whole because his territories in west-central Germany, called the Lower and Upper Palatinate, conveyed the right to be one of the seven electors who chose the emperor.

The revolt in Bohemia set off a wider war because foreign rulers also felt their interests to be involved. The English king, James I, supported Frederick because Frederick was married to his daughter. Spain's supply routes north from Italy to the Netherlands passed next to Frederick's lands in western Germany. France's first interest was its rivalry with Spain; thus, France kept its

The Defenestration of Prague This contemporary print memorializes the events of May 23, 1618. Bohemian Protestants "tried" two imperial officials for violating agreements that safeguarded their religious liberties. The two officials and their secretary were thrown out of the windows of Prague castle. (Corbis)

eye on the border principalities that were strategically important to Spain and wanted to keep Protestant, as well as Catholic, princes within the empire strong enough to thwart Austrian Habsburg ambitions. Thus, from the outset, the war was a conflict not only over the Habsburgs' power in their own lands, but also over the balance of religious and political power in the empire and in Europe (see **MAP 15.3**).

Ferdinand secured aid from Catholic princes, including his cousin, King Philip III (r. 1598–1621) of Spain, by promising them Frederick's lands in the Palatinate. By the fall of 1620, a Catholic army faced Bohemian rebels who had received little support as yet from fellow Protestants. The Battle of White Mountain, in November, was a complete Catholic victory.

Despite the rout, fighting did not end, but instead became more widespread. The 1609 truce between Spain and the Netherlands expired in 1621, and the nearby Lower Palatinate, now in Spanish hands, offered a staging point for Spanish forces and thus threatened the peace in that corner of the empire. Claiming to be a Protestant champion, the Protestant king of Denmark, Christian IV (r. 1588–1648), who was also duke of Holstein in northern Germany, entered the fight. He wanted to gain greater control over German Baltic seaports and to defend his northern German territories against any Catholic aggressors. Christian received little help from fellow Protestants, however. The Dutch were busy with Spain, the English were wary of fighting after Frederick's defeat, and Denmark's rival, the Swedes, were not interested in helping Danish ambitions in the Baltic.

Just as Protestant powers did not always support each other, neither did Catholic ones. When imperial forces defeated Denmark's armies in 1626, Catholic princes became alarmed at the possibility of greater imperial power in northern Germany. Led by the duke of Bavaria, they arranged a truce that resulted in Denmark's withdrawal from the fighting on relatively generous terms.

The Danish king's rival, Gustav Adolf, king of Sweden (r. 1611–1632), hoping to gain territory along the Baltic seacoast, now assumed the role of Protestant leader. Gustav Adolf was an innovative commander and his campaigns were capped by a victory over an imperial army at Breitenfeld, in Saxony, in 1631. However, the tide turned in favor of Ferdinand's forces when Gustav Adolf was killed in battle the following year; further imperial victories led to the Peace of Prague (1635), a general peace treaty favorable to Catholics.

The Peace of Prague brought only a temporary peace, however, because Ferdinand died shortly afterwards and French involvement increased now that other anti-Habsburg forces had been eclipsed. France seized imperial territory along its own eastern border and subsidized continued war within the empire by channeling monies to Protestant princes and mercenaries there. The fighting dragged on. By the end of the Thirty Years' War, order had disintegrated so completely in the wake of the marauding armies that both Catholic and Protestant rulers willingly allied with any power necessary, even religious enemies, to safeguard their states.

A comprehensive peace treaty became possible when France withdrew its sponsorship of the fighting in order to concentrate on its conflict with Spain, namely, the continued rivalry with the Spanish Habsburgs for control of territory along France's eastern and northern borders and in Italy. The French wanted only a workable balance of power in the empire, which had been achieved with a convincing defeat of imperial forces in 1645. Negotiations for peace began among war-weary states of the empire in 1643 and resulted in a group of agreements known as the **Peace of Westphalia** (west-FAIL-yuh) in 1648.

Peace of Westphalia
Treaty that ended the Thirty Years' War in 1648. The principalities within the Holy Roman Empire were recognized as virtually autonomous, severely weakening the power of the emperor.

The Effects of the War

The Thirty Years' War ruined the economy and decimated the population in many parts of the empire and had long-term political consequences for the empire as a whole. One reason for the war's devastation was a novel application of firepower to warfare that increased both the size of armies and their deadly force in battle. This was the use of volley fire, the arrangement of foot soldiers in parallel lines so that one line of men could fire while another reloaded. This tactic, pioneered in the Netherlands around the turn of the century, was refined by Gustav Adolf of Sweden. He amassed large numbers of troops and increased the rate of fire so that a virtually continuous barrage was maintained. He also used maneuverable field artillery to protect the massed infantry from cavalry charges.

Following Gustav Adolf's lead, armies of all the major states adopted these new offensive tactics. But defensive expertise—as in holding fortresses—also remained important, and pitched battles still tended to be part of sieges. The costs in resources and human life of this kind of warfare reached unheard-of dimensions. Compounding these effects of battle was the behavior of troops hired by enterprising mercenary generals, for whom loyalty to the princes who paid them took a back seat to personal advancement. They were contracted to provide and supply troops and thus were more willing than the princes would have been to allow armies to live "economically" on plunder. European states could field large armies but had not yet evolved the mechanisms fully to fund, and thus control, them. Popular printed literature and court drama both condemned the horrors of the war.

Where fighting had been concentrated, as in parts of Saxony, between one-third and one-half of the inhabitants of rural villages and major towns may have disappeared. Many starved, were caught in the fighting, or were killed by marauding soldiers. Some people migrated to other regions or joined the armies simply in order to survive.

The Peace of Westphalia was one of the most important outcomes of the war. The various individual treaties composing the Peace effectively put an end to religious war in the empire. Calvinism was recognized as a tolerated religion. The requirement that all subjects must follow their ruler's faith was retained, but some leeway was allowed for those who now found themselves under new rulers.

In political matters, the treaties reflected Swedish successes by granting them territory on the Baltic coast. France gained the important towns of Metz, Toul, and Verdun on its eastern border. Spain formally recognized the independence of the Netherlands. The son of Frederick, Protestant king of Bohemia, received back the smaller of the two Palatine territories that his father had held. The Upper Palatinate—as well as

The Horrors of War   The painter of this scene of soldiers plundering a farm in the Thirty Years' War was himself a veteran of Spanish campaigns in the Netherlands. The scene he depicts was commonplace in this era of poorly-supplied troops: soldiers loot a household, killing peasants who refused to hand over their own stores of food   (Soldiers Plundering a Farm during the Thirty Years' War, 1620 (oil on wood), Vrancx, Sebastian (1573–1647)/Deutsches Historisches Museum, Berlin, Germany/©DHM/The Bridgeman Art Library)

SECTION SUMMARY

- The Holy Roman Empire was relatively peaceful until destabilized by the spread of Calvinism and the ambition of the Austrian Habsburgs to extend their political and religious control within the empire.

- The Thirty Years' War started in Bohemia (modern Czech Republic) when local leaders challenged Habsburg policies.

- The Bohemian revolt led to a wider war because many rulers, inside and outside Germany, had a stake in the balance of religious and political power there.

- Large armies of mercenaries caused widespread devastation in certain areas of Germany.

- The Peace of Westphalia established a new balance of power between states within the Holy Roman Empire, but the empire itself declined as a political entity.

the right to be a new elector of the emperor—was given to the Catholic duke of Bavaria.

The most important political outcome of the peace, however, was a new balance of power in the empire. Most of the major Catholic and Protestant rulers extended their territories at the expense of smaller principalities and cities. The principalities within the empire were acknowledged, in the peace, to be virtually autonomous, both from the emperor and from one another. In addition, the constitution of the empire was changed to make it very difficult for one prince or a group of princes to disrupt the peace in their own interests. As a result, the agreements at Westphalia were the beginning of one hundred years of peace within the Holy Roman Empire.

Another outcome was that the Habsburgs, though weakened as emperors, were strengthened as rulers of their own hereditary lands on the eastern fringes of the empire. They moved their capital back to Vienna from Prague, and the government of their hereditary lands gained in importance as administration of the empire waned.

ECONOMIC CHANGE AND SOCIAL TENSIONS

What caused the economic stresses of these decades and how did ordinary people cope with them?

Religious strife disrupted the everyday lives of whole communities in the late sixteenth and early seventeenth centuries. Wars devastated many areas of western Europe and contributed to severe economic decline in parts of the Low Countries (the Netherlands), France, and the Holy Roman Empire. But other factors, most notably a steady rise in prices, also played a role in the dramatic economic and social changes of the century after 1550. Economic changes altered power relations in cities, in the countryside, and in the relationship of both to central governments. Ordinary people managed their economic difficulties in a variety of ways: they sought new sources of work; they protested against burdensome taxes; sometimes they found scapegoats for their distress among their neighbors.

Economic Transformation and Social Change

The most obvious economic change was an unrelenting rise in prices. Sixteenth-century observers attributed rising prices to the inflationary effects of the influx of silver from Spanish territories in the New World. Historians now believe that European causes may also have helped trigger this **price revolution**. Steady population growth caused a relative shortage of goods, particularly food, and the result was higher prices. Between 1550 and 1600, with local variations, the price of grain may have risen between 50 and 100 percent, and sometimes more, in cities throughout Europe. Wages did not keep pace with prices; historians estimate that wages lost between one-tenth and one-fourth of their value by the end of the century.

price revolution Steady rise in prices in the sixteenth and seventeenth centuries, resulting from population growth and the importation of precious metals from Spain's New World territories.

Wealth in the countryside was also becoming more stratified. Population growth caused many peasant farms to be subdivided for numerous children, creating tiny plots that could not support the families who lived on them. Countless peasants lost what lands they had to wealthy investors who lent them money to rent more land or to buy seed and tools and then reclaimed the land when the peasants failed to repay. Land rents rose because of high demand and some peasants were unable to rent land at all. To survive, they sought work as day laborers for rich landlords or more prosperous farmers. Many found their way to cities, where they swelled the ranks of the poor. In eastern Europe, peasants faced other dilemmas, for their lands had a different relationship to the wider European economy. The more densely urbanized western Europe, whose wealth controlled the patterns of trade, sought bulk goods, particularly grain, from eastern Germany,

Poland, and Lithuania. Thus, there was an economic incentive for landowners in eastern Europe to bind peasants to the land, just as the desire of their rulers for greater cooperation had granted the landlords more power. Serfdom now spread in eastern Europe, while precisely the opposite condition—a more mobile labor force—grew in the West.

The growth of markets around Europe and in Spanish possessions overseas, as well as population growth within Europe, had a marked effect on patterns of production and the lives of artisans. Production of cloth on a large scale for export, for example, now required large amounts of capital—much more than a typical guild craftsman could amass. Cloth production was increasingly controlled by new investor-producers with access to distant markets. These entrepreneurs bought up large amounts of wool and hired it out to be cleaned, spun into thread, and woven into cloth by wage laborers in urban workshops or by pieceworkers in their homes. Thousands of poor women and men in the countryside around towns supported their families in this way. In towns, guilds still regulated most trades but, as their share of production declined, they could not accommodate the numbers of artisans who sought to join them. Fewer and fewer apprentices and journeymen could expect to become master artisans. The masters began to treat apprentices virtually as wage laborers, at times, letting them go during slow periods.

Another consequence of the circumstances guild members faced was the effort to reduce competition at the expense of the artisans' own mothers, sisters, and daughters. Increasingly, widows were forbidden to continue their husbands' enterprises, though they headed from 10 to 15 percent of households in many trades. Women had traditionally practiced many trades, but rarely followed the formal progress from apprenticeship to master status, since they usually combined work of this kind with household production. Outright exclusion of women from guilds occurred as early as the thirteenth century, but now began regularly to appear in guild statutes. Town governments also restricted women's participation even in work they had long dominated, such as selling in markets. Working women thus began to have difficulty supporting themselves if single or widowed and difficulty supporting their children.

Profits from expanding production and trade and from higher land values made more capital available to wealthy urban or landholding families to invest in the countryside, by buying land outright on which to live like **gentry** or by making loans to desperate peasants. Enterprising landholders raised rents on farming and grazing land wherever they could, or they converted land to the production of wool, grain, and other cash crops destined for distant markets.

As a result, a stratum of wealthy, educated, and socially ambitious "new gentry," as these families were called in England, began to grow. Many of the men of these families were royal officeholders. Many bought titles of nobility or were granted nobility as a benefit of their offices. They often lent money to royal governments. The monumental expense of wars made becoming a lender to government, as well as to individuals, an attractive way to live off personal capital.

No one would have confused these up-and-coming gentry with warrior-aristocrats from old families, but the social distinctions between them are less important (to us) than what they had in common: legal privilege, the security of landownership, and a cooperative relationship with the monarchy. Monarchs deliberately favored the new gentry as counterweights to independent aristocrats.

City governments also changed character. Town councils became dominated by small numbers of privileged families, now more likely to live from landed wealth, like gentry, than from trade or manufacture. By the beginning of the seventeenth century, traditional guild control of government had been eliminated in many places. The long medieval tradition of towns serving as independent corporate bodies had come to an end.

gentry   Class of wealthy, educated, and socially ambitious families in western Europe, especially England, whose political and economic power was greatly enhanced during the sixteenth century.

Coping with Poverty and Violence

The common people of Europe did not submit passively to either the economic difficulties or the religious and political crises of their day. Whatever their religion, common people took the initiative in attacking members of other faiths to rid their communities of them. Heretics were considered to be spiritual pollution that might provoke God's wrath, and ordinary citizens believed that it was up to them to eliminate heretics if the state failed to do so.

Ordinary people fought in wars not only from conviction, but also from the need for self-defense and from economic choice. It was ordinary people who defended the walls of towns, dug siege works, and manned artillery batteries. Although nobles remained military leaders, armies consisted mostly of infantry made up of common people, not mounted knights. Women were part of armies, too. Much of the day-to-day work of finding food and firewood, cleaning guns, and repairing clothing was done by women looking after their husbands and lovers among the troops. Landless farm hands, day laborers, and out-of-work artisans joined armies because having work was attractive enough to outweigh the dangers of military life. Desertion was common; nothing more than the rumor that a soldier's home village was threatened might prompt a man to abandon his post. Battle-hardened troops could threaten their commanders, not only with desertion, but with mutiny. Occasionally, mutinies were brutally suppressed; more often, they were successful and troops received some of their back wages.

The devastation of religious war led to both peasant rebellions and urban uprisings. Peasants and townspeople rebelled because of high taxes and food shortages. Elites participated too; former soldiers, prosperous farmers, or even noble landlords whose economic fortunes were tied to peasant profits led some rural revolts. Rebels sometimes seized property—for example, they might distribute looted bread among themselves—and occasionally killed officials. Their protests rarely generated lasting political change and were usually brutally quashed.

Governments at all levels tried to cope with the increasing problem of poverty by changing the administration and scale of poor relief. In both Catholic and Protestant Europe, caring for the poor became more institutionalized and systematic, and more removed from religious impulses. Governments established public almshouses and poorhouses to dispense food or to care for orphans or the destitute in towns throughout Catholic and Protestant Europe. At first, these institutions reflected an optimistic vision of an ideal Christian community caring for its neediest members. But by 1600, the distribution of food was accompanied by attempts to distinguish "deserving" from "undeserving" poor, by an insistence that the poor work for their ration of food, and even by an effort to force the poor to live apart, in poorhouses.

A Beggar is Whipped Through the Streets   In this sixteenth-century woodcut, probably made in England, a poor man is tied up and led through the streets of a town while being whipped on his bare back. The gallows in the distance, just outside the city gates, imply that the poor were now thought of as dangerous outlaws.   ("A beggar is tied and whipped through the streets," c.1567 (woodcut) (b/w photo), English School, (16th century)/Private Collection/The Bridgeman Art Library)

These efforts were not uniformly successful. Although begging was outlawed by Catholic and Protestant city governments alike, it was never thoroughly suppressed. Catholic religious orders often resisted efforts at regulating their charitable work, even when they were imposed by Catholic governments. Nonetheless, the trend was clear. From viewing poverty as a fact of life and a lesson in Christian humility, European elites began to see it as a social problem and poor people as needing to be controlled.

The Hunt for Witches

Between approximately 1550 and 1650, Europe saw a dramatic increase in the persecution of women and men for witchcraft. Approximately one hundred thousand people were tried and about sixty thousand executed. The surge in witch-hunting was closely linked to communities' religious concerns and also to the social tensions that resulted from economic difficulties.

Certain types of witchcraft had long existed in Europe. So-called black magic of various kinds—one peasant casting a spell on another peasant's cow—had been common since the Middle Ages. The practice now seemed dangerous, especially to elites, who linked black magic to Devil worship. Catholic leaders and legal scholars began to advance such theories in the fifteenth century, and by the late sixteenth century, both Catholic and Protestant elites viewed a witch not only as someone who might cast harmful spells, but also as a heretic.

The impetus for most individual accusations of witchcraft came from within the communities where the "witch" lived— that is, from common people. Usually targeted were solitary or unpopular people whose difficult relationships with fellow villagers made them seem likely sources of evil. Often, such a person had practiced black magic (or had been suspected of doing so) for years, and the villagers took action only when faced with a community crisis, such as an epidemic.

Because they were often prompted by village disasters, individual accusations of witchcraft increased in this period in response to the crises that beset many communities. In addition, isolated accusations often started localized frenzies of active hunting for other witches. These more widespread hunts were driven, in part, by the anxieties of local elites about disorder and heresy and were facilitated by contemporary legal procedures that they applied. These procedures permitted lax rules of evidence and the use of torture to extract confessions. Torture or the threat of torture led most accused witches to "confess" and to name accomplices or other "witches." In this way, a single initial accusation could lead to dozens of prosecutions. In regions where procedures for appealing convictions were fragile or nonexistent, witch-hunts could expand with alarming speed and dozens of "witches" might be identified and executed before the whirlwind subsided. Aggressive hunts were common, for example, in the small principalities and imperial cities of the Holy Roman Empire, which were largely independent of higher political and judicial authority. (See the box, "The Written Record: A City Official Worries About Witch-Hunting.")

The majority of accused witches were women. Lacking legal, social, and political resources, women may have been more likely than men to use black magic for self-protection or advancement. Women's work often made them vulnerable to charges of witchcraft, since families' food supplies and routine medicines passed through women's hands. The deaths of young children or of domestic animals, such as a milk cow, were among the most common triggers for witchcraft accusation. The increase in poverty during the late sixteenth and early seventeenth centuries made poor women frequent targets of witch-hunts.

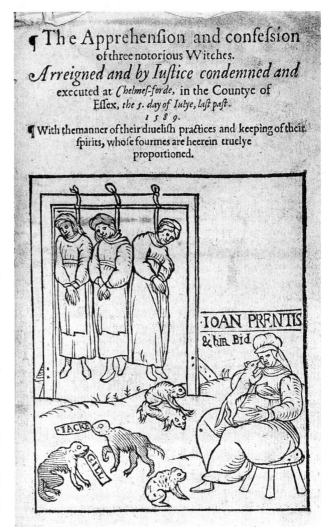

Publicizing Witch Trials Printed pamphlets, such as this one describing the execution of three women in Essex, England, spread the news of local "outbreaks" of witchcraft. One of the women, Joan Prentis, is also depicted surrounded by her animal familiars. The ferret in Joan's lap, the pamphlet relates, was the Devil himself in animal form. (Lambeth Palace Library)

A City Official Worries About Witch-Hunting

In this letter written to a friend in 1629, the chancellor to the prince-bishop of the German city of Würzburg describes the witch-hunt in his community.

As to the affair of the witches, which Your Grace thinks brought to an end before this, it has started up afresh, and no words can do justice to it. Ah, the woe and misery of it—there are still four hundred in the city, high and low, of every rank and sex, nay, even clerics, so strongly accused that they may be arrested at any hour. It is true that, of the people of my Gracious Prince here, some out of all the offices and faculties must be executed: clerics, elected councilors and doctors, city officials, court assessors several of whom Your Grace knows. There are law students to be arrested. The Prince-Bishop has over forty students who are soon to be pastors; among them thirteen or fourteen are said to be witches. A few days ago a Dean was arrested; two others who were summoned have fled.

The notary of our Church consistory, a very learned man, was yesterday arrested and put to the torture. In a word, a third part of the city is surely involved. The richest, most attractive, most prominent of the clergy are already executed. A week ago a maiden of nineteen was executed, of whom it is everywhere said that she was the fairest in the whole city, and was held by everybody a girl of singular modesty and purity. She will be followed by seven or eight others of the best and most attractive persons. . . . And thus many are put to death for renouncing God and being at the witch-dances, against whom nobody has ever else spoken a word.

To conclude this wretched matter, there are children of three or four years, to the number of three hundred, who are said to have had intercourse with the Devil. I have seen put to death children of seven, promising students of ten, twelve, fourteen and fifteen of the nobles—but I cannot and must not write more of this misery. There are persons of yet higher rank, whom you know, and would marvel to hear of, nay, would scarcely believe it; let justice be done. . . .

P.S. Though there are many wonderful and terrible things happening it is beyond doubt that, at a place called the Fraw-Rengberg, the Devil in person, with eight thousand of his followers, held an assembly and celebrated mass before them all, administering to his audience (that is, the witches) turnip-rinds and pairings in place of the Holy Eucharist. There took place not only foul but most horrible and hideous blasphemies, whereof I shudder to write. It is also true that they all vowed not to be enrolled in the Book of Life, but all agreed to be inscribed by a notary who is well known to me and my colleagues. We hope, too, that the book in which they are enrolled will yet be found, and there is no little search being made for it.

QUESTIONS

1. Which townspeople are victims of the witch-hunt?

2. Does the document reveal why the hunt is continuing? Who is in charge?

3. What is the author's attitude toward the events he describes? Does the chancellor believe that witchcraft exists?

Source: Alan C. Kors and Edward Peters, eds., *Witchcraft in Europe, 1100–1700: A Documentary History* (Philadelphia: University of Pennsylvania, 1972), pp. 251–252. Reprinted by permission of the University of Pennsylvania Press.

Both Christian dogma and humanistic writing portrayed women as morally weaker than men and thus more susceptible to the Devil's enticements. Writings on witchcraft described Devil worship in sexual terms, and the prosecution of witches had a voyeuristic, sexual dimension. The bodies of accused witches were searched for the "Devil's mark"—a blemish thought to be Satan's imprint. In some regions, women accounted for 80 percent of those prosecuted and executed. A dynamic of gender stereotyping was not always at work, however; in other regions, prosecutions were more evenly divided between men and women, and occasionally, men made up the majority of those accused.

The widespread witch-hunts virtually ended by the late seventeenth century, in part, because the intellectual energies of elites shifted from religious to scientific thought. The practice of witchcraft continued among common folk, although accusations of one neighbor by another never again reached the level of these crisis-ridden decades.

SECTION SUMMARY

- A price revolution caused a decline in the value of wages in the sixteenth century.

- Elites, particularly new gentry families, could grow rich by controlling increasingly scarce and valuable land.

- Economic hardship led common people to seek jobs in cities, join armies, and protest taxation.

- Persecutions for witchcraft dramatically increased between 1550 and 1650, reflecting both common people's search for scapegoats for their hard lives and elites' anxiety about controlling common people's religion.

WRITING, DRAMA, AND ART IN AN AGE OF UPHEAVAL

In what ways do the literature and art of this period reflect the political, social, and religious conflicts of the age?

Both imaginative literature and speculative writing, such as political theory, bear the stamp of their times. In the late sixteenth and early seventeenth centuries, political speculation concerned questions of the legitimacy of rulers and of the relationship of political power to divine authority—urgent problems in an age when religious division threatened the very foundations of states. Authors and rulers alike often relied on still-prevalent oral modes of communication to convey their ideas. Indeed, some of the greatest literature and some of the most effective political statements of the period were presented as drama and not conveyed in print. Nevertheless, literacy continued to spread and led to greater opportunities for knowledge and reflection. The medium of print became increasingly important to political life. In the visual arts, the dramatic impulse combined with religious purposes to create works that conveyed both power and emotion.

Literacy and Literature

Traditional oral culture changed slowly under the impact of the spread of printing, education, and literacy. Works of literature from the late sixteenth and early seventeenth centuries incorporate material from traditional folktales and reflect the coexistence of oral and literate culture. In *Don Quixote* (key-HO-tay), by Spain's Miguel de Cervantes (sair-VAHN-tayz) (1547–1616), the title character and his companion, Sancho Panza, have a long discussion about oral and literate traditions. The squire Panza speaks in the style that was customary in oral culture—a rather roundabout and repetitive style, which enabled the speaker and listener to remember what was said. Much of the richness of *Don Quixote* is due to the interweaving of prose styles and topical concerns from throughout Cervantes' culture—from the oral world of peasants to the refined world of court life. Yet, what enabled Cervantes to create this rich portrayal was his own highly developed literacy and the awareness of language that literacy made possible.

Much literature in this period stressed the value of education—particularly, by means of the humanist recovery of ancient wisdom, a new vision of what it meant to be a cultivated and disciplined man of the world. The French author Michel de Montaigne (1533–1592) was the epitome of the reflective gentleman. Montaigne (mon-TEN-yuh) was a judge in the parlement (law court) of Bordeaux. In 1570, he resigned from the court and retired to his small château, where he wrote his *Essais* (from which we derive the word *essays*), a collection of short reflections that were revolutionary in both form and content. Montaigne invented writing in the form of a sketch, an "attempt" (the literal meaning of *essai*) that enabled him to combine self-reflection with formal analysis.

Owing to the spread of printing, Montaigne had a virtually unparalleled opportunity to compare different events, values, and cultures through reading a wide variety of printed texts. His reflections range from the destructiveness of the French civil wars to the consequences of European exploration of the New World. Toward all of these events, Montaigne was able to achieve an analytic detachment remarkable for his day. For example, he noted ironically that Europeans labeled New World peoples "savages," yet, they committed seemingly endless and wanton violence against those "savages" and one another. (See the box "The Global Record: Montaigne Discusses Barbarity in the New World and the Old.") Montaigne's essays also reveal self-reflection—a distancing from himself. This distancing was also the result of literacy and leisure, which enabled him to enjoy long periods of solitude and reflection in the company of other solitary, book-bound voices. Montaigne's works mark the beginning of what we know as the "invention" of private life, in which an individual is defined more by internal character and personality traits than by social role.

The Great Age of Theater

The works of the great English poet and playwright William Shakespeare (1564–1616) are still compelling to us because of the profundity of the questions asked about love, honor, and political legitimacy; he asked these questions in terms appropriate to his own own day. One of his favorite

Montaigne Discusses Barbarity in the New World and the Old

In one of his most famous essays, the French jurist and essayist Michel de Montaigne (1533–1592) ironically compares the customs of Native Americans with the customs of his own society. Information about Native Americans came from published reports of European voyages and from news of individual Native Americans who had journeyed (usually forcibly) to Europe. Europeans' encounters with peoples in the New World gave Montaigne a vantage point from which to criticize his own society.

They have their wars with [other] nations, to which they go quite naked, with no other arms than bows or wooden spears. . . . It is astonishing that firmness they show in their combats, which never end but in slaughter and bloodshed; for, as to routs and terror, they know nothing of either.

Each man brings back as his trophy the head of the enemy he has killed. . . . After they have treated their prisoner well for a long time with all the hospitality they can think of . . . they kill him with their swords. This done, they roast him and eat him in common and send some pieces to their absent friends.

I am not sorry that we notice the barbarous horror of such acts, but am heartily sorry that . . . we should be so blind to our own. I think there is more barbarity . . . in tearing by tortures and the rack a body still full of feeling, in roasting a man bit by bit, having him bitten and mangled by dogs (as we have not only read but seen within fresh memory . . . among neighbors and fellow citizens, and what is worse, on the pretext of piety and religion).

Three of these men (were brought to France) . . . and [someone] wanted to know what they had found most amazing. . . . They said that in the first place they thought it very strange that so many grown men, bearded, strong and armed who were around the king . . . should submit to obey a child [the young French king]. . . . Second (they have a way in their language of speaking of men as halves of one another), they had noticed that there were among us men full and gorged with all sorts of good things, and that their other halves were beggars at their doors, emaciated with hunger and poverty; and they thought it strange that these needy halves could endure such injustice.

QUESTIONS

1. What practices in the two cultures is Montaigne commenting on in this excerpt?

2. In what ways does he find Native American culture admirable by comparison to his own? What aspects of his own culture is he criticizing?

3. How are contemporary events and conditions in France reflected in Montaigne's remarks?

Source: Donald M. Frame, trans., *The Complete Essays of Montaigne* (Stanford, Calif.: Stanford University Press, 1948), pp. 153, 155–159. Reprinted by permission of the publisher.

themes—evident in *Hamlet* and *Macbeth*—is the legitimacy of rulers. He also explored the contradictions in values between the growing commercial world he saw around him and the older, seemingly more stable world of feudal society. Subtle political commentary distinguishes Shakespeare's later writings near and shortly after the death of Elizabeth in 1603, when political and economic problems were becoming increasingly troublesome. In *Coriolanus*, he portrays commoners as poor but not ignorant; they are in fact fully rational and capable of analyzing their situation—perhaps more capable, Shakespeare hints, than their ruler. The play is safely set in ancient Rome, but the social and political tensions it depicts clearly applied to the Elizabethan present.

Shakespeare's extraordinary career was possible because his life coincided with the rise of professional theater. In the capitals of England and Spain, professional theaters first opened in the 1570s. Some drama was produced at court or in aristocratic households, but most public theaters drew large and very mixed audiences, including the poorest city dwellers. Playwrights, including Shakespeare, often wrote in teams, under great pressure to keep acting companies supplied with material. The best-known dramatist in Spain, Lope de Vega (LOW-pah day VAY-guh) (1562–1635), wrote more than fifteen hundred works on a wide range of topics. Although religious themes remained popular in Spanish theater, as an echo of medieval drama, most plays in England and Spain treated secular subjects and, as in *Coriolanus*, disguised political commentary.

Over time, theater became increasingly restricted to aristocratic circles. In England, Puritan criticism of the "immorality" of public performance drove actors and playwrights to seek royal patronage. The first professional theater to open in Paris, in 1629, quickly became dependent on Cardinal Richelieu's patronage. Inevitably, as court patronage grew in importance, the wide range of subjects treated in plays began to narrow to those of aristocratic concern, such as family honor and martial glory. These themes are depicted in the works of the Spaniard Pedro Calderón (kall-day-ROHN) (1600–1681), who wrote for his enthusiastic patron, Philip IV, and of the Frenchman Pierre Corneille (kore-NAY) (1606–1684), whose great tragedy of aristocratic life, *Le Cid*, was one of the early successes of the seventeenth-century French theater.

Drama's significance as an art form is reflected in its impact on the development of music: The opera, which weds drama to music, was invented in Italy in the early seventeenth century. The first great work in this genre is generally acknowledged to be *Orfeo* (*Orpheus*, 1607) by Claudio Monteverdi (mon-tay-VAIR-dee) (1567–1643). Opera, like drama, reflected the influence of humanism in its secular themes and in its emulation of Greek drama, which had used both words and music. The practice of music itself changed under the dramatic impulse. Monteverdi was the first master of a new musical style known as "monody," which emphasizes the progression of chords. Monodic music is inherently dramatic, creating a sense of forward movement, expectation, and resolution.

Drama, Art, and Political Thought

Whether produced on a public stage or at court or in a less formal setting, drama was a favored method of communication in this era because people responded to and made extensive use of the spoken word. Dramatic gesture and storytelling to get a message across were commonplace and were important components of politics.

What we might call "street drama" was a common event. When aristocratic governors entered major towns, such as when Margaret of Parma entered Brussels, an ostentatious formal "entry" was often staged. The dignitary would ride through the main gate, usually beneath a canopy made of luxurious cloth. Costumed townspeople staged brief symbolic dramas, such as of the story of David and Goliath, on the streets; the event might end with an elaborate banquet. A remnant of these proceedings survives today in the ceremony of giving distinguished visitors "the keys to the city," which, in the sixteenth century, really were functional.

Royalty made artful use of ceremony. Royal entries into towns took on an added weight, as did royal funerals and other such occasions. These dramas reinforced political and constitutional assumptions in the minds of witnesses and participants and, over time, there were revealing changes in the representations of royal power. In France, for example, the ritual entry of the king into Paris had originally stressed the participation of the leading guilds, judges, and administrators, symbolizing their active role in governing the city and the kingdom. But in the last half of the sixteenth century, the procession began to glorify the king alone.

Speculation about and celebration of power, as well as dramatic emotion, also occurred in the visual arts—most notably in painting and architecture, in the style now known as **baroque**. Baroque (ba-ROKE) style was a new kind of visual language that could project power and grandeur and simultaneously engage viewers' senses. (See the feature "The Visual Record: Baroque Art.")

The very fact that rulers experimented with self-representation suggests that questions about the nature and extent of royal power were far from settled. Queen Elizabeth I had the particular burden of assuming the throne in a period of great instability. Hence, she paid a great deal of attention to the image of herself that she conveyed in words and authorized to be fashioned in painting. Elizabeth styled herself variously as mother to her people and as a warrior-queen (drawing on ancient myths of Amazon women). More formal speculation about constitutional matters also resulted from the tumult

baroque Style of European art and architecture popular from the late sixteenth to early eighteenth centuries. Baroque art modified Renaissance techniques, adding dynamism and emotional energy, which resulted in works that were both impressively grand and emotionally engaging.

An Image of Royalty This dramatic painting of Charles I on horseback was one of several likenesses of the king painted by the baroque artist Anthony Van Dyck. This painting was originally hung at the end of a long gallery in one of the royal palaces, next to similarly triumphal images of Roman emperors. (The Royal Collection © 2003, Her Majesty Queen Elizabeth II)

Baroque Art

If today, you were to walk through the cathedral in the Belgian city of Antwerp and notice this painting, titled The Raising of the Cross, it might not strike you as remarkable. The crucifixion of Jesus is a frequent subject of religious painting, after all. But let us look at the image more carefully. First of all, this is a portrayal not of Jesus on the cross, but rather of the raising of the cross. In other words, it captures a moment of action, not its aftermath. The frame of the painting is filled with action as well. The figures on the left and at the center support the cross and push it up. At the bottom right, we see figures straining at ropes as they pull the cross upright. Our eye is drawn to the movement in the painting, partly by the use of light, which floods the figure of Jesus. We also note the unexpected diagonal position of the crucified figure, and we survey the image in order to make sense of it.

This is a dynamic painting, and simultaneously, an emotionally engaging one. We encounter Jesus not as a static, perhaps already dying, figure on the cross, but at the very moment of his crucifixion. There is also a striking similarity between the figure of Jesus and those of the men who are working hard to accomplish his crucifixion: They are all men, whose muscled bodies are more alike than not. The human pathos of the moment is brought to life.

The image you see before you is one of three panels in a triptych, or three-paneled altarpiece. The left-hand panel depicts Saint John, the Virgin Mary, and others witnessing Jesus' crucifixion. The panel on the right shows a Roman officer watching over his soldiers as they crucify two thieves. Whereas most triptychs of the period contained three unrelated images, here the panels combine to form a single story of the crucifixion.

This altarpiece was executed in 1610 by the influential painter Peter Paul Rubens (1577–1640), a native of Antwerp, in the southern Netherlands. Rubens was one of the great masters of what came to be called the baroque style. Baroque techniques were pioneered in the late sixteenth century in Italy, first in church design, and spread slowly, with many regional variations, especially throughout Catholic Europe, during the seventeenth century. The origin of the term baroque has been debated; it may have come from the Portuguese barroco, used to describe irregularly shaped pearls. The term, as applied to the arts, was initially derogatory, denoting distortion, illogic, and irregularity. Baroque painting was distinguished by the dramatic use of color and shading and by the dynamic energy of figures.

Baroque artists based their work on Renaissance achievements in representing the human form in a convincing three-dimensional space. But with the strong use of light, movement, and more robust and realistic human figures, these artists enhanced the drama and emotional impact of what they depicted.

Like baroque artists, baroque architects modified the precision, symmetry, and orderliness of Renaissance architecture to produce a sense of greater dynamism in space. Baroque churches, for example, were impressively grand and monumental, yet emotionally engaging at the same time. Façades and interiors were both massive and, through the clever use of architectural and decorative components, suggestive of movement. A good example of this is the work of Gianlorenzo Bernini (bare-NEE-nee) (1598–1680), who designed the portico outside Saint Peter's Basilica in Rome, as well as the highly ornate bronze canopy over the altar inside the basilica. Dramatic illusion in the interior of buildings—such as painting a chapel ceiling with figures receding as if ascending to heaven—was a common device in baroque architecture. One of the primary purposes of baroque architecture and art was to create simultaneously a display of power and an invitation to sensory experience. Baroque art encouraged piety that was not only emotionally involved, and thus satisfying, but also awe-inspired. In this way, it reflected the aims of the Counter-Reformation church, whose leaders were among its most important patrons.

Peter Paul Rubens's early training in Italy shaped him as an artist and established his secondary career as a diplomat. Throughout his life, he undertook diplomatic missions for the Habsburg viceroys in the Spanish Netherlands, gaining artistic commissions wherever he went. Rubens's subject matter varied widely, including church design and decoration, portraiture, and landscape painting, reflecting the fact that baroque art also had important secular applications. Indeed, magnificent baroque palaces symbolized the wealth and power of the elites (see the photos on pages 450 and 458).

Rulers began to employ artists as portrait painters, such as Rubens's pupil Anthony Van Dyck (1599–1641), whose painting of Charles I of England appears on page 435. Because portraits have become so common, we cannot fully appreciate how arresting this image would have been in its day. Like Rubens's Raising of the Cross, Van Dyck's image of Charles was an innovative rendering of familiar elements.

of the sixteenth and seventeenth centuries. As we have seen, the Protestant faction in France advanced arguments for the limitation of royal power. Alternative theories enhancing royal authority were offered, principally in support of the Catholic position, though also simply to buttress the beleaguered monarchy itself. The most famous of these appeared in The Six Books of the Republic (1576), by the legal scholar Jean Bodin (bo-DAHN) (1530–1596). Bodin was a Catholic, but offered a fundamentally secular perspective on the purposes and source of power within a

Rubens: The Raising of the Cross

(*Onze Lieve Vrouwkwerk*, *Antwerp Cathedral*, *Belgium/ Peter Willi/Bridgeman Art Library*)

The image of a ruler on horseback was well known, but it had never been exploited as fully by English monarchs as it had been by rulers on the Continent. This large portrait of the king was designed to be hung at the end of a long palace corridor so that, from a distance, a courtier would have the illusion of actually seeing the king riding proudly through a triumphal arch.* Compare this portrait with the much more stilted one of Elizabeth I on page 422. It is striking how effective the technical and stylistic innovations of baroque art and architecture were in expressing secular, as well as spiritual, power.

QUESTIONS

1. How does baroque art involve the viewer by appealing to senses and emotions?

2. Why was baroque painting effective for conveying political messages, as in Van Dyck's portrait of Charles I?

* This discussion draws on the work of Roy Strong, *Van Dyck: Charles I on Horseback* (New York: Viking, 1972), pp. 20–25.

state. His special contribution was a vision of a truly sovereign monarch. Bodin offered a theoretical understanding that is essential to states today and is the ground on which people can claim rights and protection from the state—namely, that there is a final sovereign authority. For Bodin, that authority was the king. Contract theory, devised by French Protestants to legitimize resistance to the monarchy, was abandoned when Henry IV granted toleration to the Huguenots in 1598. In England, theoretical justification of resistance to Charles I was initially limited to

SECTION SUMMARY

- Literacy and access to printed books enabled new levels of self-consciousness and self-reflection, as in the work of Montaigne.

- The rise of professional theater began in the 1570s; drama was a favored means of communication by writers as well as political leaders.

- Shakespeare and other writers and artists reflected on many of the current concerns about legitimate authority, religion, and human life in this period.

- Baroque art appealed to viewers' emotions, but also expressed power and grandeur.

- Political theorist Bodin developed the notion of sovereign authority within the state.

invoking tradition and precedent. Contract theory, as well as other sweeping claims regarding subjects' rights, would be more fully developed later in the century.

Bodin's theory of sovereignty, however, was immediately echoed in other theoretical works, most notably, that of Hugo Grotius (GROW-shus) (1583–1645). A Dutch jurist and diplomat, Grotius developed the first principles of modern international law. He accepted the existence of sovereign states that owed no loyalty to higher authority (such as the papacy) and thus needed new principles to govern their interactions. His major work, *De Jure Belli ac Pacis* (*On the Law of War and Peace*, 1625), was written in response to the turmoil of the Thirty Years' War. Grotius argued that relations between states could be based on respect for treaties voluntarily reached between them. In perhaps his boldest move, he argued that war must be justified, and he developed criteria to distinguish just wars from unjust ones.

CHAPTER SUMMARY

The late sixteenth and early seventeenth centuries were an era of intense struggle over political and religious authority. Rulers everywhere, through a variety of means, tried to buttress and expand their power. They were resisted by traditional centers of power, such as independent-minded nobles and wealthy townspeople. But they were also resisted by the novel challenge of religious dissent, which empowered even common people both to claim a greater right to question authority and to risk more in their attempts to oppose it.

FOCUS QUESTIONS

- What circumstances permitted Spain's ambitious policies and to what degree were they successful?

- What conditions led to civil war in France? How did religious and political conflict develop differently in England?

- Why did war erupt again within the Holy Roman Empire and what was the significance of the conflict?

- What caused the economic stresses of these decades and how did ordinary people cope with them?

- In what ways do the literature and art of this period reflect the political, social, and religious conflicts of the age?

The most powerful monarch of the day, the king of Spain, could not defeat a religious and political rebellion in the prosperous Netherlands, even with the resources of treasure from the New World. France was torn apart by decades of civil war before the Crown was able to impose a workable peace and reassert royal authority. In England, political and religiously inspired challenges to royal authority were contained by Elizabeth I, but not as effectively addressed by her successors. Meanwhile, the various states of the Holy Roman Empire were engulfed in a thirty-year war that also had political and religious roots and which became one of the most bitter and complex conflicts of the period.

War itself became more destructive, owing to new technologies and increasing resources devoted to it. Ordinary people also coped with the price revolution, which caused their wages to lose value and many to lose their land. The difficult economic circumstances of these decades meant that working people, desperate for secure livelihood, rioted or took up arms out of economic, as well as religious, concerns.

Yet, however grim the circumstances people faced, the technology of print and the spread of literacy helped spur speculative and creative works by providing the means for reflection and the audiences to receive and appreciate it. Ironically, the increased importance and grandeur of court life, though a cause of political strain, resulted in a new wave of patronage for art, literature, and drama. Other works, such as Shakespeare's plays, both reflect and reflect on the conflicts in the society of the day. Baroque art expressed both the religious passions of the era and the claims to authority by rulers.

KEY TERMS

Philip II   (p. 410)   Edict of Nantes   (p. 419)   Peace of Westphalia   (p. 429)
United Provinces   (p. 414)   Elizabeth I   (p. 421)   price revolution   (p. 430)
Armada   (p. 414)   Puritans   (p. 421)   gentry   (p. 431)
Huguenots   (p. 417)   Thirty Years' War   (p. 425)   baroque   (p. 437)

 This icon will direct you to additional materials on the website: www .cengage.com/history/ noble/westciv6e.

See our interactive eBook for map and primary source activities.

NOTES

1. Geoffrey Parker, *The Dutch Revolt* (London: Penguin, 1985), p. 288, n. 5.

2. Quoted in A. W. Lovett, *Early Habsburg Spain, 1517–1598* (Oxford: Oxford University Press, 1986), p. 212.

3. Quoted in R. J. Knecht, *The French Wars of Religion, 1559–1598* (London: Longman, 1989), p. 109.

4. Quoted in Jean Berenger, *A History of the Habsburg Empire, 1273–1700*, trans. C. A. Simpson (London and New York: Longman, 1990), p. 239.

16

CHAPTER OUTLINE

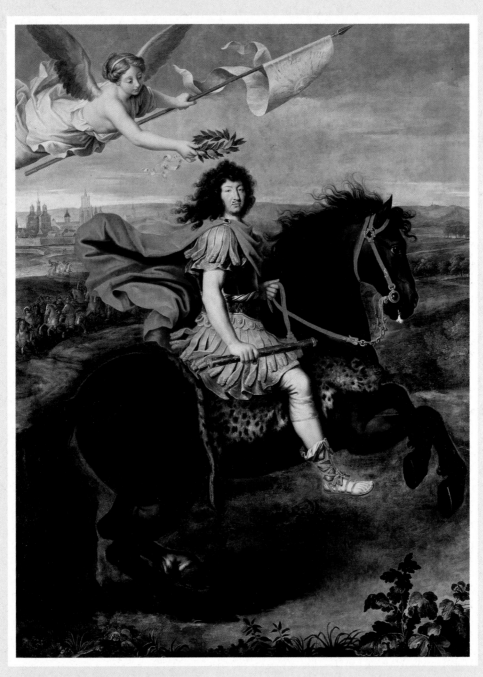

Louis XIV in Roman Armor
(Scala/Art Resource, NY)

Europe in the Age of Louis XIV, ca. 1640–1715

The portrait of King Louis XIV of France as a triumphant warrior, to the left, was one of hundreds of such images of the king that decorated his palace at Versailles and other sites around his kingdom—where they made his subjects aware of his presence, regardless of whether he was in residence. In this painting, the contemporary artist Charles Le Brun depicts Louis as a Roman warrior, and his power is represented by a mixture of other symbols—Christian and pagan, ancient and contemporary. An angel crowns him with a victor's laurel wreath and carries a banner bearing the image of the sun. In his hand, Louis holds a marshal's baton—a symbol of military command—covered with the royal emblem of the fleur-de-lys (flur-duh-LEE). In the background, behind the "Roman" troops following Louis, is an idealized city.

FOCUS QUESTIONS

- How did Louis XIV successfully expand royal power in France and what were some of the achievements of his reign?

- What were the long-term consequences of the English civil war?

- Which states began to dominate central and eastern Europe and why were they successful?

- How and why did Europe's overseas trade and colonization expand in the seventeenth century and what effects did this expansion have on Europe itself?

These trappings symbolized the significant expansion of royal power during Louis's reign. He faced down the challenges of warrior-nobles, suppressed religious dissent, and tapped the nation's wealth to wage a series of wars of conquest. A period of cultural brilliance early in his reign and the spectacle of an elaborate court life crowned his achievements. In his prime, his regime was supported by a consensus of elites; such harmony was made possible by the lack of institutional brakes on royal authority. However, as his attention to symbolism suggests, Louis's power was not unchallenged. By the end of the Sun King's reign, the glow was fading: France was struggling under economic distress brought on by the many wars fought for his glory and had missed opportunities for commercial success abroad. Elites throughout France who had once accepted, even welcomed, his rule became critics, and common people outright rebels.

In England, by contrast, the Crown faced successful rebellion by subjects claiming religious authority and political legitimacy for their causes. Resistance to the expansion of royal authority, led by Parliament, resulted in the execution of the king and the establishment of a short-lived republic, the Commonwealth. Although the monarchy was restored, it became permanently weaker after the civil war. After the Thirty Years' War, vigorous rulers in central and eastern Europe undertook a program of territorial expansion and state building that led to the dominance in the region of Austria, Brandenburg-Prussia, and Russia. The power of these states derived, in part, from the economic relationship of their lands to the wider European economy. In all the major states of continental Europe, princely governments were able to monopolize military power for the first time, in return for economic and political concessions to noble landholders.

The seventeenth century also witnessed a dynamic phase of European expansion overseas, following on the successes of the Portuguese and the Spanish in the

 This icon will direct you to additional materials on the website: www.cengage.com/history/noble/westciv6e.

 See our interactive eBook for map and primary source activities.

fifteenth and sixteenth centuries. The Dutch created the most successful trading empire. Eager migrants settled in the Americas in ever-increasing numbers, while forced migrants—enslaved Africans—were transported by the thousands to work on the profitable plantations of European colonizers. Aristocrats, merchants, and peasants back in Europe jockeyed to take advantage of—or to mitigate the effects of—the local political and economic impact of Europe's expansion.

FRANCE IN THE AGE OF ABSOLUTISM

How did Louis XIV successfully expand royal power in France and what were some of the achievements of his reign?

Absolutism Extraordinary concentration of power and symbolic authority in royal hands, achieved particularly by the king of France (Louis XIV) in the seventeenth century.

Louis XIV Longest-reigning ruler in European history, he imposed "absolute" rule in France and his reign witnessed a great flowering of French culture.

Absolutism is a term often used to describe the extraordinary concentration of power in royal hands achieved by the kings of France, most notably **Louis XIV** (r. 1643–1715), in the seventeenth century. Louis continued the expansion of state power begun by his father's minister, Cardinal Richelieu (see page 421). The extension of royal power, under Louis as well as his predecessor, was accelerated by his desire to sustain an expensive and aggressive foreign policy. The policy itself was partly traditional—fighting the perpetual enemy, the Habsburgs, and seeking military glory—and partly new—expanding the borders of France. Louis XIV's successes in these undertakings made him both envied and emulated by other rulers: The French court became a model of culture and refinement. But increased royal authority was not accepted without protest: Common French people as well as elites dug in their heels over the cost of Louis's policies to them.

The Last Challenge to Absolutism: The Fronde, 1648–1653

Louis inherited the throne at the age of five in 1643. His mother, Anne of Austria (1601–1666), acted as regent, together with her chief minister and personal friend, Cardinal Jules Mazarin (mah-zah-RAHN) (1602–1661). They immediately faced revolts against the concentration of power in royal hands and the exorbitant taxation that had prevailed under Louis's father. The most serious revolt began in 1648, led by the Parlement (par-luh-MAWNH) of Paris and the other sovereign law courts in the capital.

The source of the Parlement's leverage over the monarchy was its traditional right to register laws and edicts, which amounted to judicial review. Now, the Parlement attempted to extend this power by debating and even initiating government policy. The sovereign courts sitting together drew up a reform program abolishing most of the machinery of government established under Richelieu and calling for consent to future taxation. The citizens of Paris rose to defend the courts when royal troops were sent against them in October.

Civil war waxed and waned around France from 1648 to 1653. Fighting was led by great aristocrats in the name of the parlements and other law courts. At the same time, further reform proposals were offered. For example, middling nobles in the region around Paris worked on their own reform program and made preparations for a meeting of the Estates General—a representative assembly—to enact it.

These revolts begun in 1648 were derided with the name "Fronde," which was a popular children's game. However, the Fronde (FRAWND) was not child's play; it constituted a serious challenge to the legacy of royal government as it had developed under Richelieu. It ended without a noteworthy impact on the growth of royal power for several reasons. First, Mazarin made strategic concessions to individual aristocrats, who were always eager to trade their loyalty for the fruits of royal service. Meanwhile, the Parlement of Paris accepted a return to royal authority when the civil war caused starvation as well as threatened its control of reform.

Moreover, the Parlement of Paris was a law court, not a representative assembly. Its legitimacy derived from its role as upholder of royal law, and it could not, over time, challenge the king on the pretext of upholding royal tradition in his name. Parlementaires saw the Estates General as a rival institution and helped quash the proposed meeting of representatives. They especially wanted to avoid reform that included abolition of the paulette, a fee guaranteeing the hereditary right to royal office (see page 420).

Unlike England, France had no single institutional focus for resistance to royal power. A strong-willed and able ruler, as Louis XIV proved to be, could counter challenges to royal power, particularly when he satisfied the ambitions of aristocrats and those bureaucrats who profited from the expansion of royal power.

France Under Louis XIV, 1661–1715

Louis XIV fully assumed control of government in 1661, at a propitious moment. The Peace of the Pyrenees in 1659 had ended, in France's favor, the wars with Spain that had dragged on since the end of the Thirty Years' War. As part of the peace agreement, Louis married a Spanish princess, Maria Theresa. In the first ten years of his active reign, Louis achieved a degree of control over the mechanisms of government unparalleled in the history of monarchy in France or anywhere else in Europe. Louis was an extremely vigorous and diligent king. He put in hours a day at a desk, while sustaining the ceremonial life of the court, with its elaborate hunts, balls, and other public events.

GOVERNMENT REFORMS

Louis did not invent any new bureaucratic devices, but rather used existing ranks of officials in new ways that increased government efficiency and further centralized control. He radically reduced the number of men in his High Council, the advisory body closest to the king, to include only three or four great ministers of state affairs. This intimate group, with Louis's active participation, handled all policymaking. The ministers of state, war, and finance were chosen exclusively from nonnoble men of bourgeois origin, whose training and experience fitted them for such positions. Jean-Baptiste Colbert (coal-BEAR) (1619–1683), perhaps the greatest of them, served as minister of finance and supervised most domestic policy from 1665 until his death. He was from a merchant family and had served for years under Mazarin.

Several dozen other officials, picked from the ranks of up-and-coming lawyers and administrators, drew up laws and regulations and passed them to the intendants for execution at the provincial level. Sometimes these officials at the center were sent to the provinces on short-term supervisory missions. The effect of this system was to bypass many entrenched provincial bureaucrats, particularly those known as tax farmers. Tax farmers were freelance businessmen who bid for the right to collect taxes in a region in return for a negotiated fee they paid to the Crown. The Crown, in short, did not control its own tax revenues. The money Louis's regime saved by the more efficient collection of taxes (revenues almost doubled in some areas) enabled the government to streamline the bureaucracy: Dozens of the offices created over the years to bring cash in were bought back by the Crown from their owners.

The system still relied on the bonds of patronage and personal service—political bonds borrowed from aristocratic life. Officials rose through the ranks by means of service to the great, and family connection and personal loyalty still were essential. Of the seventeen different men who were part of Louis XIV's High Council during his reign, five were members of the Colbert family, for example.

CHRONOLOGY

1602	Dutch East India Company formed
1607	Jamestown colony founded in Virginia
1608	Champlain founds Quebec City
1613	Michael becomes first Romanov tsar in Russia
1620	Pilgrims settle at Plymouth (Massachusetts)
1642–1648	Civil war in England
1643	Louis XIV becomes king of France
1648–1653	Fronde revolts in France
1649	Execution of Charles I
1649–1660	English Commonwealth
1659	Peace of the Pyrenees
1660	Monarchy restored in England
1661	Louis XIV assumes full control of government
1672–1678	Dutch War
1682	Peter the Great becomes tsar of Russia
1685	Edict of Nantes revoked
1688	Glorious Revolution
1699	Treaty of Carlowitz
1700–1721	Great Northern War
1701–1714	War of the Spanish Succession
1713	Peace of Utrecht
1715	Death of Louis XIV

ECONOMIC DEVELOPMENT

Colbert and the other ministers began to develop the kind of planned government policymaking that we now take for granted. Partly by means of their itinerant supervisory officials, they tried to formulate policy based on carefully collected information. How many men of military age were available? How abundant was this year's harvest? Answers to such questions enabled not only the formulation of economic policy, but also the deliberate management of production and services to achieve certain goals—above all, the recruitment and supply of the king's vast armies.

Colbert actively encouraged France's economic development in other ways. He reduced the internal tolls and customs barriers, which were relics of medieval landholders' rights. He encouraged industry with state subsidies and protective tariffs. He set up state-sponsored trading companies—the two most important being the East India Company and the West India Company, established in 1664.

mercantilism Economic policy pursued by western European states in the seventeenth and eighteenth centuries that stressed self-sufficiency in manufactured goods, tight government control of trade, and the absolute value of bullion.

Mercantilism is the term historians use to describe the theory behind Colbert's efforts. This economic theory stressed self-sufficiency in manufactured goods, tight control of trade to foster the domestic economy, and the absolute value of bullion. Both capital for development—in the form of hard currency, known as bullion—and the amount of world trade were presumed to be limited in quantity. Therefore, state intervention in the form of protectionist policies was believed necessary to guarantee a favorable balance of payments.

This static model of national wealth did not wholly fit the facts of growing international trade in the seventeenth century. Nevertheless, mercantilist philosophy was helpful to France. France became self-sufficient in the all-important production of woolen cloth, and French industry expanded notably in other sectors. Colbert's greatest success was the systematic expansion of the navy and merchant marine. By the end of Louis XIV's reign, the French navy was virtually the equal of the English navy.

RELIGIOUS LIFE

Beginning in 1673, Louis tried to bring the religious life of the realm more fully under royal control. He claimed some of the church revenues and powers of ecclesiastical appointment within France that the pope still exercised. Partly to bolster his position with the pope, he also began to attack the Huguenot community in France. First, he offered financial rewards for conversion to Catholicism. Then, he took more drastic steps, such as destroying Protestant churches and quartering troops in Huguenots' homes to force them to convert. In 1685, he revoked the Edict of Nantes. A hundred thousand Protestant subjects—including some six hundred army and navy officers—refused even nominal conversion to Catholicism and chose to emigrate.

Meanwhile, Louis faced resistance to his claims against the pope from within the ranks of French Catholics. These laypeople and clerics represented a movement within French Catholicism known as Jansenism, after Cornelius Jansen, a professor of theology whose writings inspired it. Jansenists practiced an austere style of Catholic religiosity that was akin to some Protestant doctrine in its notions about human will and sinfulness. Louis was wary of any challenge to either the institutional or symbolic unity of his regime and was particularly suspicious of Jansenism because its adherents included many of his political enemies, particularly among families of parlement officials. Late in Louis's reign, another pope obligingly declared many Jansenist doctrines to be heretical as part of a compromise agreement with Louis on matters of church governance and finance.

Despite these successes, the power of the Crown was still greatly limited by modern standards. The "divine right" of kingship, a notion formulated by Louis's chief apologist, Bishop Jacques Bossuet (BOS-soo-way) (1627–1704), did not mean unlimited power to rule; rather, it meant that hereditary monarchy was the divinely ordained form of government, best suited to human needs. *Absolutism* was not iron-fisted control of the realm, but rather the successful focusing of energy, loyalties, and symbolic authority in the Crown. The government functioned well in the opening decades of Louis's reign because his role as the focal point of power and loyalty was both logical, after the preceding years of unrest, and skillfully exploited. Much of the glue holding together the absolutist state lay in informal mechanisms, such as patronage and court life, as well as in the traditional hunt for military glory—all of which Louis amply supplied.

The Life of the Court

An observer comparing the lives of prominent noble families in the mid-sixteenth and mid-seventeenth centuries would have noticed striking differences. By the second half of the seventeenth century, most sovereigns or territorial princes had the power to crush revolts. The nobility relinquished its former independence but retained economic and social supremacy and, as a consequence, considerable political clout. Nobles also developed new ways to symbolize their privilege by means of cultural refinement. This process was particularly dramatic in France.

One sign of Louis's success in marshaling the loyalty of the aristocracy was the brilliant court life that his regime sustained. No longer able to wield independent political power, aristocrats lived at court whenever they could. There, they competed for patronage and prestige—for commands in the royal army and for honorific positions at court itself. A favored courtier might, for example, participate in the elaborate daily *lever* (LEV-ay) (arising) of the king; he might be allowed to hand the king his shirt—a demeaning task, yet a coveted one for the access to the king that it guaranteed. Courtiers now defended their honor with private duels, not warfare, and relied on precise etiquette and clever conversation to mark their political and social distinctiveness. (See the feature, "The Visual Record: Table Manners.")

Noblewomen and noblemen alike began to reflect on their new roles in letters, memoirs, and the first novels. A prominent theme of these works is the increasing need for a truly private life of affection and trust, with which to counterbalance the public façade necessary to an aspiring courtier. The most influential early French novel was *The Princess of Cleves* by Marie-Madeleine Pioche de la Vergne (1634–1693), best known by her title, Madame de Lafayette. Mme. de Lafayette's novel treats the particular difficulties faced by aristocratic women who, without military careers to bring glory and provide distraction, were more vulnerable than men to gossip and slander at court and more trapped by their arranged marriages.

Louis XIV's court is usually associated with the palace he built at Versailles (vare-SIGH), southwest of Paris. Some of the greatest talent of the day worked on the design and construction of Versailles from 1670 through the 1680s. It became a masterpiece of luxurious, but restrained, baroque style—a model for royal and aristocratic palaces throughout Europe for the next one hundred years.

Before Louis's court, in his later years, withdrew to Versailles, it traveled among the king's other châteaux around the kingdom, and in this itinerant period, court life was actually at its most creative. These early years of Louis's personal reign were the heyday of French drama. The comedian Jean-Baptiste Poquelin, known as Molière (mole-YARE) (1622–1673), impressed the young Louis with his productions in the late 1650s and was rewarded with the use of a theater in the main royal palace in Paris. Like Shakespeare earlier in the century, Molière explored the social and political tensions of his day. He satirized the pretensions of the aristocracy and the social climbing of the bourgeoisie. Some of his plays were banned, but most were not only tolerated, but extremely popular with the elite audiences they mocked. Their popularity is testimony to the confidence of Louis's regime in its early days.

Also popular at court were the tragedies of Jean Racine (rah-SEEN) (1639–1699), who was to the French theater what Shakespeare was to the English: the master of poetic language. His plays focus on the emotional and psychological lives of the characters and stress the unpredictable, usually unhappy, role of fate, even among royalty. The pessimism in Racine foreshadowed the less successful second half of Louis's reign.

The Burdens of War and the Limits of Power

Louis XIV started wars that dominated the attention of most European states in the second half of the seventeenth century. His wars sprang from traditional causes: the importance of the glory and dynastic aggrandizement of the king and the preoccupation of the aristocracy with military life. But if Louis's wars had familiar motives, they were far more demanding on state resources than any previous wars.

The new offensive tactics developed during the Thirty Years' War (see page 429) changed the character of armies in ways that demanded more resources for training. A higher proportion of soldiers became gunners, and their effectiveness lay in how well they operated as a unit. Armies began to train seriously off the field of battle because drill and discipline were vital to success. France's victories in the second half of the seventeenth century are partly traceable to the regime's attention to these tasks, as well as to recruitment and supply, which together constituted another phase of the "military revolution." The numbers of men on the battlefield increased somewhat as training increased the effectiveness of large numbers of infantry, but the total numbers of men in arms supported by the state at any time increased dramatically once the organization to support them was in place. Late in the century, France kept more than 300,000 men in arms when at war (which was most of the time).

THE VISUAL RECORD

Table Manners

If you were to sit down in a fancy restaurant, order a juicy steak, and then eat it with your bare hands, other diners would undoubtedly stare, shocked by your bad manners. It has not always been the case that table manners meant very much—were able to signal social status, for example. In fact, table manners did not always exist at all in the sense that we know them. How did they evolve? How did they come to have the importance that they do? And why should historians pay any attention to them?

Imagine that you have been invited to dinner at a noble estate in the year 1500. As you sit down, you notice that there are no knives, forks, and spoons at your place, and no napkins either. A servant (a young girl from a neighboring village) sets a roast of meat in front of you and your fellow diners.

Table Manners of the Upper Class in the Seventeenth Century
(Courtesy of the Trustees of the British Museum)

In 1667, Louis invoked rather dubious dynastic claims to demand from Spain lands in the Spanish Netherlands and the large independent county on France's eastern border called the Franche-Comté (FRAWNSH–con-TAY) (see **Map 16.1**). After a brief conflict, the French obtained only some towns in the Spanish Netherlands.

Louis's focus then shifted to a new enemy, the Dutch. The Dutch had been allied with France since the beginning of their existence as provinces in rebellion against Spain. But the French now turned against them because of Dutch dominance of seaborne trade in the growing international economy. At first, the French tried to offset the Dutch advantage with tariff barriers against Dutch goods. But confidence in the French army led Louis's generals to urge action against the vulnerable Dutch lands. "It is impossible that his Majesty should tolerate any longer the insolence and arrogance of that nation," rationalized the usually pragmatic Colbert in 1670.[1]

The lords and ladies on either side of you hack off pieces of meat with the knives that they always carry with them, and then, they eat the meat with their fingers. Hunks of bread on the table in front of them catch the dripping juices.

One hundred fifty years later, in 1650, dinner is a much more "civilized" meal. Notice the well-to-do women dining in this engraving by the French artist Abraham Bosse (1602–1676). The table setting, with tablecloths, napkins, plates, and silverware, is recognizable to us. The lady at the extreme right holds up her fork and napkin in a somewhat forced and obvious gesture. These diners have the utensils that we take for granted, but the artist does not take them for granted: They are intended to be noticed by Bosse's elite audience.

In the seventeenth century, aristocrats and gentry signaled their political and social privilege with behavior that distinguished them from the lower classes in ways their more powerful ancestors had found unnecessary. Historians have called this the invention of civility. As we have seen, proper courtesy to one's superiors at court was considered essential. Rituals of honor and deference were increasingly taking the place of armed conflict as the routine behavior of the upper classes. Also essential, however, were certain standards of physical privacy and delicacy. Something as seemingly trivial as the use of a fork became charged with symbolic significance. As the actual power of the aristocrats was circumscribed by the state, they found new expressions of status. Since the sixteenth century, new kinds of manners had been touted in handbooks, reflecting changes that already had occurred at Italian courts. During the seventeenth century, these practices became more widespread and opened up a gulf between upper- and lower-class behavior.

Some of the new behaviors concerned bodily privacy and discretion. A nobleman now used a handkerchief instead of his fingers or coat sleeve, and he did not urinate in public. The new "rules" about eating are particularly interesting. Why did eating with a fork seem refined and desirable to aristocrats trying to buttress their own self-images? As any 3-year-old knows, eating with a fork is remarkably inefficient.

Using a fork kept you at a distance—literal and symbolic—from the animal you were eating. Napkins wiped away all trace of bloody juices from your lips. Interestingly, as diners began to use utensils, other eating arrangements changed in parallel ways. Sideboards had been in use for a long time, but pieces of meat were now discreetly carved on the sideboard and presented to diners in individual portions. The carcass was brought to the sideboard cut into roasts instead of unmistakably whole, and it was often decorated—as it is today—to further disguise it.

The new aristocrat was increasingly separated from the world of brute physical force, both in daily life and on the battlefield. In warfare, brute force was no longer adequate. Training, discipline, and tactical knowledge were more important and heightened the significance of rank, which separated officers from the vast numbers of common soldiers. Aristocrats now lived in a privileged world where violence—except for an occasional duel—was no longer a fact of life. Their new behavior codes signaled their new invulnerability to others. Above all, they worked to transform a loss—of the independence that had gone hand in hand with a more violent life—into a gain: a privileged immunity to violence.

Specific manners became important, then, because they were symbols of power. The symbolic distance between the powerful and the humble was reinforced by other changes in habits and behavior. A sixteenth-century warrior customarily traveled on horseback and often went from place to place within a city on foot, attended by his retinue. A seventeenth-century aristocrat was more likely to travel in a horse-drawn carriage. The presence of special commodities from abroad—such as sugar—in the seventeenth century created further possibilities for signaling status.

It is interesting to note that other personal habits still diverged dramatically from what we would consider acceptable today. Notice the large, stately bed in the same room as the dining table in Bosse's engraving. Interior space was still undifferentiated by our standards, and it was common for eating, talking, sleeping, and estate management all to go on in a single room. The grand bed is in the picture because, like the fork, it is a mark of status. Like virtually everything else, what is "proper" varies with historical circumstance.

QUESTIONS

1. Why did elites become interested in table manners in the seventeenth century?
2. How did manners function as effective symbols of power?

The Dutch War began in 1672, with Louis personally leading one of the largest armies ever fielded in Europe—perhaps 120,000 men. The English had also fought the Dutch over trade in the 1650s and now Louis secretly paid the English king, Charles II, to join an alliance against the Dutch.

At first, the French were spectacularly successful, but the Dutch opened dikes and flooded the countryside, and the land war became a soggy stalemate. At the same time, the Dutch beat combined English and French forces at sea and gathered allies who felt threatened by Louis's aggression. The French soon faced German and Austrian forces along their frontier, and by 1674, the English had joined the alliance against France as well. A negotiated peace in 1678 gave France further territory areas in the Spanish Netherlands, as well as control of the Franche-Comté, but it was an illusion of victory only.

Ensconced at Versailles since 1682, Louis seemed to be at the height of his powers. Yet, the Dutch War had in fact cost him more than he had gained. Reforms in government and finance ended under the pressure of paying for war, and old habits of borrowing money and selling offices were revived.

Versailles Palace, The Hall of Mirrors   This ornate gallery, more than 75 yards long, connects the two wings of the palace. Seventeen huge windows and opposing walled mirrors flood the gallery with light. In addition to these dramatic effects, the designers included many thematic details, such as miniature fleur-de-lys entwined with suns to symbolize the union of France and Louis, in the gilded work near the ceiling.   (Réunion des musées nationaux/Art Resource, NY)

Other government obligations, such as encouraging overseas trade, were neglected. Colbert's death in 1683 dramatically symbolized the end of an era of innovation in the French regime.

THE NINE YEARS' WAR

A new war, now known as the Nine Years' War, or King William's War, was touched off late in 1688 by a French invasion of Germany to claim an inheritance there. In his ongoing dispute with the pope, Louis also seized the papal territory of Avignon (ah-veen-YOHN) in southern France. Boldest of all, he helped the exiled Catholic claimant to the English crown, James II, mount an invasion to reclaim his throne (see page 455). Louis's unforgiving Dutch opponent, William of Orange, king of England from 1689 to 1702, led an alliance of all the major powers—Spain, the Netherlands, England, Austria, and the major German states—against the French. As with the Dutch War, the Nine Years' War was costly and, on most fronts, inconclusive. This time, though, there was no illusion of victory for Louis. In the Treaty of Ryswick (1697), Louis gave up most of the territories he had claimed or seized, as well as his contentious claim to papal revenues. The terrible burden of war taxes, combined with crop failures in 1693 and 1694, caused widespread starvation in the countryside. French courtiers began to criticize Louis openly.

THE WAR OF THE SPANISH SUCCESSION

The final and most devastating war of Louis's reign, called the War of the Spanish Succession, broke out in 1701. It was a straightforward dynastic clash between France and its perennial enemy, the Habsburgs. Both Louis and Habsburg Holy Roman emperor Leopold I (r. 1657–1705) hoped to claim, for their heirs, the throne of Spain, left open at the death in 1700 of the last Spanish Habsburg, Charles II. Charles II bequeathed the throne to Louis's grandson, Philip of Anjou, by reason of Louis's marriage to the Spanish princess Maria Theresa and Philip had quickly entered Spain to claim his new kingdom. War was made inevitable when, in an act of sheer belligerence, Louis

MAP 16.1—Territorial Gains of Louis XIV, 1667–1715
Louis's wars, though enormously expensive for France, produced only modest gains of
territory along France's eastern and northern frontiers.

renounced one of the conditions of Charles's will: Philip's accession to the throne of Spain, Louis
insisted, did not prevent his becoming king of France as well. The Dutch and English responded to
the prospect of so great a disruption of the balance of power in Europe by allying with the emperor
against France. The Dutch and English also wanted to defend their colonial interests, since the
French had already begun to profit from new trading opportunities with the Spanish colonies.

Again, the French fought a major war on several fronts on land and at sea. Again, the people
of France felt the cost in crushing taxes that multiplied the effects of harvest failures. Major revolts
inside France forced Louis to divert troops from the war. For a time, it seemed that the French
would be soundly defeated, but they were saved by the superior organization of their forces and
by dynastic accident: Unexpected deaths in the Habsburg family meant that the Austrian claimant
to the Spanish throne suddenly was poised to inherit rule of Austria and the empire as well. The
English, more afraid of a revival of unified Habsburg control of Spain and Austria than of French
domination of Spain, quickly called for peace negotiations.

The Peace of Utrecht in 1713 helped to set the agenda of European politics for the eighteenth
century. Philip of Anjou was recognized as Philip V, the first Bourbon king of Spain, but on the condition that the Spanish and French crowns would never be worn by the same monarch. To maintain
the balance of power against French interests, the Spanish Netherlands and Spanish territories in
Italy were ceded by a second treaty in 1714 to Austria, which for many decades would be France's
major continental rival. The Peace of Utrecht also marked the beginning of England's dominance
of overseas trade and colonization. The French gave to England certain lands in Canada and the
Caribbean and renounced any privileged relationship with Spanish colonies. England was allowed
to control the highly profitable slave trade with Spanish colonies.

SECTION SUMMARY

- The Fronde were revolts against royal power early in Louis XIV's reign.

- Louis successfully rebuilt royal power using control of taxation, a reformed bureaucracy, and traditional political bonds, such as aristocratic patronage.

- The power Louis wielded has been labeled "absolutism" because there were no formal institutional limits on his authority.

- Court life in Louis's reign sponsored artistic creativity and encouraged a new emphasis on cultural refinement in the aristocracy.

- Louis started a series of costly wars from which the French state gained little.

Louis XIV had added small pieces of territory along France's eastern border (see **MAP 16.1**), and a Bourbon ruled in Spain. But the costs in human life and resources were great for the slim results achieved. The army and navy had swallowed up capital that might have fueled investment and trade; strategic opportunities overseas were lost, never to be regained. Louis's government had been innovative in its early years, but remained constrained by traditional ways of imagining the interest of the state.

THE ENGLISH CIVIL WAR AND ITS AFTERMATH

What were the long-term consequences of the English civil war?

Parliament English legislative institution, which used control over monies to bargain with the Crown over foreign and domestic policies, leading to civil war and the deposition of Charles I.

In England, unlike in France, a representative institution—**Parliament**—became an effective, permanent brake on royal authority. The process by which Parliament gained a secure role in governing the kingdom was neither easy nor peaceful, however. As we saw in Chapter 15, conflicts between the English crown and its subjects, culminating in the Crown-Parliament conflict, concerned control over taxation and the direction of religious reform. Beginning in 1642, England was beset by civil war between royal and parliamentary forces. The king was eventually defeated and executed, and for a time, the monarchy was abolished altogether. It was restored in 1660, but Parliament retained a crucial role in governing the kingdom—a role that was confirmed when, in 1688, it again deposed a monarch and established limits on future monarchs' power.

Civil War, 1642–1649

Fighting broke out between the armies of Charles I and parliamentary armies in the late summer of 1642. The Long Parliament (see page 424) continued to represent a broad coalition of critics and opponents of the monarchy, ranging from aristocrats, concerned primarily with abuses of royal prerogative, to radical Puritans, eager for thorough religious reform and determined to defeat the king. Fighting was halfhearted initially, and the tide of war at first favored Charles.

In 1643, however, the scope of the war broadened. Charles made peace with Irish rebels and brought Irish troops to England to bolster his armies. Parliament, in turn, received military aid from the Scots in exchange for promises that Presbyterianism would become the religion of England.

Oliver Cromwell English Puritan general, during the English civil war, who governed as Lord Protector during the interregnum from 1653 to 1658.

Meanwhile, **Oliver Cromwell** (1599–1658), a Puritan member of the Long Parliament and a cavalry officer, helped reorganize parliamentary forces. The eleven-hundred-man cavalry, trained by Cromwell and known as the "Ironsides" and supported by parliamentary and Scottish infantry, defeated the king's troops at Marston Moor in July 1644. The victory made Cromwell famous.

Shortly afterward, Parliament further improved its forces by creating the New Model Army, rigorously trained like Cromwell's Ironsides. Sitting members of Parliament were barred from commanding troops; hence, upper-class control of the army was reduced. This army played a decisive role not only in the war, but also in the political settlement that followed the fighting.

The New Model Army won a convincing victory over royal forces at Naseby in 1645. In the spring of 1646, Charles surrendered to a Scottish army in the north. In January 1647, Parliament paid the Scots for their services in the war and took the king into custody. In the negotiations that followed, Charles tried to play his opponents off against one another, and, as he had hoped, divisions among them widened.

Most members of Parliament were Presbyterians, Puritan gentry who favored a strongly unified and state-controlled church along Calvinist lines. They wanted peace with the king in return for acceptance of the new church structure and parliamentary control of standing militias for a specified period. They did not favor wider political changes, such as extending the right to vote to ordinary people. These men were increasingly alarmed by the appearance of multiple religious sects and by the actual religious freedom that many ordinary people were claiming for themselves. With the weakening of royal authority and the disruption of civil war, censorship was relaxed, and public preaching by ordinary men, and even women, who felt divinely inspired was becoming commonplace.

Above all, Presbyterian gentry in Parliament feared more radical groups in the army and in London who had supported them up to this point, but who favored more sweeping political and religious change. Most officers of the New Model Army, such as Cromwell, were Independents, Puritans who, unlike the Presbyterians, favored a decentralized church, a degree of religious toleration, and a wider sharing of political power among men of property, not just among the very wealthy gentry. In London, a well-organized artisans' movement known as the "Levellers" went even further; Levellers favored universal manhood suffrage, equality under the law, better access to education, and decentralized churches—in short, the separation of political power from wealth and virtual freedom of religion. Many of the rank and file of the army were deeply influenced by Leveller ideas.

In May 1647, the majority in Parliament voted to offer terms to the king and to disband the New Model Army—without first paying most of the soldiers' back wages. This move provoked the first direct intervention by the army in politics. Representatives of the soldiers were chosen to present grievances to Parliament; when this failed, the army seized the king and, in August, occupied Westminster, Parliament's meeting place. Independent and Leveller elements in the army debated the direction of possible reform to be imposed on Parliament. One Leveller argued for universal manhood suffrage: "Every man that is to live under a government ought first by his own consent to put himself under that government; and I do think that the poorest man in England is not at all bound ... to that government that he hath not had a voice to put himself under."[2]

In November, however, their common enemy Charles escaped from his captors and raised a new army with his former enemies, the Scots, who were also alarmed by the growing radicalism in England. Civil war began again early in 1648. Although it ended quickly with a victory by Cromwell and the New Model Army in August, the renewed war further hardened political divisions and enhanced the power of the army. The king was widely blamed for the renewed bloodshed, and the army did not trust him to keep any agreement he might now sign. When Parliament, still dominated by Presbyterians, once again voted to negotiate with the king, army troops, led by Colonel Thomas Pride, prevented members who favored Presbyterianism or negotiating with the king from attending sessions. The "Rump" Parliament that remained after "Pride's Purge" voted to try the king. A hasty trial followed and, on January 30, 1649, Charles I was executed for "treason, tyranny and bloodshed" against his people.

The Interregnum, 1649–1660

A Commonwealth—a republic—was declared. Executive power resided in a council of state. The House of Lords was abolished and legislative power resided in the one-chamber Rump Parliament. Declaring a republic proved far easier than running one, however. The execution of the king shocked most English and Scots and alienated many elites from the new regime. The legitimacy of the Commonwealth government would always be in question.

The tasks of making and implementing policy were hindered by the narrow political base on which the government now rested. Excluded were the majority of the reformist Presbyterian or Anglican gentry who had been purged from Parliament. Also excluded were the more radical Levellers; Leveller leaders in London were arrested when they published tracts critical of the new government. Within a few years, many disillusioned Levellers would join a new religious movement called the Society of Friends, or Quakers, which espoused complete religious autonomy. Quakers declined all oaths or service to the state, and they refused to acknowledge social rank.

Above all, the new government was vulnerable to the power of the army, which had created it. In 1649 and 1650, Cromwell led punitive expeditions to Ireland and Scotland, partly for sheer revenge and partly to put down resistance to Commonwealth authority. In Ireland, where Cromwell's forces were particularly ruthless, the English dispossessed more Irish landholders, which

Popular Preaching in England Many women took advantage of the collapse of royal authority to preach in public—a radical activity for women at the time. This print satirizes the Quakers, a religious movement that attracted many women. (Mary Evans Picture Library)

served to pay off the army's wages. Meanwhile, Parliament could not agree on systematic reforms, particularly the one reform Independents in the army insisted on: more broadly based elections for a new Parliament. Fresh from his victories, Cromwell led his armies to London and dissolved Parliament in the spring of 1652.

In 1653, a cadre of army officers drew up the "Instrument of Government," England's first—and still, today, only—written constitution. It provided for an executive, the Lord Protector, and a Parliament to be based on somewhat wider male suffrage. Cromwell was the natural choice for Lord Protector. Cromwell was an extremely able leader who was not averse to compromise, either in politics or religion. He believed in a state church, but, unlike his Presbyterian opponents, one that allowed for local control, including choice of minister, by individual congregations. He also believed in toleration for Catholics and Jews, as long as no one disturbed the peace.

As Lord Protector, Cromwell oversaw impressive reforms in law that reflected his belief in the limits of governing authority. For example, contrary to the practice of his day, he opposed capital punishment for petty crimes. The government of the Protectorate, however, accomplished little, given Parliament's internal divisions. The population at large still harbored royalist sympathizers; after a royalist uprising in 1655, Cromwell divided England into military districts and vested governing authority in army generals.

After Cromwell died of a sudden illness in September 1658, the Protectorate could not survive the strains over policy and the challenges to its legitimacy. In February 1660, the decisive action of one army general enabled all the surviving members of the Long Parliament to rejoin the Rump. The Parliament summarily dissolved itself and called for new elections. The newly elected Parliament recalled Charles II, son of Charles I, from exile abroad and restored the monarchy. The chaos and radicalism of the late civil war and "interregnum"—the period between reigns, as the years from 1649 to 1660 came to be called—now spawned a conservative reaction.

The Restoration, 1660–1685

Charles II (r. 1660–1685) claimed his throne at the age of 30. He had learned from his years of uncertain exile and from the fate of his father. He did not seek retribution, but rather offered a general pardon to all but a few rebels (mostly those who had signed his father's death warrant), and he suggested to Parliament a relatively tolerant religious settlement that would include Anglicans as well as Presbyterians.

That the reestablished royal government was not more tolerant than it turned out to be was not Charles's doing, initially, but Parliament's. During the 1660s, the "Cavalier" Parliament, named for royalists in the civil war, passed harsh laws aimed at religious dissenters. Anglican orthodoxy was reimposed, including the reestablishment of bishops and the Anglican Book of Common Prayer. All officeholders and clergy were required to swear oaths of obedience to the king and to the established church. As a result, hundreds of non-Anglican Protestants were forced out of office. Holding nonconformist religious services became illegal, and Parliament passed a "five-mile" act to prevent dissenting ministers even from traveling near their former churches. Property laws were tightened and the criminal codes made more severe.

The king's behavior, however, began to mimic prerevolutionary royalist positions. Charles II began to flirt with Catholicism, and his brother and heir, James, openly converted. Charles promulgated a declaration of tolerance that would have included Catholics, as well as nonconformist Protestants, but Parliament would not accept it. In 1678, Charles's secret treaties with the French became known (see page 449), and rumors of a Catholic plot to murder Charles and reimpose Catholicism became widespread. No firm evidence of the "Popish Plot" was ever unearthed, although thirty-five people were executed for alleged participation. Parliament passed the Test Act, which barred all but Anglicans from public office. As a result, the Catholic James was forced to resign as Lord High Admiral.

When Parliament then moved to exclude James from succession to the throne, Charles dissolved it. A subsequent Parliament, worried by the possibility of a new civil war, backed down. But the legacy of the previous civil war and interregnum was a potent one. After two decades of religious pluralism and broadly based political activity, it was impossible to reimpose religious conformity or to silence all dissent, even with harsh new laws on the books. It was also impossible to silence Parliament. Though reluctant to press too far, Parliament tried to assert its policies against the desires of the king.

However, by the end of his reign, Charles was financially independent of Parliament, thanks to increased revenue from overseas trade and secret subsidies from France, his recent ally against the Dutch. If he had been followed by an able successor, Parliament might have lost a good measure of its confidence and independence. But his brother James's reign and its aftermath further enhanced Parliament's power.

The Glorious Revolution, 1688

When James II (r. 1685–1689) succeeded Charles, Parliament was wary but initially cooperative. For example, it granted James customs duties for life, as well as funds to suppress a rebellion by one of Charles's illegitimate sons. James did not try to impose Catholicism on England as some had feared, but he did try to achieve toleration for Catholics in two declarations of indulgence in 1687 and 1688. However admirable his goal—toleration—he had essentially changed the law of the realm without Parliament's consent. He further undermined his position with heavy-handed tactics. When several leading Anglican bishops refused to read the declarations from their pulpits, he had them imprisoned and tried for seditious libel. However, a sympathetic jury acquitted them.

James also failed because of the coincidence of other events. In 1685, at the outset of James's reign, Louis XIV of France had revoked the Edict of Nantes. The possibility that subjects and monarchs in France and, by extension, elsewhere could be of different faiths seemed increasingly unlikely. Popular fears of James's Catholicism were thus heightened early in his reign, and his later declarations of tolerance, though they benefited Protestant dissenters too, were viewed with suspicion. Then, in 1688, the king's second wife, who was Catholic, gave birth to a son. The birth raised the specter of a Catholic succession.

In June 1688, to put pressure on James, leading members of Parliament invited William of Orange, husband of James's Protestant daughter, Mary, to come to England. William mounted an invasion that became a rout and James sought protection in France. William called Parliament, which declared James to have abdicated and offered the throne jointly to William and Mary. With French support, James invaded the British Isles in 1690, but was defeated by William at the Battle of Boyne, in Ireland, that year.

The substitution of William (r. 1689–1702) and Mary (r. 1689–1694) for James, known as the **Glorious Revolution**, was engineered by Parliament and confirmed its power. Parliament presented the new sovereigns with a Declaration of Rights upon their accession and, later that year, with a Bill of Rights that defended freedom of speech, called for frequent Parliaments, and required all future monarchs to be Protestant (see the feature, "The Written Record: The English Bill of Rights"). Parliament's role in the political process was ensured by its power of the purse, since William sought funds for his ambitious military efforts, particularly the Netherlands' ongoing wars with France.

The issues that had faced the English since the beginning of the century were common to all European states: religious division and elite power, fiscal strains and resistance to taxation.

Glorious Revolution
Bloodless English revolution in 1688 in which Parliament replaced the Catholic King James II with William (of Orange) and his wife, Mary (James's Protestant daughter), and imposed, on the new rulers, a Bill of Rights that confirmed Parliament's power.

SECTION SUMMARY

- In England, unlike in France, a representative institution controlled taxation and could effectively challenge royal policies.

- A civil war between Charles I and parliamentary forces ended with the defeat and execution of the king in 1649.

- Several groups, including wealthy gentry and ordinary townspeople, had allied to support Parliament, but they did not agree on a program of political and religious reform.

- The government of the interregnum did not last after the death of the Lord Protector, Oliver Cromwell, because too few of the original supporters of Parliament believed it legitimate or approved of its policies.

- The Crown was restored under Charles II but began to conflict again with Parliament over political and religious policy under his successor James II.

- The role of Parliament in English government was confirmed when William and Mary accepted the Crown under conditions stated in the Bill of Rights.

The English Bill of Rights

After King William and Queen Mary accepted the throne, they signed this Bill of Rights presented to them by Parliament in 1689. They therefore accepted not only the limits of royal power enshrined in the document but also the fact that Parliament could legislate how the monarchy was to function.

Whereas the Lords Spiritual and Temporal and Commons assembled at Westminster, lawfully, fully and freely representing all the estates of the people of this realm, did upon the thirteenth of February ... present unto their Majesties, then called and known by the names and style of William and Mary, prince and princess of Orange, being present in their proper persons, a certain declaration in writing made by the said Lords and Commons in the words following, viz.:

Whereas the late King James the Second, by the assistance of diverse evil counselors, judges and ministers employed by him, did endeavor to subvert and extirpate the Protestant religion and the laws and liberties of this kingdom;

By assuming and exercising a power of dispensing with and suspending of laws and the execution of laws without consent of Parliament; ...

By levying money for and to the use of the Crown by pretense of prerogative for other time and in other manner than the same was granted by Parliament;

By raising and keeping a standing army within this kingdom in time of peace without consent of Parliament, and quartering soldiers contrary to law;

By causing several good subjects being Protestants to be disarmed at the same time when papists were both armed and employed contrary to law;

By violating the freedom of election of members to serve in Parliament;

By prosecutions in the Court of King's Bench for matters and causes cognizable only in Parliament, and by diverse other arbitrary and illegal courses; ...

And excessive bail hath been required of persons committed in criminal cases to elude the benefit of the laws made for the liberty of the subjects;

And excessive fines have been imposed;

And illegal and cruel punishments inflicted; ...

All which are utterly and directly contrary to the known laws and statutes and freedom of this realm;

And whereas the said late King James the Second having abdicated the government and the throne being thereby vacant, his Highness the prince of Orange (whom it hath pleased Almighty God to make the glorious instrument of delivering this kingdom from popery and arbitrary power) did ... cause letters to be written to the Lords Spiritual and Temporal being Protestants, and other letters to the several counties, cities, universities, boroughs and cinque ports,

Yet, the cataclysmic events in England—the interregnum, the Commonwealth, the Restoration, the Glorious Revolution—had set it apart from other states. A representative institution had become a partner of the monarchy.

NEW POWERS IN CENTRAL AND EASTERN EUROPE

Which states began to dominate central and eastern Europe and why were they successful?

By the end of the seventeenth century, three states dominated central and eastern Europe: Austria, Brandenburg-Prussia, and Russia. After the Thirty Years' War, the Habsburgs' dominance in the splintering empire waned, and they focused on expanding and consolidating their power in their hereditary possessions, centered in what became modern Austria. Brandenburg-Prussia, in northeastern Germany, emerged from obscurity to rival the Habsburg state. The rulers of Brandenburg-Prussia had gained lands in the Peace of Westphalia, and astute management transformed their relatively small and scattered holdings into one of the most powerful states in Europe. Russia's new stature in eastern Europe resulted in part from the weakness of its greatest rival, Poland, and the determination of one leader, Peter the Great, to assume a major role in European affairs. Sweden controlled valuable Baltic territory through much of the century, but eventually was also eclipsed by Russia as a force in the region.

The internal political development of states was dramatically shaped by their relationship to the wider European economy: They were sources of grain and raw materials for the more densely urbanized West. The development of and the competition among states in central and eastern Europe were closely linked to developments in western Europe.

for the choosing of such persons to represent them as were of right to be sent to Parliament. ...

And thereupon the said Lords Spiritual and Temporal and Commons, pursuant to their respective letters and elections, being now assembled in a full and free representative of this nation, taking into their most serious consideration the best means for attaining the ends aforesaid, do in the first place (as their ancestors in like case have usually done) for the vindicating and asserting their ancient rights and liberties declare;

That the pretended power of suspending of laws or the execution of laws by regal authority without consent of Parliament is illegal;

That the pretended power of dispensing with laws or the execution of laws by regal authority, as it hath been assumed and exercised of late, is illegal; ...

That levying money for or to the use of the Crown by pretense of prerogative, without grant of Parliament, for longer time, or in other manner than the same is or shall be granted, is illegal;

That it is the right of the Subjects to petition the king, and all commitments and prosecutions for such petitioning are illegal;

That the raising or keeping a standing army within the kingdom in time of peace, unless it be with consent of Parliament, is against law;

That the subjects which are Protestants may have arms for their defense suitable to their conditions and as allowed by law;

That election of members of Parliament ought to be free;

That the freedom of speech and debates or proceedings in Parliament ought not to be impeached or questioned in any court or place out of Parliament;

That excessive bail ought not to be required, nor excessive fines imposed nor cruel and unusual punishments inflicted; ...

And that for redress of all grievances, and for the amending, strengthening and preserving of the laws, Parliaments ought to be held frequently.

QUESTIONS

1. How, specifically, does this document limit royal power?
2. What rights were the creators of this document most concerned to protect, in your view?
3. Would any of the rights protected here have been useful to common English people?

Source: *The Statutes: Revised Edition*, vol. 1 (London: Eyre and Spottiswoode, 1871), pp. 10–12.

The Consolidation of Austria

The Thirty Years' War (see pages 427–430) weakened the Habsburgs as emperors but strengthened them in their own lands. The main Habsburg lands in 1648 were a collection of principalities comprising modern Austria, the kingdom of Hungary (largely in Turkish hands), and the kingdom of Bohemia (see **Map 16.2**). In 1714, Austria acquired the Spanish Netherlands (modern Belgium), which were renamed the Austrian Netherlands. Although language and ethnic differences prevented an absolutist state along French lines, Leopold I (r. 1657–1705) made political and institutional changes that enabled the Habsburg state to become one of the most powerful in Europe through the eighteenth century.

Much of the coherence that already existed in Leopold's lands had been achieved by his predecessors after the Thirty Years' War. The lands of rebels in Bohemia had been confiscated and redistributed among loyal, mostly Austrian, families. In return for political and military support for the emperor, these families were given the right to exploit their newly acquired land and the peasants who worked it. The desire to recover population and productivity after the destruction of the Thirty Years' War gave landlords further incentive to curtail peasants' autonomy, particularly in devastated Bohemia. Austrian landlords throughout the Habsburg domains provided grain and timber for the export market and foodstuffs for the Austrian armies, while elite families provided the army with officers. This political-economic arrangement provoked numerous serious peasant revolts, but the peasants were not able to force changes in a system that suited both the elites and the central authority.

Although Leopold had lost much influence within the empire itself, an imperial government including a war ministry, financial bureaucracy, and the like still functioned in his capital, Vienna. Leopold worked to extricate the government of his own lands from the apparatus of imperial institutions, which were staffed largely by Germans more loyal to imperial, than to Habsburg, interests.

Baroque Splendor in Austria The Belvedere Palace (whose name means "beautiful view") was built near Vienna as the summer residence of the great aristocratic general Prince Eugene of Savoy, who had successfully led Habsburg armies against the Turks and had reaped many rewards from Leopold and his successors. The palace shares many features in common with Louis XIV's palace of Versailles. (Erich Lessing/Art Resource, NY)

In addition, Leopold used the Catholic Church as an institutional and ideological support for his state. Leopold's personal ambition was to reestablish devout Catholicism throughout his territories. Acceptance of Catholicism became the litmus test of loyalty to the Habsburg regime, and Protestantism vanished among elites. Leopold encouraged the work of Jesuit teachers and members of other Catholic religious orders. These men and women helped staff his government and administered religious life down to the most local levels.

Leopold's most dramatic success, as a Habsburg and a religious leader, was his reconquest of the kingdom of Hungary from the Ottoman Empire. Since the mid-sixteenth century, the Habsburgs had controlled only a narrow strip of the kingdom. Preoccupied with fighting France, Leopold did not himself choose to begin a reconquest. His centralizing policies, however, alienated nobles and townspeople in the portion of Hungary he did control, as did his repression of Protestantism, which had flourished in Hungary. Hungarian nobles began a revolt, aided by the Turks, aiming for a reunited Hungary under Ottoman protection.

The Habsburgs won, instead, in part because they received help from the Venetians, the Russians, and especially the Poles, whose lands in Ukraine were threatened by the Turks. The Turks overreached their supply lines to besiege Vienna in 1683. When the siege failed, Habsburg armies slowly pressed east and south, recovering Buda, the capital of Hungary, in 1686 and Belgrade (modern Serbia) in 1688. The **Treaty of Carlowitz** ended the fighting in 1699, after the first conference where European allies jointly dictated terms to a weakening Ottoman Empire. Austria's allies had also gained at the Ottomans' expense: The Poles recovered the threatened Ukraine, and the Russians gained a vital foothold on the Black Sea.

Leopold gave control of reclaimed lands to loyal Austrian officers but could not fully break the traditions of Hungarian separatism. Hungary's great aristocrats—whether they had defended the Habsburgs against Turkish encroachment or guarded the frontier for Turkish overlords—retained their independence. The peasantry, as elsewhere, suffered a decline in status as a result of the Crown's efforts to ensure the loyalty of elites. In the long run, Hungarian independence weakened the Habsburg state, but in the short run, Leopold's victory over the Turks and the recovery of Hungary were momentous events, confirming the Habsburgs as the preeminent power in central Europe.

The Rise of Brandenburg-Prussia

Several German states, in addition to Austria, gained territory and stature after the Thirty Years' War. By the end of the seventeenth century, the strongest was **Brandenburg-Prussia**, a conglomeration of small territories held, by dynastic accident, by the Hohenzollern family. The two principal territories were electoral Brandenburg, in northeastern Germany, with its capital, Berlin, and the duchy of Prussia, a fief of the Polish crown along the Baltic coast east of Poland proper (see **MAP 16.2**). In addition, the Hohenzollerns ruled a handful of small principalities near the Netherlands. These unpromising lands became a powerful state, primarily because of the work of Frederick William, known as "the Great Elector" (r. 1640–1688).

Frederick William used the occasion of a war to effect a permanent change in the structure of government. He took advantage of a war between Poland and its rivals, Sweden and Russia (described in the next section), to win independence for the duchy of Prussia from Polish overlordship. When his involvement in the war ended in 1657, he kept intact the general war commissariat, a combined civilian and military body that had efficiently directed the war effort, bypassing traditional councils and representative bodies. He also used the standing army to force the payment of high taxes. Most significantly, he established a positive relationship with the Junkers (YUNG-kurz), hereditary landholders, which ensured him both revenue and loyalty. The Junkers surrendered their accustomed political independence in return for greater economic and social power over the peasants who worked their lands. The freedom to control their estates led many nobles to invest in profitable agriculture for the export market. The peasants were serfs who received no benefits from the increased productivity of the land.

Frederick William further enhanced his state's power by sponsoring industry. These industries did not have to fear competition from urban producers because the towns had been frozen out of the political process and saddled with heavy taxes. Though an oppressive place for many Germans, Brandenburg-Prussia attracted many skilled refugees, such as Huguenot artisans fleeing Louis XIV's France.

Other German states, such as Bavaria and Saxony, had vibrant towns, largely free peasantries, and weaker aristocracies but were relative nonentities in international affairs. Power on the European stage depended on military force. Whether in a large state like France or in a small one like Brandenburg-Prussia, that power usually came at the expense of the people.

Competition Around the Baltic

The rivers and port cities of the Baltic coast were conduits for the growing trade between the Baltic hinterland and the rest of Europe. Trade in grain, timber, furs, iron, and copper was vital to the entire European economy and caused intense competition, especially between Poland-Lithuania and Sweden, to control the coast and inland regions. In 1600, a large portion of the Baltic hinterland lay under the control of Poland-Lithuania, a vast state at the height of its power, but one that would prove an exception to the pattern of expanding royal power in the seventeenth century.

Poland and Lithuania had been jointly governed since a marriage united their ruling families in the late Middle Ages. Even so, the two states retained distinct traditions. Like some of the Habsburgs' territories, Poland-Lithuania was a multiethnic state, particularly the huge duchy of Lithuania, which included Ruthenia (modern Belarus and Ukraine). Poles spoke Polish, a Slavic language, and were primarily Catholic, although there were also large minorities of Protestants,

Treaty of Carlowitz
Treaty imposed by the European allies on the Ottoman Empire, by which the Austrians, Venetians, Russians, and Poles gained territory at the Turks' expense.

Brandenburg-Prussia
Group of German territories ruled by the Hohenzollern family that became one of Europe's most powerful states in the seventeenth century.

● **MAP 16.2 — New Powers in Central and Eastern Europe, to 1725**

The balance of power in central and eastern Europe shifted with the strengthening of Austria, the rise of Brandenburg-Prussia, and the expansion of Russia at the expense of Poland and Sweden.

Legend:
- French Bourbon lands
- Spanish Bourbon lands
- Austrian Habsburg lands
- Prussian lands
- Great Britain
- Boundary of the Holy Roman Empire
- Russian Empire
- Russian gains, by 1725
- Ottoman Empire, 1722

ATLANTIC OCEAN

North Sea

GREAT BRITAIN
SCOTLAND
Edinburgh
ENGLAND
London
Thames R.
IRELAND
Dublin

Baltic Sea

KINGDOM OF SWEDEN
NORWAY
Oslo
SWEDEN
FINLAND
St. Petersburg
INGRIA
ESTONIA
LIVONIA
Riga

RUSSIAN EMPIRE
Moscow
Smolensk

KINGDOM OF DENMARK
DENMARK

BELARUS
Minsk
LITHUANIA

POLAND-LITHUANIA
Warsaw

PRUSSIA
Königsberg
Gdansk
Vistula R.

BRANDENBURG
Berlin
Elbe R.
Oder R.
SILESIA
SAXONY
BOHEMIA

HANOVER

UNITED NETHERLANDS
Utrecht

HOLY ROMAN EMPIRE
PALATINATE
Strasbourg
Rhine R.
LORRAINE
Danube R.
BAVARIA
AUSTRIA
Vienna

FRANCE
Paris
Seine R.
Loire R.
Toulouse
Garonne R.
Marseilles
Rhône R.

SWITZERLAND
ALPS
SAVOY
MILAN
MODENA
GENOA
Po R.
Genoa

SPAIN
Madrid
Duero R.
Tagus R.
Ebro R.
CATALONIA
GIBRALTAR (Gr. Br.)

PORTUGAL
Lisbon

Corsica (Genoa)
Sardinia (Austria)
Minorca (Gr. Br.)
Balearic Is.
Sicily (Savoy)

Mediterranean Sea

PAPAL STATES
TUSCANY
Rome
KINGDOM OF NAPLES
Naples

REPUBLIC OF VENICE
Adriatic Sea

CROATIA
SLAVONIA
BOSNIA
HERZEGOVINA
MONTENEGRO
ALBANIA
SERBIA
Belgrade

HUNGARY
Buda
Pest
Danube R.
TRANSYLVANIA
CARPATHIAN MTS.
WALLACHIA
MOLDAVIA
BULGARIA

Dniester R.

UKRAINE
Kiev
Dnieper R.
Poltava
COSSACKS
DON COSSACKS
Don R.

CRIMEA

Black Sea

OTTOMAN EMPIRE
Constantinople
Aegean Sea
GREECE
ANATOLIA
ARMENIA
KURDISTAN

0   150   300 Mi.
0   150   300 Km.

N

Orthodox Christians, and Jews in Poland. Lithuanians, whose language was only distantly related to the Slavic languages, were mostly Catholic as well, although Orthodox Christianity predominated among the Ruthenians, who spoke a Slavic language related to both Russian and Polish.

The state commanded considerable resources, including the ports of Gdansk and Riga on the Baltic and grain-producing lands in the interior. However, Poland-Lithuania had internal weaknesses. It was a republic of the nobility, with a weak elected king at its head. The great nobles, whose fortunes increased with the grain trade, ran the affairs of state through the national parliament, the Sejm (SAME). They drastically limited the ability of the Crown to tax and to grant new titles of nobility, as was the practice throughout Europe. These limitations meant that the king could not reward the loyalty of wealthy gentry or the small numbers of urban elites, so that they might be a counterweight to noble power. Limited funds also meant that the Polish crown would be hard put to defend its vast territories when challenged by its rivals.

Strains began to mount within Poland-Lithuania in the late sixteenth century. The spread of the Counter-Reformation, encouraged by the Crown, created tensions with both Protestant and Orthodox subjects in the diverse kingdom. As the power of landholding nobles grew with Poland's expanding grain exports, impoverished peasants were bound to the land, and lesser gentry, particularly in Lithuania, were shut out of political power. In Ukraine, communities of **Cossacks**, nomadic farmer-warriors, grew as Polish and Lithuanian peasants fled harsh conditions to join them. The Cossacks had long been tolerated because they served as a military buffer against the Ottoman Turks to the south, but now Polish landlords wanted to reincorporate the Cossacks into the profitable political-economic system they controlled.

In 1648, the Polish crown faced revolt and invasion that it could not fully counter. The Cossacks led a major uprising, which included Ukrainian gentry as well as peasants. In 1654, the Cossacks tried to assure their autonomy by transferring their allegiance to Moscow. They became part of a Russian invasion of Poland-Lithuania that, by the next year, had engulfed much of the eastern half of the dual state. At the same time, Poland's perennial rival, Sweden, seized central Poland in a military campaign marked by extreme brutality. Many Polish and Lithuanian aristocrats continued to act like independent warlords and cooperated with the invaders to preserve their own local power.

Operating with slim resources, Polish royal armies eventually managed to recover much territory—most important, the western half of Ukraine (see **MAP 16.2**). But the invasions and subsequent fighting were disastrous. The population of Poland declined by as much as 40 percent, and vital urban economies were in ruins. The Catholic identity of the Polish heartland had been a rallying point for resistance to the Protestant Swedes and the Orthodox Russians, but the religious tolerance that had distinguished the diverse Polish kingdom and had been mandated in its constitution was now abandoned. In addition, much of its recovery of Lithuanian territory was only nominal.

The elective Polish crown passed in 1674 to the military hero Jan Sobieski (so-BYESS-key) (r. 1674–1696), known as "Vanquisher of the Turks" for his role in raising the siege of Vienna in 1683. Given Poland's internal weakness, however, Sobieski's victories, in the long run, helped the Ottomans' other foes—Austria and Russia—more than they helped the Poles. After his death, Poland would be vulnerable to the political ambitions of its more powerful neighbors. The next elected king, Augustus II of Saxony (r. 1697–1704, 1709–1733), dragged Poland back into war, from which Russia would emerge the clear winner in the power struggle in eastern Europe.

The Swedes, meanwhile, successfully vied with the Poles for control of the lucrative Baltic coast. Swedish efforts to control Baltic territory had begun in the sixteenth century, first to counter the power of its perennial rival, Denmark, in the western Baltic. Sweden then competed with Poland to control Livonia (modern Latvia) and its major port city, Riga. By 1617, under Gustav Adolf, the Swedes gained the lands to the north of Livonia surrounding the Gulf of Finland (the most direct outlet for Russian goods), and in 1621, they displaced the Poles in Livonia itself. Swedish intervention in the Thirty Years' War (see page 428) had been part of this campaign to secure Baltic territory. And the Treaty of Westphalia (1648, see page 429) confirmed Sweden's gains on the Baltic.

The port cities held by Sweden were profitable but simply served to pay for the costly wars necessary to seize and defend them. Indeed, Sweden did not have the resources to hold Baltic territory over the long term, and it gained little from its aggression against Poland in the 1650s. Owing to its earlier gains, Sweden managed to reign supreme on the Baltic coast until the end of the century, when it was supplanted by the powerful Russian state.

Cossacks Russian term meaning "free men" originally applied to people of central Asian origin in the hinterland of the Black Sea. After 1500, many peasants escaping serfdom in Poland-Lithuania and Russia fled and became "Cossacks."

Russia Under Peter the Great

The Russian state grew dramatically in the sixteenth century, under Ivan IV (r. 1533–1584), the first Russian ruler to routinely use the title "Tsar" (Russian for "Caesar"). Ivan's use of the title reflected his imperial intentions. He expanded the territory under Moscow's control south to the Caspian Sea and east into Siberia. Within his expanding empire, Ivan ruled as an autocrat. The need to gather tribute money for Mongol overlords in medieval times had concentrated many resources in the hands of Muscovite princes. Ivan was able to bypass noble participation and create ranks of officials loyal only to him.

Ivan came to be called "the Terrible," from a Russian word meaning "awe-inspiring." Although a period of disputed succession to the throne, known as the "Time of Troubles," followed Ivan's death in 1584, the foundations of the large and cohesive state he had built survived until a new dynasty of rulers was established in the seventeenth century.

The Romanovs, an aristocratic family related to Ivan's, became the new ruling dynasty in 1613. Michael (r. 1613–1645) was named tsar by an assembly of aristocrats, gentry, and commoners who were more alarmed by the civil wars and recent Polish invasions than by a return to strong tsarist rule. Michael was succeeded by his son, Alexis (r. 1645–1676), who presided over the extension of Russian control to eastern Ukraine in 1654, following the wars in Poland, and developed an interest in cultivating relationships with the West.

Peter the Great Energetic and tyrannical Russian tsar who forcibly westernized Russian state and society and made Russia into a great power.

A complete shift of the balance of power in eastern Europe and the Baltic, in Russia's favor, was achieved by Alexis's son, Peter I (r. 1682–1725), "the Great." **Peter the Great** accomplished this by military successes against his enemies and by forcibly reorienting Russian government and society toward involvement with the rest of Europe.

Peter was almost literally larger than life. Nearly 7 feet tall, he towered over most of his contemporaries and had physical and mental energy to match his size. He set himself to learning trades and studied soldiering by rising through the ranks of the military like a common soldier. He traveled abroad to learn as much as he could about western European economies and governments. He wanted the revenue, manufacturing output, technology and trade, and, above all, up-to-date army and navy that other rulers enjoyed.

Immediately on his accession to power, Peter initiated a bold series of changes in Russian society. His travels had taught him that European monarchs coexisted with a privileged, but educated, aristocracy and that a brilliant court life symbolized and reinforced their authority. So, he set out to refashion Russian society in what amounted to an enforced cultural revolution. He provoked a direct confrontation with Russia's traditional aristocracy over everything from education to matters of dress. He elevated numerous new families to the ranks of gentry and created an official ranking system for the nobility to encourage and reward service to his government.

Peter's effort to reorient his nation culturally, economically, and politically toward Europe was most obvious in the construction of the city of St. Petersburg on the Gulf of Finland, which provided access to the Baltic Sea (see **MAP 16.2**). In stark contrast to Moscow, dominated by the medieval fortress of the Kremlin, St. Petersburg was a modern European city with wide avenues and palaces designed for a sophisticated court life.

Although Peter was highly intelligent, practical, and determined to create a more productive and better governed society, he was also cruel and authoritarian. Peasants already bore the brunt of taxation, but their tax burden worsened when they were assessed arbitrarily by head and not by output of the land. The building of St. Petersburg cost staggering sums in both money and workers' lives. Peter's entire reform system was carried out tyrannically; resistance was brutally suppressed. Victims included his own son, who died after torture while awaiting execution for questioning his father's policies. Peter faced rebellions by elites, as well as common people, against the exactions and the cultural changes of his regime.

Peter the Great This portrait by a Dutch artist captures the tsar's "westernizing" mission by showing Peter in military dress according to European fashions of the day.
(Bildarchiv Preussischer Kulturbesitz/Art Resource, NY)

A major reason for the high cost of Peter's government to the Russian people was his ambition for territorial gain—hence, his emphasis on an improved, and costly, army and navy. He recruited experienced foreign technicians and created the Russian navy from scratch. At first, ships were built in the south to contest Turkish control of the Black Sea. Later, they were built in the north to secure and defend the Baltic. Peter also modernized the Russian army by employing tactics, training, and discipline he had observed in the West. He introduced military conscription and built munitions plants. By 1709, Russia was able to manufacture most of the up-to-date firearms its army needed.

Russia waged war virtually throughout Peter's reign. He struck at the Ottomans and their client state in the Crimea. Peter was most successful against his northern competitor, Sweden, for control of the weakened Polish state and the Baltic Sea. The conflicts between Sweden and Russia, known as the Great Northern War, raged from 1700 to 1709 and, in a less intense phase, lasted until 1721. By the Treaty of Nystadt in 1721, Russia gained its present-day territory in the Gulf of Finland near St. Petersburg, plus Livonia and Estonia. These acquisitions gave Russia a secure window on the Baltic and, in combination with its gains of Lithuanian territory earlier in the century, made Russia the preeminent Baltic power, at Sweden's and Poland's expense.

SECTION SUMMARY

- After the Thirty Years' War, Austria, Brandenburg-Prussia, and Russia became the dominant states in central and eastern Europe.

- Central and eastern Europe provided raw materials for the wider European economy, which enhanced elites' power over peasants, increased revenues to states, and caused wars between states over these resources.

- The Austrian Habsburgs consolidated their power in their territories within the Holy Roman Empire and reconquered Hungary from the Ottoman Turks.

- Although composed of a collection of small principalities, Brandenburg-Prussia became a powerful state.

- Poland-Lithuania declined in the seventeenth century because the elective monarchy could not defend itself against independent aristocrats, rebellious Cossacks, or powerful neighboring states.

- Russia was forcibly modernized by Peter the Great and became the most powerful state in eastern Europe under his reign, eclipsing Sweden in control of Baltic territories.

THE EXPANSION OF OVERSEAS TRADE AND SETTLEMENT

How and why did Europe's overseas trade and colonization expand in the seventeenth century and what effects did this expansion have on Europe itself?

By the beginning of the seventeenth century, competition from the Dutch, French, and English was disrupting the Spanish and Portuguese trading empires in the New World and in Asia. During the seventeenth century, the Dutch not only became masters of the spice trade, but broadened the market to include many other commodities. In the Americas, a new trading system linking Europe, Africa, and the New World came into being with the expansion of tobacco and, later, sugar production. French and English colonists began settling in North America in increasing numbers. Overseas trade also had a crucial impact on life within Europe: on patterns of production and consumption, on social stratification, and on the distribution of wealth.

The Growth of Trading Empires: The Success of the Dutch

By the end of the sixteenth century, the Dutch and the English were making incursions into the Portuguese-controlled spice trade with areas of India, Ceylon, and the East Indies. Spain had annexed Portugal in 1580, but the drain on Spain's resources, from its wars with the Dutch and French, prevented Spain from adequately defending its enlarged trading empire in Asia. The Dutch and, to a lesser degree, the English rapidly supplanted Portuguese control of this lucrative trade (see **Map 16.3**).

The Dutch were particularly well placed to dominate overseas trade. They already dominated seaborne trade within Europe, including the most important long-distance trade, which linked Spain and Portugal—with their wine and salt, as well as spices, hides, and gold from abroad—with the Baltic seacoast, where these products were sold for grain and timber produced in Germany, Poland-Lithuania, and Scandinavia. The geographic position of the Netherlands and the fact that the Dutch consumed more Baltic grain than any other area, because of their large urban population, help to explain their dominance of this trade. In addition, the Dutch had improved the design of their merchant ships to maximize their profits. By 1600, they had

🌐 **MAP 16.3—Dutch Commerce in the Seventeenth Century**
The Dutch supplanted Portuguese control of trade with Asia and dominated seaborne trade within Europe.

developed the *fluitschip* (flyship), a cheaply built vessel with a long, flat hull and simple rigging, that carried goods economically.

Dutch East India Company Commercially innovative Dutch company, formed in 1602, that combined government management of trade with both public and private investment.

The Dutch succeeded in Asia because of institutional, as well as technological, innovations. In 1602, the **Dutch East India Company** was formed. The company combined government management of trade, typical of the period, with both public and private investment. In the past, groups of investors had funded single voyages or small numbers of ships on a one-time basis. The formation of the Dutch East India Company created a permanent pool of capital to sustain trade. After 1612, investments in the company were negotiable as stock. These greater assets allowed proprietors to spread the risks and delays of longer voyages among larger numbers of investors. In addition, more money was available for warehouses, docks, and ships. The English East India Company, founded in 1607, also supported trade, but more modestly. It had one-tenth the capital of the Dutch company and did not use the same system of permanent capital held as stock by investors until 1657. The Bank of Amsterdam, founded in 1609, became the depository for the bullion that flowed into the Netherlands with the flood of trade. The bank established currency exchange rates and issued paper money and instruments of credit to facilitate commerce.

A dramatic expansion of trade with Asia resulted from the Dutch innovations, so much so that by 1650, the European market for spices was glutted, and traders' profits had begun to fall. To control the supply of spices, the Dutch seized some of the areas where they were produced. The Dutch and English also responded to the oversupply of spices by diversifying their trade. The proportion of spices in cargoes from the East fell from about 70 percent at mid-century to just over 20 percent by the century's end. New consumer goods, such as tea, coffee, and silk and cotton fabrics, took their place. Eventually, the Dutch and the English, alert for fresh opportunities, entered the local carrying trade among Asian states. This enabled them to make profits even without purchasing goods, and it slowed the drain of hard currency from Europe—currency in increasingly short supply, as silver mines in the Americas were depleted.

The "Golden Age" of the Netherlands

The prosperity occasioned by the Dutch trading empire created social and political conditions within the Netherlands unique among European states. The concentration of trade and shipping sustained a healthy merchant oligarchy and also a prosperous artisanal sector. Disparities of wealth were smaller here than anywhere else in Europe. The shipbuilding and fishing trades, among others, supported large numbers of workers with a high standard of living for the age.

The Netherlands appeared to contemporaries to be an astonishing exception to the normal structures of politics. Political decentralization in the Netherlands persisted. The Estates General (representative assembly) for the Netherlands as a whole had no independent powers of taxation. Each of the seven provinces retained considerable autonomy. Wealthy merchants in the Estates of the province of Holland, in fact, constituted the government for the entire nation for long periods because of Holland's economic dominance. The head of government was the executive secretary, known as the pensionary, of Holland's Estates.

Holland's only competition in the running of affairs came from the House of Orange, aristocratic leaders of the revolt against Spain (see pages 410–413). They exercised what control they had by means of the office of *stadtholder* (STAHT-hole-der)—a kind of military governorship—to which they were elected in individual provinces. Their principal interest, traditional military glory and dynastic power, accounted for some of their influence, since they led the Netherlands' defense against Spanish attacks until the Peace of Westphalia in 1648 and against French aggression after 1672. Their power also came from their status as the only counterweight within the Netherlands to the dominance of Amsterdam's (in Holland) mercantile interests. Small towns, dependent on land-based trade or rural areas dominated by farmers and gentry, looked to the stadtholders of the Orange family to defend their interests.

As elsewhere, religion was a source of political conflict. The stadtholders and the leading families of Holland, known as regents, vied for control of the state church. Regents of Holland generally favored a less rigid and austere form of Calvinism than did the stadtholders. Their view reflected the needs of the diverse urban communities of Holland, where thousands of Jews, as well as Catholics and various Protestants, lived. Dutch commercial dominance involved the Netherlands in costly wars throughout the second half of the century. Between 1657 and 1660, the Dutch fought the Swedes to safeguard the sea-lanes and port cities of the Baltic. The most costly conflicts came from the rivalry of England and France. Under Cromwell, the English attempted to close their ports to the Dutch carrying trade. In 1672, the English, under Charles II, allied with the French, hoping that together they could destroy Dutch commercial power and even divide the Netherlands' territory between them. The Dutch navy, rebuilt since Cromwell's challenge, soon forced England out of the alliance.

But there were long-term consequences of these wars for the Dutch state. As a result of the land war with France, the Estates in Holland lost control of policy to William of Nassau (d. 1702), prince of Orange, after 1672. William drew the Netherlands into his family's long-standing close relationship with England. Like previous members of his family, William had married into the English royal family: His wife was Mary, daughter of James II. After William and Mary assumed the English throne, Dutch commerce actually suffered more when allied with England than in its previous rivalry. William used Dutch resources for the land war against Louis XIV and reserved, for the English navy, the fight at sea. By the end of the century, Dutch maritime strength was being eclipsed by English sea power.

The Growth of Atlantic Commerce

In the seventeenth century, the Dutch, the English, and the French joined the Spanish as colonial and commercial powers in the Americas. The Spanish colonial empire, in theory a trading system closed to outsiders, was in fact vulnerable to other European traders. Spanish treasure fleets were themselves a glittering attraction. In 1628, for example, a Dutch captain seized the entire fleet. But by then, Spain's goals and those of its competitors had begun to shift. The limits of an economy based on the extraction, rather than the production, of wealth became clear with the declining output of the Spanish silver mines during the 1620s. In response, the Spanish and their Dutch, French, and English competitors expanded the production of cash crops: tobacco, dyestuffs, and, above all, sugar.

Vermeer: The Letter
This is a later work by one of the great artists of the Dutch "Golden Age." Dutch art was distinguished by common, rather than heroic, subjects–here, a merchant-class woman writes a letter. The masterful use of lighting and perspective in paintings such as this one would not be equaled until the age of photography. (Bridgeman-Giraudon/Art Resource, NY)

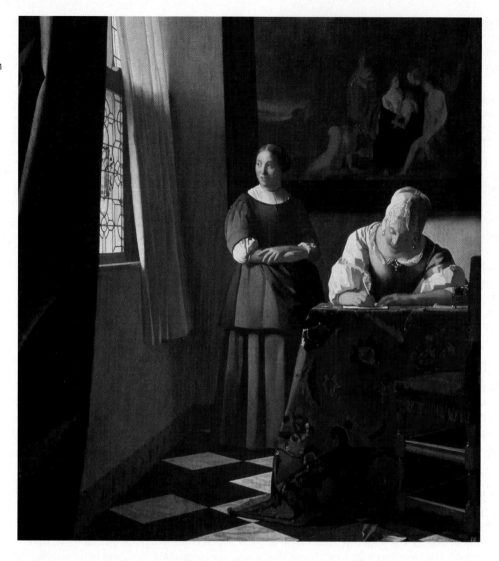

plantation system
Agricultural system, first developed by the Portuguese, in which forced labor produced cash crops on large estates owned by absentee landlords.

The European demand for tobacco and sugar, both addictive substances, grew steadily in the seventeenth century. The **plantation system**—the use of forced labor to produce cash crops on vast tracts of land—had been developed on Mediterranean islands in the Middle Ages by European entrepreneurs, using slaves procured in Black Sea ports by Venetian and Genoese traders. Sugar production by this system had been established on Atlantic islands, such as the Cape Verde Islands, using African labor, and then in the Americas, by the Spanish and Portuguese. Sugar production in the New World grew from about 20,000 tons a year in 1600 to about 200,000 tons by 1770.

In the 1620s, while the Dutch were exploiting Portuguese weakness in the Eastern spice trade, they were also seizing sugar regions in Brazil and replacing Portuguese slave traders in African ports. The Portuguese were able to retake most of their Brazilian territory in the 1650s. But the Dutch, because they monopolized the carrying trade, were able to become the official supplier of slaves to Spanish plantations in the New World and the chief supplier of slaves, as well as other goods, to most other regions. (See the feature, "The Global Record: Journal of a Dutch Slave Ship.") The Dutch made handsome profits dealing in human cargo until the end of the seventeenth century, when they were supplanted by the British.

The Dutch introduced sugar cultivation to the French and English after learning it themselves in Brazil. Sugar plantations began to supplant tobacco cultivation, as well as subsistence farming, on the Caribbean islands the English and French controlled. Beginning in the late sixteenth century, English and French seamen had seized islands in the Caribbean to use as provisioning stations and staging points for raids against or commerce with Spanish colonies. Some island outposts had expanded into colonies and attracted European settlers—some, as in North America, coming as indentured servants—to work the land. Sugar cultivation drastically transformed the character of these island settlements because it demanded huge outlays of capital

Sugar Manufacture in Caribbean Colonies Production of sugar required large capital outlays, in part because the raw cane had to be processed quickly, on-site, to avoid spoilage. This scene depicts enslaved workers operating a small sugar mill on the island of Barbados in the seventeenth century. In the background, a press crushes the cane; in the foreground, the juice from the cane is boiled down until sugar begins to crystallize. (Mary Evans Picture Library)

and continual supplies of unskilled labor. Large plantations, owned by wealthy, often absentee landlords and dependent on slave labor, replaced smaller-scale independent farms. The most profitable sugar colonies were, for the French, the islands of Martinique and Guadeloupe and, for the English, Barbados and Jamaica.

Early Colonies in North America

Aware of the overwhelming Spanish advantage in the New World, and still hoping for treasures, such as the Spanish had found, the English, French, and Dutch were also eager to explore and settle North America. From the early sixteenth century on, French, Dutch, English, and Portuguese seamen had fished and traded off Newfoundland. By 1630, small French and Scottish settlements in Acadia (near modern Nova Scotia) and on the St. Lawrence River and English settlements in Newfoundland were established to systematically exploit the timber, fish, and fur of the North Atlantic coasts.

In England, rising unemployment and religious discontent created a large pool of potential colonists, some of whom were initially attracted to early farming and trading settlements in the Caribbean. The first of the English settlements to endure, in what was to become the United States, was established at Jamestown, named for James I, in Virginia in 1607. ("Virginia," named for Elizabeth I, the "Virgin Queen," was an extremely vague designation for the Atlantic coast of North America and its hinterland.)

ENGLISH SETTLEMENTS

The Crown encouraged colonization, but a private company, similar to those that financed long-distance trade, was established to organize the enterprise. The directors of the Virginia Company were London businessmen. Investors and would-be colonists purchased shares. Shareholders among the colonists could participate in a colonial assembly, although the governor appointed by the company was the final authority.

The colonists arrived in Virginia with ambitious and optimistic instructions: to open mines, establish profitable agriculture, and search for sea routes to Asia. But at first, the colonists struggled even to survive in the unfamiliar environment. "Though there be fish in the seas … and beasts in the woods … they are so wild and we so weak and ignorant, we cannot trouble them much," wrote Captain John Smith from Virginia to the directors in London.[3] The native peoples in Virginia, unlike those in Spanish-held territories, were not organized in urbanized, rigidly

Journal of a Dutch Slave Ship

These excerpts from a journal kept by the captain of the Dutch ship St. Jan record a 1659 slave-trading voyage that began in Africa and ended on Curaçao, a Dutch island colony in the Caribbean.

The 8th [of March]. We arrived with our ship on Saturday before Arda [in modern Benin] to take onboard the surgeon's mate, and tamarinds as refreshment for the slaves. We set sail the next day to continue our voyage to Rio Reael.

The 22nd [of May]. We weighed anchor again and sailed out of the Rio Reael. … We acquired there in trade two hundred and nineteen slaves, men and women, boys as well as girls; and we set our course for [islands in the Gulf of Biafra] in order to seek food for the slaves, because nothing was to be had in Rio Reael.

The 26th ditto. On Monday we arrived [on the islands]. We spent seven days there looking but barely obtained enough for the slaves' daily consumption; therefore we decided to sail [up a nearby river] to see whether any food could be found there.

The 29th [of June]. On Sunday we decided to continue our voyage because there was also little food [up the river mouth] for the slaves because of the heavy rain which we had daily and because many slaves were suffering from dysentery caused by the bad food supplied to us at [St. George del Mina, a Dutch fort established to serve the slave trade]. …

The 11th [of August]. We lay sixteen days at Cape Lopez [modern Gabon] in order to take on water and firewood. Among the water barrels some forty were taken apart to be repaired because our cooper died … [and] we had no one who could repair them.

The 24th [of September]. On Friday we arrived at the island of Tobago [in the Caribbean] where we took on water and also bought some bread for our crew because for three weeks they have had no rations.

The 1st of November. We lost our ship on the reef [east of Curaçao] and our crew fled in the boat immediately. There was no chance to save the slaves because we had to abandon the ship on account of heavy surf.

The 4th ditto. We arrived with the boat at … Curaçao. The [governor] dispatched two sloops to retrieve the slaves from the shipwreck. One of the sloops was taken by a pirate together with eighty-four slaves.

QUESTIONS

1. Note the dates in the captain's journal. How much time was devoted to trade and provisioning in Africa? How much time to the transatlantic journey?

2. Note the details the captain includes. What do these details reveal about how the voyage was planned? For whom is he recording these details, and why?

3. A companion document reveals that 110 of the 219 captive men, women, and children died during the voyage across the Atlantic. Does knowing this information change how you interpret this document? What happened to the captives who survived the journey?

Source: Charles T. Gehring and J. A. Schiltkamp, eds., *New Netherlands Documents*, vol. 17 (Interlaken, N.Y.: Heart of the Lakes Publishing, 1987), pp. 128–131. Used by permission from the *New Netherlands Project*, The New York State Library.

---

hierarchical societies that, after conquest, could provide the invaders with a labor force. In fact, most of the native population was quickly wiped out by European diseases. The introduction of tobacco as a cash crop a few years later saved the colonists economically—although the Virginia Company had already gone bankrupt and the Crown had assumed control of the colony. With the cultivation of tobacco, the Virginia colony, like the Caribbean islands, became dependent on forced, eventually slave, labor.

Among the Virginia colonists were impoverished men and women who came as servants, indentured to those who had paid their passage—that is, they were bound by contract to pay off their debts by several years of labor. Colonies established to the north, in what was called "New England," also drew people from the margins of English society. Early settlers there were religious dissidents. The first to arrive were the Pilgrims, who arrived at Plymouth (modern Massachusetts) in 1620. They were a community of religious Separatists who had originally immigrated to the Netherlands from England for freedom of conscience.

Following the Pilgrims, came Puritans, escaping escalating persecution under Charles I. The first, in 1629, settled under the auspices of another royally chartered company, the Massachusetts Bay Company. Among their number were many prosperous Puritan merchants and landholders. Independence from investors in London allowed them an unprecedented degree of self-government once the Massachusetts Bay colony was established.

Nevertheless, the colonies in North America were disappointments to England because they generated much less wealth than expected. Shipping timber back to Europe proved too expensive, although New England forests did supply some of the Caribbean colonists' needs. The fur trade became less lucrative, as English settlement pushed the Native Americans, who did most of the trapping, west and as French trappers to the north encroached on the trade. Certain colonists profited enormously from the tobacco economy, but the mother country did so only moderately because the demand in Europe for tobacco never matched the demand for sugar. The English settlements did continue to attract more migrants than other colonizers' outposts. By 1640, Massachusetts had some fourteen thousand European inhabitants. Through most of the next century, the growth of colonial populations in North America would result in an English advantage over the French in control of New World territory.

FRENCH SETTLEMENTS

The French began their settlement of North America at the same time as the English, in the same push to compensate for their mutual weakness in comparison to the Spanish (see **MAP 16.4**). The French efforts, however, had very different results, owing partly to the sites of their settlements, but mostly to the relationship between the mother country and the colonies. The French hold on territory was always tenuous because of the scant number of colonists who could be lured from home. There seems to have been less economic impetus for colonization from France than from England. After the French crown took over the colonies, the religious impetus also evaporated, since only Catholics were allowed to settle in New France. Moreover, the Crown forced a hierarchical political organization on the French colonies. A royal governor directed the colony, and large tracts of land were set aside for privileged investors. Thus, North America offered little to tempt French people of modest means who were seeking a better life.

The first successful French colony was established in Acadia in 1605. This settlement was an exception among the French efforts because it was founded by Huguenots, not by Catholics. A few years later, the explorer Samuel de Champlain (1567?–1635) navigated the St. Lawrence River and founded Quebec City (1608). He convinced the royal government, emerging from its preoccupations with religious wars at home, to promote the development of the colony. French explorers went on to establish Montreal, farther up the St. Lawrence (1642), and to explore the Great Lakes and the Mississippi River basin (see **MAP 16.4**).

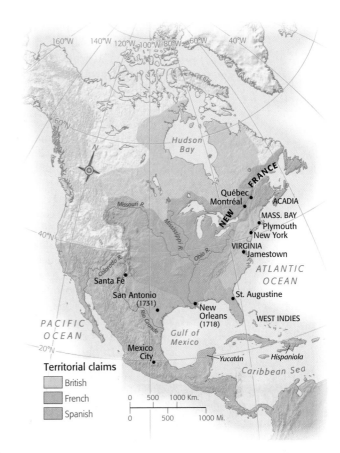

MAP 16.4—The English and French in North America, ca. 1700

By 1700, a veritable ring of French-claimed territory encircled the coastal colonies of England. English-claimed areas, however, were more densely settled and more economically viable.

Such investment as the French crown was able to attract went into profitable trade, mainly in furs, and not into the difficult business of colonization. French trappers and traders who ventured into wilderness areas were renowned for their hardiness and adaptability, but they did not bring their families and establish settled, European-style towns. Quebec remained more of a trading station, dependent on shipments of food from France, than a growing urban community. Much of the energy of French colonization was expended by men and women of religious orders—the "Black Robes"—bringing their zeal to new frontiers. By the middle of the seventeenth century, all of New France had only about three thousand European inhabitants.

The seeming weakness of the French colonial effort in North America was not much noticed at the time. French and English fishermen, trappers, and traders competed intensely, and the French often reaped the greater share of profits, owing to their closer ties with Native American trading systems. Outright battles occasionally erupted between English and French settlements. But for both England and France, indeed for all colonial powers, the major profits and strategic interests in the New World lay to the south, in the sugar-producing Caribbean. For example, in 1674, the Dutch gave up their trading center, New Amsterdam (modern-day New York City) to the English in return for recognition of the Dutch claims to sugar-producing Guiana (modern Suriname) in South America.

The growth of the plantation system meant that, by far, the largest group of migrants to European-held territories in the Americas was forced migrants: African men and women sold into slavery and shipped, like other cargo, across the Atlantic to work on Caribbean islands, in South America and southern North America. A conservative estimate is that approximately 1.35 million Africans were forcibly transported as slave labor to the New World during the seventeenth century.

The Impact of Trade and Warfare Within Europe

Within Europe, the economic impact of overseas trade was profound. Merchants and investors in a few of Europe's largest cities reaped great profits. Mediterranean ports, such as Venice, once the heart of European trade, did not share in the bonanza from the new trade with Asia or the Americas. Atlantic ports, such as Seville, through which most Spanish commerce with the New World flowed, and, above all, Amsterdam began to flourish. The population of Amsterdam increased from about 30,000 to 200,000 in the course of the seventeenth century.

All capital cities, however, not just seaports, grew substantially during the 1600s. Increasing numbers of government officials, courtiers and their hangers-on, and people involved in trade lived and worked in capital cities. These cities also grew indirectly from the demand such people generated for workers, such as carters and domestic servants, and products, ranging from fashionable clothing to exotic foodstuffs. For the first time, large numbers of country people found work in cities. Perhaps as much as one-fifth of the population of England passed through London at one time or another, creating the mobile, volatile community so active in the English civil war and its aftermath.

But social stratification intensified despite the expanding economy. Poverty increased in cities, even in vibrant Amsterdam, because cities attracted people fleeing rural unemployment with few skills and fewer resources. As growing central governments heaped tax burdens on peasants, many rural people were caught in a cycle of debt; the only escape was to abandon farming and flock to cities. Patterns of consumption reflected the economic gulf between city dwellers; most people could not afford to buy the spices or sugar that generated such profits.

Peasant rebellions occurred throughout the century as a result of depressed economic conditions and the heavy taxation that accompanied expanded royal power and extensive warfare. Some small-scale revolts involved direct action, such as seizing the tax collector's grain or stopping the movement of grain to the great cities. Urban demand often caused severe food shortages in rural areas in western Europe, despite the booming trade in grain with eastern Europe via the Baltic.

The scale of popular revolts, especially against taxation, meant that thousands of troops sometimes had to be diverted from a state's foreign wars. As a matter of routine, soldiers accompanied tax officials and enforced collection all over Europe. As the ambitions of rulers grew, so too did the resistance of ordinary people to the exactions of the state.

SECTION SUMMARY

- The Dutch innovations in ship design and forms of investment helped them dominate overseas trade.

- The wealth from trade supported a higher standard of living, wider political participation, and more religious tolerance in the Netherlands than elsewhere in Europe.

- The Dutch, the English, and the French expanded their trade and colonization in the Americas, following Spain and Portugal's earlier successes.

- Most European profits from trade and settlement in the Americas came from plantation agriculture, using slave labor, established on Caribbean islands.

- Overseas trade, together with more centralized governments, resulted in the spectacular growth of coastal and capital cities, wider divisions between rich and poor, and increased peasant rebellions.

CHAPTER SUMMARY

Following the most powerful monarchy in Europe, France, most states had moved from internal division—with independent provinces and aristocrats going their own way—to greater coherence. In France, Louis XIV's brand of government, which has been labeled "absolutism," arose from successful use of traditional political mechanisms, such as patronage, plus the defeat of any institutional brakes on his authority. Court life in Louis's reign sponsored artistic creativity and encouraged a new emphasis on cultural refinement in the aristocracy. In the military realm, however, Louis started a series of costly wars from which the French state gained little.

In England, a civil war over the very issue of parliamentary participation in government led to the temporary abolition of the monarchy itself. The Crown was restored under Charles

II, but conflicts arose again over political and religious policy under his successor James II. The year 1688 marked the "Glorious Revolution," in which Parliament helped bring William and Mary to the throne. Parliament's power was ensured by the Declaration of Rights and Bill of Rights, which have lasting significance today.

States, troubled by religious and political turmoil or on the political margins early in the century, evolved into secure and dynamic centers of power: the Netherlands, the Habsburg domains, Brandenburg-Prussia, and Russia. This stability was both cause and consequence of rulers' desires to make war on an ever larger scale. The Austrian Habsburgs reconquered Hungary from the Ottoman Turks, while the power of Poland-Lithuania declined in the seventeenth century because it was unable to defend itself against independent aristocrats, rebellious Cossacks, or powerful neighboring states. Russia was forcibly modernized by Peter the Great and became the most powerful state in eastern Europe, eclipsing Sweden in control of Baltic territories. By the end of the century, only those states able to field massive armies were competitive on the European stage. The Netherlands, a stark exception to the pattern of centralized royal control, began more closely to resemble other states under the pressure of warfare by century's end.

At the beginning of the century, overseas trade and colonization had been the near monopoly of Spain and Portugal. At the end of the century, the English, French, and Dutch had supplanted them in controlling trade with Asia and were reaping many profits in the Americas, especially from the extension of plantation agriculture. The Dutch were a successful trading empire because of their innovations in ship design and forms of investment. With their wealth from trade, they supported a higher standard of living, wider political participation, and more religious tolerance. Beneath all these developments lay significant economic, social, and cultural shifts. One effect of the increased wealth generated by overseas trade and the increased power of governments to tax their subjects was a widening gulf between rich and poor. New styles of behavior and patterns of consumption highlighted differences between social classes.

FOCUS QUESTIONS

- How did Louis XIV successfully expand royal power in France and what were some of the achievements of his reign?

- What were the long-term consequences of the English civil war?

- Which states began to dominate central and eastern Europe and why were they successful?

- How and why did Europe's overseas trade and colonization expand in the seventeenth century and what effects did this expansion have on Europe itself?

KEY TERMS

absolutism (p.444)

Louis XIV (p. 444)

mercantilism (p.446)

Parliament (p. 452)

Oliver Cromwell (p. 452)

Glorious Revolution (p. 455)

Treaty of Carlowitz (p. 459)

Brandenburg-Prussia (p. 459)

Cossacks (p. 461)

Peter the Great (p. 462)

Dutch East India Company (p. 464)

plantation system (p. 466)

 This icon will direct you to additional materials on the website: www.cengage.com/history/noble/westciv6e.

See our interactive eBook for map and primary source activities.

NOTES

1. Quoted in D. H. Pennington, *Europe in the Seventeenth Century*, 2d ed. (London: Longman, 1989), p. 508.

2. G. E. Aylmer, ed., *The Levellers in the English Revolution* (Ithaca, N.Y.: Cornell University Press, 1975), pp. 100–101.

3. Philip A. Barbour, ed., *The Complete Works of Captain John Smith (1580–1631)*, vol. 2 (Chapel Hill: University of North Carolina Press, 1986), p. 189.

CHAPTER OUTLINE

The Revolution in Astronomy, 1543–1632

The Scientific Revolution Expands, ca. 1600–1700

The New Science in Context: Society, Politics, and Religion

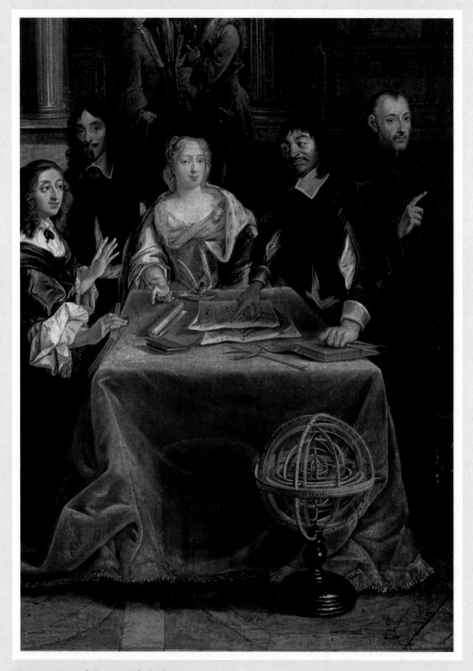

Descartes and Queen Christina
René Descartes (*second from the right*) instructs Queen Christina of Sweden and her courtiers. (Réunion des musées nationaux/Art Resource, NY)

A Revolution in Worldview

The year is 1649. Queen Christina of Sweden welcomes us with her gaze and her gesture to witness a science lesson at her court. Her instructor, the French philosopher René Descartes, clutches a compass and points to an astronomical drawing. The young queen, 23 years old at the time, was already well known as a patron of artists and scholars. Christina had invited Descartes to her court because of his achievements in physics and philosophy. This painting depicts the fact that during Christina's lifetime, new theories in the field of astronomy revolutionized the sciences and required new definitions of matter to explain them. Descartes earned fame both for his new theories about matter and for his systematic approach to using human reason to understand the universe. This painting celebrates both Descartes's work and Christina's sponsorship of it.

FOCUS QUESTIONS

- How did the Copernican theory challenge traditional views of the universe?

- How and why did new theories about astronomy lead to a broader Scientific Revolution?

- How did the new scientific worldview lead people to challenge traditional notions of society, the state, and religion?

This icon will direct you to additional materials on the website: www .cengage.com/history/ noble/westciv6e.

See our interactive eBook for map and primary source activities.

The revolution within the sciences had been initiated in the sixteenth century by the astronomical calculations and hypotheses of Nicholas Copernicus, who theorized that the earth moves around the sun. The work of the Italian mathematician and astronomer Galileo Galilei, as well as others, added evidence to support this hypothesis. Their work overturned principles of physics and philosophy that had held sway since ancient times. Later generations of scientists and philosophers, beginning with Descartes, labored to construct new principles to explain the way nature behaves. The readiness of scientists, their patrons, and educated laypeople to push Copernicus's hypothesis to these conclusions came from several sources: their exposure to the intellectual innovations of Renaissance thought, the intellectual challenges and material opportunities represented by the discovery of the New World, and the challenge to authority embodied in the Reformation. They advanced and discussed scientific theories in print for the first time. Also, the new science offered prestige and technological advances to the rulers, such as Christina, who sponsored it.

By the end of the seventeenth century, a vision of an infinite but orderly cosmos appealing to human reason had, among educated Europeans, largely replaced the medieval vision of a closed universe centered on the earth and suffused with Christian purpose. Religion became an increasingly subordinate ally of science as confidence in an open-ended, experimental approach to knowledge came to be as strongly held as religious conviction. It is because of this larger shift in worldview, not simply because of particular scientific discoveries, that the seventeenth century can be called the era of the Scientific Revolution.

Because religious significance had been attached to previous scientific explanations and religious authority had defended them, the new astronomy automatically led to an enduring debate about the compatibility of science and religion. But the revolution in worldview was not confined to astronomy or even to science generally. As philosophers gained confidence in human reason and the intelligibility of the world, they turned to new speculation about human affairs. They began to challenge traditional justifications for the hierarchical nature of society and the sanctity of authority, just as energetically as Copernicus and his followers had overthrown old views about the cosmos.

THE REVOLUTION IN ASTRONOMY, 1543–1632

How did the Copernican theory challenge traditional views of the universe?

The origins of the seventeenth-century revolution in worldview lie, for the most part, in developments in astronomy. Because of astronomy's role in the explanations of the world and human life that had been devised by ancient and medieval scientists and philosophers, any advances in astronomy were bound to have widespread intellectual repercussions. By the early part of the seventeenth century, fundamental astronomical beliefs had been successfully challenged. The consequence was the undermining of both the material (physics) and the philosophical (metaphysics) explanations of the world that had been standing for centuries.

The Inherited Worldview

Most ancient and medieval astronomers accepted the perspective on the universe that unaided human senses support—namely, that the earth is fixed at the center of the universe and the celestial bodies, such as the sun and the planets, rotate around it. The regular movements of heavenly bodies and the obvious importance of the sun for life on earth made astronomy a vital undertaking for both scientific and religious purposes in many ancient societies. Astronomers in ancient Greece carefully observed the heavens and learned to calculate and to predict the seemingly circular motion of the stars and the sun about the earth. The orbits of the planets were more difficult to explain, for the planets seemed to travel both east and west across the sky at various times and with no regularity that could be mathematically understood. Indeed, the word *planet* comes from a Greek word meaning "wanderer."

We now know that all the planets simultaneously orbit the sun at different speeds in paths that are at different distances from the sun. The relative positions of the planets constantly change; sometimes other planets are "ahead" of the earth and sometimes "behind." In the second century A.D., the Greek astronomer Ptolemy (TAHL-eh-mee) attempted to explain the planets' occasional "backward" motion by attributing it to "epicycles"—small circular orbits within the larger orbit. Ptolemy's mathematical explanations of the imagined epicycles were extremely complex, but neither Ptolemy nor medieval mathematicians and astronomers were ever able fully to account for planetary motion.

Ancient physics, most notably the work of the Greek philosopher Aristotle (384–322 B.C.), explained the fact that some objects (such as cannonballs) fall to earth but others (stars and planets) seem weightless relative to earth because of their composition: Different kinds of matter have different inherent tendencies and properties. In this view, all earthbound matter (like cannonballs) falls because it is naturally attracted to earth—heaviness being a property of earthbound things.

In the Christian era, the Aristotelian explanation of the universe was infused with Christian meaning and purpose. The heavens were said to be made of different, pure matter because they were the abode of the angels. Both the earth and the humans who inhabited it were changeable and corruptible. Yet, God had given human beings a unique and special place in the universe, which was thought to be a closed world with the stationary earth at the center. Revolving around the earth in circular orbits were the sun, moon, stars, and planets. The motion of all lesser bodies was caused by the rotation of all the stars together in the vast crystal-like sphere in which they were embedded.

A few ancient astronomers theorized that the earth moved about the sun. Some medieval philosophers also adopted this heliocentric thesis (*helios* is the Greek word for "sun"), but it remained a minority view because it seemed to contradict both common sense and observed data. The sun and stars *appeared* to move around the earth with great regularity. Moreover, how could objects fall to earth if the earth was moving beneath them? Also, astronomers detected no difference in angles from which observers on earth viewed the stars at different times. Such differences would exist, they thought, if the earth changed positions by moving around the sun. It was inconceivable that the universe could be so large and the stars so distant that the earth's movement would produce no measurable change in the earth's position with respect to the stars.

Several conditions of intellectual life in the sixteenth century encouraged new work in astronomy and led to the revision of the earth-centered worldview. The most important was the work of Renaissance humanists in recovering and interpreting ancient texts. Now able to work with new Greek versions of Ptolemy, mathematicians and astronomers noted that his explanations for the motion of the planets were imperfect and not simply inadequately transmitted, as they had long believed. Also, the discovery of the New World dramatically undercut the assumption that ancient knowledge was superior. The existence of the Americas specifically undermined Ptolemy's authority once again, for it disproved many of the assertions in his *Geography*, which had just been recovered in Europe the previous century.

The desire to explain heavenly movements better was still loaded with religious significance in the sixteenth century and was heightened by the immediate need for reform of the Julian calendar (named for Julius Caesar). Ancient observations of the movement of the sun, though remarkably accurate, could not measure the precise length of the solar year. By the sixteenth century, the cumulative error of this calendar had resulted in a change of ten days: The spring equinox fell on March 11 instead of March 21. An accurate and uniform system of dating was necessary for all rulers and their tax collectors and record keepers. And because the calculation of the date of Easter was at stake, a reliable calendar was the particular project of the church.

Impetus for new and better astronomical observations and calculations arose from other features of the intellectual and political landscape as well. Increasingly, as the century went on, princely courts became important sources of patronage for and sites of scientific activity. Rulers, eager to buttress their own power by symbolically linking it to dominion over nature, sponsored investigations of the world, as Ferdinand and Isabella had so successfully done, and displayed the marvels of nature at their courts. Sponsorship of science also yielded practical benefits: better mapping of the ruler's domains and better technology for mining, gunnery, and navigation.

Finally, schools of thought fashionable at the time, encouraged by the humanists' critique of tradition, hinted at the possibilities of alternative physical and metaphysical systems. The ancient doctrine of Hermeticism (named for the mythical originator of the ideas, Hermes Trismegistos), revived since the Renaissance, claimed that matter is universally imbued with divine (or magical) spirit. Drawing on Hermeticism was Paracelsianism, named for the Swiss physician Philippus von Hohenheim (1493–1541), who called himself Paracelsus (literally "beyond Celsus," an acclaimed Roman physician whose works had just been recovered). Paracelsus (pair-uh-SEL-sus) scoffed at the notion that ancient authorities were the final word on the workings of nature. Paracelsus offered an alternative to accepted medical theory, put forth by the ancient physician Galen (ca. 131–201), who was as revered as Aristotle. Galen (GAY-len) believed that an imbalance of bodily "humors" caused illness. Paracelsus substituted a theory of chemical imbalance that anticipated our modern understanding of pathology. He was wildly popular wherever he taught because he successfully treated many illnesses and lectured openly to laymen.

Neo-Platonism, another school of thought, had a more systematic and far-reaching impact. Neo-Platonism was a revival, primarily in Italian humanist circles, of certain aspects of Plato's thought. It contributed directly to innovation in science because it emphasized the abstract nature of true knowledge and thus encouraged mathematical investigation. This provided a spur to astronomical studies, which, since ancient times, had been concerned more with mathematical analysis of heavenly movements than with physical explanations for them. Also, like Hermeticism and Paracelsianism, Neo-Platonism had a mystical dimension that encouraged creative speculation about the nature of matter and the organization of the universe. Neo-Platonists were particularly fascinated by the sun as a symbol of the one divine mind or soul at the heart of all creation.

CHRONOLOGY

1543	Copernicus, *De Revolutionibus Orbium Caelestium* Vesalius, *On the Fabric of the Human Body*
1576	Construction of Brahe's observatory begins
1603	Accadèmia dei Lincei founded in Rome
1609	Kepler's third law of motion
1610	Galileo, *The Starry Messenger*
1620	Bacon, *Novum Organum*
1628	Harvey, *On the Motion of the Heart*
1632	Galileo, *Dialogue on the Two Chief Systems of the World*
1633	Galileo condemned and sentenced to house arrest
1637	Descartes, *Discourse on Method*
1651	Hobbes, *Leviathan*
1660	Boyle, *New Experiments Physico-Mechanical* Royal Society of London founded
1666	Académie Royale des Sciences founded in France
1686	Fontenelle, *Conversations on the Plurality of Worlds*
1687	Newton, *Principia (Mathematical Principles of Natural Philosophy)*
1690	Locke, *Two Treatises of Government and Essay on Human Understanding*
1702	Bayle, *Historical and Critical Dictionary*

The Traditional Universe
In this print from around 1600, heavenly bodies are depicted orbiting the earth in perfectly circular paths. Notice the horse-drawn chariot near the top of the image, which represents the Greek god of the sun circling the earth. (Bettmann/Corbis)

The Challenge by Copernicus

Nicholas Copernicus
Polish astronomer who initiated the Scientific Revolution by proposing that the earth and other planets orbit the sun.

Nicholas Copernicus (1473–1543), son of a German merchant family in Poland, pursued wide-ranging university studies in philosophy, law, astronomy, mathematics, and medicine—first in Cracow in Poland and then in Bologna and Padua in Italy. In Italy, he was exposed to Neo-Platonic ideas. Copernicus (kuh-PURR-nih-kus) took a degree in canon (church) law in 1503 and became a cathedral canon (a member of the cathedral staff) in the city of Frauenburg (modern Poland), where he pursued his own interests in astronomy, while carrying out administrative duties. When the pope asked Copernicus to assist with the reform of the Julian calendar, he replied that reform of the calendar required reform in astronomy. His major work, *De Revolutionibus Orbium Caelestium (On the Revolution of Heavenly Bodies*, 1543), was dedicated to the pope in the hopes that it would help with the task of calendar reform—as indeed it did. The Gregorian calendar, issued in 1582 during the pontificate of Gregory XIII (r. 1572–1585), was based on Copernicus's calculations.

Copernicus postulated that the earth and all the other planets orbit the sun. He did not assert that the earth does in fact move around the sun, but offered the heliocentric system as a mathematical construct, useful for predicting the movements of planets, stars, and the sun. However, he walked a thin line between making claims for a mathematical construct, on the one hand, and physical reality, on the other. Scholars now believe that Copernicus was himself persuaded that the **heliocentric theory** was correct. He had searched in ancient sources for thinkers who believed the earth moved. Other astronomers, familiar with his work and reputation, urged him to publish the results of his calculations. But not until 1542, twelve years after finishing the work, did he send *De Revolutionibus* to be published. He received a copy just before his death the next year.

heliocentric theory
Means "sun-centered." Theory of Nicholas Copernicus that the earth and other planets orbit the sun.

By affirming the earth's movement around the sun, while also salvaging features of the old system, Copernicus faced burdens of explanation not faced by Ptolemy. For example, Copernicus still assumed that the planets traveled in circular orbits, so he was forced to retain some epicycles in his schema to account for the circular motion. In general, however, the Copernican account of planetary motion was simpler than the Ptolemaic account. But his work only slowly led to conceptual revolution, as scientists worked with his calculations and assembled other evidence to support the heliocentric theory.

The most important reason that fundamental conceptual change followed Copernican theory so gradually was that Copernicus did not resolve the physical problems his ideas raised. If Copernicus were right, the earth would have to be made of the same material as other planets. How, then, would Copernicus explain the motion of objects on earth—the fact that they fall to earth—if it was not in their nature to fall toward the heavy, stationary earth? In Copernicus's system, the movement of the earth caused the *apparent* motion of the stars. But if the stars did not rotate in their crystalline sphere, what made all other heavenly bodies move?

Copernicus was not as troubled by these questions as we might expect him to have been. Since ancient times, mathematical astronomy—the science of measuring and predicting the movements of heavenly bodies—had been far more important than, and had proceeded independently of, physical explanations of observed motion. Nevertheless, as Copernicus's own efforts to support his hypothesis reveal, his theories directly contradicted many of the supposed laws of motion. The usefulness of his theories to other astronomers meant that the contradictions between mathematical and physical models for the universe would have to be resolved. Copernicus himself might be best understood as the last Ptolemaic astronomer, working within inherited questions and with known tools. His work itself did not constitute a revolution, but it did start one.

The First Copernican Astronomers

In the first generation of astronomers after the publication of *De Revolutionibus* in 1543, we can see the effects of Copernicus's work. His impressive computations rapidly won converts among fellow astronomers who continued to develop Copernican theories. By the second quarter of the seventeenth century, they and many others accepted the heliocentric theory as a reality and not just as a useful mathematical fiction. The three most important astronomers to build on Copernican assumptions, and on the work of one another, were the Dane Tycho Brahe (1546–1601), the German Johannes Kepler (1571–1630), and the Italian Galileo Galilei (1564–1642).

Like generations of observers before him, **Tycho Brahe** (BRAH) had been stirred by the majesty of the regular movements of heavenly bodies. After witnessing a partial eclipse of the sun, he abandoned a career in government, befitting his noble status, and became an astronomer. Brahe was the first truly post-Ptolemaic astronomer because he was the first to improve on the data that the ancients and all subsequent astronomers had used. Ironically, no theory of planetary motion could have reconciled the data that Copernicus had used: They were simply too inaccurate, based, as they were, on naked-eye observations, even when errors of translation and copying, accumulated over centuries, had been corrected.

In 1576, the king of Denmark showered Brahe with properties and pensions enabling him to build an observatory, Uraniborg, on an island near the capital, Copenhagen. At Uraniborg, Brahe improved on ancient observations with large and very finely calibrated instruments that permitted precise measurements of celestial movements by the naked eye. His attention to precision and frequency of observation produced results that were twice as accurate as any previous data had been.

As a result of his observations, Brahe agreed with Copernicus that the various planets did rotate around the sun, not around the earth. He still could not be persuaded that the earth itself moved, for none of his data supported such a notion. Brahe's lasting and crucial contribution was his astronomical data. They would become obsolete as soon as observations from telescopes were accumulated about a century later. But in the meantime, they were used by **Johannes Kepler** to further develop Copernicus's model and arrive at a more accurate heliocentric theory.

Kepler was young enough to be exposed to Copernican ideas from the outset of his training, and he quickly recognized in Brahe's data the means of resolving the problems in Copernican analysis. Though trained in his native Germany, Kepler went to Prague, where Brahe spent the last years of his life at the court of the Holy Roman emperor after a quarrel with the Danish king. There, Kepler became something of an apprentice to Brahe. After Brahe's death in 1601, Kepler kept his mentor's records of astronomical observations and continued to work at the imperial court as Rudolf II's court mathematician.

TYCHO BRAHE

Tycho Brahe   Danish astronomer and first European to collect new astronomical data by using instruments to observe the celestial bodies.

Johannes Kepler   German astronomer who developed three laws of planetary motion, known as Kepler's laws, which mathematically confirmed the Copernican heliocentric theory.

JOHANNES KEPLER

Tycho Brahe's Observatory Brahe gathered the best talent, including German instrument makers and Italian architects, to build his state-of-the-art observatory near Copenhagen. Brahe named the complex Uraniborg, for Urania, the muse of astronomy. (General View of the Observatory of Uraniborg, constructed c. 1584 by Tycho Brahe (1546–1601) on the island of Hven, Denmark from 'Le Theatre du Monde' or 'Nouvel Atlas', published in Amsterdam, 1645 (coloured engraving) by Willem Blaeu (1571–1638) and Joan (1596–1673)/Private Collection/Archives Charmet/The Bridgeman Art Library)

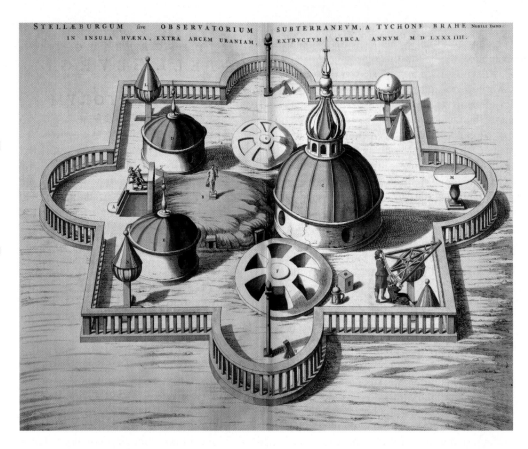

Kepler's contribution to the new astronomy, like that of Copernicus, was fundamentally mathematical. In it, we can see the stamp of the Neo-Platonic conviction about the purity of mathematical explanation. Kepler spent ten years working to apply Brahe's data to the most intricate of all the celestial movements—the motion of the planet Mars—as a key to explaining all planetary motion. Mars is close to the earth, but its orbital path is farther from the sun. This combination produces dramatic and puzzling variations in the apparent movement of Mars to an earthly observer.

The result of Kepler's work was laws of planetary motion that, in the main, are still in use. First, Kepler eliminated the need for epicycles by correctly asserting that planets follow elliptical, and not circular, orbits. Elliptical orbits could account, both mathematically and visually, for the motion of the planets when combined with Kepler's second law, which describes the *rate* of a planet's motion around its orbital path. Kepler noted that the speed of a planet in its orbit slows proportionally as the planet's distance from the sun increases. A third law demonstrates that the distance of each planet from the sun and the time it takes each planet to orbit the sun are in a constant ratio.

Kepler's work was a breakthrough because it mathematically confirmed the Copernican heliocentric hypothesis. In so doing, the work directly challenged the ancient worldview, in which heavenly bodies constantly moved in circular orbits around a stationary earth. Kepler's laws invited speculation about the properties of heavenly and terrestrial bodies alike. In fact, a new physics would be required to explain the novel motion that Kepler had posited. Kepler himself, in Neo-Platonic fashion, attributed planetary motion to the sun: "[The sun] is a fountain of light, rich in fruitful heat, most fair, limpid and pure … called king of the planets for his motion, heart of the world for his power … Who would hesitate to confer the votes of the celestial motions on him who has been administering all other movements and changes by the benefit of the light which is entirely his possession?"[1]

Galileo Galilei Italian physicist and astronomer who provided evidence supporting the heliocentric theory and helped develop the science of mechanics.

Galileo and the Triumph of Copernicanism

Galileo Galilei holds a preeminent position in the development of astronomy because, first, he provided compelling new evidence to support Copernican theory and, second, he contributed to the development of a new physics—or, more precisely, mechanics—that could account for the movements of bodies in new terms. In short, he began to close the gap between the new astronomy and new explanations for the behavior of matter. Just as important, his efforts to publicize his findings and his condemnation by the church spurred popular debate about Copernican ideas in literate society and helped to determine the course science would take.

Galileo's career also illustrates, in dramatic fashion, the dependence of scientists on and their vulnerability to patronage relationships. Born to a minor Florentine noble family, Galileo began studying medicine at the nearby University of Pisa at the age of 17, but became intrigued by problems of mechanics and mathematics. He began studying those disciplines at Pisa under the tutelage of a Florentine court mathematician and became a lecturer in mathematics there in 1589, at age 25, after publishing promising work in mechanics. Three years later, well-connected fellow mathematicians helped him secure a more prestigious professorship at the University of Padua, where Copernicus had once studied. Galileo skillfully cultivated the learned Venetian aristocrats (Venice ruled Padua at this time) who controlled academic appointments and secured renewals and salary raises over the next eighteen years.

During his years at Pisa and Padua, Galileo pursued his revolutionary work in mechanics, although he did not publish the results of his experiments until much later. Galileo's principal contribution to mechanics lay in his working out of an early theory of inertia. As a result of a number of experiments with falling bodies (balls rolling on carefully constructed inclines—not free-falling objects that, according to myth, he dropped from the Leaning Tower of Pisa), Galileo ventured a new view of what is "natural" to objects. Galileo's view was that uniform motion is as natural as a state of rest. In the ancient and medieval universe, all motion needed a cause, and all motion could be explained in terms of purpose. "I hold," Galileo countered, "that there exists nothing in external bodies … but size, shape, quantity and motion."[2] Galileo retained the old assumption that motion was somehow naturally circular. Nevertheless, his theory was a crucial step in explaining motion according to new principles and in fashioning a worldview that accepted a mechanical universe devoid of metaphysical purpose.

The results of this work were, for the most part, not published until the end of his life. In the meantime, Galileo became famous for his astronomical observations, which he began in 1609 and which he parlayed into a position back at the Florentine court. Early that year, Galileo learned of the invention of a primitive telescope (which could magnify distant objects only three times) and quickly improved on it to make the first astronomically useful instrument. In *Sidereus Nuncius (The Starry Messenger*, 1610), he described his scrutiny of the heavens with his telescope in lay language. He documented sighting previously undetectable stars, as well as moons orbiting the planet Jupiter. In another blow to ancient descriptions of the universe, he noted craters and other "imperfections" on the surface of the moon. Three years later, he published his solar observations in *Letters on Sunspots*. Sunspots are regions of relatively cool gaseous material that appear as dark spots on the sun's surface. For Galileo, sunspots and craters on the moon proved that the heavens are not perfect and changeless, but rather are like the supposedly "corrupt" and changeable earth. His telescopic observations also provided further support for Copernican heliocentrism. Indeed, Galileo's own acceptance of Copernicanism can be dated to this point because magnification revealed that each heavenly body rotates on its axis: Sunspots, for example, can be tracked across the visible surface of the sun as the sun rotates.

Galileo had already been approached by various Italian princes and in turn sought to woo their support with gifts of some of his earlier inventions, such as a military compass. He aimed his *Starry Messenger* at the Medici dukes of Florence, naming Jupiter's moons the "Medicean Stars" and publishing the work to coincide with the accession of the young Cosimo II, whom he had tutored as a youth. In 1610, he returned in triumph to his native Tuscany as court philosopher to the grand duke. Soon, however, his own fame and the increasing acceptance of Copernicanism aroused opposition. In 1615, Galileo was denounced to the Inquisition by a Florentine friar. Galileo defended himself to his patrons and to the wider scientific community by arguing, in print, that the new science did not challenge religion. (See the feature, "The Written Record: Galileo Asserts Science and Religion Are Compatible.") After an investigation, the geokinetic theory (that the earth moves) was declared heretical, but Galileo himself was allowed to continue to use Copernican theory, but only as a theory. Indeed, a number of the most fervent practitioners of the new science continued to be clergymen who followed Galileo's work with interest. A new pope, elected in 1623, was a Tuscan aristocrat and an old friend of Galileo. Galileo dedicated his work on comets, *The Assayer* (1624), to Urban VIII in honor of his election.

Galileo Asserts Science and Religion are Compatible

After Galileo Galilei's work on sunspots was released, many learned followers grew anxious about the implications of the new science. In the letter excerpted here, published in 1615 and widely circulated, Galileo reassures the mother of Cosimo II, the dowager grand duchess of Tuscany, that the new science does not contradict Christianity. The Catholic Church would eventually condemn Galileo for his beliefs, arguing that it was wrong to contradict established knowledge about the heavens. Although the church's actions constrained the development of science in some (predominantly Catholic) regions, throughout Europe investigators continued to find ways to make the new science fully compatible with their faiths.

Some years ago, as Your Serene Highness well knows, I discovered in the heavens many things that had not been seen there before our own age. The novelty of these things, as well as some consequences which followed from them ... stirred up against me no small number of professors—as if I had placed these things in the sky with my own hands in order to upset nature and overturn the sciences ... [These professors] go about invoking the Bible, which they would have minister to their deceitful purposes. Contrary to the sense of the Bible and the intention of the holy Fathers, if I am not mistaken, they would extend such authorities until even in purely physical matters—where faith is not involved—they would have us altogether abandon reason and the evidence of our own senses in favor of some biblical passage, though under the surface meaning of its words this passage may contain a different sense. ...

I think that in discussions of physical problems we ought to begin not from the authority of scriptural passages, but from sense experience and necessary demonstrations. ... I should judge that the authority of the Bible was designed to persuade men of those articles and propositions which, surpassing all human reasoning, could not be made credible by science, or by any means other than through the very mouth of the Holy Spirit. ...

But I do not feel obliged to believe that the same God who has endowed us with senses, reason and intellect has intended to forgo their use and by some other means to give us knowledge which we can attain by them. He would not require us to deny sense and reason in physical matters which are set before our eyes and minds by direct experience or necessary demonstrations. This must be especially true in those sciences of which but the faintest trace ... is to be found in the Bible. Of astronomy, for instance, so little is found that none of the planets except Venus are so much as mentioned. ...

Now, if the Holy Spirit has purposely neglected to teach us propositions of this sort as irrelevant to the highest goal (that is, to our salvation), how can anyone affirm that it is obligatory to take sides on them, and that one belief is required by faith, while another side is erroneous? ... I would assert here something that was heard from [a respected cleric]: ... "the intention of the Holy Ghost is to teach us how to go to heaven, not how heaven goes." ... [And] in St. Augustine we read: "If anyone shall set the authority of Holy Writ against clear and manifest reason, ... he opposes to the truth not the meaning of the Bible, which is beyond his comprehension, but rather his own interpretation. ... "

Moreover, we are unable to affirm that all interpreters of the Bible speak with divine inspiration, for if that were so there would exist no differences between them about the sense of a given passage. Hence [it would be wise] not to permit anyone to usurp scriptural texts and force them in some way to maintain any physical conclusion to be true, when at some future time the senses ... may show the contrary. Who indeed will set bounds to human ingenuity? Who will assert that everything in the universe capable of being perceived is already discovered and known?

QUESTIONS

1. How does Galileo justify pursuing scientific investigation against certain claims of faith?

2. Do you think that Galileo's arguments would have been reassuring to the grand duchess? Why or why not?

3. Why might the arguments have further angered those church officials already hostile toward Galileo's work?

Source: *Discoveries and Opinions of Galileo*, by Galileo Galilei, translated by Stillman Drake, copyright © 1957 by Stillman Drake. Used by permission of Doubleday, a division of Random House, Inc.

Now in his 60s, Galileo began to work on a book that summarized his life's work—*Dialogue on the Two Chief Systems of the World* (1632), structured as a conversation among three characters debating the merits of Copernican theory. Given the work's sensitive subject matter, Galileo obtained explicit permission from the pope to write it and cleared some portions with censors before publication. The work was the most important single source in its day for the popularization of Copernican theory, but it led to renewed concerns in Rome. Galileo had clearly overstepped the bounds of discussing Copernicanism in theory only and appeared to advocate it. Simplicio, the character representing the old worldview, was, as his name suggests, an example of ignorance, not wisdom.

Moreover, the larger political context affecting Galileo's patrons and friends had changed. The pope was being threatened by the Spanish and Austrian Habsburg rulers for his tepid support in the Thirty Years' War, in which Catholic forces were now losing to Protestant armies (see page 428). He could no longer be indulgent towards his friend, Galileo. Galileo was forced to stand trial for heresy in Rome in 1633. When, in a kind of plea-bargain arrangement, he pled guilty to a lesser charge of inadvertently advocating Copernicanism, Pope Urban intervened to insist on a weightier penalty. Galileo's book was banned, he was forced to formally renounce his "error," and he was sentenced to house arrest. Galileo lived confined and guarded, continuing his investigations of mechanics, until his death eight years later.

SECTION SUMMARY

- The Scientific Revolution began in 1543 with the publication of Copernicus's mathematical calculations supporting the heliocentric theory.

- Tycho Brahe and Johannes Kepler confirmed Copernicus's hypothesis with new data and more thorough mathematical explanations of the motions of planets.

- Galileo's observations with his telescope provided new evidence to support Copernican theory; his experiments in mechanics contributed to new explanations for the behavior of matter.

- Galileo's advocacy of Copernicanism led to his condemnation by the church.

THE SCIENTIFIC REVOLUTION EXPANDS, CA. 1600–1700

How and why did new theories about astronomy lead to a broader Scientific Revolution?

Galileo's work found such a willing audience in part because Galileo, like Kepler and Brahe, was not working alone. Dozens of other scientists were examining old problems from the fresh perspective offered by the breakthroughs in astronomy. Some analyzed the nature of matter, now that it appeared that all matter in the universe was somehow the same, despite its varying appearances. Many of these thinkers addressed the metaphysical issues that their investigations inevitably raised. They began the complex intellectual and psychological journey toward a new worldview, one that accepted the existence of an infinitely large universe of undifferentiated matter with no obvious place in it for humans.

The Uses of the New Science

No less a man than **Francis Bacon** (1561–1626), lord chancellor of England during the reign of James I, wrote a utopian essay extolling the benefits of science for a peaceful society and for human happiness. In *New Atlantis*, published one year after his death, Bacon argued that science would produce "things of use and practice for man's life."[3] In *New Atlantis* and *Novum Organum* (1620), Bacon reveals his faith in science by advocating patient, systematic observation and experimentation to accumulate knowledge about the world. He argues that the proper method of investigation "derives axioms from . . . particulars, rising by gradual and unbroken ascent, so that it arrives at the most general axioms of all. This is the true way but untried."[4]

Bacon did not undertake experiments himself, although his widely read works were influential in encouraging both the **empirical method** (relying on observation and experimentation) and inductive reasoning (deriving general principles from particular facts). Given the early date of his writings, it might seem difficult to account for his confidence in the benefits of science. Bacon was a visionary, but his writings reflect the widespread interest in science within his elite milieu, an interest actively encouraged by the state. In another of his writings, he argues that a successful state should concentrate on effective "rule in religion *and nature,* as well as civil administration."[5]

Bacon's pronouncements reflect the fact that an interest in exploring nature's secrets and exercising "dominion over nature" had become an indispensable part of princely rule. Princely courts were the main sources of financial support for science and the primary sites of scientific work during Bacon's lifetime. Part of the impetus for this development had come from the civic humanism of the Italian Renaissance, which had celebrated the state and service to it and had provided models both for educated rulers and for cultivated courtiers. Attention to science and to its benefits for the state also reflects the scope, and pragmatism, of princely resources and ambitions: the desire of rulers for technical expertise in armaments, fortification, construction, navigation, and mapmaking. (See the feature, "The Visual Record: Modern Maps.")

Francis Bacon England's lord chancellor during the reign of James I and author of influential works encouraging the empirical scientific method and inductive reasoning.

empirical method Philosophical view developed by Bacon and Locke, which holds that all knowledge is based on observation and experimentation and that general principles should be derived from particular facts.

The lure of the New World and the drive for overseas trade and exploration especially encouraged princely support of scientific investigation. A renowned patron of geographic investigation, from mapmaking to navigation, was Henry, prince of Wales (d. 1612), eldest son of James I. Prince Henry patronized technical experts such as gunners and seamen, as well as those with broader and more theoretical expertise. One geographer at his court worked on the vital problem of calculating longitude, sketched the moon after reading and emulating Galileo's work with the telescope, and, in the spirit of empiricism associated with Bacon, compiled information about the new territory Virginia, including the first dictionary of any Native American language.

Science was an ideological, as well as a practical, tool for power. Most courts housed collections of marvels, specimens of exotic plants and animals, and mechanical contrivances. These collections demonstrated the ruler's interest in investigation of the world—in other words, his or her status as an educated individual. Collections and the work of court experts also enhanced the ruler's reputation as a patron and person of power. Galileo was playing off such expectations when he named his newly discovered moons of Jupiter "Medicean Stars." Like all patronage relationships, the status was shared by both partners; indeed, the attention of a patron was a guarantee of the researcher's scientific credibility.

By the beginning of the seventeenth century, private salons and academies where investigators might meet on their own were another significant milieu of scientific investigation. These, too, had their roots in the humanist culture of Italy, where circles of scholars without university affiliations had formed. Though also dependent on private resources, these associations were an important alternative to princely patronage, since a ruler's funds might wax and wane according to his or her other commitments. Private organizations could avoid the stark distinctions of rank that were inevitable at courts, yet mimicked courts in the blend of scholars and educated courtiers they included. This more collegial, but still privileged, environment also fostered a sense of legitimacy for the science pursued there: Legitimacy came from the recognition of fellow members and, in many cases, from publication of work by the society itself.

The earliest academy dedicated to scientific study was the *Accadèmia Segreta* (Secret Academy), founded in Naples in the 1540s. The members pursued experiments together in order, in the words of one member, "to make a true anatomy of the things and operations of nature itself."[6] During the remainder of the sixteenth century and on into the seventeenth, such academies sprang up in many cities. The most celebrated was the *Accadèmia dei Lincei* (ack-uh-DAY-mee-uh day-ee lin-CHAY-ee), founded in Rome by an aristocrat in 1603. Its most famous member, Galileo, joined in 1611. The name "Lincei," from *lynx*, was chosen because of the legendary keen sight of that animal, an appropriate mascot for "searchers of secrets." Galileo's fame and the importance of his discoveries forced all such learned societies to take a stand for or against Copernicanism. Throughout the seventeenth century, the investigation of nature would continue in increasingly sophisticated institutional settings.

Scientific Thought in France

René Descartes   French philosopher and mathematician who emphasized skepticism and deductive reasoning in his most influential treatise, *Discourse on Method*. He offered the first alternative physical explanation of matter after the Copernican revolution.

Philosophers, mathematicians, and educated elites thus engaged in lively debate and practical investigation throughout Europe in the first half of the seventeenth century. In France, the great questions about cosmic order were being posed, ironically, at a time of political disorder. The years following the religious wars saw the murder of Henry IV, another regency, and further civil war in the 1620s (see pages 419–420). In this environment, questions about order in the universe and the possibilities of human knowledge took on particular urgency. It is not surprising that a Frenchman, **René Descartes** (1596–1650), created the first fully articulated alternative worldview.

DESCARTES AND A NEW WORLDVIEW

Descartes (day-KART) developed and refined his thinking in dialogue with a circle of other French thinkers. His work became more influential among philosophers and laypeople than the work of some of his equally talented contemporaries because of its thoroughness and rigor, grounded in Descartes's mathematical expertise, and because of his graceful, readable French. His system was fully presented in his *Discours de la méthode* (*Discourse on Method*, 1637). Descartes described some of his intellectual crises in his later work, *Meditations* (1641).

Descartes accepted Galileo's conclusion that the heavens and the earth are made of the same elements. He drew on ancient atomic models (that had not, then, been generally accepted) to create a new theory about the nature of matter. His theory that all matter is made up of identical bits, which he named "corpuscles," is a forerunner of modern atomic and quantum theories. Descartes believed that all the different appearances and behaviors of matter (for example, why stone is always hard and water is always wet) could be explained solely by the size, shape,

A Collection of Naturalia   Collections of exotic specimens, such as this display in Naples, symbolized the ruler's authority by suggesting his or her power over nature.   (From *Hevelius, Machinae coelestis.* By permission of the Houghton Library, Harvard University)

and motion of these "corpuscles." Descartes's was an extremely mechanistic explanation of the universe. It nevertheless permitted new, more specific observations and hypotheses and greater understanding of inertia. For example, because he reimagined the universe as being filled with "corpuscles" free to move in any direction, "natural" motion no longer seemed either circular (Galileo's idea) or toward the center of the earth (Aristotle's idea). The new understanding of motion would be crucial to Isaac Newton's work later in the century.

In his works, Descartes tries to resolve the crisis of confidence that the new discoveries about the universe had produced. The collapse of the old explanations about the world made Descartes and other investigators doubt not only what they knew, but also their capacity to know anything at all. Their physical senses—which denied that the earth moved, for example—had been proved untrustworthy. Descartes's solution was to reenvision the human rational capacity, the mind, as completely distinct from the world—that is, as distinct from the human body and its unreliable sense perceptions. In a leap of faith, Descartes presumed that God would not have given humans a mind if that mind consistently misled them. For Descartes, God became the guarantor of human reasoning capacity, and humans were distinguished by that capacity. This is the significance of his famous claim "I think, therefore I am."

Descartes thus achieved a resolution of the terrifying doubt about the world—a resolution that exalted the role of the human knower. The Cartesian universe was one of mechanical motion, not purpose or mystical meaning, and the Cartesian human being was preeminently a mind that could apprehend that universe. In what came to be known as "Cartesian dualism," Descartes proposed that the human mind is detached from the world and yet, at the same time, can objectively analyze the world.

Modern Maps

Modern mapping was developed during the Scientific Revolution. Like most of the changes associated with the Scientific Revolution, changes in mapping were the result of several influences: innovations in Renaissance art, knowledge gleaned from voyages of exploration, the impact of new astronomical discoveries, the interest and support of princely patrons, and the spread of new ideas by means of print. All of these factors enabled Europeans of this era to have a literally new view of their world. Yet, as in the work of Copernicus, developments in mapping also depended on the continued use of data accumulated in previous centuries. In the examples shown here, we can see the dramatic progress in mapmaking over the course of the sixteenth and seventeenth centuries.

Consider the brightly colored map of western Europe and North Africa reproduced here. It is a reproduction from a 1584 atlas of printed sea charts made by a Dutchman, Lucas Waghenauer. To our eye, the map may look decorative, even quaint. Sailing ships and sea monsters, not drawn to scale, populate the oceans. Most of the major states, such as England and France, are adorned with a crest identifying their ruling dynasties.

Because some of its features appear decorative to us, we may not realize the considerable innovation that the map represented in its day. First, it is an example of the revolutionary method of depicting space achieved in the Renaissance. The discovery of linear perspective by Renaissance artists enabled them to create the illusion of three-dimensional space in their paintings and to likewise depict territory, on a map, as imagined from the perspective of a distanced observer. In addition, the landforms appear in relatively accurate relationship to one another because mapmakers, following the newly recovered *Geography* by Ptolemy, used increasingly accurate projections of the globe to represent landforms on a two-dimensional map.*

The projection used for this map was particularly useful because compass bearings could be represented as straight lines. The many straight lines that crisscross this map are called "rhumb" lines; they represent compass headings that could be used to navigate between two points. Compass bearings between points on coastlines appeared on hand-drawn medieval sea charts (after the invention of the compass in about 1250). So, this sixteenth-century map combines medieval knowledge with new knowledge of geography and of how to depict landforms accurately. In addition, the information in this map was all the more useful because it was published, along with many other sea charts, in book form.

Europe and North Africa, 1584   (The Art Archive/John Webb/Picture Desk)

Now, let us look at the apparently simpler map of the coastline of France, made about one hundred years later, in 1693. We immediately note that virtually all the decorative elements are gone. There are no sea monsters and no ships to sail the abundant seas. The map is a line drawing; it is not even colored. The simplified style of the map by itself testifies to further progress in mapmaking, and to the ability of users to absorb information from maps. To make sense of this map, the viewer would need to be familiar with the representation of France from other maps since, for example, the land borders are not sketched in.

Indeed, the map conveys abundant information, all of which reflects scientific advancement over the intervening 100 years. The figure of a compass marks the Paris meridian, advertising that the site of the city has been precisely determined by means of its longitude. A horizontal line

Descartes's ambitious view of human reason emphasizes deductive reasoning (a process of reasoning in which the conclusion follows necessarily from the stated premises), a natural consequence of his philosophical rejection of sense data. The limits of deductive reasoning for scientific investigation would be realized and much of Cartesian physics rejected by the end of the century. Nevertheless, Descartes's assumption about the objectivity of the observer would become an enduring part of scientific practice. In Descartes's day, the most radical aspect of his thought was the reduction of God to the role of guarantor of knowledge. Many fellow scientists

The French Coastline, 1693 (Bibliothèque nationale de France)

marks its latitude. More accurate calculation of longitude had been made possible by the work of Johannes Kepler and Galileo Galilei, whose mapping of heavenly bodies provided known points in the night sky from which to calculate the longitude of the observer's position on earth. Calculation of latitude had always been easier, since it involved only determining the angle of the sun above the horizon, but it also became more precise by use of better instrumentation in the seventeenth century. (Note: Above and to the right of the compass symbol are modern circular and oval stamps identifying the archive where the map is housed; these marks would not have appeared when the map was originally published.)

After 1650, French cartographers, among others, systematically collected astronomical observations from around the world so they could map all known lands more precisely. In addition to claiming the correct coordinates for Paris, this map also dramatically corrects earlier maps of the coastline of France. The map superimposes a corrected view (the darker line) of the coastline over an older rendering (the fainter line, mostly outside of the darker line). Thus, this map not only provides information, but also boldly demonstrates the progress of mapmaking itself.

The legend of the map calls attention to this progress. It reads, "Map of France, corrected by order of the King by the observations of Messieurs of the Academy of Sciences." The map thus also documented royal patronage of scientific work. It is interesting, however, that the king is mentioned discreetly, in what is coming to be a standardized label on the map. The information in the map stands alone, without royal crests or decorations, because the public that viewed the map by now accepted and expected updated knowledge about the world.

QUESTIONS

1. What different types of information does the first map supply? Identify as many as you can.

2. What would have appeared most impressive about the second map, to a contemporary?

---

*This discussion of the evolution of mapmaking and of these examples draws on the work of Norman J. W. Thrower, *Maps and Civilization* (Chicago: University of Chicago Press, 1996). chaps. 5 and 6.

and interested laypeople were fearful of Descartes's system because it seemed to encourage "atheism." In fact, Descartes's faith had been necessary for the construction of his new world system—but the system did work without God.

Descartes would have been surprised and offended by charges of atheism, but he knew that his work would antagonize the church. He moved to the Netherlands to study in 1628, and his *Discourse* was first published there. His long residence in the Netherlands led him to advocate religious toleration late in his life. In 1649, at the urging of an influential friend with contacts at the Swedish court, Descartes accepted the invitation of Queen Christina to visit there. Christina was an eager but demanding patron, who required Descartes to lecture on scientific topics at 5:00 a.m. each day. The long hours of work and harsh winter weather took their toll on his health, and Descartes died of pneumonia after only a few months in Sweden.

PASCAL AND THE LIMITS OF SCIENTIFIC KNOWLEDGE

A contemporary of Descartes, fellow Frenchman Blaise Pascal (1623–1662), drew attention in his writings and in his life to the limits of scientific knowledge. The son of a royal official, Pascal (pahss-KAHL) was perhaps the most brilliant mind of his generation. A mathematician like Descartes, he stressed the importance of mathematical representations of phenomena, built one of the first calculating machines, and invented probability theory. He also carried out experiments to investigate air pressure, the behavior of liquids, and the existence of vacuums.

Pascal's career alternated between periods of intense scientific work and religious retreat. Today, he is well known for his writings justifying the austere Catholicism known as Jansenism (see page 446) and for his explorations of the human soul and psyche. His *Pensées* (*Thoughts*, 1657) consists of the published fragments of his defense of Christian faith, which remained unfinished at the time of his death. Pascal's appeal for generations after him may lie in his attention to matters of faith and of feeling. His most famous statement, "The heart has its reasons which reason knows not," can be read as a declaration of the limits of the Cartesian worldview.

Science and Revolution in England

The new science had adherents and practitioners throughout Europe by 1650. Dutch scientists in the commercial milieu of the Netherlands, for example, had the freedom to pursue practical and experimental interests. The Dutch investigator Christiaan Huygens (HI-ghenz) (1629–1695) worked on a variety of problems, including air pressure and optics. In 1657, he invented and patented the pendulum clock, the first device to measure accurately small units of time, essential for a variety of measurements.

England proved a unique environment for the development of science in the middle of the century. In a society torn by civil war, differing positions on science became part and parcel of disputes over Puritanism, church hierarchy, and royal power. Scientific, along with political and religious, debate was generally encouraged by the collapse of censorship, beginning in the 1640s.

During the 1640s, natural philosophers with Puritan leanings were encouraged in their investigations by dreams that science, of the practical Baconian sort, could be the means by which the perfection of life on earth could be brought about and the end of history—the reign of the saints preceding the return of Christ—could be accelerated. Their concerns ranged from improved production of gunpowder (for the armies fighting against Charles I) to surveying and mapmaking. Perhaps the best-known member of this group was Robert Boyle (1627–1691). In his career, we can trace the evolution of English science through the second half of the seventeenth century.

Boyle and his colleagues were theoretically eclectic, drawing on Cartesian mechanics and even Paracelsian chemical theories. They attacked the English university system, still under the sway of Aristotelianism, and proposed widespread reform of education. They were forced to moderate many of their positions, however, as the English civil wars proceeded. Radical groups, such as the Levellers, used Hermeticism and the related Paracelsianism as part of their political and religious tenets. The Levellers and other radical groups drew on the Hermetic notion that matter is imbued with divine spirit; they believed that each person was capable of divine knowledge and a godly life without the coercive hierarchy of church and royal officials.

Boyle and his colleagues responded to these challenges. They gained institutional power when they accepted positions at Oxford and Cambridge. They formed the core of the Royal Society of London, which they persuaded Charles II to recognize and charter on his accession to the throne in 1660. They worked out a theoretical position that combined the orderliness of mechanism, a continued divine presence in the world, and a Baconian belief in scientific progress. This unwieldy set of notions was attractive to the educated elite of the day, who wanted the certainties of science, but did not want to give up certain authoritarian aspects of the old Christian worldview.

Their most creative contribution, both to their own cause and to the advancement of science, was their refinement of experimental philosophy and practice. In 1660, Boyle published *New Experiments Physico-Mechanical*. The work describes the results of his experiments with an air pump he had designed, and it lays out general rules for experimental procedure. Descartes had accounted for motion by postulating that "corpuscles" of matter interact, thereby eliminating the possibility of a vacuum in nature. Recent experiments on air pressure suggested otherwise, however, and Boyle tried to confirm their findings with his air pump.

Boyle's efforts to demonstrate that a vacuum could exist—by evacuating a sealed chamber with his pump—were not successes by modern standards because his experiments could not readily be duplicated. Boyle tied the validity of experimental results to the agreement of witnesses to the experiment—a problematic solution, since only investigators sympathetic to his hypothesis and convinced of his credibility usually witnessed the results. In response to a Cambridge scholar who criticized his interpretation of one experiment, Boyle replied that he could not understand his critic's objections, "the experiment having been tried both before our whole society [the Royal Society of London], and very critically, by its royal founder, his majesty himself."[7] In other words, rather than debate differing interpretations, Boyle appealed to the authority and prestige of the participants. In English science of the mid-seventeenth century, therefore, we have a further example of the fact that new truths, new procedures for determining truth, and new criteria for practitioners were all being established simultaneously.

The Achievement of Isaac Newton

The Copernican revolution reached its high point with the work of the Englishman **Isaac Newton** (1643–1727), born one year almost to the day after Galileo died. Newton completed the new explanation for motion in the heavens and on earth that Copernicus's work had required and that Kepler, Galileo, and others had sought.

After a difficult childhood and an indifferent education, Newton entered Cambridge University as a student in 1661. Copernicanism and Cartesianism were being hotly debated, though not yet officially studied. Newton made use of Descartes's work in mathematics to develop his skill on his own, and by 1669, he had invented calculus. (He did not publish his work at the time, and another mathematician, Gottfried von Leibniz [LIBE-nits], later independently developed calculus and vied with Newton for credit.)

Newton won a fellowship at Cambridge in 1667 and became a professor of mathematics in 1669, at the recommendation of a retiring professor with whom he had shared his work on calculus. With less demanding teaching assignments, he was able to devote much of the next decade to work on optics—an important area of study for testing Descartes's corpuscular theory of matter.

In the 1680s, Newton experienced a period of self-imposed isolation from other scientists after a particularly heated exchange with one colleague, provoked by Newton's difficult temperament. During this decade, he returned to the study of alternative theories about matter. As a student at Cambridge, he had been strongly influenced by the work of a group of Neo-Platonists who were critical of Cartesian theory that posited God as a cause of all matter and motion but removed God, or any other unknown or unknowable force, as an explanation for the behavior of matter. The Neo-Platonists' concerns were both religious and scientific. As Newton says in some of his early writing, while a student, "However we cast about we find almost no other reason for atheism than this [Cartesian] notion of bodies having . . . a complete, absolute and independent reality."[9]

Newton now read treatises in alchemy and Hermetic tracts and began to imagine explanations for the behavior of matter (such as for bits of cloth fluttered from a distance by static electricity) that Cartesian corpuscular theory could not readily explain. Precisely what the forces were that caused such behavior, he was not sure, but his eclectic mind and his religious convictions enabled him to accept their existence.

It was this leap that allowed him to propose the existence of gravity—a mysterious force that accounts for the movements of heavenly bodies in the vacuum of space. Others had speculated about the existence of gravity; indeed, the concept of inertia worked out by Galileo, Descartes, and others suggested the need for the concept of gravity. Otherwise, if a planet

Isaac Newton English physicist, mathematician, and natural philosopher. His mathematical computation of the laws of gravity and planetary motion, which he combined with a fully developed theory of inertia, completed the explanation for motion initiated by Nicholas Copernicus.

Isaac Newton Pictured here about fifteen years after the publication of *Principia*, Newton was also one of the developers of calculus. The cumbersome mathematics he still relied on, however, has led one scholar to ponder: "What manner of man he was who could use as a weapon what we can scarcely lift as a burden."[8] (By courtesy of the National Portrait Gallery, London)

were "pushed" (say, in Kepler's view, by the "motive force" of the sun), it would continue along that course forever unless "pulled back" by something else.

Newton's extraordinary contribution to a new mechanistic understanding of the universe was the mathematical computation of the laws of gravity and planetary motion, which he combined with a fully developed concept of inertia. In 1687, Newton published *Philosophia Naturalis Principia Mathematica* (*Mathematical Principles of Natural Philosophy;* usually called *Principia*). In this mathematical treatise—so intricate that it was baffling to laypeople, even those able to read Latin—Newton laid out his **laws of motion** and expressed them as mathematical theorems that can be used to test future observations of moving bodies. Then he demonstrated that these laws also apply to the solar system, confirming the data already gathered about the planets and even predicting the existence of an, as yet, unseen planet. His supreme achievement was his law of gravitation, with which he could predict the discovery of the invisible planet. This law states that every body, indeed every bit of matter, in the universe exerts over every other body an attractive force proportional to the product of their masses and inversely proportional to the square of the distance between them. Newton not only accounted for motion, but definitively united heaven and earth in a single scheme and created a convincing picture of an orderly nature.

Neither Newton nor anyone else claimed that his theorems resolved all questions about motion and matter. Exactly what gravity is and how it operates were not clear, as they still are not. Newton's laws of motion are taught today because they still adequately account for most problems of motion. The fact that so fundamental a principle as gravity remains unexplained in no way diminishes Newton's achievement but is clear evidence of the nature of scientific understanding: Science provides explanatory schemas that account for many—but not all—observed phenomena. No schema explains everything, and each schema contains open doorways that lead both to further discoveries and to blind alleys. Newton, for example, assumed that the forces that accounted for gravity would mysteriously work on metals so that, as alchemists predicted, they might "quickly pass into gold."[10]

After the publication of *Principia*, Newton was more of a celebrated public figure than a practicing scientist. He helped lead resistance to James II's Catholicizing policies in the university, and he became the familiar of many other leading minds of his day, such as John Locke (see page 495). Newton became the president of the Royal Academy of Sciences in 1703 and was knighted in 1705, the first scientist to be so distinguished. By the end of his life, universities in England were dominated by men who acclaimed and built on his work. The transformation of the institutional structure of science in England was complete.

laws of motion The laws of gravity, planetary motion, and inertia first laid out in the seventeenth century by Isaac Newton.

Developments In Chemistry, Biology, and Medicine

The innovations in astronomy that led to the new mechanistic view of the behavior of matter did not automatically spill over to other branches of science. In astronomy, innovation came after the ancient and medieval inheritance had been fully assimilated and its errors disclosed. Other branches of science followed their own paths, though all were strongly influenced by the **mechanistic worldview**.

In chemistry, the mechanistic assumption that all matter was composed of small, equivalent parts was crucial to understanding the properties and behaviors of compounds (combinations of elements). But knowledge of these small units of matter was not yet precise enough to be of much use in advancing chemistry conceptually. Nevertheless, the flawed conceptual schema did not hold back all chemical discovery and development. Lack of understanding of gases, and of the specific elements in their makeup, for example, did not prevent the improvement of gunpowder. Indeed, unlike the innovations in astronomy, conceptual breakthroughs in chemistry and biology owed a great deal to the results of plodding experiment and the slow accumulation of data.

A conceptual leap forward was made in biology in the sixteenth and seventeenth centuries as a result of practical knowledge, because biological knowledge was mostly a by-product of the practice of medicine. The recent discovery of *On Anatomical Procedures*, a treatise by the ancient physician Galen, encouraged dissection and other research. Andreas Vesalius (1514–1564), in particular, made important advances by following Galen's example. Born in Brussels, Vesalius (vuh-SAY-lee-us) studied at the nearby University of Louvain and then at Padua, where he was appointed professor of surgery. He ended his career as physician to Emperor Charles V and his son, Philip II of Spain. In his teaching at Padua, Vesalius acted on the newly recovered Galenic teachings by doing dissections himself rather than giving the work to technicians. In 1543, he

mechanistic worldview Seventeenth-century philosophical view that saw the world as a machine that functions in strict obedience to physical laws, without purpose or will.

Vesalius on Human Anatomy The meticulous illustrations in Vesalius's work helped ensure its success. The medium of print was essential for accurate reproduction of scientific drawings. Note also the way the human body, in this drawing of musculature, is depicted as dominating the landscape. (Terri Torretto/Dover Publications)

published versions of his lectures as an illustrated compendium of anatomy, *De Humani Corporis Fabrica* (*On the Fabric of the Human Body*).

The results of his dissections of human corpses, revealed in this work, demonstrated a number of errors in Galen's knowledge of human anatomy, much of which had been derived from dissection of animals. Neither Vesalius nor his immediate successors, however, questioned overall Galenic theory about the functioning of the human body, any more than Copernicus had utterly rejected Aristotelian physics.

The slow movement from new observation to changed explanation is clearly illustrated in the career of the Englishman William Harvey (1578–1657). Much like Vesalius, Harvey was educated first in his own land and then at Padua, where he benefited from the tradition of anatomical research. Also like Vesalius, he had a career as a physician, first in London and later at the courts of James I and Charles I.

Harvey postulated the circulation of the blood—postulated rather than discovered, because owing to the technology of the day, he could not observe the tiny capillaries where the movement of arterial blood into the veins occurs. After conducting vivisectional experiments on animals that revealed the actual functioning of the heart and lungs, he reasoned that circulation of the blood must occur. He carefully described his experiments and his conclusions in *Exercitatio Anatomica de Motu Cordis et Sanguinis in Animalibus* (1628), usually shortened to *De Motu Cordis* (*On the Motion of the Heart*).

Harvey's work challenged Galenic anatomy and, like Copernicus's discoveries, created new burdens of explanation. According to Galenic theory, the heart and lungs helped each other to function. The heart sent nourishment to the lungs through the pulmonary artery, and the lungs provided raw material for the "vital spirit," which the heart gave to the blood to sustain life. The lungs also helped the heart sustain its "heat." This heat was understood to be an innate property of organs, just as "heaviness," in traditional physics, had been considered an innate property of earthbound objects.

From his observations, Harvey came to think of the heart in mechanistic terms: as a pump to circulate the blood. But he adjusted, rather than abandoned, Galenic theories concerning "heat" and "vital spirit." The lungs had been thought to "ventilate" the heart by providing air to maintain "heat," just as a bellows blows air on a fire. In light of his discovery of the pulmonary transit (that all of the blood is pumped through the lungs and back through the heart), Harvey suggested instead that the lungs carried out some of these functions for the blood, helping it to concoct the "vital spirit." Only in this sense did he think of the heart as a machine, circulating this life-giving material throughout the body.

Harvey's explanation of bodily functions, in light of his new knowledge, did not constitute a rupture with Galenic tradition. But by the end of his life, Harvey's own adjustments of Galenic theory were suggesting new conceptual possibilities. His work inspired additional research in physiology, chemistry, and physics. Robert Boyle's efforts to understand vacuums can be traced in part to questions Harvey raised about the function of the lungs and the properties of air.

SECTION SUMMARY

- Interest in the new science spread in the seventeenth century as many scholars accepted Copernican theory and as rulers realized the possible advantages of scientific advances.

- René Descartes built on the work of Galileo to formulate a new theory about the nature of matter.

- Descartes believed that humans could understand nature by using reason, not by trusting sensory data.

- English scientists, such as Robert Boyle, began to use experimental methods.

- Isaac Newton developed new laws of motion, still in use today, that explain the behavior of matter on earth and in space with a single set of mathematical principles.

- Advances in the life sciences included new anatomical discoveries by Andreas Vesalius and work by William Harvey on the circulation of the blood.

THE NEW SCIENCE IN CONTEXT: SOCIETY, POLITICS, AND RELIGION

How did the new scientific worldview lead people to challenge traditional notions of society, the state, and religion?

Scientists wrestled with questions about God and human capacity every bit as intently as they attempted to find new explanations for the behavior of matter and the motion of the heavens. Eventually, the profound implications of the new scientific worldview would affect thought and behavior throughout society. Once people no longer thought of the universe in hierarchical terms, they could question the hierarchical organization of society. Once people questioned the authority of traditional knowledge about the universe, the way was clear for them to begin to question traditional views of the state, the social order, and even the divine order. Such profound changes of perspective took hold very gradually, however. The advances in science did lead to revolutionary cultural change, but until the end of the seventeenth century, traditional institutions and ideologies limited its extent.

The Beginnings of Scientific Professionalism

Institutions both old and new supported the new science developing in the sixteenth and seventeenth centuries. Some universities were the setting for scientific breakthroughs, but court patronage, a well-established institution, also sponsored scientific activity. The development of the Accadèmia dei Lincei, to which Galileo belonged, and of other academies was a step toward modern professional societies of scholars, although these new organizations depended on patronage.

In England and France, royally sponsored scientific societies were founded in the third quarter of the century, reflecting rulers' keen interest in science. The Royal Society of London, though charted by the king in 1660, received no money. It remained an informal institution sponsoring amateur scientific interests, as well as specialized independent research. The Académie Royale des Sciences in France, established in 1666 by Jean-Baptiste Colbert, Louis XIV's minister of finance (see page 445), sponsored research but also supported chosen scientists with pensions. These associations were extensions to science of traditional kinds of royal recognition and patronage. Thus, the French Académie was well funded but tightly controlled by the government of Louis XIV, while the Royal Society of London received little of Charles II's scarce resources or precious political capital. Like the earlier academies, these royally sponsored societies published their fellows' work; in England, the *Philosophical Transactions of the Royal Society* began in 1665.

The practice of seventeenth-century science took place in so many diverse institutions—academies, universities, royal courts—that neither *science* nor *scientist* was rigorously defined. Science, as a discipline, was not yet detached from broad metaphysical questions. Boyle, Newton, Pascal, and Descartes all concerned themselves with questions of religion, and all thought of themselves not as scientists but, like their medieval forebears, as natural philosophers. These natural philosophers were still members of an elite who met in aristocratic salons to discuss literature, politics, or science with equal ease and interest. Nevertheless, the beginnings of a narrowing of the practice of science to a tightly defined, truly professional community are evident in these institutions.

Women Scientists and Institutional Constraints

The importance of court life and patronage to the new science had, at first, enabled women to be actively involved in the development of science. Women ran important salons in France; aristocratic women everywhere were indispensable sources of patronage for scientists; and women themselves were scientists, combining, as did men, science with other pursuits. Noblewomen and daughters of gentry families had access to education in their homes, and a number of such women were active scientists—astronomers, mathematicians, and botanists. The astronomer Maria Cunitz (KOO-nits) (1610–1664), from Silesia (a Habsburg-controlled province, now in modern Poland), learned six languages with the encouragement of her father, a physician. Later, she published a useful simplification of some of Kepler's mathematical calculations. Women from some artisanal families also received useful training at home. Such was the case of the German entomologist Maria Sibylla Merian (1647–1717). Merian learned the techniques of illustration in the workshop of her father, an artist in Frankfurt. She later used her artistic training and her refined powers of observation to study and record the features and behaviors of insects and plants in the New World.

Margaret Cavendish, duchess of Newcastle (1623–1673), wrote several major philosophical works, including *Grounds of Natural Philosophy* (1668). She was a Cartesian but was influenced by Neo-Platonism. She believed matter to have "intelligence" and thus disagreed with Descartes's views on matter, but she criticized fellow English philosophers on the grounds that, like Descartes, she distrusted sensory knowledge as a guide to philosophy.

Margaret Cavendish was aware of the degree to which her participation in scientific life depended on informal networks and on the resources available to her because of her aristocratic status. Women scientists from more modest backgrounds, without Cavendish's resources, had to fight for the right to employment, as public institutions gained importance as settings for the pursuit of science. The German astronomer Maria Winkelman (VINK-el-mahn) (1670–1720), for example, tried to succeed her late husband in an official position in the Berlin Academy of Sciences in 1710, after working as his unofficial partner during his tenure as astronomer to the academy. The academy withheld an official position from Winkelman after her husband's death, however, despite her experience and accomplishments (she had discovered a new comet, for example, in 1702). The secretary of the academy stated: "That she be kept on in an offcial capacity to work on the calendar or to continue with observations simply will not do. Already during her husband's lifetime the society was burdened with ridicule because its calendar was prepared by a woman. If she were now to be kept on in such a capacity, mouths would gape even wider."[11] Winkelman worked in

Astronomers Elisabetha and Johannes Hevelius The Heveliuses were one of many collaborating couples among the scientists of the seventeenth century. Women were usually denied pensions and support for their research when they worked alone, however. (Houghton Library)

private observatories but was able to return to the Berlin Academy only as the unofficial assistant to her own son, whose training she herself had supervised. As the new science gained in prestige, women scientists often found themselves marginalized. While women were routinely accepted as members of Italian academies, they were excluded from formal membership in the academies in London and Paris, although they could use the academies' facilities and received prizes from the societies for their work.

The New Science, the State, and the Church

The new natural philosophy had implications for traditional notions about the state. The new worldview that all matter, whether in the heavens or on earth, was identical and answerable to discernible natural laws gradually undermined political systems resting on a belief in the inherent inequality of persons and on royal prerogative. By the middle of the eighteenth century, a fully formed alternative political philosophy would argue for more "rational" government in keeping with the rational, natural order of things. But the change came slowly, and while it was coming, traditional rulers found much to admire and utilize in the new science.

Technological possibilities of the new science were very attractive to governments. Experiments with vacuum pumps had important applications in the mining industry, for example. Governments also sponsored pure, and not only applied, scientific research. A French naval expedition to Cayenne, in French Guiana, led to refinements of the pendulum clock but had, as its main purpose, progressive observations of the sun to permit the calculation of the earth's distance from the sun. Members of the elite saw the opportunity not only for practical advances, but also for prestige and, most important, confirmation of the orderliness of nature. It is hard to overestimate the psychological impact and intellectual power of this fundamental tenet of the new science—namely, that nature is an inanimate machine that reflects God's design not through its purposes, but simply by its orderliness. Thus, in the short run, the new science supported a vision of order that was very pleasing even to an absolute monarch, such as Louis XIV.

As we have seen, scientists themselves flourished in close relationships with princes and actively sought their patronage. Christiaan Huygens left the Netherlands to accept the patronage of Louis XIV and produced, in France, some of his most important work in optics and mechanics. Huygens had learned from his father, secretary to the princes of Orange in the Netherlands, that a princely court not only offered steady support, but also opened doors to other royal academies and salons. Huygens published some of his early research through the Royal Society in London, thanks to contacts his father had established. When Galileo left his position at Padua for the Medici court in Florence, he wrote to a friend, "It is not possible to receive a salary from a Republic [Venice] ... without serving the public, because to get something from the public one must satisfy it and not just one particular person; ... no one can exempt me from the burden while leaving me the income; and in sum I cannot hope for such a benefit from anyone but an absolute prince."[12]

Scientists and scientific thought also remained closely tied to religion in both practical and institutional ways during the seventeenth century. Both religion and the Catholic Church, as an institution, were involved with scientific advancement from the time of Copernicus. Copernicus himself was a cleric, as were many philosophers and scientists after him. This is not surprising, for most research in the sciences to this point had occurred within universities sponsored and staffed by members of religious orders, who had the education, time, and resources necessary for scientific investigation. Some of Descartes's closest collaborators were clerics, as were certain of Galileo's aristocratic patrons and his own protégés. Moreover, religious and metaphysical concerns were central to the work of virtually every scientist. The entire Cartesian process of reasoning about the world, for example, was grounded in Descartes's certainty about God. Copernicus, Kepler, Newton, and others believed they perceived God's purpose in the mathematical regularity of nature.

The notion that religion was the opponent of science in this era is a result of Galileo's trial and represents a distortion even of that event. It is true that the new astronomy and mechanics challenged traditional interpretations of Scripture, as well as the fundamentals of physics and metaphysics that were taught in universities. Thus, in its sponsorship of universities, the church was literally invested in the old view, even though individual churchmen investigated and taught Copernican ideas. The rigid response of the church hierarchy to Galileo is partially explained by the aftermath of the Protestant Reformation, which, in the minds of many churchmen—including Galileo's accusers and some of his judges—had demonstrated the need for a firm response to any challenge to the church's authority. Galileo seemed particularly threatening because he was well known, wrote for a wide audience, and, like the Protestants, presumed to interpret the Scriptures. Galileo may well have escaped punishment entirely had it not been for the political predicament faced by the pope at the time of his trial, however.

The condemnation of Galileo shocked many clerics, including the three who had voted for leniency at his trial. Clerics who were also scientists continued to study and teach the new science where and when they could. Copernicanism was taught by Catholic missionaries abroad. (See the feature, "The Global Record: Jesuits and Astronomy in China.") To be sure, Galileo's trial did have a chilling effect on scientific investigation in many Catholic regions of Europe. Investigators could and did continue their research, but many could publish results only by smuggling manuscripts to Protestant lands. After the middle of the seventeenth century, many of the most important empirical and theoretical innovations in science occurred in Protestant regions. However, Protestant leaders had also not been receptive to Copernican ideas at first because the ideas seemed to defy scriptural authority as well as common sense. In 1549, one of Martin Luther's associates wrote: "The eyes are witnesses that the heavens revolve in the space of twenty four hours. But certain men, either from love of novelty or to make a display of ingenuity, have concluded that the earth moves. . . . Now it is want of honesty and decency to assert such notions. . . . It is part of a good mind to accept the truth as revealed by God and to acquiesce in it."[13]

Protestant thinkers were also as troubled as Catholics by the metaphysical dilemmas that the new theories seemed to raise. In 1611, one year after Galileo's *Starry Messenger* appeared,

Science and Royal Power This painting memorializes the founding of the French Académie des Sciences and the building of the royal observatory in Paris. Louis himself is at the center of the painting, reflecting the symbolic importance of royal power in the sponsorship of science. (Erich lessing/Art Resource, NY)

the English poet John Donne (1573–1631) reflected on the confusion that now reigned in human affairs, with the heavenly hierarchy dismantled:

> *[The] new Philosophy calls all in doubt,*
> *The Element of fire is quite put out,*
> *The Sun is lost, and th'earth, and no man's wit*
> *Can well direct him where to look for it*
> *… … … …*
> *Tis all in pieces, all coherence gone;*
> *All just supply, and all Relation:*
> *Prince, Subject, Father, Son, are things forgot,*
> *For every man alone thinks he hath got*
> *To be a Phoenix, and that then can be*
> *None of that kinde, of which he is, but he.*[14]

The challenge of accounting, in religious terms, for the ideas of Copernicus and Descartes became more urgent for Protestants as the ideas acquired an anti-Catholic status after the trial of Galileo in 1633 and as they became common scientific currency by about 1640. As we have seen, Newton was able to develop his theories on motion and gravity in part because of a religious certainty about divine force that could account for the motion of bodies in a vacuum. In short, religion did not merely remain in the scientists' toolbox of explanations; it remained a

Jesuits and Astronomy in China

The Italian Matteo Ricci (1552–1610) was one of the first Jesuit missionaries to establish himself at the imperial court in China. Ricci's willingness to learn the Chinese language and his own scientific knowledge was crucial to his acceptance at the Chinese court. Jesuit missionaries who followed Ricci in the seventeenth century found their scientific expertise equally valued, and several openly taught Copernican theory in the East. Chinese interest in European knowledge was itself new. In previous centuries, Europeans had eagerly borrowed from China, including knowledge of papermaking and printing.

The Chinese have not only made considerable progress in moral philosophy but in astronomy and in many branches of mathematics as well. At one time they were quite proficient in arithmetic and geometry, but in the study and teaching of these branches of learning they labored with more or less confusion. They divide the heavens into constellations in a manner somewhat different from that which we employ. Their count of the stars outnumbers the calculations of our astronomers by fully four hundred, because they include in it many of the fainter stars which are not always visible. And yet with all this, the Chinese astronomers take no pains whatever to reduce the phenomena of celestial bodies to the discipline of mathematics. Much of their time is spent in determining the moment of eclipses and the mass of the planets and the stars, but here, too, their deductions are spoiled by innumerable errors. Finally they center their whole attention on that phase of astronomy which our scientists term astrology, which may be accounted for by the fact that they believe that everything happening on this terrestrial globe of ours depends upon the stars.

Some knowledge of the science of mathematics was given to the Chinese by the Saracens [Mongols], who penetrated into their country from the West, but very little of this knowledge was based upon definite mathematical proofs. What the Saracens left them, for the most part, consisted of certain tables of rules by which the Chinese regulated their calendar and to which they reduced their calculations of planets and the movements of the heavenly bodies in general. The founder of the family which at present regulates the study of astrology prohibited anyone from indulging in the study of this science unless he were chosen for it by hereditary right. The prohibition was founded upon fear, lest he who should acquire a knowledge of the stars might become capable of disrupting the order of the empire and seek an opportunity to do so.

QUESTIONS

1. In what ways is Ricci both appreciative and critical of Chinese science?

2. What do Ricci's comments about Chinese science reveal about his own assumptions concerning astronomy and mathematics and how to study them appropriately?

Source: Louis J. Gallagher, trans., *China in the Sixteenth Century: The Journals of Matthew Ricci: 1583–1610* (New York: Random House, 1953), pp. 30–31. Copyright 1942, 1953 and renewed 1970 by Louis J. Gallagher, S.J. Used by permission of Random House, Inc.

fundamental building block of scientific thought and central to most scientists' lives, whether they were Catholic or Protestant.

Thomas Hobbes English philosopher who argued in *Leviathan* that people are made up of mechanistic appetites and so need a strong ruler to govern them. However, he also envisioned citizens as potentially equal and constrained neither by morality nor by natural obedience to authority.

The New Science and Political Thought at the End of the Seventeenth Century

Traditional institutions and ideologies checked the potential effects of the new science for a time, but by the middle of the seventeenth century, political theory was beginning to reflect the impact of the mechanistic worldview. Political philosophers began to doubt that either the world or human society was an organic whole in which each part was distinguished in nature and function from the rest. Thomas Hobbes, John Locke, and others reimagined the bonds that link citizens to one another and to their rulers.

THOMAS HOBBES Because of the political turmoil in England, **Thomas Hobbes** (1588–1679) spent much of his productive life on the Continent. After the beginnings of the parliamentary rebellion, he joined a group of royalist émigrés in France. He met Galileo and lived for extended periods in Paris, in contact with the circle of French thinkers that included Descartes. Like Descartes, he theorized about the nature and behavior of matter and published a treatise on his views in 1655.

Hobbes is best known today for *Leviathan* (1651), his treatise on political philosophy. In *Leviathan*, Hobbes applies to the world of human beings his largely Cartesian view of nature as composed of "self-motivated," atom-like bits of matter. Hobbes viewed people as mechanistically as he viewed the rest of nature. In his view, people are made up of appetites of various sorts—the same kind of innate forces that drive all matter. The ideal political system, he concluded, is one in which a strong ruler controls the disorder that inevitably arises from the clash of people's desires. Unlike medieval philosophers, Hobbes did not draw analogies between the state and the human body (the king as head, judges and magistrates as arms, and so forth). Instead, he compared the state to a machine that "ran" by means of laws and was kept in good working order by a skilled technician—the ruler.

Hobbes's pessimism about human behavior and his insistence on the need for restraint imposed from above reflect, as does the work of Descartes, a concern for order in the wake of upheaval—in Hobbes's case, civil war in his native England. This concern was one reason he was welcomed into the community of French philosophers, who were naturally comfortable with royalty as a powerful guarantor of order. But Hobbes's work, like theirs, was a radical departure because it envisioned citizens as potentially equal and constrained neither by morality nor by natural obedience to authority.

Another Englishman, **John Locke** (1632–1704), offered an entirely different vision of natural equality among people and, consequently, of social order. Locke's major works, *Essay on Human Understanding* (1690) and *Two Treatises of Government* (1690), reflect the experimentalism of Robert Boyle, the systematizing rationality of Descartes, and other strands of the new scientific thought. In his *Essay*, Locke provides a view of human knowledge more pragmatic and utilitarian than the rigorous mathematical model of certainty used by many other philosophers. He argues that human knowledge is largely the product of experience. He agrees with Descartes that reason orders and explains human experience, but unlike Descartes, he doubts that human reason has unlimited potential to comprehend the universe. Locke, however, offered a more optimistic vision of the possible uses of reason. Whereas Descartes was interested in mentally ordering and understanding the world, Locke was interested in actually functioning *in* the world.

Locke's treatises on government reflect his notion of knowledge based on experience, as well as his particular experiences as a member of elite circles following the Restoration in England. Trained in medicine, he served as personal physician and general political assistant to one of the members of Parliament most opposed to Charles II's pretensions to absolutist government. When James II acceded to the throne in 1685, Locke remained in the Netherlands, where he had fled to avoid prosecution for treason. He became an adviser to William of Orange and returned to England with William and Mary in 1688. Locke's view of the principles of good government came to reflect the pro-parliamentary stance of his political milieu.

Unlike Hobbes, Locke argued that people are capable of self-restraint and mutual respect in their pursuit of self-interest. The state arises, he believed, from a contract that individuals freely enter into to protect themselves, their property, and their happiness from possible aggression by others. They can invest the executive and legislative authority to carry out this protection in monarchy or any other governing institution, though Locke believed that the English Parliament was the best available model. Because sovereignty resides with the people who enter into the contract, rebellion against the abuse of power is justified. At the core of Locke's schema is thus a revolutionary vision of political society based on human rights.

Locke's experience as an English gentleman is apparent in his emphasis on private property, which he considered a fundamental human right. Nature, he believed, cannot benefit humankind unless it is worked by human hands, as on a farm, for example. Private ownership of property guarantees its productivity and entitles the owner to participate in Locke's imagined contract. Indeed, Locke's political vision is unequivocal, and unbending, on the nature of property. Locke even found a justification for slavery. He also did not consider women to be independent beings in the same way as men. The family, he felt, is a separate domain from the state, not bound by the same contractual obligations. Locke and many other seventeenth-century thinkers were unable to imagine a new physical or political reality without invoking a notion of gender as a "natural" principle of order and hierarchy. Margaret Cavendish, among others, disputed the validity of such arbitrary distinctions in capacities and rights between men and women; nevertheless, men frequently used them. Locke's use of gender as an arbitrary organizing principle gave his bold new vision of rights for certain men a claim to being "natural." The use of gender-specific vocabulary to describe nature itself had the effect of making the new objective attitude toward the world seem "natural." Works by seventeenth-century scientists are filled with references to nature as a woman who must be "conquered," "subdued," or "penetrated."

JOHN LOCKE

John Locke English philosopher who asserted that the state arises from a contract that individuals freely endorse. Therefore, because sovereignty resides with the people, rebellion against abuse of power is justified—a revolutionary vision of a political society based on human rights.

SKEPTICISM AND THE SPREAD OF SCIENTIFIC RATIONALITY

Although traditional gender distinctions limited and reinforced most facets of political thought, in other areas, the fact of uncertainty and the need for tolerance were embraced. In another of Locke's influential works, the impassioned *Letter on Toleration* (1689), he argues that religious belief is fundamentally private and that only the most basic Christian principles need be accepted by everyone. Others went further than Locke by entirely removing traditional religion as necessary to morality and public order. Fostering this climate of religious skepticism were religious pluralism in England and the self-defeating religious intolerance of Louis XIV's persecution of Protestants.

Pierre Bayle (1647–1706), a Frenchman of Protestant origins, argued that morality can be wholly detached from traditional religion. Indeed, Bayle concluded, one need not be a Christian at all to be a moral being. Bayle cited as an example of morality the philosopher Baruch Spinoza (1632–1677), a Dutch Jew who had been cast out of his local synagogue for supposed atheism. Even so, Spinoza believed the state to have a moral purpose and human happiness to have spiritual roots.

Bayle's skepticism toward traditional knowledge was more wide-ranging than his views on religion. His best-known work, *Dictionnaire historique et critique* (*Historical and Critical Dictionary*, 1702), was a compendium of observations about and criticisms of virtually every thinker whose works were known at the time, including such recent and lionized figures as Descartes and Newton. Bayle was the first systematic skeptic, and he relentlessly exposed errors and shortcomings in all received knowledge. His works were very popular with elite lay readers. Bayle's countryman Bernard de Fontenelle (fon-tuh-NEL) (1657–1757), secretary to the Académie des Sciences from 1699 to 1741, was the greatest popularizer of the new science of his time. His *Entretiens sur la Pluralités des Mondes* (*Conversations on the Plurality of Worlds*, 1686) went through numerous editions and translations. It was, as the title implies, an informally presented description of the infinite universe of matter. He also helped spread the new science by publishing descriptions of the work of the Académie's scientists. Fontenelle is a fitting figure with whom to end a discussion of the Scientific Revolution because he represents, and worked to accomplish, the transfer of the new science into political and social philosophy—a movement we know as the "Enlightenment." A fully developed secular worldview, with revolutionary implications for human affairs, would be the product of the Enlightenment in the next century.

SECTION SUMMARY

- New institutions, such as academies, supported scientific work and were forerunners of modern scientific associations.

- European rulers were eager to sponsor scientific work both for its practical benefits and for its symbolic importance for their power.

- Scientific work remained closely tied to religion in both intellectual and institutional ways. Political thought in the seventeenth century, as represented by Locke and Bayle, began to reflect the new science's confidence in human reason.

- Women scientists were disadvantaged by the institutional settings for the new science and by the way notions about gender were used in the new science and political philosophy.

CHAPTER SUMMARY

The Scientific Revolution began with developments in astronomy. Because of astronomy's role in explanations of the world and human life that prevailed in the Middle Ages, changes in astronomical theory were bound to have widespread effects on other knowledge and beliefs. Copernicus's heliocentric theory led to wider scientific and philosophical innovation also because of the context in which it was received. Recent recoveries of new ancient texts in the Renaissance and the discovery of previously unknown lands in the New World made it possible to imagine challenging ancient scientific authority. The interest of princes in both the prestige and the practical use of science helped support the work of scientists. Other scientists, following Copernicus, built on his theories, culminating in the work of Galileo, who supported Copernican theory with additional data and widely published his findings.

The Frenchman Descartes was the first to fashion a systematic explanation for the operations of nature to replace the

FOCUS QUESTIONS

- How did the Copernican theory challenge traditional views of the universe?

- How and why did new theories about astronomy lead to a broader Scientific Revolution?

- How did the new scientific worldview lead people to challenge traditional notions of society, the state, and religion?

medieval view. The political and intellectual climate in England, meanwhile, encouraged the development of experimental science and inductive reasoning. Isaac Newton provided new theories to explain the behavior of matter and expressed them in mathematical terms that could apply to either the earth or the cosmos. With his work, traditional astronomy and physics were overturned, replaced by a vision of a universe of matter that behaves not according to a higher purpose, but rather as a machine.

New institutions in the form of private, as well as officially sponsored, scientific societies rose up to support scientists' work. These societies were particularly important before the new science became accepted in universities, although they excluded some practitioners of the new science, particularly women. Rulers made use of the new science for the practical results it offered, despite the ideological challenges it presented to their power. The relationship of religion to the new science was equally complex and contrary. Some religious leaders scorned the new science; most scientists, whether Catholic or Protestant, worked to accommodate both the new science and their religious beliefs. Indeed, religious faith—in the case of Newton, for example—was a spur to innovation. By the end of the seventeenth century, the hierarchical Christian worldview, grounded in the old science, was being challenged on many fronts, most notably in the work of the political philosophers Hobbes and Locke, who both challenged traditional justifications for royal authority. Locke's work was particularly important for the future because he argued that governments can exist only with the consent of the governed.

KEY TERMS

Nicholas Copernicus (p. 476)

heliocentric theory (p. 476)

Tycho Brahe (p. 477)

Johannes Kepler (p. 477)

Galileo Galilei (p. 478)

Francis Bacon (p. 481)

empirical method (p. 481)

René Descartes (p. 482)

Isaac Newton (p. 487)

laws of motion (p. 488)

mechanistic worldview (p. 488)

Thomas Hobbes (p. 494)

John Locke (p. 495)

 This icon will direct you to additional materials on the website: www .cengage.com/history/ noble/westciv6e.

NOTES

1. Quoted in Thomas S. Kuhn, *The Copernican Revolution* (Cambridge, Mass.: Harvard University Press, 1985), p. 131.

2. Quoted in Margaret C. Jacob, *The Cultural Meaning of the Scientific Revolution* (Philadelphia: Temple University Press, 1988), p. 18.

3. Quoted ibid., p. 33.

4. Quoted in Alan G. R. Smith, *Science and Society in the Sixteenth and Seventeenth Centuries* (New York: Science History Publications, 1972), p. 72.

5. Quoted in Jacob, p. 32 (emphasis added).

6. Quoted in Bruce T. Moran, ed., *Patronage and Institutions: Science, Technology and Medicine at the European Court* (Rochester, N.Y.: Boyden Press, 1991), p. 43.

7. Quoted in Steven Shapin, *A Social History of Truth* (Chicago: University of Chicago Press, 1994), p. 298.

8. Quoted in Smith, p. 130.

9. Quoted in Jacob, p. 89.

10. Quoted ibid., p. 25.

11. Quoted in Londa Schiebinger, *The Mind Has No Sex?* (Cambridge, Mass.: Harvard University Press, 1989), p. 92.

12. Quoted in Richard S. Westfall, "Science and Patronage," *ISIS* 76 (1985): 16.

13. Quoted in Kuhn, p. 191.

14. *Complete Poetry and Selected Prose of John Donne*, ed. John Hayward (Bloomsbury, England: Nonesuch Press, 1929), p. 365, quoted in Kuhn, p. 194.

See our interactive eBook for map and primary source activities.

18

CHAPTER OUTLINE

The Enlightenment

European States in the Age of Enlightenment

The Widening World of Trade and Production

The Widening World of Warfare

Café Society in the Eighteenth Century
(G. Dagli Orti/The Art Archive)

Europe on the Threshold of Modernity, ca. 1715–1789

Drinks are set before these gentlemen on their table, but this is more than just a social gathering. The men are absorbed in intense conversation. One man raises his hand, perhaps to emphasize his point, while another listens with a skeptical smirk. Several others eagerly follow their conversation. Other animated discussions go on at nearby tables. The setting depicted here was altogether new in the eighteenth century, when this picture was made, and a caption that originally accompanied the illustration reveals its importance: "Establishment of the new philosophy: our cradle was the café."

Cafés—coffeehouses—were as revolutionary in their day as the Internet is in our own. They were one of the principal places where educated people could debate the "new philosophy"—what we now call Enlightenment philosophy—and could explore its implications for social and political life. Men gathered in clubs and cafés; women directed private gatherings known as salons. Both men and women read more widely than ever before.

What the new science did to physics, the Enlightenment did to politics. The Enlightenment transferred into political and social thought the intellectual revolution that had already occurred in the physical sciences. Hence, it constituted a revolution in political philosophy, but it was also much more. The era witnessed the emergence of an informed body of public opinion, critical of the prevailing political system. The relationship between governments and the governed had begun to change: Subjects of monarchs were becoming citizens of nations.

The notion that human beings, using their rational faculties, could not only understand nature but might also transform their societies was appealing to rulers as well, in part for the traditional reason—strengthening state power. Frederick the Great of Prussia, Catherine the Great of Russia, and other monarchs self-consciously tried to use Enlightenment precepts to guide their efforts at governing. They had mixed success because powerful interests opposed their efforts at reform and because, ultimately, their own hereditary and autocratic power was incompatible with Enlightenment ideals.

Profound changes in economic and social life accompanied this revolution in intellectual and political spheres. The increasing economic and strategic importance of overseas colonies made them important focal points of international conflict. Economic growth spurred population growth, which in turn stimulated industry and trade. As the century closed, Europe was on the threshold of truly revolutionary changes in politics and production that had their roots in the intellectual, economic, and social ferment of eighteenth-century life.

FOCUS QUESTIONS

- What were the most important ideas in Enlightenment thought, and what were some of the intellectual, social, and political conditions that favored its development?

- To what extent did the activities of rulers, particularly "enlightened despots," reflect Enlightenment ideals, and to what extent did they reflect traditional concerns of state power?

- How and why did trade and production increase in the eighteenth century?

- How did warfare and its consequences change in the eighteenth century?

 This icon will direct you to additional materials on the website: www .cengage.com/history/ noble/westciv6e.

 See our interactive eBook for map and primary source activities.

THE ENLIGHTENMENT

What were the most important ideas in Enlightenment thought, and what were some of the intellectual, social, and political conditions that favored its development?

The Enlightenment was an intellectual movement that brought to political and social questions the confidence in the intelligibility of natural law that Newton and other scientists had recently achieved. Following Descartes and Locke, Enlightenment thinkers believed that human beings could discern and work in concert with the laws of nature for the betterment of human life. Above all, Enlightenment thought gave people the confidence to question tradition. A belief grew that society must be grounded on rational foundations to be determined by humans, not arbitrary foundations determined by tradition and justified by religious authority.

Enlightenment thought was debated in increasingly widespread publications, such as newspapers. There were new opportunities for exchanging views in literary societies, salons, and cafés. These new means of sharing information ensured that informed public opinion would become a new force in political and cultural life. Given this broad base, Enlightenment thinking was certain to challenge the very foundations of social and political order.

Voltaire: The Quintessential Philosophe

philosophes French term referring to thinkers and critics of the Enlightenment era, including Voltaire and Rousseau.

Voltaire French writer, critic, and reformer who embodied the spirit of eighteenth-century rationalism: its confidence, its increasingly practical bent, its wit and sophistication.

In France, Enlightenment thinkers were known as **philosophes** (fee-low-ZOHFS), a term meaning not a formal philosopher but rather a thinker and critic. The most famous of the philosophes was **Voltaire** (1694-1778). A prolific writer, critic, and reformer, Voltaire embodied the spirit of eighteenth-century rationalism: its confidence, its increasingly practical bent, its wit and sophistication. He was widely admired throughout Europe, including by several rulers. Born François-Marie Arouet to a middle-class family, he took the pen name Voltaire in 1718, after one of his early plays was a critical success. Like many philosophes, Voltaire moved in courtly circles but was often on its margins. His mockery of the regent for the young French king earned him a year's imprisonment in 1717, and an exchange of insults with a leading courtier some years later led to enforced exile in Great Britain for two years.

After returning from Britain, Voltaire published his first major philosophical work. *Lettres philosophiques (Philosophical Letters*, 1734) revealed the influence of his British sojourn and helped to popularize Isaac Newton's achievements in mathematics and science. To confidence in the laws governing nature, Voltaire added cautious confidence in humans' attempts to discern truth. From the Englishman Locke's work, he was persuaded to value education. These elements gave Voltaire's philosophy both its passionate conviction and its sensible practicality.

Voltaire portrayed Great Britain as a more rational society than France. The British government had a more workable set of institutions; the economy was less crippled by the remnants of feudal privilege, and education was not in the hands of the church. He was particularly impressed with the relative religious and intellectual toleration evident across the Channel. Voltaire was one of many French thinkers who singled out the Catholic Church as the archenemy of progressive thought. Philosophes constantly collided with the church's negative views of human nature and resented its control over most education and its influence in political life. Typical of Voltaire's criticism of the church is his stinging satire of the clerics who had condemned Galileo: "I desire that there be engraved on the door of your holy office: Here seven cardinals assisted by minor brethren had the master of thought of Italy thrown into prison at the age of seventy, made him fast on bread and water, because he instructed the human race."

After the publication of his audacious *Letters*, Voltaire was again forced into exile from Paris, and he lived for some years in the country home of a woman with whom he shared a remarkable intellectual and emotional relationship: Emilie, marquise du Châtelet (shot-uh-LAY) (1706–1749). Châtelet was a mathematician and a scientist. She prepared a French translation of Newton's *Principia*, while Voltaire worked on his own writing projects, which included a commentary on Newton's work. Because of Châtelet's influence, Voltaire became more knowledgeable about the sciences and more serious in his efforts to apply scientific rationality to human affairs. He was devastated by her sudden death in 1749.

Shortly afterward he accepted the invitation of the king of Prussia, Frederick II, to visit Berlin. His stay was stormy and brief because of disagreements with other court philosophers. He then lived for a time in Geneva, Switzerland, until his criticisms of the city's moral codes forced yet another exile on him. He spent most of the last twenty years of his life at his estates on the Franco-Swiss border, where he could be relatively free from interference by any government. These were productive years. He produced his best-known satirical novelette, *Candide*, in 1758. It criticized aristocratic privilege and the power of the church as well as the naiveté of philosophers who took "natural law" to mean that the world was already operating as it should.

In contrast, Voltaire believed that only by struggle could the accumulated habits of centuries be overturned. This belief led to his political activities. He became involved in several celebrated legal cases in which individuals were pitted against the authority of the church, which was still backed by the authority of the state. Voltaire's pursuit of justice in these cases was relentless. In addition to writing plays, novelettes, and essays, he published a stream of political tracts to champion specific causes and to argue for reform. He also worked close to home, initiating agricultural reform on his estates and working to improve the status of peasants in the vicinity.

Voltaire died in Paris in May 1778, after a triumphal welcome for the staging of one of his plays. By then, he was no longer leader of the Enlightenment in strictly intellectual terms. Thinkers and writers more radical than he had become prominent during his long life. They dismissed some of his beliefs, such as the notion that a monarch could introduce reform. But Voltaire had provided a crucial stimulus to French thought with his *Philosophical Letters* and through the example of his own prolific writing and political involvement. Until the end of his life, Voltaire remained a bridge between the increasingly diverse body of Enlightenment thought and the literate elite audience.

CHRONOLOGY	
1715–1774	Reign of Louis XV in France
1722–1742	Walpole first British "prime minister"
1734	Voltaire, *Philosophical Letters*
1740–1748	War of the Austrian Succession
1740–1780	Reign of Maria Theresa of Austria
1740–1786	Reign of Frederick the Great of Prussia
1746	Battle of Culloden
1748	Montesquieu, *The Spirit of the Laws* Hume, *An Enquiry Concerning Human Understanding*
1751–1765	Diderot, *Encyclopedia*
1756–1763	Seven Years' War
1758	Voltaire, *Candide*
1762	Rousseau, *The Social Contract*
1762–1796	Reign of Catherine the Great of Russia
1772	First partition of Poland
1776	Smith, *The Wealth of Nations*
1780–1790	Reign of Joseph II of Austria
1792	Wollstonecraft, *A Vindication of the Rights of Woman*

The Variety of Enlightenment Thought

A variety of thinkers contributed to the development of Enlightenment ideas. There were differences among philosophes about major issues. For example, though there was virtual unanimity in criticism of the Catholic Church, there was no unanimity about the existence or nature of God. Voltaire was a theist who believed in a creator of the universe, but not a specifically Christian God. Some philosophes were outright atheists, arguing that a universe operating according to discoverable laws needs no divine presence to explain or justify its existence. In spite of—and partly because of—their disagreements, a number of the philosophes remain among the most important political thinkers in modern times.

MONTESQUIEU

Charles de Secondat (1689–1755), baron of Montesquieu (mawn-tess-KYUH), a French judge and legal philosopher, combined the belief that human institutions must be rational with Locke's assumption of human educability. Montesquieu's treatise, *De L'Esprit des lois (The Spirit of the Laws*, 1748), published in twenty-two printings within two years, argued that laws were not meant to be arbitrary rules but derived naturally from human society: The more evolved a society was, the more liberal were its laws. This notion that progress is possible within society and government deflated Europeans' pretensions with regard to other societies, for a variety of laws could be equally "rational" given different conditions. Montesquieu is perhaps best known to Americans as the advocate of the separation of legislative, executive, and judicial powers that became enshrined in the U.S. Constitution later in the century. To Montesquieu, this scheme seemed to parallel in human government the balance of forces observable in nature; moreover, the arrangement seemed best to guarantee liberty.

Voltaire Visits Frederick the Great of Prussia   Voltaire leans forward, at left, to discuss a point of philosophy with Frederick. Skill at witty conversation enabled philosophes such as Voltaire to advance fundamental criticisms of society even to elite audiences.   (Bildarchiv Preussischer Kulturbesitz/Art Resource, NY)

ECONOMIC THOUGHT AND THE SCOTTISH ENLIGHTENMENT

Adam Smith   Scottish economist who developed the doctrine of "laissez-faire" in his treatise, *The Wealth of Nations* (1776).

Enlightenment philosophers also investigated the "laws" of economic life. For example, French thinkers, known as *physiocrats*, proposed ending "artificial" control over land in order to free productive capacity and permit the flow of crops to market. Their target was traditional forms of land tenure, including collective control of village lands by peasants and traditional rights over land and labor by landlords. The freeing of restrictions on manufacture and trade, as well as agriculture, was proposed by the Scotsman **Adam Smith** in his treatise, *An Inquiry into the Nature and Causes of the Wealth of Nations* (1776).

Smith (1723–1790) was a professor at the University of Glasgow. Scottish universities did not require specialization in subject matter and were open to ideas from abroad, enabling Smith's and others' unique contributions to Enlightenment thought.

Smith is best known in modern times as the originator of "laissez-faire" economics. *Laissez-faire* (LESS-ay-fair), or "let it run on its own," assumes that an economy will regulate itself, without interference by government and, of more concern to Smith, without the monopolies and other economic privileges common in his day. But this schema was not merely a rigid application of natural law to economics. His ideas grew out of an optimistic view of human nature and rationality that was heavily indebted to Locke. Humans, Smith believed, have drives and passions that they can direct and govern by means of reason and inherent mutual sympathy. Thus, Smith suggested, in seeking their own achievement and well-being, people are often "led by an invisible hand" simultaneously to benefit society as a whole. Smith's countryman and friend David Hume (1711–1776) investigated economics, politics, and religion but is best known today for his radical critique of the human capacity for knowing. He was the archskeptic, taking Locke's view of the limitations on human reason to the point of doubting the efficacy of any sensory data. His major exposition of these views, *An Enquiry Concerning Human Understanding* (1748), led to important innovations later in the century in the work of the German philosopher Immanuel Kant. At the time, though, Hume's arguments were almost contrary to the prevailing spirit that embraced empirical knowledge. Hume himself separated this work from his other writings on moral, political, and economic philosophy, which were more in tune with contemporary views.

Mainstream confidence in empirical knowledge and in the intelligibility of the world is evident in the multiauthored *Encyclopédie (Encyclopedia)*. This seventeen-volume compendium of knowledge, criticism, and philosophy was assembled by leading philosophes in France and published there between 1751 and 1765. The volumes were designed to contain state-of-the-art knowledge about arts, sciences, technology, and philosophy. The guiding philosophy of the project, set forth by its chief editor, Denis Diderot (DEED-uh-row) (1713–1784), was a belief in the advancement of human happiness through the advancement of knowledge. The *Encyclopedia* was revolutionary in that it not only intrigued and inspired intellectuals, but also assisted thousands of government officials and professionals.

THE ENCYCLOPEDIA

The encyclopedia project illustrates the political context of Enlightenment thought as well as its philosophical premises. The Catholic Church placed the work on the *Index of Prohibited Books*, and the French government might have barred its publication but for the fact that the official who would have made the decision was himself drawn to Enlightenment thinking. Many other officials, however, worked to suppress it. Thus, like Voltaire, the contributors to the *Encyclopedia* were admired by certain segments of the elite and persecuted by others in their official functions.

The *Encyclopedia* reflects the complexities and limitations of Enlightenment thought on another issue: the position of women. One might expect that challenging accepted knowledge and traditional power arrangements would lead to arguments for the equality of women with men, and thus, for extending women's rights. Indeed, some contributors to the *Encyclopedia* blamed women's inequality with men not on inherent gender differences, but rather on laws and customs that had excluded women from education. However, other contributors blamed women, and not society, for their plight, or they argued that women had talents that fit them only for the domestic sphere.

GENDER INEQUALITIES

Both positions were represented in Enlightenment thought as a whole. The assumption of the natural equality of all people provided a powerful ground for arguing the equality of women with men. Some thinkers, such as Mary Astell (1666–1731), challenged Locke's separation of family life from the public world of free, contractual relationships. "If absolute authority be not necessary in a state," she reasoned, "how comes it to be so in a family?" Most such thinkers advocated increased education for women, if only to make them fit to raise enlightened children. By 1800, the most radical thinkers were advocating full citizenship rights for women and equal rights to property, along with enhanced education.

The best-known proponent of those views was an Englishwoman, Mary Wollstonecraft (1759–1797), who wrote *A Vindication of the Rights of Woman* (1792). She assumed that most elite women would devote themselves to domestic duties, but she argued that without the responsibilities of citizenship, the leavening of education, and economic independence, women could be neither fully formed individuals nor worthy of their duties. "[F]or how can a being be generous who has nothing of its own? Or virtuous, who is not free?" she asked.[1] Working women, she concluded, needed political and economic rights simply to survive.

A notion of women's limited capacities was one element in the deeply influential writings of **Jean-Jacques Rousseau** (1712–1778). Like Locke, Rousseau (roo-SO) could conceive of the free individual only as male, and he grounded both his criticism of the old order and his novel political ideas in an arbitrary division of gender roles. Rousseau's view of women was linked to a critique of the artificiality of elite, cosmopolitan society in which Enlightenment thought was then flourishing, and in which aristocratic women were fully involved. Rousseau believed in the educability of men but was as concerned with issues of character and emotional life as with cognitive knowledge. Society—particularly artificial courtly society—was corrupting, he believed. The

ROUSSEAU

Jean-Jacques Rousseau
French philosophe who imagined an egalitarian society governed by the "general will" in *The Social Contract* and was a sharp critic of aristocratic society.

Rousseau Discusses the Benefits of Submitting to the General Will

In this excerpt from his Social Contract, Rousseau describes the relationship of individuals to the general will. Notice the wider-ranging benefits Rousseau believes men will enjoy in society as he envisions it. Rousseau is clearly interested in intellectual, moral, and emotional well-being.

I assume that men reach a point where the obstacles to their preservation in a state of nature prove greater than the strength that each man has to preserve himself in that state. Beyond this point, the primitive condition cannot endure, for then the human race will perish if it does not change its mode of existence ...

"How to find a form of association which will defend the person and goods of each member with the collective force of all, and under which each individual, while uniting himself with the others, obeys no one but himself, and remains as free as before." This is the fundamental problem to which the social contract holds the solution. ...

The passing from the state of nature to the civil society produces a remarkable change in man; it puts justice as a rule of conduct in the place of instinct, and gives his actions the moral quality they previously lacked. ... And although in civil society man surrenders some of the advantages that belong to the state of nature, he gains in return far greater ones; his faculties are so exercised and developed, his mind is so enlarged, his sentiments so ennobled, and his whole spirit so elevated that ... he should constantly bless the happy hour that lifted him for ever from the state of nature and from a stupid, limited animal made a creature of intelligence and a man. ...

For every individual as a man may have a private will contrary to, or different from, the general will that he has as a citizen. His private interest may speak with a very different voice from that of the public interest; his absolute and naturally independent existence may make him regard what he owes to the common cause as a gratuitous contribution, the loss of which would be less painful for others than the payment is onerous for him; and fancying that the artificial person which constitutes the state is a mere fictitious entity (since it is not a man), he might seek to enjoy the rights of a citizen without doing the duties of a subject. The growth of this kind of injustice would bring about the ruin of the body politic.

Hence, in order that the social pact shall not be an empty formula, it is tacitly implied in that commitment—which alone can give force to all others—that whoever refuses to obey the general will shall be constrained to do so by the whole body, which means nothing other than that he shall be forced to be free; for this is the necessary condition which, by giving each citizen to the nation, secures him against all personal dependence, it is the condition which shapes both the design and the working of the political machine, and which alone bestows justice on civil contracts—without it, such contracts would be absurd, tyrannical and liable to the grossest abuse.

QUESTIONS

1. What benefits will citizens find in society as Rousseau envisions it?

2. In what ways is Rousseau concerned with freedom?

Source: Jean-Jacques Rousseau, *The Social Contract*, translated by Maurice Cranston. Reprinted by permission of PFD on behalf of The Estate of Maurice Cranston. Copyright © 1968 by Maurice Cranston.

worthy citizen had to cultivate virtue and sensibility, not manners or refinement as courtiers do. Rousseau believed women should be the guarantors of the "natural" virtues of children and nurturers of the emotional life and character of men.

Rousseau's emphasis on the education and virtue of citizens was the underpinning of his larger political vision, set forth in *Du Contrat social (The Social Contract,* 1762). He imagined an egalitarian republic—possible particularly in small states, such as his native Geneva—in which men would consent to be governed because the government would determine and act in accordance with the "general will" of the citizens. The "general will" was not majority opinion, but rather what each citizen *would* want if he were fully informed and were acting in accordance with his highest nature. The "general will" became apparent whenever the citizens met as a body and made collective decisions, and it could be imposed on all inhabitants. (See the feature, "The Written Record: Rousseau Discusses the Benefits of Submitting to the General Will.") This was a breathtaking vision of direct democracy—but one with ominous possibilities, for Rousseau rejected the institutional checks on state authority proposed by Locke and Montesquieu.

Rousseau's work reflects, to an extreme degree, a central tension in Enlightenment thought: It was part of elite culture as well as its principal critic. The son of a humble family, Rousseau always sensed himself an outcast in the sophisticated world of Parisian salons. However, he depended on the patronage of several aristocratic women, even as he criticized the influence of such women. His own personal life did not match his prescriptions for others. He completely neglected to give his four children the education that he argued was vital; indeed, he abandoned them all to an orphanage. He was nevertheless profoundly important as a critic of an elite society still dominated by status and privilege.

The Growth of Public Opinion

It is impossible to appreciate the significance of the Enlightenment without understanding the degree to which it was a part of public life. Most of the philosophes came from modest backgrounds. They influenced the privileged elite of their day because of the social and political environment in which their ideas were elaborated. Indeed, one of the most important features of the Enlightenment was the creation of an informed body of public opinion that stood apart from court society.

THE READING PUBLIC

Increased literacy and access to books and other printed materials are an important part of the story. Perhaps more important, the kinds of reading that people favored began to change. We know from inventories made of people's belongings at the time of their deaths (required for inheritance laws) that books in the homes of ordinary people were no longer just traditional works such as devotional literature. Ordinary people now read secular and contemporary philosophical works. As the availability of such works increased, reading itself evolved from a reverential encounter with old ideas to a critical encounter with new ideas. Solitary reading for reflection and pleasure became more widespread.

New kinds of reading material were available. Regularly published periodicals in Great Britain, France, and Italy served as important means for the spread of enlightened opinion in the form of reviews, essays, and published correspondence. Some of these journals had been in existence since the second half of the seventeenth century, when they had begun as a means to circulate the new scientific work. Now subscribers included Americans anxious to keep up with intellectual life in Europe. In addition to newsletters and journals, newspapers, which were regularly published even in small cities throughout western and central Europe, circulated ideas. Newspapers were uniquely responsive to their readers. They began to carry advertisements, which both produced revenue for papers and widened readers' exposure to their own communities. Even more important was the inauguration of letters to the editor. Newspapers thus became venues for the often rapid exchange of news and opinions.

Habits of reading and responding to written material changed not only because of this increased and changing reading matter, but also because of changes in the social environment. In the eighteenth century, forerunners of the modern lending libraries made their debut. In Paris, for a fee, one could join a *salle de lecture* (sahl duh lek-TOOR) (literally, a "reading room") where the latest works were available to any member. Booksellers, whose numbers increased dramatically, found ways to meet readers' demands for inexpensive access to reading matter. One might pay for the right to read a book in the bookshop itself. Newspapers were available in such shops and in cafés. In short, new sites encouraged people to see themselves not just as readers, but as members of a reading public.

THE SALONS

Among the most famous and most important of these venues were the Parisian **salons**, regular gatherings in private homes, where Voltaire and others read their works-in-progress aloud and discussed them. Several Parisian women—mostly wealthy, but of modest social status—invited courtiers, bureaucrats, and intellectuals to meet in their homes at regular times each week. The *salonnières* (sal-on-YAIR) (salon leaders) themselves read widely in order to facilitate the exchange of ideas among their guests. This mediating function was crucial to the success of the salons. Manners and polite conversation had been a defining feature of aristocratic life since the seventeenth century, but they had largely been means of displaying status and safeguarding honor. The leadership of the salonnières and the protected environment they provided away from court life enabled a further evolution of "polite society" to occur: Anyone with appropriate manners could participate in conversation as an equal. The assumption of equality in turn enabled conversation to turn away from maintaining the status quo to questioning it.

The influence of salons was extended by the wide correspondence networks the salonnières maintained. Perhaps the most famous salonnière in her day, Marie-Thérèse Geoffrin (zhoh-FRAN) (1699–1777) corresponded with Catherine the Great, the reform-minded empress of Russia, as well as with philosophes outside Paris and with interested would-be members of her circle. The

salons Regular gatherings in eighteenth-century Parisian private homes, where Voltaire and other philosophes read and discussed their works; the exchange of ideas was facilitated by female *salonnières* (salon leaders).

The Growth of the Book Trade Book ownership dramatically increased in the eighteenth century, and a wide range of secular works—from racy novelettes to philosophical tracts—was available in print. In this rendering of a bookshop, shipments of books have arrived from around Europe. Notice the artist's optimism in the great variety of persons, from the peasant with a scythe to a white-robed cleric, who are drawn to the shop by "Minerva" (the Roman goddess of wisdom). (Musée des Beaux-Arts de Dijon)

ambassador of Naples regularly attended her salon while in Paris and exchanged weekly letters with her when home in Italy. He reflected on the importance of salon leaders such as Geoffrin when he wrote from Naples lamenting, "[Our gatherings here] are getting farther away from the character and tone of those of France, despite all [our] efforts. … There is no way to make Naples resemble Paris unless we find a woman to guide us, organize us, *Geoffrinise* us."[2]

Various clubs, local academies, and learned and secret societies, such as Masonic lodges, copied some features of the salons of Paris. Hardly any town was without a private society that functioned both as a forum for political and philosophical discussion and as an elite social club. Here mingled doctors, lawyers, and local officials—some of whom enjoyed the fruits of the political system in offices and patronage. In Scotland, universities were flourishing centers of Enlightenment thought, but political clubs in Glasgow and Edinburgh also were centers of debate.

Ideas circulated beyond the membership of salons and clubs, in turn, by means of print. Newsletters reporting the goings-on at salons in Paris were produced by some participants. The exchange and spread of Enlightenment ideas, regardless of the method used, encouraged a type of far-reaching political debate that had never before existed, except possibly in seventeenth-century England. The greatest impact of the Enlightenment, particularly in France, was not the creation of any specific program for political or social change. Rather, its supreme legacy was an informed body of public opinion that could generate change.

The Arts in the Age of Reason

The Enlightenment reverberated throughout all aspects of cultural life. Just as the market for books and the reading public expanded, so did the audience for works of art in the growing leisured urban circles of Paris and other great cities. The modern cultured public—a public of concertgoers and art gallery enthusiasts—began to make its first appearance and constituted another arena in which public opinion was shaped. Courts around Europe continued to sponsor composers, musicians, and painters by providing both patronage and audiences. Yet some performances began to take place in theaters and halls outside the courts in venues more accessible to the public. And, beginning in 1737, one section of the Louvre (LOO-vruh) palace in Paris was devoted annually to public exhibitions of painting and sculpture (though by royally sponsored and approved artists). In both France and Britain, public discussion of art began to occur in published reviews and criticisms: The role of art critic was born. Works of art were also sold by public means, such as auctions. As works became more available, demand grew and production increased.

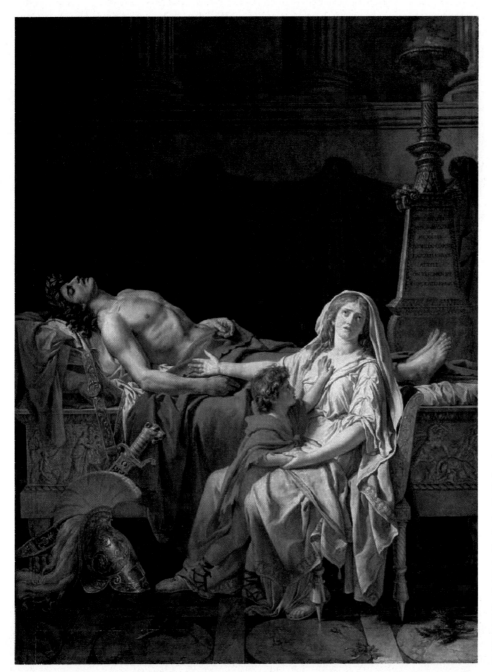

The Moralizing Message of Neoclassical Art   The French painter Jacques-Louis David portrays the mourning of the Trojan hero Hector by his wife, Andromache. This kind of art tried to depict and encourage virtuous feelings. David was well known for depicting his subjects with simple gestures—such as the extended arm of Andromache here—that were intended to portray sincere emotion.   (Private Collection/The Stapleton Collection/Bridgeman Art Library International)

In subject matter and style, these various art forms exhibited great variety. A favorite theme of painters was an exploration of private life and emotion sometimes called the "cult of sensibility." Frequently, these works depicted private scenes of upper-class life, especially moments of intimate conversation or flirtation.

The cult of sensibility was also nurtured by increased literacy, greater access to books, and the need to retreat from the elaborate artifice of court life. The novel became an increasingly important genre for exploring social problems and human relationships. Daniel Defoe, in *Robinson Crusoe* (1717), used realism for purposes of social commentary, while the novels of Samuel Richardson (1689-1761)—*Pamela* (1740) and *Clarissa* (1747-1748)—explored personal psychology and passion. The cult of sensibility was not mere entertainment; it also carried the political and philosophical message, echoing Rousseau's work, that honest emotion was a "natural" virtue and that courtly manners, by contrast, were both irrational and degrading. The enormous popularity of Rousseau's own novels, *La Nouvelle Héloïse* (1761) and *Emile* (1762), for example, came from the fact that their intense emotional appeal was simultaneously felt to be uplifting.

A revival of classical subjects and styles after the middle of the century evoked what were thought to be the pure and timeless values of classical heroes. This revival revealed the influence of Enlightenment thought because the artists assumed the educability of their audience by means of example. Classical revival architecture illustrated a belief in order, symmetry, and proportion. Americans are familiar with its evocations because it became the architecture of their public buildings, but even churches were built in this style in eighteenth-century Europe. The classical movement in music reflected both the cult of sensibility and the classicizing styles in the visual arts. Embodied in the works of Austrians Franz Josef Haydn (1732-1809) and Wolfgang Amadeus Mozart (1756-1791), this movement saw the clarification of musical structures, such as the modern sonata and symphony, and enabled melody to take center stage.

Another trend in art and literature was a fascination with nature and with the seemingly "natural" in human culture—less "developed" or more historically distant societies. One of the most popular printed works in the middle of the century was the alleged translation of the poems of Ossian (AHSH-un), a third-century Scots Highland poet. Early English, German, Norse, and other folktales were also "discovered" (in some cases invented) and published, some in several editions during the century. Folk life, other cultures, and untamed nature itself thus began to be celebrated at the very time they were being more definitively conquered. (See the feature, "The Visual Record: Gardens.") Ossian, for example, was celebrated just as the Scottish Highlands were being pillaged and pacified by the English after the clans' support for a rival claimant to the English throne. Once purged of any threat, the exotic image of another culture (even the folk culture of one's own society) could be a spur to the imagination. The remote became romantic and offered a sense of distance from which to measure one's own sophistication and superiority.

SECTION SUMMARY

- The "Enlightenment" was an intellectual movement that brought confidence in human reason and the workings of natural law from the sciences into political and social thought.

- A wide range of thinkers, known as philosophes, contributed to Enlightenment thought; opinions about religion, the limits of human reason, the equality of the sexes, and other issues were energetically debated.

- Enlightenment ideas were spread by publications, such as newspapers, and were discussed in cafés and salons; an informed body of public opinion independent of government and the court was created for the first time.

- Art became more accessible to the public; works of art became more thematically varied than before, though many explored "natural" emotion.

EUROPEAN STATES IN THE AGE OF ENLIGHTENMENT

To what extent did the activities of rulers, particularly "enlightened despots," reflect Enlightenment ideals, and to what extent did they reflect traditional concerns of state power?

Mindful of the lessons to be learned from the civil war in England, and eager to repeat the achievements of Louis XIV, European rulers in the eighteenth century continued their efforts to govern with greater effectiveness. Some, like the rulers of Prussia and Russia, were encouraged in their efforts by Enlightenment ideas that stressed the need for reforms in law, economy, and government. Like Voltaire, they believed that monarchs could be agents for change. The changes were uneven, however, and at times, owed as much to traditional efforts at better government as to "enlightened" opinion. However limited their "enlightened" policies, monarchs were changing their views of themselves and their public images from self-aggrandizing absolutist to diligent servant of the state. The state was increasingly seen as separate from the ruler, with dramatic consequences for the future.

France During the Enlightenment

It is one of the seeming paradoxes of the era of the Enlightenment that critical thought about society and politics flourished in France, an autocratic state. Yet France was blessed with a well-educated elite, a tradition of scientific inquiry, and a legacy of cultured court life that, since the early days of Louis XIV, had become the model for all Europe (see pages 446–447). French was the international intellectual language, and France was the most fertile center of cultural life. Both Adam Smith and David Hume, for example, spent portions of their careers in Paris and were welcomed into Parisian salons. In fact, the French capital was an environment that encouraged debate precisely because of the juxtaposition of the vibrant new intellectual climate with the institutional rigidities of its political system. In France, patronage and privilege were the sole avenues to power, a system that excluded many talented and eager members of the elite.

The French state continued to embody fundamental contradictions. As under Louis XIV, the Crown sponsored scientific research, subsidized commerce and exploration, and tried to rationalize the royal administration. Royal administrators tried to chip away at the traditional privileges that hampered effective government—such as the exemption most nobles enjoyed from taxation. However, the Crown also continued to claim the right to govern autocratically, and the king was supported both ideologically and institutionally by the Catholic Church. A merchant in the bustling port of Bordeaux might be glad of the royal navy's protection of the colonies, and of the Crown's efforts to build better roads for trade within France. However, with his fellow Masons, he would fume when church officials publicly burned the works of Rousseau and resent his exclusion from any formal voice in politics.

The problems facing the French government were made worse by two circumstances: first, the strength of the elites' defense of their privileges, and second, mounting government debt from foreign wars. Fiscal reform was increasingly urgent, yet entrenched elites stood in the way of change. Louis XIV was followed on the throne by his 5-year-old great-grandson, Louis XV (r. 1715–1774). During the regency early in his reign, the supreme law courts, the parlements, reclaimed the right to object to royal edicts and thus to exercise some control over the enactment of law. Throughout Louis XV's reign, his administration often locked horns with the parlements, particularly as royal ministers tried various schemes to cope with financial crises.

The power of the parlements came not only from their routine role in government, but also from the fact that parlementaires were all legally noble and owned their offices, just as a great nobleman owned his country estate. In addition, the parlements were the only institutions that could legitimately check royal power. As such, they were often supported in their opposition to royal policies by the weight of public opinion. On the one hand, enlightened opinion believed in the rationality of doing away with privileges, such as the ownership of offices. On the other hand, the role of consultative bodies and the separation of powers touted by Montesquieu, himself a parlementaire, were much prized. And even our Bordeaux merchant, who had little in common with privileged officeholders, might nevertheless see the parlementaires' resistance as his best protection from royal tyranny. The parlementaires, however, usually used their power for protecting the status quo.

A further check on reform was the character of the king himself. Louis XV displayed none of the kingly qualities of his great-grandfather. He was neither pleasant nor affable, and he was lazy. He did not give the "rationality" of royal government a good name. By the end of his reign, he was roundly despised. By the late 1760s, the weight of government debt from foreign wars finally forced the king into action. He threw his support behind the reforming schemes of his chancellor, Nicolas de Maupeou (mo-POO), who dissolved the parlements early in 1771 and created new law courts whose judges would not enjoy independent power.

The Crown lost control of reform when Louis died soon after, in 1774. His 20-year-old grandson, Louis XVI, well-meaning but insecure, allowed the complete restoration of the parlements. Further reform efforts, sponsored by the king and several talented ministers, came to nothing because of parlementary opposition. Not surprisingly, from about the middle of the century,

Gardens

What is a garden? Like most of the art forms that we see habitually, the garden is difficult to analyze or even to think of as an art form. Like the buildings they surround, however, gardens have much to tell us about human habits and values. Let us examine these eighteenth-century gardens for evidence of contemporaries' attitudes toward nature and their relationship with it.

Look at the two English-style gardens illustrated here. The first is next to the Governor's Mansion in Williamsburg, the capital of the English colony of Virginia. Construction of this garden began at the end of the seventeenth century; the photograph shows the restored gardens that tourists may visit today. The second garden, from the private estate of West Wycombe in England, looks very different—much more like a natural landscape. The engraving reproduced here dates from the 1770s. The two gardens represent distinct epochs in the development of the garden, hence the differences between them. However, each of these gardens in its own way celebrates human domination of nature.

This symbolic domination of nature is more obvious to us in the Williamsburg garden. The lawns and hedges are trimmed in precise geometrical shapes and are laid out, with the walkways, in straight lines. This "palace garden"

was a small English variant of the classical garden developed in France—most spectacularly at the Versailles Palace—and then imitated throughout Europe during the seventeenth century. The garden at Versailles is so vast that at many points, all of nature visible to the eye is nature disciplined by humans.

We can think of such gardens as pieces of architecture, because that is how they were originally conceived. The design originated in the enclosed courtyard gardens of the homes of classical antiquity. The straight lines and square shapes of these gardens mimic the buildings they are attached to. In fact, these seventeenth- and eighteenth-century gardens were usually laid out as an extension of the buildings themselves. Notice the wide staircase that descends from the central axis of the Governor's Mansion into the central walkway of the garden. Other architectural details, such as the benches positioned at the ends of various walkways, add to the sense of the garden as an exterior room. The garden symbolizes the taming of nature into a pleasing vision of order and regularity.

However, the later eighteenth-century garden represents even greater confidence in the human relationship with nature, although it does not appear to do so at first glance. The extensive garden at first seems to be nature itself

Governor's Mansion and Formal Gardens at Williamsburg, Virginia (© Robert Llewellyn)

Landscape Garden at West Wycombe, England (Courtesy of the Trustees of the British Museum)

plus a few added details, such as the statuary, and a few improvements, such as the grass kept trim by the workers in the foreground. Our familiarity with such landscapes—in our own suburban yards—keeps us from immediately perceiving how contrived such a landscape is. Nature, however, does not intersperse dense stands of trees or clumps of shrubbery with green expanses of lawns. Nor does nature conveniently leave portions of a hillside bare of trees to provide a view of the water from a palatial house on the hill (to the left). Note also that the waterfall cascading over rocks and statuary flows from an artificial lake, neatly bordered by a path.

This kind of garden reflects Enlightenment optimism about humans' ability to understand and work with nature. Such gardens were asymmetrical: Paths were usually curved, and lakes and ponds were irregularly shaped, as they would be in nature. Trees and shrubs were allowed to maintain their natural form. Nevertheless, this landscaping conveys a powerful message of confidence and order. Humans cannot bend or distort nature to their own ends, but they can live in harmony with it as they manage it and enjoy its beneficence. People were freed from regarding nature as hostile and needing to be fought. In this garden, one lives with nature but improves on it. The workers cutting the grass do not detract from the engraving but rather make the scene more compelling.

This brand of landscape gardening appeared in the English colonies across the Atlantic by the end of the eighteenth century. One of the best examples is at Monticello, Thomas Jefferson's Virginia estate, first designed in the 1770s and constructed and improved over the remainder of Jefferson's life (1743–1826). If you tour Monticello, you will notice a curving garden path bordered by flowers in season, with mature trees scattered here and there. Jefferson planned every inch of this largely random-looking outdoor space, just as he planned the regimented fruit and vegetable garden that borders it. The older, classical style of the Williamsburg garden is partly explained by its earlier date and also because this more aggressively controlling style lasted longer in the American colonies than in Europe, perhaps because "nature" seemed more wild and more formidable in the New World.

QUESTIONS

1. How do the two gardens depicted here reflect two different visions of human power over nature?

2. What explains the evolution of styles, over the eighteenth century, in this art form?

there had been calls to revive the Estates General, the representative assembly last convened in 1614. By the time an Estates General was finally called in the wake of further financial problems in 1788, the enlightened elites' habit of carrying on political debate and criticism outside the actual corridors of power, as well as their accumulated mistrust of the Crown, had created a volatile situation.

Monarchy and Parliament in Great Britain

After the deaths of William (d. 1702) and Mary (d. 1694), the British crown passed to Mary's sister, Anne (r. 1702–1714), and then to a collateral line descended from Elizabeth Stuart (d. 1662), sister of the beheaded Charles I. Elizabeth had married Frederick, elector of the Palatinate (and had reigned with him briefly in Bohemia at the start of the Thirty Years' War; see page 427), and her descendants were Germans, now electors of Hanover. The new British sovereign in 1714, George I (r. 1714–1727), was both a foreigner and a man of mediocre abilities. Moreover, his claim to the throne was immediately contested by Catholic descendants of James II (see page 455), who attempted to depose him in 1715 and later his son, George II (r. 1727–1760), in 1745.

The 1745 uprising was the more serious threat. The son of the rival Stuart claimant to the throne, Charles (known in legend as Bonnie Prince Charlie), landed on the west coast of Scotland, with French assistance. He led his forces south into England. Most of the British army and George II himself were on the Continent, fighting in the War of the Austrian Succession (see page 522). Scotland had been formally united with England in 1707 (hence, the term *Great Britain* after that time), and Charles had found some support among Scots dissatisfied with the economic and political results of that union.

But the vast majority of Britons, Scottish or English, did not want the civil war that Charles's challenge inevitably meant, especially on behalf of a Catholic claimant who relied on support from Britain's great rival, France. Charles's army, made up mostly of poor Highland clansmen, was destroyed at the Battle of Culloden (cull-UH-dun) in April 1746 by British army units, hastily returned from abroad. Charles fled back to France, and the British government used the failed uprising as justification for the brutal and forceful integration of the still-remote Scottish Highlands into the British state.

Despite this serious challenge to the new dynasty and the harsh response it occasioned, the British state, overall, enjoyed a period of relative stability as well as innovation in the eighteenth century. The civil war of the seventeenth century had reaffirmed both the need for a strong monarchy and the role of Parliament in defending elite interests. The power of Parliament had recently been reinforced by the Act of Settlement, by which the German Protestant heir to Queen Anne had been chosen in 1701. By excluding the Catholic Stuarts from the throne and establishing the line of succession, this document reasserted that Parliament determined the legitimacy of the monarchy. In fact, the act claimed greater parliamentary authority over foreign and domestic policy in the aftermath of William's constant involvement in war (see page 450).

In the eighteenth century, cooperation between monarchy and Parliament evolved further as Parliament became a more sophisticated and secure institution. Political parties—that is, distinct groups within the elite favoring certain foreign and domestic policies—came into existence. Two groups, the Whigs and the Tories, had begun to form during the reign of Charles II (d. 1685). The Whigs (named derisively by their opponents with a Scottish term for horse thieves) had resisted Charles's pro-French policies and his efforts to tolerate Catholicism. They had wholly opposed his brother and successor, James II. Initially, the Whigs favored an aggressive foreign policy against continental opponents, particularly France. The Tories (whose name was also a taunt, referring to Irish cattle rustlers) leaned toward a conservative view of their own role, favoring isolationism in foreign affairs and deference toward monarchical authority. Whigs generally represented the interests of the great aristocrats or wealthy merchants or gentry. Tories more often represented the interests of provincial gentry and the traditional concerns of landholding and local administration.

The Whigs were the dominant influence in government through most of the century to 1770. William and Mary, as well as Queen Anne, favored Whig religious and foreign policies. The loyalty of many Tories was called into question by their support for a Stuart, not Hanoverian, succession at Anne's death in 1714. The long Whig dominance of government was also ensured by the talents of Robert Walpole, a member of Parliament who functioned virtually as a prime minister from 1722 to 1742.

Walpole (1676–1745) was from a minor gentry family and was brought into government in 1714 with other Whig ministers in George I's new regime. An extremely talented politician, he took advantage of the mistakes of other ministers over the years and, in 1722, became both the first lord of the treasury and chancellor of the exchequer. No post or title of "prime minister" yet existed, but the great contribution of Walpole's tenure was to create that office in fact, if not officially. He chose to maintain peace abroad when and where he could and thus presided over a period of recovery and relative prosperity.

Initially, Walpole was helped in his role as go-between for king and Parliament by George I's own limitations. The king rarely attended meetings of his own council of ministers and was hampered by his limited command of English. Gradually, the Privy Council of the king became something resembling a modern cabinet dominated by a prime minister. By the end of the century, the notions of "loyal opposition" to the Crown within Parliament and parliamentary responsibility for policy had taken root.

In some respects, the maturation of political life in Parliament resembled the lively political debates in the salons of Paris. In both cases, political life was being legitimized on a new basis. In England, however, that legitimation was enshrined in a legislative institution, which made it especially effective and resilient. Parliament was not yet in any sense representative of the British population, however. Because of strict property qualifications, only about 200,000 adult men could vote. In addition, representation was very uneven and heavily favored traditional landed wealth. Some constituencies with only a few dozen voters sent members to Parliament. Many of these "pocket boroughs" were under the control of (in the pockets of) powerful local families who could intimidate the local electorate, particularly in the absence of secret ballots.

Movements for reform of representation in Parliament began in the late 1760s as professionals, such as doctors and lawyers, with movable (as opposed to landed) property and merchants in booming but underrepresented cities began to demand the vote. As the burden of taxation grew—the result of the recently concluded Seven Years' War (discussed later in this chapter)—these groups felt increasingly deprived of representation. Indeed, many felt kinship with the American colonists who opposed increased taxation by the British government on these same grounds and revolted in 1775.

However, the reform movement faltered over the issue of religion. In 1780, a tentative effort by Parliament to extend some civil rights to British Catholics provoked rioting in London (known as the Gordon Riots, after one of the leaders). The riots lasted for eight days and claimed three hundred lives. Pressure for parliamentary reform had been building, but this specter of a popular movement out of control temporarily ended the drive for reform by disenfranchised elites.

Political Satire in England   This gruesome image, showing England being disemboweled by members of the government, criticizes the government's acceptance of a treaty with France. Satirical images such as this one were increasingly part of the lively and more open political life in eighteenth-century England.   (Courtesy of the Trustees of the British Museum)

"Enlightened" Monarchy

Arbitrary monarchical power might seem antithetical to Enlightenment thought. After all, the Enlightenment stressed the reasonableness of human beings and their capacity to discern and act in accord with natural law. Yet, monarchy seemed an ideal instrument of reform to Voltaire and to many of his contemporaries. The work of curtailing the influence of the church, reforming legal codes, and eliminating barriers to economic activity might be done more efficiently by a powerful monarch than by other available means. Historians have labeled a number of rulers of this era "enlightened despots" because of the arbitrary nature of their power, yet the enlightened or reformist uses to which they put it.

SCANDINAVIA

In Denmark, in 1784, a reform-minded group of nobles, led by the young crown prince Frederick (governing on behalf of his mentally ill father), began to apply Enlightenment remedies to the kingdom's economic problems. This move was a bold departure from the past because, in Denmark, the Crown had governed without significant challenge from the landholding nobility since the mid-seventeenth century and the nobility enjoyed ironclad domination of the peasantry. The reformers encouraged freer trade and sought, above all, to improve agriculture by elevating the status of the peasantry. With improved legal status and with land reform, which enabled some peasants to own the land they worked for the first time, agricultural productivity in Denmark rose dramatically. These reforms constitute some of the clearest achievements of any of the "enlightened" rulers.

In contrast to Denmark, Sweden had a relatively unbroken tradition of noble involvement in government, stemming in part from its marginal economy and the consequent stake of the nobility in the Crown's aggressive foreign policy. Since Sweden's eclipse as a major power after the Great Northern War (see page 462), factions of the Swedish parliament, the Diet, had fought over the reins of government, somewhat like the emerging political parties in Britain. Ironically, it was in Sweden, and not Denmark, that an "enlightened despot" emerged. King Gustav III (r. 1771–1796) staged a coup to regain control of policy from the Diet and began an ambitious program of reform of the government. Restrictions on trade in grain and other economic controls were liberalized, the legal system was rationalized, the death penalty was strictly limited, and legal torture was abolished.

Despite his achievements, Gustav III suffered the consequences of advancing reform by autocratic means in a kingdom with a strong tradition of representative government. Gustav eventually tried to deflect the criticisms of the nobility by reviving grandiose—but completely unrealistic—schemes for the reconquest of Baltic territory. In 1796, he was mortally wounded by an assassin hired by disgruntled nobles.

PRUSSIA

Enlightened despotism
Term for the reform-oriented rule of eighteenth-century monarchs. Enlightened despots applied Enlightenment remedies to economic problems and encouraged education and legal reform, but did not dismantle elites' privileges or share their own power.

Frederick the Great
Autocratic king of Prussia who transformed the country into a major military power and also sponsored "enlightened" reforms.

"Enlightened despotism" aptly describes the rule of Frederick II of Prussia (r. 1740–1786), known as **Frederick the Great**. Much of the time, Frederick resided in his imperial electorate of Brandenburg, near its capital, Berlin. His scattered states, which he extended by seizing new lands, are referred to as Prussia rather than Brandenburg-Prussia because members of his family were now kings of Prussia thanks to their ambitions and the weakness of the Polish state, of which Prussia had once been a dependent duchy. In many ways, the Prussian state *was* its military victories, for Frederick's bold moves and the policies of his father, grandfather, and great-grandfather committed the state's resources to a military presence of dramatic proportions. Prussia was on the European stage at all only because of that driving commitment.

The institutions that constituted the state and linked the various provinces under one administration were dominated by the needs of the military. Frederick II's father, Frederick William (r. 1713–1740), had added an efficient provincial recruiting system to the state's central institutions, which he also further consolidated. But in many other respects, the Prussian state was in its infancy. There was no tradition of political participation—even by elites—and little chance of cultivating any. Nor was there any political or social room for maneuver at the lower part of the social scale. The rulers of Prussia had long ago given in to the aristocracy's demand for tighter control over peasant labor on their own lands in return for their support of the monarchy. The rulers relied on the nobles for local administration and army commands. Thus, the kinds of social, judicial, or political reforms that Frederick could hope to carry out without undermining his own power were starkly limited.

Frederick tried to modernize agricultural methods and simultaneously to improve the condition of the peasants, but he met stiff resistance from the noble landholders. He did succeed in abolishing serfdom in some regions. He tried to stimulate the economy by sponsoring state industries and trading monopolies, but too few resources and too little initiative from the tightly controlled merchant communities stymied his plans. Simplifying and codifying the inherited jumble of local laws was a goal of every ruler. A law code published in 1794, after Frederick's death, was partly the product of his efforts.

Frederick's views of the role of Enlightenment thought reflect the limitations of his situation. One doesn't have to lead a frontal assault on prejudices consecrated by time, he believed; instead, one must be tolerant of superstition because it will always have a hold on the masses. Perhaps his most distinctive "enlightened" characteristic was the seriousness with which he took his task as ruler. He was energetic and disciplined to a fault. In his book, *Anti-Machiavel* (1741), he argued that a ruler has a moral obligation to work for the betterment of the state. He styled himself as the "first servant" or steward of the state. However superficial this claim may appear, Frederick compares favorably with Louis XV of France, who, having a far more wealthy and flexible society to work with, did much less.

The Habsburg ruler **Maria Theresa** of Austria (r. 1740–1780) was guided more by traditional concerns for effective rule and compassion for her subjects than by Enlightenment ideas. After surviving the near dismemberment of Austrian territories in the War of the Austrian Succession (see page 522), she embarked on an energetic program of reform to improve the administration of her territories. "Austria," it must be remembered, is a term of convenience; the state was a very medieval-looking hodgepodge that included present-day Austria, the kingdoms of Bohemia and Hungary, the Austrian Netherlands, and lands in northern Italy. Among her more successful reforms were improved assessment and collection of taxes to tap the wealth of her subjects more effectively and thus better defend all her domains. She improved her subjects' access to justice and limited the exploitation of serfs by landlords. She made primary schooling universal and compulsory, in order to better train peasants for the army. Although the policy was far from fully implemented at the time of her death, hers was the first European state with so ambitious an education policy. Maria Theresa accomplished all of this without being particularly "enlightened" personally. She was a devout Catholic who cherished orthodoxy in religious matters. She did not welcome Enlightenment philosophy to her court and feared freedom of the press.

Many of the ministers and bureaucrats who implemented Maria Theresa's reforms were themselves well versed in "enlightened" ideas. The diverse character of the Habsburg lands meant that some members of the governing elite came from the Netherlands and from Italy, where sympathy for the Enlightenment was well rooted by comparison with the relatively poorer and more rural society of the Austrian hinterland. Moreover, the language of the Habsburg court was French (Maria Theresa spoke it fluently); thus, no amount of local censorship—which, in any case, Maria Theresa relaxed—could prevent the governing class from reading and absorbing Enlightenment philosophy in its original language.

Maria Theresa was followed on the throne by her two sons, Joseph II (r. 1780–1790) and Leopold II (r. 1790–1792), each of whom counted himself a follower of the Enlightenment. After his mother's death, Joseph II carried out bold initiatives that she had not attempted, including freedom of the press, significant freedom of religion, and the abolition of serfdom in Habsburg lands.

Like Frederick the Great, Joseph regarded himself as a servant of the state. Also like Frederick, he was limited in his reform program by the economic and social rigidities of the society he ruled; he could not directly assault the privileges of great landholders, on whose wealth the state depended. His despotic methods—he imposed reforms autocratically—antagonized many of these powerful subjects. His more able brother, Leopold, spent much of his two-year reign dexterously saving reforms enacted by his mother and, especially, his brother in the face of mounting opposition.

Perhaps the most powerful ruler with a claim to the title "enlightened despot" was Catherine, empress of Russia (r. 1762–1796). **Catherine the Great**, as she came to be called, was the true heir of Peter the Great in her abilities, policies, and ambitions. Her determination and political acumen were evident soon after she was brought to the Russian court from her native Germany in 1745. After enduring brutal treatment by her husband, Tsar Peter III, Catherine engineered a coup in which he was killed, and then ruled alone for more than thirty years.

Like any successful ruler of her age, Catherine counted territorial aggrandizement among her chief achievements: she expanded Russian territory at the expense of the Ottoman Empire and Poland-Lithuania.

Nevertheless, Catherine counted herself a sincere follower of the Enlightenment. Like Frederick, she attempted to take an active role in the European intellectual community; she corresponded with Voltaire over the course of many years and acted as patron to the encyclopedist Diderot. One of Catherine's boldest political moves was the secularization of church lands. Although Peter the Great had extended government control of the Russian Orthodox Church, he had not touched church lands. Catherine also licensed private publishing houses; the number of books published in Russia tripled during her reign. This enriched cultural life was one of the principal causes of the flowering of Russian literature that began in the early nineteenth century.

The stamp of the Enlightenment on Catherine's policies is also clearly visible in her attempts at legal reform. In 1767, she convened a legislative commission and provided it with a guiding

AUSTRIA

Maria Theresa Habsburg archduchess of Austria and queen of Hungary and Bohemia who reformed and centralized the administration of her Austrian and Bohemian lands.

RUSSIA

Catherine the Great Empress of Russia who, through an astute policy of wars and alliances, expanded her country's borders. An "enlightened despot," she advanced the westernizing reforms begun by Peter the Great.

Catherine the Great as a young woman This portrait of Catherine was painted when she first came to the Russian court from her native Germany in 1745. Catherine wears formal court dress and the portrait introduces her as a "Grand Duchess," a Russian title reserved for the royal family. (Portrait of Grand Duchess Yekatrina Alexeyevna, later Catherine II, c.1745, Grooth, Georg Christoph (1716-49)/Hermitage, St. Petersburg, Russia/The Bridgeman Art Library)

document, the *Instruction*, which she had written herself. The commission was remarkable because it included representatives of all classes, including peasants. Catherine hoped for a general codification of law as well as reforms, such as the abolition of torture and capital punishment—reforms that made the *Instruction* radical enough to be banned from publication in other countries. She did not propose changing the legal status of serfs, however, and class conflict made the commission unworkable in the end. Most legal reforms were eventually accomplished piecemeal and favored the interests of landed gentry.

Like the Austrian rulers, Catherine undertook far-reaching administrative reform to create more effective local units of government but, again, political imperatives were fundamental, and reforms in local government strengthened the hand of the gentry. The legal subjection of peasants in serfdom was also extended as a matter of state policy to help win the allegiance of landholders in newly acquired areas. In Russia, as in Prussia and Austria, oppression of the peasantry continued because the monarch wanted to ensure the allegiance of the elites who lived from the peasants' labor. Catherine particularly valued the cooperation of elites because the expanding Russian state was incorporating new peoples, such as the Tatars in the Crimea, and attempting to manage its relationships with border peoples such as the Cossacks. Catherine's reign witnessed one of the most massive and best-organized peasant rebellions of the century. Occurring in 1773, the rebellion expressed the grievances of the thousands of peasants who joined its ranks and called for the abolition of serfdom. The revolt took its name, however, from its Cossack leader, Emelian Pugachev (poo-guh-CHOFF) (d. 1775), and reflected also the Cossacks' resistance to centralized control. The dramatic dilemmas faced by Catherine illustrate both the promise and the costs of state formation throughout Europe. State consolidation permitted the imposition of internal peace, coordinated economic policy, and reform of justice, but it came at the price of greater—in some cases much greater—control and coercion of the population.

SECTION SUMMARY

- In France, the royal government tried unsuccessfully to eliminate the privileges of nobility, which limited state revenue and kept most people shut out of the political process.

- The Parliament in England was securely established as a part of government; political parties, representing differing interests among the elite, began to develop.

- "Enlightened despots," such as Frederick the Great in Prussia, ruled autocratically but used their power for some reforms in law, education, and public welfare.

THE WIDENING WORLD OF TRADE AND PRODUCTION

How and why did trade and production increase in the eighteenth century?

The importance of international trade and colonial possessions to the states of western Europe grew enormously in the eighteenth century (see **MAP 18.2**). Between 1715 and 1785, Britain's trade with North America rose from 19 to 34 percent of its total trade, and its trade with Asia and Africa rose from 7 to 19 percent of the total. By the end of the century, more than half of all British trade was carried on outside Europe; for France, the figure was more than a third. Plantation agriculture based on slave labor in European colonies created profits and products that drove much of this trade. Equally profound changes were occurring in the European countryside. Population, production, and consumption were beginning to grow beyond the bounds that all preceding generations had lived within and taken for granted.

🌐 Map 18.1—The Atlantic Economy, ca. 1750

The triangle trade linked Europe, Africa, and European colonies in the Americas. The most important component of this trade for Europe was the plantation agriculture of the Caribbean islands, which depended on enslaved Africans for labor.

The Atlantic World: Expanding Commerce and the Slave Trade

European commercial and colonial energies were concentrated in the Atlantic world in the eighteenth century because the profits were greatest there. The colonial population of British North America grew from about 250,000 in 1700 to about 1.7 million by 1760. The densely settled New England colonies provided a market for manufactured goods from the mother country, although

The Treatment of Slaves on Caribbean Plantations
These images of the brutal treatment of slaves on West Indian plantations come from a report published in England designed to convince the British public of the horrors of slavery. At top, a husband and wife are violently separated after being sold to different slave owners. At bottom, a mouthpiece and neck guard are used to prevent escape. The treatment of slaves described here is also documented in other surviving accounts from the eighteenth century.
(New York Public Library/Art Resource, NY)

they produced little by way of raw materials or bulk goods on which traders could make a profit. The colonies of Maryland and Virginia produced tobacco, the Carolinas rice and indigo (a dyestuff). England re-exported all three throughout Europe at considerable profit.

The French in New France, only 56,000 in 1740, were vastly outnumbered by British colonists. Nevertheless, the French had successfully expanded their control of territory in Canada. Settlements sprang up between the outposts of Montreal and Quebec on the St. Lawrence River. Despite resistance, the French extended their fur trapping—the source of most of the profits New France generated—west and north along the Great Lakes, consolidating their hold by building forts at strategic points. They penetrated as far as the modern Canadian province of Manitoba, where they cut into the British trade run out of Hudson Bay. The French also contested the mouth of the St. Lawrence River and the Gulf of St. Lawrence with the British. The British held Nova Scotia and Newfoundland, the French controlled parts of Cape Breton Island, and both states fished the surrounding waters.

The commercial importance of these North American holdings, as well as those in Asia, was dwarfed by the European states' Caribbean possessions, however. The British held Jamaica, Barbados, and the Leeward Islands; the French, Guadeloupe and Martinique; the Spanish, Cuba and Santo Domingo; and the Dutch, a few small islands. Sugar, produced on plantations by slave labor, was the major source of profits, along with other cash crops such as coffee, indigo, and cochineal (another dyestuff). The concentration of shipping to this region indicates the region's importance in the European trading system. For example, by the 1760s, the British China trade occupied seven or eight ships a year. In the 1730s, British trade with Jamaica alone drew three hundred ships.

The economic dependence of the colonies on slave labor meant that the colonies were tied to their home countries not with a two-way commercial exchange, but with a three-way, or "triangle," trade (see **Map 18.1**). Certain European manufactures were shipped to ports in western Africa, where they were traded for slaves. Captive Africans were transported to South America, the Caribbean, or North America, where planters bought and paid for them with profits from their sugar and tobacco plantations. (See the feature, "The Global Record: An African Recalls the Horrors of the Slave Ship.") Sugar and tobacco were then shipped back to the mother country to be re-exported at great profit throughout Europe.

This plantation economy in the Caribbean was vulnerable to slave revolts, as well as to competition among the Europeans. Often, wars over control of the islands significantly disrupted production and lessened profits for the European planters on the islands and for their trading partners back in Europe. The growing demands by Europeans for sugar and other products kept the plantation system expanding, despite these challenges, throughout the eighteenth century. The **slave trade** grew dramatically as a result. Approximately five times as many Africans— perhaps as many as seven million people—were forcibly transported to the Americas as slaves in the eighteenth century as in the seventeenth.

The slave trade became an increasingly specialized form of oceangoing commerce (for example, slave traders throughout Europe adopted a standardized ship design) and, at the same time, one increasingly linked to the rest of European commerce by complex trade and financial ties. In England, London merchants who imported Asian goods, exported European manufactures, or distributed Caribbean sugar could provide credit for slave traders based in the northern city of Liverpool to fund their journeys to Africa and then the Americas.

slave trade Europeans' trade with Africa in which involuntary laborers were shipped to the Americas to be sold to owners of, especially, sugar plantations. The trade reached its peak in the eighteenth century, when approximately seven million Africans were shipped across the Atlantic.

An African Recalls the Horrors of the Slave Ship

Olaudah Equiano (ca. 1750-1797) was an Ibo from the Niger region of West Africa. He first experienced slavery as a boy when kidnapped from his village by other Africans, but nothing prepared him for the brutality of the Europeans who bought and shipped him to Barbados, in the British West Indies. His narration of the horrors of the "Middle Passage" between Africa and the Americas may represent a composite story of others' experiences as well as his own. Nevertheless, his account remains one of the few written records by an African survivor of a slave ship.

The first object which saluted my eyes when I arrived on the [African] coast was the sea and a slave ship, which was then riding at anchor, and waiting for its cargo. ... When I was carried on board I was immediately handled, and tossed up, to see if I were sound, by some of the crew. ... When I looked around the ship ... and saw ... a multitude of black people of every description chained together, every one of their countenances expressing dejection and sorrow, I no longer doubted of my fate. ...

I was not long suffered to indulge my grief; I was soon put down under the decks, and there I received such a salutation in the nostrils as I had never experienced in my life; so that with the loathsomeness of the stench ... I became so sick and low that I was not able to eat. ... I now wished for the last friend, death, to relieve me; but soon, to my grief, two of the white men offered me eatables; and, on my refusing to eat, one of them held me fast by the hands and laid me across, I think, the windlass, and tied my feet while the other flogged me severely.

One day, when we had a smooth sea and a moderate wind, two of my wearied countrymen, who were chained together ..., preferring death to such a life of misery, somehow made through the nettings and jumped into the sea; immediately another dejected fellow who [was ill and so not in irons] followed their example; and I believe many more would very soon have done the same, if they had not been prevented by the ship's crew who were instantly alarmed. Those of us that were the most active were in a minute put down under the deck; and there was such a noise and confusion amongst the people of the ship as I have never heard before, to stop her, and get the boat to go after the slaves. However, two of the wretches were drowned, but they got the other and afterwards flogged him unmercifully for thus attempting to prefer death to slavery. In this manner we continued to undergo more hardships than I can now relate; hardships which are inseparable from this accursed trade.

QUESTIONS

1. What particular horrors of the Middle Passage seem to stand out in Equiano's mind? What is the significance of these vignettes?

2. What clues in this excerpt reveal the audience Equiano had in mind for his narrative?

Source: *The Interesting Narrative of the Life of Olaudah Equiano, or Gustavus Vassa, the African* (London, 1793); reprinted in David Northrup, ed., *The Atlantic Slave Trade* (Boston: Houghton Mifflin, 2002), pp. 68–70.

MORE FOOD AND MORE PEOPLE

Throughout European history, there had been a delicate balance between available food and numbers of people to feed. Population growth had accompanied increases in the amount of land under cultivation. From time to time, however, population growth surpassed the ability of the land to produce food, and people became malnourished and prey to disease. In 1348, the epidemic known as the Black Death struck just such a vulnerable population in decline. After this catastrophic decline in the fourteenth century, the European population experienced a prolonged recovery, and in the eighteenth century, the limits that had previously been reached began to be exceeded for the first time.

The cause was not a decline in infant mortality, which remained as high as ever. Even Queen Anne of England outlived every one of the seventeen children she bore (and all but one of them died in infancy). Instead, population growth occurred because of a decline in the death rate for adults and a simultaneous increase in the birthrate in some areas, owing to earlier marriages. Adults began to live longer partly because of a decline in the incidence of plague. However, the primary reason adults were living longer was that more and different kinds of food began to be produced. Adults were better nourished and thus better able to resist disease. The increase in the food supply also meant that more new families could be started.

Food production increased because new crops were introduced and agricultural methods changed. The cumulative effect of these changes was so dramatic that historians have called them an **agricultural revolution**. In the past, peasants safeguarded the fertility of the land by alternately cultivating some portions while letting others lie fallow or using them as pasture. Manure provided fertilizer, but during the winter, livestock could not be kept alive in large numbers. Limited food for livestock meant limited fertilizer, which in turn meant limited production of food for both humans and animals.

agricultural revolution
Dramatic increase in food production from the sixteenth to eighteenth centuries, brought about by changes in agricultural practices and cultivation of new crops. The agricultural revolution allowed the population of Europe to expand beyond historic limits.

519

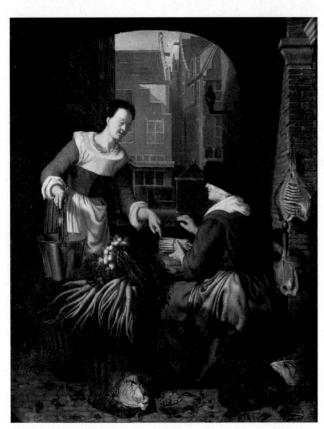

Gérard Dou: The Vegetable Seller   The specialization of agriculture meant that a more varied diet was available to increasing numbers of Europeans.   (Musée des Beaux-Arts, Nimes/Giraudon/Art Resource, NY)

The new crops now being planted included fodder, such as clover, legumes, and turnips, that did not deplete the soil and could be fed to livestock over the winter. The greater availability of animal manure in turn boosted grain production. In addition, the nutrient-dense potato was introduced from the Americas in the sixteenth century. It could feed more people per acre than could grain. In certain areas, farming families produced potatoes to feed themselves, while they grew grain to be sold and shipped elsewhere.

More food being produced meant more food available for purchase. The opportunity to buy food freed up land and labor. A family that could purchase food might decide to convert its farm to specialized use, such as raising dairy cattle, which meant, in turn, that several families might be supported by a piece of land that had previously supported only one. Over a generation or two, a number of children might share the inheritance of what had previously been a single farm, yet each could make a living from his or her share, and population could grow as it had not done before.

Farmers had known about and experimented with many of the crops used for fodder for centuries. However, widespread planting of these crops and other changes were long in coming and happened in scattered areas because a farmer had to have control over land in order to make changes. In the traditional open-field system, peasants had split up all the land in the community so that each family might have a piece of each field. Dramatic change was unlikely when an entire community had to act together. Only prosperous farmers had spare capital to invest in new crops and few were inclined to take risks with the production of food and to trust the workings of the market. The bad condition of roads was reason enough not to rely on distant markets.

Yet, where both decent roads and growing urban markets existed, some farmers—even entire villages working together—were willing to produce for urban populations. Booming capital cities, such as London and Amsterdam, and trading centers, such as Glasgow and Bordeaux, demanded not only grain, but also specialized produce, such as dairy products and fruits and vegetables. Urbanization and improved transportation networks also encouraged agriculture because human waste produced by city dwellers—known as "night soil"—could be collected and distributed in the surrounding agricultural regions as fertilizer. By the late eighteenth century, pockets of intensive, diversified agriculture existed in England, northern France, the Rhineland in Germany, the Po Valley in Italy, and Catalonia in Spain.

In some areas, changes in agriculture were accompanied by a shift in power in the countryside. Where the traditional authority of the village to regulate agriculture was weak, peasants were vulnerable to wealthy landlords who wanted to reap the profits of producing for the new markets. In England, a combination of weak village structure and high demand from urban centers created a climate that encouraged landlords to treat land speculatively. They raised the rents that farmers paid for land and changed cultivation patterns on the land that they controlled directly. They appropriated the village common lands, a process known as "enclosure," and used them for cash crops such as sheep (raised for their wool) or beef cattle.

As a result, although the agricultural revolution increased the food supply to sustain more people in Europe, it did not create general prosperity. Many rural people were driven off the land or made destitute by the loss of the resources of common lands. Charitable institutions run by cities, churches, and central governments expanded to care for them—often in poorhouses where people received food and shelter but were forced to work and to live isolated against their will. Peasants in eastern Europe produced grain for export to the growing urban centers in western Europe, but usually by traditional methods. In both eastern and western Europe, the power and profits of landlords were a major force in structuring the rural economy.

The Growth of Industry

Agricultural changes led to further changes in economic and social life. As more food was grown with less labor, that labor was freed to take on other productive work. If enough people could be kept employed making useful commodities, the nonagricultural population could continue to grow. If population grew, more and more consumers would be born, and the demand for more goods would help continue the cycle of population growth, changes in production, and economic expansion. This is precisely what happened in the eighteenth century: A combination of forces increased the numbers of people who worked at producing a few key materials and products (see **MAP 18.2**).

Especially significant was the expansion of the putting-out system. Also known as cottage industry, putting out involved the production of thread and cloth by spinners and weavers working in their own homes, usually in a farming village. An entrepreneur bought the raw materials and "put them out" to be finished by these workers. The putting-out system expanded in the eighteenth century, as the agricultural economy was transformed. All agricultural work was seasonal, demanding intensive effort and many hands at certain times but not others. The labor demands of the new crops meant that an even larger number of people periodically needed work away from the fields to make ends meet.

🌐 MAP 18.2—Population and Production in Eighteenth-Century Europe

The growth of cottage industry helped to support a growing population. With changes in agriculture, more land-poor workers were available in the countryside to accept work as spinners, knitters, and weavers.

SECTION SUMMARY

- The involvement of European states in international trade and overseas colonization grew markedly in the eighteenth century.

- Approximately seven million Africans were forcibly transported to work on plantations producing cash crops in the Americas.

- The introduction of new crops and changes in cultivation led to increases in food production and what has been called the "agricultural revolution."

- Changes in agriculture enabled the European population to grow beyond previous limits.

- Industrial production, especially of cloth, increased because more people were available for the work, markets for the products expanded, and new technologies arose to meet the demand.

Overseas trade also stimulated production by increasing both the demand in Europe's colonies for cloth and other finished products and the demand at home for manufactured items, such as nails to build the ships that carried the trade. The production of cloth expanded, particularly, because heightened demand led to changes in the way cloth was made. Wool was increasingly combined with other fibers to make less expensive fabrics. By the end of the century, wholly cotton fabrics were being made cheaply in Europe from cotton grown in America by slave labor.

The invention of machines to spin thread, also in the late eighteenth century, markedly increased the rate of production. Cloth production became a spur to a transformed industrial economy because cheaper kinds of cloth could be made for mass consumption. The regions of England, France, and the Low Countries where the new technologies were introduced stood, by the end of the century, on the verge of a massive industrial transformation that would have unprecedented social consequences.

THE WIDENING WORLD OF WARFARE

How did warfare and its consequences change in the eighteenth century?

In the eighteenth century, a new constellation of states emerged to dominate politics in Europe. Alongside the traditional powers of England, France, and Austria were Prussia in central Europe and Russia to the east (see **MAP 18.3**); these five states would dominate European politics until the twentieth century. Common to all these states was their ability to field effective armies and, especially in the case of Britain, navies. Eighteenth-century rulers launched most wars to satisfy traditional territorial ambitions. Now, however, the increasing significance of overseas trade and colonization also made international expansion an important source of conflict, particularly between England and France. As warfare widened in scope, governments increasingly focused on recruiting and maintaining large navies and armies, with increasingly serious effects on ordinary people.

The Pattern of War Within Europe

Wars between European states in the eighteenth century still reflected a dynastic, rather than wholly strategic, view of territory. Although rational and defensible "national" borders were important, collecting isolated bits of territory was also still the norm. The wars between European powers thus became extremely complex strategically. France, for example, might choose to strike a blow against Austria by invading an Italian state in order to use the conquered Italian territory as a bargaining chip in eventual negotiations. Wars were carried out with complex systems of alliances and were followed by the adjustments of many borders and the changing control of small, scattered territories. Rulers of lesser states in Germany and Italy, particularly, remained important as allies and as potential rivals of the Great Powers.

Major wars during the mid-eighteenth century decided the balance of power in German-speaking Europe for the next hundred years. Prussia emerged as the equal of Austria in the region. The first of these wars, now known as the War of the Austrian Succession, began after the death of the Habsburg emperor Charles VI in 1740. Charles died without a male heir, and his daughter, Maria Theresa, succeeded him. Charles had worked to shore up his daughter's position as his heir by means of a treaty of sorts called the Pragmatic Sanction, which he had persuaded allies and potential opponents to accept. Nevertheless, when Charles VI died, rival heiresses and their husbands challenged Maria Theresa for control of her various lands. They were supported by France, the Habsburgs' perennial rival. Worst of all, Prussia, Austria's rival to the north, seized

🌐 MAP 18.3—The Partition of Poland and the Expansion of Russia

Catherine the Great acquired present-day Lithuania, Belarus, and Ukraine, which had once constituted the duchy of Lithuania, part of the multiethnic Polish kingdom.

the wealthy Bohemian province of Silesia (sigh-LEE-zhuh). Austrian lands were threatened with dismemberment.

Though her father had not left his armies or his treasury well equipped to fight a war, Maria Theresa proved a more tenacious opponent than anyone had anticipated. She was helped by Great Britain, which saw the possibility of gains against its colonial rival, France. Fighting eventually spread throughout Habsburg territories, including the Netherlands and in Italy, as well as abroad to British and French colonies. In a preliminary peace signed in 1745, Frederick the Great of Prussia was confirmed in possession of Silesia, but the throne of the Holy Roman Empire was returned to the Habsburgs—given to Maria Theresa's husband, Francis (Franz) I (r. 1745–1765). A final treaty in 1748 ended all the fighting that had continued since 1745, mostly by France and Britain overseas. The Austrian state had survived dismemberment, and Maria Theresa now embarked on the administrative and military reforms necessary to make her state less vulnerable in the future. Prussia, because of the annexation of Silesia and the psychological imprint of victory, emerged as a power of virtually equal rank to the Habsburgs.

The unprecedented threat that Austria now felt from Prussia led to a revolution in alliances across Europe. To isolate Prussia, Maria Theresa agreed to an alliance with France, the Habsburgs' long-standing enemy. Sweden and Russia, with territory to gain at Prussia's expense, joined as well.

Frederick the Great initiated the land phase of what came to be known as the Seven Years' War in 1756, hoping to prevent consolidation of the new alliances. Instead, he found that he had started a war against overwhelming odds. What saved him in part was limited English aid. The English, engaged with France in the overseas conflict that Americans call the French and Indian War, wanted France to be heavily committed on the Continent. Prussia managed to emerge intact—though strained economically and demographically. Prussia and Austria were confirmed as the two states of European rank in German-speaking Europe. Yet, their narrow escapes from being reduced to second-class status reveal how fragile even successful states could be and how dependent on successful armies.

Later in the century, Prussia further expanded its territory by working in concert with Russian expansion. In 1768, Catherine the Great initiated a war against the Ottoman Turks, from which Russia gained much of the Crimean coast. She also continued her predecessors' efforts to dominate the weakened Poland. She was aided in this goal by Frederick the Great, who proposed the deliberate partitioning of Poland to satisfy his own territorial ambitions as well as those of his competitors, Russia and Austria. In 1772, portions of Poland were gobbled up in the first of three successive "grabs" of territory (see **Map 18.3**). Warsaw eventually landed in Prussian hands, but Catherine gained all of Belarus, Ukraine, and modern Lithuania—which had constituted the duchy of Lithuania.

Great Britain and France: Wars Overseas

The expansion of European trade and settlement abroad in the eighteenth century led to wars between major powers, particularly the British and the French, which were fought primarily overseas. The growth and the proximity of French and British settlements in North America ensured conflict (see **Map 18.4**). The Caribbean and the coasts of Central and South America were strategic flashpoints as well. At the beginning of the eighteenth century, several substantial islands remained unclaimed by any power. The British were making incursions along the coastline of Central America claimed by Spain and were trying to break into the monopoly of trade between Spain and its vast possessions in the region. Public opinion in both Britain and France became increasingly sensitive to colonial issues.

During the century, England became the dominant naval power in Europe. Its navy protected its far-flung trading networks, its merchant fleet, and the coast of England itself. Within Europe, England's strategic interest lay in promoting a variety of powers there, none of which (or no combination of which) posed too great a threat to England or to its widespread trading system. A second, dynastic consideration in continental affairs was the electorate of Hanover, the large principality in western Germany that was the native territory of the Hanoverian kings of England. Early in the century especially, the interests of this German territory were a significant factor in British foreign policy. Unable to field a large army, given their maritime interests, the British sought protection for Hanover in alliances and subsidies for allies' armies on the Continent and paid for these ventures with the profits on trade. France, on the other hand, was inevitably more committed to affairs on the Continent than were the British. The French were able to hold their own successfully in both arenas during the 1740s, but by 1763, though preeminent on the Continent, they had lost many of their colonial possessions to the English. Conflict between England and France in colonial regions played out in three major phases. The first two coincided with the major land wars in Europe: the War of the Austrian Succession (1740–1748) and the **Seven Years' War** (1756–1763). The third phase coincided with the rebellion of British colonies in North America—the American Revolution—beginning in the 1770s.

In the 1740s, France was heavily involved in the War of the Austrian Succession, while Britain vied with Spain for certain Caribbean territories. Both France and England also tested each other's strength in scattered colonial fighting, which produced a few well-balanced gains and losses. Their conquests were traded back when peace was made in 1748.

Tension was renewed almost immediately at many of the strategic points in North America. The French and British navies harassed each other's merchant shipping in the Gulf of St. Lawrence. The French reinforced their encirclement of British colonies with more forts along the Great Lakes and the Ohio River. When British troops (at one point led by the colonial commander George Washington) attempted to strike at these forts beginning in 1754, open fighting between the French and the English began.

Seven Years' War The first major war between European nations (Britain and France) started and fought largely in their overseas empires.

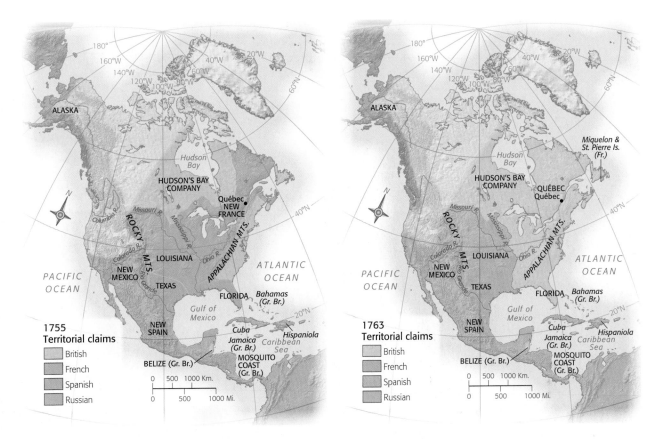

🌐 Map 18.4—British Gains in North America

The British colonies on the Atlantic coast were effective staging posts for the armies that ousted the French from North America by 1763. However, taxes imposed on the colonies to pay the costs of the Seven Years' War helped spark revolt—the American Revolution—a decade later.

In India, meanwhile, both the French and the British attempted to strengthen their commercial footholds by making military and political alliances with local Indian rulers. The disintegration of the Mogul Empire heightened competition among regional Indian rulers and sparked a new level of ambition on the part of the European powers to gain territorial footholds for the purposes of trade. A British attack on a French convoy provoked a declaration of war by France in May 1756, three months before fighting in the Seven Years' War broke out in Europe. For the first time, a major war between European nations had started in their empires, signifying a profound change in the relation of these nations to the world.

The French had already committed themselves to an alliance with Austria and were increasingly involved on the Continent after Frederick II initiated war there in August 1756. Slowly, the drain of sustaining war both on the Continent and abroad began to tell, and Britain scored major victories against French forces. The cost of involvement on so many fronts meant that French troops were short of money and supplies. They were vulnerable to both supply and personnel shortages—especially in North America—because they were weaker than the British at sea and because New France remained sparsely settled and dependent on the mother country for food.

The French lost a number of fortresses on the Mississippi and Ohio Rivers and on the Great Lakes, and then, they also lost the interior of Canada with the fall of Quebec and of Montreal in 1759 and 1760, respectively (see **Map 18.4**). In the Caribbean, the British seized the French island of Guadeloupe, a vital sugar-producer. Superior resources in India enabled the British to take several French outposts there, including Pondicherry (pon-dih-CHAIR-ee), the most important. By the terms of the Peace of Paris in 1763, France regained Guadeloupe, the most profitable of its American

The Death of General Wolfe at Quebec   General Wolfe commanded British troops that in 1759 defeated the French at Quebec in Canada. Wolfe's death at the battle was memorialized ten years later by American-born artist Benjamin West. This image became widely popular after West sold cheap engraved versions. Notice West's sympathetic treatment of the Native American earnestly focused, like his British allies, on the death of the commander.   (Private Collection/Phillips, Fine Art Auctioneers, New York, USA/The Bridgeman Art Library)

colonies, although Britain gained control of several smaller, previously neutral Caribbean islands to add to its own sugar-producing colonies of Jamaica and Barbados. In India, France retained many of its trading stations but lost its political and military clout. British power in India was dramatically enhanced not only by French losses, but also by victories over Indian rulers who had allied with the French. In the interior, Britain now controlled lands that had never before been under the control of any European power. British political rule in India, as opposed to merely a mercantile presence, began at this time. The British also held Canada. They emerged from the Seven Years' War as the preeminent world power among European states. The dramatic gains led some Britons to speak of the "British Empire" overseas.

The Costs of Warfare

In the eighteenth century, weapons and tactics became increasingly refined and armies more expensive to train and maintain. More reliable muskets were introduced. A bayonet that could slip over a musket barrel without blocking the muzzle was invented. Coordinated use of bayonets required even more careful drill of troops than did volley fire alone to ensure disciplined action in the face of enemy fire and charges. Artillery and cavalry forces also were subjected to greater standardization of training and discipline in action. Increased discipline of forces meant that commanders could exercise meaningful control over a battle for the first time. But such battles were not necessarily decisive, especially when waged against a comparable force. Indeed, training now was so costly that commanders were at times ironically reluctant to hazard their fine troops in battle at all.

In addition, wars could still be won or lost not on the battlefield, but on the supply line. Incentive still existed to bleed civilian populations and exploit the countryside. Moreover, when supply lines were disrupted and soldiers not equipped or fed, the armies of a major power could be vulnerable to smaller, less disciplined armies of minor states. Finally, even supplies, training, and sophisticated tactics could not guarantee success. Not until 1746, at Culloden, could the British army decisively defeat the fierce charge and hand-to-hand fighting of Highland clansmen by holding its position and using disciplined volley fire and bayonet tactics. Warfare became increasingly professional but was still an uncertain business with unpredictable results, despite its staggering cost.

One sure result of the new equipment, discipline, and high costs was that war became an ever greater burden on a state's resources and administration. It became increasingly difficult for small states, such as Sweden, to compete with the forces that others could mount. Small and relatively poor states, such as Prussia, that were able to support large forces did so by means of an extraordinary bending of civil society to the economic and social needs of the army. In Prussia, twice as many people were in the armed forces, proportionally, as in other states, and a staggering 80 percent of its meager state revenue went to sustain the army.

Warfare on this scale also represented an increased burden on common people. Most states introduced some form of conscription in the eighteenth century. Although the very poor often volunteered for army service to improve their lives, conscription of peasants (throughout Europe but particularly in Prussia and Russia) imposed a significant burden on peasant communities and a sacrifice of productive members to the state. Governments everywhere supplemented volunteers and conscripts with mercenaries and even criminals, as necessary, to fill the ranks without tapping the wealthier elements of the community. Men were sometimes taken out of poorhouses and forced to become soldiers. Thus, common soldiers were increasingly seen not as members of society, but as its rejects. Said Frederick II, "useful hardworking people should [not be conscripted but rather] be guarded as the apple of one's eye," and a French war minister agreed that armies had to consist of the "scum of people and of all those for whom society has no use."[3] Brutality became an accepted tool for governments to use to manage such groups of men, and the army increasingly became an instrument of social control used to contain individuals who otherwise might disrupt their own communities.

On the high seas, governments used their navies to suppress piracy. Piracy had been a way of life for hundreds of Europeans and colonial settlers since the sixteenth century. Indentured servants fleeing their obligations, runaway slaves, out-of-work laborers, and adventurers could take up the pirating life, which at least offered autonomy and a chance of some comforts. From the earliest days of exploration, European rulers had authorized men known as privateers to commit acts of war against specific enemies. The Crown took little risk and was spared the cost of arming the ships but shared in the plunder. True piracy—outright robbery on the high seas— was illegal, but in practice, the difference between piracy and privateering was negligible. As governments and merchants grew to prefer regular trade over the irregular profits of plunder, and as national navies developed in the late seventeenth century, a concerted effort to eliminate piracy began.

Because life on the seas was an increasingly vital part of European economic life in the eighteenth century, sea life began to resemble life on land in the amount of compulsion it entailed. Sailors in port were always vulnerable to forcible enlistment in the navy by impressment gangs, particularly during wartime. A drowsy sailor sleeping off a rowdy night could wake up to find himself aboard a navy ship. Press gangs operated throughout England and not just in major ports, for authorities were as interested in controlling "vagrancy" as in staffing the navy.

Like soldiers in the growing eighteenth-century armies, sailors in the merchant marine, as well as the navy, could be subjected to brutal discipline and appalling conditions. Merchant seamen attempted to improve their lot by trying to regulate their relationship with ships' captains. Contracts for pay on merchant ships became more regularized, and seamen often negotiated their terms very carefully, including, for example, details about how rations were to be allotted. Sailors might even take bold collective action aboard ship. The modern term for a work stoppage, *strike*, comes from the sailing expression "to strike sail," meaning to loosen the sails so that they cannot fill with wind. Its use dates from the eighteenth century, from "strikes" of sailors protesting unfair shipboard conditions.

The Idle Apprentice Is Sent to Sea, 1747. In one of a series of moralizing engravings by William Hogarth, the lazy apprentice is sent away to a life at sea. The experienced seamen in the boat introduce him to some of its terrors: one of them dangles a cat-o'nine tails (used for flogging), while another points out the distant gallows, where pirates and mutineers meet their fate. (*The Idle 'Prentice Turned Away and Sent to Sea*, plate V of 'Industry and Idleness', published 1833 (engraving), Hogarth, William (1697-1764)/Guildhall Library, City of London/The Bridgeman Art Library)

SECTION SUMMARY

- Prussia fought two major wars and emerged as the equal of Austria in German-speaking Europe.

- Russia expanded to the south and partitioned Poland together with Austria and Prussia.

- Britain and France fought over colonial possessions around the world; Britain won many of France's colonies by the end of the Seven Years' War in 1763.

- States recruited soldiers and equipped and trained their armies better than ever before, making war more costly and more demanding on their populations.

- Soldiers, sailors, and peasants found new ways to resist the burdens of forced labor, brutal conditions, and heavy taxation.

Seafaring men were an unusually large and somewhat self-conscious community of wage workers. But economic and political protests by ordinary people also showed interesting parallel changes. Peasant revolts—directly or indirectly a reaction to the costs of armies—had, in the past, ranged from small-scale practical actions against local tax collectors to massive uprisings that only a state's own army could suppress, such as the Pugachev rebellion. Peasant revolts continued to follow these patterns in the eighteenth century but in certain cases, peasants, like sailors, began to confront authority in new ways. They increasingly marshaled legal devices to maintain control over their land and to thwart landlords' efforts to enclose fields and cultivate cash crops. This change, though subtle, was important because it represented an effort to bring permanent structural change to the system and was not simply a temporary redress of grievances. In part, this trend toward "enlightened" revolt reflects increased access to information and the circulation of ideas about reform.

CHAPTER SUMMARY

The Enlightenment was an intellectual movement that applied to political and social thought the confidence in the intelligibility of natural law that Newton and other scientists had recently achieved. Prominent thinkers, called "philosophes," included influential individuals, such as Voltaire and Rousseau. But the Enlightenment was also a more general movement and one of its features was the growth of an informed body of public opinion outside the realm of government. The revolutionary potential of Enlightenment thought came from belief in its rationality and from the fact that it was both critical of its society and fashionable for educated elites to practice.

European rulers in the eighteenth century continued their efforts to govern with greater effectiveness; some self-consciously borrowed Enlightenment ideas to guide their policies, though they remained unwilling to share governing power. In France, although it was the center of the Enlightenment, the Crown failed to eliminate the privileges of nobility and could not adequately tap the wealth of the kingdom. In England, Parliament's role in government was securely established in this century, and new elites wanted to be represented in it.

Though some rulers were inspired by precepts of the Enlightenment, all were guided by traditional concerns of dynastic aggrandizement and strategic advantage. After dramatic expansion of trade, colonization, and the plantation system, conflict over colonial possessions became increasingly important, particularly between England and France. Partly as a result of growing commerce, the European economy was expanding, the population was growing beyond previous limits, and the system of production was being restructured.

KEY TERMS

philosophes (p. 500)

Voltaire (p. 500)

Adam Smith (p. 502)

Jean-Jacques Rousseau (p. 503)

salons (p. 505)

Enlightened despotism (p. 514)

Frederick the Great (p. 514)

Maria Theresa (p. 515)

Catherine the Great (p. 515)

slave trade (p. 518)

agricultural revolution (p. 519)

Seven Years' War (p. 524)

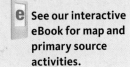 This icon will direct you to additional materials on the website: www .cengage.com/history/ noble/westciv6e.

NOTES

1. Moira Ferguson, ed., *First Feminists: British Women Writers, 1578–1799* (Bloomington: Indiana University Press, 1985), p. 426.

2. Quoted in Dena Goodman, *The Republic of Letters: A Cultural History of the French Enlightenment* (Ithaca, N.Y.: Cornell University Press, 1994), p. 89.

3. Quoted in M. S. Anderson, *Europe in the Eighteenth Century, 1713–1783*, 3d ed. (London: Longman, 1987), pp. 218–219.

See our interactive eBook for map and primary source activities.

19

CHAPTER OUTLINE

The Origins of Revolution, 1775–1789

The Phases of the Revolution, 1789–1799

The Napoleonic Era and the Legacy of Revolution, 1799–1815

A French Citizen Army
The National Guard of Paris leaves to join the army, September 1792
(detail). (Photos12.com-ARJ)

An Age of Revolution, 1789–1815

These militiamen marching off to defend France against the invader in September 1792 appear to be heroes already. Adoring women in the crowd hand them laurel wreaths as they pass; the men march by, resolute and triumphant. Symbols of the ongoing revolution stand out as well: the prominent tricolor flag, the tricolor cockade in each man's hat. In fact, that September, France's citizen armies, for the first time, defeated the army of a foreign monarch poised to breach its borders and snuff out its revolution. The painting celebrates this triumph about to happen and thereby inspires confidence in the Revolution and pride in its citizen-soldiers.

Today the French Revolution is considered the beginning of modern European, as well as modern French, history. The most powerful monarch in Europe was forced to accept constitutional limits to his power by subjects convinced of their rights. Eventually, the king was overthrown and executed, and the monarchy abolished. Events in France reverberated throughout Europe because the overthrow of one absolute monarchy threatened fellow royals elsewhere. Revolutionary fervor on the part of ordinary soldiers enabled France's armies unexpectedly to best many of their opponents. By the late 1790s, the armies of France would be led in outright conquest of other European states by one of the most talented generals in European history: Napoleon Bonaparte. He brought to the continental European nations that his armies eventually conquered a mixture of imperial aggression and revolutionary change. Europe was transformed both by the shifting balance of power and by the spread of revolutionary ideas.

Understanding the French Revolution means understanding not only its origins, but also its complicated course of events and their significance. Challenging the king's power was not new, but overthrowing the king was revolutionary. A new understanding of the people became irresistible; they were the nation and, as citizens, had the right to representation in government. Louis XVI was transformed from the divinely appointed father of his people to an enemy of the people, worthy only of execution. Central to the Revolution was the complex process by which public opinion was shaped and, in turn, shaped events. Change was driven in part by the power of symbols—flags, rallying cries, inspiring art—to challenge an old political order and legitimize a new one.

FOCUS QUESTIONS

- What factors led to revolution in France in 1789?

- Why did several phases of revolutionary change occur after 1789 and what were the characteristics of each phase?

- What impact did the Revolution and Napoleonic rule have on France, the rest of Europe, and the wider world?

This icon will direct you to additional materials on the website: www .cengage.com/history/ noble/westciv6e.

See our interactive eBook for map and primary source activities.

THE ORIGINS OF REVOLUTION, 1775–1789

What factors led to revolution in France in 1789?

"I am a citizen of the world," wrote John Paul Jones, captain in the fledgling U.S. Navy, in 1778. He was writing to a Scottish aristocrat, apologizing for raiding the lord's estate while marauding along the British coast during the American Revolution. Jones (1747–1792), born a Scotsman himself, was one of the thousands of cosmopolitan Europeans who were familiar with European cultures on both sides of the Atlantic. As a sailor, Jones literally knew his way around the Atlantic world, but he was a "citizen of the world" in another sense as well. The Scotsman replied to Jones, surprised by the raid, since he was sympathetic to the American colonists; he was a man of "liberal sentiments" like Jones himself.[1] Both Jones and the Scottish lord felt they belonged to an international society of gentlemen who recognized certain Enlightenment principles regarding just and rational government.

The Atlantic world of the late eighteenth century was united both by practical links of commerce and shared ideals about liberty. The strategic interests of the great European powers were also always in play, however. Thus, when the American colonists actively resisted British rule and then in 1776 declared their independence from Britain, the consequences were wide-ranging: British trading interests were challenged, French appetites for gains at British expense were whetted, and illusive notions about liberty seemed more plausible. The victory of the American colonies in 1783, followed by the creation of the U.S. Constitution in 1787, further heightened the appeal of liberal ideas elsewhere. Attempts at liberal reform were mounted in several states, including Ireland, the Netherlands, and Poland. However, the American Revolution had the most direct impact on later events in France because the French had been directly involved in the American effort.

Revolutionary Movements in Europe

While the British government faced the revolt of the American colonies, it also confronted trouble closer to home. Many Britons had divided loyalties, and many who did favor armed force to subdue the American rebellion were convinced that the war was being mismanaged; they demanded reform of the ministerial government. The American rebellion also had ripple effects in other parts of Europe.

A reform movement sprang up in Ireland in 1779. The reformers demanded greater autonomy from Britain. Like the Americans, Irish elites—mostly of English or Scottish origin—felt like disadvantaged junior partners in the British Empire. They objected to policies that favored British imperial interests over those of the Irish ruling class: for example, the exclusion of Irish ports from overseas commerce in favor of English and Scottish ones and the grant of political rights to Irish Catholics so that they might fight in Britain's overseas armies.

The reformers expressed their opposition to British policies not only in parliamentary debates, but also in military defiance. Following the example of the American rebels, they set up a system of local voluntary militia to resist British troops if necessary. The Volunteer Movement was neutralized when greater parliamentary autonomy for Ireland was granted in 1782, following the repeal of many restrictions on Irish commerce. Unlike the Americans, the Irish elites faced an internal challenge to their own authority—the Catholic population whom they had for centuries dominated—which forced them to reach an accommodation with the British government.

Meanwhile, a political crisis with constitutional overtones was also brewing in the Netherlands. The United Provinces (the Netherlands) was governed by a narrow oligarchy of old merchant families, particularly in Amsterdam, and a military governor, the "stadtholder," from the princely House of Orange. The interests of the merchants and of the stadtholder frequently conflicted. Tensions between them deepened during the American Revolution, as merchants favored trade with the colonists and the prince favored maintaining an English alliance.

The conflict changed character when the representatives of the various cities, calling themselves the Dutch "Patriot" Party, defended their positions not merely on the grounds of their traditional political influence within the Netherlands, but also with wider claims to American-style liberty. The Patriots, in turn, were quickly challenged by newly wealthy traders and professionals, long disenfranchised by their closed merchant oligarchy, who demanded liberty too. These challengers briefly took over the Patriot movement. Just as many Irish rebels accepted the concessions of 1782, the Patriot oligarchs in the Netherlands did nothing to resist an invasion in 1787 that restored the power of the stadtholder, the prince of Orange, because it also ended the challenge to their own control of urban government.

Both the Irish volunteers and the Dutch Patriots, though members of very limited movements, echoed the American rebels in practical and ideological ways. Both were influenced by the economic and political consequences of Britain's relationship with its colonies. Both were inspired by the success of the American rebels and their thoroughgoing claims for political self-determination.

Desire for political reform flared in Poland as well during this period. Government reform was accepted as a necessity by Polish leaders after the first partition of Poland in 1772 had left the remnant state without some of its wealthiest territories (see **MAP 18.3** on page 523). Beginning in 1788, however, reforming gentry in the *Sejm* (representative assembly) went further; they established a commission to write a constitution, following the American example. The resulting document, known as the May 3 (1791) Constitution, was the first codified constitution in Europe; it was read and admired by George Washington.

Poles thus established a constitutional monarchy in which representatives of major towns, as well as gentry and nobility, could sit as deputies. The *liberum veto*, or individual veto power, which had allowed great nobles to obstruct royal authority, was abolished. However, Catherine the Great, empress of Russia, would not tolerate a constitutional government operating so close to her own autocratic regime; she ordered an invasion of Poland in 1792. The unsuccessful defense of Poland was led by, among others, a Polish veteran of the American Revolution, Tadeusz Kosciuszko (tah-DAY-oosh kos-USE-ko) (1746–1817). The second, more extensive partition of Poland followed, to be answered in turn in 1794 by a widespread insurrection against Russian rule, spearheaded by Kosciuszko. The uprising was mercilessly suppressed by an alliance of Russian and Prussian troops. Unlike the U.S. Constitution, from which they drew inspiration, the Poles' constitutional experiment was doomed by the power of its neighbors.

The American Revolution and the Kingdom of France

As Britain's greatest commercial and political rival, France naturally was drawn into Britain's struggle with its North American colonies. In the Seven Years' War (1756–1763), the French had lost many of their colonial settlements and trading outposts to the English (see page 526). Stung by this outcome, certain French courtiers and ministers pressed for an aggressive colonial policy that would regain for France some of the riches in trade that Britain now threatened to monopolize. The American Revolution seemed to offer the perfect opportunity. The French extended covert aid to the Americans from the very beginning of the conflict in 1775. After the first major defeat of British troops by the Americans—at the Battle of Saratoga in 1777—France formally recognized the independent United States and committed troops, as well as funds, to the American cause. John Paul Jones's famous ship, the *Bonhomme Richard* (bon-OHM ree-SHARD), was purchased and outfitted by the French government, as were many other American naval vessels. French support was decisive. In 1781, the French fleet kept reinforcements from reaching the British force besieged by George Washington at Yorktown. The American victory at Yorktown effectively ended the war; the colonies' independence was formally recognized by the Treaty of Paris in 1783.

The consequences for France of its American alliance were momentous. Aid for the Americans saddled France with a debt of about 1 billion *livres* (pounds), which represented as much as one-quarter of the total debt that the French government was trying to service. A less tangible impact of the American Revolution came from the direct participation of about nine thousand French soldiers, sailors, and aristocrats. The best known is the Marquis de Lafayette, who became an aide to George Washington and helped command American troops. For many

CHRONOLOGY

1775–1783	American Revolutionary War
1779–1782	Irish Volunteer Movement
1788	U.S. Constitution ratified; Reform movement begins in Poland; "Patriot" movement ends in the Netherlands
1789	French Estates General meets at Versailles (May); Third Estate declares itself the National Assembly (June); Storming of the Bastille (July)
1791	Polish constitution French king Louis XVI captured attempting to flee (June) Slave revolt begins in Saint Domingue
1792	France declares war on Austria; revolutionary wars begin (April); Louis XVI arrested; France declared a republic (August–September)
1793	Louis XVI guillotined
1793–1794	Reign of Terror in France
1799	Napoleon seizes power in France
1801	Concordat with pope
1804	Napoleon crowned emperor Napoleonic Civil Code Independence of Haiti (Saint Domingue) declared
1805	Battle of Trafalgar; Battle of Austerlitz
1806	Dissolution of Holy Roman Empire
1812	French invasion of Russia
1814	Napoleon abdicates and is exiled French monarchy restored
1815	Hundred Days (February–June) Battle of Waterloo

humble men, the war was simply employment. For others, it was a quest of sorts. For them, the promise of the Enlightenment—belief in human rationality, natural rights, and universal laws by which society should be organized—was brought to life in America.

Exposure to the American conflict occurred at the French court, too. Beginning in 1775, a permanent American mission to Versailles lobbied hard for aid. The chief emissary of the Americans was Benjamin Franklin (1706–1790), a philosophe by French standards whose writings and scientific experiments were already known to European elites. His talents—among them, a skillful exploitation of a simple, Quaker-like demeanor—succeeded in promoting the idealization of America at the French court.

The U.S. Constitution, the various state constitutions, and the debates surrounding their ratification were all published in Paris and much discussed in salons and at court, where lively debate about reform of French institutions had been going on for decades. America became the prototype of the rational republic—the embodiment of Enlightenment philosophy. It was hailed as the place where the irrationalities of inherited privilege did not prevail. A British observer, Arthur Young (1741–1820), believed that "the American revolution has laid the foundation of another in France, if [the French] government does not take care of itself."[2]

By the mid-1780s, there was no longer a question of whether the French regime would experience reform but rather a question of what form the reform would take. The royal government was almost bankrupt. A significant minority of the politically active elite was convinced that France's system of government was irrational. Nevertheless, a dissatisfied elite and a financial crisis—even fanned by a successful revolt elsewhere—do not necessarily lead to revolution. Why did the French government—the *Ancien Régime* (ahn-SYEN ray-ZHEEM) or "Old Regime," as it became known after the Revolution—not "take care of itself"?

The Crisis of the Old Regime

The Old Regime was brought to the point of crisis in the late 1780s by three factors: (1) heavy debts that dwarfed an antiquated system for collecting revenue; (2) institutional constraints on the monarchy that defended privileged interests; and (3) public opinion that envisioned thoroughgoing reform and pushed the monarchy in that direction. Another factor was the ineptitude of the king, Louis XVI (r. 1774–1793).

Louis came to the throne in 1774, a year before the American Revolution began. He was a kind, well-meaning man better suited to be a petty bureaucrat than a king. The queen, the Austrian Marie Antoinette (1755–1793), was regarded with suspicion by the many who despised the "unnatural" alliance with Austria the marriage had sealed. She, too, was politically inept, unable to negotiate the complexities of court life, and widely rumored to be selfishly wasteful of royal resources despite the realm's financial crises.

The fiscal crisis of the monarchy had been a long time in the making and was an outgrowth of the system by which the greatest wealth was protected by traditional privileges. At the top of the social and political pyramid were the nobles, a legal grouping that included warriors and royal officials. In France, nobility conferred exemption from much taxation. Thus, the royal government could not directly tax its wealthiest subjects.

This situation existed throughout much of Europe, a legacy of the power of the nobility in medieval times. Unique to France, however, was the strength of the institutions that defended this system. Of particular importance were the royal law courts, the parlements (par-luh-MAWHN), which claimed a right of judicial review over royal edicts. All the parlementaires—well-educated lawyers and judges—were technically noble and loudly defended the traditional privileges of all nobles. Louis XV (d. 1774), near the end of his life, had successfully undermined the power of the parlements by a bold series of moves. Louis XVI, immediately after coming to the throne, buckled under pressure and restored the parlements to full strength.

Deficit financing had been a way of life for the monarchy for centuries. After early efforts at reform, Louis XIV (d. 1715) had reverted to common fund-raising expedients, such as selling offices, which only added to the weight of privileged investment in the old order. England had established a national bank to free its government from the problem, but the comparable French effort early in the century had been undercapitalized and had failed. Late in the 1780s, under Louis XVI, one-fourth of the annual operating expenses of the government was borrowed, and half of all government expenditure went to paying interest on its debt. Short-term economic crises, such as disastrous harvests, added to the cumulative problem of government finance.

The Common People Crushed by Privilege
In this contemporary cartoon, a nobleman in military dress and a clergyman crush a commoner under the rock of burdensome taxes and forced labor *(corvées)*. The victim's situation reflects that of the peasantry, but his stylish clothes would allow affluent townspeople to identify with him.   (Musée Carnavalet, Paris/Giraudon/Art Resource, NY)

The king employed able finance ministers who tried to institute fundamental reforms, such as replacing the tangle of taxes with a simpler system in which all would pay and eliminating local tariffs, which were stifling commerce. The parlements and many courtiers and aristocrats, as well as ordinary people, resisted these policies. Peasants and townsfolk did not trust the "free market" (free from traditional trade controls) for grain; most feared that speculators would buy up the grain supply and people would starve. Trying to implement such reforms in times of grain shortage almost guaranteed their failure. Moreover, many supported the parlements simply because they were the only institution capable of standing up to the monarchy. But not all members of the elite joined the parlements in opposing reform. The imprint of "enlightened" public opinion was apparent in the thinking of some courtiers and thousands of educated commoners who believed that the government and the economy had to change. They openly debated the nature and extent of reform at court, in salons, cafes, and other gathering places.

In 1787, the king called an "Assembly of Notables"—an ad hoc group of elites—to support him in facing down the parlements and proceeding with some changes. But he found little support. Some notables, even men sympathetic to reform, either did not support particular proposals or were reluctant to allow the monarchy free rein. Others, reflecting the influence of the American Revolution, maintained that a "constitutional" body such as the Estates General, which had not been called since 1614, needed to make these decisions.

Ironically, nobles and clergy who were opposed to reform supported the call for the Estates General too, confident they could control its deliberations. The three Estates met and voted separately by "order"—clergy (First Estate), nobles (Second Estate), and commoners (**Third Estate**). The combined votes of the clergy and nobles would presumably nullify whatever the Third Estate might propose.

Third Estate   In France, the common people, as distinct from the clergy (First Estate) and nobles (Second Estate), in the representative body the Estates General.

The Estates General

In 1788, mounting pressure from common people, as well as courtiers, led Louis to summon the Estates General. On Louis's orders, deputies were to be elected by local assemblies, which were chosen in turn by wide male suffrage. Louis mistakenly assumed he had widespread support in the provinces and wished to tap it by means of this grassroots voting. Louis also agreed that the Third Estate should have twice as many deputies as the other two Estates, but he did not authorize voting by head rather than by order, which would have brought about the dominance of the Third Estate. Nevertheless, the king hoped that the specter of drastic proposals put forth by the Third Estate would frighten the aristocrats and clergy into accepting some of his reforms.

Louis's situation was precarious when the Estates General convened in May 1789. Already a groundswell of sentiment confirmed the legitimacy of the Estates General and the authority of the Third Estate to enact change. Political pamphlets circulated arguing that the Third Estate deserved enhanced power because it carried the mandate of the people. The most important of these was *What Is the Third Estate?* (1789) by Joseph Emmanuel Sieyès (1748–1836), a church official from the diocese of Chartres. The sympathies of Abbé Sieyès (say-EZ), as he was known, were with the Third Estate: His career had stalled because he was not noble. Sieyès argued that the Third Estate represented the nation because it did not reflect special privilege.

Among the deputies of the first two Estates—clergy and nobility—were men, such as the Marquis de Lafayette (1757–1834), who were sympathetic to reform. In the Third Estate, a large majority of deputies reflected the most radical political thought possible for men of their standing. Most were lawyers and other professionals who were functionaries in the government but, like Sieyès, of low social rank. They frequented provincial academies, salons, and political societies. They were convinced of the validity of their viewpoints and determined on reform, and they had little stake in the system as it was. When this group convened and met with resistance from the First and Second Estates, and from Louis himself, it seized the reins of government and a revolution began.

1789: A Revolution Begins

As soon as the three Estates convened at the royal palace at Versailles, conflicts surfaced. The ineptness of the Crown was immediately clear. On the first day of the meetings in May, Louis and his ministers failed to introduce a program of reforms for the deputies to consider. This failure raised doubt about the monarchy's commitment to reform. More important, it allowed the political initiative to pass to the Third Estate. The deputies challenged the Crown's insistence that the three Estates meet and vote separately. Deputies to the Third Estate refused to be certified (that is, to have their credentials officially recognized) as members of only the Third Estate rather than as members of the Estates General as a whole.

For six weeks, the Estates General was unable to meet officially, and the king did nothing to break the impasse. During this interlude, the determination of the deputies of the Third Estate strengthened. More and more deputies were won over to the notion that the three Estates must begin in the most systematic way: France must have a written constitution.

THE NATIONAL ASSEMBLY

By the middle of June, more than thirty reformist members of the clergy were sitting jointly with the Third Estate, which had invited all deputies from all three Estates to meet and be certified together. On June 17, the Third Estate simply declared itself the **National Assembly** of France. At first, the king did nothing, but when the deputies arrived to meet on the morning of June 20, they discovered they had been locked out of the hall. Undaunted, they assembled instead in a nearby indoor tennis court and produced the document that has come to be known as the **Tennis Court Oath**. It was a collective pledge to meet until a written constitution had been achieved. Only one deputy refused to support it. Sure of their mandate, the deputies had assumed the reins of government.

The king continued to handle the situation with both ill-timed self-assertion and feeble attempts at compromise. As more and more deputies from the First and Second Estates joined the National Assembly, Louis "ordered" the remaining loyal deputies to join it, too. Simultaneously, however, he ordered troops to come to Paris. He feared disorder in the wake of the recent disturbances throughout France and believed that any challenge to the legitimacy of arbitrary monarchical authority would be disastrous.

The king's call for troops aroused Parisians' suspicions. Some assumed a plot was afoot to starve Paris and destroy the National Assembly. With a population of about 600,000, Paris was one of the largest cities in Europe and it was the political nerve center of the nation—the site of the publishing industry, salons, and the homes of parlementaires and royal ministers. It was also

National Assembly
Legislative body formed in France in June 1789, when members of the Third Estate in the Estates General, joined by some deputies from the clergy, declared themselves the representatives of the nation.

Tennis Court Oath
Pledge signed by all but one deputy of the National Assembly in France on June 20, 1789, to meet until a constitution was drafted.

The Tennis Court Oath It was raining on June 20, 1789, when the deputies found themselves barred from their meeting hall and sought shelter in the royal tennis court. Their defiance created one of the turning points of the Revolution; the significance was recognized several years later by the creator of this painting. (Réunion des Musées Nationaux/Art Resource, NY)

a working city, with thousands of laborers of all trades plus thousands more—perhaps one-tenth of the inhabitants—jobless recent immigrants from the countryside. The city was both extremely volatile and extremely important to the stability of royal power.

It took little—news of the dismissal of a reformist finance minister—for Paris to erupt in demonstrations and looting. Crowds besieged City Hall and the royal armory, where they seized thousands of weapons. A popular militia formed as citizens armed themselves. Armed crowds attacked other sites of royal authority, including the huge fortified prison, the Bastille, on the morning of July 14. The Bastille now held only a handful of petty criminals, but it still remained a potent symbol of royal power and, the crowd assumed, held large supplies of arms. The garrison commander at first mounted a hesitant defense, then decided to surrender after citizens managed to secure cannons and drag them to face the prison. Most of the garrison were allowed to go free, although the commander and several officers were murdered by the crowd.

The citizens' victory was a great embarrassment to royal authority. The king immediately had to embrace the popular movement. He came to Paris and, in front of crowds at City Hall, donned the red and blue cockade worn by the militia and ordinary folk as a badge of resolve and defiance. This symbolic action signaled the reversal of the Old Regime—politics would now be based on new principles.

Encouraged by events in Paris, inhabitants of cities and towns around France staged similar uprisings. In many areas, the machinery of royal government completely broke down. City councils, officials, and even parlementaires were thrown out of office. Popular militias took control of the streets. A simultaneous wave of uprisings shook the countryside. Most of them

THE STORMING OF THE BASTILLE

Women's March on Versailles, October 1789   Parisian marketwomen marched the 12 miles to the king's palace at Versailles, some provisioning themselves with tools or weapons as they left the capital.   (Réunion des Musées Nationaux/Art Resource, NY)

were the result of food shortages, but their timing added momentum to the more strictly political protests in cities.

TOWARD CONSTITUTIONAL GOVERNMENT

These events forced the members of the National Assembly to work energetically on the constitution and to pass legislation to satisfy popular protests against economic and political privileges. On August 4, the Assembly abolished the remnants of powers that landlords had enjoyed since the Middle Ages, including the right to force peasants to labor on the lord's land and the bondage of serfdom itself. Although largely symbolic, because serfdom and forced labor had been eliminated in much of France, these changes were hailed as the "end of feudalism." A blow was also struck at established religion by eliminating the tithe, the forced payment of one-tenth of a person's income to the church. At the end of August, the Assembly issued the **Declaration of the Rights of Man and the Citizen**. It was a bold assertion of the foundations of a newly conceived government, closely modeled on portions of the U.S. Constitution. Its preamble declared "that [since] the ignorance, neglect or contempt of the rights of man are the sole cause of public calamities and the corruption of governments," the deputies were "determined to set forth in a solemn declaration the natural, inalienable and sacred rights of man."[3]

Declaration of the Rights of Man and the Citizen Document issued by the National Assembly of France in August 1789. Modeled on the U.S. Constitution, it asserted "the natural, inalienable and sacred rights of man."

In September, the deputies debated the king's role in a new constitutional government. Monarchists favored a government rather like England's, with a two-house legislature, including an upper house representing the hereditary aristocracy and a royal right to veto legislation. More radical deputies favored a single legislative chamber and no veto power for the king. The Assembly compromised: The king was given a three-year suspensive veto—the power to suspend legislation for the sitting of two legislatures. This was still a formidable amount of power but a drastic curtailment of his formerly absolute sovereignty.

THE WOMEN'S MARCH TO VERSAILLES

Again Louis resorted to troops. This time he called them directly to Versailles, where the Assembly sat. News of the troops' arrival provoked outrage, which heightened with the threat of another grain shortage. Early on the morning of October 5, women in the Paris street markets saw the empty grocers' stalls and took immediate collective action. "We want bread!" they shouted at the steps of City Hall. Because they were responsible for procuring their families' food, women often led protests over bread shortages. This protest, however, went far beyond the ordinary. A crowd of thousands gathered and decided to walk all the way to Versailles, accompanied by the popular militia (now called the "National Guard"), to petition the king directly for sustenance.

At Versailles, a joint delegation of the women and deputies from the National Assembly was dispatched to see the king. Some of the women fell at the feet of the king with their tales of hardship, certain that the "father of the people" would alleviate their suffering. He did order stored grain supplies distributed in Paris, and he agreed to accept the constitutional role that the Assembly had voted for him. The king also agreed to return to Paris to reassure the people and was escorted back to the capital by both popular militia and bread protesters. Already, dramatic change had occurred as a result of a complex dynamic among the three Estates, the Crown, and the people of Paris. The king was still assumed to be the fatherly guardian of his people's well-being, but his powers were now limited and his authority badly shaken. The Assembly had begun to govern in the name of the "nation," and so far, it had the support of the people.

SECTION SUMMARY

- Inspired by events in America, elites in Ireland, the Netherlands, and Poland pushed for greater political liberty.

- France's support for the American colonies against Great Britain increased French government debt and exposed French soldiers and courtiers to revolutionary ideas.

- By the late 1780s, French royal government was in crisis owing to bankruptcy, institutions that impeded reform, and agitation for reform within elite society.

- The French Revolution began in 1789 when the Estates General convened, and commoners in the Third Estate claimed a mandate to write a constitution and enact major changes in law.

- French citizens, led by the Parisians, formed popular militias, attacked royal fortresses, and marched to Versailles to confront the king.

THE PHASES OF THE REVOLUTION, 1789–1799

Why did several phases of revolutionary change occur after 1789 and what were the characteristics of each phase?

The French Revolution was a complicated affair. It was a series of changes, in a sense, a series of revolutions, driven not by one group of people but by several groups. Even among elites convinced of the need for reform, the range of opinion was wide. The people of Paris continued to be an important force for change. Country people also became active, primarily in resisting changes forced on them by the central government.

All of the wrangling within France was complicated by foreign reaction to events there. Defending the revolution against foreign enemies soon became a routine burden for the fragile revolutionary governments. In addition, they had to cope with the continuing problems that had precipitated the Revolution in the first place, including the government's chronic indebtedness and frequent grain shortages. Finally, the Revolution itself was an issue in that, once the traditional arrangements of royal government had been altered, momentum for further change was unleashed.

The First Phase Completed, 1789–1791

At the end of 1789, Paris was in ferment, but for a time, forward progress blunted the threat of disastrous divisions between king and Assembly and between either of them and the people of Paris. The capital continued to be the center of lively political debate. Salons continued to meet; academies and private societies proliferated. Deputies to the Assembly joined existing societies or helped to found new ones. Several would be important throughout the Revolution— particularly the Jacobin (JACK-oh-bin) Club, named for the monastic order whose buildings the members used as a meeting hall.

These clubs represented the gamut of revolutionary opinion. Some, in which ordinary Parisians were well represented, focused on economic policies that would directly benefit common people. Women were active in a few of the more radical groups. Monarchists dominated other clubs. At first, similar to the salons and debating societies of the Enlightenment era, the clubs quickly became sources of political pressure on the government. A bevy of popular newspapers also contributed to the vigorous political life in the capital.

The broad front of revolutionary consensus began to break apart as the Assembly made decisions about the constitution and about policies to address France's still-desperate financial situation. The largest portion of the untapped wealth of the nation lay with the Catholic Church, an obvious target of anticlerical reformers. The deputies made sweeping changes: They kept church buildings intact and retained the clergy as salaried officials of the state. They abolished all monasteries, though they pensioned the monks and nuns to permit them to continue as nurses and teachers where possible. Boldest of all, the Assembly seized most of the vast lands of the church and declared them national property *(biens nationaux)* to be sold for revenue for the state.

However, revenue was needed faster than the property could be inventoried and sold, so government bonds *(assignats* [ah-see-NYAH]) were issued against the eventual sale of church lands. Unfortunately, in the cash-strapped economy, the bonds were treated like money, their value became inflated, and the government never realized the hoped-for profits. A greater problem was the political divisiveness generated by the restructuring of the church. Many members of the lower clergy, living as they did near ordinary citizens, were among the most reform-minded of the deputies. These clergy were willing to go along with many changes, but the required oath of loyalty to the state made a mockery of clerical independence.

The Civil Constitution of the Clergy, as these measures were called, was passed by the Assembly in July 1790 because the clerical deputies opposing it were outvoted. More than half of the churchmen did take the oath of loyalty. Those who refused, concentrated among the higher clergy, were in theory thrown out of their offices. A year later (April 1791), the pope declared that clergy who had taken the oath were suspended from their offices. Antirevolutionary sentiment grew among thousands of French people, particularly in outlying regions, to whom the church was still vital as a source of charity and a center of community life.

Meanwhile, the Assembly proceeded with administrative and judicial reform. The deputies abolished the medieval provinces as administrative districts and replaced them with uniform *départements* (departments). They declared that local officials would be elected—a revolutionary dispersal of power that had previously belonged to the king.

As work on the constitution drew to a close in the spring of 1791, the king decided that he had had enough. Royal authority, as he knew it, had been virtually dismantled and Louis himself was now a virtual prisoner in the Tuileries (TWEE-lair-ee) Palace in central Paris. The king and his family attempted to flee France. On June 20, 1791, they set out in disguise. However, the party was stopped—and recognized—in the town of Varennes (vah-REN) near the eastern border of the kingdom.

Louis and his family were returned to Paris under lightly disguised house arrest. It was discovered that he had left behind a document that condemned the constitution and revealed his intention was to invade France with Austrian troops, if necessary. He and the queen had sent money abroad ahead of themselves. Thus, in July 1791, just as the Assembly was completing its proposal for a constitutional monarchy, the monarch himself could no longer be trusted.

Editorials and street protests against the monarchy increased. In one incident, known as the Massacre of the Champ (Field) de Mars (SHOM duh MARSS), government troops led by Lafayette fired on citizens at an antimonarchy demonstration that certain Parisian clubs had organized; about fifty men and women died. This inflammatory incident heightened tensions between moderate reformers satisfied with the constitutional monarchy, such as Lafayette, and outspoken republicans who wanted to eliminate the monarchy altogether.

Nevertheless, on September 14, the king formally swore to uphold the constitution. He had no choice. The event became an occasion for celebration, but suspicion of the monarchy continued. Also, the tension between the interests of common Parisians and the provisions of the new constitution could not be glossed over. Though a liberal document for its day, the constitution reflected the views of the elite deputies who had created it. The right to vote, based on a minimal property qualification, was given to about half of all adult men. However, these men only chose electors, for whom the property qualifications were higher. The electors in turn chose deputies to national bodies as well as local officials. Although, in theory, any eligible voter could be an elected deputy or official, in fact, few ordinary citizens would become deputies or local administrators. A new Declaration of Rights accompanied the constitution; it reflected a fear of the masses that had not existed when the Declaration of the Rights of Man and the Citizen was first promulgated in 1789. Freedom of the press and freedom of assembly, for example, were not fully guaranteed.

Educated women had joined some of the Parisian clubs and had attempted to influence the Assembly to consider women's rights, but the constitution granted neither political rights nor legal equality to women. Nor had the Assembly passed laws beneficial to women, such as the legalization of divorce. A Declaration of the Rights of Woman was drafted by a woman named Olympe de Gouges (oh-LAMP duh GOOZH) to draw attention to the treatment of women in the new constitution.

In any case, very soon after the constitution was implemented, the fragility of the new system became clear. The National Assembly declared that its members could not serve in the first assembly to be elected under the constitution. Thus, the members of the newly elected Legislative Assembly, which began to meet in October 1791, lacked any of the cohesiveness that would have come from collective experience. Also, unlike the previous National Assembly, they did not represent a broad range of opinion but were mostly republicans.

In fact, the Legislative Assembly was dominated by republican members of the Jacobin Club. They were known as Girondins (zhih-ron-DEHN), after the region in southwestern France from which many of the club's leaders came. The policies of these new deputies and continued pressure from the ordinary citizens of Paris would cause the constitutional monarchy to collapse in less than a year.

The Second Phase and Foreign War, 1791–1793

An additional pressure on the new regime soon appeared: a threat of foreign invasion and a war to respond to the threat. Aristocratic émigrés, including the king's brothers, had taken refuge in nearby German states and were planning to invade France. The emperor and other German rulers did little actively to aid the plotters. Austria and Prussia, however, in the Declaration of Pillnitz of August 1791, declared, as a concession to the émigrés, that they would intervene if necessary to support the monarchy in France.

CHRONOLOGY	
The French Revolution	
May 5, 1789	Estates General meets in Versailles
June 17, 1789	Third Estate declares itself the National Assembly
June 20, 1789	Tennis Court Oath
July 14, 1789	Storming of the Bastille
August 27, 1789	Declaration of the Rights of Man and the Citizen
October 5–6, 1789	Women's march on Versailles Louis XVI returns to Paris
July 1790	Civil Constitution of the Clergy
June 1791	Louis XVI captured attempting to flee
August 1791	Declaration of Pillnitz
September 1791	New constitution implemented
October 1791	Legislative Assembly begins to meet
April 1792	France declares war on Austria
August 10, 1792	Storming of the Tuileries; Louis XVI arrested
September 21, 1792	National Convention declares France a republic
January 21, 1793	Louis XVI guillotined
May 1793	First Law of the Maximum
July 1793	Terror inaugurated
July 1794	Robespierre guillotined; Terror ends
October 1795	Directory established
November 1799	Napoleon seizes power

The threat of invasion, when coupled with distrust of the royal family, seemed more real to the revolutionaries in Paris than it may actually have been. But many deputies hoped for war. They assumed that the outcome would be a French defeat, which would lead to a popular uprising that would rid them, at last, of the monarchy. In April 1792, under pressure from the Assembly, Louis XVI declared war against Austria. From this point on, foreign war would be an ongoing factor in the Revolution.

At first, the war was indeed a disaster for France. The army had not been reorganized into an effective fighting force after the loss of many aristocratic officers and the addition of newly self-aware citizens. On one occasion, troops insisted on putting an officer's command to a vote. Early defeats further emboldened critics of the monarchy. Under the direction of the Girondins, the Legislative Assembly began to press for the deportation of priests who had been leading demonstrations against the government. The Assembly abolished the personal guard of the king and summoned provincial National Guardsmen to Paris.

The king's resistance to these measures, as well as fears of acute grain shortages owing to a poor harvest and the needs of the armies, created further unrest. Crowds staged boisterous marches near the royal palace, physically confronted the king, and forced him to don the "liberty cap," a symbol of republicanism. The king's authority and prestige were now thoroughly undermined.

Louis XVI in 1792 The king, though a kindly man, had neither the character nor the convictions necessary to refashion royal authority symbolically as the Revolution proceeded. When Parisian crowds forced him to wear the "liberty cap," the monarchy was close to collapse. (Metropolitan Museum of Art, The Elisha Whittelsey Collection, The Elisha Whittelsey Fund, 1962 [62.520.333]. Image © The Metropolitan Museum of Art)

By July 1792, tensions had become acute. The grain shortage was severe; Austrian and Prussian troops, committed to saving the royal family, were threatening to invade; and, most important, Parisian citizens were better organized and more determined than ever before. In each of the forty-eight "sections"—administrative wards—of Paris, a miniature popular assembly thrashed out all the events and issues of the day, just as deputies in the nationwide Legislative Assembly did. Derisively called **sans-culottes** (sahn-koo-LOT) ("without knee pants") because they could not afford elite fashions, the ordinary Parisians in the section assemblies included shopkeepers, artisans, and laborers. Their political organization enhanced their influence with the Assembly, the clubs, and Parisian newspapers. By late July, most sections of the city had approved a petition calling for the exile of the king, the election of new city officials, the exemption of the poor from taxation, and other radical measures.

In August, the sans-culottes took matters into their own hands. On the night of August 9, after careful preparations, representatives of the section assemblies constituted themselves as a new city government with the aim of "saving the state." The next day, August 10, they assaulted the Tuileries Palace, where the royal family was living. Hundreds of royal guards and citizens died in the bloody confrontation. The king and his family were imprisoned in one of the fortified towers in the city, under guard of the popularly controlled city government.

sans-culottes Ordinary citizens of revolutionary Paris, whose derisive nickname referred to their inability to afford fashionable knee pants ("culottes").

With the storming of the Tuileries Palace, the second major phase of the Revolution began: the establishment of republican government in place of the monarchy. By their intimidating numbers, the people of Paris now controlled the Legislative Assembly. Some deputies fled. Those who remained agreed under pressure to dissolve the Assembly and make way for another body to be elected by universal manhood suffrage. On September 20, that assembly, known as the National Convention, began to meet. The next day, the Convention declared the end of the monarchy and set to work crafting a constitution for the new republic.

Coincidentally, that same September day, French forces won their first genuine victory over the allied Austrian and Prussian invasion forces. Though not a decisive battle, it was a profound psychological victory. A citizen army had defeated the professional force of a ruling prince. The victory bolstered the republican government and encouraged it to put more energy into the wars. Indeed, maintaining armies in the field became a weighty factor in the delicate equilibrium of revolutionary government. The new republican regime let it be known that its armies were not merely for self-defense but for the liberation of all peoples in the "name of the French Nation."

Meanwhile, the Convention faced the divisive issue of what to do with the king. Some of the king's correspondence, discovered after the storming of the Tuileries, provided the pretext for charges of treason. The Convention held a trial for him, which lasted from December 11, 1792, to January 15, 1793. He was found guilty of treason by an overwhelming vote (683 to 39); the republican government would not compromise with monarchy. Less lopsided was the sentence: Louis was condemned to death by a narrow majority, 387 to 334.

The consequences for the king were immediate. On January 21, 1793, Louis mounted the scaffold in a public square near the Tuileries and was beheaded. The execution split the ranks of the Convention and soon resulted in the breakdown of the institution itself.

The Faltering Republic and the Terror, 1793–1794

In February 1793, the republic was at war with virtually every state in Europe; the only exceptions were the Scandinavian kingdoms and Russia. Moreover, the regime faced widespread counterrevolutionary uprisings within France. Vigilance against internal and external enemies became a top priority. The Convention established an executive body, the Committee of Public Safety. In theory, this executive council was answerable to the Convention as a whole. But as the months passed, it acted with greater and greater autonomy not only to govern, but also to eliminate enemies. The broadly based republican government represented by the Convention began to disintegrate.

In June 1793, pushed by the Parisian sections, a group of extreme **Jacobins** purged the Girondin deputies from the Convention, arresting many of them. The Girondins were republicans who favored an activist government in the people's behalf, but they were less radical than their fellow Jacobins who now moved against them, less insistent on central control of the Revolution, and less willing to share power with the citizens of Paris. After the purge, the Convention still met, but most authority lay with the Committee of Public Safety.

Now, new uprisings against the regime began as revolts by Girondin sympathizers added to counterrevolutionary revolts by peasants and aristocrats. As resistance to the government mounted and the foreign threat continued, a dramatic event in Paris led the Committee of Public Safety officially to adopt a policy of political repression. A well-known figure of the Revolution, Jean Paul Marat (1743–1793), publisher of a radical newspaper very popular with ordinary Parisians, was murdered on July 13 by Charlotte Corday (1768–1793), an aristocratic woman. Shortly afterward, a longtime member of the Jacobin Club, **Maximilien Robespierre** (ROBES-pee-air) (1758–1794), joined the Committee and called for "Terror"—the systematic repression of internal enemies. He was not alone in his views. Members of the section assemblies of Paris led demonstrations to pressure the government into making Terror the order of the day.

Since the previous autumn, the guillotine had been at work against identified enemies of the regime, but now a more systematic apparatus of Terror was put in place. A Law of Suspects allowed citizens to be arrested simply on vague suspicion of counterrevolutionary sympathies. Revolutionary tribunals and an oversight committee made arbitrary arrests and rendered summary judgments. In October, a steady stream of executions began, beginning with the queen, imprisoned since the storming of the Tuileries the year before. The imprisoned Girondin deputies followed, and then the beheadings continued relentlessly. Paris witnessed about 2,600 executions from 1793 to 1794.

Around France, the verdicts of revolutionary tribunals led to approximately 14,000 executions. Another 10,000 to 12,000 people died in prison. Ten thousand or more were killed, usually by summary execution, after the defeat of counterrevolutionary uprisings. The aim of **the Terror** was not merely to crush active resistance; it was also to silence simple dissent. The victims in Paris included not only aristocrats and former deputies, but also sans-culottes. The radical Jacobins wanted to seize control of the Revolution from the Parisian citizens who had lifted them to power.

ROBESPIERRE AND THE COMMITTEE FOR PUBLIC SAFETY

Jacobins In revolutionary France, a republican political club named for a monastic order.

A Victim of the Terror Manon Phlipon (1754–1793), known as Madame Roland, led an influential Parisian salon and was married to an important Girondin deputy. She was arrested and guillotined with other Girondins in 1793. Her last words on the scaffold were: "Oh Liberty, what crimes are committed in thy name!" (Portrait of a Woman, c.1787 (oil on canvas), Labille-Guiard, Adelaide (c.1749-1803)/Musee des Beaux-Arts, Quimper, France/The Bridgeman Art Library)

Robespierre Justifies Terror Against Enemies of the Revolution

In this excerpt from a speech before the National Convention in December 1793, Robespierre justifies the revolutionary government's need to act in a vigorous manner in order to defend itself from challenges within and without.

The defenders of the Republic must adopt Caesar's maxim, for they believe that "nothing has been done so long as anything remains to be done." Enough dangers still face us to engage all our efforts. It has not fully extended the valor of our Republican soldiers to conquer a few Englishmen and a few traitors. A task no less important, and one more difficult, now awaits us: to sustain an energy sufficient to defeat the constant intrigues of all the enemies of our freedom and to bring to a triumphant realization the principles that must be the cornerstone of public welfare. ... Revolution is the war waged by liberty against its enemies; a constitution is that which crowns the edifice of freedom once victory has been won and the nation is at peace. The revolutionary government has to summon extraordinary activity to its aid precisely because it is at war. It is subjected to less binding and less uniform regulations, because the circumstances in which it finds itself are tempestuous and shifting, above all because it is compelled to deploy, swiftly and incessantly, new resources to meet new and pressing dangers. The principal concern of a constitutional government is civil liberty; that of a revolutionary government, public liberty. [A] revolutionary government is obliged to defend the state itself against the factions that assail it from every quarter. To good citizens revolutionary government owes the full protection of the state; to the enemies of the people it owes only death. ...

Is a revolutionary government the less just and the less legitimate because it must be more vigorous in its actions and freer in its movement than ordinary government? No! For it rests on the most sacred of all laws, the safety of the people, and on necessity, which is the most indisputable of all rights. It also has its rules, all based on justice and on public order. It has nothing in common with anarchy or disorder; on the contrary, its purpose is to repress them and to establish and consolidate the rule of law. It has nothing in common with arbitrary rule; it is public interest which governs it and not the whims of private individuals.

QUESTIONS

1. How does Robespierre describe the differences between constitutional and revolutionary government?

2. How does Robespierre defend the legitimacy of revolutionary government?

Source: "Robespierre Justifies the Terror" from *Robespierre*, edited by George Rudé, 1967, 1995, pp. 58–63

Maximilien Robespierre French lawyer and revolutionary leader, influential member of the Committee of Public Safety (1793-1794); advocated Terror to suppress internal dissent.

the Terror Systematic repression of internal enemies undertaken by French revolutionary government from 1793 to 1794. Approximately fourteen thousand people were executed, including aristocrats, Girondins, and sans-culottes.

Robespierre embodied all the contradictions of the policy of Terror. He was an austere, almost prim man who lived very modestly—a model, of sorts, of the virtuous, disinterested citizen. His unbending loyalty to his political principles earned him the nickname "the Incorruptible." The policies followed by the government during the year of his greatest influence, from July 1793 to July 1794, included generous and humane policies to benefit ordinary citizens as well as the atrocities of official Terror. (See the feature, "The Written Record: Robespierre Justifies Terror Against Enemies of the Revolution.") In May 1793, the Convention had instituted the Law of the Maximum, which controlled the price of grain so that city people could afford their staple food—bread. In September, the Committee extended the law to apply to other necessary commodities. Extensive plans were made for a system of free and universal primary education. Slavery in the French colonies was abolished in February 1794. Divorce, first legalized in 1792, was made easier for women to obtain. In addition, the government of the Committee of Public Safety was effective in providing direction for the nation at a critical time. In August 1793, it instituted the first mass conscription of citizens into the army *(levée en masse* [leh-VAY ohn MAHSS]), and a consistently effective popular army came into existence. In the autumn of 1793, this army won impressive victories.

SOCIAL REFORMS IN THE NAME OF REASON

In the name of "reason," traditional rituals and rhythms of life were changed. One reform of long-term significance was the introduction of the metric system of weights and measures. Although people continued to use the old, familiar measures for a very long time, the change was eventually accomplished, leading the way for standardization throughout Europe. Equally "rational," but not as successful, was the elimination of the traditional calendar;

weeks and months were replaced by uniform thirty-day months and *decadi* (ten-day weeks with one day of rest), and all saints' days and Christian holidays were eliminated. The years had already been changed—Year I had been declared with the founding of the republic in the autumn of 1792.

Churches were rededicated as "temples of reason." Robespierre believed that outright atheism left people with no basis for personal or national morality; he promoted a cult of the Supreme Being. New public festivals were solemn civic ceremonies intended to ritualize and legitimize the new political order. But the French people generally resented the elimination of the traditional calendar and the attacks on the church. In the countryside, massive peasant uprisings protested the loss of poor relief, community life, and familiar ritual.

Divorce law and economic regulation were a boon, especially to urban women, but women's participation in section assemblies and in all organized political activity—which had been energetic and widespread—was banned in October 1793. The particular target of the regime was the **Society of Revolutionary Republican Women**, a powerful club representing the interests of female sans-culottes. By banning women from political life, the regime helped to ground its legitimacy, since the seemingly "natural" exclusion of women might make the new system of government appear part of the "natural" order. (See the feature, "The Visual Record: Political Symbols.") Outlawing women's clubs and barring women from section assemblies also eliminated one source of popular power, from which the regime was now trying to distance itself.

Society of Revolutionary Republican Women In revolutionary Paris, a powerful political club that represented the interests of female sans-culottes.

THE END OF THE TERROR

The main policy differences between the Committee and members of the Convention concerned economic matters: how far to go to assist the poor, the unemployed, and the landless. Several of the moderate critics of Robespierre and his allies were guillotined for disagreeing about policy and for doubting the continuing need for the Terror itself. Their deaths helped precipitate the end of the Terror by causing Robespierre's power base to shrink so much that it had no further legitimacy. Also, French armies had soundly defeated Austrian troops on June 26, so there was no longer any need for the emergency status that the Terror had thrived on.

Deputies to the Convention finally dared to move against Robespierre in July 1794. In late July, the Convention voted to arrest Robespierre, the head of the revolutionary tribunal in Paris, and their closest associates and allies in the city government. On July 28 and 29, Robespierre and the others—about a hundred in all—were guillotined, and the Terror ended.

The Thermidorian Reaction and the Directory, 1794–1799

After Robespierre's death, the Convention reclaimed the executive powers that the Committee of Public Safety had seized. It dismantled the apparatus of the Terror, repealed the Law of Suspects, and forced the revolutionary tribunals to adopt ordinary legal procedures. The Convention also passed into law reforms, such as expanded public education, that had been proposed the year before but not enacted. This post-Terror phase of the Revolution is called the "Thermidorian Reaction" because it began in the revolutionary month of Thermidor (July 19–August 17).

Lacking the weapons of the Terror, the Convention was unable to enforce controls on the supply and price of bread. Thus, economic difficulties and a hard winter produced famine by the spring of 1795. The people of Paris tried to retain influence with the new government. In May, crowds marched on the Convention chanting "Bread and the Constitution of '93," referring to the republican constitution drafted by the Convention but never implemented because of the Terror. The demonstrations were met with force and were dispersed.

Members of the Convention remained fearful of a renewed, popularly supported Terror, on the one hand, and royalist uprisings on the other. Counterrevolutionary uprisings had erupted in the fall of 1794, and landings on French territory by émigré forces occurred the following spring. The Convention drafted a new constitution that limited popular participation in government, as had the first constitution of 1791. The new plan allowed fairly widespread (but not universal) male suffrage, but only for electors, who would choose deputies for the two houses of the legislature. The property qualifications for being an elector were very high, so all but elite citizens were effectively disenfranchised. The Convention also decreed that

Political Symbols

During the French Revolution, thousands of illustrations in support of various revolutionary (or counterrevolutionary) ideas were reproduced on posters, on handbills, and in pamphlets. Some satirized their subjects, such as Marie Antoinette, or celebrated revolutionary milestones, such as the fall of the Bastille. The etching here of the woman armed with a pike, dating from 1792, falls into this category. Other pictures, such as the representation from 1795 of Liberty as a young woman wearing the liberty cap, symbolized or reinforced various revolutionary ideals.

Political images like these are an invaluable though problematic source for historians. Let us examine these two images of women and consider how French people during the Revolution might have responded to them. To understand what they meant to contemporaries, we must know something about the other images that these would have been compared to. We must also view the images in the context of the events of the Revolution itself. Immediately, then, we are presented with an interpretive agenda. How ordinary and acceptable was this image of an armed woman? If women were not citizens coequal with men, how could a woman be a symbol of liberty? What, in short, do these political images reveal about the spectrum of political life in their society?

The woman holding the pike stares determinedly at the viewer. Many details confirm what the original caption announced: This is a French woman who has become free. In her hat she wears one of the symbols of revolutionary nationhood: the tricolor cockade. The badge around her waist celebrates a defining moment for the revolutionary nation: the fall of the Bastille. Her pike itself is inscribed with the words "Liberty or death."

The woman appears to be serving not merely as a symbol of free women. She comes close to being the generic image of a free citizen, willing and able to fight for liberty—an astonishing symbolic possibility in a time when women were not yet treated equally under the law or granted the same political rights as the men of their class. Other images prevalent at the time echo this possibility. Many contemporary representations of the women's march on Versailles in 1789 show women carrying arms, active in advancing the Revolution. By the time this image was created (most likely in 1792), many other demonstrations and violent confrontations by ordinary people had

An Armed Citizen, ca. 1792 (Bibliothèque nationale de France)

Directory French revolutionary government from 1795 to 1799, consisting of an executive council of five men chosen by the upper house of the legislature.

two-thirds of its members must serve in the new legislature, regardless of the outcome of elections. Although this maneuver enhanced the stability of the new regime, it undermined the credibility of the new vote.

The government under the new constitution, beginning in the fall of 1795, was called the **Directory**, for the executive council of five men chosen by the upper house of the new legislature. To avoid the concentration of authority that had produced the Terror, the members of the Convention had tried to enshrine separation of powers in the new system.

resulted in the creation of dozens of popular prints and engravings that showed women acting in the same ways as men.

Repeatedly during 1792, women proposed to the revolutionary government that they be granted the right to bear arms. Their request was denied, but it was not dismissed out of hand. There was debate, and the issue was in effect tabled. Nevertheless, women's actions in the Revolution had created at least the possibility of envisaging citizenship with a female face.

The image of Liberty from 1795 does not reflect the actions of women but rather represents their exclusion from political participation. It is one of a number of images of Liberty that portray this ideal as a passive, innocent woman, here garbed in ancient dress, surrounded by a glow that in the past had been reserved for saints. Liberty here is envisaged as a pure and lofty goal, symbolized as a pure young woman.

Late in 1793, during the Terror, women were excluded from formal participation in politics with the disbanding of women's organizations. Nor did they gain political rights under the Directory, which reestablished some of the limited gains of the first phase of the Revolution. The justification offered for their exclusion in 1793 was borrowed from Jean-Jacques Rousseau: it is contrary to nature for women to be in public life (see page 503). Women "belong" in the private world of the family, where they will nurture male citizens. Women embody ideal qualities such as patience and self-sacrifice; they are not fully formed beings capable of action in their own right.

Such notions made it easy to use images of women to embody ideals for public purposes. A woman could represent liberty precisely because actual women were not able to be political players.

The two images shown here thus demonstrate that political symbols can have varying relationships to "reality." The pike-bearing citizen is the more "real." Her image reflects the way of thinking about politics that became possible for the first time because of their actions. The other woman reflects not the attributes of actual women, but an ideal type spawned by the use of arbitrary gender distinctions to legitimize political power. In these images, we can see modern political life taking shape: the sophistication of its symbolic language, the importance of abstract ideas, such as liberty and nationhood—as well as the grounding of much political life in rigid distinctions between public and private, male and female.

Liberty as a Young Woman, ca. 1795 (S. P. Avery Collection, Miriam and Ira D. Wallach Division of Arts, Prints, and Photographs, The New York Public Library, Astor, Lenox, and Tilden Foundations/Art Resource, NY)

QUESTIONS

1. What circumstances explain the 1792 image of a woman as an armed citizen?

2. How would an idealized image of a young woman be useful as a symbol of liberty?

---

* This discussion draws on the work of Joan Landes, "Representing the Body Politic: The Paradox of Gender in the Graphic Politics of the French Revolution," and Darlene Gay Levy and Harriet B. Applewhite, "Women and Militant Citizenship in Revolutionary Paris," in Sara E. Melzer and Leslie W. Rabine, eds., *Rebel Daughters: Women and the French Revolution* (New York: Oxford University Press, 1992), pp. 15–37, 79–101.

However, the governments under the Directory were never free from outside plots or from their own extra-constitutional maneuvering. The most spectacular challenge was an attempted coup by the "Conspiracy of Equals," a group of extreme Jacobins who wanted to restore popular government and aggressive economic and social policy on behalf of the common people. The conspiracy ended with arrests and executions in 1797. When elections in 1797 and 1798 returned many royalist, as well as Jacobin deputies, the Directory itself abrogated the constitution: many "undesirable" deputies were arrested, exiled, or denied seats.

SECTION SUMMARY

- The phases of the French Revolution were shaped by elites' desires for change, demands of common people, and the need to defend France against foreign monarchs.

- Between 1789 and 1791, the National Assembly wrote a constitution, seized and sold church property, ended traditional obligations of peasants, and reorganized local government.

- In 1791, the constitution was implemented and a Legislative Assembly elected.

- In 1792, Parisian citizens overthrew the monarchy; the Convention, elected by universal manhood suffrage, governed the republic.

- Control of the government passed to the Committee of Public Safety, which defended France from foreign invasion and gave economic assistance to common people, but also implemented a policy of official Terror in which thousands of French people were killed.

- After the Terror, suffrage was again restricted, but the government of the Directory could not bring stability.

The armies of the republic did enjoy some spectacular successes during these years, for the first time carrying the fighting—and the effects of the Revolution—onto foreign soil. French armies conquered the Dutch in 1795. In 1796–1797, French armies led by the young general **Napoleon Bonaparte** seized control of northern Italy from the Austrians. Both regions were transformed into "sister" republics, governed by local revolutionaries but under French protection. By 1799, however, conditions had once again reached a crisis point. The demands of the war effort, together with rising prices and the continued decline in the value of the assignats, brought the government again to the brink of bankruptcy. The government also seemed to be losing control of the French countryside; there were continued royalist uprisings, local political vendettas between moderates and Jacobins, and outright banditry.

Members of the Directory had often turned to sympathetic army commanders to suppress dissent and to carry out purges of the legislature. They now invited General Bonaparte to help them form a government that they could more strictly control. Two members of the Directory plotted with Napoleon and his brother, Lucien Bonaparte, to seize power on November 9, 1799.

THE NAPOLEONIC ERA AND THE LEGACY OF REVOLUTION, 1799–1815

What impact did the Revolution and Napoleonic rule have on France, the rest of Europe, and the wider world?

Napoleon Bonaparte
French general who took part in a coup in 1799 against the Directory, Napoleon consolidated power as first consul and ruled as emperor from 1804 to 1815.

Talented, charming, and ruthless, Napoleon Bonaparte (1769–1821) was the kind of person who gives rise to myths. His audacity, determination, and personal magnetism enabled him to profit from the political instability in France and to establish himself in power. Once in power, he temporarily stabilized the political scene by fixing in law the more conservative gains of the Revolution. He also used his power and his abilities as a general to continue wars of conquest against France's neighbors, which helped deflect political tensions at home.

Napoleon's troops exported the Revolution as they conquered most of Europe. In most states that came under French control, law codes were reformed, governing elites were opened to talent, and public works were upgraded. Yet French conquest also meant domination, pure and simple, and involvement in France's rivalry with Britain. The Napoleonic era left Europe an ambiguous legacy—war and its enormous costs, yet also revolution and its impetus to positive change.

Napoleon: From Soldier to Emperor, 1799–1804

Napoleon was from Corsica, a Mediterranean island that had passed from Genoese to French control in the eighteenth century. The second son of a large gentry family, he was educated at military academies in France, and he married the politically well-connected widow Joséphine de Beauharnais (Bow-are-NAY) (1763–1814), whose aristocratic husband had been a victim of the Terror.

Napoleon steered a careful course through the political turmoil of the Revolution. By 1799, his military victories had won him much praise and fame. He had demonstrated his ruthlessness in 1795, when he ordered troops guarding the Convention to fire on a Parisian crowd. He had capped his successful Italian campaign of 1796–1797 with an invasion of Egypt in an attempt to strike at British influence and trade connections in the eastern Mediterranean. The Egyptian campaign failed in its goals, but individual victories during the campaign ensured Napoleon's military reputation.

Napoleon's partners in the new government after the November 1799 coup soon learned of his great political skill and ambition. In theory, the new system was a streamlined version of the Directory: Napoleon was to be first among equals in a three-man executive— "First Consul," according to borrowed Roman terminology. But Napoleon quickly asserted his primacy among them and began not only to dominate executive functions, but also to bypass the authority of the regime's various legislative bodies.

His increasingly authoritarian rule was successful in part because he included, among his advisors and ministers, men of many political stripes—Jacobins, reforming liberals, even former Old Regime bureaucrats. He welcomed many exiles back to France, including all but the most ardent royalists. He thus stabilized his regime by healing some of the rifts among ruling elites. Napoleon combined toleration with ruthlessness, however. Between 1800 and 1804, he imprisoned, executed, or exiled dozens of individuals for alleged Jacobin agitation or royalist sympathies, including a prince of the royal family, whom he had kidnapped and coldly murdered.

Under Napoleon's regime, any semblance of free political life ended. Legislative bodies lost all initiative in the governing process, becoming rubber stamps for the consuls' policies. There were no meaningful elections. Voters chose only candidates for a kind of pool of potential legislators, from which occasional replacements were chosen by members of the Senate, an advisory body entirely appointed by Napoleon himself. Political clubs were banned; the vibrant press of the revolutionary years wilted under heavy censorship. Napoleon also further centralized the administrative system, set up by the first wave of revolutionaries in 1789, by establishing the office of prefect to govern the départements. All prefects and their subordinates were appointed by Napoleon, thus extending the range of his power and undermining local government.

Certain administrative changes that enhanced central control, such as for tax collection, had more positive effects. Napoleon oversaw the establishment of the Bank of France, modeled on the Bank of England. The bank provided capital for investment and helped stabilize French currency. Perhaps the most important achievement early in his regime was the Concordat of 1801. This treaty with the pope solved the problem of church-state relations that for years had provoked counterrevolutionary rebellions. The agreement allowed for the resumption of Catholic worship and the continued support of the clergy by the state, but also accepted the more dramatic changes accomplished by the Revolution. Church lands that had been sold were guaranteed to their new owners. Although Catholicism was recognized as the "religion of the majority of Frenchmen," Protestant churches also were allowed, and their clergy were paid. Later, Napoleon granted new rights to Jews as well.

The law code that Napoleon established in 1804 was much like his accommodation with the church in its limited acceptance of revolutionary gains. His **Civil Code** (also known as the *code napoléon*, or Napoleonic Code) honored the revolutionary legacy in its guarantee of equality before the law and its requirement for the taxation of all social classes; it also enshrined modern forms of property ownership and civil contracts. Neither the code nor Napoleon's political regime fostered individual rights, especially for women. Divorce was no longer permitted except in rare instances. Women lost all property rights when they married, and they generally faced legal domination by fathers and husbands.

Napoleon was careful to avoid heavy-handed displays of power. He cleverly sought ratification of each stage of his assumption of power through national plebiscites (referendums in which all eligible voters could vote for or against proposals)—one plebiscite (pleb-ih-SIGHT) for a new constitution in 1800 and another when he claimed consulship for life in 1802. He approached his final political coup—declaring himself emperor—with similar dexterity. Long before he claimed the imperial title, Napoleon had begun to sponsor an active court life appropriate to imperial pretensions. The empire

Napoleon Crossing the Alps This stirring portrait by the great neoclassical painter Jacques-Louis David memorializes Napoleon's 1796 crossing of the Alps before his victorious Italian campaign, as a general under the Directory. In part because it was executed in 1801–1802, the painting depicts the moment heroically rather than realistically. (In truth, Napoleon wisely crossed the Alps on a sure-footed mule, not a stallion.) Napoleon, as First Consul, wanted images of himself that would justify his increasingly ambitious claims to power. (Réunion des Musées Nationaux/Art Resource, NY)

Civil Code Law code established under Napoleon in 1804 that included limited acceptance of revolutionary gains, such as a guarantee of equality before the law and taxation of all social classes.

was proclaimed in May 1804 with the approval of the Senate; it was also endorsed by another plebi-scite. Napoleon rewarded members of his family and political favorites with noble titles that allowed no legal privilege but carried significant prestige. Old nobles were allowed to use their titles on this basis. Many members of the elite, whatever their origins, tolerated Napoleon's claims to power because he safeguarded fundamental revolutionary gains yet reconfirmed their status.

Conquering Europe, 1805–1810

Napoleon maintained relatively peaceful relations with other nations, while he consoli-dated power within France, but war soon resumed against political and economic enemies—principally Britain, Austria, and Russia. Tensions with the British quickly reescalated when Britain resumed aggression against French shipping in 1803, and Napoleon countered by seizing Hanover, the ancestral German home of the English king. England was at war at sea with Spain and the Netherlands, client states that Napoleon had forced to support him. Napoleon began to gather a large force on the northern coast of France; his objective was to invade England.

The British fleet, commanded by Horatio Nelson (1758–1805), intercepted a combined French and Spanish fleet that was to have been the invasion force and inflicted a devastating defeat off Cape Trafalgar in southern Spain (see **Map 19.1**) on October 21, 1805. The victory ensured British mastery of the seas and, in the long run, contributed to Napoleon's demise. In the short run, the defeat at Trafalgar paled for the French beside Napoleon's impressive victories on land. Napoleon abandoned the plans to invade England and, in August, marched his army east through Germany to confront the great continental powers, Austria and Russia.

In December 1805, Napoleon's army routed a combined Austrian and Russian force near Austerlitz (AW-stir-lits), north of Vienna (see **Map 19.1**). The Battle of Austerlitz was his most spec-tacular victory. Austria sued for peace. In further battles in 1806, French forces defeated Prussian, as well as Russian, armies once again. Prussia was virtually dismembered, but Napoleon tried to remake Russia into a contented ally. His hold on central Europe would not be secure with a

🌐 **Map 19.1—Napoleonic Europe, ca. 1810**
France dominated continental Europe after Napoleon's victories.

hostile Russia, nor would the anti-British economic system that he envisioned—the Continental System (see page 552)—be workable without Russian participation.

French forces were still trying to prevail in Spain, which had been a client state since its defeat by revolutionary armies in 1795 but was resisting outright rule by a French-imposed king, one of Napoleon's brothers. In 1808, however, Napoleon turned his attention to fully subduing Austria. After another loss to French forces in 1809, Austria, like Russia, accepted French political and economic hegemony in a sort of alliance. Thus, by 1810, Napoleon had transformed most of Europe into allied or dependent states (see **Map 19.1**). The only exceptions were Britain and the parts of Spain and Portugal that continued, with British help, to resist France.

The states least affected by French hegemony were its reluctant allies: Austria, Russia, and the Scandinavian countries. At the other extreme were territories that had been incorporated into France. These included the Austrian Netherlands, territory along the Rhineland, and sections of Italy that bordered France. These regions were occupied by French troops and were treated as though they were départements of France itself.

In most other areas, some form of French-controlled government was in place, usually headed by a member of Napoleon's family. In both northern Italy and the Netherlands, where "sister" republics had been established after French conquests under the Directory, Napoleon imposed monarchies. Rulers were also installed in the kingdom of Naples and in Spain. Western German states of the Holy Roman Empire that had allied with Napoleon against Austria were organized into the Confederation of the Rhine, with Napoleon as its "Protector." Two further states were created, largely out of the defeated Prussia's territory: the kingdom of Westphalia in western Germany and the Grand Duchy of Warsaw in the east (see **Map 19.1**).

Napoleon's domination of these various regions had complex, and at times contradictory, consequences. On the one hand, Napoleonic armies essentially exported the French Revolution, in that French domination brought with it the Napoleonic Civil Code, and with it political and economic reform like that of the early phases of the Revolution. Equality before the law was decreed following the French example. This meant the end of noble exemption from taxation in the areas where it existed. The complex snarl of medieval taxes and tolls was replaced with straightforward property taxes that were universally applied. As a consequence, tax revenues rose dramatically—by 50 percent in the kingdom of Italy, for example. Serfdom and forced labor also were abolished, as they had been in France in August 1789.

"And It Cannot Be Changed"   This horrifying scene of an execution of rebels against French rule in Spain was one of a series of etchings by Madrid artist Francisco Goya. In the 1810 series, titled "The Disasters of War," Goya was severely critical of French actions, as well as of barbarities committed by the British-backed Spaniards.   (Foto Marburg/Art Resource, NY)

In most Catholic regions, the church was subjected to the terms of the Concordat of 1801. The tithe (forced contributions to support the church) was abolished, church property seized and sold, and monasteries closed. Although Catholicism remained the state-supported religion in these areas, Protestantism was tolerated, and Jews were granted rights of citizenship. Secular education, at least for males, was encouraged.

On the other hand, Napoleon would allow in the empire only those aspects of France's revolutionary legacy that he tolerated in France itself. Just as he had suppressed any meaningful participatory government in France, so too did he suppress it in conquered regions. This came as a blow in states such as the Netherlands, which had experienced its own democratizing "Patriot" movement and which had enjoyed republican self-government after invasion by France during the Revolution itself. Throughout Napoleon's empire, many of the benefits of streamlined administration and taxation were offset by the drain of continual warfare. Deficits rose three- and fourfold, despite increased revenues. And throughout Europe, Napoleon gave away land to reward his greatest generals and ministers, thereby exempting those lands from taxation and control by his own bureaucracy.

If true self-government was not allowed, a broad segment of the elite in all regions was nevertheless won over to cooperation with Napoleon by being welcomed into his bureaucracy or into the large multinational army, called the *Grande Armée* (grawnd are-MAY). Their loyalty was cemented when they bought confiscated church lands.

The impact of Napoleon's Continental System was equally mixed. Under this system, the Continent was in theory closed to all British shipping and goods. The effects were uneven, and smuggling to evade controls on British goods became a major enterprise. Regions heavily involved in trade with Britain or its colonies suffered in the new system, as did overseas trade in general when Britain gained dominance of the seas after Trafalgar. However, the closing of the Continent to British trade, combined with increases in demand to supply Napoleon's armies, spurred the development of continental industries, at least in the short run.

Defeat and Abdication, 1812–1815

Whatever its achievements, Napoleon's empire was ultimately fragile because of the hostility of Austria and Russia, as well as the power of Britain. Russia was a particularly weak link in the chain of alliances and subject states because Russian landowners and merchants objected when their vital trade in timber for the British navy was interrupted and when supplies of luxury goods, brought in British ships, began to dwindle. A century of close alliances with German ruling houses made alliance with a French ruler an extremely difficult political option for Tsar Alexander I.

It was Napoleon, however, who ended the alliance by provoking a breach with Russia. He suddenly backed away from an arrangement to marry one of Alexander's sisters and accepted an Austrian princess instead. (He had divorced Joséphine because their marriage had not produced an heir.) Also, he seized lands in Germany belonging to a member of Alexander's family. When Alexander threatened rupture of the alliance if the lands were not returned, Napoleon mounted an invasion. Advisers warned him about the magnitude of the task he seemed so eager to undertake—particularly about winter fighting in Russia—but their alarms went unheard.

Napoleon's previous military successes had stemmed from a combination of strategic innovations and pure audacity. Napoleon divided his forces into independent corps. Each corps included infantry, cavalry, and artillery. Organized in these workable units, his armies could travel quickly by several separate routes and converge in massive force to face the enemy. Leadership on the battlefield came from a loyal and talented officer corps that had grown up since army commands had been thrown open to nonaristocrats during the Revolution. The final ingredient for success was the high morale of French troops. Since the first victory of the revolutionary armies in September 1792, citizen-soldiers had proved their worth. Complicated troop movements and bravery on the battlefield were possible when troops felt they were fighting for their *nation*, not merely their ruling dynasty. Napoleon's reputation as a winning general added a further measure of self-confidence.

The campaign against Russia began in June 1812. It was a spectacular failure. Napoleon had gathered a force of about 700,000 men—about half from France and half from allied states—a force twice as large as Russia's. But the strategy of quickly moving independent corps and assembling massive forces could not be implemented. Bold victories had often enabled Napoleon's troops to live off the countryside while they waited for supplies to catch up to the front line. But when the enemy attacked supply lines, the distances traveled were very great, the countryside was impoverished, or battles were not decisive, Napoleon's ambitious strategies proved futile. In varying degrees, these conditions prevailed in Russia.

By the time the French faced the Russians in the principal battle of the Russian campaign—at Borodino (bore-uh-DEE-no), west of Moscow (see **Map 19.1**)—the Grande Armée had been on the march for two and a half months and was already less than half its original strength. After the indecisive but bloody battle, the French occupied and pillaged Moscow but found scarcely enough food and supplies to sustain them. When Napoleon finally retreated from Moscow late in October, the fate of the French forces was all but sealed. As they retreated, the soldiers who had not died in battle died of exposure or starvation or were picked off by Russian peasants as they scavenged for food or fuel. Of the original 700,000 troops of the Grand Armée, fewer than 100,000 made it out of Russia.

Napoleon left his army before it was fully out of Russia to counter a coup attempt in Paris. The collapse of his reign had begun, spurred by a coincidental defeat in Spain. In Spain, a rebel Cortes (national representative assembly) had continued to meet in territory that the French did not control, and British troops supported resistance to the French. In 1812, as Napoleon was advancing against Russia, the collapse of French control accelerated. By the time Napoleon reached Paris at the turn of the new year, an Anglo-Spanish force led by the duke of Wellington was poised to invade France.

Napoleon lost his last chance to stave off a coalition of all major powers against him when he refused an Austrian offer of peace for the return of conquered Austrian territories. With Britain willing to subsidize the allied armies, Tsar Alexander determined to destroy Napoleon, and the Austrians now anxious to share the spoils, Napoleon's empire collapsed. The allies invaded France and forced Napoleon to abdicate on April 6, 1814.

Napoleon was exiled to the island of Elba, off France's Mediterranean coast. He was installed as the island's ruler and was given an income drawn on the French treasury. Meanwhile, however, the restored French king was having his own troubles. Louis XVIII (r. 1814–1824) was the brother of the executed Louis XVI (he took the number eighteen out of respect for Louis XVI's son, who had died in prison in 1795). The new monarch had been out of the country and out of touch with its circumstances since the beginning of the Revolution. In addition to the delicate task of establishing his own legitimacy, he faced enormous practical problems, including pensioning off thousands of soldiers now unemployed and still loyal to Napoleon.

Napoleon, bored and almost penniless in his island kingdom (the promised French pension never materialized), took advantage of the circumstances and returned surreptitiously to France on February 26, 1815. His small band of attendants was joined by the soldiers sent by the king to halt his progress. Louis XVIII abandoned Paris to the returned emperor. Napoleon's triumphant return lasted only one hundred days, however. Though some soldiers welcomed his return, many members of the elite were reluctant to throw in their lot with Napoleon again, and many ordinary French citizens were disenchanted, especially since the defeat in Russia, with the high costs, in conscription and taxation, of his armies. In any case, Napoleon's reappearance galvanized the divided allies, who had been haggling over a peace settlement, into unity. Napoleon tried to strike decisively against the allies, but he lost against English and Prussian troops in his first major battle, at Waterloo (in modern Belgium; see **Map 19.1**) on June 18, 1815. When Napoleon arrived in Paris after the defeat, he discovered the government in the hands of an ad hoc committee that included the Marquis de Lafayette. Under pressure, he abdicated once again. This time, he was exiled to the tiny, remote island of St. Helena in the South Atlantic, where he died in 1821.

The Legacy of Revolution for France and the World

The process of change in France between 1789 and 1815 was so complex that it is easy to overlook the overall impact of the Revolution. Superficially, the changes seemed to come full circle—with first Louis XVI on the throne, then Napoleon as emperor, and then Louis XVIII on the throne. Even though the monarchy was restored, however, the Revolution had discredited absolute monarchy in theory and practice.

Louis XVIII had to recognize the right of "the people," however narrowly defined, to participate in government and to enjoy due process of law. Another critical legacy of the Revolution and the Napoleonic era was a centralized political system of départements rather than a patchwork of provinces. For the first time, a single code of law applied to all French people. Most officials—from département administrators to city mayors—were appointed by the central government until the late twentieth century. This centralization had a positive side: the government sponsored national

FRANCE

scientific societies, a national library and archives, and a system of teachers' colleges and universities. Particularly under Napoleon, canal- and road-building projects improved transport systems.

Napoleon's legacy, like that of the Revolution itself, was mixed. His self-serving reconciliation of aristocratic pretensions with the opening of careers to men of talent ensured the long-term success of revolutionary principles from which the elite as a whole profited. His reconciliation of the state with the Catholic Church helped to stabilize his regime and cemented some revolutionary gains. The restored monarchy could not renege on these gains. Yet, whatever his achievements, Napoleon's overthrow of constitutional principles worsened the problem of political instability. His brief return to power in 1815 reflects the degree to which his power had always been rooted in military adventurism and in the loyalty of soldiers and officers. Similarly, the swiftness of his collapse suggests that the empire under Napoleon was not an enduring solution to the political instability of the late 1790s; indeed, it was no more secure than any of the other revolutionary governments.

Although Louis XVIII acknowledged the principle of constitutionalism at the end of the Revolution, his regime rested on fragile footing. Indeed, the fragility of new political systems was one of the most profound legacies of the Revolution. There was division over policies, but even greater division over legitimacy—that is, the acceptance by a significant portion of the politically active citizenry of a particular government's right to rule. Before the Revolution started, notions about political legitimacy had undergone a significant shift. The deputies who declared themselves to be the National Assembly in June 1789 already believed that they had a right to do so. In their view, they represented "the nation," and their voice had legitimacy for that reason. These deputies brought to Versailles not only their individual convictions that "reason" should be applied to the political system, but also their experience in social settings where those ideas were well received. In their salons, clubs, and literary societies, they had experienced the familiarity, trust, and sense of community that are essential to effective political action. The deputies' attempt to transplant their sense of community into national politics, however, was not wholly successful, in part because of their naïve refusal to stand for election under the new constitution. The king also actively undermined the system because he disagreed with it in principle. The British parliamentary system, by comparison, though representative only of a tiny elite, had a long history as a workable institution for lords, wealthy commoners, and rulers. This shared experience was an important counterweight to differences over fundamental issues, so that Parliament as an institution both survived political crises and helped resolve them. In France, politics was established on new principles, yet still lacking were the practical means to achieve the promise inherent in those principles.

EUROPE AND ITS COLONIES

France's conquests in Europe were the least enduring of the changes of the revolutionary era. Nevertheless, French domination of Europe had certain lasting effects: Elites were exposed to modern bureaucratic management, and equality under the law transformed social and political relationships. The breakdown of ancient political divisions provided important practical grounding for later cooperation among elites in nationalist movements. In Napoleon's kingdom of Italy, for example, a tax collector from Florence for the first time worked side by side with one from Milan.

The most important legacy of the French Revolution in Europe was the very success of the Revolution. The most powerful absolute monarchy in Europe had succumbed to the demands of its people for dramatic social and political reforms. Throughout Europe in the nineteenth century, ruling dynasties faced revolutionary movements that demanded constitutional government and resorted to force to achieve it.

The most important legacy of the revolutionary wars, however, was the change in warfare itself, made possible by the citizen armies of the French. Citizen-soldiers, who identified closely with their nation, even when conscripts, proved able to maneuver and attack on the battlefield in ways that the brutally disciplined poor conscripts in royal armies would not. In response, other states tried to build competing armies; the mass national armies that fought the world wars of the twentieth century were the result.

European colonial possessions changed hands during the revolutionary wars. The British took advantage of Napoleon's preoccupation with continental affairs by seizing French colonies and the colonies of the French-dominated Dutch. In 1806, they seized the Dutch colony of Cape Town in southern Africa—crucial for support of trade around Africa—as well as French bases along the African coast. In 1811, they grabbed the island of Java (modern Indonesia).

Indeed, one clear legacy of the Revolution was the expansion of British trade and colonial control, made possible by Britain's sea power. Britain's maritime supremacy and seizure of French possessions expanded British trading networks overseas—though in some cases only temporarily—and closer to home, particularly in the Mediterranean. As long as the British had

Napoleon's Letter to Toussaint-Louverture

In November 1801, Napoleon sent this letter to the governor of the colony of Saint Domingue, Toussaint-Louverture. Toussaint, a former slave, had commanded an army, composed largely of ex-slaves, which had restored order in Saint Domingue following a complicated civil war. As he mentions in the letter, Napoleon had dispatched a force to reestablish French control of the formerly profitable colony. Although Toussaint was captured and later died in a French prison, Napoleon's forces were not successful in reestablishing French control.

To Citizen General Toussaint Louverture, commander in chief of the armies of Saint-Domingue, Peace with England and with other powers in Europe [now] enables France to pay attention to its colony of Saint-Domingue. We are sending General Leclerc, our brother-in-law, to serve as captain general and governor of the colony. He is accompanied by forces suitable to make the sovereignty of France respected. In these circumstances, it pleases us to hope that you will demonstrate to us and to all of France the sincerity of the sentiments that you have continually expressed in your letters to us. We hold you in very high esteem and it pleases us to acknowledge the great service you have rendered to the French people. ... Called by your talents and by the force of circumstance to command, you have ended civil war. ... The constitution you have made contains many good things but also things which are contrary to the dignity and the sovereignty of the French people, of which the people of Saint-Domingue form only a part. The circumstances in which you found yourself, surrounded on all sides by enemies, perhaps made some provisions of the constitution necessary and legitimate. But, happily, now that things have changed you will be able to render homage to the sovereignty of the Nation of which you are one of the most illustrious citizens. ... Any contrary conduct ... would lead you to lose the many rights you have earned to the recognition and the benefits of the Republic [and] would bring you to the edge of a precipice which, in swallowing you up, would contribute to the misery of the brave blacks, whose courage we admire and whose rebellion we would be sorry to have to punish.

Help the new captain general with your counsel, your influence and your talents. What could you want? The freedom of blacks? You know that in every country we have entered we have given liberty to the people who did not have it. Do you want respect, honors and fortune? ... Given the services you have rendered and our esteem for you, you cannot be in doubt that respect, honors and fortune await you.

Make known to the peoples of Saint-Domingue that our concerns for their well-being were often impotent because of the demands of war that we faced. But now, peace and the force of our government will assure them prosperity and liberty. Tell them that if liberty is to them the most important right, that it cannot be enjoyed without the title of "French citizen" and that all acts contrary to the nation, and contrary to the obedience they owe its government and to its representative, the captain general, will be crimes against the national sovereignty. ... And you, General, consider that if you are the first man of color to have arrived at such a pinnacle of power ... you are also, before God and before us, responsible for their good conduct. ...

QUESTIONS

1. What, in your opinion, was Napoleon trying to accomplish with this letter?

2. How would Toussaint-Louverture have interpreted Napoleon's words?

Source: Paul Rossier, ed., *Lettres du Général Leclerc* (Paris: Société de l'Histoire des Colonies Françaises, 1937). Translated by Kristen B. Neuschel.

---

been involved in trade with India, the Mediterranean had been important for economic and strategic reasons because it lay at the end of the land route for trade from the Indian Ocean. Especially after Napoleon's aggression in Egypt in the 1790s, the British redoubled their efforts to control strategic outposts in the Mediterranean.

The British economy would expand dramatically in the nineteenth century as industrial production soared. The roots for growth were laid in this period in the countryside of Britain, where changes in agriculture and in production were occurring. These roots were also laid in Britain's overseas possessions as tighter control of foreign sources of raw materials, notably raw Indian cotton, meant rising fortunes back in Britain. In regions of India, the East India Company was increasing its political domination, and hence, its economic stranglehold on Indian commodities. The export of Indian cotton rose significantly during the revolutionary period as part of an expanding trading system that included China, the source of tea.

On the most productive of the French-controlled Caribbean islands, Saint Domingue (SAHN dome-ANGUE), the French Revolution inspired a successful rebellion by the enslaved plantation workers.

The National Assembly in Paris had delayed abolishing slavery in French colonies, despite the moral appeal of such a move, because of pressure from the white planters and out of fear

François Dominique Toussaint-Louverture
Former slave who governed the island of Saint Domingue (Haiti) as an independent state after the slave revolt of 1791.

REVOLUTION IN THE ATLANTIC WORLD

Haitian Leader Toussaint-Louverture   Son of an educated slave, Toussaint-Louverture had himself been freed in 1777 but took on a leadership role when the slave revolt began on Saint Domingue in 1791. His military skill and political acumen were vital to the success of the revolt and to ruling the island's diverse population afterward.   (Stock Montage, Inc.)

SECTION SUMMARY

- General Napoleon Bonaparte and two other men seized power from the Directory in a coup in 1799; Napoleon carefully expanded his power and finally declared himself emperor of France in 1804.

- Napoleon's law code and his agreement with the Catholic Church made permanent some of the key changes from the first phase of the Revolution.

- Napoleon recruited former royal officials, old nobility, and recent revolutionaries into his government, thereby resolving some of the political tensions that had resulted from the Revolution.

- The costs associated with Napoleon's foreign conquests resulted in the overthrow of his regime and contributed to the long-term problems of the French government.

- The export of revolution by French armies brought economic costs from war itself and from Napoleon's continental trading system, but also political reform that led, in many cases, to further political liberty.

- In the Americas, the French Revolution inspired movements for independence from colonial rule; in Haiti, slaves and free persons without political rights allied to successfully overthrow French rule.

that the financially strapped French government would lose some of its profitable sugar trade. But the example of revolutionary daring in Paris and confusion about ruling authority as the Assembly and the king wrangled did not go unnoticed in the colonies—in either plantation mansions or slave quarters. White planters on Saint Domingue simply hoped for political and economic "liberty" from the French government and its mercantilist trade policies. White planter rule was challenged, in turn, by wealthy people of mixed European and African descent who wanted equal citizenship, hitherto denied them. A civil war broke out between these upper classes and was followed by a full-fledged slave rebellion, beginning in 1791. Britain sent aid to the rebels when it went to war against the French revolutionary government in 1793. Only when the republic was declared in Paris and the Convention abolished slavery did the rebels abandon alliances with France's enemies and attempt to govern in concert with the mother country.

Although it recovered other colonies from the British, France never regained control of Saint Domingue. Led by a former slave, **François Dominique Toussaint-Louverture** (too-SAHN-loo-ver-TOUR) (1743–1803), the new government of the island tried to run its own affairs, though without formally declaring independence from France. (See the feature, "The Global Record: Napoleon's Letter to Toussaint-Louverture.") Napoleon decided to tighten control of the profitable colonies by reinstituting slavery and ousting the independent government of Saint Domingue. In 1802, French forces fought their way onto the island. They captured Toussaint-Louverture, who died shortly thereafter in prison. But in 1803, another rebellion, provoked by the threat of renewed slavery, expelled French forces for good. A former aide of Toussaint's declared the independence of the colony under the name Haiti—the island's Native American name—on January 1, 1804.

The French Revolution and Napoleonic rule, and the example of the Haitian revolution, had a notable impact on Spanish colonies in the Americas. Like other American colonies, the Spanish colonies wanted to loosen the closed economic relationships with the mother country. In addition, the liberal ideas that had helped spawn the French Revolution spurred moves toward independence in Spanish America. Because of the confusion of authority in Spain, some of these colonies were already governing themselves independently in all but name. Echoes of radical republican ideology and of the Haitian experience were present in two major rebellions in Mexico; participants espoused the end of slavery and championed the interests of the poor against local and Spanish elites. The leaders of these self-declared revolutions were executed (in 1811 and 1815), and their movements were crushed by local elites in alliance with Spanish troops. The efforts of local elites to become self-governing—the attempted liberal revolutions—were little more successful. Only Argentina and Paraguay broke away from Spain at this time.

But as in Europe, a legacy remained of both limited and more radical revolutionary activity. Slave rebellions rocked British Caribbean islands in subsequent decades. On islands dominated by plantation agriculture, such as some British possessions and the Spanish island of Cuba, planters were reluctant to disturb the prevailing order with any liberal political demands on the mother country.

CHAPTER SUMMARY

The French Revolution was a watershed in European history because it successfully challenged the principles of hereditary rule and political privilege by which all European states had previously been governed. The Revolution began when a financial crisis forced the monarchy to confront the desire for political reform by a segment of the French elite. Political philosophy emerging from the Enlightenment and the example of the American Revolution moved the French reformers to action. In its initial phase, the French Revolution established the principle of constitutional government and ended many of the traditional political privileges of the Old Regime.

Then, because of the intransigence of the king, the threat of foreign invasion, and the actions of republican legislators and Parisian citizens, the Revolution moved in more radical directions. Its most extreme phase, the Terror, produced the most effective legislation for ordinary citizens, but also the worst violence of the Revolution. A period of unstable conservative rule that followed the Terror ended when Napoleon seized power.

Although Napoleonic rule solidified some of the gains of the Revolution, it also subjected France and most of Europe to costly wars of conquest. After Napoleon, the French monarchy was restored, but its power would no longer be absolute—and the people would not be refused a voice in government—as a result of the Revolution. The impact of events in France also continued beyond its borders; political and legal reform had been imposed in many parts of Europe and even, in more limited ways, had been embraced in European colonies.

FOCUS QUESTIONS

- What factors led to revolution in France in 1789?

- Why did several phases of revolutionary change occur after 1789 and what were the characteristics of each phase?

- What impact did the Revolution and Napoleonic rule have on France, the rest of Europe, and the wider world?

KEY TERMS

Third Estate (p. 535)

National Assembly (p. 536)

Tennis Court Oath (p. 536)

Declaration of the Rights of Man and the Citizen (p. 538)

sans-culottes (p. 542)

Jacobins (p. 543)

Maximilien Robespierre (p. 544)

the Terror (p. 544)

Society of Revolutionary Republican Women (p. 545)

Directory (p. 546)

Napoleon Bonaparte (p. 548)

Civil Code (p. 549)

François Dominique Toussaint-Louverture (p. 555)

This icon will direct you to additional materials on the website: www.cengage.com/history/noble/westciv6e.

NOTES

1. Quoted in Samuel Eliot Morrison, *John Paul Jones: A Sailor's Biography* (Boston: Little, Brown, 1959), pp. 149–154.

2. Quoted in Owen Connelly, *The French Revolution and the Napoleonic Era* (New York: Holt, Rinehart, and Winston, 1979), p. 32.

3. James Harvey Robinson, *Readings in European History* (Boston: Ginn, 1906), p. 409.

See our interactive eBook for map and primary source activities.

CHAPTER OUTLINE

George Robertson: Nat-Y-Glo Iron Works

(National Museums & Galleries of Wales)

The Industrial Transformation of Europe, 1750–1850

As the French Revolution gave way to the fires of war in continental Europe, across the Channel, fires belched flame and smoke from England's factory chimneys, lighting the night sky and blocking the day's sun. The painting on the left depicts Shropshire, England, in 1788, a region previously renowned for its natural beauty. Industrial activity had already transformed its landscape beyond recognition. Abraham Darby (1676–1717) and his descendants built one of the largest and most important concentrations of ironworks in Shropshire because it contained the ideal combination of coal and iron deposits. In the 1830s, the French socialist Louis Blanqui (blahn-KEE) (see page 600) suggested that just as France had recently experienced a political revolution, so Britain was undergoing an "industrial revolution." Eventually, that expression entered the general vocabulary to describe the advances in production that occurred first in England and then dominated most of western Europe by the end of the nineteenth century. Although mechanization transformed Europe, it did so unevenly. In many areas, the changes were gradual, suggesting the term *revolution* was not always appropriate. Great Britain offered a model of economic change because it was the first to industrialize; each nation subsequently took its own path and pace in a continuous process of economic transformation.

Industrial development left its mark on just about every sphere of human activity. Scientific and rational methods altered production processes, removing them from the home—where entire families had often participated—to less personal workshops and factories. Significant numbers of workers left farming to enter mining and manufacturing, and major portions of the population moved from rural to urban environments. Machines replaced or supplemented manual labor.[1]

Mechanical production often meant that skilled artisans lost not only their livelihood, but their craft identity as well; it also drew women and children out of the home and into factories. New modes of production offered unprecedented opportunities for manufacturers, merchants, and entrepreneurs to create and amass wealth at levels previously unimaginable. Mechanization also caused pollution and environmental destruction. Miners in search of coal, iron ore, and other minerals cut deep gashes into the earth. The rapid growth of cities resulted in crowded slums, poor sanitation, filth, and visible poverty.

Industrialization simultaneously created unprecedented advancement and opportunity as well as unprecedented hardships and social problems. The social gap between the rich and the working poor increased. The latter, with a growing sense of solidarity, struggled to protect and advance their interests.

FOCUS QUESTIONS

- What factors allowed Europe to industrialize before the rest of the world?

- Which inventions appear to have been the most important in launching industrialization?

- What impact did industrialization have on the environment and on social classes?

- What did workers gain and lose as a result of industrialization, and how did they respond?

 This icon will direct you to additional materials on the website: www.cengage.com/history/noble/westciv6e

 See our interactive eBook for map and primary source activities.

industrialization A system of mass production of goods in which specialization, mechanization, and new sources of mineral energy made manufacturing efficient and profitable.

PRECONDITIONS FOR INDUSTRIALIZATION

What factors allowed Europe to industrialize before the rest of the world?

Industrialization—the substitution of human and animal power by mineral power—required a massive shift of labor and capital resources from agriculture to manufacturing and services. Europe was endowed with a unique combination of conditions—geographic, cultural, economic, demographic—that made this shift and its timing possible. Industrialization did not simply consist of mechanization. It consisted of, and required, simultaneous growth in commerce, population, and agricultural production. Capital accumulation for investment in industry required an entrepreneurial spirit and government support for banking and trading. As farmers applied new scientific methods to food production, less expensive and more abundant food caused the population to grow. This growth created a higher demand for manufactured goods. More efficient food production reduced the need for agricultural labor, allowing or forcing migration to urban manufacturing centers.

Why Europe?

A unique set of circumstances in Europe favored its potential for rapid economic development. Centralized state power and highly developed legal systems protected merchant trade and facilitated the accumulation of wealth for further investment. Such security was nonexistent in other parts of the world, such as the Ottoman Empire, where corruption hampered the development of a commercial spirit. Europe's greater cultural, political, and social diversity also favored its economic development. Challenges to dominant religious and political powers that had come from the Reformation, Counter-Reformation, and the Enlightenment promoted innovation. Toleration for such freedom was a rarity in Asia, where large territories tended to be dominated by a single ruler and faith. International competition among European states drove them to try to outdo one another. Governments actively encouraged industries and commerce to enrich their countries and make them more powerful than their neighbors. None of these factors alone explains why industrialization occurred, but their combination facilitated the process as well as its timing.[2] Finally, it is important to emphasize that industrialization radically transformed power relationships between the West and nonindustrial Africa, Asia, and South America. By 1900, the West had economically and militarily overwhelmed the other parts of the world. (See the feature, "The Global Record: Alexis de Tocqueville's Thoughts on Colonization.")

Transformations Accompanying Industrialization

A number of other transformations favored economic innovation in Europe. In the agricultural sector, farmers learned to rotate crops rather than leaving a portion of their land fallow when soil became depleted. In addition, they began using fertilizers, and introduced new crops from the Americas—such as the potato and maize—which not only flourished in poor soil, but replenished the soil with nitrogen. New, more efficient plows enabled farmers to cultivate more land with less labor. Most important, the new crops and the more efficient cultivation of traditional ones increased the capacity to feed a growing population and freed many people to migrate to urban industries. Until these changes began occurring in the eighteenth century, food production required the work of 80 percent of the European population.

Population growth also helped promote industrialization. The population of Europe increased dramatically throughout the industrial era, doubling between 1750 and 1850. This growth was partly due to a lowering of the death rate. Infant mortality had been very high from illness and disease, such as gastrointestinal disorders, smallpox, diphtheria, and tuberculosis. Although none of these diseases had been medically conquered, slow improvement in sanitation and food intake after 1750 enabled children to better resist them. New employment opportunities led to earlier marriages and thus higher fertility. This growing population supplied the labor force for the new industries and provided the large surge in consumers of various industrial goods.

In the countryside, industrialization was foreshadowed by a form of production that had developed beginning in the seventeenth century—the **putting-out system**, or cottage industry. During the winter, and at other slack times, peasants took in handwork such as spinning, weaving, or dyeing. Often they were marginal agriculturists, frequently women, who, on a part-time basis, could augment the family income. Entrepreneurs discovered that some individuals were better than others at specific tasks. Rather than have one household process the wool through all the steps of production until it was a finished piece, the entrepreneur would buy wool produced by one family, then take it to another to spin, a third to dye, a fourth to weave, and so on. This system of production allowed merchants to ignore guild restrictions and accumulate greater wealth, which later became a basis for investment in full-scale industrialization.

Transportation improved significantly in the eighteenth century, particularly in response to expanding markets for agricultural and manufactured products. Better roads were built; new coaches and carriages could travel faster and carry heavier loads. Government and private companies built canals linking rivers to each other or to lakes. Road- and canal-building hastened and cheapened transportation, which facilitated the movement of raw materials to factories and finished goods to local and distant markets.

Britain's Lead in Industrial Innovation

Britain was the first to industrialize for many reasons. It was the first European country to have a standard currency, tax, and tariff system. Although Britain was by no means an egalitarian society, it accommodated some movement between the classes. Ideas and experiments were readily communicated among entrepreneurs, workers, and scientists.

In addition, England had gained an increasing share of international trade since the seventeenth century. This trade provided capital for investment in industrial plants. The world trade network also ensured that Britain had a market beyond its borders; high demand from foreign markets made mass manufacture feasible. The international trade network also enabled Britain to import raw materials for its industry, the most important of which was cotton.

Earlier than its competitors, Britain had a national banking system that could finance industries in areas where private funding fell short. In addition to numerous London banks, six hundred provincial banks serviced the economy by 1810. Banking could flourish because Britons had wide experience in trade, had accumulated considerable wealth, and found a constant demand for credit.

Britain's geography also favored industrial development. It was rich in coal and iron, whose deposits were in close proximity to one another—an important advantage because coal was used to process iron (see **MAP 20.1**). A relatively narrow island, Britain had easy access to water, which was by far the cheapest means of transportation. Compared with the Continent, it had few toll roads, so moving goods was relatively easy and inexpensive.

British workers were generally more skilled and earned higher wages than their continental counterparts. As food prices fell, they also had more discretionary income to spend on manufactured goods. But because labor was more costly than on the Continent, British business owners had an incentive to find labor-saving devices and reduce the number of workers needed for production.

CHRONOLOGY

1712	Newcomen invents steam-operated water pump
1733	Kay invents flying shuttle
1750–1800	Three million Africans are brought to the Americas as slaves
1753	First steam engine in the Americas
1760s	Hargreaves invents spinning jenny
1765	Watt improves steam engine with separate condenser
1769	Arkwright patents water frame for spinning
1785	Cartwright patents power loom
1793	Whitney invents cotton gin
1804	Jacquard invents automatic loom
1811–1812	Luddites organize
1825	Börsig builds first steam engine in Germany
1831, 1834	Workers' uprising in Lyon
1832	Cholera epidemic
1834	Creation of German customs union, the Zollverein
1844	Workers' uprising in Silesia
1851	Majority of Britain's population becomes urban

putting-out system
Sometimes called "cottage industry," the production in country homes of items like thread and cloth by spinners and weavers for an entrepreneur who furnished raw materials and sold the finished product.

Alexis de Tocqueville's Thoughts on Colonization

The French military conquest of Algeria, beginning in 1830, provides an example of how economic modernization gave Europeans a sense of superiority and changed their relationship with the rest of the world. Charles X, king of France, sent the French military to the town of Algiers in response to a perceived insult from the dey (Algerian governor). Alexis de Tocqueville (1805–1859), member of the French parliament and author of the famous Democracy in America, like many Europeans, thought that industrial progress not only enabled but legitimized the military and economic takeover of undeveloped regions inhabited by people of color. He also argued that white settlement would facilitate military conquest. In the first excerpt below, Tocqueville shares his awe at the vibrancy of urban culture in Algiers, and he describes how the French have begun to tear down and rebuild sections of the town. In the second excerpt, he observes how the effort to force European civilization on Muslims had unfortunate consequences.

From "Notes on the Voyage to Algeria in 1841"

First appearance of [Algiers]: I have never seen anything like it. Prodigious mix of races and costumes, Arab, Kabyle, Moor, Negro, Mahonais, … French. Each of these races, tossed together in a space much too tight to contain them, speaks its language, wears its attire, displays different mores … The entire lower town seems in a state of destruction and reconstruction. On all sides, one sees nothing but recent ruins, buildings going up; one hears nothing but the noise of the hammer. It is Cincinnati transported onto the soil of Africa.

The French are substituting broad arcaded streets for the Moors' tortuous little alleys. This is a necessity of our civilization. But they are also substituting their architecture for that of the Moors, and this is wrong; for the latter is very appropriate to the needs of the country, and besides, it is charming. …

From "First Report on Algeria," 1847

The indigenous towns were invaded, turned upside down, and sacked by our administration even more than by our arms. … In the vicinity of Algiers itself, the very fertile areas were torn from the hands of the Arabs and given to Europeans who, not being able or not wanting to cultivate them themselves, rented them to these same indigenous people, who thus became the mere farmers of the domains that had belonged to their fathers. Elsewhere, tribes or factions of tribes that were not hostile to us, or even more who had fought with us and sometimes without us, were pushed off their territory. We accepted conditions we did not fulfill, we promised indemnities we did not pay, thus allowing our honor to suffer even more than the interests of these indigenous peoples. …

Muslim society in Africa was not uncivilized; it was merely a backward and imperfect civilization. There existed within it a large number of pious foundations, whose object was to provide for the needs of charity or for public instruction. We laid our hands on these revenues everywhere, partly diverting them from their former uses; we reduced the charitable establishments and let the schools decay, we disbanded seminaries. Around us knowledge has been extinguished, and recruitment of men of religion and men of law has ceased; that is to say, we have made Muslim society much more miserable, more disordered, more ignorant, and more barbarous than it had been before knowing us. …

It is not along the road of our European civilization that they must, for the present, be pushed, but in the direction proper to them; we must demand of them things that suit their ways, and not those contrary to them. Individual property, industry, and sedentary dwelling [as opposed to nomadic lifestyle] are in no way contrary to the religion of Muhammad. Arabs know or have known these things elsewhere; they are known and appreciated by some in Algeria itself. Why do we despair of making them familiar to a greater number? … Islam is not absolutely impenetrable to enlightenment.

… If our arms have decimated certain tribes, there are others whom our commerce has enriched and strengthened considerably, and who feel and understand this. Everywhere the prices that the indigenous people can get for their wares and their labor have increased greatly by our presence. In addition, our agriculturalists gladly make use of indigenous manpower. The European needs the Arab to make his lands valuable; the Arab needs the European to obtain a high salary.

QUESTIONS

1. How does Tocqueville react to Algerian culture? Why does he compare Algiers with Cincinnati? How are the French attempting to remake Algeria in their own image?

2. What are Tocqueville's assumptions about economic modernization in Algeria and its appropriateness for indigenous culture?

Source: de Tocqueville, Alexis. Edited and translated by Jennifer Pitts. *Writings on Empire and Slavery.* pp. 36, 140, 142, 145. © 2000 Jennifer Pitts. Reprinted with permission of The Johns Hopkins University Press.

First Railroad, from Manchester to Liverpool, England   The engineer George Stephenson (1781–1848) first built engines that could pull coal at mines; in 1821, he constructed the first "locomotive" for public transportation. Four years later, the first regular railroad line, connecting Manchester with Liverpool, was erected.   (Private Collection/The Stapleton Collection/Bridgeman Art Library)

The population of Great Britain increased by 8 percent in each decade from 1750 to 1800, partly as a result of industrial growth. This swelling population, in turn, expanded the market for goods. The most rapid population growth occurred in the countryside, causing a steady movement of people from rural to urban areas. The presence of this workforce was another contributing factor in Britain's readiness for change.

Britain was far more open to dissent than were other European countries at the time. A large proportion of British entrepreneurs was Quaker or belonged to one of the dissenting (non-Anglican) religious groups. Perhaps **dissenters** were accustomed to questioning authority and treading new paths. They were also well educated and, as a result of common religious bonds, inclined to provide mutual aid, including financial support.

Plentiful harvests in the years 1715 to 1750 also favored Britain and influenced the timing of industrial change. Farmers with good earnings could afford to order the new manufactured iron plows, and demand for industrial goods generally rose with population growth, improvements to the transportation system, and the growing availability of capital for investment. Thus, each change triggered more change; the cumulative effect was staggering.

SECTION SUMMARY

- Europe, and especially Great Britain, was endowed with rich iron and coal deposits, one of the most important factors that gave them the lead in industrialization.

- Improvements in agricultural production during the eighteenth century contributed to population growth, which in turn created a surplus labor force available for industrial production in urban areas and as well as a market for mass-produced goods.

- Toleration of religious diversity and dissent, especially in Great Britain, helped inspire innovation and an entrepreneurial spirit.

- The expansion of overseas trade from the seventeenth century onward created new sources of raw materials for manufacture, such as cotton.

- Merchants brought raw materials to the countryside for processing, leading to the development of cottage industry (the putting-out system), the division of labor, and specialization of tasks—all precursors of and steps toward industrialization.

- Centralized governments supported national banks and encouraged commerce, which in turn led to improved transportation.

🌐 **MAP 20.1—The Industrial Transformation in England, ca. 1850**
Industry developed in the areas rich in coal and iron fields. Important cities sprang up nearby and were soon linked by a growing rail network.

NEW MODES OF PRODUCTION

Which inventions appear to have been the most important in launching industrialization?

dissenters In England, a person belonging to a sect other than the Church of England.

mass production System in which great numbers of people work in centralized factories to mechanically produce large quantities of goods. The steam engine led to mass-produced textiles.

Several important technological advances powered European industry, and breakthroughs in one field often led to breakthroughs in others. Major technological innovations first transformed textiles and iron. At first limited to the British Isles, industry spread to the Continent, a development that occurred unevenly in various regions and at different times.

Mass Production

A series of inventions in the eighteenth century led to the **mass production** of textiles. One of the earliest was the flying shuttle (a shuttle carries the thread back and forth on a loom),

British Cotton Manufacture   Machines simultaneously performed various functions. The carding machine *(front left)* separated cotton fibers, readying them for spinning. The roving machine *(front right)* wound the cotton onto spools. The drawing machine *(rear left)* wove patterns into the cloth. Rich in machines, this factory needed relatively few employees; most were women and children.   (The Granger Collection, New York)

introduced in Britain in 1733 by John Kay (1704–1764). Kay's flying shuttle accelerated the weaving process to such an extent that it increased the demand for thread. James Hargreaves (1720–1778) met this need in the 1760s with his invention of the spinning jenny, a device that spun thread from wool or cotton. Improvements in spinning thread, such as the mule of Samuel Crompton (1753–1827), made the spinning jenny increasingly efficient, and by 1812, one jenny could produce as much yarn as two hundred hand spinners. In 1769, Richard Arkwright (1732–1792) patented the water frame, a machine capable of simultaneously spinning multiple threads. The frame was originally powered by waterfall, but in the 1780s, Arkwright began operating it with a steam engine. This mode of production created a glut of thread for hand weavers, which then led to the development of the power loom by Richard Cartwright in 1785. These innovations in turn increased the demand for raw cotton, inspiring American Eli Whitney (1765–1825) to invent the cotton gin, which sped up the removal of seeds from raw cotton. These innovations mechanized cotton manufacturing, moving most production from the home to factories. The industry's output increased 130-fold between 1770 and 1841.

The cotton manufacturing industry in Great Britain initiated an important departure from traditional production. For the first time in history, a staple industry was based on a natural resource that was not domestically produced—Britain's imports of cotton, mostly from the U.S. South, multiplied fivefold after 1790. Manufactured cotton became so cheap that it competed effectively with all handmade textiles. Comfortable and easy to wash, the popularity of cotton may have improved public health as well, for it enabled people to own several changes of clothing and keep them clean. Everyone was eager to buy British cottons. The enormous growth in the demand for raw cotton had a collateral impact: By making cotton production

A French Woman Goes to Work

The new cotton mills presented several obstacles to women workers. They had to negotiate the machinery while wearing the petticoats and aprons that custom required. Such dress could catch in the machinery, causing broken limbs and loss of a job, if not of life. At work and on their way to and from the British mills or at the less mechanized garment workshops of France, women had to pass dangerous places, where some experienced sexual harassment. Suzanne Voilquin (ca. 1801–ca. 1876) went to work to help her family after her mother had died. She took a job not at a mill or a factory, as was common in England, but as an embroiderer in a small workshop in Paris. In this selection, she writes of her experiences as a young woman from about 1823 to 1825.

We had to be at our looms at seven o'clock sharp and, even before setting out on the long race to get there on time, we had to carry out all our little household duties as quickly as we could. If certain details made us late, Mrs. Martin [her employer] would accept no excuses and offer no reprieve. We had to pay in kind, that is to say, make good those few minutes at the end of the day's work. When our days were prolonged in this way, I had a horrible fear of meeting on my return one of those contemptible men who makes a game of accosting young working women and frightening them with disgraceful remarks. When this happened, my nerves were always on edge and I lacked all physical courage. It was quite otherwise with … Adrienne [her younger sister]. She would say to me, … "Dear Sister, aren't I here?" (She was barely fifteen.) "If the occasion arises, why then you'll see that *a person's worth is not measured in years!*" And indeed, one evening, she gave me positive proof. Around nine o'clock … we were stopped by the vulgar words and filthy gestures of some poor wretch. As always, I stood there trembling and unable to speak before this reviler. Adrienne, on the contrary, experienced a moment

of sublime energy. She managed to find such a tone of resolve, while brandishing an enormous key before his eyes, that he backed away, and, when we reached the corner of the main street, we were delivered from his insolent remarks.

Mrs. Martin seemed satisfied with our work, and we were accepted as regular employees. And so, at the end of the first week, we were very proud to deposit on our father's mantelpiece the eighteen francs we earned as wages. It was the same each week, for he had made himself the provisioner of our little group.

That cruel year was brought to an end by an accident that nearly caused my sister the loss of her right hand. My father's wail when he thought his child had been maimed for life was heart-rending. He cried!

… Around this time, my father wanted to marry us off. … The widower whom my father begged me to marry was fairly well established but neither handsome nor pleasant nor witty. Moreover, he came with a son twelve or thirteen years old, a charming Parisian street urchin who had been very badly raised. As a result, my mind, my senses, my whole being rebelled against the thought of such a match.

QUESTIONS

1. What is Suzanne Voilquin's attitude toward work? What hardships does she face?

2. What does this excerpt tell you about family relations? Why does Suzanne's father want to "marry her off"?

Source: From Mark Traugott, ed. and trans., *The French Worker: Autobiographies from the Early Industrial Era*, Copyright © 1993 The Regents of the University of California. Reprinted by permission of The University of California Press.

---

more profitable, it also made slave labor in the U.S. South more attractive. Between 1750 and 1800, approximately three million Africans were forcibly transported to the New World. The slave economy in the Americas influenced Britain's economy in several ways. Slave-produced sugar in the West Indies and cotton in the American South shifted Britain's trade patterns from Asia to the Atlantic. The cotton trade, and later, other products, linked the economies of various nations and peoples. No longer, as in preindustrial trade, were all goods locally made, nor did the consumers have personal contact with the producers of goods they purchased. Increasingly, specialization became the norm. The results were high production and low prices for finished textile products. Hand sewing and needlework, usually done by young women, completed the garment-making process. (See the feature, "The Written Record: A French Woman Goes to Work.")

New Energy Sources and Their Impacts

Before the age of industrialization, humans, animals, wind, and water provided the power sources for production. Humans and animals were limited in their capacities to drive the large mills needed to grind grain or cut wood. Wind was unreliable because it was not constant. Water-driven mills depended on the seasons—streams dried up in the summer and froze in the winter. And water mills could be placed only where a strong current of water flowed. Clearly, the infant industries needed a power source that was constant and not confined to riverbanks. In the eighteenth and nineteenth centuries, two new sources of energy fueled industrial production: coal and steam.

Coal, long in use for heating households, for the first time came to be used for metal processing. Traditionally, smelters used charcoal to extract iron from ore. Eventually, however, the source of charcoal—wood—became depleted in Britain. Abraham Darby's invention of coke (refined coal) smelting in 1708 allowed coal to substitute for charcoal in the process of refining metals. Although coal was plentiful, the increased demand for it depleted the surface seams in mines, and it became necessary to go farther underground. But as pits deepened, they reached pools of ground water, and drainage became a critical obstacle to coal mining. In 1709, Thomas Newcomen (1663–1729) patented a **steam engine** that, within a few years, was able to pump water from the pit bottom to the surface of the mine shaft. James Watt (1736–1819) improved it, and by developing a separate condenser, Watt devised an engine that could power a variety of machines. Thus, steam engines could also operate textile mills that had previously been powered by water or wind.

steam engine The steam engine provided mechanized power for manufacturing and made factories and mass production possible.

The steam engine, initially used to meet the increased demand for coal, by the late 1700s, also powered the blast furnaces in the coke smelting process, as well as driving the forge hammers that shaped iron. Iron output increased dramatically by 1800. The greater supply of iron and the use of steam stimulated other changes. Wooden machines, which wore out rapidly, were replaced by relatively cheap and durable iron machines. The steam engine made it practical to organize work in a factory. Locating a manufacturing plant where it was most convenient eliminated the expense of transporting raw materials to be worked on at a natural but fixed power source, such as a waterfall. The central factory also reinforced work discipline. These **factories** were large, austere edifices, sometimes inspired by military architecture and therefore resembling barracks. With the introduction of blast furnaces and other heat-producing manufacturing methods, the tall factory chimney became a common sight on the industrial landscape.

factories Centralized workplaces where a number of people cooperate to mass-produce goods. The steam engine as a central power source in factories led to huge productivity increases.

The steam engine powered a dramatic growth in production. It increased the mechanical power of machinery used to forge iron and to produce equipment for spinning and weaving. Assisted by machines, workers were enormously more productive than when they depended solely on hand-operated tools. In the year 1700, spinning 100 pounds of cotton took 50,000 worker-hours; by 1825 it took only 135—a 370-fold increase in productivity capacity per worker.

Improvements in manufacturing methods and techniques increased the production of a large variety of goods, usually at lower prices. Industrial change started with cotton, but breakthroughs in the use of iron and coal continued and sustained these changes.

Inventors and Entrepreneurs

Inventions triggered the industrial age, and the continued flow of new ones sustained it. Rather than cling to traditional methods, many **entrepreneurs** persistently challenged tradition and attempted to find new ways of improving production. In this age of invention, innovation was prized as never before. The early inventors and industrialists came from various backgrounds. Jean Marie Jacquard, for example, whose invention is illustrated below, was a craftsman. Other inventors came from the merchant class, since the possession of capital was a distinct advantage in launching an industrial enterprise.

entrepreneurs People who assume the risks of organizing and investing in new business ventures, inventions, and innovations.

Entrepreneurs took the financial risk of investing in new types of enterprises. Most industrialists ran a single plant by themselves or with a partner, but even in the early stages, some ran several plants. Some enterprises were vertically integrated, controlling production at many stages. The Peels in Britain owned operations ranging from spinning to printing and even banking. The entrepreneurs' dynamism and boldness fostered the growth of the British industrial system, making that small nation the workshop of the world.

The Spread of Industry to the Continent

As the first to industrialize, Britain not only gained an economic edge over the Continent, but it offered a model for economic change. Visitors, such as German engineer August Börsig

The Jacquard Loom   Joseph-Marie Jacquard (1752–1834) invented this loom in 1804, and it was widely adopted in both France and England. While it was not "industrial" in the sense that its source of power was the human energy of a skilled craftsman, it nonetheless embodied a significant modern advancement. The pasteboard punch cards controlled the action of the loom to create complex designs automatically, making it possible for amateur weavers to produce highly prized fabrics. The punch card was an important precursor to computing hardware and programming. The looms' cards were interchangeable. They could also be stolen—an early instance of software piracy.
(Loom designed by Joseph Marie Jacquard (1752-1834) 2nd half of 19th century (engraving) (b/w photo), French School, (19th century)/Private Collection/Archives Charmet/The Bridgeman Art Library)

(BEUR-sick), came to Britain, studied local methods of production, and returned home to set up blast furnaces and spinning works inspired by British design. Some visitors even resorted to industrial espionage, smuggling blueprints of machines out of Britain. Despite a British law that forbade local artisans to emigrate, some did leave, including entrepreneurs who helped set up industrial plants in France and Belgium. By the 1820s, British technicians were all over Europe.

The Börsig Ironworks in the 1840s August Börsig (1804–1854), an artisan and engineer, founded these ironworks in Berlin after studying steam engines in Britain. He built the first German steam engine in 1825 and the first locomotive in 1842. The factory expanded to meet the needs of the burgeoning German rail system. By the time of Börsig's death, his factory had built five hundred locomotives. (Preussischer Kulturbesitz Bildarchiv/Art Resource, NY)

Even though engineers and entrepreneurs wished to emulate British methods, no other country could replicate the British pattern of industrialization, and the various paths taken toward modernization demonstrate how the "revolutionary" nature of these changes was contingent upon a precise combination of factors. Wars and revolutions of the late eighteenth century had not only slowed economic growth in France, but they cut off the flow of information and new techniques coming from Britain. France also lacked the rapid population growth that had made possible, if not necessitated, economic change in Britain. Moreover, revolutionary and Napoleonic legislation had relieved French peasants of some of the misery that drove their British counterparts to leave the land for urban industry. The Napoleonic Code of 1804 abolished **primogeniture**, so that when a peasant died, all of his children, at least in principle, enjoyed equal inheritance, which enabled many to remain on the land.

Because French labor was still quite cheap, many goods could be manufactured inexpensively by hand; thus, the incentive to invest in laborsaving devices was absent. French entrepreneurs who did seek to emulate British accomplishments faced serious cultural and geographical challenges. France had traditionally produced high quality luxury goods that were not well disposed to the methods of mass production; it also had fewer iron and coal deposits that, unlike in Britain, were geographically dispersed (see **MAP 20.2**). Soon, however, French manufacturers found themselves facing British competition; they were the first to feel the negative effects of being industrial latecomers.

The situation in Germany was quite different from that of both Britain and France. The Napoleonic invasions caused considerable destruction, but they also brought some positive

primogeniture A legal inheritance system that provided the firstborn, usually the firstborn son, the right to inherit all the family land and farm.

🌐 Map 20.2—Continental Industrialization, ca. 1850

Industry was still sparse on the Continent, but important regions had developed near major coal deposits in Liège, the Ruhr, and Silesia.

economic, social, and administrative benefits. Restrictive guilds declined. The French occupiers suppressed many tariffs and taxes that had hindered trade between German states; they also reduced the number of separate states, established a single unified legal system, and introduced a single standard of measurement based on the metric system. These changes remained intact after Napoleon's defeat in 1815.

Government in the German states played an important role in the adoption of improved methods of manufacturing. Eager for industrial development, the Prussian state sent an official to Britain to observe the puddling process (the method by which iron is freed of carbon) and bring that expertise back home. The Prussian government promoted industrial growth by investing in a transportation network to carry raw materials for processing and finished goods to their markets. To spur both trade and industrial growth, Prussia took the lead in creating a customs union, the *Zollverein* (TZOLL-fair-eyn), which abolished tariffs among its members. By 1834, a market embracing eighteen German states with a population of 23 million had been created. German industrial growth accelerated dramatically in the 1850s. Massive expenditures on railways created a large demand for metal, which pressured German manufacturers to enlarge their plant capacities and increase efficiency. The German states were not yet politically unified, but the German middle classes saw economic growth as the means by which their country could win a prominent place among Europe's nation-states.

■ **FIGURE 20.1—The Increase in Gross National Product per Capita in Principal European Countries, 1830–1913**

The countries that industrialized rapidly—such as the United Kingdom in particular, and also Belgium, France, and Germany—experienced dramatic increases in per capita income during the nineteenth century. Other countries, such as Greece and Portugal, economically trailed the industrial leaders, and per capita income there remained essentially flat.

(Source: From Norman J. G. Pounds, *An Historical Geography of Europe, 1800–1914*. Cambridge University Press, 1985. Used by permission of the publisher.)

Germany successfully emulated Britain and overtook France's rate of economic growth. Toward the end of the nineteenth century, Germany pioneered in the electrical engineering and chemical industries. If France experienced the disadvantages of being a latecomer to industrialization, Germany reaped the benefits of that status. The Germans were able to avoid costly and inefficient early experimentation and adopted the latest, proven methods; moreover, Germany entered fields that Britain had neglected.

Elsewhere in Europe, economic progress remained slow, even by the end of the nineteenth century. As long as Russia retained serfdom (until 1861), it would lack the mobile labor force needed for industrial growth. And until late in the century, the ruling Russian aristocracy hesitated to adopt an economic system in which wealth was not based on labor-intensive agriculture. With the exception of its only important industrial center in Bohemia, Austria remained heavily agrarian (see **MAP 20.2**).

The impoverished southern Mediterranean countries experienced little economic growth. With mostly poor soil, their agriculture yielded only a meager surplus. Spain, lacking coal and access to other energy sources, could not easily diversify its economic base. Some industry emerged in Catalonia, especially around Barcelona, but it was limited in scope and did not have much impact on the rest of the country. The Italian peninsula was still industrially underdeveloped in the middle of the nineteenth century. There were modest advances, but growth was too slow to have a measurable positive impact on the Italian economy. In 1871, 61 percent of Italy's population was still agrarian.

Although by midcentury only a few European nations had experienced industrialization to any great extent, many more would do so by the end of the century, pressured by vigorous competition from their more advanced neighbors (see **FIGURE 20.1**). Economic modernization had political and international implications as well, for industrialized nations had the backing of military might and superiority. Compared with the rest of the world, the European continent in the nineteenth century had acquired a distinct material culture that was increasingly based on machine manufacture or was in the process of becoming so. The possession of "skillful industry," one Victorian writer exulted, was "ever a proof of superior civilization." Although only some regions of Europe were industrialized, many Europeans came to view themselves as obviously "superior," while deeming all other races inferior. (See the feature, "The Global Record: Alexis de Tocqueville's Thoughts on Colonization.")

SECTION SUMMARY

- The influx of raw cotton into Britain, innovations that sped up the processes of spinning and weaving, as well as the mechanical removal of cotton seeds, led the revolution in textile production.

- The introduction of the blast furnace and steam engine doubled iron production at the end of the eighteenth century, leading to the production of less expensive and more durable machines, such as those used for textiles. Steam-driven machines led to the centralization of production into factories.

- The innovations that came with industrial production also depended upon entrepreneurs who were hungry for profits and willing to take investment risks.

- The pace of industrialization varied among nations and changed the nature of competition among them; the material culture produced by machine manufacture led Europeans to view themselves as a superior civilization with the military capability for colonial conquest.

SOCIAL, CULTURAL, AND ENVIRONMENTAL IMPACTS

What impact did industrialization have on the environment and on social classes?

Industry transformed people's lives, individually and collectively. It altered how they made a livelihood, where and how they lived, even how they thought of themselves. Because industry required new specialized skills, the range of occupations that people adopted expanded dramatically.

Industrialization also transformed the way society functioned. Until the eighteenth century, power and influence derived from hereditary privilege, which meant aristocratic birth and possession of land. From the late eighteenth century on, however, an emerging social class, whose wealth was self-made and whose influence was based on economic contributions to society, began to challenge the aristocracy. Industrialization also caused extraordinary growth of cities and dramatically altered the natural environment. Europeans faced not only new urban social problems, but also the dangerous pollution of their air and water.

Urbanization and Its Discontents

A sociologist at the end of the nineteenth century observed, "The most remarkable social phenomenon of the present century is the concentration of population in cities."[3] The number and size of cities grew as never before. The major impetus for urban growth was the concentration of industry in cities and the resulting need of large numbers of urban workers and their families for goods and services (see **MAP 20.3**).

Industrialization was not the only catalyst. Increased commercial, administrative, and other service functions drew people to cities, even in countries that had not yet witnessed much industrialization, such as France, Holland, Italy, and Switzerland. Urban growth in some places was explosive. In the entire eighteenth century, London grew by only 200,000; but in the first half of the nineteenth century, it grew by 1.4 million, more than doubling its size. Census figures show that by 1851, Britain was the first country to have as many people living in cities as in the countryside. For Germany, that date was 1891, and for France, it was not until 1931. In addition to industry, **urbanization** transformed cities and the way they grew. Large concentrations of people provided convenient markets for goods, services, and a labor pool. But they also encouraged a more intense social and cultural engagement, which could support, for example, scientific societies and laboratories where engineers and scientists could share new ideas.

urbanization Term related to the growth of cities, largely connected to the industrialization of the late eighteenth and nineteenth centuries.

Larger cities attracted migrants from great distances, including from beyond the nation's borders. The Irish arrived in large numbers to work in the factories of Lancashire, in northwestern England; Belgians came for mine work in northern France; and Poles sought employment in the Ruhr Valley of western Germany. Industrial activity stimulated the growth of world trade and shipping across the seas, taking merchant sailors far from home. Many large cities were marked by diverse populations, which included people with different native languages, religions, and national origins and, increasingly, of different races. Africans and Asians inhabited port cities, such as Amsterdam, Marseille, and Liverpool.

A multitude of ills accompanied urban growth and caused mortality rates to rise dramatically in some locations. In mid-nineteenth century France and Britain, annual death rates averaged about 22 per thousand, but in some industrial cities, it rose to 39.2, with infants dying at especially high rates. Social inequality in the face of death was startling. Including the high child mortality rate, the average age at death among upper-class Liverpool families in 1842 was 35; for members of laborers' families, it was 15. In 1800, boys living in urban slums were on average 8 inches shorter than the sons of rich urban dwellers.

The early stages of industrialization created severe conditions for the poor, especially in rapidly growing cities, where they lived in urban slums. The squalor of St. Giles—London's most notorious slum—had such shock value that it became a tourist attraction. (See the feature, "The Visual Record: St. Giles.") Housing shortages in many cities forced large numbers of people to cram into small areas. To accommodate the influx of workers, houses were built back to back on small lots and had insufficient lighting and ventilation. The dizzying pace of

- ● 100,000 in 1750
- ● Reached 100,000 by 1800
- ● Reached 100,000 by 1850

🌐 MAP 20.3—Cities Reaching Population Level of 100,000 by 1750, 1800, and 1850

In 1750, the largest cities owed their existence primarily to commerce, but industrialization caused populations to concentrate more in cities. England, the leading industrial nation, contained many of the largest cities.

(Source: Data from Tertius Chandler, Four Thousand Years of Urban Growth: An Historical Census [Lewistown, N.Y.: St. David's University Press, 1987], pp. 22–24.)

urban growth made it impossible for cities to provide basic sanitary facilities. The causes of many diseases, such as typhus, cholera, and tuberculosis, were unknown; the dirt, dampness, and darkness of crowded tenements and polluted streets created the conditions that fostered disease.

In manufacturing towns, factory chimneys spewed soot, and everything was covered with dirt and grime. Smoke was a major ingredient of the famous London fog, which not only reduced visibility, but posed serious health risks. Refuse, including the rotting corpses of dogs and horses, littered city streets. In 1858, the stench from sewage and other rot in London was so putrid that the British House of Commons was forced to suspend its sessions.

It is not surprising that cholera, a highly infectious disease transmitted through contaminated water, swept London and other European urban centers. In the 1830s, one of the first epidemics of modern times struck Europe, killing 100,000 in France, 50,000 in Britain, and 238,000 in Russia. Typhoid fever, also an acute infectious disease, struck mostly the poor but did not spare the privileged. Queen Victoria of Great Britain nearly died of it; her husband, Prince Albert, did.

Social Class and Family Life

A French countess, using the pen name Daniel Stern, wrote in the 1830s and 1840s about the emergence of "a class apart, as if it were a nation within the nation," working in factories and mines, called "by a new name: the industrial **proletariat**."[7] Originally used to designate the poorest propertyless wretches in Roman society, the term *proletariat* became synonymous with the

proletariat Karl Marx's term for the new class of industrial workers who owned none of the means of production and were dependent on factory owners for their livelihoods.

St. Giles

This woodcut first appeared in the *Illustrated London News* in the early 1840s, and then in Thomas Beames's, *The Rookeries of London* (1852). It is difficult to overestimate the power of such imagery, particularly in the press. Such visual portrayals did not necessarily exaggerate slum conditions, but they did help create and disseminate distinct impressions about the poor. Note the implied promiscuousness of the disheveled couple, and the indifferent attitude of the mother (who might be single), with her arm draped lackadaisically over her nursing infant.

Surrounded by the well-to-do neighborhoods of Oxford Street, Regent Street, Trafalgar Square, and the Strand, St. Giles had once been a village outside London,

inhabited by wealthy people. But London's rapid expansion swallowed it; by 1740, dwellings to accommodate the poor—called "rookeries"—were built in courtyards and alleys between the original streets, and the wealthier population moved out. The rapid degeneration of neighborhoods, such as St. Giles, in fast-growing urban centers of Britain, France, and Germany took local authorities by surprise. Overcrowding worsened the already poor sanitary conditions. A single privy in a courtyard was likely to serve dozens, sometimes even a few hundred, tenants. Waste from the privy might contaminate nearby wells, or drain through open sewers to a nearby river, which was likely to be the local source of drinking water—and a breeding ground for cholera. Some

St. Giles   (From Thomas Beames, The Rookeries of London. Photo: Harvard Imaging Service)

class of workers developing in the burgeoning factories. What distinguished this growing class throughout the nineteenth century was that it was relatively unskilled and totally dependent on the factory owners for its livelihood. Even lowly apprentices of earlier eras never occupied such a precarious status because guild rules and traditions protected them from arbitrariness. The guild system also made it possible for apprentices to become journeymen and then master artisans, owning their own tools and working on their own time and on their own premises. Improvement in status and owning the means of production would never be a possibility for the new proletariat.

tenants lacked toilets and relieved themselves in the streets. The practice of storing human waste in heaps alongside houses for sale as manure also contributed to the pervasive stench and the spread of bacteria. Water in the cities was scarce and filthy. Only the rich had piped water. The poor had to supply themselves from public fountains or wells and were often obliged to carry water a considerable distance.

Social Reformers and medical experts who visited St. Giles and other urban slums in European cities tended to focus repeatedly on the dangers of promiscuity, disease, crime, and moral contagion, often employing the same words and metaphors to describe what they had seen or what others had written. They especially decried what they perceived to be the immoral conditions in which families lived. Physician James Philips Kay, for example, who practiced medicine in Manchester, England, wrote in 1832 of how "A whole family is often accommodated on a single bed, and sometimes a heap of filthy straw and a covering of old sacking hide them in one undistinguished heap, debased alike by penury, want of economy and dissolute habits. Frequently, the inspectors found [that] ... more than one family lived in a damp cellar, containing only one room, in whose pestilential atmosphere from twelve to sixteen persons were crowded. To these fertile sources of disease were sometimes added the keeping of pigs and other animals in the house, with other nuisances of the most revolting character."[4] Inspectors often dwelled on the mixture of sexes across generations sharing beds, implying incest and animal-like behavior.

In his *Condition of the Working Class in England* (1845), Friedrich Engels described St. Giles as a place where "no human being" would wish to live: broken windows, crumbling walls, stinking piles of garbage and filth that "surpassed description." He might have been referring to the printed image of St. Giles when he emphasized how overcrowding produced "brutal indifference" and "unfeeling isolation," where humankind dissolved into "monads, of which each one has a separate essence, and a separate purpose, the world of atoms. ... "[5] Indeed, with the possible exception of the little girl (whose back is to the viewer) and the middle-class woman (on the right, in the back) toward whom she might be approaching for a handout, there is not a single mutual gaze among those portrayed in this print—each individual is looking outward or downward. Note as well that the middle-class woman's gaze is disapproving, not sympathetic. Middle-class women often ventured into slums for charitable works—one of the few excuses respectable women had to be in public. But the charity was limited by morals; providers wanted to be certain that only the "worthy" poor received it.

Beames, who included the same print in his book, seems to draw his description of St. Giles from the image as much as from his own visit there:

> ... squalid children, haggard men, with long uncombed hair, in rags, most of them smoking, many speaking Irish; women without shoes or stockings—a babe perhaps at the breast, with a single garment, confined to the waist by a bit of string; wolfish looking dogs; decayed vegetables strewing the pavement; low public houses; linen hanging across the street to dry; the population stagnant in the midst of activity; lounging about in remnants of shooting jackets, leaning on the window frames, blocking up the courts and alleys; with young boys gathered round them, looking exhausted as though they had not been to bed. Never was there so little connection between masses of living beings and their means of livelihood.[6]

Engels and Beames both expressed deep concern about how the working class became mixed with "prostitutes, thieves, and criminals." Indeed, a closer look at the couple in the print suggests the woman is a prostitute, and the figure lying prone is probably drunk. Not only are the numerous children subject to terrible influences, but so are honest laborers. Beames feared that because workers could not live on their low wages, criminal temptations would spread like a "plague." But the contagion of crime was not the only threat. If the working poor ever united to challenge social injustice, they might foment violent revolution.

QUESTIONS

1. Study more closely the details in the wood block. What do you think are the intentions of the artist?

2. Do you think this wood block is an accurate representation of St. Giles's entire population?

3. What were the dangers, real or perceived, of ignoring the plight of the poor in neighborhoods like St. Giles?

As industry advanced and spread, more and more people depended on it for a livelihood. In the putting-out system, during an agricultural downturn, a cottager could spend more time on hand labor; when demand for piecework slacked off, the cottager could devote more time to cultivating the land. But people living in industrial cities had no such backup: Any downturn in the economy translated into layoffs or job losses. In addition, the introduction of new industries often devastated laborers in older forms of production. The mechanization of cotton production reduced the earning power of weavers. Cheap cotton production also drove down workers' wages in other textiles with higher production costs, such as linen, because of competition.

Children Toiling in Mines   Able to crawl in narrow mine shafts, many children were employed underground. In this woodcut, a woman joins a child in his labor. Often, whole families worked together and were paid a fixed price for the amount of coal extracted.   (Rischgitz/Hulton Archive/Getty Images)

Most factory work was dirty and laborious and took place in grim plants with heavy, noisy machinery. Sixteen-hour workdays were common. Child labor was widespread. With no safety provisions, the workers were prone to accidents and exposed to dangerous substances or circumstances. Mercury, used in hat manufacturing, gradually poisoned the hatmakers and often led to dementia, hence, the term *mad hatters*. Lead, used in paints and pottery, also had a devastating impact on workers' health.

Young girls especially suffered poor health from heavy labor. In 1842, 18-year-old Ann Eggley testified to a parliamentary commission that she had been a mineworker since the age of 7 and hauled carriages loaded with ore weighing 800 pounds for twelve hours a day. Isabel Wilson, another mineworker, testified that she had given birth to ten children and had suffered five miscarriages. These women—overworked, exhausted, and vulnerable to disease—faced premature death.

Did industrialization improve the workers' lot? Until the mid-nineteenth century, information about workers' standard of living, measured by income and expenses, is incomplete. Generally, incomes were so low that workers usually spent between two-thirds and three-fourths of their budget on food. The best evidence comes from Britain, where an average family of five needed at least 21 shillings a week to fend off poverty. Skilled workers might earn as much as 30 shillings a week, but most were unskilled and earned substantially less. All workers faced the insecurity of illness or old age resulting in lost wages or unemployment. Women and children usually had to pitch in. Even when women were the main breadwinners, they almost never received wages sufficient to meet the needs of their own subsistence, let alone those of an entire family. Regardless of what work they performed, women always earned a fraction of men's wages. Employers based women's wages on the assumption that they supplemented the income of a husband or father.

From the beginning, industrialization increased society's wealth, but historians continue to debate whether and at what point it benefited workers. "Optimist" historians argue that some of the new wealth trickled down to the lower levels of society. "Pessimist" historians say that a downward flow did not necessarily occur. Statistics suggest that by the 1840s, workers' lives in Britain did improve. Their real income rose by 40 percent between 1800 and 1850 because of relatively low prices of many basic goods. As the cost of cloth declined, the dress of working-class people noticeably improved. Nonetheless, the general trend in real wages meant little when workers faced frequent cycles of unemployment or underemployment, when they lived in crowded, unsanitary conditions, or when a major economic downturn, such as occurred in the 1840s, made their situation even more precarious.

Industrialization also had dramatic impacts on the character of family and household among both the middle and working classes. Industrial capitalism gave rise to a new middle class or **bourgeoisie**, whose wealth derived from the capitalistic activities of trade, finance, and manufacturing. Previously, the wives and daughters of small shopkeepers readily performed tasks, such as bookkeeping or serving customers, because the businesses were in or near the home. But as small businesses became public companies with venues outside the home, women ceased participating. Family life came to reflect these new economic realities, justified and reinforced by a new set of cultural values. In more than any other social class, new family values based on gender distinctions became just as important a signifier of class identity as wealth itself. Catherine Hall notes that "A man's dignity lay in his occupation; a woman's gentility was destroyed if she had one."[8] The nineteenth-century world of market capitalism made wealth—rather than aristocratic bloodlines—the sign of success and power. Conspicuous consumption on homes, home furnishings, and clothing offered visible proof of success.

With business affairs removed from the home and enough wealth that women's employment was not required, motherhood and women's devotion to it became more idealized in the middle class than it ever had been in the past. Women developed a "cult of domesticity" in which they devoted themselves to their children and to home décor—or supervised servants who did—as men became preoccupied with work and with male sociability. While bourgeois men and women did not always live up to these ideals, they did generally embrace them as a prescription appropriate for family life in the new industrial world. These ideals also became a basis for judgment of those who did not live up to them—the lower classes and errant women of all classes.

Industrialization transformed working-class life in ways very different from the middle classes. Many families could not afford to keep women and children at home as production became mechanized and left the household. The textile industries especially employed children and women in the lowliest positions, where they tended machines, tied broken threads, and performed menial tasks. Factory work often undermined the ability of working women to take care of their children. As farmers or cottagers, they had been able to work and supervise children simultaneously. When women had to leave the home to work, it was not uncommon for an older child, sometimes only 5 or 6 years of age, to be entrusted with the care of infants and toddlers. Urban and rural women sometimes resorted to more dangerous methods of child-care. Many mothers sent their children to wet nurses in the countryside, where—if they survived—they stayed for up to two years. The mortality of these babies was high, as they were often neglected. In France and Italy, the poorest of mothers—especially single mothers—abandoned their infants at foundling homes, which in turn sent them out to be wet nursed. In many cases, baby-farming was no more than a camouflaged form of infanticide. Mothers who kept their children, but were obliged to leave them unwatched at home during factory hours, sometimes pacified them with mixtures of opium, readily available from the local apothecary.

Women's work patterns, however, were sporadic; many only worked before their children were born, or after they grew older. Overall, relatively few women were in the wage market—by 1850, only about a quarter in both Britain and France. Of that quarter, few worked in factories; far more were in agriculture, crafts industries (which still flourished despite poor working conditions), and domestic service.

The textile industry employed children once they were over the age of 5 or 6. Their size and agility made them useful for certain jobs, such as reaching under machines to pick up loose cotton and replacing bobbins. Elizabeth Bentley began work as a doffer (bobbin replacer) in 1815 at the age of 6. At the age of 23, she testified before a parliamentary commission that she normally worked from 6:00 A.M. to 7:00 P.M., but for six months, worked sixteen-hour days, beginning at 5:00 A.M. She told the commission that children were strapped if they arrived late. She had only forty minutes at noon to eat, but said "I had not much to eat, and the little I had I could not eat it, my appetite was so poor. . . . " The commission noted that she was "considerably deformed . . . in consequence of this labor."[9] Child labor certainly did not start with the industrial transformation;

bourgeoisie   another word for the middle class, commonly associated with the rise of capitalism, industrialization, and the accumulation of wealth.

The Iron Forge　This 1772 painting by Joseph Wright of Derby depicts forge men converting pig iron to wrought iron. It glorifies the human power required to cast heavy objects. It also suggests the pride, dignity, and independence of the preindustrial forger, whose work not only allowed him to support his family, but blended with his unregimented everyday family life. This romanticized portrayal starkly contrasts with the much less dignified factory labor that would dominate textile and iron production.　(Wright of Derby, Joseph (1734–97)/Broadlands Trust, Hampshire, UK/The Bridgeman Art Library)

it had always existed. The stern industrial discipline imposed on the very young, however, was new. Children were subject to the clock, closely supervised and prevented from taking long breaks or mixing work and play—as had been possible in an earlier era. Although children commonly worked in British textile industries, overall, less than 10 percent of working children were employed in industrial work. Most were in agriculture or the service sector.

If not participating in the wage market, wives and children contributed in other ways to the household budget—by making clothes, raising a pig, tending a potato patch, and performing daily household chores. Grandparents often moved from the country to live with the family and take care of the children. When industrial workers married, they frequently settled with their spouses on the same street or in the same neighborhood as their own parents. Moreover, as in the putting-out system, whole families were often hired as a group to perform a specific function. Thus, although industry had the potential to break up traditional family bonds and structures, the historical evidence shows that the family generally adjusted and survived the challenges posed by the new economic system.

The Land, the Water, and the Air

Industrialization seriously disturbed the environment, transforming the surface of the earth, the water, and the air. The exploitation of coal, whose production rose fifteen-fold (see **TABLE 20.1**) ushered in the modern age of energy use, in which massive amounts of nonrenewable resources are consumed.

TABLE 20.1

Coal Production in Industrializing Nations

	Millions of Tons	Kilograms per Inhabitant
1700	4	26
1750	7	16
1800	16	76
1830	30	120
1860	129	390

Source: Based on B. R. Mitchell, "Statistical Appendix, 1700-1914," in *The Fontana Economic History of Europe*, ed. Carlo Cippola, vol. 4 (London: Collins, 1973), pp. 747, 770; and Norman J. G. Pounds, *An Historical Geography of Europe, 1500-1840* (New York: Cambridge University Press, 1979), pp. 268-269.

To meet the growing demand for coal, iron, and other minerals, miners dug deep tunnels, removing millions of tons of earth, rock, and other debris. This material, plus slag and other waste from the factories, was heaped up in mounds that at times covered acres, transforming the landscape into geological blight. Mining also increased the demand for wood to build shafts or to convert to charcoal. Between 1750 and 1900, industrial and agricultural needs led to the clearing of 50 percent of all the forests ever cleared. Deforestation in turn sped up soil erosion.

Forests, lakes, rivers, and air—as well as people themselves—displayed the scars of industry. Centrifugal pumps drained large marshes in eastern England. A contemporary lamented, "The wind which, in the autumn of 1851 was curling the blue water of the lake, in the autumn of 1853 was blowing in the same place over fields of yellow corn." Factory odors and chemicals fouled the air at several miles' distance, sometimes killing trees. Waste ash, dumped into rivers, changed their channels and made them considerably shallower. Because of pollution from industrial and human waste, by 1850, no fish could survive in the lower Thames River. Not merely unpleasant, these various pollutants caused cancer and lung diseases, though the connection between pollutants and disease was not yet understood.

A Changing Sense of Time

In agrarian societies, time was measured in terms of natural occurrences, such as sunrise and sunset, or the time it might take to milk a cow. With industrialization, punctuality became essential. Shifts of labor had to be rotated to keep the smelters going; they could not stop, or the molten iron would harden at the bottom of the hearths. The interactive nature of industrial production, in which workers with differing specialties each performed a particular task in finishing a product, made it necessary for employees to be at the factory at an appointed time. Factory rules often reflected an obsession with the efficient use of time. Lateness or idleness, and even conversation between workers, could be cause for dismissal.

Clocks in church towers and municipal buildings were installed as early as the fourteenth century, but they were not very reliable until the eighteenth century. Men of property and even some artisans commonly owned watches; as their prices dropped by the mid-nineteenth century, many workers could afford them. And even when workers did not own timepieces, they were intensely aware of time. Those who ignored time were fined or fired from their jobs. People listened for the church bell or factory whistle or asked a neighbor or passerby for the time. Western societies increasingly regularized and internalized the sense of time.

SECTION SUMMARY

- Industrialization, as well as commerce and the growth of administrative bureaucracy, caused urbanization; overcrowded and unsanitary conditions spread infectious diseases and gave rise to fears about the poor becoming criminal.

- Industrialization ultimately raised living standards, but its early stages disrupted workers' lives by mechanizing traditional forms of production, which rendered some artisanal skills obsolete and caused systematic unemployment and poverty.

- By removing production from the home, industrialization reshaped middle-class families by making gender roles more distinct; it also often forced women and children of the lower classes into low-paying factory jobs.

- Industrial production, particularly the consumption of nonrenewable resources such as coal, transformed the environment and polluted the earth, water, and air.

- Mechanical modes of production transformed the sense of time; they allowed work to be organized in long shifts that required discipline and rigid punctuality.

RESPONSES TO INDUSTRIALIZATION

What did workers gain and lose as a result of industrialization, and how did they respond?

People living at subsistence levels in urban slums offered visible and disquieting evidence of industrialization's social consequences. As middle-class reformers wondered how to contend with social ills, the working classes developed their own sense of a common interest and fate. The result was a resounding cry for political and social democracy that began in the first half of the nineteenth century and became increasingly insistent—and sometimes violent.

The Growth of Working-Class Solidarity

Hardest hit by economic changes, workers sought to improve their conditions by organizing and articulating their needs. In the preindustrial economy, artisans and craftsmen lived in an accepted hierarchy with prescribed rules. They began by serving for a certain number of years as apprentices to a master, next became journeymen, and finally, with hard work and good fortune, became masters of their trades. As tradesmen with common interests, they tended to band together into brotherhoods, promising one another help and trying to improve their working conditions.

Guilds, already weakened by the putting-out system, declined further with industrialization. Unlike the skilled handicrafts that required years of apprenticeship, few aspects of industrial production demanded extensive training. The system of dependence between apprentice and master became irrelevant. Guilds, trying to protect their members, often resisted new technologies and came to be seen as a hindrance to economic development. Liberal economists viewed them as constraints on trade and on the free flow of labor. For this reason, the French abolished guilds during the Revolution of 1789. Throughout the eighteenth century, the British Parliament also passed various acts against "combinations" by workmen. While guilds faded in importance, the solidarity and language born of the guild continued to shape workers' attitudes throughout much of the nineteenth century. New experiences also reinforced the sense of belonging to a group and sharing common aspirations.

Cultural forces, such as shared religious practice, further fostered workers' sense of solidarity. Religious sects flourished in an environment of despair punctuated by hopes of deliverance. Some historians believe that the growth of Methodism in England in the 1790s (see page 594) was a response to grim economic conditions. Emphasis on equality before God fueled the sense of injustice in a world where a privileged few lived in luxury, while others were condemned to work along with their children for a pittance. In France, workers believed the new society would come about by their martyrdom; like Jesus, the workers would suffer, and from their suffering would emerge a new, better society. Religious themes and language continued to be important in labor organization for many years.

Other cultural and social factors created bonds among workers. Urban workers lived close together, in similar conditions, either in the center of cities or in the outlying areas near factories. They grew close by spending their leisure time together, drinking in pubs, attending theaters and new forms of popular entertainment, such as the circus, or watching traditional blood sports, such as boxing or cockfights. Sports became popular as both spectator and participatory events in the 1880s. Soccer, which developed in England at this time, drew players and fans overwhelmingly from the working classes.

friendly societies
Nineteenth-century organizations formed by workers; members pooled their resources to provide mutual aid.

Faced with the uncertainties of unemployment and job-related accidents, in addition to disease and other natural catastrophes, workers formed so-called **friendly societies** in which they pooled their resources to provide mutual aid. These societies, descendants of benefit organizations of the Middle Ages and Renaissance, combined business activity with feasts, drinking bouts, and other social functions.

Friendly societies had existed as early as the seventeenth century, but they became increasingly popular with industrialization. Initially organized to provide aid for workers in a particular trade, they soon included members from several crafts. In time, they federated into national organizations, so that a worker who moved to a new town could continue membership

Leisure Activity for the Working Poor   With few outlets for leisure in the early nineteenth century, the lower classes turned to some harsh forms of entertainment. Scores of working-class spectators came to see the celebrated dog "Billy" kill a hundred rats at one time at the Westminster Pit in London in 1822.   (© Courtesy of the Trustees of the British Library)

in the new locale. Connected by common membership in friendly societies, workers came to identify with the difficulties of those outside their own occupation; a self-conscious working class was in the making.

Collective Action

Militant and in some cases violent action strengthened workers' solidarity. Since they did not have the vote, they could not express their grievances through official political channels, and their frustrated efforts to improve their own work and living conditions underscored their common plight.

In 1811 and 1812, British hand weavers, in reaction against mechanized looms, organized in groups claiming to be led by a mythical General Ned Ludd. In the name of economic justice and to protect their livelihood, the **Luddites**, as the general's followers were called, smashed machines or threatened to do so. German weavers went on machine-crushing campaigns in the 1830s and 1840s.

In Lyon, France, in 1831 and 1834, workers led insurrections to demand fair wages for piecework. Angered when the silk merchants lowered the amount they would pay, the workers marched in the streets bearing banners proclaiming "Live Working or Die Fighting." The government sent troops to restore order to the riot-torn city. Although conditions of the silk trade had been the immediate impetus for the uprising, the workers appealed for help to their fellow workers in other trades, who joined in the protests.

Labor agitation in much of Europe increased in the 1840s. A major strike wave involving twenty thousand workers broke out in Paris in 1840. In the summer of 1842, an industrial downturn in England led to massive unemployment and rioting. During the summer of 1844, in Silesia, in eastern Prussia, linen hand-loom weavers, desperate because of worsening

Luddites   Organized groups of British workers who smashed machines that threatened their livelihood. The name comes from their mythical leader, General Ned Ludd.

Unionization Membership Certificate Pictured here is an elaborate certificate for membership in the Amalgamated Society of Engineers. Note the wide array of symbolism and allegory on which it draws, with images of classical antiquity, Greek mythology, and the modern material culture of the nineteenth century. (Eileen Tweedy/The Art Archive/Picture Desk)

conditions brought on by competition from machine-made cotton fabrics, attacked the homes of the wealthy. In 1855, in Barcelona, the government tried to dissolve unions, and fifty thousand workers went on strike, carrying placards that warned "Association or Death."

Economic problems were not the only concern of laboring people. Some employers compelled workers to conform to severe discipline even outside the workplace. In some cases, they were forbidden to read certain newspapers, compelled to attend religious services, and could marry only with the employer's permission. Workers resented the intrusiveness into their private lives and resisted these attempts at control. Unions provided a means to resist unreasonable regulation and secure decent wages and working conditions by organizing strikes and supporting members during work stoppages.

Although there were early attempts in Britain to organize unions on a national basis, most were centered on a single craft or a single industry. Because labor unions originated in the crafts tradition, the earliest members were skilled craftsmen who organized to protect their livelihoods from the challenge that industrialization posed. These craftsmen were usually literate and longtime residents of their communities. They provided the labor movement with much of its leadership and organization. Skilled craft workers also played a strong role in developing a sense of class-consciousness. The language and institutions that they had developed over decades, and sometimes over centuries, became the common heritage of workers in general.

Workers increasingly understood the powerful potential of organized labor. As a French workers' paper declared in 1847, "If workers came together and organized . . . nothing would be able to stop them." But unionization nonetheless faced formidable obstacles throughout the nineteenth century. Unions were illegal in Britain until 1825, in Prussia until 1859, and in France until the 1860s. Even where they were legal, authorities often used press censorship and armed force against strikers. Moreover, population growth made it difficult for workers to withhold labor lest they be replaced by others only too willing to take their places.

The working classes were, moreover, never a monolithic group. They consisted of people with varying skills, responsibilities, and incomes. Artisans, more highly paid and respected by employers, often looked upon unskilled workers with contempt. Most often work was segregated by sex, making it more difficult for women and men to share a common cause. Even when they worked side by side in the industrial workplace, male and female laborers usually felt little common identity. Men worried that women were undermining their earning power by accepting lower wages. They often excluded women from their unions. Men sometimes even went on strike to force employers to discharge women. Nor was there solidarity across nationalities. Foreign workers were not well informed about local conditions, or so desperate for work they were willing to overlook them. British workers were hostile toward the Irish, the French toward the Belgian and Italian immigrants. The hostility often led to anti-immigrant riots. Many forces fostered dissension among the working classes in the nineteenth century, undermining the potential effectiveness of unions.

Political action offered another means to seek justice. In the 1830s and 1840s, British and French workers agitated for the right to vote as a way to put themselves on equal footing with the privileged and to win better conditions. Their anger over their failure to win political representation strengthened working-class solidarity against the upper classes. Politically organized workers played a major role in the revolutions that would rock Europe in 1848 (see pages 607–612). They showed that their organizations were legitimate representatives of the people and that the government needed to concern itself with the workers' lot. In general, advocates of the lower classes upheld the ideal of a moral economy—one in which all who labored received a just wage and every person was assured a minimum level of well-being.

By the mid-nineteenth century, as noted in the "Visual Record" illustration of St. Giles on pages 574–575, the middle classes had developed a clear fear of workers and viewed them as a single class that threatened society. It was not unusual for members of the elite to refer to workers as "the swinish multitude" or, as the title of a popular English book put it, *The Great Unwashed* (1868). In France, reference was alternately made to "the dangerous classes" and "the laboring classes." Not just workers, but even the privileged, seemed to see relations between the groups as a form of class war.

SECTION SUMMARY

- As guilds declined (or were prohibited), new worker solidarities based on religion, language, a sense of social justice, and shared experiences provided the foundation for the emergence of trade unions.

- Workers at times resorted to violence in their effort to preserve more traditional modes of production and protect their right to work.

- Friendly societies and unions sought to provide health, accident, unemployment, and funeral benefits.

- Professional unionization faced the obstacles of government repression as well as the diversity of the labor force itself: skilled workers versus the unskilled; men versus women; nationals versus foreigners.

CHAPTER SUMMARY

Industrial transformation, which started around 1750 in parts of England, spread by 1850 to the Continent. The proximity of coal and iron, the relative ease of domestic transportation, a culture open to innovation and entrepreneurship, and the existence of an already relatively dynamic economy help explain why Britain was the first nation to industrialize, and why industrialization spread—at varying paces—to much of Europe. The new industrial economy changed power relations among European states and altered the relationship of Europe to the rest of the world.

FOCUS QUESTIONS

- What factors allowed Europe to industrialize before the rest of the world?

- Which inventions appear to have been the most important in launching industrialization?

- What impact did industrialization have on the environment and on social classes?

- What did workers gain and lose as a result of industrialization, and how did they respond?

A number of key inventions gave impetus to industrialization: John Kay's flying shuttle increased the production of weaving; James Hargreave's spinning jenny and Samuel Crompton's mule more than met the increased need for thread production; and power looms soon followed. The use of coal to process iron made possible the creation of iron machinery that could be powered by James Watt's steam engine, as well as stronger blast furnaces that could, in turn, improve iron processing.

The extraction and use of energy resources, such as coal, permanently transformed the human relationship with the environment, with consequences for land, air, and water. Industry also changed the nature of work for large numbers of Europeans. A decreasing number of people worked in agriculture, and more entered manufacturing, where machines replaced human energy. For the first time, European cities grew to more than one million inhabitants.

Industrialization created new social classes and transformed family lives, changing the roles of men, women, and children. It ultimately raised the standard of living across social classes, but in the short term, a large portion of the lower classes suffered low wages, geographical displacement, periodic unemployment, and overcrowding in the cramped, unsanitary housing of fast-growing towns and cities. Eager to improve their lives, workers began to organize into associations. The new proletarian class, shaped by industrialization, was a growing force that would challenge the existing order throughout the nineteenth century and much of the next.

 This icon will direct you to additional materials on the website: www .cengage.com/history/ noble/westciv6e

KEY TERMS

industrialization (p. 559)

putting-out system (p. 561)

dissenters (p. 564)

mass production (p. 564)

steam engine (p. 567)

factories (p. 567)

entrepreneurs (p. 567)

primogeniture (p. 569)

urbanization (p. 572)

proletariat (p. 573)

bourgeoisie (p. 577)

friendly societies (p. 580)

Luddites (p. 581)

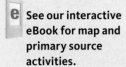 See our interactive eBook for map and primary source activities.

NOTES

1. Phyllis Deane, *The First Industrial Revolution* (Cambridge: Cambridge University Press, 1965), p. 1.

2. These ideas are provocatively developed in E. L. Jones, *The European Miracle: Environments, Economies and Geopolitics of Europe and Asia* (Cambridge: Cambridge University Press, 1981).

3. Adna Ferrin Weber, *The Growth of Cities in the Nineteenth Century: A Study in Statistics* (New York: Macmillan, 1899; repr., Ithaca, N.Y.: Cornell University Press, 1963), p. 1.

4. J. P. Kay, *The Moral and Physical Condition of the Working Classes Employed in the Cotton Manufacture in Manchester* (London: James Ridgway, 1832), pp. 6, 14–15, 19.

5. Friedrich Engels, *The Condition of the Working Class in England* (New York: Penguin, 1987; first published 1845).

6. Source: *http://www.victorianlondon.org/publications5/rookeries-03.htm*

7. Marie de Flavigny d'Agoult [Daniel Stern], *Histoire de la Révolution de 1848*, 2d ed., vol. 1 (Paris, 1862), p. 7, quoted in Theodore S. Hamerow, *The Birth of a New Europe: State and Society in the Nineteenth Century* (Chapel Hill: University of North Carolina Press, 1983), pp. 206–207.

8. Catherine Hall, "The Sweet Delights of Home," in *A History of Private Life: From the Fires of Revolution to the Great War*, ed. Michelle Perrot (Cambridge: Belknap Press, 1990), p. 74.

9. House of Commons, *Sessional Papers, 1831–32*, hearing of 4 June 1932, vol. 15, pp. 195–197.

21

Barricades in Vienna, Austria, May 1848

(Historisches Museum (Museen der Stadt Wien) Vienna/Gianni Dagli Orti/The Art Archive/Picture Desk)

Restoration, Reform, and Revolution, 1814–1848

In 1848, Europe experienced a revolutionary wave, unprecedented in over a half century since the heady days of the French Revolution. Workers, artisans, and even members of the middle classes poured into the streets to challenge authoritarian rulers and the militaries that tried to repress rebellion. As illustrated in the painting at the left, they built street barricades to defend themselves and to trap and attack military troops. Barricades, long a part of urban insurrectionary history, had almost become an art form. Revolutionaries systematically tore the paving stones from streets and beams from the façades of houses. To build the barricade, they confiscated passing omnibuses, carriages, and carts to pile rubble, along with empty barrels and casks. The barricades they built sometimes rose as high as nine feet.

In addition to its material reality, this painting represents the spirit present at the barricades, as well as in the revolutions as a whole. Its mixture of social classes and genders shows the inclusive camaraderie in conquering the streets, as even fraternizing soldiers listen attentively to the speaker atop the rubble. The neatly piled shovels and signs of meal preparation suggest a systematic order in the midst of a chaos that is only apparent. The figure hung in effigy reminds the viewer of the seriousness of the event. Scenes such as this burst forth in major cities throughout western and eastern Europe.

The revolutions of 1848 had their ideological origins in the irrepressible forces unleashed in the Revolution of 1789. With the end of the Napoleonic Wars in 1815, the victorious Great Powers—Austria, Great Britain, Prussia, and Russia—tried to reestablish as much of the old European state system as possible. The international arrangements they carved out at the Congress of Vienna were soon shaken by outbreaks of nationalist fervor. Nationalists aimed either to create larger political units, as in Italy and Germany, or to win independence from foreign rule, as in Greece. In addition to nationalism, which had in part been sparked by Napoleonic reforms, other new ideologies, such as romanticism, liberalism, and socialism, born of the Enlightenment and French Revolution, prevented a complete restoration of the old order. (An ideology is a structured, organized set of ideas that reflects a group's thinking about life or society.) The ideologies that helped promote revolution continued to shape development in the second half of the century, as well as throughout the twentieth.

As revolution swept through Europe, a similar pattern took place: After the first exhilarating moments of emancipation from authoritarian monarchies, conflict, disappointment, and failure allowed the forces of reaction and repression to take control. Revolutionaries did not win all their goals, and in many cases, the forces of order crushed them. Yet by midcentury, major intellectual, social, and political changes had occurred.

FOCUS QUESTIONS

- What were the goals of the Restoration, and the sources of resistance to it?

- What major ideologies developed in the first half of the nineteenth century?

- How did the restorations that followed the Napoleonic era give way to reform?

- What were the main causes of the revolutions of 1848, and what roles did nationalism, liberalism, and socialism play in inciting and sustaining revolution?

This icon will direct you to additional materials on the website: www .cengage.com/history/ noble/westciv6e.

See our interactive eBook for map and primary source activities.

RESTORATION AND REACTION, 1814–1830

What were the goals of the Restoration, and the sources of resistance to it?

Bby the end of the French Revolution and Napoleonic wars, the ruling elite believed that the upheavals of the previous twenty-five years had proved that human beings could not rely on reason, on man-made constitutions, or on laws to govern themselves. They therefore sought to restore the order of the past by redrawing territorial boundaries to establish a balance of power among the Great Powers, and reinstating the traditional foundations of hierarchy that would assure stability: religion, monarchy, and aristocracy. But members of the middle and working classes, especially in cities, resisted the effort to turn the clock back.

The Congress of Vienna, 1814–1815

Congress of Vienna
Conference called by the Great Powers after Napoleon's defeat. They sought long-term stability as they drew new territorial boundaries and restored some of the rulers who had been overthrown.

The defeat of Napoleon put an end to French dominance in Europe. In September 1814, the victorious Great Powers—Austria, Great Britain, Prussia, and Russia—convened an international conference, the **Congress of Vienna**, to negotiate the terms of peace. The victors sought to draw territorial boundaries advantageous to themselves and to provide long-term stability on the European continent. Having faced a powerful France, which had mobilized popular forces with revolutionary principles, the victors decided to erect an international system that would remove such threats. Following principles of "legitimacy and compensation," they redrew the map of Europe (see **MAP 21.1**). Rulers who had been overthrown were restored to their thrones. The eldest surviving brother of Louis XVI of France became King Louis XVIII. In Spain, Ferdinand VII was restored to the throne from which Napoleon had toppled him and his father. The restoration, however, was not as complete as its proponents claimed. After the French Revolution, certain new realities had to be recognized. For example, Napoleon had consolidated the German and Italian states; the process was acknowledged in the former with the creation of a loose German Confederation. In Italy, the number of independent states had shrunk to nine. Also, unlike earlier French kings, Louis XVIII could not rule as an absolute monarch after a generation without one.

Negotiations at the Congress of Vienna strengthened the territories bordering France, enlarged Prussia and created the kingdom of Piedmont-Sardinia, joined Belgium to Holland, and provided the victors with spoils and compensation for territories bartered away. Austria received Venetia and Lombardy in northern Italy to strengthen its position and to redress the loss of Belgium (to the Netherlands) and parts of Poland (to Russia). Prussia was allowed to annex part of Saxony, Posen, and the port city of Danzig in return for giving up parts of Poland. England acquired a number of colonies and naval out posts. Thus, with one hand, these conservative statesmen swore their loyalty to the prerevolutionary past, and with the other, they redrew national boundaries with no consideration for the inhabitants whose territories changed.

The leading personality at the Congress of Vienna was the Austrian foreign minister, Prince Clemens von Metternich (MEH-ter-nick) (1773–1859). An aristocrat in exile from the Rhineland, which had been annexed by revolutionary France, he had gone into the service of the Habsburg Empire and risen to become its highest official. Personal charm, tact, and representation of a state that, for the time being, was satisfied with its territories made Metternich seem a disinterested statesman and enabled him to wield enormous influence on the congress's proceedings.

Because it was Napoleon's belligerent imperialism that had brought the powers together in Vienna, France was at first treated as an enemy at the conference. By the end, however, France was included as one of the five Great Powers jointly known as the "Concert of Europe." The Concert continued to function for nearly forty years, meeting and resolving international crises and preventing any major European war from breaking out. Underlying the states' cooperation was the principle of a common European destiny.

Restored Monarchs in Western Europe

The most dramatic restoration of the older order occurred in France. The restored Bourbons turned the clock back, not to 1789 but closer to 1791, when the country had briefly enjoyed a constitutional monarchy. Moreover, it maintained the Napoleonic Code with its provisions of legal equality.

The Bourbon constitution provided for a parliament with an elected lower house, the Chamber of Deputies, and an appointed upper house, the Chamber of Peers. Although suffrage to the Chamber of Deputies was limited to a small elite of men with landed property—only 100,000 voters, about 0.2 percent of the population—this constitution was a concession to representative government that had not existed in the Old Regime (see page 534). Louis XVIII (r. 1814–1824) stands out among European rulers because he realized that it would be necessary to compromise on the principles of popular sovereignty proclaimed by the French Revolution.

Compared with the rest of Europe, Great Britain enjoyed considerable constitutional guarantees and a parliamentary regime. Social unrest beset Britain as it faced serious economic dislocation with the arrival of peace in 1815. The sudden drop in government expenditures, the return into the economy of several hundred thousand war veterans, financial disarray, and plummeting prices caused disruption for the poor and the middle classes. They were especially incensed over the clear economic advantages that the landed classes, who dominated Parliament, had secured for themselves. In 1815, the Parliament passed legislation—known as the **Corn Laws**—that imposed high tariffs on various forms of imported grain. These laws shielded landowning grain producers from international competition and allowed them to reap huge profits at the expense of consumers.

All these issues caused various forms of protest. Workers and the urban middle classes found their government retrograde and repressive. Traumatized by the French Revolution, the ruling class clung to the past, certain that advocates for change were Jacobins in disguise wishing to foment revolution.

In August 1819, sixty thousand people gathered in St. Peter's Fields in Manchester to demand universal suffrage for men and women alike, an annual Parliament, and other democratic reforms. The crowd was peaceful and unarmed, yet mounted soldiers charged, killing eleven and wounding four hundred. The use of military force against the peaceful demonstrators as if they were the French at Waterloo shocked and outraged the British public, and they branded the confrontation "the Peterloo Massacre." Parliament responded by passing the so-called Six Acts, which outlawed freedom of assembly and effectively imposed censorship. Through much of the 1820s, Britain appeared resistant to reform.

CHRONOLOGY

1808	Beethoven, *Pastoral* Symphony
1814–1815	Congress of Vienna
1819	Peterloo Massacre
	Carlsbad Decrees
1821	Spanish revolt
	Greek Revolution
1821–1825	Spanish colonies in the Americas win independence
1823	Monroe Doctrine
1824	Owen establishes New Harmony
1825	Decembrists in Russia
1830	July Revolution in France
	Ottoman Empire recognizes Serbian autonomy
1832	Great Reform Bill in Britain
1833	Abolition of slavery in British colonies
1834	Turner, *Fire at Sea*
1838	"People's charter" in Great Britain
1839	Anti-Corn Law League
1845–1848	Hungry '40s
1848	Marx and Engels, *Communist Manifesto*
	Revolutions of 1848

Corn Laws Laws passed by the British Parliament in 1815 that placed tariffs on imported foreign grains to protect domestic grain producers from international competition.

Eastern Europe

Having seen the turmoil unleashed by the French Revolution and having suffered at the hands of Napoleon's Grande Armée, the states of central and eastern Europe were particularly committed to maintaining absolute government. The Austrian Empire's far-flung territories seemed to its Habsburg rulers to require a firm hand (see **Map 21.1**); they could countenance no challenge or threat to their imperial power in the wake of French revolutionary rhetoric about liberty. Nor, in this multinational empire, could rulers tolerate a sense of national identity provoked by the Napoleonic wars. The emperor, Francis I (r. 1792–1835), clung to his motto, "Rule and change nothing." Prince Metternich, Francis's chief minister and key figure in the "Concert of Europe" from 1815, viewed the French Revolution of 1789 as a disaster and believed his task was to hold the line against the threat of revolution. Quick to interpret protests or the desire for change as a threat to the fundamental order, Metternich established a network of secret police and informers to spy on the imperial subjects and keep them in check.

🌐 MAP 21.1—Europe in 1815

Intent on regaining the security and stability of prerevolutionary years, the Great Powers redrew the map of Europe at the Congress of Vienna.

In most of the German states, the political order was similarly authoritarian and inflexible. The states of Baden, Württemberg, and Bavaria had granted their subjects constitutions, although effective power remained in the hands of the ruling houses. Prussia was ruled by an alliance of the king and the *Junkers* (YUNG-kurz), the landowning aristocrats who staffed the officer corps and the bureaucracy. Their administrative efficiency earned widespread admiration in Europe. But throughout the German states, the urban middle classes, intellectuals, journalists, university professors, and students were frustrated with the existing system. They were disappointed by the lack of free institutions and the failure of the patriotic wars against Napoleon to create a united Germany. University students formed *Burschenschaften* (BOOR-shen-shaft-en), or brotherhoods, whose slogan was "Honor, Liberty, Fatherland." Metternich reacted swiftly in July 1819 with the Carlsbad Decrees; these decrees established close supervision over the universities, censorship of the press, and dissolution of the youth groups. Wholesale persecution of people who advocated representative government or nationalistic ideas followed. The Prussian king dismissed his more enlightened officials.

Italy, by the end of Napoleon's reign, consisted of nine political states; the consolidation of states and the influence of Napoleonic rule had begun to inspire among some Italians a notion of national identity. At the same time, Austria exercised considerable power over Italy through its possession, from the Congress of Vienna, of its northern territories, Lombardy and Venetia. Austria also had dynastic ties to several ruling houses in the central part of the peninsula, and had political alliances with the papacy. The only ruling house free of Austrian ties—and hence, eventually looked to by nationalists as a possible rallying point for the independence of the peninsula—was the Savoy dynasty of Piedmont-Sardinia. But it was in Austria's interest to maintain disunity.

By far the most autocratic of the European states was tsarist Russia. Alexander I (r. 1801–1825) was an enigmatic character who puzzled his contemporaries. His domestic policy vacillated between liberalism and reaction; his foreign policy wavered between brutal power politics and apparently selfless idealism. When the Congress of Vienna gave additional Polish lands to the tsar, establishing the kingdom of Poland, he demonstrated his liberalism to the world (and curried favor with his new subjects) by granting Poland a liberal constitution. But he offered no such constitution to his own people. Within a few years, moreover, he violated the same Polish constitution he had approved, by refusing

Metternich　A consummate statesman and aristocrat, the Austrian prince Metternich tried to quell revolution at home and abroad. Some called his era the Metternichean age. (Réunion des Musées Nationaux/Art Resource, NY)

"Peterloo" Massacre　In August 1819 at St. Peter's Fields in Manchester, England, a crowd demanding parliamentary reform was charged by government troops, leading to bloodshed.　(The National Archives, Public Record Office)

to call the Diet into session. His planned efforts to abolish serfdom between 1803 and 1812 also failed. As much as he desired freedom for serfs, he was unwilling to impose the necessary policies toward that end because they would be detrimental to the interests and privileges of the landed gentry.

Toward the end of his rule, Alexander became increasingly authoritarian and repressive, probably in response to growing opposition. Myriad groups—Russian military officers who had served in western Europe, Russian Freemasons who had corresponded with Masonic lodges in western Europe, and Russian intellectuals who read Western liberal political tracts—had warmed to the ideals of individual freedom and constitutionalism. These groups formed secret societies with varying agendas. Some envisioned Russia as a republic, others as a constitutional monarchy, but all shared a commitment to the abolition of serfdom and the establishment of a freer society.

Alexander died in December 1825, without designating which of his brothers would succeed him. Taking advantage of the confusion, the military conspirators declared in favor of the older brother, Constantine, in the belief that he favored a constitutional government. The younger brother, Nicholas, claimed to be the legal heir. The St. Petersburg garrison, whose officers believed that the military could bring about change on its own, rallied to the conspirators' cause.

Decembrists Group of Russian military officers, later viewed as martyrs, who led the unsuccessful December 1825 rebellion seeking to install a constitutional monarchy.

The "Decembrist uprising," as it is known, quickly failed. The military revolt in the Russian capital was badly coordinated with uprisings planned in the countryside, and Nicholas moved quickly to crush the rebellion. He had the leaders, called the **Decembrists**, executed, sent to Siberia, or exiled. In spite of its tragic end, throughout the nineteenth century, the Decembrist uprising served as an inspiration to Russians resisting tsarist oppression.

Spain and Its Colonies

Spain, under the Napoleonic occupation, had in 1812 elected a national parliament, the Cortes. It issued a democratic constitution that provided for universal manhood suffrage and a unicameral legislature with control over government policy. Supporters and admirers of the constitution in Spain were known as "friends of liberty," and the term *liberal* was coined. But in 1814, Ferdinand VII (r. 1808, 1814–1833), the Bourbon king of Spain whom Napoleon had ousted, returned to power. Though he promised to respect the liberal 1812 constitution, Ferdinand believed in the divine right of kings and was hostile to the new order. With support from the aristocracy and from segments of the general population still loyal to the call of throne and altar, Ferdinand had liberals arrested or driven into exile.

Ferdinand's plan to restore Spain to its earlier prominence included a reassertion of control over its American colonies. The Spanish dominions had grown restless in the eighteenth century, for they had witnessed the advent of an independent United States and the French occupation of Spain itself. Spain's emboldened colonies had refused to recognize the Napoleonic regime in Madrid and became increasingly self-reliant. Their attitude did not change when French control of Spain ended. Ferdinand refused to compromise with the overseas territories. Instead, he gathered an army to subdue them. Some liberal junior officers, declaring the army's loyalty to the constitution of 1812, won support from the rank and file, who balked at going overseas. This military mutiny coincided with a sympathetic provincial uprising to produce the "revolution of 1820," the first major assault on the European order established in 1815 at the Congress of Vienna. Ferdinand appealed to the European powers for help. France intervened on his behalf and crushed the uprising.

Ferdinand restored his reactionary regime but could not regain Spain's American colonies. The British, sympathetic to the cause of Latin American independence and eager for commercial access to the region, opposed reconquest, and their naval dominance of the seas kept Spain in its place. By 1825, all of Spain's colonies on the mainland in Central and South America had won their freedom.

SECTION SUMMARY

- At the Congress of Vienna (1814–1815), Austria, Great Britain, Prussia, and Russia, having defeated Napoleon, redrew territorial boundaries for their own advantage and restored previous rulers to create stability.

- Western Europe had constitutional monarchies, though they faced a variety of social and political discontents.

- Eastern Europe remained committed to absolutist monarchies that took measures to repress any protest or revival of revolutionary thinking.

- Spain returned to absolute monarchy, exiling liberals, but lost its American colonies.

IDEOLOGICAL CONFRONTATIONS

What major ideologies developed in the first half of the nineteenth century?

The conservative order established in 1815 was inspired by the desire of rulers to return to the past. But the appeal of Enlightenment ideals never faded completely, nor did the promises of revolutionary reform. Those who challenged the restored order did so through a number of ideologies responding to the economic and political turmoil of the era.

Conservatism

The architects of the restoration justified their policies with doctrines based on the ideology of **conservatism**, emphasizing the need to preserve the existing order of monarchies, aristocracy, and an established church. As a coherent movement, conservatism sprang up during and after the French Revolution to resist the forces of change. Before the American and French Revolutions, the existing political institutions appeared to be permanent. When the old order faced serious challenges in the late eighteenth and early nineteenth centuries, conservatism emerged as an ideology justifying traditional authority.

Edmund Burke (1729–1797), a British statesman and political theorist, launched one of the first intellectual assaults on the French Revolution. The revolutionary National Assembly had asserted that ancient prerogatives were superseded by the rights of man and principles of human equality based on appeals to natural law. In *Reflections on the Revolution in France* (1790), Burke countered that such claims were abstract and dangerous and that the belief in human equality undermined the social order. Government should be anchored in tradition, he argued. The very longevity of Old Regime institutions proved their usefulness, and they should be preserved. Burke's writings were widely read and influential on the Continent.

Reaction against the French Revolution also inspired a moral and religious conservatism. One of the most popular authors of this new morality was Hannah More (1745–1833), who saw piety as a rampart against rebellion. In a series of pamphlets titled *Cheap Repository Tracts*, she advocated the acceptance of the existing order and the solace of religious faith. Costing but a penny, the moral tracts were often handed out by the rich together with alms or food to the poor. More was the first writer in history to sell over a million copies; within three years, her sales doubled. Conservative values thus spread to a very large audience in both Britain and the United States, where one of her works appeared in thirty editions.

A more extreme version of conservatism was the counterrevolutionary or "ultraroyalist" ideology. Unlike Burke, who was willing to tolerate some change, counterrevolutionaries wanted to restore society to its prerevolutionary condition. The most extreme counterrevolutionaries were those who personally experienced the revolutionary upheavals. Count Joseph de Maistre (MESS-treh) (1753–1821), a nobleman whose estates were occupied by the invading French, described monarchy as a God-given form of government in his *Considerations on France* (1796). Any attempt to abolish or even limit it was a violation of divine law. According to de Maistre and his fellow reactionaries, only the authority of church and state could prevent human beings from falling into evil ways. De Maistre advocated stern government control, including the generous use of the death penalty, to keep people loyal to throne and altar.

Conservative ideas were not limited to intellectual circles; at times they had mass appeal, even for the peasantry. Especially in bourgeois and aristocratic circles, conservatism extended to private life, and placed priority on family stability, with a strict separation of gender roles and a strong sense of patriarchy, in which the husband and father held exclusive authority. Conservatism was also influenced by **romanticism**, with its glorification of the past, taste for pageantry, and belief in the organic unity of society.

Romanticism

The romantic movement emerged in the 1760s as a rebellion against the rationalist values of the Enlightenment, and persisted until the 1840s. Primarily an expression of the arts, it included writers, painters, and composers. In contrast to the philosophes and their emphasis on reason (see

conservatism Ideology underlying the order established in Europe in 1815, which afterward emphasized support for the existing order of monarchy, aristocracy, and an established church.

romanticism Cultural movement, prevalent from the 1760s to 1840s, that rebelled against rationalism and its Enlightenment values and prized sentiment.

Lord Byron in Albanian Costume The British romantic poet had himself painted in exotic garb. Romantics were attracted to what were believed to be the mysteries of the East, representing a truer, more authentic existence. (National Portrait Gallery, London)

Chapter 18), the romantics praised emotion and feeling. German writer Johann Wolfgang von Goethe (GOE-teh) (1749–1832), who declared, "Feeling is everything," offers a famous and influential example of this movement. His *Sorrows of Young Werther* (1774), the most widely read book of the era—Napoleon had a copy by his bedside—depicted the passions of the hero, who, depressed over unrequited love, kills himself. Many young men dressed in "Werther clothes"—tight black pants, long blue jacket, and buff yellow leather vest—which typified the clothing of tradesmen and provided a visual protest by young intellectuals against the frivolous dress of the upper classes. In some cases, they emulated the tragic hero by committing suicide.

Goethe and other writers exalted mythical figures as embodiments of human energy, passion, and heroism. In the dramatic poem, *Faust*, Goethe retold the legend of a man who sells his soul to the Devil in exchange for worldly success. In the poetic drama, *Prometheus Unbound*, the English romantic poet Percy Bysshe Shelley (1792–1822) took up a similar theme in celebrating Prometheus, who, according to Greek mythology, stole fire from the gods and gave it to human beings. In much the same spirit, many romantics lionized Napoleon for his military feats and ability to overthrow kings and states.

Many romantics drew their inspiration from nature. In contrast to the Enlightenment, whose philosophers and scientists had studied nature for the principles it could impart, the romantics worshiped its inherent beauty and formidable power. The German composer Ludwig van Beethoven (1770–1827) wrote his *Pastoral* Symphony in praise of idyllic nature, depicting the passions one might feel in contemplating its loveliness and serenity. The English poets William Wordsworth (1770–1850) and Samuel Taylor Coleridge (1772–1834) treated untamed wilderness as a particular subject of wonder. Fellow Englishman Joseph Mallord William Turner (1775–1851) displayed the raw passions of the sea. Before painting *Snowstorm: Steamboat off a Harbour's Mouth* (1842), Turner is said to have tied himself to a ship's mast and braved a snowstorm for four hours.

Disillusionment with the French Revolution inspired many romantics to rediscover religion as an authentic source of emotion, a sensibility in accord with the revival of popular religion in regions throughout Europe. For example, the German states experienced a revival of pietism, which stressed the personal relationship between the individual and God, unimpeded by theological formalities or religious authorities. The influence of pietism, with its emphasis on spirituality and emotion, spread throughout central Europe in schools and churches.

In England, religious emotion expressed itself in Methodism. Founded in the 1730s by the English preacher John Wesley (1703–1791), this popular movement emphasized salvation by a faith made active in one's life, a method of living. Appealing especially to the poor and desperate, Methodism, by the 1790s, had gained seventy thousand members; within a generation its flock quadrupled.

Romantics also celebrated the medieval past; artists painted images of Gothic ruins and buildings, while architects replicated its style in both private and public buildings. Writers, such as Sir Walter Scott (1771–1832) in Scotland and Victor Hugo (U-go) (1802–1885), recaptured chivalry and the age of faith in such popular works as *Ivanhoe* (1819) and *The Hunchback of Notre Dame* (1831). Exotic places also had great appeal to romantics. Recently conquered Algeria in North Africa provided scenes for French painters. Senegal, in West Africa, which the French recovered from the British in 1815, offered the setting for Théodore Géricault's powerful *Raft of the "Medusa."* (See the feature, "The Visual Record: *Raft of the 'Medusa.'*")

Romantics challenged the cultural order in a number of ways. Appeals to emotion and sentiment were congenial to audiences without elite educations, especially as a new interest developed in folklore and rustic life. Viennese-born Franz Schubert (1797–1828) composed over 600 songs that echo the simplicity of folk tunes, and Frédéric Chopin (1810–1849) composed works influenced by the peasant music of his native Poland. The performance of romantic music in masses, symphonies, operas, choral groups, and even gatherings among friends in private homes grew considerably in the first half of the nineteenth century. Its popularity helped support musicians, not just in their performances, but in providing private music lessons, especially at the piano, whose presence became increasingly common in middle-class homes.

Romantic culture also found expression in relations between the sexes. The influential French writer Amandine-Aurore Dupin (1804–1876), better known by her pen name, George Sand (SAN), spoke for the emancipation of women from the oppressive supervision of their husbands, fathers, and brothers. In her personal life, Sand practiced the freedom she preached, dressing like a man, smoking cigars, and openly pursuing affairs with a number of well-known artists. But her many literary works also expressed her hopes for spiritual and political renewal, bearing the romantic era's utopian aspirations.

After the French Revolution, nobles and monarchs ceased sponsoring art on a grand scale and were expected to conduct their lives soberly. Cut off from royal patronage, artists had to depend on members of the new middle classes to buy paintings and books and attend plays and musical performances. Forced to live marginally, they cultivated the image of the artist as unconventional. In their lifestyles and their work, they deliberately rejected the norms of society. The romantic period gave rise to the notion of the starving genius, alienated from society and loyal only to his all-consuming art. Born of conservative reaction against the Enlightenment and French Revolution, romanticism also embodied the modern notions of liberty and appealed to an emerging sense of national identity. Romantics of many stripes declared their determination to overthrow the smug present and create a new world. Victor Hugo called for "no more rules, no more models" to constrain the human imagination. Romantic painters and musicians consciously turned their backs on the classical tradition in both subject matter and style. The English poet George Gordon, Lord Byron (1788–1824), declared war on kings, on established religion, and on the international order. A nationalist as well as a romantic, he died while fighting for the independence of Greece.

Nationalism

The ideology of nationalism emerged in, and partly shaped, this era. **Nationalism** is the belief that people derive their identity from their nation and owe it their primary loyalty. A list of criteria for nationhood is likely to include a common language, religion, and political authority, as well as common traditions and shared historical experiences.

In an era that saw the undermining of traditional religious values, nationalism offered a new locus of faith. To people who experienced the social turmoil brought about by the erosion of the old order, nationalism held out the promise of a new community. Nationalism became an ideal espoused as strongly as, and often in conjunction with, religion. The Italian nationalist Giuseppe Mazzini (mat-SEE-nee) (1805–1872) declared that nationalism was "a faith and mission" ordained by God. The Polish romantic poet and nationalist Adam Mickiewicz (MISS-kyev-ich) (1798–1855) compared perpetually carved-up Poland to the crucified Christ. The religious-like fervor of nationalism helps explain its widespread appeal.

The earliest manifestation of nationalism was cultural, originating in Rousseau's concept of the "general will" constituting the sovereign nation, greater than the sum of its parts. Johann Gottfried Herder (1744–1833), Rousseau's German disciple, elaborated on his mentor's ideas, declaring that every people has a "national spirit." To explore the unique nature of this spirit, intellectuals all over Europe began collecting local folk poems, songs, and tales, a trend also inspired by romanticism. In an effort to document the spirit of the German people, the Grimm brothers, Jacob (1785–1863) and Wilhelm (1786–1859), compiled fairy tales and published them between 1812 and 1818; among the better known are "Little Red Riding Hood" and "Snow White."

Political nationalism was born in the era of the French Revolution. French aristocrats resisted taxation by claiming that they embodied the rights of "the nation" and could not be taxed without its consent, which in turn gave the concept a currency that spread across all social classes. When revolutionary France was attacked by neighboring countries, which were ruled by kings and dukes, the Legislative Assembly called on the French people to rise and save the nation. The kingdom of France had become a nation of citizens who had a stake in its destiny. German and Italian intellectuals, in reaction to the French threat, developed a nationalist spirit. German philosopher Johann Gottlieb Fichte (FISH-te) (1762–1814), in a series of *Addresses to the German Nation* after the Prussian defeat at Jena, called on all Germans to stand firm against Napoleon. Germans, he claimed, were endowed with a special genius that had to be safeguarded

nationalism Belief that people derive their identity from their nation and owe it their primary loyalty. The criteria for nationhood typically included a common language, religion, and political authority, as well as common traditions and shared historical experiences.

Raft of the "Medusa"

In September 1816, the French were shocked at the news of the disaster that had befallen the government ship Méduse (Medusa) as it headed for Senegal in West Africa the previous July. Including the ship's crew, 400 passengers had boarded the vessel.

The captain of the ship was a nobleman, Duroys de Chaumareys (du-RWAH duh sho-mah-RAY), whom the restoration government had appointed solely on the basis of his family and political connections. Inexperienced as a seaman, the captain clumsily ran his ship aground on the Mauritanian coast, off West Africa, on July 2. The *Medusa* had only 6 lifeboats, capable of carrying a total of 250 people. For the rest of the passengers, a raft was rigged with planks, beams, and ropes. The captain and his officers forcibly took over the lifeboats, abandoning 150 passengers to the less secure raft. With no navigational tools and insufficient food and water, the passengers of the raft were left to the mercy of stormy seas and a brutal sun. Anger at officers for having abandoned them led seamen on the raft to murder some of their superiors. By the third day, driven by thirst and hunger, some passengers ate their dead companions—killed by exposure or drowned by huge waves. On the sixth day, the strongest among the survivors, fearing that their rations were dwindling, banded together and murdered the weaker ones. On the thirteenth day, the French frigate *Argus* spotted the raft and rescued 15 survivors. Five died soon after, leaving only 10 survivors out of the raft's original 150 passengers.

Although the government tried to suppress information about the event, the French press exposed the incompetence and cowardice of Captain de Chaumareys—reflecting the bad judgment of the Bourbon regime that had appointed him on the basis of his family status rather than experience. The selfish act of the captain and his fellow officers further suggested the narrow class interest of the restoration government, which favored aristocracy at the cost of the common people.

The French painter Théodore Géricault (1791–1824) befriended the ship's surgeon, Henri Savigny, one of the lucky ten who survived. Savigny provided Géricault (jair-ih-KO) with a direct eyewitness account of the event. The painter shared Savigny's sense of outrage against the government for having appointed the incompetent captain and for having treated the survivors callously. (At one point, the government arrested Savigny for publicizing the tragedy.) The light prison sentence imposed on the captain was another source of grievance.

The 1819 French government salon exposition of art was intended to be larger and more glorious than any previous one. Among its paintings was Géricault's huge canvas—the largest in that year's exposition—measuring 16 feet high by 24 feet wide and innocently titled "Scene of Shipwreck." The regime had wanted to gain glory for itself by exhibiting this impressive artwork without exposing the true subject. But the stratagem failed; everyone recognized the painting to be the *Raft of the "Medusa"* and an attack on the Bourbon regime.

The painting reproduced here depicts the moment the survivors spotted the frigate *Argus*, barely visible on the horizon. Notice the figure of an African standing at the fore of the raft, waving a red and white cloth to attract the ship's attention. The hope he symbolizes represents an attack on the slave trade, in which France was still engaged. The artist implicitly criticized the restoration regime for sanctioning commerce in humans. Just as the *Argus* is coming to the rescue of the shipwrecked, the painting appears to suggest, so Africans will see the day when their enslavement will be ended.

Historians often regard the *Raft of the "Medusa"* as the most important painting of French romanticism, and it includes nearly all the major themes of the movement. By locating the scene off the coast of Africa, Géricault incorporated an element of exoticism. Nature—cruel and unforgiving—is central to the scene, reflected in the turbulent sea, dark clouds, and imperiled raft. The canvas includes an extraordinary range of passions. Observe, for example, the inconsolable grief of the figure at the bottom left, a father cradling the dead body of his son. Other figures express despair and terror, and still others limitless hope. The painting evokes the dark passions lurking in the human heart. Although it does not show the scenes of insanity, murder, and cannibalism that the survivors had witnessed, they undoubtedly came to the minds of the viewers, who were familiar with the tragic events. The painting is a powerful

for the well-being of all humankind. Similarly, in reaction to French incursions, Italian writer Vittorio Alfieri (1749–1803) insisted that Italians, as the descendants and heirs of ancient Rome, should be the ones to lead the peoples of Europe.

For the most part, however, after the French Revolution and the Napoleonic era, early-nineteenth-century nationalism was generous and cosmopolitan in its outlook. Many nationalists in the 1830s and 1840s were committed to the ideal of a "Europe of free peoples." Victor Hugo even envisioned a "European republic" with its own parliament.

It is important to remember, however, that although many intellectuals found nationalism attractive, in the first half of the nineteenth century most people felt stronger local and regional affinities than national identities. Only after several decades of propaganda by nationalists and governments did Europeans begin to imagine themselves as part of a national rather than local community, and only then could they think of dying for their nations.

Géricault: Raft of the "Medusa" (Erich Lessing/Art Resource, NY)

indictment of Enlightenment faith in humans as creatures of reason and balance.

Romantic artists wanted to engage the passions of those viewing, reading, or hearing their works. The *Raft of the "Medusa"* purposely stages the events in the foreground in order to pull viewers into the picture and make them participants in the drama. They thus share in the alternating feelings of terror and hope that swept the raft.

The fate of the painting and the artist followed a romantic script. When Géricault started the painting, he intended it as an indictment of the restoration government. He poured energy into it in an effort to take his mind off a disastrous love affair. As his work proceeded, he came to see the painting as an allegory of larger human passions and concerns. Yet when it was displayed, much to his disappointment, the painting was understood mainly in political terms. Disillusioned by this reaction, Géricault thereafter painted no major works.

He grew sickly, rarely bestirred himself, and died of bone tuberculosis in 1824 at age 33. He illustrates the romantics' view of a heroic life—the genius who performs a major feat and then dies young, before realizing his potential. To the romantics, human intent and effort often appeared thwarted by larger forces. This painting, originally meant to criticize the regime, was purchased after Géricault's death by the restoration government and hung in France's national museum, the Louvre.

QUESTIONS

1. What elements in the subject matter and style of this painting typify romanticism?

2. Why was this painting seen as a brutal critique of the French restoration government? What had been the artist's intent?

Liberalism

Liberalism was a direct descendant of the Enlightenment's critique of eighteenth-century absolutism. It is important not to confuse its original meaning with left-wing connotations "liberalism" has come to represent in the twenty-first century. Nineteenth-century liberals, like modern western "conservatives," believed that individual freedom was best safeguarded by reducing government powers to a minimum. They wanted to impose constitutional limits on government, to establish the rule of law, to sweep away all restrictions on individual enterprise—specifically, state regulation of the economy—and to ensure a voice in government for men of property and education. Liberalism was influenced by romanticism, with its emphasis on individual freedom and the imperative of the human personality to develop to its full potential. Liberalism was also affected by

liberalism Nineteenth-century economic and political theory that called for reducing government powers to a minimum. Liberals sought to eliminate state regulation of the economy and ensure a voice in government for men of property and education.

nationalism, especially in multinational autocratic states, such as Austria, Russia, and the Ottoman Empire, in which free institutions could be established only if political independence were wrested from, respectively, Vienna, St. Petersburg, and Constantinople. (Nationalism challenged the established order in the first half of the century, but in the second half, conservatives were to use nationalism as a means to stabilize their rule.)

ECONOMIC LIBERALISM

Liberalism was both an economic and a political theory. In 1776, Adam Smith (1723–1790), the influential Scottish economist, published *An Inquiry into the Nature and Causes of the Wealth of Nations*. Smith advocated freeing national economies from the fetters of the state. Under the mercantilist system, prevalent throughout Europe until about 1800, the state regulated the prices and conditions of manufacture. Smith argued for letting the free forces of the marketplace shape economic decisions. He believed that economics was subject to basic unalterable laws of human behavior that could be discerned and applied in the same fashion as natural laws. Chief among them, in Smith's view, was the compatibility of economic self-interest and the general good. He argued that entrepreneurs who lower prices sell more products, thus increasing their own profits *and* providing the community with affordable wares. In this way, an individual's drive for profit benefits society as a whole. The economy is driven as if "by an invisible hand." This competitive drive for profits, Smith predicted, would expand the "wealth of nations." In France, advocates of nonintervention by government in the economy were called supporters of **laissez-faire** (meaning "to leave alone, to let run on its own").

laissez-faire French term meaning "to leave alone," to advocate freeing national economies from the fetters of the state and allowing supply and demand to shape the marketplace.

Smith and his disciples formed what came to be known as the school of classical economy, emphasizing the importance of laissez-faire. Smith had been relatively optimistic about the capacities of the free market. He warned, however, that the market tended to form monopolies, and he suggested that government intervene to prevent this occurrence. He also thought marketplace could not provide for all human needs; the government needed to supply education, road systems, and an equitable system of justice.

Those who followed Smith, and who witnessed the negative results of industrial capitalism, developed gloomier views. In 1798, Thomas Malthus (1766–1834) published *An Essay on the Principle of Population*, which suggested that the rate of population growth was much higher than the rate of food production. Unless people had fewer children, they would suffer starvation. By their failure to exercise sexual restraint, the poor, Malthus declared, "are themselves the cause of their own poverty." The laws of economics suggested to Malthus that factory owners could not improve their workers' lot by increasing wages or providing charity because higher living standards would lead to more births, which in turn would depress wages and bring greater misery. He therefore advocated abstinence (birth control was considered sinful and unnatural) and thought couples should marry only when they could afford to raise children. Malthus himself had twelve.

David Ricardo (1772–1823) made his fortune in the stock market, retired young, and wrote on economics; his best-known work was *Principles of Political Economy* (1817). Ricardo argued that the only way capitalists could make profits in a competitive market would be to pay the lowest wages possible. Like Malthus's theory of population, Ricardo's "iron law of wages" provided scientific justification for the exploitation of workers.

POLITICAL LIBERALISM

Political liberalism also represented the belief that government should refrain from regulating human affairs in order to preserve freedom. But eventually some proponents of laissez-faire changed their attitudes about the role of the government when they witnessed the alarming results of industrialization and rapid urban growth. Around midcentury, some liberals called on the state to intervene in areas of concern that would have been unthinkable a half century earlier. Jeremy Bentham (1748–1832) argued that the purpose of government is to provide "the greatest happiness of the greatest number" and that governments should be judged on that basis. Bentham and his disciples believed that the test of government is its usefulness; thus, his theory is known as **utilitarianism**.

utilitarianism Political theory of Jeremy Bentham, who argued that the purpose of government is to provide "the greatest happiness of the greatest number" and that the test of government is its usefulness.

John Stuart Mill (1806–1873), a disciple of Bentham and the leading British economic and political thinker at midcentury, initially voiced strong support for laissez-faire economics in his *Principles of Political Economy* (1848). In subsequent editions, however, he noted that the free market could not address every human need, and he argued that the state had an obligation to relieve human misery.

In his essay, *On Liberty* (1859), one of the fundamental documents of nineteenth-century liberalism, Mill argued for the free circulation of ideas—even false ideas. For in the free marketplace of ideas, false ideas will be defeated, and truth vindicated, in open debate. Mill also asserted that all members of society should have equal access to freedom. Influenced by his wife, Harriet Taylor Mill (1807–1856), he wrote in *On the Subjection of Women* (1861) that women should be permitted to vote and should have access to equal educational opportunities and the professions. Such equality not only would be just, but also would have the advantage of "doubling the mass of mental faculties available for the higher service of humanity." Mill, the foremost male proponent of women's rights in his generation, helped win a broader audience for the principle of equality between the sexes.

Despite Mill's influence, many liberals, especially in the early nineteenth century, feared the masses and therefore vigorously opposed democracy. They feared that the common people, uneducated and supposedly gullible, would easily be swayed by demagogues who might become despotic or who, in a desire to curry favor with the poor, might attack the privileges of the wealthy. The French liberal Benjamin Constant denounced democracy as "the vulgarization of despotism"; the vote, he declared, should be reserved for the affluent and educated. When less fortunate Frenchmen denounced the property requirements that prevented them from voting, the liberal statesman François Guizot (1787–1874) smugly replied, "Get rich."

Guizot's comment reflects attitudes associated with the bourgeoisie, a social class that came of age in the nineteenth century. The word *bourgeois* derives from *burgers*, a term that referred to a group of people who gained wealth and civic identity from urban occupations beginning in the twelfth and thirteenth centuries. This class fully developed in the nineteenth century. If unsympathetic to extending suffrage to the lower classes, the *bourgeoisie* championed liberalism because it justified its own right to participate in governance. Economic liberalism was also attractive to merchants and manufacturers, who wished to gather wealth without state interference. The basic tenets of liberalism—the belief in the sanctity of human rights, of the freedoms of speech and of association, and of the rule of law and equality before the law—eventually became widely accepted, even among conservatives and socialists who originally opposed them.

Socialism

A fundamental element in the pursuit of happiness, according to liberals, was the ability to accumulate property. Socialists, on the other hand, believed that the "social" ownership of property, unlike private ownership, would benefit society as a whole. The notion that human happiness can best be ensured by the common ownership of property had been suggested in earlier times by individuals as different as the Greek philosopher Plato (427?–347 B.C.) and Sir Thomas More (1478–1535), the English author *of Utopia*. In the 1820s, troubled by the harsh condition of the working classes, thinkers in Britain and France began to espouse new theories to address the social ills produced by industrial capitalism. During the first half of the nineteenth century, most workers were still artisans, even in industrializing England, where manufacturing was increasingly large scale. Only in a later era would **socialism** address the issues raised by industry.

socialism Nineteenth-century economic and social doctrine and political movement that advocated the "social" or state ownership of property in order to create a more just system.

EARLY SOCIALIST THINKERS

During the French Revolution, Gracchus Babeuf (GRAH-kus bah-BOEF) (1760–1797), a minor civil servant, participated in the Conspiracy of Equals (see page 547). He believed political equality was meaningless without economic equality. Babeuf advocated revolution to bring about a "communist" society—a society in which all property would be owned in common and private property would be abolished. Work would be provided for everyone; medical services and education would be free to all. Upon the discovery of his plot, Babeuf was guillotined, but his theories and his example of conspiratorial revolutionary action would influence later socialists.

Several other important French thinkers made contributions to European socialism. Henri de Saint-Simon (saen-see-MON) (1760–1825), a French aristocrat, emphasized the need "to ameliorate as promptly and as quickly as possible the moral and physical existence of the most numerous class," and believed the state should ensure the welfare of the masses. He argued, furthermore, that technical experts, rather than an elite derived from birth, should govern the state and formulate economic policies.

Another vital contribution to socialist thought came from thinkers who tried to imagine an ideal world. They were later derisively dismissed as builders of utopias, fantasy worlds (the Greek word *utopia* means "no place"). Their schemes varied, but they shared the view that property should be owned in common and used for the common good. They also believed that society should rest on principles of cooperation rather than on competitive individualism.

Karl Marx Through his writings and agitation, Marx transformed the socialism of his day and created an ideology that gave new direction to the course of events in the nineteenth and twentieth centuries. (Bettmann/Corbis)

One of the earliest and most notable utopians was mill owner Robert Owen (1771–1859). Beginning in 1800, he ran a prosperous cotton mill in New Lanark, Scotland. He also provided generously for his workers, guaranteeing them jobs and their children a decent education. In his writings, Owen suggested the establishment of self-governing communities owning the means of production. Essentials would be distributed to all members according to their needs. His ideas for the new society also included equal rights for women. Owen received little support from fellow manufacturers and political leaders, and his own attempt in 1824 to establish an ideal society in the United States at New Harmony, Indiana, ended in failure after four years.

Another influential contributor to early socialist theory was the Frenchman Charles Fourier (foor-YAY) (1772–1837). A clerk and salesman, Fourier wrote in great detail about his vision of the ideal future society. It would consist of cooperative organizations called "phalansteries," each with sixteen hundred inhabitants who would live in harmony with nature and with one another. Everyone would be assured gainful employment, which would be made enjoyable by rotating jobs. Because cooperative communes often faced the issue of who would carry out the distasteful tasks, everyone would share the pleasant *and* unpleasant work.

Fourier had an important female following because of his belief in the equality of the sexes, and some of these women tried to put his ideas into action. In Belgium, the activist Zoé Gatti de Gamond (1806–1854) cofounded a phalanstery for women. She believed that if women could be assured of economic well-being, other rights would follow. Also inspired by Fourier, Flora Tristan (1801–1844) was an effective advocate for workers' rights. Her book, *Union Ouvrière (Workers' Union)*, suggested that all workers should contribute funds to establish a "Workers' Palace" in every town, where the sick and disabled would have shelter, and the workers' children could receive a free education. Crossing France on foot, she spread the word of workers' solidarity and self-help.

Socialism encompassed a variety of approaches. The French journalist Louis Blanc (BLAHN) (1811–1882) thought that by securing the vote, the common people could win control over the state and require it to serve their needs. Once in control of the state by the ballot, they in turn would establish "social workshops" in which the workers would be responsible for production and for supervision of business matters. Society should be established according to the maxim, "Let each produce according to his aptitudes and strength; let each consume according to his need." Blanc's contemporary Louis Blanqui (1805–1882) suggested a more violent mode of action. He advocated seizure of the state by a small, dedicated band of men who would establish equality for all through communism. His ideas strengthened the notion of class warfare.

MARXISM   Karl Marx (1818–1883) was the most important socialist of the nineteenth century. The son of a lawyer, he grew up in the Rhineland, an industrializing area of western Germany that was particularly open to political ideas and agitation. After his education in philosophy at the University of Berlin, he edited a newspaper that spoke out for freedom and democracy in Germany. Marx's radical journalism caused him to be exiled from the Rhineland. After living briefly in Paris, then Brussels, he settled in London in 1849. There he lived for the rest of his life, dedicated to establishing his ideas on what he viewed as scientific bases.

Along with many of his contemporaries, Marx believed that human history has a direction and a goal. In his mind, it was the abolition of capitalism, the victory of the proletariat, the disappearance of the state, and the ultimate liberation of all humankind. He insisted that material conditions, rather than ideas, govern the world. According to him, the process of history was grounded on the notion of "dialectical materialism," in which the inequality of conditions existing in any economic order—such as feudalism or capitalism—would inevitably engender opposition that would create a new order based on a new set of economic relationships, which would, in turn, create opposition. The dialectical process would continue until economic equality and freedom were established.

Marx grouped human beings into classes based on their relationship to the means of production. The prevailing economic system in western Europe in his time was industrial capitalism. Capitalists constituted a class because they owned the means of production. Workers— the proletariat—were a separate class because they did not own any of the means of production, nor would they ever be able to because the "iron law of wages" would keep them perpetually impoverished. Because these two classes had different relationships to the means of production, they had different—in fact, antagonistic—interests and were destined (Marx believed) to engage in a class struggle.

Some of Marx's contemporaries lamented the increasing hostility between workers and capitalists. Marx, however, saw the conflict as necessary to advance human history, and he sought to validate his thesis by studying the past. In the Middle Ages, he pointed out, the feudal class dominated society but eventually lost the struggle to the commercial classes. Now, in turn, the capitalists were destined to be defeated by the rising proletariat. Thus, industrial capitalism, he argued, was a necessary, if painful, economic stage through which humankind had to traverse on its way to liberation.

In his study of history and economics, Marx found not only justification for, but irrefutable proof of, the "scientific" basis of his ideas. Capitalism was itself creating the forces that would supplant it. The large industrial plants necessitated an ever greater workforce with a growing sense of class interest. The inherently competitive nature of capitalism would inevitably drive an increasing number of enterprises out of business, and a form of monopoly capitalism would emerge, abusive of both consumers and workers. Ever more savage competition would force businesses to fail, creating widespread unemployment. Angered and frustrated by their lot, workers would overthrow the system that had abused them for so long: "The knell of private property has sounded. The expropriators will be expropriated." Workers would take power and, to solidify their rule, would temporarily exercise the "dictatorship of the proletariat." Once that had taken place, the state would wither away. With the coming to power of the proletariat, the history of class war would end and the ideal society would prevail. In the absences of classes and struggles between them, history would end.

Marx's study of economics and history proved to him that the coming of socialism was not only desirable, but inevitable. The laws of history dictated that capitalism, having created the rising proletariat, would collapse. By labeling his brand of socialism as scientific, Marx gave it the aura it needed to become the faith of millions of people. To declare ideas scientific in the nineteenth century, when science was held in such high esteem, was to ensure their popularity.

In 1848, Marx and Friedrich Engels (1820–1895) published the *Communist Manifesto*. A pamphlet written for the Communist League, a group of Germans living in exile, the Manifesto made an appeal to the working classes of the world. The league deliberately called itself "Communist" rather than "Socialist." Communism was a revolutionary program, bent on changing property relations by violence; socialism was associated with more peaceful means of transformation. The pamphlet laid out Marx's basic ideas. "The history of all hitherto existing society," he said, "is the history of class struggles." In this pamphlet, Marx and Engels called on the proletariat to rise—"You have nothing to lose but your chains"—and create a society that would end human exploitation. The idea of an international workers' movement contrasted with the dominant currents of capitalism and nationalism.

A number of political and polemical works flowed from Marx's pen, but most of them remained unpublished during his lifetime. The first volume of his major work, *Capital*, was published in 1867; subsequent volumes appeared posthumously. **Marxism**, the body of Marx's thought, is complex and sometimes contradictory, but certain basic concepts resound throughout and were embraced by Marx's followers.

Marxism The "scientific socialism" of Karl Marx and Friedrich Engels, which stated that the working class inevitably would rebel against the capitalist owners and build a communist society.

SECTION SUMMARY

- From 1815 to 1848, conservatism provided the ideological foundations for restored monarchies and social hierarchy; the ideologies of romanticism, nationalism, liberalism, and socialism challenged that order.

- Romanticism was based on feeling and passion rather than on reason; it inspired the arts, but also revived religion and challenged the existing political order through its influence on nationalism.

- Nationalism—the identification with one's nation based on shared language, culture, political authority, and historical past—began to emerge in the first half of the nineteenth century.

- The economic and political theory of liberalism originated with and justified middle-class interests and stressed individual freedoms.

- Socialist ideologies—"utopian" and "scientific"—emerged in response to the harsh conditions of the working classes and offered an alternative to capitalism.

THE QUEST FOR REFORM, 1830–1848

How did the restorations that followed the Napoleonic era give way to reform?

The new ideologies challenged the existing order, and by the 1830s, in western Europe, revolution and the threat of revolution helped dismantle the most reactionary features of the restored regimes. But in central and eastern Europe, from the German states to Russia and to most of the Ottoman Empire, the political systems established in 1815 would persist virtually unchanged until midcentury.

Revolution of 1830 and the July Monarchy in France

While the restored Bourbon monarch, Louis XVIII, had understood the need to incorporate some principles of popular sovereignty into his regime, his ultra-reactionary brother and successor, Charles X (r. 1824–1830), tried to reestablish an Old Regime type monarchy whose rule would be unrestricted by a constitution. He promoted the revival of Catholicism and its influence in education. The death penalty was even authorized as punishment for any desecration of the churches or religious icons. He also tried to suppress any opposition with strict press censorship.

More general disenchantment came with an economic downturn in 1827, marked by poor harvests and increased unemployment in the cities. Discontent brought to Parliament a liberal majority that refused to accept the reactionary ministers the king appointed. On July 26, 1830, after the humiliating defeat of his party at the polls, the king issued a set of decrees suspending freedom of the press, dissolving the Chamber of Deputies, and stiffening property qualifications for voters in subsequent elections. The king appeared to be engineering a coup against the existing political system.

The first to protest were the Parisian journalists and typesetters, directly threatened by the censorship laws. On July 28, others joined the protest and began erecting barricades across many streets. After killing several hundred protesters, the king's forces lost control of the city. This **July Revolution** drove the king into exile.

July Revolution Uprising in Paris in July 1830 that forced King Charles X to abdicate and signaled a victory for constitutional reform over an absolute monarchy.

Alarmed by the crowds' clamor for a republic, the liberal opposition—consisting of some of the leading newspaper editors and sympathetic deputies—quickly drafted the duke of Orléans, Louis Philippe (r. 1830–1848), known for his liberal opinions, to occupy the throne.

As a result of the 1830 revolution in Paris, a more liberal regime was installed in France. Louis Philippe proclaimed himself "King of the French" (rather than of France), thus acknowledging that he reigned at people's behest. Freedom of the press was reinstated. Suffrage was extended to 200,000 men, twice as many voters as before. The July Monarchy, named after the month in which it was established by revolution, justified itself by celebrating the great Revolution of 1789. On the site where the Bastille had been razed in 1789, the government erected a large column with the names of the victims of the July 1830 revolution, thus suggesting continuity between those who had fought tyranny in 1789 and 1830.

Identification with the Revolution appeared to legitimize the regime but also had the potential to subvert it. Fearful that the cult of revolution would encourage violence against the new monarchy, the regime censored artistic production, promoting only works that extolled the period from 1789 to 1791, when the revolutionaries had attempted to found a constitutional monarchy. Now that the revolution of 1830 had established a constitutional monarchy, the regime was suggesting, any further uprisings were illegitimate. If the July Monarchy turned out not to be as liberal as its founders had hoped, foreign visitors coming from more authoritarian societies were nonetheless impressed by France's apparently liberal institutions. (See the feature, "The Global Record: A Moroccan Describes French Freedom of the Press.") Many French liberals, however, saw the regime as a travesty of the hopes and promises it had represented on coming to power in 1830.

British Reforms

The major political problem facing Britain in the early nineteenth century was the composition of Parliament, which failed to reflect the dramatic population shifts that had occurred since the seventeenth century. Industrialization had transformed mere villages into major cities—Manchester, Birmingham, Leeds, Sheffield—but those cities had no representation in Parliament. Localities whose population had declined, however, were still represented. In districts known as "pocket boroughs," single individuals owned the right to a seat in Parliament. In districts known as "rotten boroughs," a handful of voters elected a representative. As exemplified in the causes and consequences of the "Peterloo Massacre" (see page 589), Parliament continued to represent only the interests of the traditional landed elite at the expense of the urban middle and working classes.

News of the July 1830 revolution in Paris made conservatives fear the same fate as Charles X and encouraged British liberals to push for reform. The government introduced a reform bill to abolish or reduce representation for sparsely populated areas, and grant seats for the populous and unrepresented cities. The bill also proposed lowering property qualifications for the vote, which would extend the franchise to some middle-class men. Following a prolonged, bitter political battle between the government and middle classes on one side and the aristocracy on the other, the House of Lords finally passed what came to be known as the **Great Reform Bill** of 1832.

Great Reform Bill British law that broadened the franchise and provided parliamentary seats for new urban areas that had not previously been represented.

The reform bill enfranchised only the upper layers of the male middle class, or one in seven adult men. Nonetheless, it demonstrated the willingness of the political leaders to acknowledge the increasing economic importance of manufacturing. Parliament became a more representative forum whose makeup better reflected the shift of economic power from agricultural landowners to the industrial and commercial classes. The bill passed as a result of nationwide agitation, evidence that Britain's political system could respond to grievances and bring about reform peacefully.

A series of colonial reforms also showed the British Parliament's willingness to adapt to changing circumstances. Opposition to slavery had been voiced since the 1780s. (See the feature, "The Written Record: A Plea to Abolish Slavery in the British Colonies.") Slavery, the very opposite of human freedom, was an affront to liberal principles. Moreover, its persistence threatened the empire—in 1831, sixty thousand slaves rebelled in the British colony of Jamaica. Parliament heeded the call for change and in 1833 abolished slavery throughout the British Empire.

The antislavery campaign led to the extension of British power into Africa. Britain used its navy—the largest in the world—to suppress the traffic in humans and hinder its colonial rivals from benefiting from the slave trade. Needing bases for these patrols, the British established a number of minor settlements in West Africa, and thereby became the predominant European power along the coast. These possessions foreshadowed the increasing European intrusion into African affairs.

In addition, the British began to review the imperial administration of their white settler colonies. In response to an 1837 Canadian uprising opposing British rule, self-government for Canada was promulgated in 1839 and 1841. Eventually, all the British colonies with a majority of white settlers were given similar rights of self-rule. The idea of self-government for nonwhites in the colonies was not yet imagined.

Parliament's reforming zeal, and most particularly the Reform Bill of 1832, set off a movement among those who had not been granted the right to vote. **Chartism** sought political democracy as a means for social change. In 1838, political radicals with working-class support drew up a "people's charter," a petition calling for universal male suffrage, electoral districts with equal population, salaries and the abolition of property qualifications for members of Parliament, the secret ballot, and annual general elections. The Chartists hoped that giving workers the vote would end the dominance of the much smaller upper classes in Parliament and ensure an improvement in the workers' lot.

Chartism Nineteenth-century British political movement calling for universal male suffrage, electoral districts with equal population, salaries and the abolition of property qualifications for members of Parliament, the secret ballot, and annual general elections.

Chartism won wide support among men and women in the working classes, sparking demonstrations and petition drives of unprecedented size—millions signed the petition. Women participated to a larger extent than in any other political movement of the day, founding over a hundred female Chartist chapters. Some Chartists, especially female members, asked for women's voting rights, but this demand failed to gain overall adherence from the membership. Winning mass support during particularly hard economic years, Chartism lost followers during a temporary economic upswing. The movement also fell under the sway of advocates of violence, who scared off many artisans and potential middle-class supporters. Chartism failed as a political movement; yet it drew public attention to an integrated democratic program whose main provisions (except for yearly elections) would be adopted piecemeal over the next half century.

In 1839, urban businessmen founded the Anti-Corn Law League for the purpose of abolishing the tariffs on foreign grain imports that kept food prices so high. The Corn Laws were

A Moroccan Describes French Freedom of the Press

In 1845–1846, a Moroccan diplomatic mission visited Paris. The ambassador's secretary, Muhammad as-Saffar (d. 1881), wrote an account of the visit. Impressed by many aspects of French society, he praises France's press in the following passage. The "Sultan" as-Saffar refers to is King Louis Philippe. To this Moroccan observer, the extent to which the French enjoyed constitutional government was striking.

The people of Paris, like all the French indeed, like all of [Europe] are eager to know the latest news and events that are taking place in other parts [of the world]. For this purpose they have the gazette. [In] these papers … they write all the news that has reached them that day about events in their own country and in other lands both near and far.

This is the way it is done. The owner of a newspaper dispatches his people to collect everything they see or hear in the way of important events or unusual happenings. Among the places where they collect the news are the two Chambers, the Great and the Small, where they come together to make their laws. When the members of the Chamber meet to deliberate, the men of the gazette sit nearby and write down everything that is said, for all debating and ratifying of laws is matter for the gazette and is known to everyone. No one can prevent them from doing this. …

… [I]f someone has an idea about a subject but he is not a member of the press, he may write about it in the gazette and make it known to others, so that the leaders of opinion learn about it. If the idea is worthy they may follow it, and if its author was out of favor it may bring him recognition.

No person in France is prohibited from expressing his opinion or from writing it and printing it, on condition that he does not violate the law. …

In the newspapers they write rejoinders to the men of the two Chambers about the laws they are making. If their Sultan demands gifts from the notables or goes against the law in any way, they write about that too, saying that he is a tyrant and in the wrong. He cannot confront them or cause them harm. Also, if someone behaves out of the ordinary, they write about that too, making it common knowledge among people of every rank. If his deeds were admirable, they praise and delight in him, lauding his example; but if he behaved badly, they revile him to discourage the like.

Moreover, if someone is being oppressed by another, they write about that too, so that everyone will know the story from both sides just as it happened, until it is decided in court. One can also read in it what their courts have decided.

QUESTIONS

1. Based on the diplomat's reaction to the French system, what can you deduce about freedom of the press and the expression of public opinion in Morocco?

2. Do you think this observer has a positive opinion of the French press? Why or why not?

Source: *Disorienting Encounters: Travels of a Moroccan Scholar in France in 1845–1846. The Voyage of Muhammad as-Saffar*, edited and translated by Susan Gilson Miller, © 1992 by the Regents of the University of California. Reprinted by permission of the publisher, the University of California Press.

unpopular with manufacturers, who knew that low food prices would allow them to pay low wages. It was also unpopular with workers, who wanted bread at a price they could afford. The anti-Corn Law movement proved more effective than Chartism because the middle classes supported it. Alarmed by the threat of famine after the poor harvest of 1845, Parliament repealed the Corn Laws in 1846.

The repeal of the Corn Laws was a milestone in British history, demonstrating the extent to which organized groups could bring about economic improvements. A popular, mass organization had been able to shape public policy—a far cry from the days of Peterloo, when the government had not only ignored the public but attacked it with bayonets fixed.

The Absolutist States of Central and Eastern Europe

In contrast to many parts of western Europe, which saw important political changes in the 1830s, the absolutist states in central and eastern Europe were able to preserve themselves essentially unchanged until 1848—and in some cases even beyond.

The king of Prussia had repeatedly promised a constitution, but none had materialized. A representative Diet would not meet there until 1847. Renewed nationalist agitation swept the German states in the 1840s. A mass outpouring of patriotic sentiment erupted in response to possible French ambitions on the Rhine during a diplomatic crisis in 1840. Two patriotic songs were penned: "The Watch on the Rhine" and *"Deutschland, Deutschland über alles"* ("Germany, Germany Above All"); the latter became Germany's national anthem half a century later. German

A Plea to Abolish Slavery in the British Colonies

Among the causes that British reformers embraced was the abolition of slavery. The slave trade had been abolished in 1807; one more step was left—ending in the colonies the institution of slavery itself. In this petition to Parliament in 1823, the Society for the Mitigation and Gradual Abolition of Slavery Throughout the British Dominions explains the harsh and degrading nature of the institution. Trading in slaves had been abolished as immoral and unnatural; here the petitioners remind Parliament that holding slaves is no less abhorrent. Under the pressure of this type of agitation, Parliament in 1833 abolished slavery in the British Empire.

In the colonies of Great Britain there are at this moment upwards of 800,000 human beings in a state of degrading personal slavery.

These unhappy persons, whether young or old, male or female, are the absolute property of their master, who may sell or transfer them at his pleasure, and who may also regulate according to his discretion (within certain limits) the measure of their labour, their food, and their punishment.

Many of the slaves are (and all may be) branded like cattle, by means of a hot iron, on the shoulder or other conspicuous part of the body, with the initials of their master's name; and thus bear about them in indelible characters the proof of their debased and servile state. . . .

It can hardly be alleged that any man can have a right to obtain his fellow creatures in a state so miserable and degrading as has been described. And the absence of such right will be still more apparent, if we consider how these slaves were originally obtained.

They, or their parents, were the victims of the Slave Trade. They were obtained, not by lawful means, or under any colourable pretext, but by the most undisguised rapine, and the most atrocious fraud. Torn from their homes and from every dear relation in life, barbarously manacled, driven like herds of cattle to the sea-shore, crowded into the potential holds of slave ships, they were transported to our colonies and there sold in bondage. . . .

The Government and Legislature of this country have on various occasions, and in the most solemn and unequivocal terms denounced the Slave Trade as immoral, inhuman, and unjust; but the legal perpetuation of that state of slavery, which has been produced by it, is surely, in its principle, no less immoral, inhuman and unjust, than the trade itself. . . .

QUESTIONS

1. Why would the British Parliament abolish the slave trade but allow slavery to continue in its colonies?

2. Why did it take ten years from the time of this petition for slavery to be abolished? What changes occurred in the British Parliament that might explain the timing of abolition?

Source: Reprinted in *Circular Letters of the Society for the Mitigation and Gradual Abolition of Slavery Throughout the British Dominions* (April 1823).

rulers, who in the past had been reluctant to support the national idea, now attempted to co-opt it. Cologne's unfinished cathedral, for example, became a symbol of German enthusiasm; from all over Germany donations poured in to finish it. These events suggested a broadening base for nationhood, which potentially could replace the existing system of a fragmented Germany. But with minor exceptions, the system established in 1815 prevailed until 1848.

Many Italian governments—notably the papacy, the kingdom of Naples, and the central Italian duchies—also successfully resisted aspirations for freer institutions and a unified Italy with repressive policies, knowing that they could count on Austrian assistance to squelch any uprising. Indeed, Metternich did crush rebellions, which generated hatred of Austria among Italian liberals and nationalists.

Having come to the throne by virtue of repressing the Decembrist uprising of 1825, Russia's Tsar Nicholas I (r. 1825–1855) was obsessed with the danger of revolution and determined to suppress all challenges to his authority. The declared goal of his rule was to uphold "orthodoxy, autocracy, and nationality." Nicholas created a stern, centralized bureaucracy to control all facets of Russian life. He originated the modern Russian secret police, called the "Third Section"; a state within the state, it was above the law. Believing in the divine right of monarchs, Nicholas refused to accept limits to his imperial powers. The tsar supported the primacy of the Russian Orthodox Church within Russian society; the church in turn upheld the powers of the state. Nicholas also used nationalism to strengthen the state by exalting the country's past and by trying to "Russify" non-Russian peoples. After a nationalist rebellion in 1831 in Poland attempted to shake loose Russian control, Nicholas abrogated the kingdom's constitution and tried to impose the Russian language on its Polish subjects.

Russia's single most overwhelming problem was serfdom. Economically, serfdom had little to recommend it; free labor was far more efficient. Moreover, the serfs' dissatisfaction with their lot threatened public safety. Nicholas's thirty-year reign was checkered with over six hundred peasant uprisings, half of them put down by the military. Nicholas understood that serfdom had to be abolished for Russia's own good, but also he believed emancipation would only sow further disorder. Except for a few minor reforms, he did nothing.

Ottoman Empire and Greek Independence

Although less directly affected by the events of 1789–1815, the Ottoman Empire was not immune to the forces of change unleashed by revolutions and reform in the West. In its sheer mass, the Ottoman Empire continued to be a world empire. It extended over three continents. In Africa, it ran across the whole North African coast. In Europe, it stretched from Dalmatia (on the Adriatic coast) to Constantinople. In Asia, it extended from Mesopotamia (present-day Iraq) to Anatolia (present-day Turkey) (see **MAP 24.3**, p. 688). But it was an empire in decline, seriously challenged by foreign threats and by nationalist movements from within—and its decline would ultimately have consequences for the European and world order.

The Ottoman bureaucracy, once the mainstay of the government, had fallen into decay. In the past, officials had been recruited and advanced by merit; now lacking funds, Constantinople sold government offices. Tax collectors ruthlessly squeezed the peasantry. By the eighteenth century, the Janissaries, formerly an elite military force, had become an undisciplined band that menaced the peoples of the Ottoman Empire—especially those located at great distances from the capital. The reform-minded Sultan Selim III (r. 1789–1807) sought to curb the army, but rebellious Janissaries killed him. They then forced the new ruler, Mahmud II (r. 1808–1839), to retract most of the previous improvements.

The ideas of nationalism and liberty that triggered changes in western Europe also stirred the peoples of the Balkans. Most of the Ottoman Empire was inhabited by Muslims, but in the Balkans, Christians were in the majority. Ottoman officials usually treated religious minorities, such as Jews and Orthodox Christians, with tolerance. But the Christian subject peoples found in their religion a means of collectively resisting a harsh and at times capricious rule. Some Christian peoples in the Balkans looked back nostalgically to earlier eras—the Greeks to their great Classical civilization or the Serbs to their era of self-rule.

The Serbs were the first people to revolt successfully against Ottoman rule. A poor, mountainous region, Serbia suffered greatly from the rapaciousness of the Janissaries, and revolted in 1804. By 1815, the Ottomans had to recognize one of its leaders, Milosh Obrenovich (r. 1815–1839), as governor and allow the formation of a national assembly. In 1830, under pressure from Russia, which took an interest in fellow Slavs and members of the Orthodox faith, Constantinople recognized Milosh as hereditary ruler over an autonomous Serbia.

The Greeks' struggle led to complete independence from Ottoman rule. As merchants and seafarers, Greeks traveled widely throughout the Mediterranean world and beyond. They had encountered the ideas of the French Revolution and, in the 1790s, were affected by the nationalism spreading in Europe. Adamantios Koraïs (KOOR-ay-iss) (1748–1833), an educator living in revolutionary Paris, created a new, more elegant Greek and edited Greek classics to connect his fellow countrymen with their ancient and illustrious past. Greek cultural nationalism found an echo among some intellectuals, a group of whom conspired to restore Greek independence by political means.

A parallel movement developed among Greek peasants, who were hostile to the Ottoman Turks for having accumulated vast landholdings at their expense. Greek peasants joined an anti-Turkish revolt that began in 1821 and lasted several years.

Mehemet Ali Painted by the famed British artist Sir David Wilkie, this portrait depicts the Egyptian leader at the height of his powers. Mehemet challenged the Ottoman Empire, winning for Egypt virtual independence and bringing Syria under his control. (Tate Gallery, London/Art Resource, NY)

By 1827, the Ottomans, aided by their vassal Mehemet Ali (1769–1849) of Egypt, controlled most of the Balkan peninsula. The rest of Europe, excited by the idea of an independent Greece restored to its past greatness, widely supported the Greek movement for freedom. The Great Powers intervened in 1827, sending their navies to intercept supplies intended for the Ottoman forces. Their victory ensured the independence of Greece, which was ratified by an international agreement in 1830. But in sanctioning the Greek nationalist insurrection, the allies of the Concert of Europe contradicted their own stated principles of opposing any challenge to the established order.

Losing influence in the Balkans, the Ottoman Empire also faced challenges elsewhere. Mehemet Ali, nominally subordinate to Constantinople, actually ruled Egypt as if it were independent. He wrested Syria away in 1831 and threatened to march against his overlord, the sultan. Britain and Russia, concerned that an Ottoman collapse would upset the region's balance of power, intervened on the empire's behalf. Constantinople won back Syria, but in 1841 had to acknowledge Mehemet Ali as the hereditary ruler of Egypt. The survival of the Ottoman Empire was beginning to depend on the goodwill—and self-interest—of the Great Powers.

SECTION SUMMARY

- In July 1830, the French responded to reactionary measures taken by their king with revolution, ushering in the more liberal July Monarchy; these events inspired serious opposition to other regimes.

- British liberals responded to France's July Revolution by redrawing the voting districts to reflect the growth of cities, widening the franchise to include the middle classes, and loosening colonial rule over white settler populations.

- Having suffered more directly from Napoleonic invasions, rulers in the Austrian Empire, the German states, and Russia remained determined to preserve absolute political power from 1815 to 1848; they effectively repressed agitation for liberal reform and aspirations for national unification.

- National movements from within and foreign threats from without challenged the religiously diverse Ottoman Empire, already in decay because of its corrupt bureaucracy; Serbs and Greeks successfully revolted against Ottoman rule.

THE REVOLUTIONS OF 1848

What were the main causes of the revolutions of 1848, and what roles did nationalism, liberalism, and socialism play in inciting and sustaining revolution?

From France in the west to Poland in the east, at least fifty separate revolts and uprisings shook the Continent in 1848, the most extensive outbreak of popular violence in nineteenth-century Europe (see **MAP 21.2**). The revolt had an impact far beyond Europe's borders. The revolutions inspired Brazilians to rise up against their government. In Bogota, Colombia, church bells rang, and in New York public demonstrations enthusiastically greeted the announcement of a republic in France. And as a result of the Parisian revolution, slaves in French colonies were finally emancipated.

The revolutions of 1848 also brought women into the political arena, creating new opportunities to criticize their legal status. In France, feminist clubs and newspapers proliferated as they never had before. In central, eastern, and southeastern Europe, revolution gave women political experience that promoted an emancipatory consciousness among them. The revolutions produced a long list of eloquent feminists throughout Europe who made various demands through their newspapers, magazines, and in their political participation. But just as had happened in the French Revolution of 1789, revolutionary governments eventually excluded women from politics, censored their newspapers, and disbanded their clubs.

Roots of Rebellion

The widespread outbreak of discontent occurred for many reasons, some of which stemmed from the pressure that population growth put on available resources. In the countryside, increased restrictions in access to land frustrated peasants. Although in the past many had enjoyed free access to village commons, these were coming increasingly under private control, or the peasants faced competition for their use. Also, the poor once had relatively free access to forests to forage for firewood, but restrictions on this right also now led to frequent conflicts.

MAP 21.2—Major Uprisings and Reforms, 1848–1849

In no other year had as many revolts broken out simultaneously. In many cases, the revolutions led to reforms and new constitutions.

In the urban environment, a crisis erupted in the handicrafts industry, which dominated city economies. Urban artisans were being undercut by the putting-out system or cottage industry, in which capitalists had goods produced in the countryside by cottagers—part-time artisans who supported themselves as well through agriculture and were thus willing to work for lower wages. Crises in the crafts hurt the journeymen who wanted to be masters; they had to serve far longer apprenticeships and in many cases could never expect promotion. Where the guild system still existed, it was in decline, unable to protect the economic interests of artisans anxious about their futures.

These developing concerns came to a crisis point as a result of the economic depression of 1845–1846. In 1845, a crop disaster destroyed the basic food of the poor in northern Europe. The Irish suffered the most catastrophically from this blight: One million starved to death between 1844 and 1851. As the price of food doubled from its 1840 level, an industrial downturn accompanied these agricultural disasters, creating massive unemployment. Municipal and national governments seemed unable to deal with the crowding, disease, and unsanitary conditions that were worsening already high tensions in the cities, the sites of national governments. New liberal, socialist, and nationalist ideologies had created hope for change, as well as a vision for what it should be. The insurrections seeking to overthrow existing regimes disoriented the established political and administrative elites, and they found they could not count on their traditional sources of support.

In February, 1848, a revolution in Paris overthrew the king. News of Louis Philippe's fall triggered a ripple effect, spreading turbulence to over fifty localities in Europe. In France, the revolution was for political and social rights, particularly the rights to vote and to work. In several other countries, another issue was added to the combustible situation—nationalism. Once revolution in the German states broke out, the demands arose for national unification. National unity also became a goal throughout the Italian peninsula; northern Italians also desired independence from the Habsburg Empire. The cry for national independence went out in other Habsburg lands: The Hungarians, Poles, and Czechs all wanted to be masters of their own destinies and free from Vienna's control.

Liberals: From Success to Defeat

The revolutions of 1848 went through two basic stages: unity in the shared goal of regime change, followed by disagreement about what should replace the toppled regimes. In the first stage, liberal demands for more political freedoms, such as the right to vote, joined with popular demands for social and economic justice. In France, the victors declared a republic, which provided basic constitutional freedoms and granted universal male suffrage (the first European regime to do so). The provisional government attempted to solve the problem of widespread unemployment by creating jobs through a system of "national workshops." Inspired by the example of Paris, crowds in Vienna demonstrated and petitioned the emperor. Having lost control over the capital, Metternich resigned and fled to England. On March 15, 1848, the Austrian imperial court, faced with continued agitation by students and workers, announced its willingness to issue a constitution. Even more important was Austria's decision to abolish serfdom.

The news from Paris also acted as a catalyst for change in the German states, where dukes and princes dismissed their cabinets and instituted constitutions. Prussia was initially conspicuous for being untouched by the revolutionary wave. But when news of Metternich's fall in Vienna reached Berlin on March 16, middle-class liberals and artisans demonstrated for reforms. King Friedrich Wilhelm IV (r. 1840–1861) surprised his subjects on March 21 by announcing support for a united, free, constitutional Germany. He appointed as chief minister a liberal Rhenish businessman, who in a ceremonial march through Berlin symbolically walked ahead of the king. Representative government was introduced, and suffrage was extended, though it was still restricted to men of property from the liberal professions and the business classes. As in Austria, the German countryside was appeased by reducing some of the feudal arrangements that still existed in many areas.

The second stage of the revolution marked a breakdown in the unity that had initially formed against the old regimes. With the enemy defeated or compliant, the middle classes, peasants, and workers no longer had a common goal. In France, the peasants, who at least had not opposed the revolution, by April 1848, were hostile to the new republic. They decried the additional taxes that had to be levied to pay for the national workshops supporting unemployed urban workers. Armed with the vote, the peasants elected conservative landowners, lawyers, and notaries—a group nearly identical to the pre-1848 deputies. In June, the new parliament terminated the costly national workshops that had employed thousands of workers. The latter, in despair, revolted. The government carried out a bloody repression, killing 3,000 and arresting 15,000.

The propertied classes, feeling menaced by the poor, looked to authority for security. Of the several candidates for president in 1848, Louis Napoleon (1808–1873), a nephew of Napoleon Bonaparte, appealed to the largest cross section of the population. The middle class was attracted by the promise of authority and order. Peasants, disillusioned by the tax policies of the republic, remained loyal to the memory of Napoleonic glory. Workers, embittered by the government's repression of the June uprisings, were impressed by Louis Napoleon's vaguely socialistic program. Louis Napoleon was elected president. Three years later, he dissolved the National Assembly by force and established a personal dictatorship. In 1852, he declared himself Emperor Napoleon III.

In Austria and Germany, the middle classes became wary of the lower classes; the class conflict in Paris intensified their concern. Once the peasants had won their freedom from feudal dues in Germany and from serfdom in the Austrian Empire, they were no longer interested in what was occurring in the capital. Thus, the alliance in favor of change disappeared, and it could not even serve as a bulwark against counter-revolution. In Austria, the reactionary forces around the court, led by General Windischgrätz, reconquered Vienna in October 1848 for the emperor and

King Friedrich Wilhelm IV Announcing His Devotion to German Unity This print, distributed by the thousands, shows the grateful people—well-dressed middle-class citizens and humble artisans united in their purpose—acclaiming the king *(center)* on horseback. The black, red, and gold flags, the symbol of German unity since the Napoleonic Wars, are prominently displayed. (Germanisches\National Museum Nuremberg)

suspended the liberals' constitution. In December, the king of Prussia, who had appeared to bow to liberal opinion, regained his courage and dismissed the elected assembly. Most of the liberal forces were spent and overcome by the end of the year.

The Nationalist Impulse

The revolutions did not break out because of nationalism, but once they erupted, the nationalist cause helped shape the outcome in several regions. Faced with internal turmoil, Prussia and Austria—whose rulers opposed German unification, lest it undermine their power—could not prevent the question of a united Germany from coming to the fore. In March 1848, a self-appointed national committee invited five hundred prominent German liberals to convene in Frankfurt to begin the process of unifying the German states into a single nation. In addition to fulfilling a long-standing liberal dream, a united Germany would consolidate the liberal victory over absolutism. The gathering called for suffrage based on property qualifications, thus excluding most Germans from the political process and alienating them from the evolving new order. The first all-German elected legislature met in May 1848 in Frankfurt to pursue unification. It faced the thorny issue of which regions should be included and which excluded in this new Germany. The most ambitious plan envisioned a *Grossdeutschland* (GROSE-doyt-shlant), or large Germany, consisting of all the members of the German Confederation, including the German-speaking parts of Austria and the German parts of Bohemia. Such a solution would include many non-Germans, including Poles, Czechs, and Danes. The proponents of *Kleindeutschland* (KLINE-doyt-shlant), or small Germany, which would exclude Austria and its possessions, saw their solution as a more likely scenario, although it would exclude many Germans. The proposal of a small Germany succeeded in the end, largely because the reassertion of Austrian imperial power in the fall of 1848 put the non-German areas under Vienna's control out of reach.

The Prussian reassertion of royal power, though partial, was a signal for other German rulers in late 1848 to dismiss their liberal ministers. The moment for liberalism and national unification to triumph had passed by the time the **Frankfurt Assembly** drew up a constitution in the spring of 1849. Having opted for the *Kleindeutsch* solution, the parliament offered the throne to Friedrich Wilhelm IV, king of Prussia. Although the king was not a liberal, he ruled the largest state within the designated empire. If power could promote and protect German unity, he possessed it in the form of the Prussian army. But Friedrich Wilhelm feared that accepting the throne would lead to war with Austria. Believing in the principle of monarchy, he also did not want an office offered by representatives of the people, and so he refused the offer. Lacking an alternative plan, most members of the Frankfurt Assembly went home. A rump parliament and a series of uprisings in favor of German unity were crushed by the Prussian army.

In Italy, too, nationalist aspirations emerged once a revolt, triggered by social and economic grievances, had broken out. In the years before 1848, nationalists and liberals hoped somehow to see their program of a united and free Italy implemented. News of the Paris uprising in February galvanized revolutions in Italy. Italians, under Austrian rule, forced the Austrians to evacuate their Italian possessions. Revolts and mass protests in several Italian states led rulers to grant, or at least promise, a constitution. The king of Piedmont, Charles Albert (r. 1831–1849), who hoped to play a major part in unifying Italy, did grant his people a constitution. In Austrian Italy, the middle classes, although eager to be free of foreign rule, feared radical elements among the laborers. They believed that annexation to nearby Piedmont would provide security from both Austria and the troublesome lower classes. The king of Piedmont decided to unite Italy under his throne if doing so would prevent the spread of radicalism to his kingdom. The persistent nationalist and revolutionary sentiment provoked Charles Albert to declare war on Austria, first in March 1848, and again a year later. Both times he was defeated, the second in only six days. Humiliated, the king resigned his throne to his son, Victor Emmanuel II (r. 1849–1878). The Austrians quickly reconquered their lost provinces and reinstated their puppet governments, dashing the dream of a united Italy.

In the multinational empire of the Habsburgs, nationalism manifested itself in the form of demands for national independence from foreign rule. With Austria's power temporarily weakened, as a result of revolution in Vienna, nationalist revolts broke out not only in Italy, but simultaneously in Hungary, the Czech lands, and Croatia. The Austrian emperor yielded in Hungary, giving it virtual independence. Constitutional government was established, but participation in the political process was limited to Magyars, who were the single largest ethnic group, constituting 40 percent of the population. The other nationalities in Hungary—Romanians,

Ça, c'est pour l'ennemi du dehors, pour le dedans, voici comme l'on combat loyalement les adversaires...

Ballots, Not Bullets　This print from 1848 encourages the revolutionary on the barricades to put away his rifle and trust the democratic process. Pointing to the rifle, our French revolutionary announces, "This is for the external enemy." "As for the internal ones," he says, indicating the election urn, "this is how one fights them loyally."
(Roger Viollet/Getty Images)

Frankfurt Assembly
Popularly elected national assembly that attempted to create a unified German state.

Constitutional Government in Denmark　On March 21, 1848, fifteen thousand Danes, inspired by the example of Paris, marched on the palace to demand constitutional rights. Unlike the protests at the French capital, however, this event was peaceful and led to the establishment of a constitutional government. This painting honors the new parliament that came into being after the liberal constitution was adopted in 1849.　(Photo, Statens Museum for Kunst, Copenhagen)

Slovaks, Croats, and Slovenes—preferred the more distant rule of Austrian Vienna to Magyar authority. The Czech lands also witnessed agitation, but there and elsewhere the tide favoring the nationalists turned. The revolt against the empire was not coordinated, and the various nationalisms were often in conflict with one another. Once the emperor reestablished his power in Vienna, he could move against his rebellious subjects. The Austrian Empire bombarded Prague into submission, and with Russian help, brought Hungary to heel, and then reestablished its authority in Italy. If the nationalist fires had been quenched, the dangers nationalism posed to the survival of the Habsburg Empire were also revealed.

Three major countries escaped the revolutionary wave that washed across Europe. In Great Britain, the government had proven capable of adjusting to some of the major popular demands, averting the need for revolution. In Russia, the repressive tsarist system prevented any defiance from escalating into an opposition mass movement. Spain was also spared. General Ramón Narváez (nar-VA-yes) (1799–1868) brutally ran the country from 1844 to 1851. When he was on his deathbed, the priest asked him whether he forgave his enemies. He answered, "I have no enemies. I have shot them all!"

SECTION SUMMARY

- Across the Continent, the roots for revolution lay in increasingly restricted resources among rural peasants and urban workers; the harvest failures and economic depression of 1845–1846 turned this situation into a crisis.

- The liberal impulse to revolution at first united middle classes, peasants, and workers in demands for political freedoms and economic justice.

- Once regimes gave into the challenge or were overthrown, the goals of different social classes conflicted; the divisions between them opened the path to reaction and repression.

- Liberal revolution in eastern and central Europe inspired movements of national unification in the German states and in Italy, Hungary, the Czech lands, and Croatia, all at the expense of the Austrian Empire.

CHAPTER SUMMARY

In 1814 and 1815, after more than twenty-two years of war, the powers that finally defeated Napoleon—Great Britain, Austria, Prussia, and Russia—wanted to restore the prerevolutionary Old Regime to Europe. The Congress of Vienna sought to establish international stability by creating a balance of power. To that end, the Great Powers even brought the vanquished nation of France—with its Bourbon monarchy reinstated—into the Concert of Europe on equal footing.

In reaction to the revolutionary challenges of the late eighteenth century, new ideologies—conservatism, romanticism, nationalism, liberalism, and socialism—took root, and shaped the outlook, movements, and policies of the first half of the nineteenth century. While conservatism sought to stem the tides of change through repressive measures in both eastern and western Europe, the other ideologies called for and justified it. The severe economic downturn and the social displacements of the 1840s, along with perceptions of social injustice and profound desire for representative, if not democratic institutions, culminated in the Revolutions of 1848.

Most of the aspirations of the 1848 revolutions failed to be realized as authoritarian regimes regained the upper hand by 1851. Although counterrevolutionary forces temporarily defeated both the liberal and nationalistic impulses behind the revolutions of 1848, experiments born of these events suggested new modes of political organization that would later come to fruition.

FOCUS QUESTIONS

- What were the goals of the Restoration, and the sources of resistance to it?

- What major ideologies developed in the first half of the nineteenth century?

- How did the restorations that followed the Napoleonic era give way to reform?

- What were the main causes of the revolutions of 1848, and what roles did nationalism, liberalism, and socialism play in inciting and sustaining revolution?

KEY TERMS

Congress of Vienna (p. 588)
Corn Laws (p. 589)
Decembrists (p. 592)
conservatism (p. 593)
romanticism (p. 593)

nationalism (p. 595)
liberalism (p. 597)
laissez-faire (p. 598)
utilitarianism (p. 598)
socialism (p. 599)
Marxism (p. 601)

July Revolution (p. 602)
Great Reform Bill (p. 603)
Chartism (p. 603)
Frankfurt Assembly (p. 611)

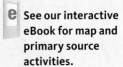 This icon will direct you to additional materials on the website: www .cengage.com/history/ noble/westciv6e.

See our interactive eBook for map and primary source activities.

22

CHAPTER OUTLINE

The Changing Nature of International Relations

Forging New Nation-States, 1850–1871

Fragile Empires

The Development of Western Democracies

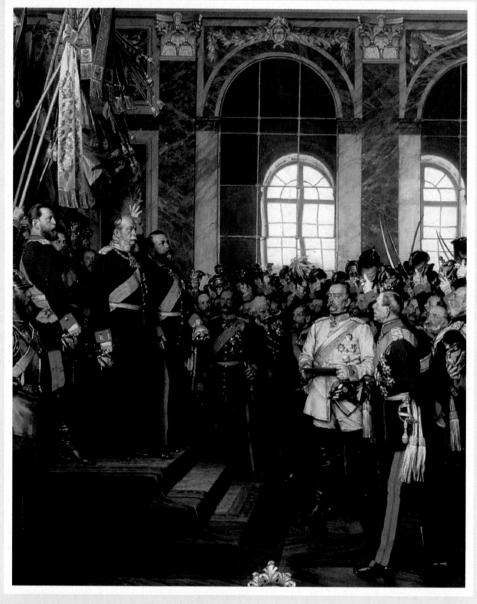

Wilhelm I at Versailles
Wilhelm is proclaimed ruler of the German Empire, 1871. (akg-images)

Nationalism and Political Reform, 1850–1880

The ceremonial occasion depicted in the painting on the left is a monumental one for European and world history: The crowned heads of different German states, without the benefit of a parliament or popular vote, proclaim the unification of all their states under one nation. On the podium, standing just behind the newly declared kaiser, Wilhelm I, is Crown Prince Friedrich Wilhelm (later Kaiser Friedrich III). To the kaiser's left, with his arm upraised, is the grand duke of Baden. In the middle of the scene, resplendent in his white uniform, is Bismarck, the political architect of German unification. On the right nearby is Field Marshal Helmuth von Moltke (von molt-KEH), the military genius who provided the series of military victories allowing Prussia to unify Germany under its aegis. The location of this ceremony also has profound symbolism as well as irony: Four months after delivering a humiliating defeat to France, a unified Germany was proclaimed in the famed Hall of Mirrors in the grandiose palace of Versailles, the former seat of French kings and royal court.

Germany had become a united nation by war. In the generation after 1850, the contours of European politics changed—new states appeared on the map, and within their national borders a good number of states reformed their political institutions. To meet the demand for popular participation in government so forcefully expressed in 1848, every European state except the Ottoman and Russian Empires found it necessary to have a parliament. Rare before midcentury, such institutions became common thereafter. No longer was the demand for popular participation seen as a threat to the existing political and social order. In fact, popular participation, or the appearance of it, gave the existing order a legitimacy it had not enjoyed since before the French Revolution. Nationalism flourished during this period, emerging as a decisive force throughout the West.

These political transformations occurred in an era of unprecedented economic growth and prosperity. Industrial production expanded the economy; the discovery of gold in California in 1848 led to the expansion of credit (since currencies were backed by gold), which in turn led to the founding of new banks and mass investments in growing industries. The standard of living rose significantly in industrializing nations. Between 1850 and 1880, industrial production increased by 90 percent in Great Britain and by 50 percent in France. The middle classes expanded dramatically.

In the first half of the century, international relations had been dominated by the congress system, in which representatives of the major European states met periodically to refine and preserve the balance of power. This system collapsed in the second half of the

 This icon will direct you to additional materials on the website: www .cengage.com/history/ noble/westciv6e.

See our interactive eBook for map and primary source activities.

Realpolitik Style of governing based on practical and material factors, rather than on ethics or ideology, and that uses all means, including war, to expand the influence and power of a state.

century, as political leaders pursued the narrow nationalist interests of their respective states. Instead of negotiating with one another, a new generation of leaders employed brute military force—or the threat of its use—to resolve international conflicts. The new age was dominated not by ideals but by force, announced Bismarck, the main practitioner of what became known as **Realpolitik**, a policy in which war became a regular instrument of statecraft.

THE CHANGING NATURE OF INTERNATIONAL RELATIONS

How did the Crimean War affect international relations?

congress system System of European international relations in the first half of the nineteenth century in which the major European states cooperated to preserve the balance of power.

Following the 1815 Congress of Vienna (see Chapter 21), European states attempted, through the **congress system**, to work out their differences by negotiation, avoiding situations in which one state triumphed at the cost of another. The Crimean War and the subsequent national realignments it caused raised mutual suspicions, leading nations to act in their own self-interests and to ignore the concerns of the other major players in the international system. This reorientation facilitated the emergence of nation-states at the expense of traditional empires.

The Crimean War, 1854–1856

The Crimean War had many causes. Principally, however, it had to do with Russia claiming the right to protect Orthodox Christians within the predominantly Muslim Ottoman Empire. This claim led to war between Russia and the Ottoman Empire in 1853, resulting in a Russian victory. The defeat of the Ottoman Empire made it more vulnerable to further Russian incursions.

British and French statesmen had considerable interest in the conflict. Britain had long feared that the collapse of the Ottoman Empire would lead Russia to seek territorial gains in the Mediterranean. Such a move would challenge Britain's naval supremacy in that region. An explosion of public sentiment against Russia's aggressiveness also obliged the British government to consider military action. Meanwhile, the French emperor, Napoleon III, believed that successful war against Russia would provide the opportunity to redraw European borders. He hoped that a new order would lead to increased French power and influence. Napoleon also imagined that fighting side by side with Britain could lay the foundation for Anglo-French friendship. And so England and France rushed to defend the Ottoman Empire and declared war on Russia in March 1854.

Florence Nightingale   This photograph was taken in 1856, shortly after Nightingale returned to England from the Crimean War. Her privileged background provided the official connections that helped her nursing services succeed.   (Florence Nightingale, c.1860 (b/w photo), English Photographer, (19th century)/Florence Nightingale Museum, London, UK/The Bridgeman Art Library)

All sides fought the war poorly, with woefully inadequate leadership. Five times more casualties resulted from disease than from enemy fire. Although the Russians had a standing army of a million men, their poor communications and supply systems prevented them from ever fielding more than a quarter of their forces. In Britain, the press and members of Parliament denounced their side's inadequate materiel and incompetent leadership. For the first time, the press played an active role in reporting war; the new technologies of the telegraph and photography brought to readers at home the gruesome realities of battle. One of the few heroic figures to emerge from this conflict was the English nurse Florence Nightingale (1820–1910), who organized a nursing service to care for the British sick and wounded. Later, her wartime experience allowed her to pioneer nursing as a professional calling. (See the feature, "The Written Record: Florence Nightingale in the Crimean War.")

After almost two years of fighting in the Balkans and the Crimean peninsula, Russia abandoned the key fortress of Sevastopol in September 1855. The conflict killed three-quarters of a million people—more than any European war between the end of the Napoleonic Wars and World War I. It was a particularly futile, senseless war whose most important consequence was political: It unleashed dramatic new changes in the international order that allowed for the emergence of the new nation-states.

The Congress of Paris, 1856

The former combatants met in Paris in February 1856 to work out a peace treaty. Their decisions—which pleased no one—shaped relations among European states for the next half century. Russian statesmen were especially discontented, as their country was forbidden to have a fleet in the Black Sea. Nor did French leaders feel that their nation had benefited, other than the prestige of holding the congress in Paris. The north Italian state of Piedmont (Kingdom of Sardinia), which had joined the allies, only gained a vague statement about the unsatisfactory nature of Italy's existing situation. Prussia was invited to attend the congress only as an afterthought and hence also felt slighted.

Although the war seemed to have sustained the integrity of the Ottoman Empire, the peace settlement weakened it indirectly by dictating reforms in the treatment of its Christian populations. These reforms impaired the empire's ability to repress the growing nationalist movements in the Balkans. British political leaders, galled by the heavy sacrifices of the war, moved toward isolationism in foreign policy. Austrian policymakers had hoped Britain and France would aid them in preserving the Habsburg Empire; instead, these powers, angry that Austria had not helped in the war, offered no assistance—a stance that would further weaken Habsburg imperial hegemony. At the time the peace treaty was signed, few people foresaw the enormous results that would flow from it.

By and large, the decisions reached in Paris would be disregarded or unilaterally revised as competition and rivalry between the major powers destabilized the international system. This new international climate also allowed new states to take shape without international sanction.

SECTION SUMMARY

- The Crimean War of 1854–1856 marked the end of the spirit of cooperation that had resulted from the Congress of Vienna in 1815.
- The Crimean War was caused by the Russian defeat of the Ottomans in 1853, British fear of Russian influence in the Mediterranean, and Napoleon III's desire to increase French influence.
- The 1856 Congress of Paris humiliated Russia and restricted its military access to the Black Sea. The postwar settlement dictated reforms in the treatment of Christians in the Ottoman Empire, which, in turn, impaired the Ottoman ability to repress nationalist movements in the Balkans.

Crimean War This photograph shows the interior of the Sevastopol fortress after it had been battered into surrender. The Crimean War was the first conflict to be documented by photographers. (The Art Archive/Picture Desk)

FORGING NEW NATION–STATES, 1850–1871

What respective processes led to the unifications of Italy and Germany into nation-states, and how did they differ?

In the aftermath of the Crimean War, both Italy and Germany became united as nation-states. These new states resulted in part from issues left unresolved in the Revolutions of 1848, and from the collapse of the congress system established in 1815. In both cases, national unification resulted from a series of wars. In Italy, the relatively liberal constitutional monarchy of Piedmont-Sardinia (Kingdom of Sardinia) initiated the unification process. Prussia, with a long tradition of militarism and authoritarianism, forged German unification. The resulting states reflected the stark differences between their respective goals and the means of realizing them.

Italian Unification, 1859–1870

The revolution of 1848 in Italy (see pages 609–611) had revealed an interest in national unification, but the attempt had failed. Idealists, such as Giuseppe Mazzini (see page 595), had preached that Italy would be unified not by its rulers but by its people, who would rise and establish a free republic. Instead, the deed was done by royalty, by war, and with the help of a foreign state. Although ideals were not absent from the process of unification, cynical manipulation and scheming also came into play.

risorgimento Italian term, beginning in the late eighteenth century, for the political and cultural renewal of Italy. It later came to be associated with Italian unification.

Since the late eighteenth century, some Italians had been calling for a *risorgimento* (ree-sor-djee-MEN-toe), a political and cultural renewal of Italy. By the mid-nineteenth century,

Florence Nightingale in the Crimean War

Florence Nightingale used her influential family connections to win an appointment to the Crimean battlefield. Once there, she organized nursing for the wounded and was able to secure additional personnel and medical supplies for her hospital. Women were supposed to be sheltered from the harsh realities of the outside world, but as this letter indicates, Nightingale was not spared war in its cruelest aspects.

We have no room for corpses in the wards. The Surgeons pass on to the next, an excision of the shoulder-joint—beautifully performed and going on well—[cannon] ball lodged just in the head of the joint, and fracture starred all round. The next poor fellow has two stumps for arms—and the next has lost an arm and leg. As for the balls, they go in where they like, and do as much harm as they can in passing. That is the only rule they have. The next case has one eye put out, and paralysis of the iris of the other. He can neither see nor understand. But all who can walk come into us for Tobacco, but I tell them that we have not a bit to put into our own mouths. Not a sponge, nor a rag of linen, not anything have I left. Everything is gone to make slings and stump pillows and shirts. These poor fellows have not had a clean shirt nor been washed for two months before they came here, and the state in which they arrive from the transport is literally crawling. I hope in a few days we shall establish a little cleanliness. But we have not a basin nor a towel nor a bit of soap nor a broom—I have ordered 300 scrubbing brushes. But one half the Barrack is so sadly out of repair that it is impossible to use a drop of water on the stone floors, which are all laid upon rotten wood, and would give our men fever in no time. . . .

I am getting a screen now for the Amputations, for when one poor fellow, who is to be amputated tomorrow, sees his comrade today die under the knife it makes an impression—and diminishes his chance. But, anyway, among these exhausted frames the mortality of the operations is frightful.

QUESTIONS

1. How did Florence Nightingale's presence on the Crimean battlefield defy Victorian middle-class gender roles? How did it reaffirm them?

2. What does her description convey about the impact that modern technology had on warfare by 1854?

Source: Letter to Dr. William Bowman, November 14, 1854, in *"I Have Done My Duty": Florence Nightingale in the Crimean War, 1854-56*, ed. Sue M. Goldie, *1987*, pp. 37-38. Copyright © 1987. Reprinted by permission of University of Iowa Press.

the idea was actively supported by a small, elite group consisting of the educated middle class, urban property owners, and members of the professions. For merchants, industrialists, and professionals, a unified state would provide a larger stage on which to pursue their ambitions.

THE PLOT TO UNIFY ITALY

After the failed 1848 revolution, most Italian rulers resorted to repression. Only the northern Italian kingdom of Piedmont-Sardinia kept the liberal constitution adopted during the 1848 revolution, and it welcomed political refugees from other Italian states. Not only politically, but economically, it was a beacon to the rest of Italy, establishing modern banks and laying half the rail lines on the peninsula.

The statesman who was to catapult Piedmont into a position of leadership in the dramatic events leading to Italian unification was Count Camillo di Cavour (1810–1861). The son of a Piedmontese nobleman and high government official, Cavour was sympathetic to the aspirations of the middle class and saw in Britain and France models of what Italy ought to become: a liberal and economically advanced society.

Cavour was ambitious, hardworking, and driven to succeed. A well-known journalist and the editor of the newspaper *Risorgimento*, he joined the government in 1850. Two years later, King Victor Emmanuel appointed him prime minister. Cavour shared the enthusiasm of the middle classes for an Italian nation, but his vision did not include all of Italy—only its north and center—which then could dominate the rest of the peninsula in a loose federation. Unifying the north and center would first require ousting Austria from the northern provinces. The failures of 1848 had taught Cavour that this task would require foreign help, especially from France.

When the Crimean War broke out in 1854, Cavour supported the British and the French, hoping to advance his cause. He sent twenty thousand troops to the Crimea, one-tenth of whom died. This act gained him a seat at the Congress of Paris, where his presence boosted Piedmont's prestige—and where he and Napoleon III had an opportunity to meet and size up each other.

Because Austria had been France's traditional opponent, Napoleon III favored the cause of Italian liberation from its rule; destroying Austria's power in Italy might strengthen France. Thus, in July 1858, the French emperor and the Piedmontese prime minister met secretly to discuss how

🌐 **Map 22.1—The Unification of Italy, 1859–1870**

Piedmontese leadership under Cavour in the north, and national-ist fervor inspired by Garibaldi in the south, united Italy.

Legend:
- Kingdom of Sardinia before 1859
- To Kingdom of Sardinia, 1859
- To Kingdom of Sardinia, 1860
- To Kingdom of Italy, 1866, 1870
- ✦ Major battle
- ▬ Boundary of Kingdom of Italy after unification

Italian unity could be achieved. They agreed that Piedmont would stir up trouble in one of Austria's Italian territories in an effort to goad the Austrians into war. According to the plan, France would join the war to help the Piedmontese expel Austria from the northern provinces of Lombardy and Venetia. In exchange, the French emperor demanded the Piedmontese provinces of Nice and Savoy, which bordered France.

War between Austria and Piedmont broke out in April 1859. By June, the combined Piedmontese and French forces had routed the Austrians at Magenta and Solferino (see **Map 22.1**). So bloody were these battles that the color magenta was named after the deep red of the soaked battlefield. The horrors of this war also inspired the founding of the Red Cross.

Shocked by the bloodshed he had witnessed, Napoleon III decided to end the fighting instead of pressing on. He was further alarmed because Prussia had begun to mobilize its army to support Austria. His plan for Italy had meanwhile begun to unravel: Several central Italian states expressed a desire to be annexed to Piedmont, which would have resulted in an independent state much larger than Napoleon III had anticipated. These factors led him to betray Cavour; he made an agreement with the Austrians, which gave Lombardy to Piedmont, but allowed Venetia to remain within the Austrian Empire.

Unification Achieved, 1860   Napoleon's betrayal outraged Cavour, but unexpected events in the south also changed his vision of national unification. The centuries-old misgovernment of the Kingdom of the Two Sicilies (Naples and Sicily) led to an uprising on the island of Sicily in April 1860. The revolutionary firebrand Giuseppe Garibaldi (1807–1882) set sail for Sicily in May 1860 with but a thousand poorly armed, red-shirted followers to help the island overthrow its Bourbon ruler. Winning that struggle, Garibaldi's forces crossed to the mainland in August. Victory followed victory, and enthusiasm for Garibaldi grew. His army swelled to 57,000 men, and he won the entire kingdom of Naples.

Threatened by the advance of Garibaldi's power and fearing its reach into the Papal States, Cavour sent his army into the area in September 1860. Although Garibaldi was a republican, he was convinced that Italy could best achieve unity under the king of Piedmont-Sardinia, and he willingly submitted the southern part of Italy, which he controlled, to the king, Victor Emmanuel II (r. 1849–1878). Thus, by November 1860, Italy had been united under the Kingdom of Sardinia (see **Map 22.1**). The united territories affirmed their desire to be part of the new Italy through plebiscites based on universal male suffrage. The 1848 constitution of Piedmont became the constitution of the newly united Italy. Cavour lived to relish his handiwork for only a few months, as he died of an undiagnosed illness in May 1861. His last words were "Italy is made—all is safe."

Still to be joined to the new state were Austrian-held Venetia in the northeast and Rome and its environs, held by the pope with the support of a French garrison. But within a decade, a favorable international situation enabled the fledgling country to acquire both key areas. Upon its defeat in the Austro-Prussian War in 1866, Austria ceded Venetia to Italy. Four years later, the Franco-Prussian War forced the French to evacuate Rome, which they had occupied since 1849. Rome was joined to Italy and became its capital in 1870. With that event, unification was complete.

National unity had been achieved, but it was frail. The uprisings that Garibaldi had led in the south were motivated more by hatred of the Bourbons than by fervor for national unification. And once the union was achieved, the north behaved like a conquering state—sending its officials to the south, raising taxes, and imposing its laws. In 1861, civil war broke out and lasted five years; it produced more casualties than the entire effort of unification.

THE PROBLEMS OF A UNIFIED ITALY

Garibaldi Leading His "Red Shirts" to Victory Over the Neapolitan Army, May 1860
Garibaldi's conquests in the south and Cavour's in the north opened the way for Italian unification. (Scala/Art Resource, NY)

Other major divisions remained. In 1861, only 2.5 percent of the population spoke the national language, Florentine Italian. Economics also divided the country. The north was far more industrialized than the rural south. In the south, child mortality was higher, life expectancy was lower, and illiteracy was close to 90 percent. The Catholic Church remained hostile to the new Italian state. The popes, left to rule a tiny domain—a few square blocks around the papal palace known as the Vatican—considered themselves prisoners. They denounced anyone who participated in elections. Thus, many Italian Catholics refused to recognize the new state for decades, thwarting its legitimacy.

In the face of such divisions, Piedmont-Sardinia imposed strong central control, resolutely refusing a federal system of government, which many Italians in an earlier era had hoped for. This choice reflected fear that any other form of government might lead to a fate similar to that of the United States, whose federal system of government led to secessionism and the Civil War in early 1861. The constitution Piedmont-Sardinia imposed on unified Italy limited suffrage to men of property and education—less than 2 percent of the population. Further, as prime minister, Cavour created and manipulated parliamentary majorities in favor of his cabinet, reversing the logic behind the parliamentary system in which cabinets were supposed to represent, and answer to, freely elected legislative bodies. Nevertheless, the new unified Italy was a liberal state that guaranteed legal equality and freedom of association, and provided more freedom for its citizens than the Italian people had seen for centuries.

German Unification, 1850–1871

Like Italy, Germany had long been a collection of states. Since 1815, the thirty-eight German states had been loosely organized in the German Confederation. Like Piedmont-Sardinia in Italy, one German state, powerful Prussia, led the unification movement. And just as Italy had in Cavour a strong leader who imposed his will, so did German unification have a ruthless and cunning champion: **Otto von Bismarck**, minister president of Prussia. But whereas Cavour, for all his wiliness, was committed to establishing a liberal state, Bismarck was wedded to autocratic rule.

Otto von Bismarck
Nineteenth-century German statesman who, through a series of aggressive wars, united Germany. Germany became the dominant power in Europe under his administration.

The revolutionaries of 1848 had failed in their attempt to achieve German unification when the king of Prussia refused to accept a throne offered by the elected Frankfurt Assembly (see page 611). As the painting at the beginning of this chapter illustrates, German unification was ratified not by the ballot, as it was in Italy, but by the acclamation of the crowned heads of Germany. The nation was united by the use of military force and the imposition of Prussian absolutism over the whole country.

THE RISE OF BISMARCK

Austria under Metternich had always treated Prussia as a privileged junior partner. After Metternich's fall in 1848, however, rivalry erupted between the two German states. Each tried to manipulate, for its own benefit, the desire for national unity that had become manifest during the revolution of 1848.

In March 1850, representatives from a number of German states met to consider unification under Prussian sponsorship. Austria opposed such a union and, with Russian support, threatened war. Since the Prussian military was not strong enough to challenge Austria, Prussia agreed to abandon the plan for unification and to accept Austrian leadership in Germany. But a decade later, the new Prussian king, Wilhelm I (r. 1861–1888), was determined to strengthen Prussia by expanding the size and effectiveness of the army. The parliament, however, refused to approve funding for a military buildup. The conflict was not simply about the budget; it was an issue of who should govern the country—the king or the elected representatives. To get his way, the king appointed Count Otto von Bismarck as minister president.

Bismarck was a Junker, a Prussian aristocrat known for his reactionary views, who had opposed the liberal movement in 1848. As Prussian emissary to the German Confederation, he had challenged Austrian primacy. Devoted to his monarch, Bismarck sought to heighten Prussian power in Germany and throughout Europe through policies based on "Realpolitik," stressing pragmatic considerations at the expense of ethics and the law. He faced down the parliament, telling the Budget Commission in 1862, "The position of Prussia in Germany will be decided not by its liberalism but by its power … not through speeches and majority decisions are the great questions of the day decided—that was the mistake of 1848 and 1849—but by iron and blood."[1]

Bismarck tried to win over the liberals by suggesting that with military force at its disposal, Prussia could lead German unification. But the liberals continued to resist, and the parliament voted against the military reforms. Unfazed, Bismarck carried out the military measures anyway and ordered the collection of the necessary taxes. The citizens acquiesced and paid to upgrade their army. Prussia would not yield to parliamentarism as Britain had.

German liberals faced a dilemma: Which did they value more—the goal of nationhood or the principles of liberty? To oppose Bismarck effectively, German liberals knew they would have to ally themselves with the working classes, but they feared the workers and forestalled forming a unified front of opposition. Germany appeared embarked on an illiberal course.

Bismarck ingeniously exploited the weakness of the liberals and the growing desire for German unification, further strengthened by the Franco-Austrian War of 1859, during which Germans had feared that the French would attack across the Rhine River. Many came to believe that only a strong, united Germany could give its inhabitants security. Prussia had already led the important move toward economic unification with the *Zollverein*, a customs union that included most German states, but excluded Austria. Founded in 1834, the customs union had become more extensive with the passage of time; even states that were politically hostile to Prussia joined the union to protect their economic interests. Economic unity led to all-German professional and cultural associations that surpassed state boundaries; it was an indispensable stage in the process toward political unity. By 1860, the idea of a united Germany had gained a substantial appeal.

Zollverein Customs union formed among states in the German Confederation beginning in 1834, creating an important step to later political unification of the German nation-state.

PRUSSIAN WARS AND GERMAN UNITY

Having built up the military and established the supremacy of royal power in Prussia, Bismarck was ready to enlarge its role in Germany—and he believed that war against Austria was the only means to do so. Conflicts over the provinces of Schleswig (SHLES-vik) and Holstein (HOLL-shteyn) served as a pretext (see **MAP 22.2**). In 1864, Prussia and Austria had successfully gone to war against Denmark to secure the independence of these two German-speaking provinces. Bismarck then used disputes over their joint administration as an excuse for war against Austria. Prussia attacked Austrian-administered Holstein in June 1866, launching the Austro-Prussian War. After a scant seven weeks, the newly reformed Prussian army won a decisive victory in the Battle of Sadowa (SAH-doe-wah). Prussia's industrial superiority had enabled it to equip its soldiers with the Dreyse needle guns, new breech-loading rifles with innovative pins capable of firing rounds at a faster rate than traditional guns. They also allowed troops to fire from a prone position, while the Austrians, with their muzzle loaders, had to stand up to shoot. With military victory, Prussia annexed its smaller neighbors, which had supported Austria. In Bismarck's scheme, this enlarged Prussia would dominate the newly formed North German Confederation, comprising all the states north of the Main (MINE) River. From now on, Austria was excluded from German affairs.

The triumph of Sadowa made Bismarck a popular hero. Elections held on the day of the battle returned a conservative pro-Bismarck majority to the Prussian parliament. The legislature, including a large number of liberals mesmerized by the military victory, voted to legalize retroactively the illegal taxes that had been levied since 1862 to upgrade the military. In making this compromise, liberals gave national unity higher priority than constitutional institutions, which they mistakenly thought could be secured later.

The unification of Germany, like that of Italy, was facilitated by a favorable international situation. The Crimean War had estranged Russia from Austria, once allies. Although it would have been opportune for France to intervene on the Austrian side in the Austro-Prussian War, the French emperor had been lulled into inaction by vague Prussian promises of support for French plans to annex Luxembourg. Once the war was won, Bismarck reneged on these promises. France was left with the problem of a strong, enlarged Prussia on its eastern border, which threatened France's position as a Great Power. British leaders likewise did not intervene in the unification process. Disillusioned by the results of the Crimean War, they were in an isolationist mood. Moreover, Britain's government was sympathetic to the rise of a fellow Protestant power.

Bismarck's design was almost complete. Only the southern German states remained outside the North German Confederation. He obliged them to sign a military treaty with Prussia and established a customs parliament for all the members of the Zollverein (the customs union), including the southern German states. The southern states, which were Catholic and sympathetic to Austria, were reluctant to see German unity advance any further. Only some dramatic event could remove their resistance.

French leaders were also determined to prevent German unity—French security had relied on a weak and divided Germany since the mid-seventeenth century.

Both Berlin and Paris anticipated war, which came soon enough, precipitated by a crisis over the Spanish succession. In 1868, a military coup had overthrown the Spanish queen Isabella, and the provisional government offered the throne to a Catholic member of the Hohenzollerns

THE FRANCO-PRUSSIAN WAR AND UNIFICATION, 1870–1871

🌐 **MAP 22.2—The Unification of Germany, 1866–1871**

A series of military victories made it possible for Prussia to unite the German states under its domain.

(HO-en-tsoll-ernz), the reigning Prussian monarch's family. The French viewed this candidacy as an unacceptable expansion of Prussian power and influence. Fearing a two-front war with Prussia in the east and Spain in the south, they insisted that the Hohenzollerns refuse the proffered throne. As passions heated, Bismarck was elated at the prospect of war, but King Wilhelm was not. On July 12, 1870, Wilhelm engineered the withdrawal of the young prince's candidacy for the Spanish throne, removing the cause for war. Bismarck was bitterly disappointed.

Not content with this diplomatic victory, the French pushed their luck further. On July 13, the French ambassador met the king of Prussia at the resort spa of Ems and demanded guarantees that no Hohenzollern would ever again be a candidate for the Spanish throne. Unable to provide any more concessions without a serious loss of prestige, the Prussian king refused the French petition.

Wilhelm telegraphed an account of his meeting to Bismarck. The chancellor immediately seized the opportunity this message provided. He edited the message to make the exchange between king and ambassador seem more curt than it actually had been; then he released it to the press. As he hoped, the French interpreted what became known as the "Ems Dispatch" to be a deliberate snub to their ambassador, and overreacted. Napoleon III was deluged with emotional demands that he avenge the imagined slight to French national honor. On July 15, he declared war.

The Prussians led a well-planned campaign. An army of 384,000 Prussians was rushed by rail to confront a force of 270,000 Frenchmen. The French had the advantage of better rifles, but the Prussians were equipped with heavier cannon, which could pulverize French positions from a distance. Within a few weeks, Prussia won a decisive victory at Sedan (seh-DAEN), taking the French emperor prisoner on September 2. The French continued the struggle, despite difficult odds. Infuriated by the continuation of the war, the Prussians resorted to extreme measures. They took hostages and burned down whole villages, and then laid siege to Paris, starving and bombarding its beleaguered population.

Throughout Germany, the outbreak of the war aroused general enthusiasm for the Prussian cause. Exploiting this popular feeling, Bismarck called on leaders of the southern German states to accept the unification of Germany under the Prussian king. Reluctant princes, such as the king of Bavaria, were bought off with bribes. On January 18, 1871, the German princes met in the Hall of Mirrors at the palace of Versailles, symbol of past French greatness. There, they acclaimed the Prussian king as Kaiser Wilhelm I, German emperor.

In May 1871, the Treaty of Frankfurt established the peace terms (see **MAP 22.1**). France was forced to give up the industrially rich provinces of Alsace and Lorraine and to pay Germany a heavy indemnity of five billion francs. These harsh terms embittered the French, leading many to desire revenge and establishing a formidable barrier to future Franco-German relations.

THE CHARACTER OF THE NEW GERMANY

German unity had been won through a series of wars—against Denmark in 1864, Austria in 1866, and France in 1870. The military had played a key role in forging German unity; victory in these wars had been due to the extraordinary leadership of Field Marshall Helmuth von Moltke and the Prussian general staff, the importance of which is represented in von Moltke's pride of place next to Bismarck in the opening illustration to this chapter. The military was established as a dominant force in the new nation. Italian unity had been sanctioned by plebiscites and a vote by an elected assembly accepting the popular verdict. The founding act of the new German state, as the illustration also shows, was the acclamation of the German emperor by German rulers on the soil of a defeated neighbor. Thus, the rulers placed themselves above elected assemblies and popular sanction.

On the surface, the constitution of the new Germany was remarkably democratic. It provided for an upper, appointed house, the *Bundesrat* (BOON-tes-raht), representing the individual German states, and a lower house, the *Reichstag* (RYSH-stak), which was elected by universal manhood suffrage. The latter might seem a surprising concession from Bismarck. But he knew the liberals lacked mass support and had confidence that he would be able to create majorities that could be manipulated for his purposes.

The authoritarianism of Prussia was projected onto all of Germany. The king of Prussia occupied the post of emperor, and the chancellor and other cabinet members were responsible only to him, and not to parliament. Only the emperor could make foreign policy and war, command the army, and interpret the constitution.

The emergence of a strong, united Germany shattered the European balance of power. In February 1871, the British political leader Benjamin Disraeli observed that the unification of Germany was a "greater political event than the French revolution of last century. … There is not a diplomatic tradition which has not been swept away. You have a new world. … The balance of power has been entirely destroyed."[2]

SECTION SUMMARY

- The reconfiguration of international relations after the Crimean War, in addition to persistent desires for national unification from 1848 among various groups, created opportunities for the unification of Italy and Germany into new nation-states. The strongest states in each achieved unification through conspiracy, war, and policies reflecting the new "Realpolitik" that characterized domestic and international relations.

- Italy's unification began with the Piedmont-Sardinian Prime Minister Cavour's plotting war against Austria with Napoleon III of France in order to free Lombardy and Venetia of Austrian rule. Giuseppe Garibaldi and his army advanced the process when rebellion against the Bourbon monarchy broke out in the south, and it was completed in 1870 as a by-product of the Franco-Prussian War.

- The Zollverein, a customs union that included most German states, but excluded Austria, helped advance support for national unification under Prussia. Prussia's reformed and expanded army, which Bismarck achieved without legislative approval, assured Prussian success in wars against Denmark (1864), Austria (1866), and France (1870), which finalized unification without Austria.

- Though Italian and German unifications each resulted from wars, the former had the benefit of plebiscites, while the latter did not, reflecting the more authoritarian character of the new German nation. Germany, henceforth, became the dominant power on the European continent, shattering the balance of power.

FRAGILE EMPIRES

How did the Austrian, Ottoman, and Russian Empires deal with the challenges they faced?

The three large empires of central and eastern Europe, battered by aggressive behavior from other European states and challenged by internal tensions, attempted to weather the endless crises they confronted. The Austrian, Ottoman, and Russian Empires labored to fortify their regimes with political reforms, but only Austria tried to accommodate democratic impulses by establishing a parliament. The Ottoman sultans and the Russian tsars clung tenaciously to their autocratic traditions.

The Dual Monarchy in Austria-Hungary

Emperor Franz Joseph (r. 1848–1916) had come to the Austrian throne as an 18-year-old in that year of crisis, 1848. He was a well-meaning monarch who took his duties seriously. His upbringing was German, he lived in German-speaking Vienna, and he headed an army and a bureaucracy that was mostly German. But Franz Joseph was markedly cosmopolitan. He spoke several of his subjects' languages and thought of himself as the emperor of all his peoples. A much-loved, regal figure, Franz Joseph provided a visible symbol of the state. He lacked imagination, however, and did little more than try to conserve a disintegrating empire coping with the modern forces of liberalism and nationalism.

February Patent
Enactment issued in 1861 by the Austrian emperor Franz Joseph that established a constitutional monarchy in the old Austrian Empire.

After the war with Piedmont and France (see page 620), Austrian statesmen sensed the vulnerability of their empire. To give the government credibility, in February 1861, Franz Joseph issued what became known as the **February Patent**, which guaranteed civil liberties and provided for local self-government and a parliament elected by eligible males.

The need to safeguard the remaining territories was clear. By 1866, the Austrian Habsburgs were no longer a German or an Italian power (Venetia had been handed over to a united Italy in return for assisting Prussia in defeating Austria). The strongest challenge to Habsburg rule came from Hungary, where the Magyars insisted on self-rule, a claim based on age-old rights and Vienna's initial acceptance of autonomy in 1848. Since Magyar cooperation was crucial for the well-being of the Habsburg Empire, the government entered into lengthy negotiations with Magyar leaders in 1867. The outcome was the **Compromise of 1867**. The agreement divided the Habsburg holdings into Austria in the west and Hungary in the east (see **MAP 22.3**). Each was independent, but they were linked by the person of the emperor of Austria, Franz Joseph, who was also king of Hungary. Hungary had full internal autonomy and participated jointly in imperial affairs—state finance, defense, and foreign relations. The new state created in 1867 was known as the dual monarchy of Austria-Hungary.

Compromise of 1867
Agreement that divided the Habsburg Empire into Austria in the west and Hungary in the east, a dual monarchy under Emperor Franz Joseph called Austria-Hungary.

The compromise confirmed Magyar dominance in Hungary. Although numerically a minority, the Magyars were nonetheless the largest of several ethnic groups; they controlled the Hungarian parliament, the army, the bureaucracy, and other state institutions. They opposed self-rule of other ethnic groups in the kingdom who spoke different languages: the Croats, Serbs, Slovaks, and Romanians. They also attempted a policy of Magyarization—teaching only Magyar in the schools, conducting all government business in Magyar, and giving access to government positions only to those fully assimilated in Magyar culture. This arrangement created frustrations and resistance among the various nationalities under their rule.

The terms of the compromise also gave the Hungarians a voice in imperial foreign policy. The Magyars feared that Slavic groups outside the empire, who planned to form independent states or had already done so, would inspire fellow Slavs in Austria-Hungary to revolt. To prevent that, the Hungarians favored an expansionist foreign policy in the Balkans, which the monarchy embraced (see **MAP 22.3**). Having lost its influence in Germany, Austria-Hungary saw the Balkans as an area in which it could assert itself—a policy that led to hostilities with other states.

The Ailing Ottoman Empire

At midcentury, the Ottoman Empire was still one of the largest European powers, but it faced unrest within its borders and threats from the expansionist designs of its neighbors. The ailing empire was commonly referred to as "the sick man of Europe." Over the next twenty-five years, the empire shed some of its territory and modernized its government, but nothing could save it from decline in the face of nationalist uprisings in its Balkan possessions.

🌐 **MAP 22.3—Austria-Hungary in 1878**

The Compromise of 1867 produced the dual monarchy of Austria-Hungary. A state of many languages and ethnicities, the Austro-Hungarian Empire occupied Bosnia in 1878, bringing more dissatisfied peoples under its rule. Tensions in the Balkans would lead to the outbreak of world war in 1914.

As early as the 1840s, the Ottoman Empire had begun various reform movements to bring more security to its subjects. Emulating Western institutions, the reforms introduced security of property, equity in taxation, and equality before the law regardless of religion. Government officials—who previously had been free to collect taxes arbitrarily, sending the required amount to the central government and keeping the rest—were given fixed salaries and subjected to regular inspections.

These reforms were strengthened after the Crimean War by further imperial edicts. Many young intellectuals were impatient with the pace of change, however, and critical of the sultan. Unable to freely express their opinions at home, some went into exile in Paris and London in the late 1860s. Their hosts called them the **Young Turks**, an expression that became synonymous with activists for change and improvement.

The failure to hold on to its empire caused further dissatisfaction with Ottoman rule among its people, and in the spring of 1876, rioters demanded and won the establishment of constitutional government. Within a year, however, the new sultan, Abdul Hamid II (r. 1876–1909), dismissed the constitutional government and reverted to personal rule. Part of the administration's problem was financial. The easy terms of foreign credit lured the sultan into taking out huge loans to finance extravagant projects. In spite of drought and famine, the authorities raised taxes to pay debts, fostering widespread discontent.

Young Turks Young intellectuals who wanted to transform the Ottoman Empire into a more modern, Westernized state. The expression has subsequently come to designate any group of activists pushing for political change.

Nationalistic Uprising in Bulgaria In this 1879 lithograph, Bulgaria is depicted in the form of a maiden—protected by the Russian eagle, breaking her chains, and winning liberty from the Ottoman Empire. (St. Cyril and Methodius National Library, Sofia)

BALKAN NATIONALISM

Nationalist fervor in the Balkans further intensified opposition to the Ottoman government. The central administration had lost control over its provincial officials, who were often corrupt and tyrannical. Christians, the majority population in the Balkans, blamed their suffering on Islamic rule, and many were inspired by the 1821 Greek war of independence and the revolutions of 1848 to seek their own independence.

The Romanians, who lived mainly in the adjoining provinces of Moldavia in the north and Wallachia (vall-AK-yah) in the south, began to express nationalist sentiments in the late eighteenth century. These sentiments were nurtured by Western-educated students, who claimed for their countrymen illustrious descent from Roman settlers of antiquity. News of the 1848 revolution in Paris helped trigger a revolt in both provinces by those demanding unification and independence. The Turks quickly crushed this uprising.

The Congress of Paris in 1856 removed Russia's right of protection over Moldavia and Wallachia and provided for a referendum to determine their future. In 1859, the two provinces chose a local military officer to rule both territories. In 1862, the Ottoman Empire recognized the union of the two principalities in the single, autonomous state of Romania. The Congress of Berlin in 1878 recognized Romania's full independence. Thus, in less than a quarter century, two provinces of the Ottoman Empire had gained full sovereignty.

The path to independence was much more violent for the Bulgarians. Revolutionary committees—encouraged by Serbia and Russia—spread propaganda and agitated against Ottoman rule. An uprising in Bulgaria broke out in May 1876. The Christian rebels attacked not only symbols of Ottoman authority, but also peaceable Muslim Turks living in their midst. The imperial army, aided by local Turkish volunteers, quickly reestablished Ottoman authority. Incensed by the massacre of fellow Muslims, the volunteers resorted to mass killing, looting, and burning of Christian villages. The "Bulgarian horrors" shocked Europe and made the continuation of Turkish rule unacceptable.

Russia, which saw itself as the protector of the Slavic peoples, reacted to the Bulgarian horrors by declaring war on the Ottoman Empire in April 1877. Russian victory resulted in the Treaty of San Stefano, signed in March 1878; it created a huge, independent Bulgaria as essentially a Russian protectorate.

THE CONGRESS OF BERLIN, 1878 The British, Austrians, and French were shocked at the extent to which the San Stefano treaty favored Russia. Under their pressure, the European Great Powers met in Berlin in 1878 to reconsider the treaty and reestablish a balance of power. The Congress of Berlin returned part of the Bulgarian territory to the Ottomans. It also removed Bosnia and Herzegovina from Ottoman rule. Henceforth, Austria-Hungary administered these provinces (see **MAP 24.3** on page 688). The sultan was forced to acknowledge the legal independence of Serbia, Montenegro, and Romania and the autonomy of Bulgaria.

Thus, Turkey was plundered not only by its enemies, but also by powers that had intervened on its behalf. When France complained that it received no compensation, it was given the chance to grab Tunisia, another land under Ottoman rule. Russia was given the Bessarabian provinces that Romania had acquired in 1856. The devious work of the Congress of Berlin reflected the power politics—Realpolitik—that now characterized international affairs. Statesmen shamelessly used force against both foe and friend for the aggrandizement of their own states. Neither morality nor international law restrained ambition. While the Great Powers attempted to appease one another to maintain peace in the short run, the settlement of 1878 led to further instability in the Balkans, which ultimately became the principal cause of the First World War.

Russia and the Great Reforms

Russia's defeat in the Crimean War and its distrust of the Western powers forced the tsar to consider ways of strengthening Russia by restructuring its institutions. In 1861, a series of measures known collectively as the Great Reforms initiated an era of structural transformation.

Many educated Russians felt that the defeat in the Crimea had revealed Russia's general backwardness. The critique of its archaic institutions, underway since the 1840s, widened—and serfdom was considered a central problem. Educated opinion had long denounced serfdom as immoral, but it also presented clear disadvantages in both the domestic and international domains.

THE ABOLITION OF SERFDOM

Serfdom held Russia back in its competition with the rest of the world. Defeat in the Crimean War by Britain and France suggested that soldiers with a stake in their society fought harder than men bound to lifetime servitude. In addition, the victorious Western states had won in part because their industrial might translated into more and better guns, ammunition, and transportation. Industrial progress required a mobile labor force, not one tied to the soil by serfdom. With a free labor force, rural populations, as in the West, could become the abundant labor supply that drove industrial production. Many Russians believed economic progress would be impossible unless serfdom were abolished.

The new tsar, Alexander II (r. 1855–1881), feared that if serfdom were not abolished from above, it would be overthrown by a serf rebellion that would destroy the aristocracy itself. In April 1861, he issued a decree freeing the serfs. With one stroke of a pen, he emancipated 22 million people from a system that allowed them to be bought and sold, separated from their families, and treated in the cruelest ways imaginable. Emancipation represented a compromise with the gentry; they insisted on compensation for their reluctant agreement to liberate the serfs. As a result, the newly liberated peasants had to reimburse the government with mortgage payments lasting fifty years. The peasants

A Critique of Russian Serfdom   The French artist Gustave Doré reveals how landowners inhumanely viewed their serfs as mere property that could be won and lost with a draw of the cards.   (Miriam and Ira D. Wallach Division of Art, Prints and Photographs, The New York Public Library, Astor, Lenox and Tilden Foundations/Art Resource, NY)

received some land, but its value was vastly overrated and its quantity insufficient for peasant families. To make ends meet, most freed peasants continued working for their former masters.

mir   Russian peasant commune. After Tsar Alexander II freed the serfs in 1861, the mir determined land use and paid the government mortgages and taxes.

The local commune, or **mir**, handled the mortgage payments and taxes that the central government imposed on the peasants. The mir (MEER) determined how the land was to be used, and it paid collectively for the mortgages and taxes on the land. As a consequence, the commune needed peasants to remain on the land, and they could leave only with its permission. Freed from serfdom, the peasants still suffered many constraints. In fact, the emancipation declaration was accompanied by massive peasant uprisings that had to be put down by force.

The tsar and his advisers feared the large mass of uneducated peasants as a potential source of anarchy and rebellion. They depended on the mir to preserve control, even though the commune system had some inherent economic disadvantages. Since increased productivity benefited the commune as much as the individual peasant, there was little incentive for peasants to improve their land, and agricultural yields remained low.

GOVERNMENT REFORM

Between 1800 and 1850, the Russian population had increased from 36 million to 59 million, and administering this vast country had become increasingly difficult. Overcentralized, with a poorly trained civil service, the government was unable to cope effectively with the problems of its people. Emancipation of the serfs greatly exacerbated this situation, as suddenly 22 million illiterate peasants threatened to overwhelm existing institutions. To address these problems, an 1864 law created village or regional governments, or **zemstvos** (SEMST-vose), which gave Russians the authority and the opportunity to use initiative in local matters.

zemstvos   Village or district assemblies created by Tsar Alexander II in 1864 as part of the Great Reform; they elected delegates to regional assemblies.

The zemstvos were largely controlled by the gentry and not particularly democratic. They were forbidden to debate political issues, and their decisions could be overridden or ignored by local officials appointed by the tsar. Some hoped that zemstvos could become the basis for self-government at the national level and looked for the creation of an all-Russian zemstvo, but the tsar firmly squelched such hopes. He jealously continued to insist and depend on an undivided and undiminished autocracy. Nonetheless, the zemstvos were a viable attempt to modernize an overburdened central government and created an important precedent for self-government.

The tsar also created an independent judiciary that ensured equality before the law, public jury trials, and uniform sentences. Russian political leaders recognized that growth in commerce and industry required public confidence in the judiciary and the rule of law. Businessmen would no longer fear arbitrary intervention by capricious officials and could develop enterprises in greater security.

In addition, censorship of the press was abolished. Under the previous tsar, Nicholas I, all ideas that did not conform to government policy were censored. Such censorship prevented the central government from being well informed about public opinion or about the effects of its policies on the country. Under Alexander, openness in the press was viewed as a remedy for corruption and misuse of power.

Reform also extended to the Russian army. Its structure and methods became more Western. Military service, previously limited to peasants, became the obligation of all Russian men, who submitted to a lottery. Those with an "unlucky" number entered the service. In an effort to make military service more attractive, the length of service was drastically cut and corporal punishment was abolished. Access to the officer corps was to be by merit rather than by social connection. The Ministry of War also improved the system of reserves, enabling Russia to mobilize a larger army with more modern weapons in case of war.

The Great Reforms represented considerable change for Russia. Nonetheless, Alexander remained wedded to the principles of autocracy. His aim in abolishing serfdom and introducing other reforms was to modernize and strengthen Russia and stabilize his divinely mandated rule. Like most Russians, Alexander believed that only the firm hand of autocracy could hold together a large, ethnically diverse country. The tsarist regime thus remained repressive, flexible only to the degree that its rulers had the will and wisdom to be.

SECTION SUMMARY

- Internal tensions and aggressive behavior of the European powers, as well as nationalist aspirations in the Balkan provinces, forced the Austrian, Ottoman, and Russian Empires to reform.

- Loss of the Italian territories and Magyar desire for self-rule in Hungary weakened Austrian rule. The Compromise of 1867 divided Habsburg territories into the dual monarchy of Austria-Hungary.

- The Ottoman Empire became weakened by nationalist uprisings in its Balkan possessions, making it prey to Western imperialistic ambitions. Territorial shifts, such as the transfer of Bosnia and Herzegovina to Austrian administration, created conditions for further instability and war in the Balkans.

- Russia undertook a series of reforms beginning in 1861: the abolition of serfdom, establishment of local governments, equality before the law, abolition of press censorship, and improvements in military service.

THE DEVELOPMENT OF WESTERN DEMOCRACIES

How did western European states create democracies?

In the generation after 1850, Britain, France, and several smaller states in northern Europe made major strides forward in creating democratic political systems and cultures. Although universal manhood suffrage had been instituted only in France, all these countries' governments were responsible to elected representatives of the voters.

Victorian Britain

The mid-nineteenth century was a period of exceptional wealth and security for Britain, as the population as a whole began to share in the economic benefits of industrialization. Britain enjoyed both social and political peace. The political system was not challenged as it had been in the generation after the Napoleonic Wars. A self-assured, even smug, elite—merchants, industrialists, and landowners—developed a political system reflecting liberal values.

Although suffrage was still restricted to propertied Christian men before the 1850s, the parliamentary system was firmly established, with government clearly responsible to the electorate. The importance of Parliament was symbolized by the new building in which it met, finished in 1850 and of unprecedented splendor and size. The form of government developed in its halls after midcentury aroused the curiosity and envy of much of the world. (See the feature, "The Global Record: A Japanese View of the British Parliament.")

In the twenty years after 1846, five different political parties vied for power. Depending on the issue, parties and factions coalesced to support particular policies. After 1867, however, a clear two-party system emerged: Liberal and Conservative (Tory), both with strong leadership. This development gave the electorate a distinct choice. The Conservatives were committed to preserving traditional institutions and practices, whereas the Liberals were more open to change.

Two strong-minded individuals headed these parties and dominated British political life for over a generation: William E. Gladstone (1809–1898), a Liberal, and Benjamin Disraeli (1804–1881), a Conservative. Both Gladstone and Disraeli were master debaters; Parliament and the press hung on their every word. Each was capable of making speeches lasting five hours or more and of conducting debates that kept the house in session until 4:00 A.M. The rivalry between the two men thrilled the nation and made politics a popular pastime.

The Conservatives' electoral base came from the landed classes, from Anglicans, and from England, rather than the rest of the United Kingdom (consisting of Scotland, Wales, and Ireland). The Liberals' base came from the middle classes, from Christian groups other than the Church of England, and from Scotland and Wales. In the House of Commons, both parties had a large number of members from the landed aristocracy, but cabinet members were increasingly chosen for political competence rather than family background. Aristocratic birth was no longer a requirement for reaching the pinnacle of power.

The competition for power between the Liberals and the Conservatives led to an extension of suffrage in 1867. The

Disraeli and Gladstone: Victorian Political Rivals This 1868 cartoon from *Punch* magazine captures the politicians' personalities. Disraeli was known as vain and theatrical, while Gladstone was dour and moralistic. (Mary Evans Picture Library)

A Japanese View of the British Parliament

In 1862, the Japanese government sent its first diplomatic mission to Europe. Accompanying the delegation was a young translator, Fukuzawa Yukichi (1835–1901). Intrigued by what he saw and eager to interest his fellow Japanese in the West, Fukuzawa published several books. In fact, all books about the West in Japan came to be known as "Fukuzawa-bon." Toward the end of his life, in his Autobiography, he described how, while in London, he had tried to understand the workings of the British Parliament.

Of political situations at that time, I tried to learn as much as I could from various persons that I met in London . . . though it was often difficult to understand things clearly as I was as yet unfamiliar with the history of Europe. . . . A perplexing institution was representative government. When I asked a gentleman what the "election law" was and what kind of an institution the Parliament really was, he simply replied with a smile, meaning I suppose that no intelligent person was expected to ask such questions. But these were the things most difficult of all for me to understand. In this connection, I learned that there were different political parties—the Liberal and the Conservative—who were always "fighting" against each other in the government.

For some time it was beyond my comprehension to understand what they were "fighting" for, and what was meant, anyway, by "fighting" in peace time. "This man and that man are 'enemies' in the House," they would tell me. But these "enemies" were to be seen at the same table, eating and drinking with each other. I felt as if I could not make much out of this. It took me a long time, with some tedious thinking, before I could gather a general notion of these separate mysterious facts. In some of the more complicated matters, I might achieve an understanding five or ten days after they were explained to me. But all in all, I learned much from this initial tour of Europe.

QUESTIONS

1. Why might the Japanese visitor have been puzzled by the use of the words *fighting* and *enemies* in this context?

2. Would Japanese readers have obtained a good idea of the British parliamentary system based on this report?

Source: *The Autobiography of Fukuzawa Yukichi*, trans. Eiizhi Kiyooka. Copyright 1948, 2007 by Columbia University Press. Reproduced with permission of Columbia University Press via Copyright Clearance Center.

Second Reform Bill
British legislation that extended suffrage to clerks, artisans, and other skilled workers by lowering property qualifications.

Second Reform Bill lowered property qualifications for the vote, thus extending it from 1.4 million to 2.5 million men out of a population of 22 million. The bill also equalized electoral districts, which gave new urban areas better representation. Although some in Parliament feared that these changes would lead to the masses capturing political power—"a leap into the dark," one member called it—in fact, no radical change ensued. Extending the vote to clerks, artisans, and other skilled workers made them feel more a part of society and thus bolstered the existing system rather than undermining it. John Stuart Mill, then a member of Parliament, along with his colleague and wife, Harriet Taylor Mill (1807–1856), championed the cause of women's suffrage; but he had few allies in Parliament, and that effort failed.

As the extension of voting rights increased the size of the electorate, parties became larger and stronger. Strong party systems meant alternation of power between the Liberals and the Conservatives. With an obvious majority and minority party, the monarch could no longer play favorites in choosing a prime minister. The leader of the majority party had to be asked to form a government. Thus, even though Queen Victoria (r. 1837–1901) detested Gladstone, she had to ask him to form governments when the Liberals won parliamentary elections. (See the feature, "The Visual Record: An Engraving of the British Royal Family.")

The creation of a broad-based electorate also meant that politicians had to make clear appeals to the public and its interests. In the past, oratory had been limited to the halls of Parliament, but after the electoral reforms, it occurred in the public arena as well. Public election campaigns increasingly had to appeal to the common man. The adoption of the secret ballot in 1872 protected lower-class voters from intimidation by their employers, landowners, or other social superiors. In 1874, the first two working-class members of Parliament were elected, sitting as Liberals.

France: From Empire to Republic

France took a more tumultuous path to parliamentary democracy than Britain. Revolutions and wars overthrew existing political systems and inaugurated new ones. Each time the French seemed to have democracy within reach, the opportunity slipped away.

The constitution of the Second French Republic (1848–1852) provided for a single four-year presidential term. Frustrated by this limitation of power, Louis Napoleon engineered a coup d'état in 1851 to extend his presidency to a ten-year term. The following year, he called for a plebiscite to confirm him as Napoleon III (r. 1852–1870), emperor of the French. Both of these moves were resisted in the countryside, particularly in the south, but massive repression defeated all opposition.

In the rest of the country, huge majorities of voters endorsed first the prolonged presidency and then the imperial title. Much of the populace genuinely supported Louis Napoleon in these two plebiscites. But prefects—local administrators appointed by the government—had helped produce the favorable majorities by manipulating elections. As emperor, Napoleon III made no claim to divine right and kept in place the apparatus of parliamentary government—including universal male suffrage. He could not, however, tolerate any opposition and used police force to repress it. He also suppressed freedom of assembly and regulated the press. In subsequent legislative elections, local prefects also assured that "official" candidates—those loyal to the regime—were elected to the legislature.

Napoleon III never enjoyed deep support, but his most vociferous opponents either fell silent or, like poet Victor Hugo, were driven into exile. Many republicans continued to harbor resentment because he had usurped the constitution of 1848. But economic growth in the 1850s and 1860s, some of which resulted from his own business-expanding policies, helped stabilize his regime. Most Frenchmen, including urban workers and peasants, generally enjoyed better living standards, and many of those who initially opposed him came to support him. With his power consolidated by 1859, Napoleon III began to relax his dictatorial rule, and a more liberal atmosphere prevailed in the 1860s. In an attempt to win over the opposition, Napoleon made some concessions, easing censorship and making his government more accountable to the parliament. But instead of winning him new support, liberalization allowed the expression of mounting opposition.

Republican candidates were elected to the legislature. Workers won limited rights to strike, and labor unions were virtually legalized. A number of issues—including opposition to policies of free trade, widespread hostility toward the influence of the Catholic Church, and the desire for more extensive freedom of expression and assembly—helped forge a republican alliance of the middle classes and workers. This alliance was strongest in the large cities and in some southern regions notorious for their opposition to central government control. Republicanism was better organized than in earlier years and had a more explicit program. Moreover, its proponents were now better prepared to take over the government, if the opportunity arose.

By 1869, the regime of Napoleon III, which declared itself a "liberal empire," had evolved into a constitutional monarchy, responsible to the parliament. In a plebiscite in May 1870, Frenchmen supported the liberal empire by a vote of five to one. It might have endured had Napoleon III not rashly declared war against Prussia two months later in a huff over the supposedly insulting Ems dispatch (see page 625). Rapid defeat at the hands of Bismarck brought down the empire. In September, at news of the emperor's capture, the republican opposition in the parliament declared a republic. It continued the war but had to sign an armistice in January 1871.

The leader of the new government was an old prime minister of Louis Philippe, Adolphe Thiers (tee-YAIR) (1797–1877). Before signing a definitive peace, the provisional government held elections. The liberals, known as republicans, since they favored a republic, were identified with continuing the war; the conservatives, mostly royalists, favored peace. Mainly because of their position on this issue, the royalists won a majority from a country discouraged by defeat.

The new regime had no time to establish itself before a workers' uprising in the spring of 1871 shook France, reminding the rest of Europe of revolutionary dangers. The uprising was called the **Paris Commune**—a name referring to the municipal government that harked back to 1792 to 1794, when the Paris crowds had dictated to the national government. The Commune insisted on its right to local rule. Radicals and conservatives greeted the Commune as a workers' revolt intended to establish a workers' government. Marx described it as the "bold champion of the emancipation of labor." Women took an active part, fighting on the barricades, pouring scalding water on soldiers, posting revolutionary broadsides. Louise Michel (1830–1905) was a schoolteacher who became famous for her leadership in active fighting and for her agitation for socialism and women's rights.

Although labor discontent played a role in the Paris Commune, other forces also contributed, notably the earlier Prussian siege of Paris during the Franco-Prussian War. Paris had become radicalized during the siege: The rich had evacuated the city, leaving a power vacuum quickly filled by the lower classes. Parisians suffered much because of the siege; angered that their economic needs went unmet and their courage against the Prussians unnoticed, they rose up against the new French government. The paramount issue of food sparked the massive women's participation in the uprising. The Commune, composed largely of artisans, now governed the city.

Paris Commune Parisian workers' uprising intended to establish a workers' government under home rule. It was violently suppressed by the army of the conservative French government.

An Engraving of the British Royal Family

This illustration of the British royal family might have been that of any upper-middle-class family. Queen Victoria is plainly dressed; her husband, Prince Albert, wears a dark business suit; the children are clothed in simple outfits. The simplicity conveyed by the family extends to the image of the rest of England, depicted as a quaint farm with a grouping of common people. Notice the crown hovering over this idyllic pastoral scene.

Illustrations of this type—appearing in a song book that would find its way into British homes—familiarized the British with their monarch. Surrounded by her husband and children, the queen focuses her gaze not on the viewer—a British subject—but on her children. It is her husband, the prince, who, protective of his family, gazes outward. In the past, representations of the monarchy had suggested power and intimidation. The aura of the close-knit, nuclear royal family suggested a reassuring serenity to British subjects. It also offered a model for the family and gender very much like those to which middle-class families aspired.

Victoria cultivated the image of herself as contented mother, but in reality, she resented much about motherhood. She complained of the extent to which her pregnancies interfered with her daily routines and prevented her from traveling and from being with her beloved Albert. She lamented, "I think our sex a most unenviable one." She described childbearing as an "annoyance" that made her feel "so pinned down—one's wings clipped." She also refused to romanticize birthing, seeing it as an animal-like act that reduced a woman to "a cow or a dog." For the births of her seventh and eighth children, she resorted to the uncommon practice of using chloroform to alleviate the pain of labor—the first public figure to do so openly. Even after their infancy, Victoria continued to describe her children as "an awful plague and anxiety" who showed no gratitude. But such views were expressed privately, and the public never suspected Victoria's ambivalence about motherhood.

Despite her complaints, the highly moral image of Victoria's family life contrasted with that of her predecessors. Her grandfather George III (r. 1760–1820) had been plagued with bouts of insanity. Her uncle George IV (r. 1820-1830) was a notorious philanderer. George IV and his brothers, the duke of Clarence (later to be William IV [r. 1830-1837]) and the duke of Kent (Victoria's father), were bigamists. They fathered a large brood of children out of wedlock and were implicated in numerous public scandals.

Public outrage at the excesses of Victoria's predecessors had produced a call to abolish the institution of monarchy. Given the disrepute into which the monarchy had fallen and the rise of republican sentiment, the crowning of a woman in 1837 may have substantially lessened antimonarchical sentiment. Victoria, as a young, seemingly frail woman coming to the throne at age 18, lent a certain gallantry to the royal household. Moreover, as a female monarch, she was seen as less of a threat to constitutional liberties.

The image of Victoria shown here intentionally contrasts her reign with those of her predecessors. The simple terms in which she and her family are depicted appealed to the growing middle class of the second half of the nineteenth century. The portrayal also fit the emerging democratic spirit—and electoral power—of the lower classes. Henceforth, monarchs would not be able to ignore public opinion. This image marks a historical departure in other ways. Victoria is surrounded by four of her children (eventually, she would have nine). Her royal predecessors had died without leaving any legitimate direct heirs, thus endangering the regular succession to the throne. This engraving sent the message that the royal line was assured. British people, wary of a female ruler, could find solace, not only from her husband's confident gaze outward, but in knowing that Victoria would be succeeded by one of her sons.

Unlike Victoria's uncles and father, who were wastrels and bankrupts, the queen and her husband lived frugally by royal standards and conducted an exemplary family life. Royal wealth increased under Prince Albert's careful administration. Instead of being subject to various debtors, the British royal house became one of the wealthiest and most prominent landowners in Great Britain. It is most telling that by the time of her death in 1901, Victoria had considerably strengthened the institution of monarchy, having restored confidence in and respect for it.

Under Victoria's rule, Britain completed the process of becoming a constitutional monarchy. The queen cultivated the image of being above politics and a symbol of national unity. Fellow monarchs in central and eastern Europe exercised greater power, but after World War I, they were all toppled. In Britain, monarchy in its constitutional form endured. Victoria established a pattern of public and private behavior by which members of subsequent generations of the British royal family were to be judged. This portrayal of the royal family also suggests the important role that visual imagery played in creating public support for state power in the nineteenth century.

In March 1871, the Commune declared itself free to carry out policies independent of the central government, temporarily located in Versailles. It sought free universal education, a fairer taxation system, a minimum wage, and disestablishment of the official Catholic Church. Finding these goals too radical, the conservative French government sent the army to suppress the Commune. It massacred 25,000 people, arrested 40,000, and deported several thousand more.

Illustration from the Illustrated Book of British Song (Visual Connection Archive)

QUESTIONS

1. Why did it make sense for the British royal family to have itself portrayed so simplistically? What values does this engraving communicate to British subjects?

2. How does this engraving exemplify the importance of visual imagery in conveying the meaning of monarchy to British subjects?

The crushing of the Paris Commune and some of its sister communes in southern France, which had also asserted local autonomy, signified the increasing power of centralized government. One mark of the emerging modern state was its capacity to squelch popular revolts that, in the past, had constituted serious threats. Western Europe would never again witness a popular uprising of this magnitude.

Despite its brutality, the suppression of the Commune reassured many Frenchmen. The question now at hand was what form the new government would take. The monarchist majority in the democratically elected parliament offered the throne to the Bourbon pretender. However, he insisted he would become king only if the *tricouleur*—the blue, white, and red flag of the Revolution, which long since had become a cherished national symbol—were discarded and replaced by the white flag of the house of Bourbon. This was unacceptable, so France remained a republic. The republic, as Thiers put it, "is the regime which divides us the least."

By 1875, the parliament had approved a set of basic laws that became the constitution of the Third Republic. Ironically, a monarchist parliament had created a liberal, democratic parliamentary regime. A century after the French Revolution, the republican system of government in France was firmly launched.

Scandinavia and the Low Countries

France and especially Britain served as models of parliamentary democracy for the smaller states in northern Europe. Denmark, Sweden, Norway, Holland, and Belgium recast their political institutions at midcentury. Several of the states were affected by the revolutions of 1848. That year, protesters in Denmark demanded enlarged political participation (see page 612), Sweden saw minor riots, and the king of the Netherlands (after 1830, Holland and the Netherlands refer to the same country) feared revolution in the neighboring German states would spill into his country. In Copenhagen, King Frederick VII (r. 1848–1863), who had no stomach for a confrontation, accepted a constitution providing for parliamentary government. "Now I can sleep as long as I like," he is reputed to have said.

Sweden's parliamentary system, in place since the Middle Ages, had representation by estates—noble, clergy, burgher, and peasant. The 11,000 nobles were given the same weight as the 2.5 million to 3 million peasants. After the riots of 1848, liberal aristocrats recognized that abolition of the estates system would best preserve their privileges, removing the major issue that had provoked popular resentments. In 1866, the estates were finally replaced by a parliament with two houses. The upper house was restricted to the wealthiest landowners and the lower house to men of property, providing the vote to 20 percent of adult men. Norway had been joined to Sweden in 1814 under the Swedish king, but it had a separate parliament and made its own laws. Swedish rule rankled the Norwegians, however, and in the 1850s, the Norwegian Liberal Party began to insist that the king should not have the final word in governance. Instead, they argued, the parliament, representative of the Norwegian people, should be supreme. In 1883, the principle that government officials are responsible to parliament won out. In 1905, Norway peacefully separated from Sweden and became an independent state.

In the Netherlands, as a result of the revolutions of 1848, the king recognized the need to strengthen support for his crown by acceding to liberals' demands for parliamentary government. By midcentury, government officials in the Netherlands were responsible to the parliament rather than to the king. A new constitution guaranteed the principles of freedom of speech, assembly, and religion.

Belgium had enjoyed a liberal constitution from the time it became an independent state after its revolution in 1830, but because no strong party system materialized, the king was able to appoint to government whomever he pleased. In the 1840s, the liberals organized, and the king, reluctantly, had to invite them to govern in 1848. The new government reduced property qualifications for voting, thus increasing the electorate.

Contrary to the conservative backlashes that rescinded reform following the revolutions of 1848 elsewhere, the sweeping reforms in northern European states became the basis for their evolution into full democracies. For full democracy to take hold, the electorate had to be broadened. These years witnessed much agitation for universal male suffrage. Property qualifications, wherever they were instituted, were questioned and resisted. For instance, in Sweden, the stipulation that a man had to earn 800 crowns a year to be a voter unleashed a pamphlet war: What if a man earned only 799 crowns? Did that make him less qualified? Although suffrage still remained limited in these countries, it was only a matter of time before democracy would be achieved.

SECTION SUMMARY

- By the late 1860s, a two-party system emerged in Britain: Conservative (Tory) and Liberal.

- The Second Reform Bill (1867) in Britain extended the vote and equalized voting districts, giving significantly more representation to urban areas.

- War and revolution continued to shape France's path to democracy. The French Second Republic, born of revolution, gave way to the authoritarian rule of Louis Napoleon, who became Napoleon III in 1852.

- The Franco-Prussian War of 1870–1871 ended the Second Empire of Napoleon III and gave birth to the French Third Republic.

- Denmark, Sweden, Norway, the Netherlands, and Belgium peacefully established governments responsible to parliaments rather than to their kings, providing the basis for their evolution toward full democracies.

CHAPTER SUMMARY

Liberal nationalists in the early nineteenth century had believed that Europe would be freer and more peaceful if each people had a separate nation, if the power between those nations could be balanced. The Crimean War proved them wrong. The Great Powers became rival states in pursuit of their own self-interests, largely at the expense of the Ottoman Empire. The postwar peace settlement impaired Ottoman efforts to repress nationalist movements in the Balkans.

The Crimean War and its aftermath also created an international climate that permitted the emergence of two newly unified nation-states, Italy and Germany. In the case of Italy, unification occurred through the leadership of Cavour in Piedmont-Sardinia (Kingdom of Sardinia). After waging war against Austria to acquire the northern provinces (with partial success), Cavour brought the revolutionary national movement of the south, led by Garibaldi, under the centralized control of Piedmont-Sardinia. Plebiscites and an elected assembly sanctioned Italian unification.

Germany, through a series of wars, became unified under the authoritarian, centralized control of Prussia. Bismarck annexed the northern German states after defeating Austria. After Prussia's victory in war against France, Bismarck was able to press the southern states into unity with the north. This process lent the German state, even with parliamentary rule, an authoritarian and militaristic character. The rulers of the various German states accepted unification by personal acclamation rather than through consent from the German people.

FOCUS QUESTIONS

- How did the Crimean War affect international relations?

- What respective processes led to the unifications of Italy and Germany into nation-states, and how did they differ?

- How did the Austrian, Ottoman, and Russian Empires deal with the challenges they faced?

- How did western European states create democracies?

The Austrian and Ottoman Empires faced the daunting challenges of nationalistic movements seeking to break away from their rule. In the effort to keep their empires intact, rulers offered various reforms from above, modeled on the West; but at the same time, they attempted to exert centralized rule to suppress breakaway movements. Austria compromised by establishing a dual monarchy with Hungary. But the empire then turned its aggressive ambitions toward the Balkans in order to exert control over Slavic people. These ambitions further challenged the Ottoman Empire, already weakened by defeat in war against Russia in 1853. The 1856 Congress of Paris and subsequent Balkan wars led to the creation of the independent and sovereign states of Romania and Bulgaria, formerly Ottoman provinces.

Russia, considering itself a protector of Slavic peoples, took advantage of the Ottoman Empire's weakness to wage war against it, further fueling Balkan nationalism and extending its influence there. In the face of its own domestic ills, Russia instituted major reforms on a Western model; nonetheless it remained autocratic, repressive, and inflexible.

Britain, France, and several northern European states became increasingly democratic, answerable to a growing electorate. Britain successfully and peacefully extended suffrage and maintained its monarchy. In France, the crushing of the Paris Commune spelled doom for those who wanted a nation of decentralized self-governing units. Indeed, strong, centralized governments increasingly became the norm. In other states, parliaments had only limited powers; but once they were in place, they gradually gained more power and expanded the electorate. Parliaments gave governments the appearance of legitimacy through the consent of their peoples. Hence, all European rulers, except those of the Ottoman and Russian Empires, found it necessary to have a parliament.

KEY TERMS

Realpolitik (p. 616)

congress system (p. 616)

risorgimento (p. 618)

Otto von Bismarck (p. 622)

Zollverein (p. 623)

February Patent (p. 626)

Compromise of 1867 (p. 626)

Young Turks (p. 627)

mir (p. 630)

zemstvos (p. 630)

Second Reform Bill (p. 632)

Paris Commune (p. 633)

 This icon will direct you to additional materials on the website: www.cengage.com/history/noble/westciv6e.

NOTES

1. Quoted in Otto Pflanze, *Bismarck and the Development of Germany*, vol. 1 (Princeton, N.J.: Princeton University Press, 1990), p. 184.

2. Quoted in William Flavelle Monypenny and George Earle Buckle, *The Life of Benjamin Disraeli: Earl of Beaconsfield*, vol. 2 (London: John Murray, 1929), pp. 473–474.

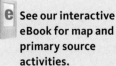 See our interactive eBook for map and primary source activities.

CHAPTER OUTLINE
Industrial Growth and Acceleration
Social Impacts of Economic Growth
Urban Problems and Solutions
Culture in an Age of Optimism

Felix Valloton: Le bon marché
(Snark/Art Resource, NY)

The Age of Optimism, 1850–1880

The Bon marché (the "good deal") was the first department store in Paris. Opening its doors in the 1850s, it served as a model for others in France and abroad. The store bought goods in mass quantities and thus could sell them at low prices. Constructed of glass and iron, the Bon marché represented the new, modern age. It combined under one roof a large range of products that previously had been available only in separate specialty shops—a time-saving convenience in an increasingly harried age. The store also had a large catalog sales department for customers too busy or distant to shop in person. Filled with toys, bed linens, furniture, crystal, and other items, the department store was a symbol of the new opulence of the middle classes.

This new type of store would not have been possible in an earlier age. It represents a culmination of the various technological and social changes that the West experienced as industrialization advanced in the second half of the nineteenth century. Industrial innovation had lowered the price of glass and steel, so that these new, huge commercial emporiums could be built at reasonable cost. Railroads brought into the city large quantities of increasingly mass-produced goods, as well as out-of-town customers. In town, trams and omnibuses transported shoppers to the store. The penny press provided advertising for the department store, which in turn supported the emergence of this new medium. The expansion of the postal system facilitated catalog sales and the mailing of parcels to customers. And the higher incomes available to many people allowed them to purchase more than just the necessities. This era gave birth to the consumer society.

To a large extent, the growing middle classes, who were filled with optimism and convinced they were living in an age of progress, shaped prevailing attitudes in the second half of the nineteenth century. John Stuart Mill proclaimed that in his era "the general tendency is and will continue to be … one of improvement—a tendency towards a better and happier state." Across the Channel in France, the social thinker Auguste Comte (1798–1857) concurred, confidently stating, "Human development brings … an ever growing amelioration." The successful application of science and technology to social problems gave many men and women confidence in the human ability to improve the world. People controlled their environments to a degree never before possible. On farms, they increased the fertility of the soil; to the burgeoning cities, they brought greater order through urban planning and dazzling architecture. Scientists used new methods to study and combat disease. Public authorities founded schools, trained teachers, and reduced illiteracy. Transportation and communication rapidly improved.

Not all of society benefited from the fruits of progress. The new wealth was far from equally shared. Eastern and southern Europe changed little, and even in the western

FOCUS QUESTIONS

- What technological changes led to the expansion of the European economy after the mid-nineteenth century?

- How did the economic expansion affect the various social classes, and city versus rural areas, differently?

- What problems did urbanization create, and what were the solutions?

- What new scientific, intellectual, and cultural trends emerged in this period, and what impact did they have on systems of belief?

This icon will direct you to additional materials on the website: www.cengage.com/history/noble/westciv6e.

See our interactive eBook for map and primary source activities.

regions a large part of the population still lived in great misery. If some cities carried out ambitious programs of urban renewal, others continued to neglect slums. Public sanitation programs did not affect the majority of Europeans who lived in rural areas. Despite spectacular advances in science, much of the population maintained a traditional belief in divine intervention. Many intellectuals strongly denounced the materialism and smugness of the age, stressing the meanness and ignorance that lay just beneath the surface.

INDUSTRIAL GROWTH AND ACCELERATION

What technological changes led to the expansion of the European economy after the mid-nineteenth century?

Beginning in the 1850s, western Europe experienced an unprecedented level of economic expansion. Manufacturers created new products and harnessed new sources of energy. An enlarged banking system provided more abundant credit to fund this expansion. Scientific research improved methods of manufacture. A revolution in transportation speedily delivered goods and services to distant places. Technological innovation profoundly changed the daily lives of many Europeans.

The "Second Industrial Revolution"

second industrial revolution Interrelated economic changes after 1850 that included new sources of energy, new products, new methods of manufacture, and new materials, such as mass-produced steel, synthetic dyes, and aluminum.

The interrelated cluster of economic changes that began in the generation after 1850 is often called the **second industrial revolution**. It was characterized by a significant speedup in production and by the introduction of new materials, such as mass-produced steel, synthetic dyes, and aluminum. Manufacturers replaced the traditional steam engine with stronger steam-powered turbines or with machines powered by new forms of energy—petroleum and electricity.

The second half of the nineteenth century has often been called the "age of steel." In 1856, Sir Henry Bessemer (1813–1898) discovered a method that produced in twenty minutes the same amount of steel previously produced in twenty-four hours. In the next two decades, further advances in steel production yielded even more dramatic results. In Great Britain, for example, steel production increased fourfold, and by the 1880s, its price fell by 50 percent. Greater steel production made possible the expansion of the rail system, the creation of a steamship fleet, and an explosive growth in the building industry. Once a rare alloy used only for the finest swords and knives, steel became the material that defined the age.

Significant changes in the supply of credit further stimulated economic expansion. Discovery of gold in California and Australia led to the inflow of huge amounts of the precious metal to Europe, expanding the supply of money and credit. This led to the establishment of the modern banking system.

Each advance made possible additional changes. Increased wealth and credit financed industrial plant expansion and an ambitious infrastructure of roads, railroads, and steamships, which in turn boosted trade. Between 1850 and 1870, the value of world trade increased by 260 percent.

By the 1880s, important scientific discoveries fueled industrial improvements. Electricity came into wider use, replacing coal as a source of energy. Synthetic dyes revolutionized the textile industry, as did alkali in the manufacture of soap and glass. Dynamite, invented by the Swedish chemist Alfred Nobel (no-BELL) (1833–1896) in the 1860s, made it possible to level hills and blast tunnels through mountains, facilitating construction. Nobel's will established a prestigious prize in his name to honor significant contributions to science and peace.

Transportation and Communication

The rail system grew dramatically in the middle decades of the nineteenth century. By 1880, total European railroad mileage reached 102,000. In 1888, the Orient Express line opened, linking Constantinople to Vienna and thus to the rest of Europe. Speed also conquered distance. By midcentury, trains ran 50 miles per hour, ten times faster than when they were invented. The cost of rail transport steadily decreased, allowing for its greater use. Between 1850 and 1880, in Germany, the number of rail passengers increased tenfold and the volume of goods eightyfold. In France and Great Britain, the increases were nearly as impressive.

Ocean transportation was also revolutionized. In 1869, the French built the Suez Canal across Egyptian territory, linking the Mediterranean to the Red Sea and the Indian Ocean. The canal reduced, by 40 percent, the thirty-five-day journey between London and Bombay. More efficient carriers—such as the clipper ship and the steamship—were developed. By 1880, European shipping carried nearly three times the cargo it had thirty years earlier.

The optimism born of conquering vast distances was reflected in a popular novel by the French writer Jules Verne (DJOOL VAIRN) (1828–1905), *Around the World in Eighty Days* (1873). The hero, Phineas Fogg, travels by balloon, llama, and ostrich, as well as by the modern steam locomotive and steamship, to accomplish in eighty days a feat that, only thirty years earlier, would have taken at least eleven months. In 1889, the New York newspaper the *World,* in a publicity gambit to increase readership, sent its reporter Nellie Bly (1867–1922) on an around-the-world trip to see if she could beat fictional Phineas Fogg's record. Readers breathlessly kept up with reports of her progress. She circled the globe in 72 days, 6 hours, 11 minutes, and 14 seconds. Such was the impact of the steamship, the locomotive, the Suez Canal—and the newspaper.

Along with the new speed, advances in refrigeration changed food transport. Formerly, refrigeration could be achieved only with natural ice, cut from frozen ponds and lakes, but this changed in the 1870s with the introduction of mechanical ice-making machines. By the 1880s, dairy products and meat were being transported vast distances by rail and even across the seas by ship. Thanks to these advances, the surplus food of the Americas and Australia, rich in grasslands, could offer Europe a cheaper and far more varied diet.

Regular postal service was also a child of the new era of improved transportation. In 1840, Britain instituted a postage system based on standard rates. Replacing the earlier practice in which the recipient paid for the delivery of a letter, the British system enabled the sender to buy a stamp—priced at just one penny— and drop the letter into a mailbox. It was collected, transported speedily by the new railroads, and delivered. The efficiency and low cost of mail led to a huge increase in use.

The reformed postal service and transoceanic telegraphs revolutionized the exchange of information. The telegraph was invented in the early 1830s, and by the 1860s, telegraph wire had been laid on both the European and North American continents; the two continents were then connected via the transatlantic cable. By the 1870s, telegraph lines extended 650,000 miles, connecting twenty thousand towns and villages around the world.

The telegraph had many uses. Newspapers prided themselves on being "wired" and thus able to provide readers the latest news. Governments found the telegraph useful in collecting information and issuing orders to subordinates, better assuring imperial authority over distant

CHRONOLOGY

Year	Event
1813	Gas streetlamps in London
1820s	Omnibuses introduced in France
1830	Lyell founds the principles of modern geology
1831	Faraday discovers electromagnetic induction
1833	Telegraph invented
1840	Penny stamp introduced
1848	England adopts first national health legislation
1850s	Age of clipper ships
	Trams added to public transportation systems
1851	Crystal Palace
1852–1870	Rebuilding of Paris
1859	Darwin, *On the Origin of Species*
1863	Europe's first underground railroad, in London
1864	Pope Pius IX issues *Syllabus of Errors*
1865	Transoceanic telegraph cable installed
	Lister initiates antiseptic surgery
	University of Zurich admits women
1869	Opening of Suez Canal
	Mendeleev produces periodic table of elements
1874	Impressionist exhibition
1875	Bell invents telephone
	Electric lights in Paris
1881	Pasteur proposes germ theory of disease
1891	Pope Leo XIII issues *Rerum novarum*

French Board Game: Around the World in 80 Days   This French board game, based on Jules Verne's novel *Around the World in Eighty Days*, illustrates with a steam locomotive the new speed with which people could travel, suggesting as well the technological power to colonize exotic territories (see Chapter 24).   ('Le Voyage Autour du Monde', cover of a box for a game based on 'Around the World in 80 Days' by Jules Verne (1828–1905) (litho), French School, (19th century)/Private Collection/Archives Charmet/The Bridgeman Art Library)

territories. In the 1840s, it took ten weeks for a message and a reply to go from London to Bombay and back. Thirty years later, the exchange took four minutes.

The telegraph was also a tool of warfare. The first conflict in which it played a crucial role was the Crimean War. The British and French high commands in London and Paris were able to communicate with their officers in the Crimea, directing operations from afar. It was also the first war whose unfolding events were communicated immediately through the telegraph to newspapers at home. Charles Dickens described the telegraph as "of all our modern wonders the most wonderful." Even more than improved transportation, it transformed the world into an instant, global village. As the governor of New York said at a commemorative event, "Men speak to one another now, though separated by the width of the earth, with lightning's speed and as if standing face to face."

To the telegraph was added another instant form of communication. In 1875, the American Alexander Graham Bell (1847–1922) invented a machine capable of transmitting the human voice by electrical impulses; in 1879, the first telephones were installed in Germany; two years later, they appeared in France. At first a curiosity, used to listen to a musical or theatrical production at a distance, the phone entered the homes of the elite and became a new form of interpersonal communication.

SECTION SUMMARY

- After 1850, steam-powered turbines and new sources of energy, such as electricity, increased the pace and quantity of industrial production.

- New methods of steel production made possible the expansion of railroads, the construction of steamships, and explosive growth in the building industry.

- The Suez Canal helped revolutionize ocean transportation by cutting travel time to India and other parts of Asia nearly in half, while ships as well became more efficient.

- The telegraph, telephone, and standardized mail systems sped up communications and collapsed global distances of time and space.

The Suez Canal Opened in 1869, the canal cut through one hundred miles of Egyptian desert to enable passage between the Mediterranean and the Red Seas. It reduced by half the voyage from Europe to India and the rest of Asia, and particularly benefited Britain. The Suez Canal exemplified the speeding up of transportation and communication in the second half of the nineteenth century. (The Inauguration Procession of the Suez Canal at El-Guisr in 1865, from 'Voyage Pittoresque a travers l'Isthme de Suez' by Marius Fontane, engraved by Jules Didier (1831-c.80) 1869–70 (colour litho), Riou, Edouard (1833–1900)/Bibliotheque des Arts Decoratifs, Paris, France/Archives Charmet/The Bridgeman Art Library International)

SOCIAL IMPACTS OF ECONOMIC GROWTH

How did the economic expansion affect the various social classes, and city versus rural areas, differently?

Industrial advances transformed the traditional structure of European society. Fewer people worked the land; more worked in manufacturing and services. Because political power no longer depended as much upon landed property ownership and inherited titles, the aristocracy had to find new channels through which they could exercise social and political influence; to varying degrees, they had to share power with the middle classes. Generally, life for both industrial and farm workers improved in this period. However, great disparities persisted, and many people continued to suffer from profound deprivation.

The Adapting Aristocracy

Always a small, exclusive group, the European aristocracy in the nineteenth century represented less than 1 percent of the population. Many of noble birth were quite poor and economically indistinguishable from their nonnoble neighbors. Others owned vast estates and were fabulously wealthy.

Distinctions between aristocrats and members of the upper middle class became increasingly blurred. Noble families in financial straits often married their children to the offspring of wealthy merchants. And many nobles who previously had shunned manufacture participated in the new economy by becoming industrialists and bankers. Idle members of the nobility became rarer. Although many aristocrats still enjoyed a lavish lifestyle, others adopted the habits of successful business people.

The power of the aristocracy surprisingly persisted through much of the nineteenth century, despite the theories of egalitarianism sweeping Europe in the aftermath of the French Revolution and the rapidly changing social structure engendered by industrialization. In Prussia, some of the wealthiest industrialists came from the highest aristocracy. The heavily aristocratic officer corps played an important role in running the Prussian state and unified Germany. In France, about 20 to 25 percent of officers and many diplomats were aristocrats. In Britain, officers, diplomats, and high-ranking civil servants were usually of noble birth. In Austria and Russia, aristocratic origin continued to be the norm for government service.

The Expanding Middle Classes

bourgeois century
Characterization of the nineteenth century. Having expanded dramatically with industrialization, the bourgeoisie helped shape western European society.

Up to the eighteenth century, society had been divided into legally separate orders on the basis of birth. In the nineteenth century, it became more customary to classify people by their economic functions, whose variety grew as the industrial and services sectors expanded. The "middle class" included such people as wealthy manufacturers, country physicians, and bank tellers. Given this diversity, it has become common to use the plural and think of all these people as forming the "middle classes." Another term frequently used to describe them is the *bourgeoisie,* which usually refers to those with higher than average wealth.

The nineteenth century has often been described as the **bourgeois century**, because, especially in western Europe, the middle classes not only expanded numerically, but had an enormous social and cultural influence. Rapidly growing trade and manufacture meant more entrepreneurs and managers, while the increasingly complex society called for more engineers, lawyers, accountants, and bankers. New standards of comfort and health increased the demand for merchants and doctors, while urban renovations required architects and contractors, among other professionals.

The middle and lower levels of middle-class society grew most rapidly. In the 1870s, about 10 percent of urban working-class people reached lower-middle-class status by becoming store-keepers, lower civil servants, clerks, or salespeople. As industries matured, the increasing use of machinery and better industrial organization created a greater need for clerks and bureaucrats rather than laborers. Large import-export businesses, insurance companies, and department stores provided opportunities of this kind. So did the expansion of government services.

The social impact of job growth was great. The men and women staffing these new positions often came from modest backgrounds. For the son or daughter of peasants to become village postmaster, schoolteacher, or clerk in a major firm signified social ascension, however modest. Accessibility to its ranks was certainly one of the strengths of the bourgeoisie, an ever-growing group whose promise of social respectability and material comfort exercised a compelling force of attraction over the lower classes.

A widening subgroup of the middle classes consisted of professionals, those whose prestige rested on the claim of exclusive expertise in a particular field. In the early nineteenth century, requirements for exercising a profession, though they varied by country, became more stringent. Medical doctors, for instance, began requiring specialized education to distinguish themselves from herbalists, midwives, bonesetters, healers, and other competitors, and they insisted on their exclusive right to exercise their profession. Doctors controlled access to their ranks by establishing powerful professional associations.

Interior of a Danish Middle-Class Home   With its stuffed furniture, lace curtains and tablecloths, and gilt-edged framed paintings, this meticulously decorated living room contrasted sharply with the grimy exterior of the industrial city from which it provided a sheltered escape.   (National Museum of Denmark (Nationalmuseet))

Similarly, other professions, such as law, architecture, and engineering, encouraged **professionalization** through the adoption of common requirements and standards of expertise. By midcentury, either professional associations or the state itself accredited members of the professions. Women had limited access to these professions; typically their opportunities were confined to lower teaching positions. After the Crimean War, as a result of Florence Nightingale's efforts (see page 617), nursing became an increasingly popular profession for women. Even so, the dominant culture generally opposed middle-class women's salaried employment outside the home.

The growing role of the state in society led to bureaucratic expansion. Civil servants were increasingly subjected to educational requirements and had to pass civil service exams, sharply reducing the role that patronage played in the assignment of government positions.

professionalization
Standardization of requirements and regulation of expertise, especially in medicine, law, architecture, and engineering.

Middle-Class Lifestyles

The standard of living among the middle classes varied considerably, ranging from the wealthy entrepreneur who bought a château, or built one, to the low-level clerk who dwelled in a modest apartment. All of them lived in new standards of comfort. Their homes increasingly had running water, upholstered furniture, and enough space to provide separate sleeping and living quarters. They owned several changes of clothing and consumed a varied diet that included meat and dairy products, sugar, coffee, and tea. They read books and subscribed to newspapers and journals. Having at least one servant was a requisite for anyone who wished to be counted among the middle classes in the mid-nineteenth century.

By 1900, servants were still common among bourgeois households, but their number was declining in proportion to the population as a whole. As service industries developed, the need for servants decreased. With the growth of cab services, for instance, a family could dispense with a coachman and groom. Toward the end of the century, domestics' wages rose as competing forms of employment vied for their service, and households below the upper layers of the bourgeoisie found it difficult to afford domestic help.

The need to escape the relentless stimulation of crowded cities gave rise to resort towns throughout Europe, devoted principally to the amusement of the well-off. Water cures—bathing in hot springs and drinking the mineral waters thought to have special attributes—became fashionable, as did gambling in resorts such as Baden-Baden in Germany and Vichy in France. For the first time, tourism became big business. Thomas Cook (1808–1892), an Englishman, organized tours to the Crystal Palace exhibition of 1851 in London, the largest world exposition, which highlighted industrial accomplishments. Discovering the large market for guided travel, Cook began running tours in England and on the Continent. Middle-class wealth and leisure time led to the construction of more hotels, restaurants, and cafés.

The middle classes, at least on the surface, sought to foster a set of values about proper conduct. They believed their successes were due not to birth, but to talent and effort. They wanted to be judged by their merits, and they expected their members to abide by strict moral principles. Their lives were supposed to be disciplined, especially with regard to sex and drink. The age was called "Victorian" because the middle classes in Britain saw in the queen, who reigned for two-thirds of the century, a reflection of their own values. (See the feature, "The Visual Record: An Engraving of the British Royal Family" on pages 634–635 in Chapter 22.) **Victorian morality**, widely preached but not always practiced, was often viewed as hypocritical by social critics. Yet as the middle classes came to dominate society, their values established social norms. Public drunkenness was discouraged, and anti-alcohol movements vigorously campaigned against drinking. Public festivals were regulated, making them more respectable and less rowdy.

Victorian morality
Nineteenth-century ethos wherein the strict moral principles of the dominant middle class became the social norm. The middle classes saw in Queen Victoria a reflection of their own values.

In spite of their differences in education, wealth, and social standing, most of the bourgeoisie resembled one another in dress, habits of speech, and deportment. Bourgeois men dressed somberly, in dark colors, avoiding any outward signs of luxury. Their clothing fit closely and lacked decoration—a symbolic adjustment to the machine age, in which elaborate dress hampered activity. It also reflected a conscious attempt to emphasize achievement-oriented attitudes, and new standards for what constituted honorable manhood. Through dress and other fashionable tastes, middle classes distinguished themselves from what they viewed as a decadent and effeminate nobility.

Bourgeois conventions regarding women's dress were the opposite of men's, further reinforcing gender distinctions—women's clothing became the material symbol of male success.

The Crystal Palace   Built in 1851, this building was the largest glass and steel structure of its time. Site of the first great international exposition, the Crystal Palace displayed the inventiveness and opulence of the age.   (Courtesy of the Trustees of the British Museum)

Extravagant amounts of colorful fabrics used to fashion huge, beribboned hoop dresses reflected the newfound wealth of the middle classes and confirmed their view of women as ornaments whose lives were to be limited to the home and made easier by servants. The language and paraphernalia of idealized domesticity dominated this era. While the man was out in the secular world earning a living and advancing his career, the bourgeois woman was supposed to provide her family with an orderly, comfortable shelter from the storms of daily life. In 1861, London housewife Isabella Mary Mayson Beeton published *Mrs. Beeton's Book of Household Management,* which provided British middle-class women with advice on running their households. This book reflected middle-class values in fostering discipline, frugality, and cleanliness. The ideal woman decorated the rooms, changed the curtains with the seasons and styles, supervised the servants, kept the accounts, oversaw the children's homework and religious education, and involved herself in charitable works. In Britain, this book was outsold only by the Bible. In the decades around midcentury, the notion of two **separate spheres**—one male and public, the other female and private—reached its height.

> **separate spheres**   Notion of two distinct sets of roles— one male and public, the other female and private. While the man was out in the world advancing his career, the bourgeois woman was to run her home.

In spite of the relatively passive role assigned to bourgeois women, many were very active. Some helped their husbands or fathers in the office, the business, or the writing of scientific treatises. Others achieved success on their own terms, running their own businesses, writing, painting, or teaching. Though advice books prescribed a world of separate spheres, in practice, the boundaries between them were not always rigid. In general, however, even bright and intellectually curious young girls most often could not receive as good an education as their brothers, nor, as a consequence, could they pursue as interesting a career.

Some liberals insisted that sexual difference should not constitute the basis for denying equal rights to women. Proponents of women's rights demanded equal access to education

Ladies' Bicycling Fashion This new mode of transportation suggested possibilities for female emancipation. Free on her bicycle, the young woman is contrasted with the man, who rides only a tricycle. (From Karin Helm [ed.], Rosinen aus der Gartenlaube [Gutersloh: Signum Verlag, n.d.]. Reproduced with permission.)

and the professions. Slowly, secondary and university education was made available to young women. On the European continent, the University of Zurich was the first university to admit women, in 1865. Although British universities admitted women, they did not initially grant them degrees. In spite of discriminatory laws, harassment by male students, and initial obstruction by professional and accrediting groups, a few female doctors and lawyers practiced in England by the 1870s and on the Continent in the following decades.

Women more easily penetrated the lower levels of middle-class occupations. Expanding school systems, civil services, and businesses provided new employment opportunities for them. By the 1890s, women comprised two-thirds of primary school teachers in England and half the post office staff in France. Some new technologies created jobs that became heavily feminized, such as the positions of typist and telephone operator.

Improving Conditions among Workers and the Poor

The increased prosperity and greater productivity of the period gradually improved the conditions of both female and male workers in the generation after 1850. Their wages and standards of living rose, and they enjoyed more job security. In Britain, the earning power of the average worker rose by one-third between 1850 and 1875. For the first time, workers were able to put money aside to tide them over in hard times. They had greater access to leisure activities that previously had been limited to the upper classes. Expanded rail connections enabled workers to visit resort towns. New music and dance halls, popular theaters, and other forms of public entertainment sprang up to claim workers' increased spending money.

Nonetheless, conditions of poverty persisted among many workers throughout Europe and a vast gulf remained between them and the middle and upper classes. In the 1880s, in the northern French industrial city of Lille, the combined property of twenty thousand workers equaled the estate of one average industrialist. Life expectancies still varied dramatically according to income. In Bordeaux in 1853, the life expectancy of a male bourgeois was twenty years greater than that of a male laborer.

The disparity between rich and poor was especially striking in the case of domestics, one of the most common sources of employment for women. Servants led tiring and restricted lives under the close supervision of their employers. They worked

Telephone Operators in London New technologies opened up new employment opportunities for women. Telephone operators formed a completely feminized profession. (Jacques Boyer/Roger Viollet/Getty Images)

overly long hours and often worked six and a half days a week. Housed in either the basement or the attic, servants experienced extremes of cold, heat, and humidity. Sometimes they were subjected to physical or sexual abuse by the master of the house, his sons, or the head of the domestic staff. And yet, for impoverished rural women with little chance of finding better work, domestic service offered an option few could refuse. It provided free housing, food, and clothing and sometimes allowed a servant to save an annual sum that might reach one-third to one-half of a worker's yearly wages. These savings could serve as a dowry, enabling a young woman to marry advantageously.

Although some members of the working class managed to enter the lower levels of the middle classes, most remained mired in the same occupations as their grandparents. Poverty was still pervasive, and workers more commonly suffered from industrial and urban diseases, such as tuberculosis.

The difficult conditions imposed on industrial workers led to debates in several countries about the need for the state to protect them. The growing militancy of organized labor, fear of social upheaval, and the rising strength of socialist political parties motivated some governments to act. Moreover, viewing populations as a national resource, states grew increasingly concerned about infant mortality and declining birthrates. While some legislators rejected government intervention in the free operation of market forces, others argued that the laws of supply and demand exploited those who ought to have been protected—especially very young children and pregnant women.

Britain led the way with the Factory Acts, regulating child and female labor. The British workweek, typically 73 hours in the 1840s, was reduced to 56 hours in 1874. In newly unified Germany, the government wanted to impress workers with state benefits so they would abandon the growing Socialist Party and back the kaiser's authoritarian government. In the 1880s, it thus provided a comprehensive welfare plan that included health insurance and old-age pensions, and then reduced the work day to 11 hours. In France, the republican government also sought to defuse class war by passing a number of laws toward the end of the century. Particularly concerned about declining fertility, they regulated female factory labor, especially that of pregnant women. Most of this legislation only applied to large-scale industrial labor, and did not improve the situations among other working poor. And in eastern Europe, where industry was still in its infancy, workers remained unprotected by the law.

Apart from state initiatives, upper- and middle-class individuals, inspired by pity and religious teachings, also became concerned about conditions among workers and the poor. Women especially engaged in charity and social reform. As many as half a million English women involved themselves in charities or efforts to enact social legislation. In Sweden, by the 1880s, women had founded shelters for the destitute, old-age homes, a children's hospital, an asylum for the mentally handicapped, and various societies to promote female industry.

Government efforts to improve conditions through the regulation of public health also resulted in oppositional movements. In Great Britain, Josephine Grey Butler (1828–1906) waged a fierce battle against the harsh laws directed against prostitutes. The Contagious Diseases Acts (beginning in 1864) empowered the police to arrest any woman suspected of prostitution and to force her to be examined for venereal disease. Largely as a result of Butler's efforts, these acts were repealed in 1886. Annie Wood Besant (1847–1933) became an active social reformer on behalf of the poor. At a time when governments were becoming concerned about falling birthrates (resulting in limits on women's rights to work), she argued that poor women suffered from excessive childbearing and that their children died too often because of their poverty. With Charles Bradlaugh (1833–1891), Besant republished a pamphlet that contained information on birth control. British authorities called the publication pornographic and brought Besant and Bradlaugh to trial in 1877. After being found guilty, Bradlaugh and Besant won the case on appeal. In 1888, Besant turned her attention to protecting the health of young women workers, and in 1893, she went to India to establish schools for girls, educate widows, and agitate for Indian home rule.

The church also intervened in social issues. Pope Leo XIII (r. 1878–1903) reflected a trend of growing religious social consciousness and reinforced it among Catholics when in 1891, he issued his encyclical *Rerum novarum* (*Of New Things*), which defined Christians' moral responsibility for the poor. He declared, "Rich men and masters should remember this—that to exercise pressure for the sake of gain upon the indigent and the destitute and to make one's profit out of the need of another is condemned by all laws, human and divine." His message was taken up in France, Italy, and Spain among activists who became known as social Catholics. In England, Protestants founded the Salvation Army to assist the poor in 1878. Religious groups also hoped to win converts to their faith through the assistance they provided.

social Catholics Catholics in western Europe who believed that society bore responsibility for the well-being of the poor.

The Transformation of the Countryside

Before the nineteenth century, the countryside had hardly changed, but beginning at midcentury, it transformed radically. Especially in western Europe, an increasing number of people left the land. In 1850, 20 percent of the British people worked in agriculture; by 1881, they constituted only 11 percent of the population. The decrease in the number of agricultural workers led in many places to labor shortages and therefore higher wages for farmhands.

The food supply grew significantly as agricultural methods became more efficient. Not only was more land cultivated, but the yield per acre increased. In 1760, an agricultural worker in England could feed himself and one other person; by 1841, he could feed himself and 2.7 others. Food production on the continent similarly became more efficient, allowing greater access to better nutrition and consequently a drop in mortality rates; the population of Europe almost doubled between 1800 and 1880.

Higher yields were the result of an increased use of manure, augmented in the 1870s by salt-peter imported from Chile and, beginning in the 1880s, by chemical fertilizers manufactured in Europe. Innovations in tools also improved productivity. In the 1850s, steam-driven threshing machinery was introduced in some parts of western Europe. Organizational techniques borrowed from industrial labor, including specialization and regular schedules, also contributed to greater productivity on the land.

New and expanded technologies began to break through the insularity of rural life. Improved roads and dramatically expanded rail lines enabled farmers to extend their markets nationally and internationally. They also brought teachers into the villages, making school systems national. Local dialects, and in some cases, even distinct languages that peasants had spoken for generations, were replaced by a standardized national language. Local provincial costumes became less

Steam-Powered Thresher   This image shows the thresher being operated in the French countryside in 1860. Its loud noise and relentlessly rhythmic speed changed the pace and sensibility of rural labor, and sometimes prolonged the hours demanded of workers. It would be decades before this kind of technology became a common sight in Europe, but it was a harbinger of the change coming to the rural world.   (Bibliothèque nationale de France)

SECTION SUMMARY

- As landed wealth and hereditary titles declined in importance during the second half of the nineteenth century, the old aristocracy adapted by participating more in manufacturing, banking, and the professions.

- New technologies of the second industrial revolution and the expansion of commerce, government bureaucracy, and the professions dramatically increased the size and influence of the middle classes.

- The middle classes (bourgeoisie) developed their own moral code, including the notion of separate spheres for men and women; but many women defied their prescribed role and sought the right to higher education and entry into the professions.

- Standards of living generally rose among workers, but stark class disparities of wealth and living conditions persisted in many areas; legislation and private charity attempted to redress social ills, often in order to undermine the potential of worker militancy and socialist politics.

- New agricultural methods and technologies greatly increased agricultural production; modernization also created competition for agricultural and cottage industry products, forcing migration from the countryside.

common as styles fashionable in the cities spread to the countryside via mail-order catalogs. The farm girls who went to the cities to work as domestic servants returned to their villages with urban and middle-class ideals. The military draft brought the young men of the village into contact with urban folk and further spread urban values to the countryside.

Many rural regions, however, suffered from modernization. The growth of urban manufacturing caused rural cottage industry to decline, depriving agricultural workers of the supplementary income on which they previously relied during slack seasons. Railroads bringing goods made elsewhere wiped out some of the local markets on which cottage industries had depended. Grain brought by steamship from distant Canada and Argentina often undersold European wheat. The resultant crisis caused millions to emigrate; they left the land for towns and cities or even migrated across the seas to the Americas and Australia (see page 668).

These trends had a striking effect in the rural areas of western Europe. Eastern Europe, in contrast, was hardly touched by them. In Russia, agriculture remained backward; the average yield per acre in 1880 was one-quarter that in Great Britain. The land sheltered a large surplus population that was underemployed and contributed little to the rural economy. In the Balkans, most peasants were landless and heavily indebted.

URBAN PROBLEMS AND SOLUTIONS

What problems did urbanization create, and what were the solutions?

Epidemics, crowding, crime, and traffic jams were among the many problems that accompanied explosive urban growth in the nineteenth century. In the second half of the century, city governments more aggressively tackled these problems by developing public health measures and urban planning. They provided amenities, such as streetlights, public transportation, and water and sewer systems, and they established large, more efficient police forces. Cities gradually became safer and more pleasant places to live, although for a long time, city dwellers continued to suffer high mortality rates.

City Planning and Urban Renovation

Most of Europe's cities, originating in the Middle Ages as walled enclaves, had grown haphazardly into major industrial centers. Their narrow, crooked streets could not accommodate the increased trade and daily movement of goods and people, and traffic snarls were common. City officials began to recognize that broad, straight avenues would help relieve the congestion and also bring sunlight and fresh air into the narrow and perpetually dank lanes and alleys. (See the feature, "The Visual Record: The Modern City and Photography.")

The most extensive program of urban rebuilding took place in midcentury Paris. Over a period of eighteen years, Napoleon III and his aide Baron Georges Haussmann (1809–1891) transformed Paris from a dirty medieval city to a beautiful modern one (see **MAP 23.1**). Haussmann and his engineers carved broad, straight avenues through what had been overcrowded areas. They built visually elegant, if uniform, apartment houses on the new tree-lined avenues. Public monuments and buildings, such as the new opera house, enhanced the city. The urban renewal program drove tens of thousands of the poorest Parisians to the outskirts of the city, leading to greater social segregation than had previously existed. The boulevards created the environment

Pissarro: *L'avenue de l'Opéra, Sunlight, Winter Morning*   Camille Pissarro, one of the leading impressionists, portrayed the broad new Parisian avenue designed by Baron Haussmann. The avenue leads to the new opera in the background, also planned during the Second Empire. Note the active pedestrian as well as equestrian traffic.   (Erich Lessing/Art Resource, NY)

that nurtured the development of department stores, and street life became bourgeois. Boulevards also provided access for quick troop movements in the event of social upheaval, and made building barricades more difficult.

Haussmann's extensive work in Paris served as a model for other cities, and although none was rebuilt as extensively, many underwent significant improvements. The cities of Europe began to display an expansive grace and sense of order, supporting the belief of the middle classes that theirs was an age of progress.

The Introduction of Public Services

Beginning at midcentury, government at the central and local levels helped make cities more livable through sanitary reforms, public transportation, and lighting. Medical practitioners in the 1820s had observed that disease and higher mortality were related to dirt and lack of clean air, water, and sunshine. Since diseases spreading from the poorer quarters of town threatened the rich and powerful, there was a general interest in improving public health by clearing slums, broadening streets, and supplying clean air and water to the cities.

City walls

—— Wall of Philippe Auguste (1180–1210)

—— Tollhouse Wall (1784–1791), razed by Haussmann to rebuild as boulevards

—— Fortress Wall (1841–1845)

▢ Paris before 1860

▢ Expanded city limits established in 1860

▢ Public parks opened during Second Empire

—— Streets constructed by Haussmann

—— Other streets

—— Railway system created by Haussmann during Second Empire

Source: *Encyclopedia Universalis*

🌐 Map 23.1—Haussmann's Paris, 1850–1870

During the reign of Napoleon III, Baron Georges Haussmann reshaped the city of Paris, replacing its narrow medieval streets with a system of broad avenues and public parks and encircling the city with a railway.

Reform began in England with the Public Health Bill of 1848. This legislation established national standards for urban sanitation and required cities to regulate the installation of sewers and the disposal of refuse. The 1875 Health Act mandated certain basic health standards for water and drainage. Armed with these laws, cities and towns took the initiative: Birmingham cleared 50 acres of slums in the 1870s, for example.

London also took the lead in supplying public water, a service later adopted by Paris and many other cities. Berlin had a municipal water system in 1850, but it would be several decades before clean water was available in every household. In Paris, which typically led France in innovations, 60 percent of the houses had running water in 1882. As running water in the home became a standard rather than a luxury, bathing became more common. The English upper classes had learned the habit of frequent bathing from their colonial experience in India; on the Continent, it did not become the custom until about the third quarter of the nineteenth century.

All these changes had a direct impact on the lives of city dwellers. Between the 1840s and 1880, London's death rate fell from 26 per thousand to 20 per thousand. During the same period, the rate in Paris declined from 29.3 per thousand to 23.7 per thousand. Improved water supplies sharply reduced the prevalence of waterborne diseases, such as cholera and typhoid.

With the provision of urban transportation, city dwellers no longer had to live within walking distance of their workplaces. In the 1850s, the French introduced the tram—a carriage drawn on a rail line by horses. It could pull larger loads of passengers faster than its predecessor, the horse-drawn omnibus. Because of the many rail stations in London and the difficulty of getting from one station to another in time to make a connection, the British built an underground railway in 1863, the predecessor of the subway system. Technological improvements made the bicycle a serious means of transportation. By the mid-1880s, nearly 100,000 bicycles were being pedaled around Great Britain; by 1900, France had 1 million bicycles.

Improvements in public transportation and urban renewal projects led workers to move out of the inner city and into the less dense and less expensive suburbs. This trend in turn led to a decrease in urban population density that eventually helped make the city a healthier place to live.

Gaslights also improved city life, making it easier and safer to be outside at night. (Prior to gaslights, city dwellers depended mainly on moonlight or, rarely, expensive and time-consuming oil lamps—which had to be lit one at a time.) In 1813, London was the first city to be illuminated by gas; Berlin followed in 1816. Electrical lights were introduced in Paris in 1875, although they were not common until the end of the century.

Cities also significantly expanded police forces to impose order, control criminal activity, and discourage behavior deemed undesirable, such as dumping garbage on the street, relieving oneself in public, and carousing late at night. In 1850, London was the best-policed city in Europe, with a 5,000-man force. Paris had around 3,000 police officers.

SECTION SUMMARY

- Rapid population growth occurred in cities that had originally been constructed in haphazard fashion; to cope with the problems of growth, city officials began programs of urban renovation.

- The most notable example of urban renewal was that of Haussmann in Paris, which became a model in cities elsewhere.

- Central and local governments introduced sanitary reforms to combat disease, such as installing sewers, regulating the disposal of refuse, and supplying public water.

- Improvement in public transportation allowed workers to leave the overcrowded conditions in urban centers, further contributing to improved health.

CULTURE IN AN AGE OF OPTIMISM

What new scientific, intellectual, and cultural trends emerged in this period, and what impact did they have on systems of belief?

The improving economic and material conditions of the second half of the nineteenth century buoyed European thinkers. Many believed that men and women were becoming more enlightened, and they expressed faith in humankind's ability to transform the world with a parade of scientific and technological breakthroughs. The world seemed knowable and perfectible, especially through expanded education. This faith advanced secularism, while it undermined the certainties of traditional religion. The arts reflected these new values, emphasizing realism and science—as well as an underlying foreboding about the dark side of this "age of optimism."

Educational and Cultural Opportunities

At the beginning of the nineteenth century, governments took little responsibility for providing education. Some upper-class children were educated with private tutors, and others attended elite schools. A few charity schools offered minimal education for the poor. In the second half of the nineteenth century, governments took direct action to establish free and mandatory primary education, largely as a result of extended voting rights. In England, the Second Reform Bill of 1867 reduced the tax-based voting qualification, extended suffrage to better-off workers, and prompted a movement to ensure that the new voters were educated. The English government provided significant subsidies for education, set educational standards, and established a national inspection system to enforce them. France joined England in establishing mandatory primary education in the 1880s for boys and girls. Other European countries did the same; by 1900, all but one percent of Germans met the standards of literacy.

The goal of public education was to instill love of country, discipline, and obedience to authority, as well as basic skills of reading, writing, and arithmetic. It also sought to instill discipline.

By insisting on punctuality and obliging students to carry out repetitive tasks, schools formed youth to fit into the emerging industrial society and the civic culture of nation-states. The obedience and respect for authority learned at school shaped the soldiers and factory workers of the future. And regardless of political inclination, each regime took advantage of its control of the educational system to inculcate the love of one's country and of its form of government.

Secondary education was, on the whole, available only to the privileged few in the upper middle classes, giving them access to the universities and the professions. A small fraction of the lower middle class attended universities; the children of workers and peasants were totally absent.

Other public institutions made culture available to the masses in new ways. Between 1840 and 1880, the number of large libraries in Europe increased from forty to five hundred. The French national public library, the *Bibliothèque nationale,* was established in Paris in the 1860s. This iron and glass building, radical for its time, was an impressive monument to the desire to make reading available to an expanded public. Beyond cities, traveling libraries allowed books to reach rural populations.

Museums and art galleries, which in the previous century had been open to only a select few, gradually became accessible to the general public, making their national cultural heritages available to the masses; even the poorer classes gained access to these temples of culture by the late nineteenth century. The dramatic rise in literacy and new sources of cultural enrichment resulted from, and contributed to, the processes of modernization; they exposed the masses to new, potentially transformative ideas, experiences, and modes of understanding the rapidly changing world.

Darwin and Evolution

By midcentury, most thinkers accepted the notion of the change and transformation of society—and, by analogy, of the natural environment. The French thinker Auguste Comte (oh-GOOST KONT) championed the notion that human development—human history—proceeded through distinct and irreversible stages. Human progress would lead inexorably upward to the final and highest stage of development, the "positive"—or scientific-stage. Widely read throughout Europe and Latin America, Comte's writings helped bolster faith in science—and scientific advances of the nineteenth century seemed to confirm his precepts. Comte's philosophy, known as **positivism**, dominated the era. Whereas the romantics had emphasized feeling, the positivists found truth in what could be measured and verified. They were confident that scientific methods would ensure the continued progress of humanity.

positivism Philosophy of the French thinker Auguste Comte who asserted that human history progressed through distinct and irreversible stages, leading to the final and highest stage of development, the positive—or scientific—stage.

Faith in science and progress helped create the intellectual environment for rethinking progress in the biological realm. While the concept of biological evolution was not new, Charles Darwin (1809–1882) was the first to offer a systematic explanation of the process. As the naturalist on an official British scientific expedition in the 1830s, he had visited the Galápagos Islands off the western coast of South America. There, he discovered species similar to but very different from those on the mainland. Could they be the results of separate creations? Or was it more likely that in varying environments they had adapted differently? Darwin proposed that closely related species compete for food and living space. In this struggle, those in each species that are better adapted to the environment have the advantage over the others and hence are more likely to survive. In the "struggle for existence," only the fittest endure. Those surviving, Darwin surmised, pass on the positive traits to their offspring. He called the mechanism that explained the evolution and development of new species "natural selection," a process that he proposed was imperceptible but continuous. Darwin's observations in the Galápagos Islands became the basis for *On the Origin of Species by Means of Natural Selection* (1859), the most important scientific work of the nineteenth century. (See the feature, "The Written Record: Darwin's Basic Laws of Evolution.")

Darwin's theory that evolution in nature was inevitable echoes the nineteenth-century conviction that the present represented an ever more developed stage of the past. Many viewed his work as confirmation that societies—like species—were preordained to evolve toward progressively higher stages. Darwin at first avoided the question of whether the laws of evolution applied to human beings as well. The notion of human evolution would throw into question humanity's uniqueness and its separation from the rest of creation by its possession (in the Christian view) of a soul. But Darwin finally did confront the issue in *The Descent of Man* (1871), in which he presented evidence that humanity, too, is subject to these natural laws. The recognition that human

Darwin's Basic Laws of Evolution

Writing in an age of vast transformations, Darwin could imagine the mutability of all nature, including species, over time. And like his contemporaries, he could imagine that evolution would lead to improvement, to increasing "perfection" of various species. A religious man who lost much of his faith as a result of his scientific investigations, Darwin was anxious to reassure Christians, hence his attempt to portray evolution as part of God's divine plan.

Nothing at first can appear more difficult to believe than that the more complex organs and instincts have been perfected, not by means superior to, though analogous with, human reason, but by the accumulation of innumerable slight variations, each good for the individual possessor. Nevertheless, this difficulty, though appearing to our imagination insuperably great, cannot be considered real if we admit the following propositions, namely, that all parts of the organisation and instincts offer, at least, individual differences—that there is a struggle for existence leading to the preservation of profitable deviations of structure or instinct and, lastly, that gradations in the state of perfection of each organ may have existed, each good of its kind. The truth of these propositions cannot, I think, be disputed....

As geology plainly proclaims that each land has undergone great physical changes, we might have expected to find that organic beings have varied under nature, in the same way as they have varied under domestication. And if there has been any variability under nature, it would be an unaccountable fact if natural selection had not come into play....

There is grandeur in this view of life, with its several powers, having been originally breathed by the Creator into a few forms or into one; and that, whilst this planet has gone cycling on according to the fixed law of gravity, from so simple a beginning endless forms most beautiful and most wonderful have been, and are being evolved.

QUESTIONS

1. What role does natural selection play in Darwin's theory, and what is the logic behind it?

2. How and why does Darwin attempt to reconcile his theory with religion?

Source: Charles Darwin, *On the Origin of Species by Means of Natural Selection*, 6th ed., vol. 2 (1872; repr., New York: Appleton, 1923), pp. 267–268, 279, 305–306.

beings are members of the animal kingdom, like other species, disturbed him, and the admission, he wrote, "is like confessing a murder." Nonetheless, for Darwin scientific evidence took precedence over all other considerations.

These assertions shocked Christians, many of whom denounced the new scientific findings. Some argued that science and faith belonged to two different worlds. Others claimed that there was no reason why God could not have created the world through natural forces. In the long run, however, **Darwinism** seemed to undermine the certainties of religious orthodoxies; many found religion incompatible with scientific discovery.

Some contemporaries took Darwin's theories beyond biology and applied them to human social development. Social Darwinists argued that human societies evolve in the same way as plants and animals. According to their logic, human societies—races, classes, nations—like species, were destined to compete for survival, and some would be condemned to fade away. And from these harsh laws, a better humanity would evolve. The British social theorist Herbert Spencer (1820–1903), who coined the expression "survival of the fittest," believed that society should be established in such a way that the strongest and most resourceful would survive. The weak, poor, and improvident were not worthy of survival, and if the state helped them survive—for instance, by providing welfare—it would only perpetuate the unfit. Poverty, according to Spencer and his followers, was a sign of biological inferiority; wealth was a sign of success in the struggle for survival. In Europe and the United States (where Spencer was extremely popular, selling hundreds of thousands of books), **Social Darwinism** justified callousness toward the poor at home and toward imperial conquest abroad. The European subjugation of Africans and Asians through colonization confirmed for Social Darwinists white racial superiority. People of color were seen as poorly endowed to compete in the race for survival (see Chapter 24). Darwin's theory was also used to justify inequality of the sexes, as men were thought to be more highly evolved than women.

Darwinism Influential theory of biological evolution, first put forth by Charles Darwin. He proposed that all forms of life continuously develop through natural selection, whereby those that are better adapted to the environment have the advantage and are more likely to survive and pass on their beneficial traits to their offspring.

Social Darwinism Theory of social evolution that states that human societies evolve in the same way as plants and animals, and that the weak, poor, and improvident are not worthy of survival.

Monkey Man Darwin's controversial theory of evolution made him a worldwide celebrity as well as an object of scorn. Caricatures of Darwin as a "monkey man" proliferated. This one is from an 1878 issue of the French satirical journal, *La Petite Lune.* (Library of Congress Prints and Photographs Division Washington, D.C. [LC-USZ62-88790])

Physics, Chemistry, and Medicine

Dramatic scientific advances in the nineteenth century confirmed the prevalent belief that human beings could understand and control nature. From the seventeenth century, scientists had studied nature through careful observation, seeking to develop theories by explaining its regularities. By the 1850s, major breakthroughs in physics established the field of electrical science. In chemistry, new elements were discovered almost every year. In 1869, Russian chemist Dmitri Mendeleev (men-del-LAY-ef) (1834–1907) developed the periodic table, which arranged the elements by their atomic weight. He left blank spaces for elements still unknown but that he was confident existed. Within ten years, three of these elements were discovered, affirming the belief that scientific knowledge not only can be experimentally tested, but also has predictive value. Such triumphs further enhanced science's prestige.

Once a practicing hobby among amateurs, science became increasingly specialized. In the nineteenth century, as the state and industry became more involved in promoting scientific research, the scientist became a professional employed by a university, a hospital, or some other institution. Scientific journals and meetings of scientific associations disseminated new discoveries and theories. Around midcentury, a number of important breakthroughs occurred in medicine. Before the development of anesthesia, surgical intervention was limited. With only alcohol to dull the patient's pain, even the swiftest surgeons could perform only modest surgical procedures. In the 1840s, however, the introduction of ether and then chloroform allowed people to undergo more extensive surgery. It also was used to relieve pain in more routine procedures and in childbirth; Queen Victoria asked for chloroform when in labor.

Increasingly, physicians applied the scientific experimental method to medicine, and as a result their concerns reached beyond the treatment of diseases to the discovery of their origins. Louis Pasteur (1822–1895) achieved notable breakthroughs when he discovered that microbes, small organisms invisible to the naked eye, cause various diseases. Pasteur found that heating milk to a certain temperature kills disease-carrying organisms. This process, called pasteurization, reduced the incidence of gastrointestinal illnesses that caused a high rate of infant deaths. Pasteur initiated other advances as well in the prevention of disease. Vaccination against smallpox had started in England in the eighteenth century, but Pasteur invented vaccines for other diseases and was able to explain the process by which the body, inoculated with a weak form of bacilli, developed antibodies that successfully overcame more serious infections. In England, the surgeon Joseph Lister (1827–1912) developed an effective disinfectant, carbolic acid, to kill the germs that cause gangrene and other infections in surgical patients. Lister's development of germ-free procedures transformed the science of surgery. By reducing the patient's risk, more ambitious surgery could be attempted. Eventually, midwives and doctors, by washing their hands and sterilizing their instruments, began to reduce the incidence of the puerperal, or "childbed," fever, a toxic infection that killed women after childbirth. The increasingly scientific base of medicine and its visible success in combating disease improved its reputation.

Birth of the Social Sciences

No field in the human sciences flourished as much in the nineteenth century as that of history. In an era undergoing vast transformations, many people became interested in change over time, particularly with regard to their own national histories. The father of modern historical writing is the German Leopold von Ranke (von RANG-kuh) (1795–1886). Departing from the tradition of earlier historians, who explained the past as the ongoing fulfillment of an overarching purpose— whether divine will, the human liberation, or some other goal—Ranke insisted that the role of the historian was to "show how things actually were." Like a scientist, the historian must be objective and dispassionate. Only by viewing humankind of all eras and environments on their own terms could historians arrive at a better understanding of humanity.

This perspective transformed the study of history into a discipline with recognizable common standards of evidence. Historians studied and interpreted original (or "primary") sources; they collected and published their findings; they founded professional organizations and published major journals.

Other social sciences also developed in this period. Anthropology, the comparative study of people in different societies, had been the subject of speculative literature for hundreds of years. Increased contacts with non-European societies in the nineteenth century—the effect of burgeoning trade, exploration, and missionary activities—stimulated anthropological curiosity. In 1844, the Society of Ethnology was founded in Paris, followed by the Anthropological Society (1859). London, Berlin, and Vienna quickly followed suit, establishing similar societies in the 1860s. Anthropologists speculated on the causes of perceived differences among human races, mainly attributing the variations to their physical structures. They offered apparent "scientific" backing to the era's racism, explaining that non-Europeans were condemned to an existence inferior to the white races.

The main anthropological theorist in Britain was Edward Tylor (1832–1917), the son of a brass manufacturer. Through his travels, Tylor came into contact with non-European peoples, who aroused his curiosity. Strongly influenced by the evolutionary doctrines of his day, Tylor believed that the various societies of humankind were subject to discoverable scientific laws. Tylor posited that if one could travel back in time, one would find humankind increasingly unsophisticated. So, too, the farther one traveled from Europe, the more primitive humankind became. Thus, according to his view, the contemporary African was at a level of development similar to that of Europeans in an earlier era.

Tylor was not technically a racist, since he argued that the conditions of non-Europeans resulted from their social and cultural institutions—not from their biology. Eventually, they would "evolve" and become akin to Europeans. Like racists, however, social evolutionists believed in European superiority. Anthropology gave "scientific" sanction to the idea of a single European people who shared either a similar biological structure or a common stage of social development, which distinguished them from non-Europeans.

The term *sociology* was coined by Auguste Comte. A number of ambitious thinkers, among them the English "social philosopher" Herbert Spencer (see page 655), considered the influence that social conditions exerted on individuals. In the 1840s, various social reformers published detailed statistical investigations that suggested relationships between, for instance, income, disease, and death rates. A few decades later, researchers spelled out the theoretical principles underlying sociology. Emile Durkheim (DIRK-hime) (1858–1917), among the first to do so, insisted that sociology was a verifiable science. His disciples, and the journal he founded, ensured the success of sociology as a professionalized discipline.

In the past, history, anthropology, and sociology were the purview of amateurs; now professional historians, anthropologists, and sociologists took over these fields, engaging in full-time research and teaching at universities or research institutes. Professionalization and specialization led to significant advances in several disciplines, but it also led to the fragmentation and compartmentalization of knowledge. People of broad learning and expertise became far less common.

The Challenge to Religion

Religion had assumed increased importance as a bulwark of order in the wake of the 1848 revolutions. In France, Napoleon III gave the Catholic Church new powers over education, and the bourgeoisie flocked to worship. In Spain, moderates who had been anticlerical (opposed to the clergy) began to support the church, and in 1851, they signed a concordat (an agreement with the papacy) declaring Roman Catholicism "the only religion of the Spanish nation." In Austria in 1855, the state surrendered powers it had acquired in the 1780s, returning to bishops full control over the clergy, the seminaries, and the administration of marriage laws.

In 1848, the papacy had been nearly overthrown by revolution, and in 1860, it lost most of its domains to Italy. Thus, Pope Pius IX became a sworn enemy of liberalism. In 1864, he issued the *Syllabus of Errors,* in which he condemned a long list of faults that included "progress," "liberalism," and "modern civilization." To establish full control over the clergy and believers, the Lateran Council in 1870 issued the controversial doctrine of papal infallibility, which declared that the pope, when speaking officially on matters of faith and morals, is incapable of error. This doctrine became a target of anticlerical opinion.

The political alliance the Catholic Church struck with reactionary forces meant that when new political groups came to power, they moved against the church. In Italy, since the church had discouraged national unification, conflict raged between the church and the new state. In Germany, Catholics had either held on to their regional loyalties or favored unification under Austrian auspices. When Protestant Prussia unified Germany, Chancellor Bismarck viewed the Catholics with suspicion as unpatriotic and launched a campaign against them, the *Kulturkampf* (KOOL-toor-kampf) ("cultural struggle"). Bismarck expelled the Jesuits and attempted to establish state control over the Catholic schools and appointment of bishops. Not satisfied, he seized church property and imprisoned or exiled eighteen hundred priests.

In France, the republicans, who finally won the upper hand over the monarchists in 1879, bitterly resented the church's support of the monarchist party. Strongly influenced by Comte's ideas of positivism, republicans believed that France would not be a free country until the power of the church was diminished and its nonscientific or antiscientific disposition was overcome. The republican regime reduced the role of the church in education as well as some other clerical privileges.

Greater tolerance, or perhaps indifference to religion in general, led to more acceptance of religious diversity. In 1854 and 1871, England opened university admission and teaching posts at all universities to non-Anglicans. In France, too, the position of religious minorities improved. Some of the highest officials of the Second Empire were Protestants, as were some early leaders of the Third Republic and some important business leaders and scientists.

Legal emancipation of Jews, started in France in 1791, subsequently spread to the rest of the Continent. The British allowed Jews to hold seats in the House of Commons in 1858, and in the House of Lords the following decade. In the 1860s, Germany and Austria-Hungary granted Jews the rights of citizenship. Although some Jews occupied high office in France and Italy, they had to convert to Christianity before they could aspire to such positions in Germany and Austria-Hungary. In other fields, such as banking and commerce, access was easier. Social discrimination continued, however—most of European society refused to accept Jews as social equals.

Because conditions for most people of western Europe improved with the expanding economy, Jews drew relatively less attention as they too took advantage of new opportunities. In other parts of the continent, Jews were not so fortunate. In eastern Europe, they incurred resentment when they moved into commerce, industry, and the professions. Outbreaks of violence against them, called *pogroms,* occurred in Bucharest, the capital of Romania, in 1866 and in the Russian seaport of Odessa in 1871. Although economic rivalries may have fueled anti-Semitism, they do not completely explain it. In most cases, anti-Jewish sentiment occurred in the areas of Europe least exposed to liberal ideas of human equality and human rights.

Culture in the Age of Material Change

Advances in technology and science became reflected in the arts, especially in the movement known as **modernism**, which rejected traditional forms of cultural expression and embraced new ones. Some artists optimistically believed they could more accurately portray reality by adopting scientific methods, objectively depicting their subjects. The materialism of the age, however, also disillusioned a minority of artists, who warned against its loss of values.

modernism A set of cultural tendencies and movements finding expression in new forms of art, architecture, and in attitudes and practices that rejected traditional forms of cultural expression.

Photography had a direct impact on artistic perspectives. The inventions of the Frenchman Louis Daguerre (dah-GAIR) (1789–1851) made the camera relatively usable by the 1830s. The introduction of celluloid film and American George Eastman's (1854–1932) invention of the Kodak camera, which became mass-produced and affordable, gave wide public access to the practice of photography by the 1890s. Photographic services were in high demand; by the 1860s, thirty thousand people in Paris made a living from photography and allied fields. (See the feature, "The Visual Record: The Modern City and Photography.")

The ability of photography to depict a scene with exactitude had a significant impact on art. On the one hand, it encouraged many artists to be true to reality, to reproduce on the canvas a visual image akin to that of a photograph. On the other hand, some artists felt that such realism was no longer necessary in their sphere. However, the great majority of the public, which now had wide access to museum exhibitions, was accustomed to photographic accuracy and desired art that was representative and intelligible. Realistic works of art met this need, at least superficially.

Courbet: *The Stone Breakers* This realistic 1849 painting depicts the rough existence of manual laborers. The bleakness of the subject matter and the style in which it was carried out characterized much of the realist school of art. (The Stone Breakers, 1849 (oil on canvas) (destroyed in 1945), Courbet, Gustave (1819–77)/Galerie Neue Meister, Dresden, Germany/© Staatliche Kunstsammlungen Dresden/The Bridgeman Art Library)

Many artists discarded myths and symbols to portray the world as it actually was, or at least as it appeared to them—a world without illusions, everyday life in all its grimness. The realist painter Gustave Courbet (koor-BAY) (1819–1877) proclaimed himself "without ideals and without religion." His fellow Frenchman Jean-François Millet (mil-LAY) (1814–1875) held a similar opinion. Instead of romanticizing peasants in the manner of earlier artists, he painted the harsh physical conditions under which they labored. In England, the so-called pre-Raphaelites took as their model those painters prior to Raphael in Renaissance Italy, who had depicted the realistic simplicity of nature. In painting historical scenes, these artists meticulously researched the landscape, architecture, fauna, and costumes of their subjects.

Photography and science also helped inspire completely new approaches to painting that abandoned traditional standards and shocked artistic sensibilities. On April 15, 1874, six French artists—Edgar Degas (1834–1917), Claude Monet (1840–1926), Camille Pissarro (1830–1903), Auguste Renoir (1840–1919), Alfred Sisley (1839–1899), and Berthe Morisot (1841–1895)—opened an exhibition in Paris that a critic disparagingly called **impressionist**, after the title of one of Monet's paintings, *Impression: Sunrise*. The impressionists were influenced by new theories of physics that claimed images were transmitted to the brain as small light particles that the brain then reconstituted. The impressionists wanted their paintings to capture what things looked like before the brain "distorted" them. Many of these painters unconventionally left their studios to paint objects exactly as they looked outdoors when light hit them at a certain angle. Monet, for example, emphasized outdoor painting and the need for spontaneity—for reproducing subjects without preconceptions about how earlier artists had depicted them—and seeking to show exactly how the colors and shapes struck the eye. Monet was particularly interested in creating multiple paintings of the same scene—from different viewpoints, under different weather

impressionist Late-nineteenth-century style of painting pioneered by the French artists Degas, Monet, Pissarro, Renoir, Sisley, and Morisot.

A Chinese Official's Views of European Material Progress

Educated in European universities, Ku Hung-Ming rose to become a high official in the Chinese court. His essays were penned under the impact of the European military intervention in China during the Boxer Rebellion in 1900 (see page 673). Ku denounced European notions of superiority over Asia by arguing that material progress was not an appropriate measure of a civilization's value.

In order to estimate the value of a civilization, it seems to me, the question we must finally ask is not what great cities, what magnificent houses, what fine roads it has built and is able to build; what beautiful and comfortable furniture, what clever and useful implements, tools and instruments it has made and is able to make; no, not even what institutions, what arts and sciences it has invested: the question we must ask, in order to estimate the value of a civilization—is what type of humanity, what kind of men and women it has been able to produce. In fact, the man and woman—the type of human beings—which a civilization produces, it is this which shows the essence, the personality, so to speak, the soul of that civilization. Now if the men and women of a civilization show the essence, the personality and soul of that civilization, the language which the men and women in that civilization speak, shows the essence, the personality, the soul of the men and women of that civilization....

To Europeans, and especially to unthinking practical Englishmen, who are accustomed to take what modern political economists call "the standard of living" as the test of the moral culture of or civilization of a people, the actual life of the Chinese and of the people of the East at the present day, will no doubt appear very sordid and undesirable. But the standard of living by itself is not a proper test of the civilization of a people. The standard of living in America at the present day, is, I believe, much higher than it is in Germany. But although the son of an American millionaire, who regards the simple and comparatively low standard of living among the professors of a German University, may doubt the value of the education in such a University, yet no educated man, I believe, who has traveled in both countries, will admit that the Germans are a less civilized people than the Americans.

QUESTIONS

1. How does the Chinese official define civilization? How does his view differ from the European view?

2. What is Ku Hung-Ming's idea of a hierarchy of civilization?

3. According to the ideas in this reading, what is the connection between progress and civilization?

Source: Ku Hung-Ming, *The Spirit of the Chinese People*, 2d ed. (Beijing: Commercial Press, 1922), pp. 1, 144–145.

conditions, at different times of day—to underscore that no single "correct" depiction could possibly capture a subject.

The school of realism also influenced literature, especially the novel. Departing from romanticism, realist novels did not glorify life or infuse it with mythical elements; they portrayed instead the stark realities of daily existence. Charles Dickens (1812–1870), who came from a poor background and had personally experienced the inhumanity of the London underworld, wrote novels depicting the lot of the poor with humor and sympathy. The appalling social conditions he described helped educate his large middle-class audience on the state of the poor.

Another realist, the French novelist Gustave Flaubert (flo-BEAR) (1821–1880), consciously debunked the romanticism of his elders. His famous novel, *Madame Bovary,* depicts middle-class life—particularly that of the married woman—as bleak, boring, and meaningless. The heroine seeks to escape the narrow confines of provincial life by adulterous and disastrous affairs.

Two Russian novelists of the realist school—arguably the greatest and most influential of all time—exploded onto the literary scene in the 1870s. Leo Tolstoy's (1828–1910) *War and Peace,* rather than portraying battle as heroic, showed individuals trapped by forces beyond their control. Small and insignificant events, as well as major ones, governed human destiny. Feodor Dostoyevsky (1821–1881) realistically portrayed the psychological dimensions of his characters in novels, such as *Crime and Punishment* (1866), *The Idiot* (1868), and *The Brothers Karamazov* (1879–1880).

The naturalist school of literature, a successor to realism, reflected positivist philosophy and grounded its methods in the natural sciences. Emile Zola (1840–1902), a Frenchman, belonged to this school. The writer, he declared, should record and represent human behavior scientifically. He described his own work as similar to "the analysis that surgeons make on cadavers."

The Modern City and Photography

This photo of Piccadilly Square in Manchester documents the modernization of the nineteenth-century city and, at the same time, conveys the sense of immediacy that photography provided as a new means of representation.

Taken in the 1880s, this photo* shows evidence of the great progress that had taken place in photography since its invention half a century earlier. In 1839, Louis Daguerre publicized the method of fixing an image on silvered copperplate. At first, the cameras and equipment were so cumbersome that photography was confined to studios. Thus, the only images were portraits of people and the occasional still life. As the camera became simpler, photographers could leave the studio and take pictures outdoors. The introduction of the dry plate method in the 1870s made film far more sensitive to light, reducing exposure time to a fraction of a second. Now a photograph could capture movement without reducing it to a blur, as in this bustling city scene.

Originally, photography had been regarded as a more exact, and less expensive, form of illustration and so was influenced by the conventions of painting. Because of the slowness of taking pictures and the obvious presence of the photographer with bulky equipment, most early photographs, even outdoor shots, were staged. But soon thereafter, thanks to technical innovations, photographers could capture a scene even without the cooperation of the subject. None of the subjects in this photo has eye contact with the camera. In fact, they seem unaware of the photographer as they go about their daily business.

This photo also conveys important visual information about the emerging modern city. A vibrant textile city, Manchester had a population that more than doubled to 600,000 inhabitants between 1830 and 1900. Piccadilly was its commercial center. As the photo here shows, it had been built as a large open square intended for the easy movement of pedestrians and wagons. City planners of the nineteenth century created squares and broad, straight avenues feeding into them, such as suggested here. Replacing old slums and narrow alleys, broad avenues eased the flow of traffic and admitted fresh air and sunlight. The square contained fancy stores with dwellings situated on the upper floors behind the elegantly crafted façades.

Piccadilly, the commercial center of Manchester, had warehouses and offices where buyers purchased textiles that they would in turn sell to retail consumers. As seen in this photo, Piccadilly Square, as a commercial center, required public transportation to move people quickly on the broad new avenues. Notice the rails for the horse-drawn tramway that had been introduced as early as the 1820s. They were the first means of mass transportation within the city. Trams on rails reduced friction and allowed a horse to pull a far greater load. In this case, the tram, located in the center of the photo, is a double-decker.

The large modern city required ease of communication at night as well as in the daytime. Street lighting not only provided that convenience, but also made the streets more secure by making potential crime more visible. Streetlamps became the norm in large cities, especially in the better neighborhoods. The elegant gaslights viewable in the photo of Piccadilly Square were replaced a few years later by electric lamps that were cheaper to operate and allowed for the spread of city lighting.

An industrial town, Manchester was not a particularly pleasant city to live in. Visitors complained of its grime, pollution, and foul smells. Many members of the commercial classes lived in wealthy suburbs and commuted by tram to work in the center. Sometime after this picture was taken, the horse-drawn tram was replaced by the electric tram, which could transport more people faster than its predecessor. Its lower cost also meant that it was accessible to most workers. With the advent of the electric tram, workers also began to move to the suburbs, making the center less crowded.

If the modern photograph was different from a painting, photography still adhered to some of the traditions of painting—notably composition. The photographer composed this image by making choices, for example, as to what to put in the foreground. Our eye centers on the harried merchant crossing the well-ordered street with its backdrop of amenities.

Compare this photograph with Camille Pissarro's *L'avenue de l'Opéra, Sunlight, Winter Morning* on page 651. Paris, known as the "city of light," was very different from Manchester, though like that industrial city, the new boulevards resulting from "Hausmannization" allowed for a larger and speedier flow of traffic and commerce. Pissarro also conveys in this painting the bustle—and perhaps alienation—some felt in modern life. Note the predominance of solitary figures in both the painting and the photograph. Wide boulevards meant that pedestrians did not "run into each other" and socialize as readily as they had on narrow streets. Indeed, Pissarro and other impressionist painters disdained the modernization of cities and turned instead to the suburbs and rural landscapes, leaving the

Zola's Rougon-Macquart (roo-ZHON-mah-KAR) series, which includes the novels *Nana* (1880) and *Germinal* (1885), describes the experience of a family over several generations. He emphasizes the impact environment and heredity had on his characters' lives of degradation and vice, in which they seem to be locked in a Darwinian struggle for survival: Some are doomed by the laws of biology to succeed, others to succumb.

Piccadilly Square, Manchester, ca. 1886   (Topham Picturepoint/The Image Works)

documentation of urban change to photographers. Pissarro thought Paris had become "ill" from all of its changes.

The chemical and optical breakthroughs that made the camera such an effective new tool were implemented by inventors in cities, such as London, Paris, and Berlin. Photographers in turn took pictures of some of the great technical feats of their era, such as the Eiffel Tower. The modern aspects of the city, such as the scene in this photo, were frequent subjects for the photographer's lens. Before the end of the century, photographs such as this were commonly used on postcards. The producers and consumers of postcards were more fascinated by the reality of representation rather than the beauty of particular sites, as postcards geared toward tourism would later embrace.

QUESTIONS

1. How did modernization—urbanization, commercialization, the design of cities, and modern means of transportation—change people's sensual experience and perceptions?

2. In its replication of "reality," how did photography both record and create our understanding of the past? How did it both replicate traditional art and create new ways of seeing?

*The advice of Thomas Prasch in the choice of this photo is gratefully acknowledged.

Although this era generally celebrated material progress, a number of intellectuals reacted against it. They were alarmed by the prospect of the popular masses achieving political power through winning the vote and by mass production and consumption. They denounced the smug and the self-satisfied, who saw happiness in acquisition and consumption. Some condemned the age in severe terms. Dostoyevsky railed against the materialism and egotism of the West,

663

SECTION SUMMARY

- Darwin's theory of evolution reinforced the belief among some of the inevitability of human progress; others found the placement of human beings in the same category as animal species profoundly disturbing.

- Social Darwinists applied Darwin's theories to human society in order to justify social and gender inequality, racial hierarchies, and "survival of the fittest."

- The application of the scientific method (experimentation) transformed fields, such as physics (especially electrical science), chemistry, and medicine.

- The scientific method also transformed the study of human society, professionalizing the fields of history, anthropology, and sociology.

- Scientific discoveries and theories undermined religious belief among some people; others, however, reacted to the harshness of the material world by embracing religion more fervently.

- Science and technology infused the arts with a new emphasis on realism and on the importance of visual representations.

branding its civilization as driven by "trade, shipping, markets, factories." In Britain—the nation that seemed to embody progress—the historian Thomas Carlyle (1795–1881) berated his age as one not of progress but of selfishness. He saw parliamentarianism as a sham, and he called for a strong leader to save the nation from endless debates and compromises. Unlike most of his contemporaries, who saw in material plenty a sign of progress, Carlyle saw the era as one of decline, bereft of spiritual values.

In France, republicans saw in the ostentation of the Second Empire a sign of depravity and decline. The 1870–1871 defeat in war and the insurrection of the Paris Commune contributed to the mood of pessimism among many intellectuals. Flaubert detested his own age, seeing it as petty and mean. The characters in Zola's Rougon-Macquart novels slide steadily downward as each generation's mental faculties, social positions, and morals degenerate. Some people abroad also were unimpressed with developments in Europe. (See the feature, "The Global Record: A Chinese Official's Views of European Material Progress.")

Not all were optimistic in this age of optimism. If many people celebrated what they viewed as an age of progress, others claimed that under the outer trappings of material comfort lay a frightening ignorance of aesthetic, moral, and spiritual values.

CHAPTER SUMMARY

During the second half of the nineteenth century, the cluster of technological innovations known as the second industrial revolution—mass-produced steel, synthetic dyes, new forms of energy, and the speedup in production—created for many Westerners an era of unprecedented material plenty. The expansion of railroads, advances in shipping, the standardization of postal service, and the inventions of the telegraph and telephone collapsed distances of time and space, and brought Europe further into a global economy.

Economic changes transformed the class structure of many European countries: the middle classes expanded, and their values and tastes defined the second half of the century. Conditions for the lower classes generally improved, but many rural and urban laborers still lived in poverty. To address problems of urban growth and threats of social upheaval, local governments took measures to improve public health and provide advice and material assistance. The need to shape a loyal citizenry inspired national governments to provide free and compulsory primary education.

Intellectual and cultural currents reflected material changes and the confidence they inspired. Scientific methods were applied to the study of human behavior. Novelists and painters, like scientists, aimed to dissect the world around them, adopting realism in the arts. Some intellectuals, however, were repulsed by the crass self-satisfaction of the bourgeoisie, and they despised their age's worship of industry and materialism.

FOCUS QUESTIONS

- What technological changes led to the expansion of the European economy after the mid-nineteenth century?

- How did the economic expansion affect the various social classes, and city versus rural areas, differently?

- What problems did urbanization create, and what were the solutions?

- What new scientific, intellectual, and cultural trends emerged in this period, and what impact did they have on systems of belief?

KEY TERMS

second industrial revolution (p. 640)

bourgeois century (p. 644)

professionalization (p. 645)

Victorian morality (p. 645)

separate spheres (p. 646)

social Catholics (p. 649)

positivism (p. 654)

Darwinism (p. 655)

Social Darwinism (p. 655)

modernism (p. 659)

impressionist (p. 660)

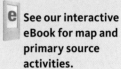 **This icon will direct you to additional materials on the website: www .cengage.com/history/ noble/westciv6e.**

See our interactive eBook for map and primary source activities.

CHAPTER OUTLINE

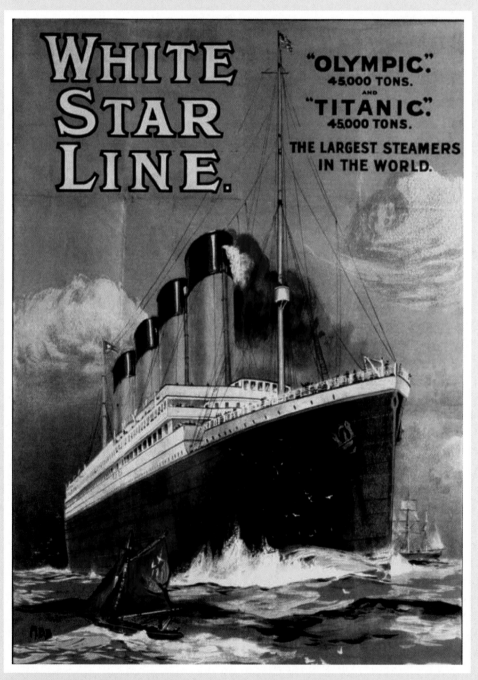

The "Unsinkable" Titanic
The *Titanic* proudly announces its maiden voyage.   (Christie's Images/CORBIS)

Imperialism and Escalating Tensions, 1880–1914

In April 1912, the *Titanic*, the largest and most techno-logically advanced passenger ship ever built, sailed from England for New York. Its owners, the White Star Line, boasted that this majestic vessel testified to "the progress of mankind" and would "rank high in the achieve-ments of the twentieth century." Though hailed as "virtu-ally unsinkable," on the night of April 12, the *Titanic* struck an iceberg south of Newfoundland and rapidly sank. More than 1,500 of the 2,100 people aboard perished in the icy North Atlantic waters. The overconfident captain had not taken warnings of icebergs in the ship's path seriously enough.

Two years later, European society was hit by a major disaster—the outbreak of a world war. That such a disas-ter would end the era that contemporaries called the *belle époque* (BELL eh-POK)—"beautiful epoch"—was as unimaginable as the *Titanic's* fate. The economy had been booming, and more nations seemed to be adapting to democracy and extending suffrage. Yet hand in hand with these trends of apparent progress appeared troubling tendencies. Forces beneath the surface threatened European social stability, which is why, in 1914, a lone assassin's bullet could set off a series of reactions that brought a whole era to a tragic close.

In the decades prior to 1914, governing became more complex as nations grew larger. The population of Europe jumped from 330 million in 1880 to 460 million by the outbreak of war. A larger population coupled with extended suffrage made reaching political con-sensus more difficult. The example of democracy in some countries led to discontent in the autocracies that failed to move toward freer institutions. Where freer institutions did exist, those excluded from them—women, ethnic minorities, and the poor—became ever more resentful.

Intellectuals no longer felt certain that the world was knowable, stable, or subject to mastery by rational human beings. Some jettisoned rationality and instead glorified emo-tion, irrationality, and in some cases violence. The works of painters and writers seemed to anticipate the impending destruction of world order.

The anxieties and tensions that beset many Europeans took a variety of forms. Ethnic minorities became targets of hatred. European states embarked on a race for empire throughout the world, forcibly subjecting non-Europeans to white domination. European states felt increasingly insecure, worried that they would be subject to attack. They established standing armies, shifted alliances, drafted war plans, and, in the end, went to war.

FOCUS QUESTIONS

- What were the main motivations for European imperialism?

- In what ways did the worldview of intellectuals living in the belle époque differ from that of a generation earlier?

- What factors made parliamentary rule in Great Britain, France, and Italy dysfunctional?

- What various crises weakened autocratic rule in Germany, Russia, and the Ottoman Empire?

- What responsibility did each of the Great Powers have for the outbreak of war in 1914?

 This icon will direct you to additional materials on the website: www .cengage.com/history/ noble/westciv6e.

 See our interactive eBook for map and primary source activities.

THE NEW IMPERIALISM AND THE SPREAD OF EUROPE'S INFLUENCE

What were the main motivations for European imperialism?

new imperialism   Era of European overseas expansion launched in the 1880s. Europeans subjugated 500 million people in Africa and Asia.

Part of Europe's self-confidence during the period from the 1880s to 1914 derived from the unchallenged sway it held over the rest of the globe. The age of empire building that started in Europe in the sixteenth century seemed to have ended by 1750. Then, in the 1880s, European states launched a new era of expansionism, conquering an unprecedented amount of territory. In only twenty-five years, Europeans subjugated 500 million people—one-half of the world's non-European population.

European expansion also marked the globe in a massive movement of people. Between 1870 and 1914, 55 million Europeans moved overseas, mainly to Australia, the United States, Canada, and Argentina. Scandinavians, Italians, Germans, Britons, Portuguese, and other groups each left a cultural and economic imprint on their adopted land, introducing new customs, tastes, and farming techniques. This phenomenal expansion of overseas migrations added to Europe's global influence.

But the more dramatic impact of European influence in this era assumed the form of ambitious conquest. The term the **new imperialism** differentiates this phase of European expansion from the earlier stage of empire building, which had focused on the Americas. Nineteenth-century imperialism centered on Africa and Asia. Unlike the earlier period, the new imperialism occurred in an age of mass participation in politics, accompanied by expressions of popular enthusiasm.

Petersen: *Emigrants Preparing to Depart*   Edward Petersen's 1890 painting depicts Danish emigrants preparing to leave their homeland. Between 1860 and 1914, 300,000 people emigrated from the small country of Denmark, most of them to the United States.   (Courtesy of the Aarhus Kunstmuseum. Reproduced with permission of Thomas, Poul, and Ole Hein Pedersen, Aarhus.)

Economic and Social Motives

The desire for huge markets and the hope for profit—much of it illusory—stirred an interest in empire. Colonies, it was believed, would provide eager buyers for European goods that would stimulate production at home. Yet colonies did not represent large markets for the metropolitan countries. France's colonies represented only 12 percent of its foreign trade, and Germany's even less. Great Britain's trade with its colonies represented a considerable one-third of its foreign trade, but most of that was with the white settlement colonies, such as Canada and Australia, not with those acquired in the era of the new imperialism.

Lack of profitability, however, mattered little to many proponents of empire. Some of them, known as social imperialists, argued that possession of an empire could resolve social as well as economic issues. An empire could offer an outlet for a variety of domestic frustrations. German and Italian imperialists often argued that their nations needed colonies in which to resettle their multiplying poor. Once the overseas territories were acquired, however, few Europeans found them attractive for settlement.

Nationalistic Motives

To a large extent, the desire to assert national power triggered empire building, particularly in the last third of the nineteenth century when the new nation-states of Italy and Germany had emerged. The latter in particular, in its rapid industrialization, became a daunting source of economic competition. Territorial expansion became a new means to compete effectively on the world stage.

The British Empire, with India as its crown jewel, constituted the largest, most powerful, and apparently wealthiest of all the European domains. Although the real source of Britain's wealth and power was the country's industrial economy, many people believed that its success came from its vast empire. The British example thus stimulated other nations to carve out empires. Their activities in turn triggered British anxieties. Britain and France unleashed a scramble for Africa and Asia; in Asia, Britain also competed with Russia.

France, defeated by Prussia in 1870, found in its colonies proof that it was still a Great Power. Germany and Italy, which formed their national identities relatively late, cast a jealous eye on the British and French empires and decided that if they were to be counted as Great Powers, they too would need overseas colonies. Belgium's King Leopold II (r. 1876–1909) spun out various plans to acquire colonies to compensate for his nation's small size. In the race for colonies, worldwide strategic concerns stimulated expansion. Because the Suez Canal ensured the route to India, the British established a protectorate over Egypt in 1882. Then, fearing a rival power might threaten their position by encroaching on the Nile, in the next decade, they extended their control all the way south to Uganda (see **MAP 24.1**). Russia, fearing a British takeover in central Asia, expanded toward Afghanistan, while the British movement northwestward to Afghanistan had a similar motivation—to prevent Russia from encroaching on India. The "great game" played by Russia and Britain in central Asia ended only in 1907, with the signing of the Anglo-Russian Entente.

The desire to control the often-turbulent frontiers of newly acquired areas drove much of this expansion. Once those frontiers had been brought under control, there were, of course, new frontiers that had to be subdued. As a Russian foreign minister said of such an incentive for expansion, "The chief difficulty is to know where to stop." The imperial powers rarely did.

CHRONOLOGY

1873	Three Emperors' League
1882	Britain seizes Egypt
	Triple Alliance of Germany, Italy, and Austria-Hungary
1884	Three Emperors' League renewed
1890	Kaiser Wilhelm II dismisses Bismarck as chancellor
1894	Franco-Russian Alliance
	Beginning of the Dreyfus affair
1900	King of Italy assassinated
1903	Emmeline Pankhurst founds the Women's Social and Political Union
1904	Anglo-French Entente
1905	Einstein proposes theory of relativity
	Revolution in Russia
1907	Anglo-Russian Entente
1908	Young Turk rebellion in Ottoman Empire
1911	Italy colonizes Libya
	Second Moroccan crisis
June 28, 1914	Assassination of Archduke Franz Ferdinand
August 4, 1914	With the entry of Britain, Europe is at war

🌐 **Map 24.1—Africa in 1914**

European powers in the late nineteenth century conquered most of Africa. Only Liberia and Ethiopia were left unoccupied at the start of World War I.

Other Ideological Motives

In addition to the search for profit and nationalistic pride, Europeans developed other strong rationalizations for imperialism. The remarkable technological and scientific advances of the nineteenth century made many imperialists believe it was Europe's duty to modernize Africa and Asia. Railroads, telegraphs, hospitals, and schools would open colonial peoples—if necessary, by brute force—to beneficent European influences.

The dramatic disparity between European material culture and that of colonial peoples in Africa and Asia offered Europeans apparent proof of their own innate superiority. They viewed Africans and Asians as primitive, inferior peoples, still in their evolutionary "infancy." Influenced by Darwin's theory of evolution (see pages 654–657), many imperialists argued that human groups competed in the struggle for survival in the same way that different species competed in nature. Dubbed "Social Darwinists," these thinkers believed that the most basic struggle occurred between the races. They also believed in a predetermined outcome: The white race, already superior, was destined to succeed, and the nonwhites to succumb.

Many Europeans paternalistically believed they had a duty to "civilize" the people they deemed inferior. The British bard of imperialism, Rudyard Kipling (1865–1936), celebrated this view in his poem "White Man's Burden" (1899):

Take up the White Man's burden—
Send forth the best ye breed—
Go bind your sons to exile
To serve your captives' need.

Each nation was certain that providence had chosen it for a colonial mission. The French Prime Minister Jules Ferry (feh-REE) declared it the duty of his country "to civilize the inferior races." Although European states rivaled each other in colonial acquisitions, they also believed they shared a common mission and a common destiny that distinguished them from the ascribed savagery and backwardness of non-Europeans. Their success at empire building reinforced those views.

Colonial acquisitions triggered public support for further expansion of the empire, much of which was expressed by the founding of various colonial societies. One million people joined the British Primrose League, which lobbied for empire as well as other patriotic goals. Though

Dutch Colonial Officials in the Dutch East Indies   In this club in an outpost of empire (in present-day Indonesia), the comforts of European bourgeois life were lovingly recreated. Absent from this photo are the countless Indonesian servants who were part of the colonial officials' lives.   (Royal Tropical Institute)

more limited in size, Germany, France, and Italy had similar organizations. Colonial societies generally drew their membership from the professional middle classes—civil servants, professors, and journalists—who were quite open to nationalist arguments. These societies produced a steady stream of propaganda favoring empire building.

Much of the literature celebrating empire building employed masculine terms to describe it. Primarily a male venture, conquest alone required "virility." But writers also contrasted the colonizer's manliness with the supposed effeminacy of the colonized peoples, as well as with the domestic passivity of European wives, sisters, or mothers. If European women did venture overseas, they went as helpmates to male colonial officials or as missionaries. Believing that they would have a positive influence on the world, women missionaries, either as members of a religious order or joining their husbands, went to the colonies to spread Western religions and European values. A few women heroically explored distant lands; the Englishwoman Mary Kingsley (1862–1900) made two exploration trips into Africa. Her popular books focused British interest on overseas territories, but they in no way shook the established view that empire was a man's enterprise.

Conquest, Administration, and Westernization

Industrialization gave Europeans the means to conquer overseas territories. Their rapid-fire weapons, steam-driven gunboats, and oceangoing vessels demonstrably assured their power overseas. Telegraphic communications tied the whole world into a single network, allowing Europeans to gather information and coordinate military and political decision making. Such advantages made Europeans virtually invincible in a colonial conflict. One remarkable exception was the 1896 Italian defeat in Adowa at the hands of an Ethiopian force, which was not only superior in numbers, but better armed.

Conquest was often brutal. In September 1898, British-led forces slaughtered 20,000 Sudanese at the Battle of Omdurman. From 1904 to 1908, an uprising in southwest Africa against German rule led to the killing of an estimated 60,000 of the Herero people. The German general, who had expressly given an order to exterminate the whole population, was awarded a medal by Kaiser Wilhelm II.

Colonial governments could be brutally insensitive to the needs of the indigenous peoples. (See the feature, "The Global Record: Chief Montshiwa Petitions Queen Victoria.") To save administrative costs in the 1890s, France put large tracts of land in the French Congo under the control of private rubber companies, which systematically and savagely coerced the local people to collect the sap of the rubber trees. When the scandal broke in Paris, the concessionary companies were abolished, and the French state reestablished its control. The most notorious example of exploitation, terror, and mass killings occurred in the Belgian Congo. Leopold II of Belgium had acquired it as a personal empire. It was his private domain, and he was accountable to no one for his actions there. To his shame, Leopold mercilessly exploited the Congo, and to expedite the collection of rubber, instituted the systematic torture and killing of its people. An international chorus of condemnation finally forced the king to surrender his empire and put it under the administration of the Belgian government, which abolished some of the worst features of Leopold's rule.

Imperialism also spread Western technologies, institutions, and values. By 1914, Great Britain had built 40,000 miles of rail lines in India—nearly twice as much as in Britain. In India and Egypt, the British erected hydraulic systems that irrigated previously arid lands. Colonials built cities, often modeled on the European grid system. In some cases, they were graced with large, tree-lined avenues, and some neighborhoods were equipped with running water and modern sanitation. Schools,

IN THE RUBBER COILS.

Scene—The Congo "Free" State.

Rubber Coils in Belgian Congo The Belgians colonized the Congo hoping to exploit its resources. This critical cartoon, published in the British satirical magazine *Punch* in 1906, shows a Congolese ensnared in the rubber coils of the Belgian king Leopold in the guise of a serpent. Rubber was the major cash crop, introduced by the Belgians to generate profits. (Punch Cartoon Library & Archive) patterned after those in Europe, taught the imperial language and spread Western ideas and scientific knowledge—though only to a small percentage of the local population.

The European empire builders created political units that had never existed before. In many parts of Africa, they ignored tribal and indigenous differences, which had serious repercussions in the postcolonial world. Although there had been many efforts in the past to join the whole Indian subcontinent under a single authority, the British were the first to accomplish this feat (see **MAP 24.2**). Through a common administration, rail network, and trade, Britain gave Indians the sense of a common condition, leading in 1885 to the founding of the India Congress Party. The Congress Party platform included the demand for constitutional government, representative assemblies, and the rule of law—concepts all based on Western theory and practice. Though initially demanding reforms within the British colonial system, the Congress Party eventually became India's major nationalist group.

In contact with Europeans, native intellectuals in colonized societies adopted a European ideology—nationalism. Indians, having studied in British schools or visited Britain, were most likely to be nationalists. They founded a movement, known as "Young India," harking back to "Young Italy" and other European nationalist movements founded during the mid-1800s (see page 595–596). Similarly, in French Algeria before World War I, a "Young Algerians" movement sprang up.

It was to be several decades before nationalism successfully challenged the European empires. In the meantime, overseas achievements confirmed Europeans' sense of themselves as agents of progress and builders of a new and better world. Europeans arrogantly believed that they knew what was best for other people, and when necessary, readily used force to implement their ideas.

The ties of empire also marked European cultures. Scenes from the colonial world often became the subjects of European art, such as Paul Gauguin's paintings of Tahiti and advertising posters for products as different as soap and whiskey. (See the feature, "The Visual Record: Imagining Empire.") A growing number of people from the colonies also came to live in European cities. By 1900, some former colonial subjects, despite various forms of discrimination, had become full participants in the lives of their host countries; two Indians won election to the British Parliament in the 1890s.

Unanticipated Consequences: Rebellion and Colonial War

The new imperialism encountered resistance from indigenous populations and caused war between colonizers. Two important examples, one of rebellion in China, the other of war in South Africa, exemplify the high material and moral costs Europe's compulsion for conquest entailed.

A prolonged decline in the effective rule of the Chinese government (the Qing dynasty), which was exacerbated by defeat in a war with Japan in 1895, opened the way to further economic incursions from western powers. By 1900, France, Britain, Russia, Germany, the United States, and Japan had exacted territorial and trading concessions from China, including rights to build railroads and control ports. The influx of Europeans included missionaries who sought to convert the Chinese to Christianity. Chinese peasants deeply resented both the economic disruptions and the contempt westerners showed for their ancient civilization. A secret society, "Righteous and Harmonious Fists" (called "Boxers" by westerners) staged a series of violent attacks in 1900–1901 against missionaries, engineers, Chinese Christians, diplomats, and merchants. They killed more than 200 westerners. In an unusual moment of cooperation, the Great Powers sent a combined expedition of 20,000 troops to crush the rebellion; they then demanded a huge indemnity from the Chinese government.

A much larger conflict unfolded in South Africa between Dutch settlers (called Afrikaners or Boers) and the British. The Boers and British had been competing with one another for African territory for nearly one hundred years. Tensions grew worse with the discovery of gold and diamonds, and the subsequent influx of 10,000 British and other foreigners to the Dutch state of Transvaal. In a series of disputes over the rights of the new arrivals, as well as over the competition for gold, the British decided to incorporate the Boer states into a federation under British control. In 1899, they goaded the Boers into war, thinking their victory would be swift.

The outnumbered Boers proved to be far more skilled in their sharpshooting and guerilla tactics than the 400,000 British troops; indeed, this war revealed to the British how physically unfit their soldiers were, many of whom had been drawn from the ranks of the poor and suffered from ailments, such as rickets. Both sides demonstrated cruelty, but the British employed methods that earned international condemnation. They adopted a "scorched earth" policy,

MAP 24.2—Asia in 1914

China, Siam (Thailand), and a portion of Persia were the only parts of Asia still independent after the Great Powers, including the United States and Japan, subjugated the continent to alien rule.

Territories held by Western powers

- Great Britain
- France
- Netherlands
- United States
- Russian Empire

- Japan and its territories
- Independent Asian states
- Ottoman Empire
- Major railroads

RUSSIAN EMPIRE

SIBERIA

JAPANESE EMPIRE

Sea of Okhotsk

Sakhalin

Karafuto (1905)

Khabarovsk (1858)

AMUR DISTRICT (1858)

Vladivostok (1860)

Sea of Japan (East Sea)

MANCHURIA

Harbin

KOREA (1905, 1910)

Lüshun (Port Arthur) (Japan 1905)

Weihai (Gr. Br. 1898)

Shenyang (Mukden)

JEHOL

Jiaozhou (Ger. 1898)

Beijing

Tianjin

Shanghai (Gr. Br. 1842)

Nanjing

Ryuku Is. (Jap.)

East China Sea

Philippine Is. (U.S. 1898)

INNER MONGOLIA

OUTER MONGOLIA (Russian Influence, 1912)

Irkutsk

Chita

Lake Baikal

CHINA

Wuhan

Fuzhou

Formosa (1895)

Xiamen

Guangzhou (Gr. Br. 1842)

Hong Kong (France 1898)

Zhanjiang (France 1898)

Manila

BRITISH NORTH BORNEO (1888)

SINKIANG

Chongqing

Kunming

Macao (Port. 1557)

Haiphong

Hainan

FRENCH INDOCHINA (1859, 1907)

Hanoi

South China Sea

SARAWAK (1888)

Borneo

DUTCH EAST INDIES

Yangzi R.

Huang He R.

TIBET

SIAM

Bangkok

Saigon

MALAY STATES (1874, 1909)

Singapore (Gr. Br. 1819)

Sumatra

Celebes

New Guinea

Timor (Portugal 1859)

Java (1619)

Batavia (Neth.)

Trans-Siberian Railway

Omsk

HIMALAYA MTS.

BHUTAN

NEPAL

BURMA (1852, 1885)

Rangoon

Calcutta

Ganges R.

Bay of Bengal

Andaman Is. (Gr. Br.)

Helsinki

Riga

St. Petersburg

Moscow

Kiev

Warsaw

Brest-Litovsk

Kazalinsk

Orenburg

Samara

Tashkent (1864)

Andizhan (1871)

KASHMIR (1846)

PUNJAB

Delhi

INDIA

Madras

Yanaon (Fr.)

Pondicherry (Fr.)

Karikal (Fr.)

Ceylon

Lake Balkash

Aral Sea

Bukhara

Samarkand (1868)

Merv (1884)

Kushka

AFGHANISTAN

BALUCHISTAN (1883)

Karachi

Diu (Port.)

Bombay

Goa (Port.)

Indus R.

INDIAN OCEAN

Kazalinsk

Krasnovodsk

Ashkhabad (1881)

BRITISH SPHERE (1907)

IRAN

RUSSIAN SPHERE (1907)

Tehran

Baghdad

OMAN (1891)

Caspian Sea

Baku

Batum (1878)

Kars (1878)

Angora

Constantinople

Beirut

Damascus

OTTOMAN EMPIRE

Persian Gulf

KUWAIT (1899)

ARABIA

Medina

HADRAMAUT (1888)

WEST ADEN (1903)

Arabian Sea

Black Sea

Mediterranean Sea

Red Sea

AFRICA

Nile R.

Danube R.

Dnieper R.

Volga R.

PACIFIC OCEAN

Tropic of Cancer

Equator 0°

20°N

40°N

80°E

100°E

60°E

40°E

N

1,000 Mi.

1,000 km.

500

500

0

0

Chief Montshiwa Petitions Queen Victoria

In 1885, Bechuanaland, in southern Africa, became a British protectorate. The Bechuana leaders saw British protection as a means to prevent takeover by the Boers, Dutch-speaking white settlers who were aggressively expanding in South Africa. The British were cavalier about their responsibilities, however, and a few years later allowed the British South Africa Company, a particularly exploitive enterprise, to take control of Bechuanaland. In protest, Chief Montshiwa (1815–1896), a major chief of the Baralong people, petitioned Queen Victoria for redress. His petition was supported by missionary lobbying, and most of Bechuanaland was saved from the clutches of the company.

Mafeking, 16 August 1895

To the Queen of England and Her Ministers:

We send greetings and pray that you are all living nicely. You will know us; we are not strangers. We have been your children since 1885.

Your Government has been good, and under it we have received much blessing, prosperity, and peace....

We Baralong are very astonished because we hear that the Queen's Government wants to give away our country in the Protectorate to the Chartered Company; we mean the B[ritish] S[outh] A[frica] Company.

Our land there is a good land, our fathers lived in it and buried in it, and we keep all our cattle in it. What will we do if you give our land away? My people are increasing very fast and are filling the land.

We keep all the laws of the great Queen; we have fought for her; we have always been the friends of her people; we are not idle; we build houses; we plough many gardens; we sow....

Why are you tired of ruling us? Why do you want to throw us away? We do not fight against your laws. We keep them and are living nicely.

Our words are No: No. The Queen's Government must not give my people's land in the Protectorate to the Chartered Company....

Peace to you all, we greet you;

Please send a good word back.

I am etc,

Montshiwa

QUESTIONS

1. What are Chief Montshiwa's grievances?

2. Why did the missionaries lend their support to the chief?

3. How does Montshiwa view the relationship between his people and the queen?

Source: S. M. Molema, *Montshiwa, 1815–1896* (Cape Town: G. Struik, 1966), pp. 181–182.

---

a military strategy that involves destruction of anything that supports the enemy. They thus burned homesteads and crops, and poisoned wells. The policy also included amassing Boer and African women, children, and workers in "concentration camps"—the first time this term was used.

The war ended with an armistice in 1902 and a toll of about 75,000 deaths, more than one-third of which occurred among Boer women and children confined in the concentration camps. Their deaths resulted from food deprivation and subjection to unhygienic conditions that fostered the spread of deadly diseases. Black Africans, many of whom also died for the same reasons in separate concentration camps, suffered famine from the massive destruction of their farmlands. Because Boers were of European descent, news of the concentration camps turned international public opinion against the British.

The Boxer Rebellion and the Boer War illustrate the degree to which pursuit of trading rights and natural resources readily resulted in violence, with permanent consequences for Europeans, indigenous cultures, and settler populations. Although the Boxers failed, peasant opposition to the corrupt Chinese government grew as a result of their rebellion, as did a movement for national independence, causing the Qing dynasty to fall in 1911. In addition to tarnishing Britain's reputation, the Boer War resulted in institutionalized racism. Joining the British Union of South Africa, Boers continued their long-term oppression of Africans by establishing Apartheid, the official policy of white supremacy and separation of blacks and whites that lasted until 1994.

SECTION SUMMARY

- Although the quest for commercial profit helped motivate imperialism, the colonies did not become large markets of the colonizing powers.

- Growing nationalism, rivalry among the Great Powers, and the need to protect the frontiers of already acquired colonies also generated empire building.

- Technological superiority, strong public support, notions of racial and cultural superiority, and a "civilizing mission" justified colonial conquest in the minds of Europeans.

- Industrialization produced powerful weaponry that made colonial conquest possible; European powers brought Western technologies, methods of administration and education, and ideologies, such as nationalism, to the colonized.

- The Boxer Rebellion and the Boer War exemplify the high costs and unintended consequences of imperialism, effecting permanent changes for European, indigenous, and settler populations.

FROM OPTIMISM TO ANXIETY: POLITICS AND CULTURE

In what ways did the worldview of intellectuals living in the belle époque differ from that of a generation earlier?

Most of the beliefs and institutions that had seemed so solid in the "age of optimism" came under attack in the next generation. Forces hostile to liberalism became increasingly vocal. In the arts and philosophy, doubt and relativism replaced the earlier confidence associated with positivism.

The Erosion of the Liberal Consensus

In 1850, liberals assumed that with the passage of time more and more people would be won over to their worldview. But the course of events in the late nineteenth century gave way to ideas and movements—some new, some rooted in the past—that chipped away at the liberal consensus. Prominent among these were socialism, anarchism, a new political right, racism, and anti-Semitism.

Liberals themselves retreated from some of their basic tenets in the face of changing circumstances. For example, a free market economy had always been one of their fundamental principles. But under the pressure of economic competition, liberals supported tariffs at home and created closed markets in their empires. To ensure workers' safety, they passed legislation requiring employers to improve working conditions. In some countries, liberals advocated income taxes and instituted welfare programs. These reforms were intended to strengthen the state by winning support from the masses and by fostering the growth of a healthy population through limited aid to mothers and children.

Historically, liberals had typically stood for an expansion of civil liberties, yet they saw nothing wrong or inconsistent in continuing to deny women both the vote and free access to education and professional advancement. In the face of labor agitation, many of them ceased supporting civil liberties for workers and favored instead the violent crushing of strikes.

In the effort to address real-life problems of the day, however, liberals encountered a paradox at the heart of their ideology: Creating rights for one group (such as workers or women) infringed on those of others (such as employers or men). Whatever action liberals took seemed to reveal a willingness to breach fundamental principles.

The Growth of Socialism and Anarchism

Among the groups challenging the power and liberal ideology of the middle classes were the socialist parties, both Marxist and non-Marxist, whose goal was to win the support of workers by espousing their causes. Socialists varied in their notions of how their goals should be achieved. Some favored pursuing objectives gradually and peacefully; others were dedicated to a violent overthrow of capitalist society.

SOCIALISM British socialists founded the Fabian Society in 1884, named after the Roman general noted for winning by avoiding open, pitched battles. The Fabians criticized the capitalist system as inefficient, wasteful, and unjust. They believed that by gradual, democratic means, Parliament could transfer factories and land from the private sector to the state, which would manage them for the benefit of society as a whole. More efficient and more just, socialism would come into being not through class war but through enlightened ideas. This gradualist approach became the hallmark of British socialism; it shaped the ideology of the Labour Party that would gain electoral success in the 1920s.

In Germany, various strands of socialism came together when a single united party was formed in 1875. But within a few years, a debate that generally divided socialism broke up the German party: Could socialism come about by gradual democratic means, or, as Marx had contended, would it require a violent revolution? The German socialist leader Eduard Bernstein (1850–1932), who had visited England and had soaked up the influence of the Fabians, argued for gradualism in a book with the telling English title *Evolutionary Socialism* (1898). Marx had been wrong, said Bernstein, to suggest that capitalism necessarily led to the increasing wretchedness of the working class. The capitalist economy had in fact expanded and been able to provide for steadily improved conditions. Rather than having to seize power by some cataclysmic act,

Jean Jaurès An ideological moderate, the French socialist leader Jean Jaurès (zhaw-REZ) (1859–1914) was one of France's greatest orators. Much of his socialism was based on ethical notions about social justice, rather than on Marxist doctrine. Here Jaurès addresses a social gathering in 1913. On the eve of World War I, he was assassinated for his efforts to prevent war. (Branger/Roger Viollet/Getty Images)

workers could win more political power through piecemeal democratic action, and achieve their goals through legislation. Since he argued for a revision of Marxist theory, Bernstein was labeled a "revisionist." Opposing him in this great debate was the party theoretician, Karl Kautsky (KOUT-skee) (1854–1938). Kautsky insisted that nothing short of a revolution would institute socialism.

Despite internal divisions, European socialists achieved some success in making their movement international. In 1864, Marx helped found the International Workers' Association, known as the First International. The more robust **Second International** succeeded it in 1889. The International met yearly and debated issues of concern to socialists, including deteriorating relations among the Great Powers. As early as 1893, the International urged European states to resolve their conflicts by mandatory arbitration. In 1907, sensing impending war, the International called on workers to strike and refuse military service in case of international conflict.

Another movement that sought to liberate the downtrodden was anarchism, which proclaimed that humans could be free only when the state had been abolished. According to anarchist theory, in a stateless society, people would naturally join together in communes and share the fruits of their labor. Some anarchists believed they could achieve their goal through education. Others hoped to speed up the process by making direct attacks on existing authority.

The Russian nobleman Michael Bakunin (bah-KOO-neen) (1814–1876), frustrated at the authoritarianism of his homeland, became a lifelong anarchist. He challenged tsarism at home and participated in the 1848 revolutions throughout Europe. He viewed all governments as repressive and declared unilateral war on them, stating, "The passion for destruction is also a creative passion." His ideas were particularly influential in Italy, Spain, and parts of France, especially among the artisan classes.

Many anarchists of this period wanted to bring about the new society by "propaganda of the deed" aimed at dissolving the state. They formed secret terrorist organizations that assassinated heads of state or those close to them. Between 1894 and 1901, anarchists killed a president of France, a prime minister of Spain, an empress of Austria, a king of Italy, and a president of the United States. These murders fixed the popular image of anarchism as a violence-prone ideology.

Without accepting the anarchists' methods, some labor activists shared their hostility toward parliamentary institutions. They argued that only a purely working-class movement, such as unionization, could achieve workers' goals. According to this line of thought, known as "syndicalism" (after the French word for unions), workers would amass their power in unions and, at the right moment, carry out a general strike, crippling capitalist society and bringing it down.

ANARCHISM

Second International International socialist organization founded in 1889 that met yearly to debate issues of broad concern. It called for workers to strike and refuse military service.

The New Right, Racism, and Anti-Semitism

Beginning in the 1880s, a "new right" emerged among conservatives, the traditional opponents of liberalism. The new right distinguished itself with populist and demagogic tactics, particularly with regard to nationalism—a sentiment that had made traditional conservatives support war. Alienated by democracy and social egalitarianism, many in this new right rejected doctrines of human equality and embraced racist ideologies.

Many Europeans believed that human races differed not only physiologically, but in their endowed intelligence and other qualities (see page 658). At midcentury, the Frenchman Arthur

Imagining Empire

In 1822, Joseph Huntley opened a small bakery in Reading, England. It was located near a coaching inn on the busy road between London and Bath. From a handbasket, he sold biscuits to hungry coach travelers passing through. In 1832, Huntley's son, an ironmonger, began producing tin boxes for the biscuits, which allowed them to "retain their freshness for years" and to travel worldwide without breaking. The bakery expanded rapidly. George Palmer joined the business in 1841; five years later, they purchased a former silk factory of 5,000 square feet that occupied more than half an acre. From this point on, Huntley & Palmers mass-produced their biscuits. By 1898, Huntley & Palmers was the largest biscuit manufacturer in the world, employing more than 5,000 men and women in a cluster of factory buildings comprising a "small city" unto itself on 24 acres.*

The image depicted here, a trade card advertising the Huntley & Palmers product, portrays a British hunting party in India around the turn of the nineteenth century. This card and the story behind the company it represents illustrate several themes inherent to nineteenth-century Western civilization: Industrial capitalism, the modernization in transportation, global commerce, and most poignantly, the interaction between imperialism and advertising.

The expansion of Huntley & Palmers in the second half of the century could not have occurred without the "second industrial revolution" (see pages 640–642). Improved modes of transportation, improved metal production for packaging, the building of the Suez Canal, and the expansion of empire brought Huntley & Palmers biscuits to ever greater distances. Export to the British colonies began in the 1840s. By 1874, the company could boast that "seldom a ship sails from England that does not bear within [its] ribs a Reading biscuit." By the end of the nineteenth century, Huntley & Palmers had sales representatives in China, Japan, India, South Africa, and North and South America. Ten percent of all its exports went to Britain's most important colony, India. Foreign companies produced biscuits under the Huntley & Palmers license in India, France, New Zealand, and Australia. The company increasingly relied on raw materials imported from overseas—eggs came from Ireland, coconuts came from Barbados and the West Indies, and cocoa came from West Africa.

An important reason for Huntley & Palmers' success lay in advertising—whose aesthetics had changed dramatically with new technologies of print and color. In addition to newspaper advertisements, handbills and multi-colored posters placarded urban surfaces. Particularly pervasive were trade cards, usually 4 x 6 inches in size, such as the one presented here. Huntley & Palmers produced hundreds of these trade cards, with vibrantly colored images on the front and a description of their latest products on the back. They showed not only how the biscuits could be found all over the world, but how they were transported, such as by camel, hot air balloon, elephant, and ship. Retailers distributed the cards, which were so appealing that they became collectors' items.

The card shown here depicts a tiger hunt in India, to which only those who had power and authority—royalty and senior imperial officials—were given the honor of attending. Members of the hunting party sit atop the crates in which 10-pound tins of Huntley & Palmers' biscuits have been shipped, transported by a British-built railroad, and then carried on elephants. Retaining their civilized British custom, the hunters take their tea break after killing tigers, whose carcasses hang from the elephants. The Indians function not only as their guides, but also as servants to them, performing functions women would perform at home. The relationship the colonizer had to native men was one that effeminized the latter. The scene also suggests the successful and safe insertion of British civilization into an exotic, adventurous, and potentially dangerous context.

In addition to cards, images such as this were placed on the biscuit tins themselves and on calendars, on posters, and in catalogs. Advertisements that included colonial themes conveyed the message that biscuits could bring a "taste of home" to British who found themselves anywhere on the globe; their images made imperialism seem safe, adventurous, and appealing.

Advertising also targeted the colonies. One image from 1902, for example, depicts an Indian market located in a narrow shadowy street where two upper-class British ladies negotiate with a turbaned figure. Once again, the portrayal suggests potential danger lurking in the shadows; but a tin of Huntley & Palmers biscuits is displayed on the stall, with more stacked in the background, bringing a sense of safety and familiarity to an otherwise strange scene. This 1902 image was used for trade cards, as well as for pocket calendars that were placed inside the tins as a promotional gift.

Similar images on the tins made them into collectable objects that are of great value today. One of the most elaborate is an "Arabian Nights" tin from 1888 featuring the adventures of Ali Baba and his encounter with the

---

anti-Semitism
Centuries-old prejudice against and demonization of Jews that became virulent in the 1880s with the emergence of the ultranationalist and racist ideologies and political movements.

de Gobineau (1816–1882) published his *Essay on the Inequality of Human Races*, declaring that race "dominates all other problems and is the key to it." Biologists and early anthropologists made similar statements, which gave racism a "scientific" aura. Race came to be the principle explanation for social, cultural, and ethnic differences among human groups.

The pseudo-scientific concepts of race helped fuel **anti-Semitism**. For centuries, Jews had been the object of suspicion and bigotry. Originally, the basis of the prejudice was religious. As early as the Middle Ages, however, the argument emerged that "Jewish blood" was different. And with the popularization of racist thinking in the nineteenth century, Jews were

Trade Card Advertising Huntley & Palmers Biscuits (Robert Opie Collection)

forty thieves. Stories such as these—and the distribution of images depicting such figures in exotic dress—influenced European perceptions of the Muslim world.

Huntley & Palmers iconography turned ordinary objects—trade cards, tins, calendars—into vehicles that carried multiple messages about imperial domination into the homes of ordinary people in Europe and around the globe. The images showed that Huntley & Palmers biscuits could accompany civilized British men (and occasionally women) into sites of potential danger. The biscuit represented all that was civilized about the British—from its mass production and distribution, to its ability to preserve the habit of tea time—and it offered symbolic proof of British capacity to tame nature and establish order over the "uncivilized." For consumers at home and abroad, Huntley & Palmers represented the success of British imperial dominance.

Huntley & Palmers became so associated with the export business that in 1953 a cartoon depicted their tins of biscuits arriving by spaceship to curious aliens on the planet Mars. So dependent was the company for its success on the British Empire, post-World War II decolonization was one of the factors that caused its closure in 1972.

QUESTIONS

1. What role did the British Empire play in the success of companies such as Huntley & Palmers? What role, in turn, did such a company play in the British experience of empire?

2. How did advertising contribute to the shaping of national, ethnic, and gender identities, and to the way Europeans imagined Empire?

---

*Most of the historical information on Huntley & Palmers comes from "The Huntley & Palmers Collection" on the Reading Museum website, at http://www.huntleyandpalmers.org.uk.

commonly viewed as a separate, inferior race, unworthy of the same rights as the majority of the population.

Historically, Christians had relegated Jews to marginal positions. In the Middle Ages, when land was the basis of wealth and prestige, Jews were prohibited from owning land, and thus confined to urban trades, among which was money-lending. They incurred high risks by lending money: They often were not paid back and faced unsympathetic courts when they tried to collect their debts. To counteract these risks, Jewish moneylenders charged high interest rates that earned them their unpopular reputation as usurers.

The emancipation of the Jews, which began in France with the Revolution and spread to Germany and Austria by the 1860s, provided them with unprecedented opportunities. Some members of society found it hard to adjust to the prominence that some Jews gained. Because their increased social standing and success were concurrent with the wrenching social transformations brought by industrialization and urbanization, anti-Semites pointed to the Jews as perpetrators of these unsettling changes. They became the targets for resentment toward the rich, even though most Jews were of modest means.

Anti-Semitic political movements emerged in the 1880s. Depicting Jews as dangerous and wicked, they called for their exclusion from the political arena and from certain professions. In some cases, proponents suggested that Jews be expelled from the state. In Berlin, the emperor's chaplain, Adolf Stöcker (SHTOE-kur) (1835–1909), founded an anti-Semitic party, hoping to make political inroads among the working-class supporters of socialism. In France, Edouard Drumont (1844–1917) published one of the bestsellers of the second half of the nineteenth century, *Jewish France*, in which he blamed all the nation's misfortunes on the Jews. Anti-Semitism in eastern Europe was more deadly. In Russia, organized *pogroms*, or mass attacks, killed two thousand Jews in the 1880s and one thousand in 1905, frightening two million into exile, mostly to the United States.

In the face of growing hostility, some Jews speculated that they would be safe only in their own nation. The Austrian Jewish journalist Theodore Herzl (HER-tsl) (1860–1904), outraged by the Dreyfus affair in France, in which a Jewish officer was imprisoned on trumped-up charges of treason (see pages 684–685), founded the Zionist movement. He advocated establishing a Jewish state in the Jews' ancient homeland of Palestine. At first, the Zionist movement won a following only in eastern Europe, where the Jews were particularly ill-treated—but by 1948, **Zionism** culminated in the creation of the state of Israel.

Irrationality and Uncertainty

In contrast to the confidence in reason and science that had prevailed at midcentury, a sense of irrationality and uncertainty characterized the era starting in the 1880s. The positivism of the earlier era had emphasized the surface reality of "progress" but had ignored the emotional and intuitive aspects of life. By the 1890s, a neo-romantic mood, emphasizing emotion and feeling, stirred major intellectual movements.

PHILOSOPHY

The work of the German philosopher Friedrich Nietzsche (FREED-reesh NEET-sheh) (1844–1900) vividly expressed the tension between reason and emotion. He proclaimed that rationality had led humankind into a meaningless abyss. Reason would not resolve human problems, nor would any preconceived ideas. "God is dead," Nietzsche announced. With no God, humankind was free of all outside constraints, free to overthrow all conventions. Nietzsche admonished his readers to challenge existing institutions and accepted truths, and to create new ones.

The French philosopher Henri Bergson (BERK-sohn) (1859–1940) argued that science—and indeed life—must be interpreted not rationally, but intuitively. "Science," Bergson declared, "can teach us nothing of the truth; it can only serve as a rule of action." Only a reliance on human feeling could provide access to the meaningful truths, such as those of religion, literature, and art.

SOCIAL SCIENCES

Various disciplines of knowledge subscribed to the notion that human beings are often irrational, governed by deep-seated instinctive forces. The Austro-Hungarian **Sigmund Freud** (1856–1939) believed that unconscious feelings and emotions motivated human behavior. He founded psychoanalysis, a method of treating psychic disorders by exploring the unconscious. While earlier physicians had described ailments as physical in origin, Freud saw their roots as psychological, the result of unresolved inner conflicts. He stressed that irrational forces played a significant role in human behavior.

The social theorist Gaetano Mosca (1858–1941) pessimistically argued that the desire to dominate is a basic part of human nature. His book, *Elements of Political Science* (1891), posited that in all societies—even democratic ones—an elite minority rules over the majority. Beneath slogans touting the public good lies selfish ambition, and the thirst for power is never slaked—a poor prognosis for socialist ideals.

ARTS

In the arts, the idea of being **avant-garde**—French for "forefront"—took hold among creative people. Breaking the taboos of society and the conventions of one's craft were, for them, signs of artistic creativity.

Zionism Nationalist Jewish movement beginning in the late nineteenth century. In face of anti-Semitism, Zionism advocated establishing a Jewish state in the Jews' ancient homeland of Palestine.

Sigmund Freud Austrian founder of psychoanalysis, a method of treating psychic disorders by exploring the unconscious, based on the belief that people are motivated by unconscious feelings and drives.

avant-garde French for "forefront," the term refers to early-twentieth-century artists who inspired unconventional techniques, considered themselves precursors of new styles, and called for the rejection of existing forms of expression.

Munch: *The Scream* Painted in 1893, this work reflects the fear and horror that some intellectuals experienced at the end of the nineteenth century. (© 2008 The Munch Museum/The Munch-Ellingsen Group/Artist's Rights Society (ARS), NY. Erich Lessing/Art Resource, NY)

In protest against the mass culture of their day, artists focused on images that were unique. Unlike earlier art, which had a clear message, the art of this era did not. Many artists no longer believed their role was to portray or spread ideals. Rather, they tended to be introspective and even self-absorbed. The public at large found it difficult to decipher the meaning of the new art, but a number of patrons supported the avant-garde artists' talent and insight.

Unlike the realists who preceded them, artists in the 1890s surrendered to neoromanticism, trying to investigate and express inner forces. As the French painter Paul Gauguin (1848–1903) noted, the purpose of painting is to communicate not how things look, but the emotions they convey. The Russian Wassily Kandinsky (vass-IH-lee kan-DIN-skee) (1866–1944) asked viewers of his art to "look at the picture as a graphic representation of a mood and not as a representation of objects." Artists appeared to be examining the hidden anxieties of society. The Norwegian painter Edvard Munch (MOONGK) (1863–1944) emphasized scenes of violence, fear, and sheer horror.

The era of uncertainty undermined both religious belief and confidence in science. Although large numbers of people still held traditional religious beliefs, indifference to organized **RELIGION AND SCIENCE**

religion spread. In urban areas of western Europe, church attendance declined, while various forms and practices of mysticism—such as séances—became more widespread. Some people were attracted to Eastern religions, such as Buddhism and Hinduism, perhaps reflecting a loss of faith in Western culture itself.

Scientists of this period questioned long-held commonsense beliefs. During the last week of the century, the German physicist Max Planck (1858–1947) suggested that light and other kinds of electromagnetic radiation, such as radio waves, which had always been considered continuous trains of waves, actually consist of individual packages of well-defined energy, which he called "quanta." In 1905, Albert Einstein (1879–1955) proposed the theory of relativity, which required a drastic change in fundamental ideas about space and time. To the three dimensions of space—length, breadth, and width—was added a complicating fourth dimension, that of time. The new ideas were not easily grasped. The old concept of a fixed cause tied to a fixed effect became unhinged, because even though things happen predictably, they also happen randomly.

SECTION SUMMARY

- The liberal ideology of the early nineteenth century could not address economic and social practicalities by the century's end. Civil and political liberties, some concluded, could not apply to everyone.

- Two strands of socialism emerged by the end of the nineteenth century: one that advocated violent revolution, and another—revisionism—that argued change could come through gradual, democratic means. The latter became more dominant.

- A "new right" of the late nineteenth century embraced nationalism and rejected democracy and the notion of human equality. It also adopted racist and anti-Semitic ideologies.

- By the 1890s, a neo-romantic mood emphasized the validity of feeling and emotion, while irrationality and uncertainty permeated philosophy, the social sciences, the arts, religion, and science itself.

VULNERABLE DEMOCRACIES

What factors made parliamentary rule in Great Britain, France, and Italy dysfunctional?

By the end of the nineteenth century, most of Europe's political systems floundered in crisis. The major powers with democratic institutions—Great Britain, France, and Italy—confronted volatile public opinion and had difficulty winning a broad consensus for their policies. They struggled with new challenges emerging from an expanded electorate; the latter expressed frustration over government failures to meet its competing and contradictory demands. Turning away from the democratic precept of resolving differences through the ballot and legislation, many people—both in government and out—were willing to resort to extraparliamentary means, including violence, to see their interests prevail.

Great Britain

In Great Britain, the Reform Bill of 1884 extended the vote to two of every three adult men, doubling suffrage to five million. To win votes from this enlarged electorate, some politicians made demagogic promises, which—to the exasperation of their constituents—they often later broke. Representing a population with more diverse interests and values, members of Parliament found compromise more difficult than in the past when they represented a much narrower set of interests.

The problem of Ireland persisted. The Irish seethed under British rule. In 1886, Prime Minister William Gladstone (GLAD-sten) proposed autonomy, or "home rule," for Ireland. But many opposed this plan. If Ireland, a predominantly Catholic country, ruled itself, the local Protestant majority in Ulster (the northeast part of the island) would be overwhelmed by Catholic control. In addition, the Conservative Party in England opposed changing the existing relationship with Ireland. With considerable political maneuvering, the Liberals finally pushed a home-rule bill through the House of Commons in 1911, but it was obstructed in the House of Lords and was not slated to go into effect until September 1914.

Passage of the home-rule bill did not resolve the Irish problem. Many segments of British society showed they were willing to resort to extralegal and even violent means. Fearing Catholic domination, Protestants in northern Ireland armed themselves in their determination to resist home rule. Catholic groups also took up arms, insisting on the unity of the island. The Conservative Party in Britain called on Ulster Protestants to revolt, and British officers said they would not take military action against them. The behavior of the Conservatives and the army indicated a breakdown of order and authority—a disregard for tradition by two of its major bulwarks. Only the outbreak of world war in 1914 delayed a showdown over Ireland, and then by only a few years.

Irish home rule was not the only issue that eroded civility in the British Parliament. Liberals, who dominated the House of Commons from 1906, committed themselves to an impressive array of social reforms, such as old-age pensions. To finance such measures, the feisty chancellor of the exchequer, David Lloyd George (1863–1945), proposed raising income taxes and death duties and levying a tax on landed wealth. A bill with these measures easily passed the House of Commons in 1909 but was stymied in the upper chamber. Motivated by economic self-interest and personal spite against the Liberals, a majority in the House of Lords voted against the bill. Lloyd George expressed his outrage that a handful of magnates in the upper chamber—sitting there not by election, but by hereditary right—could thwart the will of the people. A major constitutional crisis ensued.

In 1911, the government sponsored a bill to limit the legislative power in the House of Lords to a suspensive veto—meaning that any bill defeated there would simply be suspended for a predetermined period, such as two years. The House of Lords initially refused to pass the bill, but finally conceded when the king threatened to appoint four hundred new lords.

During the debate over the bill, Conservatives resorted to brawling and refused to let the prime minister speak. It was the first time in British parliamentary history that such a breach of conduct had occurred. The British Parliament, considered the model for supporters of free institutions, had shown itself unable to resolve issues in a civil manner.

Violence also broke out in another unexpected place: the women's suffrage movement. Most liberal males, when speaking of the need to extend human liberty, had excluded women because they thought public affairs an inappropriate arena for them. In 1903, Emmeline Pankhurst

A Suffragist Attempts to Chain Herself to the Gates of Buckingham Palace, London, 1914 In their effort to win the vote, women resorted to civil disobedience, and police often violently intervened. (Popperfoto/Classicstock.com/Getty Images)

(1858–1928) and her two daughters founded the Women's Social and Political Union, whose goal was immediate suffrage.

Angered and frustrated by their lack of progress, the **suffragists** (often referred to by contemporaries as "suffragettes"), led by the Pankhursts, began a more militant program of protest in 1906. They disrupted the proceedings in Parliament, broke windows at the prime minister's residence, slashed canvases at the National Gallery, burned down empty houses, dropped acid into mailboxes, and threw bombs. They even threatened the lives of the prime minister and the king. In 1913, Emily Wilding Davidson sacrificed her life to the cause of female suffrage when, before thousands of spectators at the Derby, she threw herself in front of the king's horse. These acts of violence and tragedy drew condemnation, but they also brought worldwide attention to the cause.

But these acts also incurred severe punishment. Imprisoned suffragists often engaged in hunger strikes, which provoked the authorities to force-feed them—an extremely painful and humiliating procedure that amounts to torture. Female protesters also incurred physical attacks in public. (See the feature, "The Written Record: Pankhurst Testifies on Women's Rights.") That women would resort to violence, and that men inside and outside government would retaliate in kind, demonstrated how widespread the cult of force had become.

suffragists Activists who, beginning in the late nineteenth century, organized to win the vote for women and adopted increasingly violent tactics. Also called "suffragettes."

France

The Third Republic, founded in 1870 after France's humiliating military defeat by Prussia, also struggled with an ongoing series of crises. Enemies of the Republic, on both the political left and right, continually called for the abolition of democracy.

Pankhurst Testifies on Women's Rights

In 1908, the suffragists, led by Emmeline Pankhurst, issued a handbill calling on the people of London to "rush" Parliament and win the vote for women. The legal authorities interpreted their action as a violation of the peace, and several suffragists, including Pankhurst, were put on trial. They put up a spirited defense, in which Pankhurst movingly explained her motives for leading the suffragist cause.

I want you to realise how we women feel; because we are women, because we are not men, we need some legitimate influence to bear upon our law-makers. Now, we have tried every way. We have presented larger petitions than were ever presented for any other reform, we have succeeded in holding greater public meetings than men have ever had for any reform, in spite of the difficulty which women have in throwing off their natural diffidence, that desire to escape publicity which we have inherited from generations of our fore-mothers; we have broken through that. We have faced hostile mobs at street corners, because we were told that we could not have that representation for our taxes which men have won unless we converted the whole of the country to our side. Because we have done this, we have been misrepresented, we have been ridiculed, we have had contempt poured upon us. The ignorant mob at the street corner has been incited to offer us violence, which we have faced unarmed and unprotected by the safeguards which Cabinet Ministers have. We know that we need the protection of the vote even more than men have needed it....

We believe that if we get the vote it will mean better conditions for our unfortunate sisters. We know what the condition of the woman worker is...and we have been driven to the conclusion that only through legislation can any improvement be effected, and that that legislation can never be effected until we have the same power as men have to bring pressure to bear upon our representatives and upon Governments to give us the necessary legislation....

I should never be here if I had the same kind of power that the very meanest and commonest of men have—the same power that the wife-beater has, the same power that the drunkard has. I should never be here if I had that power, and I speak for all the women who have come before you and other magistrates....

If you had power to send us to prison, not for six months, but for six years, for sixteen years, or for the whole of our lives, the Government must not think that they can stop this agitation. It will go on....

We are here not because we are law-breakers; we are here in our efforts to become lawmakers.

QUESTIONS

1. What is the logic behind Pankhurst's comment that women need the "protection of the vote" even more than men? What is her main argument here for why women should get the vote?

2. Do you think women were justified in breaking laws in order to obtain their goal? Why or why not? How did their behavior compare with that of men, both within and outside of the British Parliament?

Source: F. W. Pethick Lawrence, ed., *The Trial of the Suffragette Leaders* (London: The Women's Press, 1909), pp. 21-24.

This situation resulted in part from the French government's lack of strong leadership. The need to build coalitions among the several parties in the parliament rewarded those politicians who had moderate, but often mediocre, programs. Supporters of the republic actually found lackluster leadership appealing. They continued to fear that a strong leader might—as Louis Napoleon had in 1851—exploit his support to make himself dictator.

The regime lurched from one crisis to another. The most notorious was the Dreyfus affair. In October 1894, Captain Alfred Dreyfus (1859–1935) of the French army was arrested and charged with passing military secrets to the German embassy. Dreyfus (DRY-fooss) seems to have attracted suspicion because he was the only Jewish officer on the general staff. The evidence was flimsy—a handwritten letter that some thought Dreyfus had penned, although other experts testified that the handwriting was not his.

This letter, and materials that later turned out to be forged, led the French army to court-martial Dreyfus and sentence him to life imprisonment on Devil's Island off the coast of South America. By March 1896, the general staff had evidence that another officer, Major Esterhazy, was actually the spy. But to reopen the case would be to admit the army had made an error, and the general staff refused to do this.

By late 1897, when the apparent miscarriage of justice became widely known, French society split over "the affair." The political left argued for reopening the case. The army and its supporters—right-wing politicians, royalists, and zealous Catholics—argued that the decision should stand. They believed the army, as a bulwark against internal and foreign threats, should be above the law, and the fate of a single man—guilty or innocent—was immaterial. From the outset, Dreyfus was the target of virulent anti-Semitism.

The affair unleashed a swirl of controversy and rioting, which led the government to order a retrial in 1899. But the court again found Dreyfus guilty—this time with "extenuating circumstances" and the recommendation that he be pardoned. Finally, in 1906, Dreyfus was fully exonerated.

The strong encouragement many Catholics gave to those who supported the original verdict confirmed the republicans' belief that the church was a menace to the regime. The politicians who backed Dreyfus—anticlericals—were voted into the parliament. In 1905, they passed a law separating church and state, thus ending the privileged position the Catholic Church had enjoyed. Violent language and physical confrontations on both sides accompanied this division. Catholics trying to prevent state officials from entering churches to take required inventories sometimes resorted to force, using weapons or, in one case, a bear chained to the church. Armed soldiers broke down church doors and dragged priests away.

Labor problems also triggered repeated confrontations with the government. Increased labor militancy produced long, drawn-out strikes, which in 1904 alone led to the loss of four million workdays. Rural workers agitated as well, particularly in the Midi, the south of France. This region suffered from a crisis in the wine industry caused by a disease that attacked the vines, competition from cheap foreign wines, and fraud. The region witnessed increased rural proletarianization as landholdings became concentrated in fewer hands. Rural militancy led to a revolt in 1907. Troops were sent in; they killed dozens and won for the Radical regime the title "government of assassins."

Italy

Italy, the third major power in Europe to adopt parliamentary government, also had grave problems. Although unification took place in 1860, genuine national unity proved elusive. As in the past, the south especially challenged the central government. Assertive regionalism, crime, and poverty made this area resistant to most government programs.

The parliamentary system established in 1860 was far from democratic. Property qualifications limited suffrage to less than 3 percent of the population. Between 1870 and 1890, the Italian government introduced some important reforms, but the relatively low standard of living failed to improve. In the fifty years after unification, the population increased from 25 million to 35 million, and the country had limited resources to deal with such growth. In the south, a few wealthy landowners held large private estates, while the majority of the peasants were landless and forced to work for minimum wages. In the north, industrialization had started, but the region was not rich in coal or iron. To be competitive, industry paid very low wages, and the workers lived in abject misery.

Conditions on the land and in the factories led to widespread protests. In 1893, a Sicilian labor movement won the adherence of 300,000 members, who seized land and attacked government offices. The government responded with massive force and declared martial law. As unrest spread throughout the peninsula in 1896, the government placed half of the provinces under military rule. A cycle of violence and repression gripped the nation. In this turbulent atmosphere, an anarchist killed King Umberto I on July 29, 1900.

After the turn of the century, a new prime minister, Giovanni Giolitti (jo-VAH-nee jo-LEE-tee) (1842–1928), tried to end the upheaval. He used government force more sparingly and showed a spirit of cooperation toward the workers. Seeking to divert

SÉANCE ORAGEUSE A LA CHAMBRE ITALIENNE

Riots in Italian Parliament Party strife and conflicts between individuals in the Italian parliament were so severe that often they degenerated into fisticuffs. This illustration catches a particularly violent moment of a parliamentary debate. (Roger-Viollet/The Image Works)

SECTION SUMMARY

- Democratic governments in western Europe experienced crises that led to forceful repression. The British resorted to violence or uncivil behavior over the issues of Irish home rule, a constitutional crisis over social reform, and women's suffrage.

- Democracy in the French republic was threatened by the nation-splitting Dreyfus affair, the role of the Catholic Church, and labor militancy.

- Regionalism, poverty, social strife, violence, and unrepresentative government challenged Italy's efforts at parliamentary democracy.

attention from domestic ills and appeal to nationalist fervor, Giolitti launched an attack on Libya in 1911, wresting it from the ailing Ottoman Empire. This arid territory was bereft of economic promise, but imperialists championed the conquest as a test of national virility and the foundation of national greatness.

The government also resorted to force for its domestic problems when, in June 1914, a national strike led to rioting. Workers seized power in several municipalities, and in northern Italy, they proclaimed an independent republic. It took 100,000 government troops ten days to restore order. The workers' brazen defiance led some nationalist right-wing extremists to form groups of "volunteers for the defense of order," anticipating the vigilante thugs who were to make up the early bands of Italian fascism.

AUTOCRACIES IN CRISIS

What various crises weakened autocratic rule in Germany, Russia, and the Ottoman Empire?

Four major autocracies dominated central and eastern Europe: Germany, Austria-Hungary, the Ottoman Empire, and Russia. If the democracies encountered difficulties in these years, the autocracies faced even more vehement opposition. As the demands for more democracy grew louder, protesters resorted to violence and governments in turn used force to maintain themselves.

The severity of autocratic rule varied from state to state, ranging from the absolutism of the Ottoman Empire to the semiparliamentary regime of Germany; but in all of the states, the ruler had the final political say. Resistance to the autocracies included broad popular challenges to the German imperial system, discontent among ethnic minorities in the nearly ungovernable empire of Austria-Hungary, and revolution and war in the Russian and Ottoman Empires.

Germany

Although Germany had a parliament, the government was answerable to the kaiser, not the people's electoral representatives. To rule effectively, Chancellor Otto von Bismarck quelled opposition through manipulation and intrigue. He used an attempt to assassinate the emperor as the excuse to ban the Socialist Party in 1879. He also persecuted Catholics and their institutions in order to strengthen Protestant Prussia. These measures, however, did not prevent the growth of the Socialist and Catholic Center Parties.

Bismarck's tenure in office depended on the goodwill of the emperor, Wilhelm I, who died in 1888. He was succeeded by his son, Friedrich, who ruled only a few months, and then by his grandson, Wilhelm II (r. 1888–1918). The young Kaiser Wilhelm was ill fit to govern. He could not bear any limitation to his power, announcing, "There is only one ruler in the Reich and I am he. I tolerate no other." Intimidated by Bismarck and dismayed by his domestic and foreign policies, the kaiser dismissed him.

Wilhelm II was determined to make Germany a world power whose foreign policy would have a global impact. He

Wilhelm II The German emperor liked to be viewed in a heroic and military posture. A restless individual, Wilhelm changed uniforms eight times daily and traveled ceaselessly among his seventy-five castles and palaces. (Landesarchiv Berlin)

wanted Germany to have colonies, a navy, and major influence among the Great Powers. This policy, **Weltpolitik**—"world politics"—greatly troubled Germany's neighbors. The kaiser's bombastic threats and the prospect of a new, assertive power in central Europe made them wary. Within Germany, however, Weltpolitik won support.

Although the nationalist appeals impressed many Germans, others challenged the emperor's autocratic style and increasingly viewed his behavior as irresponsible. In the elections of 1912, one-third of all Germans voted for Socialist Party candidates. Thus, the largest single party in the Reichstag challenged both the capitalist system and autocracy. Labor militancy also reached new heights. In 1912, one million workers—a record number—went on strike. Increasingly, Germans pressed for a government accountable to the people's elected representatives.

> **Weltpolitik** Meaning "world politics," the term describes the policy pursued, with nationalistic appeals and bombastic threats, by Kaiser Wilhelm II to make Germany a world power.

Austria-Hungary

A series of crises also wracked the neighboring Austro-Hungarian Empire. In an age of intense nationalism, a multinational empire was an anomaly, as the emperor Franz Joseph (r. 1848–1916) himself acknowledged. Despite the Compromise of 1867 (see page 626) that regulated the relationship between Austria and Hungary, conflict grew, particularly over control of their joint army. Hungary increasingly saw its interests as separate from Austria's and probably would have broken loose from the dual monarchy had world war not occurred.

In the Hungarian half of the empire, the Magyar rule faced growing challenges. Other nationalities opposed Magyarization—the imposition of the Magyar language and institutions—and insisted on the right to use their own languages in their schools and administrations. The Hungarian government censored and imprisoned nationalist leaders. The Austrian half of the empire was equally strife-ridden.

These conflicts had no easy solutions. Hoping to dilute the influence of nationalist middle-class intellectuals, the Habsburg government introduced universal male suffrage in 1907. The result backfired. The extended suffrage produced a parliament that included thirty ethnically based political parties, making a workable majority nearly impossible to achieve.

The virulence of debate based on nationality and class divisions grew to unprecedented extremes. Within the parliament, deputies threw inkwells at each other, rang sleigh bells, and sounded bugles. Parliament ceased to be relevant. By 1914, the emperor had dissolved it and several regional assemblies, and ruled Austria by decree. Emperor Franz Joseph feared that the empire would not survive him.

Ottoman Empire

The Ottoman Empire suffered the most advanced case of dissolution prior to 1914, undermined by both secessionist movements within its borders and aggression from other European powers. Sultan Abdul Hamid II (r. 1876–1909) ruled the country as a despot and authorized mass carnage against those who contested his rule, earning him the title "the Great Assassin."

Young, Western-educated Turks—the so-called Young Turks—disgusted at one-man rule and the continuing loss of territory and influence, overthrew Abdul Hamid in July 1908. They set up a government responsible to an elected parliament. The Young Turks hoped to stem the loss of territory by establishing firmer central control, but their efforts had the opposite effect. The various nationalities of the empire resented the imposition of Turkish education and administration. Renewed agitation broke out in Macedonia, in Albania, and among the Armenians. The government carried out severely repressive measures to end the unrest, massacring thousands of Armenians.

To foreign powers, the moment seemed propitious to plunder the weakened empire. In 1911, Italy occupied Libya, an Ottoman province. Greece, Bulgaria, and Serbia formed the Balkan League and waged a successful war against the empire in 1912. Albania became independent, and Macedonia was partitioned among members of the League. This war stripped the empire of most of its European possessions (see **Map 24.3**).

Russia

The Great Reforms of the 1860s, intended to resolve Russia's problems, instead unleashed new forces because they coincided with major social changes. Tsarist rule became even more difficult.

🌐 **MAP 24.3—The Ottoman Empire**

The Ottoman Empire once included much of southeastern Europe, western Asia, and North Africa. Secessionist movements and European aggression caused it to lose most of its European, Caucasus, and North African territories. By 1914, it was restricted largely to parts of western Asia.

The needs of a modernizing country led to an increase in the number of universities. The newly educated Russian youths almost instantly began an ardent, sustained critique of autocracy. In the absence of a sizable middle class upholding liberal, advanced ideas, university students and graduates, who came to be known as the *intelligentsia*, saw it as their mission to transform Russia.

In the 1870s, university youths by the thousands organized a populist movement, hoping to bring change to the countryside. These young idealists, both men and women, intended to educate the peasants and make them more politically aware. But instead, they encountered peasant suspicion and government repression. Large numbers of populists were arrested and put on trial. Disaffected by such results, radicals formed the People's Will, which sought to hasten revolution by murdering public officials.

In response, the regime intensified repression. But it also sought to broaden its public support. In 1881, Tsar Alexander II decided to create an advisory committee that some thought would eventually lead to a parliamentary form of government. Just before the tsar signed the decree establishing this committee, the People's Will assassinated him. The son who succeeded him, Tsar Alexander III (r. 1881–1894), blamed the assassination on his father's leniency, and so decided to make the government even more autocratic, weakening his father's reforms and reducing local self-rule.

When Alexander's son, Nicholas II (r. 1894–1917), succeeded to the throne in 1894, he too was determined to maintain autocratic rule. However, he lacked the methodical, consistent temperament such a pledge required, as well as a coherent policy for his troubled country.

Serious problems had accumulated that threatened the stability of the regime. Conditions worsened in the countryside as explosive population growth increased pressure on the land.

Despite the abolition of serfdom, the peasants were not free to move around. Agriculture remained inefficient, far inferior to that of western Europe. Between 1861 and 1914, the peasant population grew by 50 percent, but it acquired only 10 percent more land. In 1891, famine broke out in twenty provinces, killing a quarter of a million people.

Although Russia remained largely agrarian, there were pockets of industrial growth. Some factories and mining concerns had as many as six thousand employees. When workers grew incensed at their condition and insistent on winning the same rights and protection as workers in western Europe, they engaged in massive strikes that crippled industry.

Political dissatisfaction with the autocracy grew among all social classes—the slowly expanding middle classes and aristocrats demanded the right to political participation. Various revolutionary groups committed to socialism flourished. Socialist Revolutionaries, heirs to the People's Will, emerged as a political force in the 1890s. They believed that the peasants would bring socialism to Russia.

In 1898, the Russian Social Democratic Party was founded. A Marxist party, it promoted the industrial working class as the harbinger of socialism. In 1903, that party split into the Menshevik and Bolshevik factions. The Mensheviks insisted that Russia had to go through the stages of history Marx had outlined—to witness the full development of capitalism and its subsequent collapse before the socialists could come to power. The **Bolsheviks**, a minority group, were led by Vladimir Ilich Lenin (1870–1924), a zealous revolutionary and Marxist. Rather than wait for historical forces to undermine capitalism, he insisted that a revolutionary cadre could seize power on behalf of the working class. Lenin favored a small, disciplined, conspiratorial party, like the People's Will, while the Mensheviks favored a more open, democratic party.

In February 1904, war broke out between Russia and Japan in a dispute over control of northern Korea. In the face of Russian military ineptitude, popular opposition to tsarism grew. An economic slowdown heightened social tensions.

Beginning in January 1905, a series of demonstrations, strikes, and other acts of collective violence erupted. Together they were dubbed "the revolution of 1905." On a Sunday of that month, 400,000 workers gathered in front of the tsar's St. Petersburg palace. Rather than hear their demands, officials ordered soldiers to fire on them, resulting in 150 deaths and hundreds more wounded. "Bloody Sunday" inflamed the populace, who now viewed the tsar as a murderer of his people. Unrest spread to most of the country. The regime's prestige deteriorated further with reports of increasing losses in the war with Japan. By September 1905, Russia had to sue for peace and admit defeat. Challenged in the capital, where independent workers' councils called *soviets*

Bolsheviks Faction of the Russian Socialist Democratic Party led by Marxist Vladimir Ilich Lenin (1870–1924), who insisted that an exclusive revolutionary cadre could seize power on behalf of the working class.

Workers' Demonstration in Moscow, 1905 In 1905, workers as well as peasants protested against the Russian autocracy. To bring the revolution under control, Nicholas II was obliged to grant several concessions. (Novosti/Sovfoto)

- In Germany after 1890, Wilhelm II's aggressive foreign policy menaced other European powers, while his autocratic governing style created widespread opposition to his rule.

- Parliamentary rule in Austria-Hungary failed because of ongoing conflicts between the two monarchies, as well as between the multiple nationalities within each.

- The Ottoman Empire continued to suffer from both secessionist movements within its borders and aggression from other European powers; by 1912, the empire had lost most of its European possessions.

- In Russia, the emergence of revolutionary socialist groups, deteriorating conditions of peasants, worker discontent, and defeat in war with Japan fueled opposition to tsarist rule. The revolution of 1905 and subsequent reforms failed to stem the regime's problems.

had sprung up, the government also lost control over the countryside, the site of widespread peasant uprisings.

Fearing for his regime, Nicholas hoped to disarm the opposition by meeting some of its demands. He granted major constitutional and civil liberties, including freedom of religion, speech, assembly, and association. The tsar also established an elective assembly, the Duma, with restricted male suffrage and limited political power. It quickly became an arena for criticizing autocracy. Nicholas responded by suspending the Duma and changing its electoral base and rules of operation. This blatant breach of his promise to establish constitutionalism and parliamentarianism even disillusioned many conservatives.

Although the government reduced the peasants' financial obligations, weakened the power of the commune, or *mir* (see page 630), and extended local self-rule to the peasants, these changes did little to alleviate rural poverty. Labor unrest also mounted. In 1912, 725,000 industrial workers went on strike; that number doubled in the first half of 1914. On the eve of the outbreak of the First World War, workers were building barricades.

THE COMING WAR

What responsibility did each of the Great Powers have for the outbreak of war in 1914?

Instability and upheaval characterized international relations in the years between 1880 and 1914. But the outbreak of war was by no means inevitable. Common sense dictated against it, and some intelligent people predicted that in the new modern era, war would become so destructive that it would be unthinkable. Finally, no European state wanted a war, although the Great Powers carried on policies that brought them to its brink.

Power Alignments

Triple Alliance Military alliance established in 1882 among Germany, Austria-Hungary, and Italy to counter the Franco-Russian Alliance (later the Triple Entente).

Germany enjoyed an unchallenged position in the international order of the 1870s and 1880s. It was united in an alliance with the two other eastern conservative states—Russia and Austria-Hungary—in the Three Emperors' League, formed in 1873 and renewed by treaty in 1884. It also formed part of the **Triple Alliance** with Austria and Italy. France stood alone, without allies. Britain, with little interest in continental affairs, appeared to be enjoying a "splendid isolation."

However, Germany's alliance system was not free from problems. Two of its allies, Austria-Hungary and Russia, were at loggerheads over control of the Balkans. How could Germany be the friend of both? Wary of apparent German preference for Austria, Bismarck signed the Reinsurance Treaty in 1887, assuring Russia that Germany would not honor its alliance with Austria if the latter attacked Russia. After Bismarck's resignation in 1890, Kaiser Wilhelm allowed the Reinsurance Treaty to lapse. Alarmed, the Russians turned to France and, in January 1894, signed the Franco-Russian Alliance, by which each side pledged to help the other should Germany attack either of them.

The Great Powers on the Continent were now divided into two alliances, the Triple Alliance and the Franco-Russian Alliance. Britain formally belonged to neither, but if it favored any side, it would be the German-led alliance because of colonial rivalries with France over Africa and with Russia over Asia.

In the 1890s, Germany lost British goodwill. Launching his Weltpolitik, Wilhelm II built up the German navy. An island nation dependent on international trade for its economic survival, Britain had developed a navy second to none—and it saw the German naval buildup as a threat to its security.

In the face of a mounting German menace, France and Britain decided to reconcile their differences. In 1904, they signed an understanding, or *entente*, resolving their rivalries in Egypt. In 1907, Great Britain and Russia regulated their competition for influence in Persia (present-day Iran) with the Anglo-Russian Entente. Europe was now loosely divided into a new configuration of two groups: the Triple Alliance of Germany, Austria-Hungary, and Italy, and the **Triple Entente** of Great Britain, France, and Russia.

Triple Entente Military alliance between Great Britain, France, and Russia, completed in 1907, countering the Triple Alliance.

The Momentum Toward War

Only through a series of crises did these alignments solidify to the point where their members were willing to go to war to save them. In 1905, and again in 1911, France and Germany nearly went to war over their respective interests in Morocco; both instances left Germany with the appearance of unreasonable aggressiveness. Meanwhile, the unstable situation in the Balkans sharpened tensions between Austria and Russia.

The heightened international tensions forced the European states to increase their arms expenditures, which in turn increased their sense of insecurity. In 1906, Britain launched a new class of ships—the *Dreadnought*. Powered by steam turbines, it was the fastest ship afloat; heavily armored, it could not be sunk easily, and its 12-inch guns made it a menace on the seas. The British had thought the Germans incapable of building equivalent ships. But they did, wiping out British supremacy. Britain felt less secure than at any time since the Napoleonic Wars, and it continued an expensive and feverish naval race with Germany.

Meanwhile, the growing war-making capacity of Russia created great anxieties within Germany. The Japanese defeat of the tsarist empire in 1905 had revealed the Russian military to be inferior—a lumbering giant, slow to mobilize and maneuver. As a result, Germany had not been particularly afraid of its eastern neighbor. But stung by its humiliation in 1905, Russia quickly rebuilt its army and planned an extensive rail network in the west, which would, in the event of war, be used for military purposes. Germany now felt encircled by a hostile Russia to the east and an equally unfriendly France to the west, and by 1912, some military officers and government officials began thinking about a preventive war. If war was inevitable, many Germans argued, it should occur before Russia became even stronger.

Many political leaders viewed the escalating arms race as a form of madness. Between 1904 and 1913, French and Russian arms expenditures increased by 80 percent, those of Germany by 120 percent, those of Austria-Hungary by 50 percent, and those of Italy by 100 percent. British foreign secretary Sir Edward Grey (1862–1933) warned that if the arms race continued, "it will submerge civilization."

But most Europeans did not fear warfare. The Western powers had not experienced a major conflict since the Crimean War (1854–1856). Most policymakers believed that the next war would be short. The wars that had so dramatically changed the borders of European states in the second half of the nineteenth century, notably the Austro-Prussian War of 1866 and the Franco-Prussian War of 1870, had been decided within a few weeks. Because few imagined that the next war would be either long or brutal, Europe's leaders did not make a major effort to prevent it.

The territorial rivalry between Austria and Russia triggered international disaster. For decades enmity had been growing between the two empires over control of the Balkans (see **Map 24.4**). In 1903, following a bloody military coup that killed the king and queen of Serbia, a pro-Russian party took control of the Serbian government. In 1908, Austria shocked Russia by annexing the province of Bosnia (which it had

🌐 **Map 24.4—The Balkans in 1914**

By 1914, the Ottoman Empire was much diminished, containing virtually no European territory. Political boundaries did not follow nationality lines. Serbia was committed to unite all Serbs at the expense of the Austro-Hungarian Empire.

The Shot Heard Round the World The young Serb nationalist Gavril Princip shoots Franz Ferdinand, the heir to the Austro-Hungarian throne, and his consort. The assassination led to the outbreak of World War I. (Three Lions/Hulton Archive/Getty Images)

administered since the Congress of Berlin in 1878; see page 728). Austria's action thwarted Serbia's ambition of annexing Bosnia, which had many Serb inhabitants. Still weakened from the 1905 war with Japan, Russia had to accept diplomatic defeat and abandoned its ally, Serbia. But Russia was determined not to cave in again.

Undeterred, Serbia spread anti-Austrian propaganda and sought to unify under its banner Slavs living in the Balkans—including those under Austrian rule. As a result, many Austrian officials were convinced that the survival of the Austro-Hungarian Empire required the destruction of Serbia. On June 28, 1914, the heir to the Habsburg throne, Archduke Franz Ferdinand, visited Sarajevo in Austrian-ruled Bosnia. A young Bosnian-Serb nationalist hostile to Austrian rule, who had been trained and armed by a Serb terrorist group called the Black Hand, assassinated the archduke and his wife.

The assassination of the heir to the throne provided Austria with an ideal pretext for military action. The German kaiser, fearing that failure to support Vienna would lead to Austrian collapse and a Germany bereft of any allies, urged Austria to attack Serbia. On July 23, Austria issued an ultimatum to Serbia, deliberately worded in such a way as to be unacceptable. When Serbia refused the ultimatum, Austria declared war on July 28.

Perceived self-interest motivated each state's behavior in the ensuing crisis. Russia's status as a Great Power required that it not allow its client state, Serbia, to be humiliated, much less obliterated. In the past, the French government had acted as a brake on Russian ambitions in the Balkans. On the eve of the war in 1914, France counseled restraint, but it did not withhold its promise of aid to Russia, its only ally on the Continent. Since 1911, France had increasingly feared isolation in the face of what it perceived as growing German aggression. To remain a Great Power, France needed to preserve its friendship with Russia and help that country maintain its own Great Power status.

Germany could not allow Austria, its only ally, to be destroyed. Its leaders may also have seen the crisis as a propitious moment to begin a war that they believed was going to occur anyway. The Germans no doubt thought it expedient to strike before the Entente powers, especially Russia, became stronger. After declaring war on Russia, Germany then invaded France through Belgium to prevent it from coming to Russia's aid. The British, concerned for their ally France and outraged by the violation of Belgian neutrality (to which all the Great Powers had been signatories since 1839), on August 4, declared war on Germany. Europe was at war. Eventually, so would be much of the world.

SECTION SUMMARY

- By 1907, Europe was loosely divided into the Triple Alliance of Germany, Austria-Hungary, and Italy and the Triple Entente of Great Britain, France, and Russia.

- Mounting crises solidified the alliances: France and Germany came into conflict over Morocco; all the countries, but especially Britain and Germany, engaged in an arms race; rivalry over the Balkans between Russia and Austria intensified when the latter annexed Bosnia.

- Anti-Austrian sentiments in Serbia led to the assassination of the Austrian archduke Franz Ferdinand, provoking Austria to declare war on Serbia; the system of alliances then brought all of the Great Powers into war.

CHAPTER SUMMARY

In the decades prior to 1914, Europe appeared to dominate the globe. With the intention of acquiring new sources of wealth, trade, and the trappings of international power and prestige, Europeans forcibly conquered most of Africa and much of Asia. They also conceived of their mission as one that brought civilization to inferior peoples. They introduced both technology and Western education to the colonized subjects. The scramble to build empires reflected growing competition among the Great Powers, but it also produced anxiety and tensions over them.

Between 1880 and 1914, many intellectuals abandoned the optimism of the generation that preceded them and saw in materialism and democracy the evidence of decline and decadence. They suggested that a hidden, irrational dimension of life lurked beneath the tranquil surface. Among the new nationalist right, fear of mass society gave way to racist and anti-Semitic ideologies.

In Western democracies, improved conditions also led to rising expectations. People grew more demanding, insisting in sometimes violent ways on their political and economic rights. Although mass movements, such as socialism and women's suffrage, generally used peaceful means in their campaigns to change society, some of their members advocated and employed violence. Anarchism appeared to stalk Europe. States readily used brutality in efforts to quell various protest movements, even resorting to martial law.

In central and eastern Europe, similar problems emerged. Extremist opposition to autocratic rule joined with the conflicts between national and ethnic groups to destabilize regimes. Everywhere in Europe, domestic ills raised the stakes in competition for overseas empire; at the same time, the traditional empires of Austria-Hungary and Turkey were threatened with dissolution.

Every European power had some responsibility for feeding the international tensions that led to the outbreak of war in 1914. France and Germany clashed over Morocco; Austria and Russia competed for influence over the Balkans; Britain and Germany raced each other to build warships. The Weltpolitik of Wilhelm II menaced France and Britain. Among European thinkers and leaders, force had become widely accepted as the means to an end; all the powers (except Britain) built up large standing armies with millions of men and lethal modern equipment. As rising tensions tightened the alliance system, Europe divided into two armed camps. Some leaders—notably those of Austria-Hungary and Germany—favored war over negotiation in July 1914.

FOCUS QUESTIONS

- What were the main motivations for European imperialism?

- In what ways did the worldview of intellectuals living in the belle époque differ from that of a generation earlier?

- What factors made parliamentary rule in Great Britain, France, and Italy dysfunctional?

- What various crises weakened autocratic rule in Germany, Russia, and the Ottoman Empire?

- What responsibility did each of the Great Powers have for the outbreak of war in 1914?

KEY TERMS

new imperialism (p. 668)

Second International
 (p. 677)

anti-Semitism (p. 678)

Zionism (p. 680)

Sigmund Freud (p. 680)

avant-garde (p. 680)

suffragists (p. 683)

Weltpolitik (p. 687)

Bolsheviks (p. 689)

Triple Alliance (p. 690)

Triple Entente (p. 691)

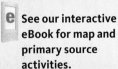 This icon will direct you to additional materials on the website: www .cengage.com/history/ noble/westciv6e.

See our interactive eBook for map and primary source activities.

CHAPTER OUTLINE

Passchendaele, Belgium, 1917
(The Art Archive/Picture Desk)

War and Revolution, 1914–1919

Mud. It was not what soldiers had in mind when they headed off to war in August 1914 amid visions of glory, gallantry—and quick victory. But after heavy rain and constant shelling, mud was a fact of life for those fighting on the western front—Belgium and northern France—during the fall of 1917. The mud was so pervasive, in fact, that soldiers literally drowned in it. These Canadian troops are holding the line on November 14, 1917, at the end of the Battle of Passchendaele (PAH-shun-dale), a British-led assault that began late in July. That assault pushed the Germans back a mere 5 miles—at the cost of 300,000 lives. There was no end to the war in sight.

Some had thought a major war impossible in rational, civilized Europe. Others had devoutly wished for war—precisely to break out of the stifling bourgeois conventions of rational, civilized Europe. When war actually began early in August 1914, the European mood was generally enthusiastic, even festive. No one was prepared for what this war would bring, including the hellish scenes of mud, smoke, artillery craters, blasted trees, decaying bodies, and ruined buildings that came to frame the daily experience of those on the western front. A far wider and more destructive war would follow within a generation, but it was World War I, known to contemporaries as "the Great War," that shattered the old European order, with its comfortable assumptions of superiority, rationality, and progress. After this war, neither Westerners nor non-Westerners could still believe in the privileged place of Western civilization in quite the same way.

The war that began in August was supposed to be over by Christmas. The British government promised "business as usual." But the fighting bogged down in a stalemate during the fall of 1914, then continued for four more years. By the time it ended, in November 1918, the war had strained the whole fabric of life, affecting everything from economic organization to literary vocabulary, from journalistic techniques to the role of women.

Partly because the war grew to become the first "world war," it proved the beginning of the end of European hegemony. The intervention of the United States in 1917 affected the military balance and seemed to give the war more idealistic and democratic purposes. The geographic reach of the war was itself unprecedented, especially after the intervention of the Ottoman Empire spread the fighting to the Middle East. Because of European colonial networks, the war also involved many other non-Europeans in combat or support roles. Although the old colonialism continued into the postwar era, the war nourished the forces that would later overthrow it.

Because of all the strains it entailed, the war had many unintended consequences. Revolutions dramatically changed the political landscape first in Russia, then in Germany.

FOCUS QUESTIONS

- How and why had the course of the war by 1917 defied the expectations that had surrounded the beginning of fighting in August 1914?

- Why did this prove a total war, making necessary new forms of socioeconomic coordination and even systematic propaganda?

- Why did the first revolution in Russia pave the way for a second, spearheaded by the Bolsheviks?

- Why did Germany and its allies end up losing the war even after forcing Russia to make a separate peace by early 1918?

- What factors shaped the peace settlement that the victors imposed on Germany and its allies in 1919–1920?

 This icon will direct you to additional materials on the website: www .cengage.com/history/ noble/westciv6e.

e **See our interactive ebook for map and primary source activities.**

The Habsburg and Ottoman Empires collapsed. So when the victors met early in 1919 to shape the peace, they confronted a situation that could not have been foreseen in 1914. Their effort to determine the contours of the postwar world, and thus the immediate meaning of the war, left much unresolved.

THE UNFORESEEN STALEMATE, 1914–1917

How and why had the course of the war by 1917 defied the expectations that had surrounded the beginning of fighting in August 1914?

When the war began in August 1914, enthusiasm and high morale, based on expectations of quick victory, marked both sides. But fighting on the crucial western front led to a stalemate by the end of 1914, and the brutal encounters of 1916 made it clear that this was not the sort of war most had expected. By early 1917, the difficulties of the war experience brought to the surface underlying questions about what all the fighting was for—and whether it was worth the price.

August 1914: The Domestic and Military Setting

Although some, including Helmuth von Moltke (MOLT-kuh), chief of the German general staff, worried that this would prove a long, destructive war testing the very fabric of Western civilization, the outbreak of fighting early in August produced a wave of euphoria and a remarkable degree of domestic unity. To many, war came almost as a relief; the issues that had produced intermittent crisis for the past decade would at last find definitive solution. Especially to educated young people, the war promised an escape from the stifling bourgeois world and the prospect of societal renewal.

An unexpected display of patriotism from the socialist left reinforced the sense of domestic unity and high morale. Forgetting their customary rhetoric about international proletarian solidarity, socialist parties rallied to their respective national war efforts almost everywhere in Europe. To socialists and workers, national defense against a more backward aggressor seemed essential to the eventual creation of socialism. When, on August 4, the German Socialist Party delegation in the Reichstag voted with the other parties to give the government the budgetary authority to wage war, it was clear that the Second International had failed in its long-standing commitment to keep the workers of Europe from slaughtering each other.

In France, the government had planned, as a precaution, to arrest roughly one thousand trade union and socialist leaders in the event of war, but no such arrests were necessary. The order of the day was **Sacred Union**, which meant that French leaders from across the political spectrum agreed to cooperate for the duration of the war. Rather than seek to sabotage the war, Socialist leaders joined the new government of national defense. Germany enjoyed a comparable "Fortress Truce," including an agreement to suspend labor conflict during the war, although no Socialist was invited to join the war cabinet.

On the eve of war, the forces of the Triple Entente outnumbered those of Germany and Austria-Hungary. Russia had an army of over 1 million men, the largest in Europe, and France had 700,000. Britain, which did not introduce conscription until 1916, had about 250,000. Germany led the Central Powers with 850,000; Austria-Hungary contributed 450,000. Though outnumbered, the Central Powers had potential advantages in equipment, coordination, and speed over their more dispersed adversaries. The outcome was hardly a foregone conclusion in August 1914.

After the fighting began, a second group of nations intervened one by one, expanding the war's scope and complicating the strategic alternatives. In November 1914, the Ottoman Empire, fearful of Russia, joined the Central Powers, thereby extending the war along the Russo-Turkish border and on to the Middle East. For Arabs disaffected with Ottoman Turkish rule, the war presented an opportunity to take up arms—with the active support of Britain and France. Italy, after dickering with both sides, committed itself to the Entente in the Treaty of London

Sacred Union An agreement between leaders of different French political groups to cooperate during World War I.

of April 1915. This secret agreement specified the territories Italy would receive—primarily the Italian-speaking areas still within Austria-Hungary—in the event of Entente victory. In September 1915, Bulgaria entered the war on the side of the Central Powers, seeking territorial advantages at the expense of Serbia, which had defeated Bulgaria in the Second Balkan War in 1913. Finally, in August 1916, Romania intervened on the side of the Entente, hoping to gain Transylvania, then part of Hungary.

Thus, the war was fought on a variety of fronts (see **MAP 25.1**). This fact, combined with uncertainties about the role of sea power, led to ongoing debate among military decision makers about strategic priorities. Some expected that Britain and Germany would quickly be drawn into a decisive naval battle. But though Britain promptly instituted an effective naval blockade on imports to Germany, the great showdown on the seas never materialized. Despite the naval rivalry of the prewar years, World War I proved fundamentally a land war.

Germany faced not only the long-anticipated two-front war against Russia in the east and France and Britain in the west; it also had to look to the southeast, given the precarious situation of its ally Austria-Hungary, which was fighting Serbia and Russia, then also Italy and Romania as well. On the eastern front, Germany was largely successful, forcing first Russia, then Romania, to seek a separate peace by mid-1918. But it was the western front that proved decisive.

Into the Nightmare, 1914–1916

With the lessons of the wars of German unification in mind, both sides had planned for a short war based on rapid offensives. According to the Schlieffen (SHLEE-fyn) Plan, drafted in 1905, Germany would concentrate first on France, devoting but one-eighth of its forces to containing the Russians, who would need longer to mobilize. After taking just six weeks to defeat France, Germany would focus on Russia. French strategy, crafted by commander-in-chief Joseph Joffre (JOFF-ruh), similarly relied on rapid offensives. The boys would be home by Christmas—or so it was thought.

Although German troops encountered more opposition than expected from the formerly neutral Belgians, they moved swiftly through Belgium into northern France during August. By the first week of September, they had reached the Marne River, threatening Paris and forcing the French government to retreat south. But French and British troops counterattacked, forcing the Germans to fall back and begin digging in along the Aisne (ENN) River. By holding off the German offensive at this first Battle of the Marne, the Entente had undercut the Schlieffen Plan—and with it, it turned out, any chance of a speedy victory by either side.

During the rest of the fall of 1914, each side tried—unsuccessfully—to outflank the other. When, by the end of November, active fighting ceased for the winter, a military front of about 300 miles had been established, all the way from Switzerland to the coast of the North Sea in Belgium (see **MAP 25.1**). This line failed to shift more than 10 miles in either direction over the next three years. The result of the first six weeks of fighting on the western front was not a gallant victory but a grim and unforeseen stalemate.

Virtually from the start, the war took a fiercely destructive turn. In northern France in September 1914, the Germans fired on the famed Gothic cathedral at Reims (RAANZ), severely damaging its roof and nave, because they believed—apparently correctly—that the French were using one of its towers as an observation post. If such a catastrophe could happen to one of the great monuments in Europe, what else might this war bring?

CHRONOLOGY

August 1914	Fighting begins
September 1914	French forces hold off the German assault at the Marne
August–September 1914	German victories repel Russian invasion on eastern front
May 1915	Italy declares war on Austria-Hungary
February–December 1916	Battle of Verdun
July–November 1916	Battle of the Somme
January 1917	Germans resume unrestricted submarine warfare
March 1917	First Russian revolution: fall of the tsar
April 1917	U.S. declaration of war
July 1917	German Reichstag war aims resolution
November 1917	Second Russian revolution: the Bolsheviks take power
March 1918	Treaty of Brest-Litovsk between Germany and Russia
March–July 1918	Germany's last western offensive
June 1918	Initial outbreak of the "Spanish flu"
July 1918	Second Battle of the Marne
November 1918	Armistice: fighting ends
January 1919	Paris Peace Conference convenes
June 1919	Victors impose Treaty of Versailles on Germany

🌐 **MAP 25.1—The War in Europe, 1914–1918**

Although World War I included engagements in East Asia and the Middle East, it was essentially a European conflict, encompassing fighting on a number of fronts. On the western front, in northern France and Belgium, trench warfare developed and the best-known battles of the war were fought. Notable sites include Verdun, Passchendaele, and the Marne and Somme Rivers.

Main map labels:

ATLANTIC OCEAN

British blockade line

NORWAY
SWEDEN
FINLAND
Helsinki
Petrograd (St. Petersburg)
Moscow

Treaty of Brest-Litovsk, March 1918

R U S S I A

Don R.
Dnieper R.

Black Sea

Armistice line, December 1917

Kiev
UKRAINE

Constantinople
O T T O M A N   E M P I R E
Gallipoli 1915
Dardanelles
Cyprus
Crete

Mediterranean Sea

GREAT BRITAIN
London
IRELAND
North Sea
Jutland 1916
DENMARK
Kiel
Elbe R.
NETHERLANDS
GERMANY
Berlin
Farthest Russian advance, 1914

ESTONIA
LATVIA
Riga
COURLAND
LITHUANIA
Wilno (Vilnius)
BELARUS
Brest-Litovsk
Masurian Lakes 1914
E. PRUSSIA
Tannenberg 1914
Warsaw
KINGDOM OF POLAND (Russia)
Bug R.
Vistula R.
MAY 1915
GALICIA
Dniester R.

Baltic Sea

AUSTRIA-HUNGARY
Vienna
Budapest
Caporetto 1917
AUG. 1917
MAR. 1918
Italian front
ITALY
Rome
Po R.
Adriatic Sea
Corsica
Sardinia
Elba
Sicily
Malta
Tunis
TUNISIA (France)

SWITZERLAND
LUXEMBOURG
ALSACE-LORRAINE
Rhine R.
BELGIUM
Louvain
Paris
Western front
FRANCE
Bordeaux
Seine R.
Loire R.
Garonne R.
Ebro R.
SPAIN
Balearic Is.
Rhône R.

ROMANIA
Bucharest
TRANSYLVANIA
Danube R.
SERBIA
BULGARIA
1911–1918
1916
1915
GREECE
MONTENEGRO
ALBANIA
Balkan front
Sarajevo

400 Mi.
400 Km.
0   200
0   200

Legend (main map):

- Triple Entente and its Allies
- Central Powers
- Neutral nations
- Greatest extent of territory gained by Germany-Austria
- — Battle line

N

Inset map labels:

English Channel
Dover
Calais
Ostend
FLANDERS
Ghent
Antwerp
Brussels
BELGIUM
Liège
ARDENNES
NETHERLANDS
Ruhr R.
Cologne
Coblenz
Rhine R.
Moselle R.
GERMANY
LUXEMBOURG
Sedan
St. Quentin
Amiens
Arras
Compiègne
Somme R.
Somme
Aisne R.
Reims
Belleau Wood
Marne R.
Marne
Chalôns-sur-Marne
Château-Thierry
Marne II
Paris
Seine R.
FRANCE
ARGONNE FOREST
Verdun
St. Mihiel
Nancy
LORRAINE
Saar R.
Strasbourg
ALSACE
Epinal
Mulhouse
Basel
Scheldt R.
Meuse R.

50 Mi.
50 Km.
0   25

Legend (inset):

- Germany, 1914
- ↓ German offensive, 1915
- Greatest extent of territory gained by Germany, Sept. 1914
- — Front at beginning of 1915
- — German offensive, Summer 1918
- ← Armistice line, November 1918
- ✦ Major battle

The two sides were forced to settle into a war of attrition relying on an elaborate network of defensive trenches. Although separated by as much as 5 miles in some places, enemy trenches were sometimes within shouting distance, so there was occasionally banter back and forth, even attempts to entertain the other side. But the trenches quickly became almost unimaginably gruesome—filthy, ridden with rats and lice, noisy and smoky from artillery fire, and foul-smelling, partly from the odor of decaying bodies.

As defensive instruments, however, the trenches proved quite effective. Each side quickly learned to take advantage of barbed wire, mines, and especially machine guns to defend its positions. A mass of barbed wire, 3 to 5 feet high and 30 yards wide, guarded a typical trench. The machine gun had been developed before the war as an offensive weapon; few foresaw the decided advantage it would give the defense. But with machine guns, soldiers could defend trenches even against massive assaults—and inflict heavy casualties on the attackers.

Despite the advantages of defensive trenches, neither side could give up the vision of a decisive offensive. Thus, the troops were periodically called on to go "over the top" and then across "no man's land" to assault the dug-in enemy. Again and again, however, such offensives proved futile, producing incredibly heavy casualties.

For the soldiers on the western front, the war became a nightmarish experience in a hellish landscape. Bombardment by new, heavier forms of artillery scarred the terrain with craters, which became muddy, turning the landscape into a near swamp. Beginning early in 1915, tear gas, chlorine gas, and finally mustard gas found use on both sides. Although the development of gas masks significantly reduced the impact of this menacing new chemical warfare, the threat of poison gas added another nightmarish element to the experience of those who fought the war.

The notions of patriotism, comradeship, duty, and glory that had been prevalent in 1914 gradually dissolved as soldiers experienced the horrors of this war. A French soldier, questioning his own reactions after battle in 1916, responded with sarcasm and irony: "What sublime emotion inspires you at the moment of assault? I thought of nothing other than dragging my feet out of the mud encasing them. What did you feel after surviving the attack? I grumbled because I would have to remain several days more without *pinard* [wine]. Is not one's first act to kneel down and thank God? No. One relieves oneself."[1]

Trench Warfare Grim though they were, the trenches proved effective for defensive purposes. Here a British soldier guards a trench at Ovillers, on the Somme, in July 1916. (The Art Archive/Picture Desk)

Although the Germans had been denied their quick victory in the west, by the end of 1914, they occupied much of Belgium and almost one-tenth of France, including major industrial areas and mines producing most of France's coal and iron. On the eastern front, as well, the Germans won some substantial advantages in 1914—but not a decisive victory.

The first season of fighting suggested that the pattern in the east would not be trench warfare, but rapid movement across a vast but thinly held front. When hostilities began in August, the Russians mustered more quickly than anticipated, confronting an outnumbered German force in a menacing, if reckless, invasion of East Prussia. But by mid-September, German forces under General Paul von Hindenburg (1847–1934) and his chief of staff, General Erich Ludendorff (1865–1937), repelled the Russian advance, taking a huge number of prisoners and seriously demoralizing the Russians.

As a result of this victory, Hindenburg and Ludendorff emerged as heroes, and they would play major roles in German public life thereafter. Hindenburg became chief of staff of the entire German army in August 1916, but the able and energetic Ludendorff proved the key figure as this duo gradually assumed undisputed control of the whole German war effort, both military and domestic.

Seeking a Breakthrough, 1915–1917

After the campaigns of 1915 proved inconclusive, German leaders decided to concentrate in 1916 on a massive offensive against the French fortress at Verdun, intending to inflict a definitive defeat on France. To assault the fortress, the Germans gathered 1,220 pieces of artillery for attack along an 8-mile front. Included were thirteen "Big Bertha" siege guns, weapons so large that nine tractors were required to position each of them; a crane was necessary to insert the shell, which weighed over a ton. The level of heavy artillery firepower that the Germans applied at Verdun was unprecedented in the history of warfare.

German forces attacked on February 21, taking the outer defenses of the fortress, and appeared poised for victory. The tide turned, however, when General Philippe Pétain (puh-TANH) (1856–1951) assumed control of the French defense. Pétain had the patience and skill necessary to organize supply networks for a long siege. Furthermore, he proved able, through considerate treatment, to inspire affection and confidence among his men. By mid-July, the French army had repelled the German offensive, although only in December did the French retake the outer defenses of the fortress. The French had held in what would prove the war's longest, most trying battle—one that killed over 700,000 people.

To relieve pressure on Verdun, the British led a major attack at the Somme River on July 1, 1916. On that day alone, the British suffered almost 60,000 casualties, including 21,000 killed. Fighting continued into the fall, but the offensive proved futile in the end. One-third of those involved, or over 1 million soldiers, ended up dead, missing, or wounded.

Dominated by the devastating battles at Verdun and the Somme, the campaigns of 1916 finally extinguished the high spirits of the summer of 1914. Both sides suffered huge losses—apparently for nothing. By the end of 1916, the front had shifted only a few miles from its location at the beginning of the year.

In light of the frustrating outcome so far, the French turned to new military leadership, replacing Joffre as commander-in-chief with Robert Nivelle (nuh-VELL), who promptly sought to prove himself with a new offensive early in 1917. Persisting even as it became clear that this effort had no chance of success, Nivelle provoked increasing resistance among French soldiers, some of whom were refusing to follow orders by the end of April.

With the French war effort in danger of collapse, the French government replaced Nivelle with General Pétain, the hero of the defense of Verdun. Pétain reestablished discipline by adopting a conciliatory approach—improving food and rest, visiting the troops in the field, offering encouragement, even dealing relatively mercifully with the resisters themselves. To be sure, many of the soldiers who had participated in this near mutiny were court-martialed, and over 3,400 were convicted. But of the 554 sentenced to death, only 49 were actually executed.

After the failure of the Nivelle offensive, the initiative fell to the British under General Douglas Haig, who was convinced, despite skepticism in the British cabinet, that Nivelle's offensive had failed simply because of tactical mistakes. Beginning near Ypres (EE-pray) in Belgium on July 31, 1917, and continuing until November, the British attacked. As before, the effort yielded only minimal territorial gains—about 50 square miles—at a horrifying cost, including 300,000 British and Canadian casualties. Known as the Battle of Passchendaele, the British offensive of 1917 ranks with the Battles of Verdun and the Somme as the bloodiest of the war.

1917 as a Turning Point

Meanwhile, the Germans decided to concentrate on the eastern front in 1917 in an effort to knock Russia out of the war. This intensified German military pressure helped spark revolution in Russia, and in December 1917, Russia's new revolutionary regime asked for a separate peace (see page 710). The defeat of Russia freed the Germans at last to concentrate on the west, but by this time, France and Britain had a new ally.

On April 6, 1917, the United States entered the war on the side of the Entente, in response to Germany's controversial use of submarines. Germany did not have enough surface ships to respond to Britain's naval blockade, whether by attacking the British fleet directly or by mounting a comparable blockade of the British Isles. So the Germans decided to use submarines to interfere with shipping to Britain. Submarines, however, were too vulnerable to be able to surface and confiscate goods, so the Germans had to settle for sinking suspect ships with torpedoes. In February 1915, they declared the waters around the British Isles a war zone and served notice that they would torpedo not only enemy ships, but also neutral ships carrying goods to Britain.

The German response was harsh, but so was the **British blockade**, which violated earlier international agreements about the rights of neutral shipping and the scope of wartime blockades. The British had agreed that only military goods, such as munitions and certain raw materials, not such everyday goods as food and clothing, were subject to confiscation. Yet, in blockading Germany, the British refused to make this distinction, prompting the sarcastic German quip that Britannia not only rules the waves but waives the rules.[2]

In May 1915, a German sub torpedoed the *Lusitania*, a British passenger liner, killing almost 1,200 people and producing widespread indignation. Partly because 128 of those killed were Americans, U.S. president Woodrow Wilson issued a severe warning, which contributed to the German decision in September 1915 to pull back from unrestricted submarine

British blockade Britain's naval blockade of Germany during World War I; it seriously impeded the German war effort.

SECTION SUMMARY

- Although the war was fought on a variety of fronts and even expanded beyond Europe, the fighting on the western front, in a relatively small chunk of Belgium and northern France, proved decisive.

- At the outset, each side expected a short war of rapid offensives, but the struggle on the western front produced a stalemate, based on defensive trench warfare, by the end of 1914.

- The defensive trenches proved difficult to attack, especially because of barbed wire and the machine gun.

- Massive assaults during 1916–1917 failed to produce the intended breakthrough for either side, though they resulted in horrifying numbers of casualties.

- Though the United States declared war in 1917, in response to Germany's resumption of unrestricted submarine warfare, it was not equipped to make an immediate difference on European battlefields.

warfare. But as German suffering under the British blockade increased, pressure mounted on Berlin to put the subs back into action.

The issue provoked bitter debate. Chancellor Theobald von Bethmann-Hollweg (BETT-mahn-HOHL-veg) (1856–1921) and the civilian authorities opposed resumption, fearing it would provoke the United States to enter the war. But Ludendorff and the military finally prevailed, arguing that even if the United States did intervene, U.S. troops could not get to Europe in time to have a major impact. Germany announced it would resume unrestricted submarine warfare on January 31, 1917, and the United States responded with a declaration of war on April 6.

Many on both sides doubted that U.S. intervention would make a pivotal difference; most assumed—correctly—that it would take at least a year for the American presence to materialize in force. Still, the entry of the United States gave the Entente at least the promise of more fighting power. And the United States seemed capable of renewing the sense of purpose on the Entente side, showing that the war had a meaning that could justify the unexpected costs and sacrifice.

THE EXPERIENCE OF TOTAL WAR

Why did this prove a total war, making necessary new forms of socioeconomic coordination and even systematic propaganda?

As the war dragged on, the distinction between the military and civilian spheres blurred. Suffering increased on the home front, and unprecedented governmental mobilization of society proved necessary to wage war on the scale required. Because it became "total" in this way, the war decisively altered not only the old political and diplomatic order, but also culture, society, and the patterns of everyday life.

Hardship on the Home Front

The war meant food shortages, and thus malnutrition, for ordinary people in the belligerent countries, although Britain and France, with their more favorable geographic positions, suffered considerably less than others. Germany was especially vulnerable, and the British naval blockade exacerbated an already dire situation. With military needs taking priority, the Germans encountered shortages of the chemical fertilizers, farm machinery, and draft animals necessary for agricultural production. The government began rationing bread, meat, and fats during 1915. The increasing scarcity of food produced sharp increases in diseases, such as rickets and tuberculosis, and in infant and childhood mortality rates.

The need to pay for the war produced economic dislocations as well. Government borrowing covered some of the cost for the short term, but to underwrite the rest, governments all over Europe found it more palatable to inflate the currency, by printing more money, than to raise taxes. The notion that the enemy would be made to pay once victory had been won seemed to justify this decision. But this way of financing the war meant rising prices and severe erosion of purchasing power for ordinary people all over Europe.

In France and Germany, the labor truces of 1914 gave way to increasing strike activity during 1916. With an especially severe winter in 1916–1917 adding to the misery, there were serious instances of domestic disorder, including strikes and food riots, in many parts of Europe during 1917. The revolution that overthrew the tsarist autocracy in Russia that same year began with comparable protests over wartime food shortages.

The strains of war even fanned the flames in Ireland, where an uneasy truce over the home-rule controversy accompanied the British decision for war in 1914. Partly because of German efforts to stir up domestic trouble for Britain, unrest built up again in Ireland, culminating in the Easter

Rebellion in Dublin in 1916. The brutality with which British forces crushed the uprising intensified demands for full independence—precisely what Britain would be forced to yield to the Irish republic shortly after the war.

Moreover, new technologies made civilians more vulnerable to wartime violence. Although bombing from aircraft began with an immediate military aim—to destroy industrial targets or to provide tactical support for other military units—it quickly became clear that night bombing, especially, might demoralize civilian populations. In 1915, German airplanes began bombing English cities, provoking British retaliation against cities in western Germany. These raids had little effect on the course of the war, but they showed that new technologies could make warfare more destructive, even for civilians.

Domestic Mobilization

Once it became clear that the war would not be over quickly, leaders on both sides realized that the outcome would not be determined on the battlefield alone. Victory required mobilizing all of the nation's resources and energies. So World War I became a **total war**, involving the entire society.

The British naval blockade on Germany, which made no distinction between military and nonmilitary goods, was a stratagem characteristic of total war. The blockade would not affect Germany's immediate strength on the battlefield, but it could damage Germany's long-term war-making capacity. Thus, Germany seemed to need stringent economic coordination and control. By the end of 1916, the country had coordinated all aspects of economic life for the war effort. Under the supervision of the military, state agencies, big business, and the trade unions were brought into close collaboration. The new system included rationing, price controls, and compulsory labor arbitration, as well as a national service law enabling the military to channel workers into jobs deemed vital to the war effort.

The Germans did not hesitate to exploit the economy of occupied Belgium, requisitioning foodstuffs even to the point of causing starvation among the Belgians themselves. They forced sixty-two thousand Belgians to work in German factories under conditions of virtual slave labor. By the time this practice was stopped in February 1917, nearly a thousand Belgian workers had died in German labor camps.

The body coordinating Germany's war economy was the **Kriegsrohstoffabteilung (KRA)** (kreegs-roh-stoff-AHB-ty-loong), or "War Raw Materials Office." Led initially by the able Jewish industrialist Walther Rathenau (RAT-un-ow) (1867–1922), this agency came to symbolize the unprecedented coordination of the German economy. Recognizing that Germany lacked the raw materials for a long war, Rathenau devised an imaginative program that included the development of synthetic substitute products and the creation of new mixed (private and government) companies to allocate raw materials. The KRA's effort was remarkably successful—a model for later economic planning and coordination in Germany and elsewhere.

Although Germany presented the most dramatic example, this sort of domestic coordination was evident everywhere. In Britain, the central figure was David Lloyd George (1863–1945), appointed to the newly created post of minister of munitions in 1915. During his year in office, ninety-five new factories opened, soon overcoming the shortage of guns and ammunition that had impeded the British war effort until then. His performance made Lloyd George seem the person who could organize Britain for victory. Succeeding Herbert Asquith as prime minister in December 1916, he would direct the British war effort to its victorious conclusion.

Accelerating Socioeconomic Change

Everywhere, the war effort quickened the long-term socioeconomic change associated with industrialization. Government orders for war materiel fueled industrial expansion. The needs of war spawned new technologies—advances in food processing and medical treatment, for example—that would carry over into peacetime.

With so many men needed for military service, women were called on to assume new economic roles—such as running farms in France, or working in the new munitions factories in Britain. During the course of the war, the number of women employed in Britain rose from 3.25 million to 5 million. In Italy, 200,000 women had war-related jobs by 1917. Women also played indispensable roles at the front, especially in nursing units.

The expanded opportunities of wartime intensified the debate over the sociopolitical role of women that the movement for women's suffrage had stimulated. The outbreak of war led some antiwar feminists to argue that women would be better able than men to prevent wars, which

total war The concept, first associated with World War I, that war requires the mobilization of all a nation's resources and energies.

Kriegsrohstoffabteilung (KRA) The "War Raw Materials Office" that coordinated Germany's World War I economy.

Working Women and the War   All over Europe, governments recruited women to work in munitions factories. This Russian government poster uses an image of working women to rally support for the war. The text reads, "Everything for the war effort! Subscribe to the war loans at $5\frac{1}{2}$ percent."   (Eileen Tweedy/The Art Archive/Picture Desk)

SECTION SUMMARY

- Partly because of the advent of new technologies, the war threatened civilian populations in unforeseen ways.

- The unexpected length of the war forced domestic mobilization, both to maintain civilian morale and to enhance the production necessary to sustain the military effort.

- Britain's naval blockade of Germany forced German leaders to adopt innovative, highly centralized forms of socioeconomic coordination, partly to spearhead the development of substitute products.

- Domestic mobilization accelerated socioeconomic change, especially by enhancing employment opportunities for women.

- Systematic attempts to discredit the enemy, by intellectuals as well as governments, made it harder to envision the scope for a lasting peace.

were essentially masculine undertakings. Women should have full access to public life, not because they could be expected to respond as men did, but because they had a distinctive—and valuable—role to play. At the same time, by giving women jobs and the opportunity to do many of the same things men did, the war undermined the stereotypes that had long justified restrictions on women's political roles and life choices.

For many women, doing a difficult job well, serving their country in this emergency situation, afforded a new sense of accomplishment, as well as a new taste of independence. Women were now much more likely to have their own residences and to go out on their own, eating in restaurants, even smoking and drinking. Yet, while many seized new opportunities and learned new skills, women frequently had to combine paid employment with housework and child rearing, and those who left home—to serve in nursing units, for example—often felt guilty about neglecting their traditional family roles.

Propaganda and the "Mobilization of Enthusiasm"

Because the domestic front was crucial to sustaining a long war of attrition, it became ever more important to shore up civilian morale as the war dragged on. The result was what the historian Elie Halévy called the "mobilization of enthusiasm"—the manipulation of collective passions by governments on an unprecedented scale. Every country instituted extensive censorship, even of soldiers' letters from the front. Because of concerns about civilian morale, the French press carried no news of the Battle of Verdun, with its horrifying numbers of casualties. In addition, systematic propaganda included not only patriotic themes, but also attempts to discredit the enemy, even through outright falsification of the news.

At the outset of the war, the brutal behavior of the German armies in Belgium made it easy for the French and the British to demonize the Germans. Having expected to pass through neutral Belgium unopposed, the Germans were infuriated by the Belgian resistance they encountered. At Louvain, late in August 1914, they responded to alleged Belgian sniping by shooting a number of hostages and setting the town on fire, destroying the famous old university library. This episode led the *London Times* to characterize the Germans as "Huns," a reference to the central Asian tribe that began invading Europe in the fourth century. Stories about German soldiers eating Belgian babies began to circulate.

In October 1914, ninety-three German intellectuals, artists, and scientists signed a manifesto, addressed to "the world of culture," justifying Germany's conduct in Belgium and its larger purposes in the war. As passions heated up, major intellectuals on both sides began denigrating the culture of the enemy and claiming a monopoly of virtue for their own side.

As the war dragged on, some came to believe that real peace with an adversary so evil, so abnormally different, was simply not possible. There must be no compromise but rather total victory, no matter what the cost. At the same time, however, war-weariness produced a countervailing tendency to seek a "white peace," a peace without victory for either side. But in 1917, as Europeans began earnestly debating war aims, the Russian Revolution and the intervention of the United States seemed to change the war's meaning.

Devastation at Louvain   Unexpected destruction at the outset of the war fanned the flames of hatred and changed the stakes of the conflict. Located in the path of the first German advance, the Belgian city of Louvain was particularly hard-hit.   (The Art Archive/Imperial War Museum/Picture Desk)

THE TWO RUSSIAN REVOLUTIONS OF 1917

Why did the first revolution in Russia pave the way for a second, spearheaded by the Bolsheviks?

Strained by war, the old European order cracked first in Russia in 1917. Initially, the overthrow of the tsarist autocracy seemed to lay the foundations for parliamentary democracy. But by the end of the year, the Bolsheviks, the smallest and most extreme of Russia's major socialist parties, had taken power, an outcome that was hardly conceivable when the revolution began.

The Wartime Crisis of the Russian Autocracy

The Russian army performed better than many had expected; as late as June 1916, it mounted a successful offensive against Austria-Hungary. Russia had industrialized sufficiently by 1914 to sustain a modern war, at least for a while, and the country's war production increased significantly by 1916. But even early in 1915, perhaps a fourth of Russia's newly conscripted troops were sent to the front without weapons; they were told to pick up rifles and supplies from the dead. Moreover, Russia suffered from problems of leadership and organization that made it less prepared for a long war than the other belligerents.

In August 1915, Tsar Nicholas II (1868–1918) assumed personal command of the army, but his absence from the capital only accelerated the deterioration in government and deepened the divisions within the ruling clique. With the tsar away, the illiterate but charismatic Siberian "holy man" Grigori Rasputin (ca. 1872–1916) emerged as the key political power within the circle of the German-born Empress Alexandra (1872–1918). He won her confidence because of his alleged ability to control the bleeding of her hemophiliac son, Alexis, the heir to the throne. Led by Rasputin, those around the empress made a shambles of the state administration. Many educated Russians, appalled at what was happening, assumed—incorrectly—that pro-German elements at court were responsible for the eclipse of the tsar and the increasing governmental chaos. One Duma deputy asked of the government's performance, "Is this stupidity, or is it treason?"

Finally, late in December 1916, Rasputin was assassinated by aristocrats seeking to save the autocracy from these apparently pro-German influences. This act indicated how desperate the situation had become, but eliminating Rasputin made little difference.

By the end of 1916, the difficulties of war had combined with the strains of rapid wartime industrialization to produce a revolutionary situation in Russia. The country's urban population had mushroomed, and now, partly because of transport problems, the cities faced severe food shortages. Strikes and demonstrations spread from Petrograd (the former St. Petersburg—a name abandoned as too German at the start of the war) to other cities during the first two months of 1917. In March, renewed demonstrations in Petrograd, spearheaded by women protesting the lack of bread and coal, led to revolution.

The March Revolution and the Fate of the Provisional Government

At first, the agitation that began in Petrograd on March 8, 1917, appeared to be just another bread riot. Even when it turned into a wave of strikes, the revolutionary parties (see page 689) expected it to be crushed by government troops. But when they were called out to help the police break up the demonstrations, the soldiers generally avoided firing at the strikers. Within days, they were sharing weapons and ammunition with the workers; the government's troops were joining what was now becoming a revolution.

Late in the afternoon of March 12, leaders of the strike committees, delegates elected by factory workers, and representatives of the socialist parties formed a *soviet*, or council, following the example of the revolution of 1905, when such soviets had first appeared. Regiments of the Petrograd garrison also began electing representatives, soon to be admitted to the **Petrograd Soviet**, which officially became the Council of Workers' and Soldiers' Deputies. This soviet was now the ruling power in the Russian capital. It had been elected and was genuinely representative— though of a limited constituency of workers and soldiers. Following the lead of Petrograd, Russians elsewhere promptly began forming soviets, so that over 350 local units were represented when the first All-Russian Council of Soviets met in Petrograd in April. The overwhelming majority of their representatives were Mensheviks and Socialist Revolutionaries; about one-sixth were Bolsheviks.

Petrograd Soviet The *soviet* (council) of leaders of strike committees and army regiments elected in March 1917, when Petrograd's workers protested in response to severe wartime shortages.

On March 14, a committee of the Duma, recognizing that the tsar's authority had been lost for good, persuaded Nicholas to abdicate, then formed a new **provisional government**. This government was to be strictly temporary, paving the way for an elected constituent assembly, which would write a constitution and establish new governmental institutions.

provisional government The body that ruled Russia from March to November 1917, in the wake of the revolution that overthrew the tsarist regime.

Considering the strains that had produced the revolution of 1905 after the Russo-Japanese War, it was hardly surprising that the autocratic system would shatter now, in light of this far more trying war and the resulting governmental disarray. Russia had apparently experienced, at last, the bourgeois political revolution necessary to develop a Western-style parliamentary democracy. Even from an orthodox Marxist perspective, the immediate priority was to help consolidate the new democratic order, which would then provide the framework for the longer-term pursuit of socialism.

Although the fall of the tsarist government produced widespread relief, Russia's new leaders faced difficult questions about priorities. Should they focus their efforts on revitalizing the Russian war effort? Or, given the widespread war-weariness in the country, should they focus on domestic political reform? For now, the Petrograd Soviet was prepared to give the provisional government a chance to govern. But the soviet was a potential rival for power if the new government failed to address Russia's immediate problems.

The provisional government took important steps toward democracy, establishing universal suffrage, civil liberties, autonomy for ethnic minorities, and labor legislation, including provision for an eight-hour workday. But the government failed in two key areas, fostering discontents that the Bolsheviks soon exploited. First, it persisted in fighting the war. Second, it dragged its feet on agrarian reform.

The provisional government's determination to renew the war effort stemmed from concern about Russia's obligations to its allies, its national honor and position among the great powers. The long-standing goal of Russian diplomacy—an outlet to the Mediterranean Sea through the Dardanelles—seemed within reach if Russia could continue the war and contribute to an Entente victory.

Although the March revolution began in the cities, the peasantry soon moved into action as well, seizing land, sometimes burning the houses of their landlords. By midsummer, a full-scale peasant war seemed to be developing in the countryside, and calls for agrarian reform became increasingly urgent. Partly from expediency, partly from genuine concern for social justice, the provisional government promised a major redistribution of land. But it insisted that the reform be carried out legally—not by the present provisional government, but by a duly elected constituent assembly.

Calling elections would thus seem to have been the first priority. The new political leaders kept delaying, however, waiting for the situation to cool off. But playing for time was a luxury they could ill afford. As unrest grew in the countryside, the authority of the provisional government diminished and the soviets gained in stature. But what role were the soviets to play?

The Bolsheviks Come to Power

In the immediate aftermath of the March revolution, the Bolsheviks had not seemed to differ substantially from their rivals within the socialist movement, at least on matters of immediate concern—the war, land reform, and the character of the revolution itself. But the situation began to change in April when Lenin, assisted by the German military, returned from exile in Switzerland. The Germans assumed—correctly, it turned out—that the Bolsheviks would help undermine the Russian war effort. Largely through the force of Lenin's leadership, the Bolsheviks soon took the initiative within the still-developing revolution in Russia.

Lenin as Leader   Although he was in exile during much of 1917, Lenin's leadership was crucial to the Bolshevik success in Russia. He is shown here addressing a May Day rally in Red Square, Moscow, on May 1, 1919. (ITAR-TASS/Sovfoto)

Born Vladimir Ilich Ulianov, **Vladimir Lenin** (1870–1924) came from a comfortable upper-middle-class family. He was university-educated and trained as a lawyer. But after an older brother was executed in 1887 for participating in a plot against the tsar's life, Lenin followed him into revolutionary activity. Arrested for the first time in 1895, he was confined to Siberia until 1900. He then lived in exile abroad for almost the entire period before his return to Russia in 1917.

The Bolshevik Party was identified with Lenin from its beginning in 1903, when it emerged from the schism in Russian Marxist socialism. Because of his emphases, Bolshevism came to mean discipline, organization, and a special leadership role for a revolutionary vanguard. Lenin proved effective because he was a stern and somewhat forbidding figure, disciplined, fiercely intelligent, sometimes ruthless. As a Bolshevik colleague put it, Lenin was "the one indisputable leader . . . a man of iron will, inexhaustible energy, combining a fanatical faith in the movement, in the cause, with an equal faith in himself."[3]

Still, Lenin's reading of the situation when he returned to Petrograd in April astonished even many Bolsheviks. He argued that the revolution was about to pass from the present bourgeois-democratic stage to a socialist phase, involving proletarian dictatorship in the form of government by the soviets. So the Bolsheviks should begin actively opposing the provisional government, especially by denouncing the war as fundamentally imperialist and by demanding the distribution of land from the large estates to the peasants. This latter measure had long been

EARLY YEARS UNDER LENIN

Vladimir Lenin   Russian revolutionary and leader of the Bolsheviks since 1903, he masterminded the November 1917 revolution that overthrew the provisional government and led to a communist regime in Russia.

identified with the Socialist Revolutionaries; most Bolsheviks had envisioned collectivization and nationalization instead.

As Lenin saw it, the strains of war had made all of Europe ripe for revolution. A revolution in Russia would provide the spark to ignite a wider proletarian revolution, especially in Germany. He did not envision backward Russia seeking to create socialism on its own. Although some remained skeptical of Lenin's strategy, he promptly won over most of his fellow Bolsheviks. And thus, the Bolsheviks began actively seeking wider support by promising peace, land, and bread.

THE BOLSHEVIK REVOLUTION

In April 1917, moderate socialists still had majority support in the soviets, so the Bolsheviks sought to build support gradually, postponing any decisive test of strength. But events escaped the control of the Bolshevik leadership in mid-July when impatient workers, largely Bolshevik in sympathy, took to the streets of Petrograd on their own. The Petrograd Soviet refused to support the uprising, and the provisional government had no difficulty getting military units to put it down, killing two hundred in the process. Though the uprising had developed spontaneously, Bolshevik leaders felt compelled to offer public support, and this gave the government an excuse to crack down on the Bolshevik leadership. Lenin managed to escape to Finland, but a number of his colleagues were arrested and jailed.

With the Bolsheviks on the defensive, counterrevolutionary elements in the Russian military decided to seize the initiative with a march on Petrograd in September. To resist this attempted coup, the provisional government, now led by the young Socialist Revolutionary Alexander Kerensky (1881–1970), had to rely on anyone who could help, including the Bolsheviks. And thanks to Bolshevik propaganda, the soldiers under the command of the counterrevolutionaries refused to fight against the upholders of the revolution in Petrograd. Thus, the coup was thwarted. Within days, the Bolsheviks won their first clear-cut majority in the Petrograd Soviet, and then shortly gained majorities in most of the other soviets as well.

During the fall of 1917, the situation became increasingly volatile, eluding control by anyone. People looted food from shops; peasants seized land, sometimes murdering their landlords. Desertions and the murder of officers increased within the Russian military.

With the Bolsheviks now the dominant power in the soviets, and with the government's control diminishing, Lenin, from his hideout in Finland, urged the Bolshevik central committee to prepare for armed insurrection. Although some found this step too risky, the majority accepted Lenin's argument that the provisional government would continue dragging its feet, inadvertently giving right-wing officers time for another coup.

Because Lenin remained in hiding, the task of organizing the seizure of power fell to Leon Trotsky (1870–1940), who skillfully modified Lenin's aggressive strategy. Lenin wanted the Bolsheviks to rise in their own name, in opposition to the provisional government, but Trotsky linked the insurrection to the cause of the soviets and played up its defensive character against the ongoing danger of a counterrevolutionary coup. With the political center at an impasse, the only alternative to such a coup seemed to be a Bolshevik initiative to preserve the Petrograd Soviet, by now the key institutional embodiment of the revolution and its promise. Trotsky's interpretation led people who wanted simply to defend the soviet to support the Bolshevik action.

During the night of November 9, armed Bolsheviks and regular army regiments occupied key points in Petrograd, including railroad stations, post offices, telephone exchanges, power stations, and the national bank. Able to muster only token resistance, the provisional government collapsed. Kerensky escaped and mounted a futile effort to rally troops at the front for a counterattack. In contrast to the March revolution, which had taken about a week, the Bolsheviks took over the capital, overthrowing the Kerensky government, literally overnight and almost without bloodshed.

But though the Bolsheviks enjoyed considerable support in the network of soviets, it was not clear that they could extend their control across the whole Russian Empire. Moreover, from their own perspective, the revolution's immediate prospects, and its potential wider impact, were bound up with the course of the war. Would the Bolshevik Revolution in Russia prove the spark for revolution elsewhere in war-weary Europe, as Lenin anticipated?

The Russian Revolution and the War

Having stood for peace throughout the revolution, the Bolsheviks promptly moved to get Russia out of the war, agreeing to an armistice with Germany in December 1917. They hoped that Russia's withdrawal would speed the collapse of the war effort on all sides and that this, in turn, would intensify the movement toward revolution elsewhere in Europe. The Russian Revolution was but a chapter in this larger story. As Lenin noted to Trotsky, "If it were necessary for us to go under to assure the success of the German revolution, we should have to do it. The German revolution is vastly more important than ours." Indeed, said Lenin to the Bolsheviks' party congress of March 1918, "It is an absolute truth that we will go under without the German revolution."[4]

After assuming control in November, the Bolsheviks published the tsarist government's secret agreements specifying how the spoils were to be divided in the event of a Russian victory. They hoped to inflame revolutionary sentiment elsewhere by demonstrating that the war had been, all along, an imperialist offensive on behalf of capitalist interests. This Bolshevik initiative added fuel to the controversy already developing in all the belligerent countries over the war's purpose and significance.

SECTION SUMMARY

- The strains of war led to a revolution that ended the tsarist order in Russia in March 1917.

- Although the soviet, or workers' and soldiers' council, was a major force in Petrograd, the first Russian revolution of 1917 was not intended to produce a socialist system.

- The provisional government proved ineffective because it dragged its feet on land reform and insisted on maintaining the war effort.

- Due partly to the leadership of Lenin and Trotsky, the Bolsheviks were able to seize the initiative and take power from the provisional government in November 1917.

- The Bolsheviks envisioned their takeover as a spark to revolution elsewhere in war-torn Europe.

THE NEW WAR AND THE ALLIED VICTORY, 1917–1918

Why did Germany and its allies end up losing the war even after forcing Russia to make a separate peace by early 1918?

Because the stakes of the war changed during 1917, the eventual outcome included consequences that Europeans could not have foreseen in 1914. German defeat brought revolution against the monarchy and the beginning of a new democracy. Austro-Hungarian defeat brought the collapse of the Habsburg monarchy and thus the opportunity for its national minorities to form nations of their own. As the old European order fell, grandiose new visions competed to shape the postwar world.

The Debate over War Aims

Allied war aims agreements, such as the Treaty of London that brought Italy into the war in 1915, had remained secret until the Bolsheviks published the tsarist documents. Products of old-style diplomacy, those agreements had been made by a restricted foreign policy elite; even members of the elected parliaments generally did not know their contents. The debate over war aims that developed in 1917 thus became a debate over decision making as well. Many assumed that a more democratic approach to foreign policy would minimize the chances of war, since the people would not agree to wars for dynastic or business interests. In addition, there were exhortations for all the parties in the present war to renounce annexations and settle for a white peace. It was time to call the whole thing off and bring the soldiers home.

Seeking to counter such sentiments, especially the Russian contention that the war was not worth continuing, the idealistic U.S. president, Woodrow Wilson (1856–1924), insisted on the great potential significance of an Allied victory. In his State of the Union speech of January 1918, and in several declarations thereafter, Wilson proposed **Fourteen Points** to guide the new international order. Notable among them were open diplomacy, free trade, reduced armaments, self-determination for nationalities, a league of nations, and a recasting of the colonial system to ensure equal rights for the indigenous populations.

Lenin and Wilson, then, offered radically different interpretations of the war, with radically different implications for present priorities. Yet, compared with the old diplomacy, they had something in common. Together, they seemed to represent a whole new approach to international relations—and the possibility of a more peaceful world. Thus, they found an eager audience among the war-weary peoples of Europe.

Despite the strains of the war, Sacred Union in France did not weaken substantially until April 1917, with General Nivelle's disastrous offensive. But then, as near mutiny began to develop within the army, rank-and-file pressures forced socialist leaders to demand clarification, and perhaps revision, of French war aims. Suddenly the French government was under pressure to

Fourteen Points
Proposals by U.S. president Woodrow Wilson to guide the new international order that would follow an Allied victory in World War I.

suggest that the war had idealistic and democratic purposes. Doubts about the government's goals were beginning to fuel active opposition to the war.

The same pressures were at work in Germany. Antiwar sentiment grew steadily within the Social Democratic Party (SPD) until the antiwar faction split off and formed the Independent Socialist Party (USPD) in April 1917. A large-scale debate over war aims, linked to considerations of domestic political reform, developed in the Reichstag by the summer of 1917. On July 19, a solid 60 percent majority passed a new war aims resolution, which affirmed that Germany's purposes were solely defensive, that Germany had no territorial ambitions. Germany, too, seemed open to a white peace.

But just as the dramatic events of 1917 interjected new pressures for moderation and peace, pressures in the opposite direction also mounted as the war dragged on. It seemed to some that this war was only the beginning of a new era of intense international competition. The current war convinced top German officials that Germany's geography and dependence on imports made it especially vulnerable. So Germany had to seize the present opportunity to conquer the means to fight the next war on a more favorable footing. Many German officials believed that Germany could achieve parity with Britain, and thus, the basis for security and peace, only if it maintained control of the Belgian coast. German expansion into Russian Poland and up the Baltic coast of Lithuania and Latvia seemed essential as well.

Treaty of Brest-Litovsk
Harsh peace terms that Germany imposed on Russia in March 1918.

When, in response to the Russian request for an armistice, Germany was able to dictate the peace terms, as specified in the **Treaty of Brest-Litovsk** of March 1918, it became clear how radically annexationist Germany's war aims had become. European Russia was to be largely dismembered, leaving Germany in direct or indirect control of 27 percent of Russia's European territory, 40 percent of its population, and 75 percent of its iron and coal. All the Reichstag parties except the Socialists accepted the terms of the treaty, which, in fact, produced a renewed determination to push on to victory.

France, less vulnerable geographically than Germany, tended to be more modest. But news of the terms the Germans had imposed at Brest-Litovsk inflamed the French, reinforcing their determination to fight on to an unqualified victory. Only thus could France secure the advantages necessary to ward off an ongoing German menace.

The Renewal of the French War Effort

Domestic division in France reached its peak during the fall of 1917. In November, with France's ability to continue fighting in doubt, President Raymond Poincaré (1860–1934) called on Georges Clemenceau (1841–1929) to lead a new government. The 76-year-old Clemenceau (klem-ahn-SOH) was known as a "hawk"; his appointment portended a stepped-up prosecution of the war. His message was simple as he appeared before the Chamber of Deputies on November 20, 1917: "If you ask me about my war aims, I reply: my aim is to be victorious." For the remainder of the war, France was under the virtual dictatorship of Clemenceau and his cabinet.

Clemenceau moved decisively on both the domestic and military fronts. By cracking down on the antiwar movement—imprisoning antiwar leaders, suppressing defeatist newspapers—he stiffened morale on the home front. Understanding that lack of coordination between French and British military leaders had hampered the Allied effort on the battlefield, Clemenceau persuaded the British to accept the French general Ferdinand Foch (FOHSH) (1851–1929) as the first supreme commander of all Allied forces in the west. In choosing Foch, known for his commitment to aggressive offensives, Clemenceau was pointedly bypassing Pétain, whom he found too passive, even defeatist. After some initial friction, Clemenceau let Foch have his way on the military level, and the two proved an effective leadership combination.

The German Gamble, 1918

As the military campaigns of 1918 began, Germany seemed in a relatively favorable position: Russia had been knocked out of the war, and American troops were yet to arrive. Moderates in Germany wanted to seize the opportunity to work out a compromise peace while there was still a chance. But military leaders persuaded Kaiser Wilhelm II that Germany could win a definitive victory on the western front if it struck quickly, before U.S. help became significant. Since Germany would be out of reserves by summer, the alternative to decisive victory in the west would be total German defeat.

The German gamble almost succeeded. From March to June 1918, German forces seized the initiative with four months of sustained and effective attacks. By May 30, they had again reached the Marne, where they had been held in 1914. Paris, only 37 miles away, had to be evacuated once more (see **MAP 25.1**). As late as mid-July, Ludendorff remained confident of victory, but by mid-August, it was becoming clear that Germany lacked the manpower to exploit the successes of the offensive.

The German advance had caused mutual suspicion between the French and the British at first, but under Foch's leadership, the Western allies eventually managed more effective coordination. And on June 4, over a year after the U.S. declaration of war, American troops went into action for the first time. As the Allied counterattack proceeded, 250,000 U.S. troops were arriving per month, considerably boosting Allied morale and battlefield strength.

By June 1918, Europe was experiencing the first outbreak of a virulent new influenza virus, promptly dubbed the "Spanish flu," though it had originated in South Africa. Because of their inferior diets, German soldiers proved far more susceptible to the disease than their adversaries, a fact that significantly affected Germany's combat performance during the crucial summer of 1918.

Germany lost the initiative for good during the second Battle of the Marne, which began on July 15 with yet another German attack. Foch launched a sustained counterattack on July 18, using tanks to good advantage, and maintained the momentum thereafter. By early August, the whole western front began to roll back. With astonishing suddenness, the outcome was no longer in doubt, although most expected the war to drag on into 1919. Few realized how desperate Germany's situation had become.

Meanwhile, Germany's allies began falling one by one. In the Balkans, an Allied offensive broke through the German-Bulgarian line in September, prompting the Bulgarians to ask for an armistice. The Turkish military effort collapsed in October. With the defeat of Russia in 1917, German troops joined the Austrians on the Italian front, breaking through the Italian line at Caporetto late in 1917 and almost inflicting a decisive defeat. But after retreating, the Italians managed to regroup and hold—and eventually to drive the Austrians back. The Italian victory at Vittorio Veneto forced Austria's unconditional surrender on November 3, 1918. But by this point, the armies of the Habsburg Empire were disintegrating along nationality lines.

Military Defeat and Political Change in Germany

By late September, it was clear to Ludendorff that his armies could not stop the Allied advance. On September 29, he informed the government that to avoid invasion, Germany would have to seek an immediate armistice. Hoping to secure favorable peace terms and to foist responsibility for the defeat onto the parliamentary politicians, Hindenburg and Ludendorff asked that a government based on greater popular support be formed. A leading moderate, Prince Max von Baden (BAH-dyn) (1867–1929), became chancellor, and he promptly replaced Ludendorff with General Wilhelm Groener (GREU-nur) (1867–1939), who seemed more democratic in orientation. By now it was clear that ending the war could not be separated from the push for political change in Germany, especially because it was widely assumed that a more democratic Germany could expect more favorable peace terms.

After securing a written request for an armistice from Hindenburg, Prince Max sent a peace note to President Wilson early in October, asking for an armistice based on Wilson's Fourteen Points. During the month that followed, Prince Max engineered a series of measures, passed by the Reichstag and approved by the emperor, that reformed the constitution, abolishing the three-class voting system in Prussia and making the chancellor responsible to the Reichstag. At last, Germany had a constitutional monarchy. Not completely satisfied, President Wilson encouraged speculation that Germany could expect better peace terms if Wilhelm II were to abdicate and Germany became a republic.

But a far more radical outcome seemed possible during late 1918 and early 1919. As negotiations for an armistice proceeded in October, the continuing war effort produced instances of mutiny in the navy and breaches of discipline in the army. By early November, workers' and soldiers' councils were being formed all over Germany, just as in Russia the year before. On November 7, antiwar socialists in Munich led an uprising of workers and soldiers that expelled the king of Bavaria and proclaimed a new Bavarian republic. Its provisional government promptly sought its own peace negotiations with the Allies. On November 9, thousands of workers took to the streets of Berlin to demand immediate peace, and the authorities could not muster enough military resources to move against them.

"stab in the back" myth
The notion, widely held among Germans after their unexpected loss in World War I, that political intrigue and revolution at home had sabotaged the German military effort.

The senior army leadership grew concerned that the collapse of government authority would undermine the ability of officers even to march their troops home. So Hindenburg and Groener persuaded the emperor to abdicate. Having lost the support of the army, Wilhelm II accepted the inevitable and left for exile in the Netherlands.

With the German right, including the military, in disarray, and with the centrist parties discredited by their support for what had become an annexationist war, the initiative passed to the socialists. They, at least, had been in the forefront of the movement for peace. But the socialists had divided in 1917, mostly over the question of response to the war. The mainstream of the SPD, by supporting the war for so long, had irrevocably alienated the party's leftist socialist wing. The most militant of these leftist socialists, led by Karl Liebknecht (1871–1919) and Rosa Luxemburg (1870–1919), envisioned using the workers' and soldiers' councils as the basis for a full-scale revolution, more or less on the Bolshevik model.

The SPD, on the other hand, clung to its reformist heritage and insisted on working within parliamentary institutions. Party leaders argued that a Bolshevik-style revolution was neither appropriate nor necessary under the circumstances. On November 9, just hours before the revolutionaries proclaimed a soviet-style republic, SPD moderates proclaimed a parliamentary republic, soon to be led by the moderate socialist Friedrich Ebert (A-bairt) (1871–1925).

Birth from military defeat was especially disabling for the new republic because the German people were so little prepared for defeat when it came. Vigorous censorship had kept the public in the dark about Germany's real situation, so the request for an armistice early in October came as a shock. At no time during the war had Germany been invaded from the west, and by mid-1918, the German army had seemed on the brink of victory. It appeared inconceivable that Germany had lost a military decision, plain and simple. Thus, the **"stab in the back" myth**, the notion that political intrigue and revolution at home had sabotaged the German military effort, developed to explain what otherwise seemed an inexplicable defeat. This notion would prove a heavy burden for Germany's new democracy to bear.

SECTION SUMMARY

- By 1917, the will to continue the war was flagging on both sides, as some began to question war aims and even to call for a "white peace."

- The idealism of U.S. president Wilson, with his Fourteen Points, suggested to Europeans that the war might indeed be worth fighting to a victorious conclusion.

- The harsh Treaty of Brest-Litovsk that Germany imposed on Russia reflected changes in German war aims.

- The leadership combination of Clemenceau and Foch was crucial to the renewal of the French war effort.

- Germany's gamble on one last massive offensive during the summer of 1918 almost succeeded, but, led by France, the Allies began forcing the Germans back, prompting Germany to ask for an armistice.

- German leaders decided to turn from Wilhelm II's imperial regime toward democracy, partly in an effort to secure more favorable peace terms.

THE OUTCOME AND THE IMPACT

What factors shaped the peace settlement that the victors imposed on Germany and its allies in 1919–1920?

After the armistice officially ended the fighting on November 11, 1918, it was up to the war's four victors—France, Britain, Italy, and the United States—to establish the terms of peace and, it was to be hoped, a new basis for order at the same time. But after all that had happened since August 1914, it was not clear what a restoration of peace and order would require. Revolution had undermined, or threatened to undermine, the old political order in much of Europe. And the involvement of non-Europeans in the war seemed to suggest that Europe would no longer dominate world affairs in quite the way it had.

The Costs of War

Raw casualty figures do not begin to convey the war's human toll, but they afford some sense of its magnitude. Estimates differ, but it is generally agreed that from 10 million to 13 million military men lost their lives, with another 20 million wounded. In addition, between 7 million and 10 million civilians died as a result of the war and its hardships. In the defeated countries especially, food shortages and malnutrition continued well after the end of the fighting. Thus, the Spanish flu that had affected the balance on the battlefield early in the summer of 1918 returned with particularly devastating results during the fall. The influenza pandemic killed perhaps 40 million people worldwide.

Germany suffered the highest number of military casualties, but France suffered the most in proportional terms. Two million Germans were killed, with another 4 million wounded. Military deaths per capita for France were roughly 15 percent higher than for Germany—and twice as severe as for Britain. Of 8 million Frenchmen mobilized, over 5 million were killed or wounded. Roughly 1.5 million French soldiers, or 10 percent of the active male population, were killed—and this in a country already concerned about demographic decline. The other belligerents suffered less, but still in great numbers. Among the military personnel killed were 2 million Russians, 500,000 Italians, and 114,000 Americans.

Economic costs were heavy as well. In addition to the privations suffered during the years of war, Europeans found themselves reeling from inflation and saddled with debt, especially to the United States, once the war was over. Although the immediate transition to a peacetime economy did not prove as difficult as many had feared, the war and its aftermath produced an economic disequilibrium that lingered, helping to produce a worldwide depression by the 1930s.

The Search for Peace in a Revolutionary Era

The war had begun because of the nationality problem in Austria-Hungary, and it led not simply to military defeat for Austria-Hungary, but to the breakup of the Habsburg system (see **MAP 25.3**). In east-central Europe, the end of the war brought bright hopes for self-determination to peoples like the Czechs, Slovaks, Poles, Serbs, and Croats. Even before the peacemakers opened deliberations in January 1919, some of these ethnic groups had begun creating a new order on their own. For example, a popular movement of Czechs and Slovaks established a Czechoslovak republic on October 29, 1918, and a new Yugoslavia and an independent Hungary similarly emerged from indigenous movements. Czechoslovakia and Yugoslavia were made up of different ethnic groups that found cooperation advantageous now but that might well disagree in the future (see **MAP 25.2**). Moreover, many of these countries lacked traditions of self-government, and they had reason to feud among themselves. With the Habsburg system no longer imposing one form of stability, a power vacuum seemed likely in this potentially volatile part of Europe.

The Bolshevik Revolution in Russia immeasurably complicated the situation. The unsettled conditions in Germany and the former Habsburg territories seemed to invite the spread of revolution—precisely according to Lenin's script. Shortly after taking power, Lenin and his party had begun calling themselves "communists," partly to jettison the provincial Russian term *bolshevik*, but especially to underline their departure from the old reformist socialism of the Second International. In adopting "communism," they wanted to make it clear that they stood for a revolutionary alternative, and they actively sought to inspire revolution elsewhere.

Outside Russia, the greatest communist success was in Hungary, where a communist regime under Béla Kun governed Budapest and other parts of the country from March to August 1919, when it was put down by Allied-sponsored

🌐 **MAP 25.2—Ethnicity in East-Central Europe, 1919**
Ethnic diversity made it hard to create homogeneous nation-states in east-central Europe. The new states that emerged after World War I mixed ethnic groups, and ethnic tensions would contribute to future problems.

forces. At about the same time, communist republics lasted for months in the Slovak part of Czechoslovakia and in the important German state of Bavaria. Even in Italy, which had shared in the victory, socialists infatuated with the Bolshevik example claimed that the substantial labor unrest during 1919 and 1920 was the beginning of full-scale revolution.

Further complicating the postwar situation were the defeat and dissolution of the Turkish Ottoman Empire, which had controlled much of the Middle East in 1914. The Arab revolt against the Turks that developed in the Arabian peninsula in 1916 did not achieve its major military aims, though it caused some disruption to the Turkish war effort. Its success was due partly to the collaboration of a young British officer, T. E. Lawrence (1888–1935), who proved an effective military leader and an impassioned advocate of the Arab cause. The support that Britain had offered the Arabs suggested that independence, perhaps even a single Arab kingdom, might follow from a defeat of the Ottoman Empire.

But British policy toward the Arabs was uncertain and contradictory. Concerned about the Suez Canal, the British government sought to tighten its control in Egypt by declaring it a protectorate in 1914, triggering increased anti-British sentiment in the region. The secret Sykes-Picot Agreement of May 1916, named for the British and French diplomats who negotiated it, projected a division of the Ottoman territories of the Middle East into colonial spheres of influence. France would control Syria and Lebanon, while Britain would rule Palestine and Mesopotamia, or present-day Iraq (see **Map 25.4**).

Potentially complicating the situation in the region was Zionism, the movement to establish a Jewish state in Palestine. Led by Chaim Weizmann (1874–1952), a remarkable Russian-born British chemist, the Zionists reached an important milestone when British foreign secretary Arthur Balfour (1848–1930) cautiously announced, in the Balfour Declaration of November 1917, that the British government "looked with favor" on the prospect of a "Jewish home" in Palestine. At this point, Jews were only 10 percent of the population in Palestine. British leaders sympathetic to Zionism saw no conflict in simultaneously embracing the cause of the Arabs against the

An Arab in Paris   Prince Faisal *(foreground)* attended the Paris Peace Conference, where he lobbied for the creation of an independent Arab kingdom from part of the former Ottoman Turkish holdings in the Middle East. Among his supporters was the British officer T. E. Lawrence *(middle row, second from the right)*, on his way to legend as "Lawrence of Arabia." (Bettmann/Corbis)

Ottoman Turks. Indeed, Arabs and Jews, each seeking self-determination, could be expected to collaborate.

In the heat of war, the British established their policy for the former Ottoman territories without careful study. Thus, they made promises and agreements that were not entirely compatible. After the war, the victors' efforts to install a new order in the Middle East would create fresh conflicts.

The Peace Settlement

The peace conference took place in Paris, beginning in January 1919. Its labors led to separate treaties with each of the five defeated states. The first and most significant was the **Treaty of Versailles** with Germany, signed in the Hall of Mirrors of the Versailles Palace on June 28, 1919. Treaties were also worked out, in turn, with Austria, Bulgaria, Hungary, and finally, in August 1920, Turkey.

Treaty of Versailles
Peace treaty that the victors in World War I imposed on a defeated Germany in 1919.

This was to be a dictated, not a negotiated, peace. Germany and its allies were excluded, as was revolutionary Russia. The passions unleashed by the long war had dissolved the possibility of a more conciliatory outcome, a genuinely negotiated peace. However, spokesmen for many groups—from Slovaks and Croats to Arabs, Jews, and pan-Africanists—were in Paris as well, seeking a hearing for their respective causes. Both the Arab Prince Faisal (1885–1933), who would later become king of Iraq, and Colonel T. E. Lawrence were on hand to plead for an independent Arab kingdom. (See the feature, "The Global Record: Prince Faisal at the Peace Conference.") The African American leader W E. B. DuBois (doo-BOYS) (1868–1963), who took his Ph.D. at Harvard in 1895, led a major pan-African congress in Paris concurrently with the peace conference.

THE PARTICIPANTS

The fundamental challenge for the peacemakers was to reconcile the conflicting visions of the postwar world that had emerged by the end of the war. U.S. president Wilson represented the promise of a new order that could give this terrible war a lasting meaning. As he toured parts of Europe on his way to the conference, Wilson was greeted as a hero. Clemenceau, in contrast, was a hard-liner concerned with French security and dismissive of Wilsonian ideals. Since becoming prime minister in 1917, he had stressed that only permanent French military superiority over Germany, and not some utopian league of nations, could guarantee a lasting peace. The negotiations at Paris centered on this fundamental difference between Wilson and Clemenceau. Although Britain's Lloyd George took a hard line on certain issues, he also sought to mediate, helping engineer the somewhat awkward compromise that resulted. When, after the peace conference, he encountered criticism for the outcome, Lloyd George replied, "I think I did as well as might be expected, seated as I was between Jesus Christ and Napoleon Bonaparte."[5]

SHIFTING POWERS

In Article 231 of the final treaty, the peacemakers sought to establish a moral basis for their treatment of Germany by assigning responsibility for the war to Germany and its allies. The Germans were required to pay reparations to reimburse the victors for the costs of the war, although

The Victors and the Peace   In June 1919, the leaders of the major victorious powers exude confidence after signing the Treaty of Versailles with Germany. From the left are David Lloyd George of Britain, Georges Clemenceau of France, and Woodrow Wilson of the United States.   (Bettmann/Corbis)

the actual amount was not established until 1921. The determination to make the loser pay was one of the factors keeping both sides from seeking a compromise peace by 1917.

Germany was also forced to dismantle much of its military apparatus. The army was to be limited to a hundred thousand men, all volunteers. The treaty severely restricted the size of the German navy as well, and Germany was forbidden to manufacture or possess military aircraft, submarines, tanks, heavy artillery, or poison gas.

France took back Alsace and Lorraine, the provinces it had lost to Germany in 1871 (see **MAP 25.3**). But for France, the crucial security provision of the peace settlement was the treatment of the adjacent Rhineland section of Germany itself. For fifteen years, Allied troops were to occupy the west bank of the Rhine River in Germany—the usual military occupation of a

🌐 MAP 25.3—Europe after the Peace Conference, 1920

With Russia, Austria-Hungary, Germany, and Ottoman Turkey defeated, the peacemakers finalized major changes in the European map. France, Italy, and Denmark gained significant territory, while a number of new countries were established in the east-central part of the continent.

defeated adversary. But this would only be temporary. The long-term advantage for France was to be the permanent demilitarization of all German territory west of the Rhine and a strip of 50 kilometers along its east bank. Germany was to maintain no troops on this part of its own soil; in the event of hostilities, French forces would be able to march into Germany unopposed.

French interests also helped shape the settlement in east-central Europe. To ensure that Germany would again face potential enemies from both the east and the west, French leaders envisioned building a network of allies in east-central Europe. The first was the new Poland, created from Polish territories formerly in the German, Russian, and Austro-Hungarian Empires. That network might come to include Czechoslovakia, Yugoslavia, and Romania as well. These states would be weak enough to remain under French influence but, taken together, strong enough to replace Russia as a significant force against Germany.

Partly as a result of French priorities, Poland, Czechoslovakia, Yugoslavia, and Romania ended up as large as possible, either by combining ethnic groups or by incorporating minorities that, on ethnic grounds, belonged with neighboring states (see **Map 25.2**). The new Czechoslovakia included not only Czechs and Slovaks, but also numerous Germans and Magyars. Indeed, Germans, mostly from the old Bohemia, made up 22 percent of the population of Czechoslovakia. By contrast, Austria, Hungary, and Bulgaria, as defeated powers, found themselves diminished (see **Map 25.3**). What remained of Austria, the German part of the old Habsburg Empire, was prohibited from choosing to join Germany, an obvious violation of the Wilsonian principle of self-determination.

Desires to contain revolutionary Russia were also at work in the settlement in east-central Europe. A band of states in east-central Europe, led by France, could serve not only as a check to Germany, but also as a shield against the Russian threat. Romania's aggrandizement came partly at the expense of the Russian Empire, as did the creation of the new Poland. Finland, Latvia, Estonia, and Lithuania, all part of the Russian Empire for over a century, became independent states (see **Map 25.3**).

The territorial settlement cost Germany almost 15 percent of its prewar territory, but German bitterness over the peace terms stemmed above all from a sense of betrayal. In requesting an armistice, German authorities had appealed to Wilson, who had not emphasized war guilt and reparations. He seemed to be saying that the whole prewar international system, not one side or the other, had been responsible for the current conflict. Yet, the peacemakers now placed the primary blame on Germany, so for Germans, the terms of the peace greatly intensified the sting of defeat.

A New International Order?

Wilson had been forced to compromise with French interests in dealing with east-central Europe, but he achieved a potentially significant success in exchange—the establishment of a **League of Nations**, embodying the widespread hope for a new international order. (See the feature, "The Written Record: The Covenant of the League of Nations.") According to the League covenant worked out by April, disputes among member states were to be settled no longer by war, but by mechanisms established by the new assembly. Other members were to participate in sanctions, from economic blockade to military action, against a member that went to war in violation of League provisions.

How could Wilsonian hopes for a new international order be squared with the imperialist system, which seemed utterly at odds with the ideal of self-determination? Elites among the colonial peoples had tended to support the war efforts of their imperial rulers, but often in the hope of winning greater autonomy or even independence. The Indian leader Mohandas Gandhi (GAHN-dee) (1869–1948), who had been educated in the West and admitted to the English bar in 1889, even helped recruit Indians to fight on the British side. But his aim was to speed Indian independence, and he led demonstrations that embarrassed the British during the war. (See the feature, "The Global Record: Gandhi Advocates Nonviolence," on page 760 in Chapter 27.)

Colonial peoples participated directly in the war on both sides. In sub-Saharan Africa, for example, German-led Africans fought against Africans under British or French command. France brought colonial subjects from West and North Africa into frontline service during the war. But one result was an expansion of political consciousness that led more of those subject to imperialism to question the whole system.

The hope that support for the Western powers in wartime would eventually be rewarded led China and Siam (now Thailand) to associate with the Allied side in 1917, in an effort to enhance

League of Nations An international organization established at the end of World War I without the membership of the United States. Though its covenant called for the peaceful settlement of disputes and for sanctions against a member that went to war in violation of League provisions, it failed to prevent the escalating violence that culminated in World War II.

Prince Faisal at the Peace Conference

With the war nearing its end in October 1918, British authorities, in line with provisions of the Sykes-Picot Agreement, permitted Faisal ibn-Husayn (1885–1933) to set up a provisional Arab state, with its capital at Damascus. As head of a delegation from this area to the Paris Peace Conference, Faisal claimed to speak for all Arab Asia, but some on the Arabian peninsula challenged his claim. In the memorandum of January 1919 that follows, he outlined the Arab position, mixing pride and assertiveness with a recognition that the Arabs would continue to need the support and help of Western powers. After the peace was concluded, Faisal found himself caught up in British and French rivalries as he was installed as king—first of Syria, then of Iraq (Mesopotamia). But his efforts were central to the eventual achievement of Arab independence in the Middle East.

We believe that our ideal of Arab unity in Asia is justified beyond need of argument. If argument is required, we would point to the general principles accepted by the Allies when the United States joined them, to our splendid past, to the tenacity with which our race has for 600 years resisted Turkish attempts to absorb us, and, in a lesser degree, to what we tried our best to do in this war as one of the Allies....

The various provinces of Arab Asia—Syria, Irak [sic], Jezireh, Hedjaz, Nejd, Yemen—are very different economically and socially, and it is impossible to constrain them into one frame of government.

We believe that Syria, an agricultural and industrial area thickly peopled with sedentary classes, is sufficiently advanced politically to manage her own internal affairs. We feel also that foreign technical advice and help will be a most valuable factor in our national growth. We are willing to pay for this help in cash; we cannot sacrifice for it any part of the freedom we have just won for ourselves by force of arms.

...The world wishes to exploit Mesopotamia rapidly, and we therefore believe that the system of government there will have to be buttressed by the men and material resources of a great foreign Power. We ask, however, that the Government be Arab, in principle and spirit, the selective rather than the elective principle being necessarily followed in the neglected districts, until time makes the broader basis possible....

In Palestine the enormous majority of the people are Arabs. The Jews are very close to the Arabs in blood, and there is no conflict of character between the two races. In principles we are absolutely at one. Nevertheless, the Arabs cannot risk assuming the responsibility of holding level the scales in the clash of races and religions that have, in this one province, so often involved the world in difficulties. They would wish for the effective super-position of a great trustee, so long as a representative local administration commended itself by actively promoting the material prosperity of the country....

In our opinion, if our independence be conceded and our local competence established, the natural influences of race, language, and interest will soon draw us together into one people; but for this the Great Powers will have to ensure us open internal frontiers, common railways and telegraphs, and uniform systems of education. To achieve this they must lay aside the thought of individual profits, and of their old jealousies. In a word, we ask you not to force your whole civilisation upon us, but to help us to pick out what serves us from your experience. In return we can offer you little but gratitude.

QUESTIONS

1. How does Prince Faisal assess the prospects for unity among the diverse Arab peoples of Asia?
2. What role does Prince Faisal envision for the Western powers in Arab Asia?

Source: Encounters: Prince Faisal at the Peace Conference from J.C. Hurewitz, *Diplomacy in the Near and Middle East: A Documentary Record: 1914–1956.* D. Van Nostrand, 1956; reprinted by Archive Editions, UK, 1987.

their international stature. Each was seeking to restore full sovereignty in the face of increasing Western influence. China sent 200,000 people to work in France to help ease France's wartime labor shortage.

At the peace conference, spokesmen for the non-Western world tended to be moderate in their demands. And prodded by Wilson, the peacemakers made some concessions. German colonies and Ottoman territories were not simply taken over by the victors, in the old-fashioned way, but were placed under the authority of the League. The League then assigned them as mandates to one of the victorious powers, which was to report to the League annually on conditions in the area in question. Classes of mandates varied, based on how prepared for sovereignty the area was judged to be. In devising this system, the Western powers formally recognized, for the first time, that non-Western peoples under Western control had rights of their own and, in principle, were progressing toward independence.

Still, the mandate approach to the colonial question was a halting departure at best. Although Britain granted considerable sovereignty to Iraq in 1932, the victorious powers generally operated

🌐 MAP 25.4—The European Peace Settlement and the Middle East

In light of the peace settlement, the end of Ottoman rule in the Middle East meant new roles for European powers, not independence for the peoples of the region. As had been envisioned with the Sykes-Picot Agreement of 1916, the British and French dominated the Middle East, although the new League of Nations mandate system was a departure from the earlier imperialism.

The Covenant of the League of Nations

In its very first part, before treating defeated Germany, the Treaty of Versailles established a new "League of Nations," outlining its aims and procedures as well as the obligations of its members. With this bold experiment, the war's victors sought to organize international relations on a radically new basis. The League's overriding aim was to settle international disputes without resort to war. But the League was also to fulfill an international responsibility, newly recognized here, for the gradual departure from colonialism. Although it instilled great hope at first, the League's inability to prevent aggression and war became clear during the 1930s. Even so, its failure prompted a still more determined effort to order international affairs with the creation of the United Nations in the aftermath of World War II.

The High Contracting Parties,

In order to promote international co-operation and to achieve international peace and security by the acceptance of obligations not to resort to war, by the prescription of open, just and honourable relations between nations, by the firm establishment of the understandings of international law as the actual rule of conduct among Governments, and by the maintenance of justice and a scrupulous respect for all treaty obligations in the dealings of organised peoples with one another,

Agree to this Covenant of the League of Nations....

Article 12.

The Members of the League agree that if there should arise between them any dispute likely to lead to a rupture, they will submit the matter either to arbitration or to inquiry by the Council, and they agree in no case to resort to war until three months after the award by the arbitrators or the report by the Council....

Article 16.

Should any Member of the League resort to war in disregard of its covenants under Articles 12, 13, or 15, it shall *ipso facto* be deemed to have committed an act of war against all other Members of the League, which hereby undertake immediately to subject it to the severance of all trade or financial relations, the prohibition of all intercourse between their nations and the nationals of the covenant-breaking State, and the prevention of all financial, commercial, or personal intercourse between the nationals of the covenant-breaking State and the nationals of any other State, whether a Member of the League or not....

Article 22.

To those colonies and territories which as a consequence of the late war have ceased to be under the sovereignty of the States which formerly governed them and which are inhabited by peoples not yet able to stand by themselves under the strenuous conditions of the modern world, there should be applied the principle that the well-being and development of such peoples form a sacred trust of civilisation and that securities for the performance of this trust should be embodied in this Covenant.

The best method of giving practical effect to this principle is that the tutelage of such peoples should be entrusted to advanced nations who by reason of their resources, their experience or their geographical position can best undertake this responsibility, and who are willing to accept it, and that this tutelage should be exercised by them as Mandatories on behalf of the League.

QUESTIONS

1. How did the League of Nations expect to minimize the resort to war?
2. On what grounds did the League assume responsibility for overseeing the development of the former colonies of the defeated German and Ottoman Empires?

Source: *The Treaties of Peace, 1919–1923*, vol. 1 (New York: The Carnegie Endowment for International Peace, 1924), pp. 10, 14, 17, 19.

---

as before, assimilating the new territories into their existing systems of colonial possessions. After the hopes for independence raised in the Arab world during the war, this outcome produced a sense of betrayal among Arab leaders (see **MAP 25.4**).

The Chinese similarly felt betrayed. Despite China's contributions to the Allied war effort, the victors acquiesced in special rights for Japan in China, causing a renewed sense of humiliation among the Chinese and provoking a boycott of Japanese goods. Although Western leaders were allowing a non-Western power, Japan, access to the imperial club, they were hardly departing from imperialism. For Chinese, Arabs, and others, the West appeared hypocritical. Those whose political consciousness had been raised by the war came to believe not only that colonialism should end, but that the colonial peoples themselves would have to take the lead in ending it.

Would the principal victors have the resolve, and the capacity, to preserve the new order they had established at Paris? Debate over the American role promptly developed in the United States as President Wilson sought Senate ratification of the Versailles treaty, which entailed U.S. membership in the League of Nations, as well as commitments to France and Britain. Wilson's opponents worried that League membership would compromise U.S. sovereignty, but other nations managed to overcome such concerns and join the new organization. American reluctance stemmed especially from the isolationist backlash that was developing against the U.S. intervention in the European war. Late in 1919, at the height of the debate, Wilson suffered a disabling stroke. The Senate then refused to ratify the peace treaty, thereby keeping the United States out of the League of Nations.

American disengagement stemmed partly from doubts about the wisdom of the peace settlement that quickly developed in both Britain and the United States. During the peace conference, a member of the British delegation, the economist John Maynard Keynes (KAINZ) (1883–1946), resigned to write *The Economic Consequences of the Peace* (1920), which helped undermine confidence in the whole settlement. Keynes charged that the shortsighted, vindictive policy of the French, by crippling Germany with a punishing reparations burden, threatened the European economy and thus the long-term peace of Europe. For some, then, the challenge was not to enforce the Versailles treaty but to revise it. This lack of consensus about the legitimacy of the peace made it especially hard to anticipate the longer-term consequences of the war.

The Cultural Impact of the Great War

Coming after a century of relative peace and apparent progress, this long and brutal war ended up shaking Europe's social and cultural foundations. The number of casualties, the advent of terrifying new weapons, and the destruction of famous old monuments—all gave the war an apocalyptic aura that heightened its psychological impact.

The war touched virtually everyone, but it marked for life those who had experienced the nightmare of the trenches. At first, traditional notions of glory, heroism, and patriotic duty combined with images of fellowship and regeneration to enable the soldiers to make a certain sense of their wartime experience. But as the war dragged on, such sentiments gradually eroded, giving way, in many cases, to resignation and cynicism. (See the feature, "The Visual Record: Max Beckmann's *The Night*.") But others, such as the young German soldier and writer Ernst Jünger (1895–1998), lauded

Severini: Armoured Train In this painting from 1915, the Italian futurist Gino Severini (1883–1966) conveys the hard, steel-like imagery and the sense of disciplined modern efficiency that became associated with war, making it attractive to some young Europeans. (© 2006 Artist's Rights Society (ARS), New York/ADAGP, Paris. Richard S. Zeisler Collection, New York/The Bridgeman Art Library)

Max Beckmann's *The Night*

"One of the most disagreeable images which the art of our century has to show," wrote the noted art historian and critic John Russell in 1981 of the painting we see here.* Max Beckmann (1884–1950) painted *The Night* during 1918–1919, as Germany was suffering military defeat, experiencing political turmoil, and encountering extreme economic hardship. And surely this unprecedented and disturbing image reflects that difficult combination of circumstances. But what are the sources of the imagery we see here, and what does this painting tell us about the war's cultural impact?

The young Beckmann established himself as an innovative painter before the war, working partly within the idiom of German expressionism. Emerging as a formal movement in 1905, expressionism became the major German contribution to the avant-garde in the visual arts. Expressionists like Ernst Ludwig Kirchner, Ernst Haeckel, and Franz Marc used unnatural colors and deformed natural appearance to convey emotion and to provoke a psychological response in the viewer. In much of their work, they sought an appropriately innovative response to the uncanniness, even the menace, of modern life—and especially the modern urban world, at once enticing and threatening.

Like so many of the educated youth of his generation, Beckmann initially welcomed the war as a source of renewal. Indeed, he was especially fascinated with its potentially cataclysmic effects, in light of his quasi-Nietzschean faith in the scope for a more intense form of life through struggle and suffering. After volunteering for service in the fall of 1914, he was assigned to the German medical corps. Working in a field hospital on the western front in 1915, Beckmann still found something grandly apocalyptic in the death, the suffering, the wounded bodies. Indeed, he welcomed the chance to observe all that up close; it inspired notes and sketches to be used as material for his art. At the same time, he began to envision conveying his ideas through images recalling the scourging of Christ.

But Beckmann's beliefs were being shaken, and his drawings during 1915 depicted suffering, pain, and death with ever greater intensity. That summer, he suffered a nervous breakdown and was sent back to Germany to recuperate. In 1917, he was finally discharged from the army as unfit for further service.

Beckmann turned back to painting in an effort to convey his increasingly disillusioning experience of the war. Like many expressionist artists, he had been influenced by late Gothic German painting, and *The Night* uses certain formal elements from that earlier tradition. Note especially the color—pure but thin, even sour—and the space—shallow and confined, with the figures almost piled atop one another. Beckmann also adapted the religious themes of German Gothic—not, however, as a believer. Rather, he valued their familiarity, as images of suffering, combined with suggestions of cruelty and guilt. Such familiar images seemed to offer the means to create the new, utterly unfamiliar imagery that, Beckmann felt, was necessary to convey what human beings had come to feel as a result of the war and its aftermath.

Here is how Beckmann put it at the end of 1918, precisely as he was working on *The Night*:

> The stronger my determination grows to grasp the unutterable things of this world, the deeper and more powerful the emotion burning inside me about our existence, the tighter I keep my mouth shut and the harder I try to capture the terrible, thrilling monster of life's vitality and to confine it, to beat it down and to strangle it with crystal-clear, razor-sharp lines and planes. ... We must be a part of all the misery which is coming. We have to surrender our heart and our nerves, we must abandon ourselves to the horrible cries of pain of a poor deluded people.†

On the immediate level, *The Night* conveys a scene of violence, torture, and suffering, for three of the figures have apparently broken into a family's home (complete with dog and phonograph) in order to torture, rape, and perhaps kidnap or murder. Yet, the complex interplay between the figures suggests that we cannot easily distinguish perpetrators from victims.

The suffering figure on the left seems to be Beckmann himself, in the pose of the suffering Christ, yet his bandaged torturer may suggest the wounded to whom Beckmann had earlier ministered on the battlefield. In performing his medical duties, he had become haunted with the ambiguity between causing and relieving suffering, especially, perhaps, because he had initially observed the suffering of the wounded with the combination of voyeuristic excitement and clinical detachment we noted earlier. His initial attitude had been symptomatic of the somewhat cavalier attitude with which so many of the educated of his generation had gone off to war.

Another of the torturers is patterned after a blind figure in a fourteenth-century Italian fresco—yet is also made to look like Lenin and/or a contemporary German worker. With bourgeois and proletarian seemingly both implicated in gratuitous violence, there seems no scope for political redemption. Yet neither is the family's home a safe refuge the war as the catalyst for a welcome new era of steel, hardness, discipline, organization, and machine precision.

Beginning in the late 1920s, a wave of writings about the war appeared. Many were memoirs, such as *Goodbye to All That* by the English writer Robert Graves (1895–1985) and *Testament of Youth* by Vera Brittain (1893–1970), who had served as a British army nurse at the front. But the

Beckmann: The Night (© 2006 Artist's Rights Society (ARS), New York/VG Bild-Kunst, Bonn. Erich Lessing/Art Resource, NY)

from the violence of politics and war. We all seem to be at once perpetrators and victims, caught in a claustrophobic space, with no place to escape, and little if any scope for action. We are even a hell unto ourselves.

Through this combination of images suggesting suffering and guilt, but seemingly precluding any hope of redemption, "Beckmann achieves," as Reinhard Spieler has put it, "a form which transcends commentary on his own time: the corruption and cruelty of postwar society is raised to a general and timeless level of human experience, to eternal night, to humanity's hell on earth."[‡]

The Night conveys not simply the disarray of a moment—the German experience of defeat and revolutionary violence—but a changed sensibility; in the wake of World War I, the world could never be the same. Although he was determined to avoid sentimentality or collective self-pity, Beckmann still thought that we might hope, through art, to come to terms with all that recent historical experience had revealed. But it had come to seem that we could do so only through "one of the most disagreeable images" in modern art.

QUESTIONS

1. Why does Beckmann place this combination of interconnected figures in such a shallow, confined space?

2. What relationship between the private domestic sphere and the public political sphere does Beckmann seem to be depicting in *The Night*?

---

* John Russell, *The Meanings of Modern Art* (New York: Harper & Row, 1981), p. 95.

† Max Beckmann, "Creative Credo," in *Art in Theory, 1900–1990: An Anthology of Changing Ideas*, edited by Charles Harrison and Paul Wood (Oxford: Blackwell, 1993), pp. 267–268.

‡ Reinhard Spieler, *Max Beckmann, 1884–1950: The Path to Myth* (Cologne: Taschen, 1995), p. 38.

most famous retrospective was the novel *All Quiet on the Western Front* (1929) by the German Erich Maria Remarque (1898–1970); it sold 2.5 million copies in twenty-five languages in its first eighteen months in print. Remarque provided a gripping portrait of the experience of ordinary soldiers on the western front, but his book also reflected the disillusionment that had come to surround the memory of the war by the late 1920s. Not only were many dead or maimed for

SECTION SUMMARY

- Although Germany suffered the highest number of wartime casualties, France's losses in proportional terms were 15 percent higher—and twice as high as Britain's.

- The breakup of the Habsburg and Ottoman Empires, together with the defeat of Russia and Germany, raised hopes for self-determination among formerly subject peoples, but also complicated the challenges of peacemaking.

- The peace settlement represented an awkward compromise between Wilson's idealistic principles and Clemenceau's hardheaded concern for long-term French interests.

- The harsh peace terms imposed on Germany not only inflamed German opinion, but also seemed counterproductive to many elsewhere, thereby compromising the moral force of the peace settlement.

- Britain and France divided the Arab parts of the former Ottoman Empire according to the secret Sykes-Picot Agreement of 1916.

life, but all the sacrifices seemed to have been largely in vain, a sentiment that fueled determination to avoid another war in the future.

What followed from the war, most fundamentally, was a new sense that Western civilization was neither as secure nor as superior as it had seemed. The celebrated French poet Paul Valéry (1871–1945), speaking at Oxford shortly after the war, observed that "we modern civilizations have learned to recognize that we are mortal like the others. We had heard … of whole worlds vanished, of empires foundered. … Elam, Nineveh, Babylon were vague and splendid names; the total ruin of these worlds, for us, meant as little as did their existence. But France, England, Russia … these names, too, are splendid. … And now we see that the abyss of history is deep enough to bury all the world. We feel that a civilization is as fragile as a life."[6] Valéry went on to warn that the coming transition to peace would be even more difficult and disorienting than the war itself. So traumatic might be the convulsion that Europe might lose its leadership and be shown up for what it was in fact—a small corner of the world, a mere cape on the Asiatic landmass. Astounding words for a European, yet even Valéry, for all his foresight, could not anticipate what Europe would experience in the decades to follow.

CHAPTER SUMMARY

The war that began in August 1914 was supposed to be over in a few months, but after the French held at the first Battle of the Marne in September, it bogged down in a stalemate on the western front, thanks partly to the unforeseen effectiveness of defensive trenches. The massive assaults of 1916–1917 yielded horrifying numbers of casualties—but not the intended breakthrough for either side.

FOCUS QUESTIONS

- How and why had the course of the war by 1917 defied the expectations that had surrounded the beginning of fighting in August 1914?

- Why did this prove a total war, making necessary new forms of socio economic coordination and even systematic propaganda?

- Why did the first revolution in Russia pave the way for a second, spearheaded by the Bolsheviks?

- Why did Germany and its allies end up losing the war even after forcing Russia to make a separate peace by early 1918?

- What factors shaped the peace settlement that the victors imposed on Germany and its allies in 1919–1920?

Because it was so much longer and more difficult than expected, this first "world war" proved a total war, calling forth new forms of socioeconomic coordination and even systematic propaganda. Partly as a result, the war accelerated processes, from economic coordination to technological development to women's suffrage, that many found progressive.

But the war also caused cracks in the old order, first and most dramatically in Russia, where war-weariness led to a revolution overthrowing the tsarist regime early in 1917. Although this was not a socialist revolution, it paved the way by the end of 1917 to a second revolution, spearheaded by the Bolsheviks, who represented the more extreme wing of Russian Marxism. Although their own tactical prowess was also a factor, they were able to seize the initiative especially because of the mistakes of the provisional government, which kept Russia in the war and balked at systematic land reform. In taking power, the Bolsheviks were seeking not simply to control Russia, but to spark the wider revolution they believed essential if a viable new socialist order was to be created.

Although war-weariness on both sides prompted calls for a white peace by 1917, the defection of revolutionary Russia and the intervention of the United States dramatically altered the lineup—and even the potential meaning of the war. In 1918, Germany mounted a last-ditch offensive in the west that came close to succeeding. But France had toughened under Georges Clemenceau, and by that point, a lack of food, provisions, and manpower was fatally weakening the German effort. U.S. intervention gave the anti-German coalition the long-term advantage in any case. Although it entailed far more sacrifice than anyone had expected at the outset, the war reached a definitive outcome with the defeat of Germany and its allies by November 1918.

Conflicting aspirations among the victors led to an awkward peace settlement. Whereas Woodrow Wilson envisioned a new era in world affairs, based on national self-determination and a new League of Nations, Clemenceau was concerned to cement French superiority on the European continent in the face of Germany's greater long-term demographic, economic, and military potential. Such security considerations even compromised the principle of self-determination at the peace conference. But the harshness of the Treaty of Versailles, which produced much resentment even outside Germany, led some observers to doubt the peace could last for long.

KEY TERMS

Sacred Union   (p. 696)

British blockade   (p. 701)

total war   (p. 703)

Kriegsrohstoffabteilung (KRA)   (p. 703)

Petrograd Soviet   (p. 706)

provisional government (p. 706)

Vladimir Lenin   (p. 707)

Fourteen Points   (p. 709)

Treaty of Brest-Litovsk (p. 710)

"stab in the back" myth (p. 712)

Treaty of Versailles   (p. 715)

League of Nations   (p. 717)

 This icon will direct you to additional materials on the website: www .cengage.com/history/ noble/westciv6e.

NOTES

1. The remarks of Raymond Joubert, as quoted in John Ellis, *Eye-Deep in Hell: Trench Warfare in World War I* (Baltimore: Johns Hopkins University Press, 1989), p. 104.

2. Brian Bond, *War and Society in Europe, 1870–1970* (New York: Oxford University Press, 1986), p. 114.

3. A. N. Potresov, quoted in Richard Pipes, *The Russian Revolution* (New York: Random House, Vintage, 1991), p. 348.

4. Both statements are quoted in Koppel S. Pinson, *Modern Germany: Its History and Civilization*, 2d ed. (New York: Macmillan, 1966), p. 337.

5. Quoted in Walter Arnstein, *Britain Yesterday and Today: 1830 to the Present*, 6th ed. (Lexington, Mass.: D. C. Heath, 1992), p. 266.

6. Paul Valéry, *Variety*, 1st series (New York: Harcourt, Brace, 1938), pp. 3–4.

See our interactive ebook for map and primary source activities.

CHAPTER OUTLINE

Kees van Dongen: Au cabaret nègre (detail)

(© Artist's Rights Society (ARS), New York. Au Cabaret Negre, 1925 (oil on canvas), Dongen, Kees van (1877–1968)/ Private Collection/© DACS/Photo © Christie's Images/The Bridgeman Art Library)

The Illusion of Stability, 1919–1930

In 1925, Josephine Baker (1906–1975), a black entertainer from St. Louis, moved from the chorus lines of New York to the music halls of Paris, where she quickly became a singing and dancing sensation. Also a favorite in Germany, she was the most famous of the African American entertainers who took the cultural capitals of Europe by storm during the 1920s. After the disillusioning experience of war, many Europeans found a valuable infusion of vitality in Baker's jazz music, exotic costumes, and "savage," uninhibited dancing (see the poster on page 741).

The European attraction to African Americans as primitive, vital, and sensual reflected a good deal of racial stereotyping, but there really *was* something fresh and uninhibited about American culture, especially its African American variant. And even as they played to those stereotypes, black performers like Baker had great fun ironically subverting them. Many realized they could enjoy opportunities in parts of Europe that were still denied them in the United States. Baker herself was a woman of great sophistication who became a French citizen in 1937, participated in progressive causes, and was decorated for her secret intelligence work in the anti-Nazi resistance during World War II.

The prominence of African Americans in European popular culture was part of a wider infatuation with things American as Europeans embraced the new during the 1920s. Lacking the cultural baggage of Europe, America seemed to offer revitalization and modernity at the same time. With so many old conventions shattered by the war, the ideal of being "modern" became widespread among Europeans, affecting everything from sex education to furniture design. "Modern" meant no-nonsense efficiency, mass production, and a vital popular culture, expressed in jazz, movies, sport, and even advertising. (See the feature, "The Visual Record: Advertising" on pages 742–743.)

But Europeans themselves had pioneered modernism in many areas of the arts and sciences, and innovation continued after the war. Paris held its own as an international cultural center, hosting a decorative arts exhibition in 1925 that produced art deco, the sleek, "modernistic" style that helped give the decade its distinctive flavor. And in the unsettled conditions of postwar Germany, Berlin emerged to rival Paris for cultural leadership during what Germans called "the Golden Twenties."

Still, there was something dizzying, even unnerving, about the eager embrace of the new during the 1920s. The war had accelerated the long-term modernization process toward large industries, cities, and bureaucracies, and toward mass politics, society, and culture. That process was positive, even liberating, in certain respects, but it was also disruptive and disturbing. Some Europeans viewed the vogue of black American entertainers as a symptom of decadence that would further undermine the best of European civilization.

FOCUS QUESTIONS

- How did the differing priorities of Britain and France affect international relations during the 1920s?

- In what ways did the advent of communism and fascism seem to expand the range of political possibilities after World War I?

- Why, and on what basis, did sexuality, gender roles, and the "new woman" provoke so much concern during the 1920s?

- What factors made the future of the new German democracy so uncertain during the 1920s?

- How did cultural and intellectual leaders differ over the place of "tradition" as they sought to suggest how to come to terms with the new situation of the 1920s?

This icon will direct you to additional materials on the website: www .cengage.com/history/ noble/westciv6e.

See our interactive eBook for map and primary source activities.

In this sense, the postwar sense of release and excitement combined with an anxious longing for stability, for a return to order. Even in embracing the new, many were seeking a new basis for order and security.

Although the immediate disruptions of wartime carried over to 1923, a more hopeful era of relative prosperity and international conciliation followed, continuing until 1929. But there was much that called into question the ideal of a "world safe for democracy" that had surrounded the end of the war. Revolutionary Russia remained an uncertain force, even as it began seeking to build socialism on its own. In Italy, the democracy that had emerged in the nineteenth century gave way to the first regime to call itself fascist, and some of the new democracies in east-central Europe did not survive the decade. The postwar efforts at economic restabilization, apparently successful for a while, masked growing strains in the international economy. In one sphere after another, postwar restabilization was fragile—and could quickly unravel.

THE WEST AND THE WORLD AFTER THE GREAT WAR

How did the differing priorities of Britain and France affect international relations during the 1920s?

The war and the peace had weakened—and to some extent discredited—the European powers, who now found themselves saddled with foreign debts and unbalanced economies. Though the United States pulled back from a direct political role in Europe in 1919, it became far more active in world affairs, helping to engineer major conferences on arms limitation and international economic relations during the 1920s. But in crucial respects, the shape of the postwar international order still depended on Europeans. And colonial concerns continued to affect the balance of power in Europe, where it fell to the two major victors in the war, France and Britain, to enforce the controversial peace settlement.

The Erosion of European Power

Emerging from the war as the principal power in East Asia was a non-Western country, Japan, whose claims to the German bases in the region and to special rights in China were formally recognized at the Paris Peace Conference. With the Washington treaty of 1922, Japan won naval parity with Britain and the United States in East Asia. The Western nations were recognizing Japan as a peer, a great power—even a threat. Aspects of the Washington agreements were intended to block Japanese expansion in East Asia. If a new international system was to emerge, it would not be centered in Europe to the extent the old one had been.

As the old Europe lost prestige, President Wilson's ideals of self-determination and democracy were greeted enthusiastically outside the West—in China, for example. At the same time, the Russian revolutionary model appealed to those in the colonial world seeking to understand the mainsprings of Western imperialism—and the means of overcoming it. To some Chinese intellectuals by the early 1920s, Leninism was attractive because it showed the scope for mass mobilization by a revolutionary vanguard.

By the 1920s, a generation of anticolonialist, nationalist intellectuals was emerging to lead the non-Western world. Some were more radical than others, but most agreed that the challenge was to learn from the West and to modernize, but without simply copying the West and losing distinctive cultural identities. It was imperative to sift through tradition, determining what needed to be changed and what was worth preserving. The pioneering Chinese nationalist Sun Yixien (Sun Yat-sen, 1866–1925) was typical in recognizing the need to adopt the science and technology of the West. But China, he insisted, could do so in its own way, without sacrificing its unique cultural and political traditions. (See the feature, "The Global Record: Sun Yixien on Chinese Nationalism.")

As the greatest imperial power, Britain was especially vulnerable to the growing anticolonial sentiment. The struggle to hang on to its empire drew British energies away from the problems of Europe after the peace settlement.

In light of the strong Indian support for the British war effort, the British government promised in 1917 to extend the scope for Indian involvement in the colonial administration in India. Growing expectations as the war was ending provoked episodes of violence against the British, whose troops retaliated brutally in April 1919, firing indiscriminately into an unarmed crowd. This Amritsar Massacre helped galvanize India's independence movement, even though the British, seeking conciliation in the aftermath, extended self-rule by entrusting certain government services to Indians. Another milestone was reached in 1921, when Mohandas Gandhi, the British-educated leader of the Indian independence movement, shed his European clothes in favor of simple Indian attire. But it was on the basis of Western egalitarianism, not some indigenous value, that Gandhi demanded political rights for the "untouchables," the lowest group in India's long-standing caste system. (See the feature, "The Global Record: Gandhi Advocates Nonviolence" on page 760 in Chapter 27.)

In Egypt, a full-scale anti-British insurrection broke out in 1919. After British troops suppressed the rebellion, British authorities offered to grant moderate concessions, as in India. But Egyptian nationalists demanded independence, which was finally granted in 1922. Egypt gradually evolved into a constitutional monarchy, with representative government and universal suffrage. But Britain retained a predominant influence in Egypt until the nationalist revolution of 1952 (see page 837–838).

At the same time, nationalism was growing among West Africans who had studied in England. In March 1919, Western-educated Africans in the Gold Coast asked the British governor to establish representative institutions so that Africans could at least be consulted about governmental affairs. The West African National Congress, formed in 1920, made similar demands. The British agreed to new constitutions for Nigeria in 1923 and the Gold Coast in 1925 that took significant steps in that direction. They also agreed to build more schools, though they tended to promote practical education, including African languages and agriculture, whereas African leaders wanted students to learn the Western classics that "made gentlemen." Such conflicting priorities indicate the complexities in the relationships between colonial rulers and the emerging elites among the colonized peoples.

CHRONOLOGY

March 1919	Founding of the Italian fascist movement
November 1920	Russian civil war ends
March 1921	New Economic Policy announced at Russian Communist Party congress
October 1922	Mussolini becomes Italian prime minister
January 1923	French-led occupation of the Ruhr
November 1923	Peak of inflation in Germany
January 1924	First Labour government in Britain
	Death of Lenin
August 1924	Acceptance of the Dawes Plan on German reparations
October 1925	Treaty of Locarno
May 1926	Pilsudski's coup d'état in Poland
	Beginning of general strike in Britain
May 1927	Lindbergh completes first transatlantic solo flight
January 1929	Stalin forces banishment of Trotsky from Soviet Union
April 1929	Soviets adopt first economic Five-Year Plan
August 1929	Acceptance of the Young Plan on German reparations
October 1929	Death of Stresemann

Enforcing the Versailles Settlement

It was up to France and Britain to make sure the new international order worked, but it was not clear that either had the will and resources to do so. Cooperation between them was essential, yet sometimes their differences—in geography, in values, and in perceptions—seemed to doom them to work at cross-purposes.

France was the dominant power on the European continent after World War I, and until well into the 1930s, it boasted the strongest army in the world. Yet even in the early 1920s, a sense of artificiality surrounded France's image of strength. Thus, the shrillness and the defensiveness that came to mark French thinking and French policy.

In light of Germany's larger population and stronger industrial base, France's long-term security seemed to require certain measures to tip the scales in its favor. By imposing German disarmament and the demilitarization of the Rhineland, the Versailles treaty gave France immediate military advantages. Yet how long could these measures be maintained, once the passions of war had died down and Germany no longer seemed such a threat? France had hoped for British help in enforcing the treaty, but Britain was pulling back from the Continent to concentrate on its empire, just as it had after other major European wars.

Reinforcing Imperialist Rule In response to episodes of anticolonialist violence in Amritsar, India, early in 1919, the British brutally cracked down, most notably in the massacre of April 1919. Here British authorities enforce a decree in the wake of the beating of a female British doctor on this road—forcing any Indian using the road to crawl along it. (Courtesy of the National Army Museum, London)

Maginot Line A 200-mile system of elaborate permanent fortifications on France's eastern border, named for war minister André Maginot and built primarily during the 1930s. It was a defense against German frontal assault; in 1940, the Germans invaded by flanking the line.

In particular, the British wanted to avoid getting dragged into the uncertain situation in east-central Europe, where its own national interests did not seem to be at stake. Yet the French, to replace their earlier link with Russia, promptly developed an alliance system with several of the new or expanded states of the region, including Poland, Czechoslovakia, Romania, and Yugoslavia. France's ties to east-central Europe made the British especially wary of binding agreements with the French.

At first, France felt confident enough to take strong steps even without British support. In response to German foot-dragging in paying reparations, Prime Minister Raymond Poincaré decided to get tough in January 1923. Declaring the Germans in default, he sent French troops at the head of an international force to occupy the Ruhr industrial area and force German compliance. But the move backfired. The Germans adopted a policy of passive resistance in response, and the costs of the occupation more than offset the increase in reparations that France received.

British leaders viewed French policy as unnecessarily vindictive and bellicose, and they increasingly saw the Versailles treaty as counterproductive. Instead, they placed great store in the League of Nations and in the international arms reduction effort gaining momentum by the later 1920s. From 1923 on, France gradually lost the advantages it had gained by defeating Germany, and self-confidence gave way to defensiveness and resignation.

The defensive mentality found physical embodiment in the **Maginot Line**, a system of fortifications on France's eastern border. Remembering the defensive warfare of World War I and determined to preclude the sort of invasion France had suffered in 1914, the military convinced

Sun Yixien on Chinese Nationalism

Sun Yixien (Sun Yat-sen), widely regarded as the father of modern China, founded the Guomindang (Kuomintang), the Chinese nationalist movement, in 1912. Educated by Western missionaries in China, he lived in the United States for extended periods and came to admire the West in important respects. But he insisted that China, to make the best use of what the West offered, had to reconnect with its own unique traditions. Variations on this argument would be heard for decades as the rest of the world sought to come to terms with the seemingly more advanced West. The following passages are from an influential series of lectures that Sun Yixien presented in China in the early 1920s.

What is the standing of our nation in the world? In comparison with other nations we have the greatest population and the oldest culture, of four thousand years' duration. We ought to be advancing in line with the nations of Europe and America. But the Chinese people have only family and clan groups; there is no national spirit. Consequently, in spite of four hundred million people gathered together in one China, we are in fact but a sheet of loose sand. We are the poorest and weakest state in the world, occupying the lowest position in international affairs; the rest of mankind is the carving knife and the serving dish, while we are the fish and the meat. Our position now is extremely perilous; if we do not earnestly promote nationalism and weld together our four hundred millions into a strong nation, we face a tragedy—the loss of our country and the destruction of our race. To ward off this danger, we must espouse nationalism and employ the national spirit to save the country....

But even if we succeed in reviving our ancient morality, learning, and powers, we will still not be able, in this modern world, to advance China to a first place among the nations.... [W]e will still need to learn the strong points of Europe and America before we can progress at an equal rate with them. Unless we do study the best from foreign countries, we will go backward. With our own fine foundation of knowledge and our age-long culture, with our own native intelligence besides, we should be able to acquire all the best things from abroad. The strongest point of the West is its science....

As soon as we learn Western machinery we can use it anytime, anywhere; electric lights, for example, can be installed and used in any kind of Chinese house. But Western social customs and sentiments are different from ours in innumerable points; if, without regard to customs and popular feelings in China, we try to apply Western methods of social control as we would Western machinery—in a hard and fast way—we shall be making a serious mistake....

...For the governmental machinery of the United States and France still has many defects, and does not satisfy the desires of the people nor give them a complete measure of happiness. So we in our proposed reconstruction must not think that if we imitate the West of today we shall reach the last stage of progress and be perfectly contented....

Only in recent times has Western culture advanced beyond ours, and the passion for this new civilization has stimulated our revolution. Now that the revolution is a reality, we naturally desire to see China excel the West and build up the newest and most progressive state in the world. We certainly possess the qualifications necessary to reach this ideal, but we must not merely imitate the democratic systems of the West.

QUESTIONS

1. Why does Sun Yixien think China, despite its ancient and sophisticated culture, has fallen behind the West?

2. On what grounds does Sun Yixien consider it necessary for China to study Western culture, as opposed to relying on its own traditions?

Source: Sun Yixien on Chinese Nationalism from Sun Yat-sen, *San Min Chu I: The Three Principles of the People* (Taipei, Taiwan: China Cultural Service, 1953).

French political leaders to adopt a defensive strategy based on a line of forts. Construction began in 1929, and the Maginot (MAH-zhih-noh) system reached preliminary completion in 1935, when it extended along France's border with Germany from Switzerland to the border with Belgium.

This defensive system was not consistent with the other major strands of French policy, especially its alliances with states in east-central Europe. If France emphasized defense behind an impregnable system of forts, what good were French security guarantees to such new allies as Poland and Czechoslovakia?

Still, the situation remained fluid during the 1920s. In France, as in Britain, national elections in 1924 produced a victory for the moderate left, ending a period of conservative nationalist dominance since the war. In each country, international relations became a major issue in the elections, and the outcome heralded a more conciliatory tack, especially in relations with Germany.

SECTION SUMMARY

- Although the prewar European colonial system remained largely in place after the war, Wilsonian ideals of self-determination spurred anticolonial sentiment in the colonized world.

- On the basis of their study in the West, intellectuals from Europe's colonies sought to combine Western values with indigenous traditions as they began spearheading the anticolonial struggle.

- More vulnerable geographically, France was initially more determined than Britain to keep Germany limited by strictly enforcing the Versailles settlement.

- France's confident, even aggressive, posture gradually gave way to the defensiveness of the "Maginot mentality," evident in the decision to build a series of defensive fortifications.

COMMUNISM, FASCISM, AND THE NEW POLITICAL SPECTRUM

In what ways did the advent of communism and fascism seem to expand the range of political possibilities after World War I?

In making their revolution in 1917, the Russian Bolsheviks had expected to spark wider revolution. Hopes—and fears—that the revolution would spread were palpable in the immediate postwar period. Although the Russian Communists initially enjoyed extraordinary prestige on the European left, some Marxists grew skeptical or hostile as the nature of Leninist communism became clearer. The Russian model eventually produced a damaging split in international socialism. By the end of the 1920s, revolution elsewhere was nowhere in sight, and it seemed that, for the foreseeable future, the communist regime in Russia would have to go it alone.

By then, a new and unexpected political movement had emerged in Italy, expanding the political spectrum in a different direction. This was the first **fascism**, which brought Benito Mussolini to power in 1922. Emerging directly from the war, Italian fascism was violent and antidemocratic—and thus disturbing to many. Stressing national solidarity and discipline, the fascists were hostile not only to liberal individualism and the parliamentary system, but also to Marxist socialism, with its emphasis on class struggle and the special role of the working class. Claiming to offer a modern alternative to both, Italian fascism quickly attracted the attention of those in other countries who were disillusioned with parliamentary politics and hostile to the Marxist left. The interplay of communism and fascism, as new political experiments, added to the uncertainties of the postwar world.

fascism A violent, antidemocratic movement founded by Benito Mussolini in Italy in 1919. The term is widely used to encompass Hitler's Nazi regime in Germany and other movements stressing disciplined national solidarity and hostile to liberal individualism, the parliamentary system, and Marxist socialism.

Changing Priorities in Communist Russia, 1918–1921

Even after leading the revolution that toppled the provisional government in November 1917, the Bolsheviks could not claim majority support in Russia. When the long-delayed elections to select a constituent assembly were held a few weeks after the revolution, the Socialist Revolutionaries won a clear majority, while the Bolsheviks ended up with fewer than one-quarter of the seats. But the Bolsheviks dispersed the assembly by force when it met in January 1918. And over the next three years, the Communists, as the Bolsheviks renamed themselves, gradually consolidated their power, establishing a centralized and nondemocratic regime. Power lay not with the soviets, nor with some coalition of socialist parties, but solely with the Communist Party.

CIVIL WAR   During its first years, the new communist regime encountered a genuine emergency that especially seemed to require such a monopoly of power. During 1918 to 1920, in what became a brutal civil war, the communist "Reds" battled counterrevolutionary "Whites," people who had been dispossessed by the revolution or who had grown disillusioned with the Communist Party. Moreover, foreigners eager to topple the communist regime began to intervene militarily. At the same time, several of the non-Russian nationalities of the old Russian Empire sought to take advantage of the unsettled situation to free themselves from Russian and communist control. Appointed "People's Commissar for War" in April 1918, Leon Trotsky forged a loyal and disciplined Red Army in an effort to master the difficult situation.

A series of thrusts, involving troops from fourteen countries, at one time or another, struck at Russia from a variety of points along its huge border. However, the Whites and the foreign troops never managed a coordinated strategy. By the end of active fighting in November 1920, the communist regime had not only survived but regained most of the territory it had lost early in the civil war (see **Map 26.1**).

The need to launch the new communist regime in this way, fighting counterrevolutionaries supported by foreign troops, inevitably affected Communists' perceptions and priorities. Separatist sentiment might continue to feed counterrevolutionary efforts, so the new regime exerted careful control over the non-Russian nationalities. Thus, when the Union of Soviet Socialist Republics (USSR) was organized in December 1922, it was only nominally a federation of autonomous republics; strong centralization from the communist regime's new capital in Moscow was the rule from the start.

Legend:

- Boundaries of Russian Empire 1914
- Area controlled by the Bolsheviks, August 1918
- Treaty of Brest-Litovsk
- → White Russian forces
- → Non-Russian anti-Bolshevik forces
- Territory lost to Russia, 1914–1921
- Soviet territory, 1922
- Boundaries, 1922

0   200   400 Km.
0   200   400 Mi.

Map labels:

Barents Sea

British, French, Canadians, Italians, Serbs — Murmansk

Canadians, Americans — Archangel

NORWAY

FINLAND (Independent 1917)

SWEDEN

Helsinki, Kronstadt, Finns

British, Petrograd (St. Petersburg)

ESTONIA, Yudenich 1918–20, Pskok

LATVIA, Riga, Latvians

LITHUANIA, Lithuanians

Danzig, GERMANY E. PRUSSIA

GERMANY

Minsk, Poles, Mogilev, Smolensk

BOLSHEVIK RUSSIA

Moscow, Kaluga, Orel

Vistula R., Warsaw, Poles, Gomel

POLAND, Brest-Litovsk, Poles

Zhitomir, Kiev, Denikin 1919, Poltava, Kharkov

CZECHOSLOVAKIA

Dniester R., UKRAINE, Dnieper R., Yekaterinoslav

HUNGARY

Romanians, BESSARABIA

ROMANIA

YUGOSLAVIA, Danube R.

Odessa, French, Simferopol

Voronezh, Don R.

Tsaritsyn (Stalingrad)

Rostov-on-Don, Novocherkassak

Penza, Tambov, Saratov

Nizhniy Novgorod, Volga R., Kazan

Kolchak 1918–19, Samara, Orenburg, Ural R.

Perm, Czechs

Cossacks 1918–20

Volga R., Astrakhan

Caspian Sea

ALBANIA, BULGARIA

Black Sea, British

Cossacks, Novorossiysk

Batum, British, Tiflis

Kars, GEORGIA

Baku, Krasnovodsk

GREECE, TURKEY

British, British

SYRIA, Tabriz, PERSIA

MAP 26.1—Foreign Intervention and Civil War in Revolutionary Russia, 1918–1920

By mid-1918, the new communist regime was under attack from many sides, by both foreign troops and anticommunist Russians. Bolshevik-held territory shrank during 1919, but over the next year, the Red Army managed to regain much of what had been lost and to secure the new communist state. Anton Denikin, Alexander Kolchak, and Nicholas Yudenich commanded the most significant counterrevolutionary forces.

(Source: Adapted from *The Times Atlas of World History*, 3d ed. Reprinted by permission of HarperCollins Publishers Ltd. © HarperCollins Publishers Ltd.)

Comintern An association founded in March 1919 by the Communists (formerly Bolsheviks) to translate their success in Russia into leadership of the international socialist movement.

In March 1919, while fighting the civil war, the Russian Communists founded the Third, or Communist, International—widely known as the **Comintern**—to make clear their break with the seemingly discredited strategies of the Second International. Through the Comintern, the Russian Communists expected to translate their success in Russia into leadership of the international socialist movement. However, many old-line Marxists refused to admit that the leadership of European socialism had passed to the Communist rulers of backward Russia. As early as 1919, the German Karl Kautsky (1854–1938), who had been the leading spokesman for orthodox Marxism after the death of Friedrich Engels in 1895, harshly criticized Leninist communism as a heretical departure that would lead to despotism and severely damage international socialism.

From its founding in March 1919 until the spring of 1920, the Comintern actively promoted the wider revolution that Lenin had envisioned. Seeking to win mass support, the organization accented leftist solidarity and reached out to the rank and file in the labor unions. By the spring of 1920, however, it seemed clear that further revolution was not imminent, so Comintern leaders began focusing on a more protracted revolutionary struggle.

The Russians felt that poor organization and planning had undermined the wider revolutionary possibility in Europe during 1919 and 1920. The Comintern would cut through all the revolutionary romanticism to show what the Leninist strategy, or communism, meant in fact. The Russians themselves would have to call the shots because what communism meant, above all, was tight organization and discipline.

By early 1921, the Comintern's aggressive claim to leadership had split the international socialist movement, for the Comintern attracted some, but not all, of the members of the existing socialist parties. Those who now called themselves "communists" accepted the Leninist model and affiliated with the Comintern. Those who retained the "socialist" label rejected Comintern leadership; they still claimed to be Marxists but declined to embrace the Bolshevik strategy for taking power.

Late in 1923, the Comintern finally concluded that revolution elsewhere could not be expected any time soon. The immediate enemy was not capitalism or the bourgeoisie, but the socialists, the Communists' rivals for working-class support. The Communists' incessant criticism of the socialists, whom they eventually dubbed "social fascists," demoralized and weakened the European left, especially in the face of the growing threat of fascism by the early 1930s. The schism on the left remained an essential fact of European political life for half a century.

From Lenin to Stalin, 1921–1929

To win the civil war, the communist regime had adopted a policy of "war communism," a rough-and-ready controlled economy in which food and supplies were commandeered for the Red Army. At the beginning of 1921, the economy was in crisis. Industrial production equaled only about one-fifth the 1913 total, workers in key factories went on strike, and peasants were resisting further requisitions of grain. In March 1921, sailors at the Kronstadt naval base near Petrograd mutinied, suffering considerable loss of life as governmental control was reestablished.

New Economic Policy (NEP) A Russian economic liberalization measure aimed at reviving an economy in crisis. The NEP restored considerable scope for private enterprise and allowed peasants to sell some of their harvest.

With the very survival of the revolution in question, Lenin replaced war communism with the **New Economic Policy (NEP)** in March 1921. Although transport, banking, heavy industry, and wholesale commerce remained under state control, the NEP restored considerable scope for private enterprise, especially in agriculture and the retail sector. The economy quickly began to revive, and by 1927, was producing at prewar levels.

But what about the longer term? If revolution elsewhere was not on the immediate horizon, could the Soviet Union—relatively backward economically and scarred by over a decade of upheaval—build a socialist order on its own? Certain measures were obvious: The new regime engineered rapid improvements in literacy, for example. But the Marxist understanding of historical progress required industrialization, and so debate focused on how to promote industrial development under Soviet conditions.

Debate about priorities became intertwined with questions about the leadership of the new regime. Lenin suffered the first of a series of strokes in May 1922 and then died in January 1924, setting off a struggle among his possible successors. Leon Trotsky, an effective organizer and powerful thinker, was by most measures Lenin's heir apparent. Although he favored tighter economic controls to speed industrial development, Trotsky insisted that the top priority should be spreading the revolution to other countries.

Rivals for the Soviet Leadership In July 1926 in Moscow, Soviet leaders carry the coffin of Feliks Dzerzhinsky, the first head of the secret police. Among them are Trotsky *(with glasses, center left)*, Stalin *(right foreground)*, and Bukharin *(with mustache, at far right)*, rivals for the Soviet leadership after Lenin's death. The winner, Stalin, would eventually have his two competitors killed. (David King Collection)

In contrast, Nikolai Bukharin (1888–1938) wanted to concentrate on the gradual development of the Soviet Union, based on a more open and conciliatory strategy. Rather than tightening controls to squeeze a surplus from agricultural producers, the government should promote purchasing power by allowing producers to profit. By the time of his death, Lenin had apparently begun thinking along the same lines. And he had come to have considerable misgivings about the man who would win this struggle to direct the fragile new Soviet regime, **Joseph Stalin** (1879–1953).

Joseph Stalin Soviet dictator who jettisoned the New Economic Policy and instituted a program of crash industrialization and agricultural collectivization. He concluded the Nazi-Soviet Pact in 1939 but joined the Allies after the German invasion of the Soviet Union in 1941.

Stalin was born Josef Djugashvili into a lower-class family in Georgia, in the Caucasus region. As an ethnic Georgian, he did not learn to speak Russian until he was 11 years old. From the position of party secretary, which he had assumed in 1922, Stalin established his control within the Soviet system by 1929. Though he lacked Trotsky's charisma and knew little of economics, he was highly intelligent and proved a master of backstage political maneuvering. Stalin first outmaneuvered Trotsky and his allies, removing them from positions of power and forcing Trotsky himself into exile in 1929. Bitterly critical of Stalin to the end, Trotsky was finally murdered by Stalin's agents in Mexico in 1940. Stalin's victory over those like Bukharin was more gradual, but ultimately just as complete. And his victory proved decisive for the fate of Soviet communism.

By the later 1920s, those who believed in the communist experiment were growing disillusioned with the compromises of the NEP. It was time for the Soviet Union to push ahead to a new order, leaving capitalism behind altogether. Even if revolution was not imminent elsewhere, the Soviet Union could show the way by building "socialism in one country." Genuine enthusiasm greeted the regime's turn to centralized economic planning in 1927 and its subsequent adoption of the first Five-Year Plan early in 1929. Central planning led to a program of crash industrialization, favoring heavy industry, by the end of that year. But this new, more radical direction was not fully thought through, and it soon caused incredible suffering.

To buy the necessary plant and equipment, the state seemed to require better control of agricultural output than had been possible under the NEP. The key was to squeeze the agricultural surplus from the peasantry on terms more favorable to the government. By forcing peasants into large, state-controlled collective farms, government leaders could more readily extract the surplus, which would then be sold abroad, earning the money to finance factories, dams, and power plants.

During the 1920s, the possibility of building a new socialist society in the Soviet Union had attracted a number of modernist artists, who assumed that artistic innovation went hand in hand with radical socioeconomic transformation. But in 1929, Soviet officials began mobilizing the

Tatlin: Monument to the Third International Vladimir Tatlin created this model for a monument to the Third International, or Comintern, during 1919 and 1920. He envisioned a revolving structure of glass and iron; it would be twice as tall as the later Empire State Building. Although the monument was never built, Tatlin's bold, dynamic form symbolizes the utopian aspirations of the early years of the communist experiment in Russia. (David King Collection)

cultural realm to serve the grandiose task of building socialism in one country. No longer welcoming modernist experiment, they demanded "socialist realism," which portrayed the achievements of the ongoing Soviet revolution in an inspiring, heroic light. Modernism, in contrast, they denounced as decadent and counterrevolutionary.

In retrospect, it is clear that a Stalinist revolution within the Soviet regime had begun by 1930, but where it was to lead was by no means certain—not even to Stalin himself. Still, the Soviet Union was pulling back, going its own way by the end of the 1920s. For the foreseeable future, the presence of a revolutionary regime in the old Russia would apparently be less disruptive for the rest of Europe than it had first appeared.

The Crisis of Liberal Italy and the Creation of Fascism, 1919–1925

Fascism emerged directly from the Italian experience of World War I, which proved especially controversial because the Italians could have avoided it altogether. No one attacked Italy in 1914, and the country could have received significant territorial benefits just by remaining neutral. Yet it seemed to many, including leading intellectuals and educated young people, that Italy could not stand idly by in a European war, especially one involving Austria-Hungary, which still controlled significant Italian-speaking areas. Participation in this major war would be the test of Italy's maturity as a nation. In May 1915, Italy finally intervened on the side of the Triple Entente. The government's decision stemmed not from vague visions of renewal, but from the commitment of tangible territorial gains that France and Britain made to Italy with the secret Treaty of London.

Despite the near collapse of the Italian armies late in 1917, Italy lasted out the war and contributed to the victory over Austria-Hungary. Supporters of the war felt that this success could lead to a thoroughgoing renewal of Italian public life. Yet many Italians had been skeptical of claims for the war from the outset, and the fact that it proved so much more difficult than expected hardly won them over. To socialists, Catholics, and many left-leaning liberals, intervention itself had been a tragic mistake. Thus, despite Italy's participation in the victory, division over the war's significance immensely complicated the postwar Italian political situation.

Skepticism was only confirmed when Italy did not secure all the gains it sought at the Paris Peace Conference. To be sure, the country got most of what it had been promised in the Treaty of London, but appetites increased with the dissolution of the Austro-Hungarian Empire. Many Italians were outraged at what seemed a denigration of the Italian contribution by France, Britain, and the United States. The outcome fanned resentment not only of Italy's allies, but also of the country's political leaders, who seemed too weak to deliver on what they had pledged.

The leaders of Italy's parliamentary democracy also failed to renew the country's political system in light of the war experience. To be sure, in a spirit of democratic reform, Italy adopted proportional representation to replace the old system of small, single-member constituencies in 1919. The new system meant a greater premium on mass parties and party discipline at the expense of the one-to-one bargaining that had characterized the earlier *trasformismo*. But the new multiparty system quickly reached an impasse—partly because of the stance of the Italian Socialist Party.

ITALIAN SOCIALISM In contrast to the French and German parties, the Italian Socialists had never supported the war, and they did not accept the notion that the war experience could yield political renewal in the aftermath. So rather than reaching out to idealistic but discontented war veterans, Socialist leaders talked of imitating the Bolshevik Revolution. And the Italian situation seemed at least potentially revolutionary during 1919 and 1920, when a wave of strikes culminated in a series of factory occupations. But despite their revolutionary rhetoric, Italy's Socialist leaders did not understand the practical aspects of Leninism and did not carry out the planning and organization that might have produced an Italian revolution.

The established parliamentary system was at an impasse, and the Socialist Party seemed at once too inflexible and too romantic to lead some sort of radical transformation. It was in this context that fascism emerged, claiming to offer a third way. It was bound to oppose the Socialists and the socialist working class because of conflict over the meaning of the war and the kind of transformation Italy needed. And this antisocialist posture made fascism open to exploitation by reactionary interests. By early 1921, landowners in northern and central Italy were footing the bill as bands of young fascists drove around the countryside in trucks, beating up workers and burning down socialist meeting halls. But fascist spokesmen claimed to offer something other than mere reaction—a new politics that all Italians, including the workers, would eventually find superior.

At the same time, important sectors of Italian industry, which had grown rapidly thanks to wartime government orders, looked with apprehension toward the more competitive international economy that loomed after the war. With its relative lack of capital and raw materials, Italy seemed to face an especially difficult situation. Nationalist thinkers and business spokesmen questioned the capacity of the parliamentary system to provide the vigorous leadership that Italy needed. Prone to short-term bickering and partisanship, ordinary politicians seemed to lack the vision to pursue Italy's international economic interests and the will to impose the necessary discipline on the domestic level. Thus, the government's response to the labor unrest of 1919 and 1920 was hesitant and weak.

Postwar Italy, then, witnessed widespread discontent with established forms of politics, but those discontented were socially disparate, and their aims were not entirely compatible. Some had been socialists before the war, others nationalists hostile to socialism. While some envisioned a more intense kind of mass politics, others thought the masses already had too much power. Still, these discontented groups agreed on the need for an alternative to both parliamentary politics and Marxist socialism. And all found the germs of that alternative in the Italian war experience.

Benito Mussolini The founder of fascism is shown with other fascist leaders in 1922, as he becomes prime minister of Italy. Standing at Mussolini's left (*with beard*) is Italo Balbo, later a pioneering aviator and fascist Italy's air force minister. (Bettmann/Corbis)

THE RISE OF MUSSOLINI

Benito Mussolini
Founder of the fascist movement and subsequently dictator within the Italian fascist regime.

The person who seemed able to translate these aspirations into a new political force was **Benito Mussolini** (1883–1945), who had been a prominent socialist journalist before the war. Indeed, he was so talented that he was made editor of the Socialist Party's national newspaper in 1912, when he was only 29 years old. At that point, many saw him as the fresh face needed to revitalize Italian socialism.

His concern with renewal made Mussolini an unorthodox socialist even before 1914, and he was prominent among those on the Italian left who began calling for Italian intervention after the war began. The Italian Socialist Party refused to follow his lead, but through his new newspaper, *Il popolo d'Italia (The People of Italy)*, Mussolini helped rally the disparate groups that advocated Italian participation in the war. He saw military service once Italy intervened, and after the war he seemed a credible spokesman for those who wanted to translate the war experience into a new form of politics. Amid growing political unrest, he founded the fascist movement in March 1919, taking the term *fascism* from the ancient Roman *fasces*, a bundle of rods surrounding an ax carried on state occasions as a symbol of power and unity.

But fascism found little success at first. Even as it gathered force in violent reaction against the socialist labor organizations by 1921, the movement's direction was uncertain. Although young fascist militants wanted to replace the established parliamentary system with a new political order, Mussolini seemed to be using fascism as his personal instrument to achieve power within the existing system. When his maneuvering finally won him the prime minister's post in October 1922, it was not at all clear that a change of regime, or a one-party dictatorship, would follow.

A crisis in 1924 forced Mussolini's hand. In June, the moderate socialist Giacomo Matteotti (mah-tay-OH-tee) rose in parliament to denounce the renewed fascist violence that had accompanied recent national elections. His murder by fascist thugs shortly thereafter produced a great public outcry, though the responsibility of Mussolini and his government was unclear. Many establishment figures who had tolerated Mussolini as the man who could keep order now deserted him as a result of the **Matteotti murder**.

Matteotti murder The 1924 killing by fascist thugs of Italian moderate socialist Giacomo Matteotti; the public outcry following the murder eventually led Mussolini to commit to a more radical direction, which included the creation of a new, fascist form of state.

Mussolini sought at first to be conciliatory, but more radical fascists saw the crisis as an opportunity to end the compromise with the old liberal order and to begin creating a whole new political system. The crisis came to a head on December 31, 1924, when thirty-three militants called on Mussolini to insist that the way out of the crisis was not to delimit the scope of fascism, but to expand it. Mussolini was not an ordinary prime minister, but *Il Duce* (eel DOO-chay), spearheading an ongoing fascist revolution.

A few days later, on January 3, 1925, Mussolini committed himself to this more radical course in a speech to the Chamber of Deputies. Defiantly claiming responsibility for all that had happened, including all the violence, he promised to accelerate the transformation that had begun, he claimed, with his agitation for intervention in 1914.[1] And now began the creation of a new fascist state, although the compromises continued and the direction was never as clear as committed fascists desired.

Innovation and Compromise in Fascist Italy, 1925–1930

Early in 1925, the fascist government began to undermine the existing democratic system by imprisoning or exiling opposition leaders and outlawing nonfascist parties and labor unions. But fascism was not seeking simply a monopoly of political power; the new fascist state was to be totalitarian, all-encompassing, limitless in its reach. Under the liberal system, the fascists charged, the state had been too weak to promote the national interest, and Italian society had been too fragmented to achieve its potential. So Mussolini's regime both expanded the state's sovereignty and mobilized society to create a deeper sense of national identity and shared purpose. New organizations—for youth, for women, for leisure-time activities—were to make possible new forms of public participation.

corporativism, corporative state The system established in fascist Italy beginning in 1926 that sought to involve people in public life not as citizens, but as producers, through their roles in the economy.

The centerpiece of the new fascist state was **corporativism**, which entailed mobilizing people as producers, through organization of the workplace. Groupings based on occupation, or economic function, were gradually to replace parliament as the basis for political participation and decision making. Beginning in 1926, corporativist institutions were established in stages until a Chamber of Fasces and Corporations at last replaced the old Chamber of Deputies in 1939.

Especially through this **corporative state**, the fascists claimed to be fulfilling their grandiose mission and providing the world with a third way, beyond both outmoded democracy and misguided communism. The practice of corporativism never lived up to such rhetoric, but the effort to devise new forms of political participation and decision making was central to fascism's self-understanding and its quest for legitimacy. And that effort attracted much attention abroad, especially with the Great Depression of the 1930s.

Despite the commitment to a new regime, however, fascism continued to compromise with preexisting elites and institutions. The accommodation was especially evident in the arrangements with the Catholic Church that Mussolini worked out in 1929, formally ending the dispute between the church and the Italian state that had festered since national unification in 1870. With the Lateran Pact, Mussolini restored a measure of sovereignty to the Vatican; with the Concordat, he gave the church significant roles in public education and marriage law.

This settlement of an old and thorny dispute afforded Mussolini a good deal of prestige among nonfascists at home and abroad. But compromise with the church displeased many committed fascists, who complained that giving this powerful, autonomous institution a role in Italian public life compromised fascism's totalitarian ideal. Such complaints led to a partial crackdown on Catholic youth organizations in 1931, as Mussolini continued trying to juggle traditionalist compromise and revolutionary pretension.

By the end of the 1920s, then, it remained unclear whether Italian fascism was a form of restoration or a form of revolution. It had restored order in Italy, overcoming the labor unrest of the immediate postwar years, but it was order on a new, antidemocratic basis. Yet the fascists still claimed to be implementing a revolution of their own. Fascism could be violent and disruptive, dictatorial and repressive, but Mussolini's regime seemed dynamic and innovative. Though its ultimate direction remained nebulous, fascism attracted those elsewhere who were discontented with liberal democracy and Marxist socialism. It thus fed the volatility and ideological polarization that marked the European political order after World War I.

SECTION SUMMARY

- The question of whether to affiliate with the new Communist International (Comintern), established by the Russian Communists in 1919, split Marxist socialist parties throughout the world.

- The struggle for the Soviet leadership with the death of Lenin became intertwined with questions about communist priorities in the wake of the New Economic Policy adopted in 1921.

- A Stalinist revolution within the Soviet communist experiment had begun by 1930, but where it would lead was not clear.

- The fascist reaction against both liberalism and socialism reflected deep divisions in Italy over the significance of the Italian war effort.

- Once Mussolini committed himself to a decisively postliberal direction, the fascists fastened upon corporativism as the basis for a new, specifically fascist form of state.

TOWARD MASS SOCIETY

Why, and on what basis, did sexuality, gender roles, and the "new woman" provoke so much concern during the 1920s?

After a few years of wild economic swings just after the war, Europe enjoyed renewed prosperity by the later 1920s. Common involvement in the war had blurred class lines and accelerated the trend toward what contemporaries began to call "mass society." As the new prosperity spread the fruits of industrialization more widely, ordinary people increasingly set the cultural tone, partly through new mass media, such as film and radio. To some, the advent of mass society portended a welcome revitalization of culture and a more authentic kind of democracy, whereas others saw only a debasement of cultural standards and a susceptibility to populist demagoguery.

Economic Readjustment and the New Prosperity

In their effort to return to normal, governments were quick to dismantle wartime planning and control mechanisms. But the needs of war had stimulated innovations that helped fuel the renewed economic growth of the 1920s. The civilian air industry, for example, developed rapidly during the decade by taking advantage of wartime work on aviation for military purposes. More generally, newer industries, such as chemicals, electricity, and advanced machinery, significantly altered patterns of life in the more industrialized parts of the West.

The automobile, a luxury plaything for the wealthy before the war, began to be mass produced in western Europe. In France, automobile production shot up dramatically, from 40,000 in 1920 to 254,000 in 1929.

But the heady pace masked problems that lay beneath the relative prosperity of the 1920s, even in victorious Britain and France. While new industries prospered, old ones declined in the face of new technologies and stronger foreign competition. The sectors responsible for Britain's earlier industrial preeminence—textiles, coal, shipbuilding, and iron and steel—now had trouble competing. Rather than investing in new technologies, companies in these industries demanded government protection and imposed lower wages and longer hours on their workers. At the same time, British labor unions resisted the mechanization necessary to make these older industries more competitive.

Whereas such structural decline in industry was clearest in Britain, inflation and its psychological impact were most prominent in Germany and France. By the summer of 1923, Germany's response to the French occupation of the Ruhr had transformed an already serious inflationary problem, stemming from wartime deficit spending, into one of the great hyperinflations in history. At its height in November, when it took 4.2 trillion marks to equal a dollar, Germans had to cart wheelbarrows of paper money to stores to buy ordinary grocery items. By the end of 1923, the government managed to stabilize prices through currency reform and drastically reduced government spending—a combination that won greater cooperation from the victors. But the rampant inflation, and the readjustment necessary to control it, had wiped out the savings of ordinary people while profiting speculators and those in debt, including some large industrialists. This inequity left scars that remained even as Germany enjoyed a measure of prosperity in the years that followed.

Inflation was less dramatic in France, but there, too, it deeply affected perceptions and priorities. For over a century, from the Napoleonic era to the outbreak of war in 1914, the value of the French franc had remained stable. But the war started France on an inflationary cycle that shattered the security of its many small savers—those, such as teachers and shopkeepers, who had been the backbone of the Third Republic. To repay war debts and rebuild war-damaged industries, the French government continued to run budget deficits, and thereby cause inflation, even after 1918. The franc was finally restabilized in 1928, though at only about one-fifth its prewar value.

On the international level, war debts and reparations strained the financial system, creating problems with the financing of trade. Still, during the course of the 1920s, experts made adjustments that seemed to be returning the international exchange system to equilibrium. Only in retrospect, after the international capitalist system fell into crisis late in 1929, did it become clear how potent those strains were—and how inadequate the efforts at readjustment.

Work, Leisure, and the New Popular Culture

The wartime spur to industrialization produced a large increase in the industrial labor force all over Europe, and a good deal of labor unrest accompanied the transition to peacetime. Some of that agitation challenged factory discipline and authority relationships. Seeking to reestablish authority on a new basis for the competitive postwar world, business advocates fostered a new cult of efficiency and productivity, partly by adapting Taylorism and Fordism, influential American ideas about mass production. On the basis of his "time-and-motion" studies of factory labor, Frederick W. Taylor (1856–1915) argued that breaking down assembly-line production into small, repetitive tasks was the key to maximizing worker efficiency. In contrast, Henry Ford (1863–1947) linked the gospel of mass production to mass consumption. In exchange for accepting the discipline of the assembly line, the workers should be paid enough to buy the products they produced—even automobiles. Sharing in the prosperity that mass production made possible, factory workers would be loyal to the companies that employed them. Not all Europeans, however, welcomed the new ideas from America. In the new cult of efficiency and mass production, some saw an unwelcome sameness and a lowering of cultural standards.

CHANGING ROLES FOR WOMEN In light of the major role women had played in the wartime labor force, the demand for women's suffrage proved irresistible in Britain, Germany, and much of Europe, though not yet in France

The Sensational Josephine Baker   After moving from the United States to Paris in 1925, Baker quickly created a sensation as a cabaret dancer and singer. Her exotic costumes played on the European association of Africa with the wild and uninhibited. This poster advertises her appearance at the Folies-Bergère, a famed Parisian music hall. (The Granger Collection, NY)

or Italy. In Britain, where calls for women's suffrage had earlier met with controversy (see page 683), the right to vote was readily conceded in 1918, though at first only to women over 30. By now, women no longer seemed a threat to the political system. And in fact, British women, once they could vote, simply flowed into the existing parties, countering earlier hopes—and fears—that a specifically feminist political agenda would follow from women's suffrage.

Although there was much discussion of the "new woman," especially in Germany, the wider place of women in society was uncertain during the 1920s, as the new sense of openness clashed with the desire to return to normal. (See the feature, "The Visual Record: Advertising.") Female employment remained higher than before the war, but many women—willingly or not—returned home, yielding their jobs to the returning soldiers. The need to replace the men killed in the war lent renewed force to the traditional notion that women served society, and fulfilled themselves, by marrying and rearing families. More generally, some men found the emancipated "new woman" threatening, and after all the disruptions of war, male leaders sometimes assumed that the very stability of the political sphere depended on conventional gender roles. Still, the decade's innovative impulse brought into the public arena subjects—largely taboo before the war—that might portend changes in gender roles later on. The desire to be "modern" produced, for example, a more open, unsentimental, even scientific discussion of sexuality and reproduction.

The new "rationalization of sexuality" fed demands that governments provide access to sex counseling, birth control, and even abortion as they assumed ever greater responsibilities for promoting social health. This trend was especially prominent in Germany, although German innovators learned from experiments in the new Soviet Union and from the birth control movement that Margaret Sanger (1883–1966) was spearheading in the United States.

The more open and tolerant attitude toward sexuality affected popular entertainment—for example, Josephine Baker's dancing and costumes, which would have been unthinkable before the war. Another result was the emergence of a more visible gay subculture, prominent especially in the vibrant cabaret scene in Berlin during the 1920s.

PROSPERITY AND THE CULTURE OF LEISURE

Mass consumption followed from the mass production bound up with the new prosperity of the 1920s. As it became possible to mass-produce the products of the second industrial transformation, more people could afford automobiles; electrical gadgets, such as radios and phonographs; and clothing of synthetic fabrics, developed through innovations in chemistry.

With the eight-hour workday increasingly the norm, growing attention was devoted to leisure as a positive source of human fulfillment—for everyone, not just the wealthy. European beach resorts grew crowded as more people had the time, and the means, to take vacations. An explosion of interest in soccer among Europeans paralleled the expansion of professional baseball and college football in the United States. Huge stadiums were built across Europe.

The growth of leisure was linked to the development of mass media and mass culture. During the early 1920s, radio became a commercial venture, reaching a mass audience in Europe, as in the United States and Canada. Although movies had begun to emerge as vehicles of popular entertainment even before the war, they came into their own during the 1920s, when the names of film stars became household words for the first time.

Advertising

A sleek new automobile. A stylish "new woman" who'd adore a Christmas gift of jewelry. These images from the 1920s catch our eye even today, but why? The designs look "modern" somehow, and they convey particular messages about efficiency and the good life. What do such advertisements tell us about the changes at work in Western culture after World War I?

Advertising, in one form or another, is as old as civilization itself. But the advent of printing expanded possibilities, and the second industrial revolution led to a big boost in advertising by the 1890s, as ads for new products like bicycles and sewing machines appeared in newspapers and magazines. But it was during the 1920s that modern advertising came into its own. As mass consumption grew, advertising budgets expanded dramatically, and professional ad agencies emerged to study tastes and determine how to shape the desires of consumers. Moreover, the advent of commercial radio in 1920 opened a whole new set of possibilities, including the scope for musical jingles.

Mass consumption required advertising to show people what to want. And during the 1920s, ad agencies began offering images of the good life, seeking to define the popular sense of what it meant to be "modern." They often drew from the United States, which stood for efficiency and a fast-paced life of fun, pleasure, and consumerist abundance. So eager were the Germans to follow the U.S. lead in advertising that they adopted the term *sex appeal*, leaving it untranslated.

The new products featured in the print and broadcast media ran the gamut from automobiles to cosmetics, from rayon apparel to chewing gum. When the Wrigley Company of Chicago opened a factory in Germany in 1925, chewing gum quickly became associated with Americanization—and its use increased dramatically. But luxury goods were prominent as well, as in elegant ads such as the two shown here. Even for the many who could not afford expensive jewelry or the six-cylinder Opel, images of the good life stimulated the desire to buy less costly versions. Automobile consumption rose sharply during the 1920s, thanks also to the new techniques of mass production that Henry Ford had pioneered in the United States.

Although advertising served the economic interests of business by stimulating consumption, many began to view it as an art form as well. Far more attention was paid to its design, so the advertising "look" of the 1920s differed dramatically from anything seen before. As in the examples here, the new ads were often self-consciously modern, using simplified typefaces and stylized images suggesting the sleek efficiency and precision of the new machine age. The jewelry ad features an elegant contemporary typeface, and the German automobile ad of 1928 relies on crisp, bold forms and a clean, modern design.

The new prominence of advertising raised issues that were debated all over, but especially in Weimar Germany, where conditions remained unsettled even as a measure of prosperity returned by 1924. From cultural standards to gender roles, much was being called into question, and the wider implications of advertising were central to the "culture wars" of the period.

At an international advertising congress in Berlin in 1929, critics charged that advertising was furthering the debasement of standards already associated with mass culture and Americanization. Defenders countered that advertising was rejuvenating the mainstream culture, which had grown either stale and conventional or overblown and elitist. The fact that advertising served a commercial purpose need not mean cultural debasement. On the contrary, they argued, this new meshing of the best design with popular culture was healthy. In 1928, G. F. Hartlaub, a leading German art dealer, summed up a widespread view when he observed that advertising was a "truly social, collective, mass art, the only one we now have. It shapes the visual habits of that anonymous collectivity, the public. Little by little an artistic attitude is hammered into the mass soul by billboards."*

A particular advertising target was the "new woman," with her bobbed hair, short skirts, and freer lifestyle. But the image of women in advertisements was controversial, especially in Weimar Germany. Partly because of the simplification of female attire, images of the new woman in popular magazines provoked much concern about the "masculinization" of women by the mid-1920s. Some men found such images aggressive, even threatening.

Yet at the same time, advertising often assumed women to be master consumers—or perhaps merely mindless shoppers. In the holiday advertisement here, the woman is chic and liberated in one sense, but she is urged to drape herself with jewelry—to indulge in conventional ornamentation. This was also an age that claimed to value efficiency purified of ornament, as with the stripped-down typeface in the automobile ad. So though gender differentiation and women's

Exploiting the new fascination with air travel, the American Charles Lindbergh (1902–1974) captured the European imagination in 1927 with the first solo flight across the Atlantic. Lindbergh's feat epitomized the affirmative side of the decade—the sense that there were new worlds to conquer and that there still were heroes to admire, despite the ironies of the war and the ambiguities of the peace.

Jewelry Ad, 1920s: "Wear jewelry—It makes you a winner. And it's the ideal Christmas gift."
(akg-images)

Car Ad, 1928: The Six-Cylinder Opel Hits the Jackpot
(From Bärbel Schrader and Jürgen Schebera, *The "Golden" Twenties: Art and Literature in the Weimar Republic* [New Haven: Yale University Press, 1990]. Reproduced with permission.)

roles were very much at issue in advertising, the relationship between portrayals of the new woman and genuine liberation remained uncertain.

Despite tensions and contradictions, advertising helped bring new issues to center stage after World War I. Although the ads of the 1920s assumed a prosperity that proved fleeting, the cultural change proved enduring. Eye-catching images of the sleek, the chic, the new—all bathed in "sex appeal"—became the staples of twentieth-century advertising, bound up with the new culture of mass consumption.

QUESTIONS

1. What factors led to the upsurge in advertising during the 1920s?

2. What seems specifically modern about the images we see here?

*Quoted in John Willett, *Art and Politics in the Weimar Period: The New Sobriety, 1917–1933* (New York: Pantheon, 1978), p. 137. Translation modified slightly.

Society and Politics in the Victorious Democracies

France and Britain seemed the best positioned of the major European countries to take advantage of renewed peace and stability to confront the sociopolitical problems of the postwar era. And during the 1920s, each seemed to return to normal. But was normal good enough, in light of the rupture of the war and the challenges of the emerging mass society?

Innovation in Cinema This poster advertises Fritz Lang's 1926 film *Metropolis*, which explored the dehumanization and exploitation of the modern city. (Schulz-Neudamm, Metropolis, 1926. Lithograph, 83" × 36½". Gift of Universum-Film-Aktiengesellschaft. Photograph © 1997 The Museum of Modern Art, New York/Art Resource, NY)

FRANCE

Victory in the Great War seemed to belie France's prewar concerns about decadence and decline. In the immediate aftermath of the war, Clemenceau and other French leaders were confident in dealing with radical labor unrest and aggressive in translating the battlefield victory into a dominant position on the European continent. But the tremendous loss of French lives had produced a new fear—that France could not withstand another such challenge. The renewed confidence thus proved hollow.

Although some in prewar France had worried about falling behind rapidly industrializing Germany, victory seemed to have vindicated France's more cautious, balanced economy, with its blend of industry and agriculture. Thus, the prewar mistrust of rapid industrial development continued. Rather than foster a program of economic modernization that might have promoted genuine security, the French pulled back even from the measure of state responsibility for the economy that had developed during the war. Although government grants helped reconstruct almost eight thousand factories, most were simply rebuilt as they had been before the war. Moreover, the working class benefited little from the relative prosperity of the 1920s.

GREAT BRITAIN

Britain made certain adjustments after the war but missed the chance to make others. The government's handling of the Easter Rebellion in Ireland in 1916 (see pages 702–703) intensified anti-British feeling and fed further violence. But the British finally forged at least a provisional resolution. The first step was to partition Ireland, creating a separate Ulster, or Northern Ireland, from those counties with Protestant majorities. Ulster then remained under the British crown when an independent Republic of Ireland was established in the larger, majority-Catholic part of the island in 1922.

The British political system remained stable between the wars, although the Labour Party supplanted the Liberals to become the dominant alternative to the Conservatives by the early 1920s. The Labour Party even got a brief taste of power when Ramsay MacDonald (1866–1937) formed Britain's first Labour government in January 1924. The coming of Labour to power resulted in a significant expansion of the governmental elite to incorporate those, like MacDonald himself, with genuinely working-class backgrounds.

However, it was the Conservative leader, Stanley Baldwin (1867–1947), who set the tone for British politics between the wars in three stints as prime minister from 1923 to 1937. Although he was the wealthy son of a steel manufacturer, Baldwin deliberately departed from the old aristocratic style of British Conservative politics. More down-to-earth and pragmatic, he was the first British prime minister to use radio effectively, and he made an effort to foster good relations with workers. Yet Baldwin's era was one of growing social tension.

With exports declining, unemployment remained high in Britain throughout the interwar period, never falling below 10 percent. The coal industry, though still the country's largest employer, had become a particular trouble spot in the British economy. As coal exports declined, British mine owners became ever more aggressive in their dealings with labor, finally, in 1926, insisting on a longer workday and a wage cut of 13 percent to restore competitiveness. The result was a coal miners' strike in May that promptly turned into a general strike, involving almost all of organized labor—about four million workers—in the most notable display of trade-union solidarity Britain had ever seen. For nine days, the economy stood at a virtual standstill. But threats of arrest and a growing public backlash forced the union leadership to accept a compromise. The miners continued the strike on their own, but they finally returned to work six months later at considerably lower wages.

Although, for somewhat different reasons, Britain and France both failed during the 1920s to take advantage of what would soon seem, in retrospect, to have been a precious opportunity to adjust their economies and heal social wounds. The lost opportunity would mean still deeper social tensions once the relative prosperity of the decade had ended.

SECTION SUMMARY

- The inflation that resulted from the war and its aftermath had long-term psychological consequences, most dramatically in Germany, but also in France.

- Adapting influential American ideas about mass production, business leaders throughout much of Europe fostered a new cult of efficiency and productivity as they sought to adjust to the more competitive postwar world economy.

- Although there was much discussion of the "new woman," reflecting a new sense of openness after the war, women were pulled in traditional as well as modernizing directions during the 1920s.

- Mass production yielded mass consumption, the growth of leisure, and the popularity of new media like movies and radio.

- Victory bred a certain complacency in Britain and France, each of which failed to take advantage of what would seem, in retrospect, to have been a precious opportunity to adjust their economies and deepen their democracies.

THE TRIALS OF THE NEW DEMOCRACIES

What factors made the future of the new German democracy so uncertain during the 1920s?

The war was supposed to have paved the way for democracy, and new democracies emerged in Germany, Poland, and elsewhere in Europe. But almost everywhere they led tortured lives and soon gave way to more authoritarian forms of government. So the postwar decade did not see the extension of the political democracy that optimistic observers associated with the emerging mass society.

The most significant test took place in Germany, where a new democracy emerged from the republic proclaimed in November 1918. Elections in January 1919 produced a constituent assembly that convened in Weimar, a town associated with what seemed the most humane German cultural traditions. The assembly gave this new Weimar Republic, as it came to be called, a fully democratic constitution. But the Weimar democracy had great difficulty establishing its legitimacy, and it was suffering serious strains by 1930.

Democracy Aborted in East-Central Europe

New democracies were established in much of central and eastern Europe after the war, but except in Czechoslovakia and Finland, the practice of parliamentary government did not match the initial promise. Democracy seemed divisive and ineffective, so one country after another adopted a more authoritarian alternative during the 1920s and early 1930s.

In Poland, for example, the democratic constitution of 1921 established a cabinet responsible to a parliamentary majority, but the parliament fragmented into so many parties that instability proved endemic from the start. Poland had fourteen different ministries from November 1918 to May 1926, when Marshal Josef Pilsudski led a coup d'état that replaced parliamentary government with an authoritarian regime stressing national unity. This suppression of democracy came as a relief to many Poles—and was welcomed even by the trade unions. After Pilsudski's death in 1935, a group of colonels ruled Poland until the country was conquered by Nazi Germany in 1939.

Democracy proved hard to manage in east-central Europe partly because of the economic difficulties resulting from the breakup of the Habsburg system. New national borders meant new economic barriers that disrupted long-standing economic relationships. Industrial centers, such as Vienna and Budapest, found themselves cut off from their traditional markets and sources of raw materials. In what was now Poland, Silesians had long been oriented toward Germany, Galicians toward Vienna, and those in eastern Poland toward Russia. Thus, the new Polish nation-state was hardly a cohesive economic unit.

The countries of east-central Europe remained overwhelmingly agrarian, and this, too, proved unconducive to democracy. Land reform accompanied the transition to democracy, making small properties the norm in much of the region. But because these units were often too small to be efficient, agricultural output actually decreased after land was redistributed, most dramatically in Romania and Yugoslavia. When agricultural prices declined in the late 1920s, many peasants had no choice but to sell out to larger landowners. What had seemed a progressive reform thus failed to provide a stable agrarian smallholder base for democracy.

Germany's Cautious Revolution, 1919–1920

Meanwhile, in Germany, the Weimar Republic began under particularly difficult circumstances. Born of military defeat, it was promptly forced to take responsibility for the harsh Treaty of Versailles in 1919. During its first years, moreover, the regime encountered severe economic dislocation, culminating in the hyperinflation of 1923, as well as ideological polarization that threatened to tear the country apart.

Although Germany had strong military and authoritarian traditions, the initial threat to the new democracy came not from the right, disoriented and discredited, but from the left, stimulated by the Russian example. Even after Karl Liebknecht and Rosa Luxemburg were captured and murdered in Berlin in January 1919, a serious chance of further revolution persisted through May 1919, and communist revolutionary agitation continued to flare up until the end of 1923.

As it turned out, there was no further revolution, partly because the parallel between Germany and Russia carried only so far. The new German government had made peace, whereas the leaders of the provisional government in Russia had sought to continue the war. Furthermore, those who ended up controlling the councils that sprang up in Germany during the fall of 1918 favored political democracy, not communist revolution; therefore, they supported the provisional government.

Even so, the revolutionary minority constituted a credible threat. And the new government made repression of the extreme left a priority—even if it meant leaving in place some of the institutions and personnel of the old imperial system. In November 1918, at the birth of the new republic, the moderate socialist leader Friedrich Ebert had agreed with General Wilhelm Groener, the new army head, to preserve the old imperial officer corps to help prevent further revolution. But when the regular army, weakened by war and defeat, proved unable to control radical agitation in Berlin in December, it seemed the republic would have to take extraordinary measures to defend itself from the revolutionary left. With the support of Ebert and Groener, Gustav Noske, the minister of national defense, began to organize "Free Corps," volunteer paramilitary groups to be used against the revolutionaries.

During the first five months of 1919, the government unleashed the Free Corps to crush leftist movements all over Germany, often with wanton brutality. In relying on right-wing paramilitary groups, the republic's leaders were playing with fire, but the immediate threat at this point came from the left. In 1920, however, the government faced a right-wing coup attempt, the Kapp Putsch. The army declined to defend the republic, but the government managed to survive thanks largely to a general strike by leftist workers. The republic's early leaders had to juggle both extremes because, as one of them put it, the Weimar Republic was "a candle burning at both ends."

Though sporadic street fighting by paramilitary groups continued, the republic survived its traumatic birth and achieved an uneasy stability by 1924. But Germany's postwar revolution had remained confined to the political level. There was no program to break up the cartels, with their concentrations of economic power. Even on the level of government personnel, continuity was more striking than change. There was no effort to build a loyal republican army, and no attempt to purge the bureaucracy and the judiciary of antidemocratic elements from the old imperial order. When right-wing extremists assassinated prominent leaders, such as the Jewish industrialist Walther Rathenau in 1922, the courts often proved unwilling to prosecute those responsible.

In light of the republic's eventual failure, the willingness of its early leaders to leave intact so much from the old order has made them easy targets of criticism. It can be argued, however, that the course they followed—heading off the extreme left, reassuring the established elites, and playing for time—was the republic's best chance for success. The new regime might establish its legitimacy by inertia, much like the Third Republic in France, which had similarly been born of defeat. Even lacking the sentimental fervor that had earlier surrounded democratic ideals, Germans might gradually become "republicans of reason," recognizing that this regime could be a framework for prosperity and renewed German prominence in international affairs. In the event of an early crisis, however, a republic consolidating itself in this cautious way might well find fewer defenders than opponents.

The constituent assembly elections of January 1919 took place before the peace conference had produced the widely detested Treaty of Versailles. By the time of the first regular parliamentary elections, in June 1920, the new government had been forced to accept the treaty. The three moderate parties that led the government suffered a major defeat, together dropping from 76 to 47 percent of the seats. These were the parties most committed to democratic institutions, but they were never again to achieve a parliamentary majority.

The 1920 elections revealed the problems of polarization and lack of consensus that would bedevil, and eventually ruin, the Weimar Republic. Because the electorate found it difficult to agree, or even to compromise, Germany settled into a multiparty system that led to unstable coalition government. And the strength, or potential strength, of the extremes immeasurably complicated political life for those trying to make the new democracy work. On the left, the Communist Party constantly criticized the more moderate Socialist Party for supporting the republic. On the right, the Nationalist Party (DNVP) played on nationalist resentments and fears of the extreme left—but the result was similarly to dilute support for the new republic. To the right, even of the Nationalists, were Adolf Hitler's National Socialists, or Nazis, who were noisy and often violent, but who attracted little electoral support before 1930.

Gustav Stresemann and the Scope for Gradual Consolidation

All was not necessarily lost for the republic when the three moderate, pro-Weimar parties were defeated in 1920. Germans who were unsupportive or hostile at first might be gradually won over. After the death of President Ebert in 1925, Paul von Hindenburg, the emperor's field marshal, was elected president. In principle, having a conservative military leader from the old order in this role could have proven advantageous, helping to persuade skeptics that the new regime was a worthy object of German patriotism. But when crisis came by 1930, Hindenburg was quick to give up on parliamentary government—with devastating results.

The individual who best exemplified the possibility of winning converts to the Weimar Republic was **Gustav Stresemann** (STRAY-zuh-mahn) (1878–1929), the leader of the German People's Party (DVP), a conservative party that did not support the republic at the outset. But the DVP was relatively flexible and offered at least the possibility of broadening the republic's base of support. As chancellor, and especially as foreign minister, Stresemann proved the republic's leading statesman.

Stresemann's background and instincts were not democratic, but by the end of 1920, Germany's postwar political volatility had convinced him that if the new republic should go under, the outcome would not be the conservative monarchy he preferred but the triumph of the extreme left. Moreover, it had become clear that the new democratic republic was not likely to

Gustav Stresemann
German statesman of the Weimar Republic, he secured a reduction of Germany's reparations payments and negotiated the Treaty of Locarno, paving the way for Germany's entry into the League of Nations in 1926.

Hopes for Peace Foreign ministers Aristide Briand (*left*) of France and Gustav Stresemann of Germany spearheaded the improved international relations that bred optimism during the late 1920s. (Corbis)

be revolutionary on the socioeconomic level. It made sense, then, to work actively to make the new regime succeed. From within this framework, Germany could pursue its international aims, negotiating modifications of the Versailles treaty and returning to great power status.

Stresemann became chancellor in August 1923, when inflation was raging out of control. Within months, his government managed to get the German economy functioning effectively again, partly because the French agreed that an international commission should review the reparations question, specifying realistic amounts based on Germany's ability to pay. New plans worked out under American leadership—the Dawes Plan of 1924 and finally the Young Plan of 1929—seemed to specify a reasonable and workable settlement.

Quite apart from the immediate economic issue, Stresemann understood that better relations with France had to be a priority if Germany was to rejoin the great powers. French foreign minister Aristide Briand (bree-AHN) (1862–1932) shared Stresemann's desire for improved relations, and together they engineered a new, more conciliatory spirit in international affairs. Its most substantial fruit was the **Treaty of Locarno** of 1925. France and Germany accepted the postwar border between the two countries, which meant that Germany gave up any claim to Alsace-Lorraine. France, for its part, renounced the sort of direct military intervention in Germany that it had attempted with the Ruhr invasion of 1923 and agreed to begin withdrawing troops from the Rhineland ahead of schedule. Germany freely accepted France's key advantage, the demilitarization of the Rhineland, and Britain and Italy now explicitly guaranteed the measure.

By accepting the status quo in the West, Stresemann was freeing Germany to concentrate on eastern Europe, where he envisioned gradual but substantial revision in the territorial settlement that had resulted from the war. Especially with the creation of Poland, that settlement had come partly at Germany's expense. Stresemann, then, was pursuing German interests, not subordinating them to some larger European vision. But he was willing to compromise and, for the most part, to play by the rules as he did so.

With the Locarno treaty, the victors accepted Germany as a diplomatic equal for the first time since the war. Germany's return to good graces culminated in its entry into the League of Nations in 1926. The new spirit of reconciliation was widely welcomed. Indeed, Stresemann and Briand were joint winners of the Nobel Peace Prize for 1926.

Still, those on the right continually exploited German resentments by criticizing Stresemann's compromises with Germany's former enemies. Even when successful, from Stresemann's own perspective, his negotiations often cost his party electoral support. The controversy that surrounded Stresemann, a German conservative pursuing conventional national interests, indicates how volatile the German political situation remained, even with the improved economic and diplomatic climate of the later 1920s. Still, Stresemann's diplomatic successes were considerable, and his death in October 1929, at the age of 51, was a severe blow to the republic.

Treaty of Locarno The 1925 treaty in which Germany, again recognized as a diplomatic equal, freely agreed with France, Britain, and Italy to accept key aspects of the Versailles peace settlement.

An Uncertain Balance Sheet

Although Weimar Germany was better off in 1929 than it had been in 1923, the political consensus remained weak, the political party system remained fragmented, and unstable coalition government remained the rule. The immediate threat from the extreme left had been overcome, but many conservatives continued to fear that the unstable Weimar democracy would eventually open the way to a socialist or communist regime.

The Weimar Republic epitomized the overall European situation during the 1920s. As long as prosperity and international cooperation continued, the new German democracy might endure, even come to thrive. But the new institutions in Germany, like the wider framework of prosperity and stability, were fragile indeed. At the first opportunity, antidemocratic elites, taking advantage of their access to President Hindenburg, would begin plotting to replace the Weimar Republic with a more authoritarian alternative.

SECTION SUMMARY

- Although new democracies were established in central and eastern Europe after the war, parliamentary government proved divisive and ineffective in much of the region, so one country after another adopted a more authoritarian alternative.

- Germany's democratic political revolution was not accompanied by major changes in socioeconomic relations—or even in the administrative structures inherited from Wilhelm II's government.

- Because of polarization and lack of consensus in the electorate, the Weimar Republic quickly fell into a multiparty system that led to unstable coalition government.

- A conservative monarchist by instinct, Gustav Stresemann rallied to the Weimar Republic because he found it the best framework for restoring Germany to prosperity and international influence—and for heading off leftist revolution.

- Although many Germans continued to resent the peace settlement, the Treaty of Locarno of 1925 seemed to suggest a hopeful new spirit of reconciliation between France and Germany

THE SEARCH FOR MEANING IN A DISORDERED WORLD

How did cultural and intellectual leaders differ over the place of "tradition" as they sought to suggest how to come to terms with the new situation of the 1920s?

For all its vitality, the new culture of the 1920s had something brittle about it. The forces that produced a sense of openness, liberation, and innovation were disruptive and disturbing at the same time. Perhaps the frenetic pace only masked a deeper sense that things had started to come apart and might well get worse. The era called forth some notable diagnoses and prescriptions, but, not surprisingly, they differed dramatically.

Anxiety, Alienation, and Disillusionment

Concern about the dangers of the emerging mass civilization was especially clear in *The Revolt of the Masses* (1930), by the influential Spanish thinker José Ortega y Gasset (1883–1955). In his view, contemporary experience had shown that ordinary people, incapable of creating standards, remained content with the least common denominator. Communism and fascism indicated the violent, intolerant, and ultimately barbaric quality of the new mass age. But Ortega found the same tendencies in American-style democracy. The fact that much of Europe seemed to be moving toward the mass politics and culture of the United States was a symptom of the deeper problem, not a solution.

Concern with cultural decline was part of a wider pessimism about the condition of the West, which stood in stark contrast to the belief in progress, and the attendant confidence in Western superiority, that had been essential to Western self-understanding before 1914. The German thinker Oswald Spengler (1880–1936) made concern with decline almost fashionable with his bestseller of the immediate postwar years, *The Decline of the West* (1918), which offered a cyclical theory purporting to explain how spirituality and creativity were giving way to a materialistic mass-based culture in the West.

To Sigmund Freud (1856–1939), the eruption of violence and hatred during and after the war indicated a deep, instinctual problem in the human makeup (see page 680). In his gloomy essay, *Civilization and Its Discontents* (1930), Freud suggested that the progress of civilization requires individuals to bottle up their aggressive instincts, which are directed inward as guilt, but which may erupt in violent outbursts. This notion raised questions not only about the scope for continued progress, but also about the plausibility of the Wilsonian ideals that had surrounded the end of the war. Perhaps, with civilization growing more complex, the Great War had been only the beginning of a new era of hatred and violence.

The sense that something incomprehensible, even nightmarish, haunted modern civilization, with its ever more complex bureaucracies, technologies, and cities, found vivid expression in the work of the Czech Jewish writer Franz Kafka (1883–1924), most notably in the novels *The Trial* and *The Castle*, published posthumously in the mid-1920s. In a world that claimed to be increasingly rational, Kafka's individual is the lonely, fragile plaything of forces utterly beyond reason, comprehension, and control. In such a world, the quest for law, or meaning, or God, is futile, ridiculous.

Especially in the unsettled conditions of Weimar Germany, the anxiety of the 1920s tended to take extreme forms, from irrational activism to a preoccupation with death. Suicides among students increased dramatically. Youthful alienation prompted the novelist Jakob Wassermann (1873–1934) to caution German young people in 1932 that not all action is good simply because it is action, that feeling is not always better than reason and discipline, and that youth is not in itself a badge of superiority.

Recasting the Tradition

Expressions of disillusionment revealed something about human experience in the unsettled new world, but they were sometimes morbid and self-indulgent. Other cultural leaders sought to be more positive; the challenge was not to give vent to new anxieties, but to find antidotes to them. One direction was to recast traditional categories—in the arts, in religion, in politics—to make them relevant to contemporary experience. Although not all were optimistic about human prospects, many found such a renewal of tradition to be the best hope for responding to the disarray of the postwar world.

Among artists, even those who had been prominent in the modernist avant-garde before the war now pulled back from headlong experimentation and sought to pull things back together, though on a new basis. In music, composers as different as Igor Stravinsky (1882–1971) and Paul Hindemith (1895–1963) adapted earlier styles, though sometimes in an ironic spirit, as they sought to weave new means of expression into familiar forms. The overall tendency toward neoclassicism during the period was an effort to give musical composition a renewed basis of order.

One of the most striking responses to the anxieties of this increasingly secular age was a wave of neo-orthodox religious thinking, most prominent in Protestants like the German-Swiss theologian Karl Barth (1886–1968). In his *Epistle to the Romans* (1919), Barth reacted against the liberal theology, the attempt to marry religious categories to secular progress, that had become prominent by the later nineteenth century. The war, especially, had seemed to shatter the liberal notion that the hand of God was at work in history, and Barth emphasized the radical cleft between God and our human, historical world, sunken in sin. Recalling the arguments of Augustine and Luther, he portrayed humanity as utterly lost, capable at best of a difficult relationship with God through faith, grace, and revelation.

With democracy faring poorly in parts of Europe, and with fascism and communism claiming to offer superior alternatives, some sought to make new sense of the liberal democratic tradition. In Italy, Benedetto Croce (CROH-chay) (1866–1952) agreed with critics that the old justifications, based on natural law or utilitarianism, were deeply inadequate, but he also became one of Europe's most influential antifascists. The most significant innovations in modern thought, he argued, show us why democratic values, institutions, and practices are precisely what we need. We human beings are free, creative agents of a history that we make as best we can, without quite understanding what will result from what we do. Humility, tolerance, and equal access to political participation are essential to the process whereby the world is endlessly remade.

The new political challenges also stimulated fresh thinking within the Marxist tradition. By showing that Marxism could encompass consciousness as well as economic relationships, the Hungarian Georg Lukács (LOO-kash) (1885–1971) invited a far more sophisticated Marxist analysis of capitalist culture than had been possible before. Lukács accented the progressive role of realistic fiction and attacked the disordered fictional world of Kafka, which seemed to abandon all hope for human understanding of the forces of history. Though more eclectic, the Institute for Social Research, founded in Frankfurt, Germany, in 1923, gave rise to an influential tradition of criticism of capitalist civilization in what came to be known as the Frankfurt School. These innovations helped give the Marxist tradition a new lease on life in the West, even as it was developing in unforeseen ways in the Soviet Union.

The Search for a New Tradition

While some intellectuals sought renewal from within the European tradition, others insisted that a more radical break was needed—but also that the elements for a viable new cultural tradition were available.

Reflecting on the situation of women writers in 1928, the British novelist Virginia Woolf (1882–1941) showed how women in the past had suffered from the absence of a tradition of writing by women. By the 1920s, women had made important strides, but Woolf suggested that further advance required a more self-conscious effort by women to develop their own tradition. Most basically, women needed greater financial independence so that they could have the time for scholarship, the leisure for cultivated conversation and travel, and the privacy of "a room of one's own." Woolf also envisioned a new sort of historical inquiry, focusing on how ordinary women lived their lives, that could show contemporary women where they came from—and thus deepen their sense of identity. (See the feature, "The Written Record: Tradition and Women: The Conditions of Independence.")

surrealism A literary and artistic movement that emerged in Paris in the early 1920s, it sought to explore the subconscious, which it believed to hold something liberating for human beings.

A very different effort to establish a new tradition developed in Paris, where the poet André Breton (1896–1966) spearheaded the surrealist movement in literature and the visual arts. **Surrealism** grew directly from Dada, an artistic movement that had emerged in neutral Zurich, Switzerland, and elsewhere during the war. Radically hostile to the war, Dada artists developed shocking, sometimes nihilistic forms to deal with a reality that now seemed senseless and out of control. Some made collages from gutter trash; others indulged in nonsense or relied on chance to guide their art. By the

Tradition and Women: The Conditions of Independence

Speaking in 1928 about the situation of women writers, the British novelist Virginia Woolf raised questions that were relevant to all women seeking the opportunity to realize their potential. Indeed, her reflections about the value of difference and the need for particular traditions inspired those seeking equal opportunity for decades to come. And her question about why we know so little about women's lives in the past helped stimulate later historians to investigate the experiences of ordinary people.

Woman ... pervades poetry from cover to cover; she is all but absent from history.... Occasionally an individual woman is mentioned, an Elizabeth, or a Mary; a queen or a great lady. But by no possible means could middle-class women with nothing but brains and character at their command have taken part in any one of the great movements which, brought together, constitute the historian's view of the past. ... What one wants ... is a mass of information; at what age did she marry; how many children had she as a rule; what was her house like; had she a room to herself; did she do the cooking; would she be likely to have a servant? All these facts lie somewhere, presumably, in parish registers and account books; the life of the average Elizabethan woman must be scattered about somewhere, could one collect it and make a book of it. It would be ambitious beyond my daring, I thought, looking about the shelves for books that were not there, to suggest to the students of those famous colleges that they should rewrite history, though I own that it often seems a little queer as it is, unreal, lop-sided. ...

But whatever effect discouragement and criticism had upon their writing—and I believe they had a very great effect—that was unimportant compared with the other difficulty which faced them (I was still considering those early nineteenth-century novelists) when they came to set their thoughts on paper—that is that they had no tradition behind them, or one so short and partial that it was of little help. For we think back through our mothers if we are women. It is useless to go to the great men writers for help, however much one may go to them for pleasure. ...

... Women have sat indoors all these millions of years, so that by this time the very walls are permeated by their creative force, which has, indeed, so overcharged the capacity of bricks and mortar that it must needs harness itself to pens and brushes and business and politics. But this creative power differs greatly from the creative power of men. And one must conclude that it would be a thousand pities if it were hindered or wasted, for it was won by centuries of the most drastic discipline, and there is nothing to take its place. It would be a thousand pities if women wrote like men, or lived like men, or looked like men.... Ought not education to bring out and fortify the differences rather than the similarities?

QUESTIONS

1. Why does Woolf find something "lop-sided" about the body of historical writing available in her own time, and how does she believe the problem might be overcome?

2. Why does Woolf suggest that education ought to nurture a distinctive female voice?

Source: Virginia Woolf, *A Room of One's Own* (San Diego: Harcourt Brace Jovanovich, Harvest/HBJ, 1989), pp 43–45, 76, 87–88.

---

early 1920s, however, the surrealists felt it was time to create a new and deeper basis of order after the willful disordering of Dada. Having learned from Freud about the subconscious, they sought to adapt Dada's novel techniques—especially the use of chance—to gain access to the subconscious mind, which they believed contains a deeper truth, without the overlay of logic, reason, and conscious control.

But other artists, seeking to embrace the modern industrial world in a more positive spirit, found surrealism merely escapist. Among them was Walter Gropius (1883–1969), a pioneering modernist architect and leader of an influential German art school, the Bauhaus, during the 1920s. Gropius held that it was possible to establish new forms of culture, even a new tradition, that could be affirmative and reassuring in the face of the postwar cultural disarray. Rather than putting up familiar neoclassical or neo-Gothic buildings, "feigning a culture that has long since disappeared," the West had to face up to the kind of civilization it had become—industrial, technological, efficient, urban, mass-based. If people chose carefully from among the elements of this new machine-based civilization, they could again have a culture that worked, an "integrated pattern for living."[2]

This "constructive," pro-modern impulse was particularly prominent in Germany, but it could be found all over—in the

SECTION SUMMARY

- The shock of the war produced a sense of disillusionment and even decline that took many forms in the culture of the 1920s.

- Some accented the scope for recasting traditions during the 1920s, but others insisted on the need to form new traditions if the era's challenges were to be met.

- The contrast between surrealism and the German Bauhaus suggested a wider disagreement over whether Western culture was excessively rational or not rational enough.

- Whereas some, like Ortega y Gasset, were at best ambivalent about the advent of modern mass society, others welcomed it and sought to devise cultural forms that seemed more appropriate to a mass machine age.

Bauhaus An influential German art school, founded in 1919, that sought to adopt contemporary materials to develop new forms of architecture, design, and urban planning in response to the cultural uncertainty that followed World War I.

modernists of the Russian Revolution, in the French painter Fernand Léger (leh-ZHAY) (1881–1955), in the Swiss architect Le Corbusier (luh cor-BOO-zee-ay) (1887–1965). Whereas many of their contemporaries were at best ambivalent about the masses, these artists sought to bring high art and mass society together in the interests of both. And they welcomed the new patterns of life that seemed to be emerging in the modern world of mass production and fast-paced cities.

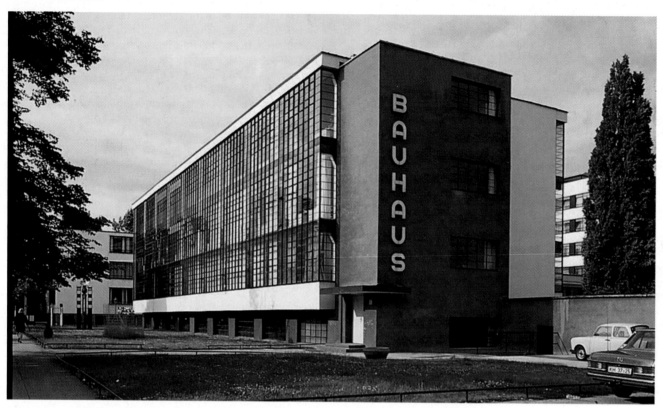

The Bauhaus Building, Dessau   The Bauhaus, an influential but controversial German art school, was established in Weimar in 1919 and then moved to Dessau in 1925. Walter Gropius, its founding director, spearheaded the design of its headquarters building. Constructed in 1925–1926, it immediately became a symbol of the Weimar modernism that some admired and others detested.   (Vanni/Art Resource, NY)

CHAPTER SUMMARY

FOCUS QUESTIONS

- How did the differing priorities of Britain and France affect international relations during the 1920s?

- Why did Italy turn from parliamentary democracy to fascism even after sharing in the victory in World War I?

- Why, and on what basis, did sexuality, gender roles, and the "new woman" provoke so much concern during the 1920s?

- What factors made the future of the new German democracy so uncertain during the 1920s?

- How did cultural and intellectual leaders differ over the place of "tradition" as they sought to suggest how to come to terms with the new situation of the 1920s?

In the wake of the most destructive war in history, questions about the new international framework, established at the peace conference of 1919–1920, were bound to be central. Although they bore the major responsibility for enforcing the peace, France and Britain seemed to drift apart as the British, preoccupied with colonial concerns, distanced themselves from politics on the Continent. Whereas France was willing to intervene actively to enforce the Versailles treaty, Britain placed greater faith in reconciliation and the new League of Nations.

The threat of leftist revolution was a major factor in the emergence of fascism in Italy, although the fascists claimed to offer a "third way," a modern alternative to *both* Marxist socialism and liberal democracy. Once Mussolini committed himself to a decisively postliberal direction, the fascists fastened upon corporativism as the basis for a new fascist form of state. Corporativism, they claimed, offered a way of transcending the class divisions accented by Marxism while also involving people in public life in more constant and direct ways than democracy had made possible.

The war had seemingly enhanced opportunities for women, and a new sense of openness carried into the postwar period. During the 1920s, sexuality, reproductive choices, gender roles, and family life were open to discussion as never before in the West. But in light of demographic losses and the brutalizing effects of the war, women encountered considerable pressure to conform to traditional roles of mothering and nurturing. Although the image of the liberated "new woman" was central to the era, women themselves were sometimes torn between conflicting roles and expectations.

Germany's Weimar Republic provided the central test of the bright hopes for democracy that marked the beginning of the postwar era. Yet the new German democracy was launched under the difficult circumstances of defeat, harsh peace terms, and ongoing revolutionary unrest. Moreover, the limits of political consensus in Germany meant a fragmented electorate, a complicated multiparty system, and a reliance on unstable coalition governments. Although the improved economic and diplomatic situation by 1925 enhanced the prospects for democracy, the Weimar Republic remained fragile and vulnerable.

In light of the cultural disruptions of the war and its aftermath, many intellectuals insisted that certain traditions could be recast to provide the sense of direction that people needed. But there was wide disagreement over which traditions were relevant. Whereas some pointed to religion, others fastened upon Marxism. Still others found it essential to return to more accessible forms in the arts, turning from the avant-garde experiment that had marked the prewar period. At the same time, however, figures as disparate as Virginia Woolf, André Breton, and Walter Gropius insisted that the means were available to develop *new* traditions, more appropriate to the needs and possibilities of the postwar world.

KEY TERMS

Maginot Line (p. 730)

fascism (p. 732)

Comintern (Third, or Communist, International) (p. 734)

New Economic Policy (NEP) (p. 734)

Joseph Stalin (p. 735)

Benito Mussolini (p. 738)

Matteotti murder (p. 738)

corporativism, corporative state (p. 738)

Gustav Stresemann (p. 747)

Treaty of Locarno (p. 748)

surrealism (p. 750)

Bauhaus (p. 752)

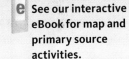 **This icon will direct you to additional materials on the website: www .cengage.com/history/ noble/westciv6e.**

See our interactive eBook for map and primary source activities.

NOTES

1. Benito Mussolini, speech to the Italian Chamber of Deputies, January 3, 1925, from Charles F. Delzell, ed., *Mediterranean Fascism, 1919–1945* (New York: Harper & Row, 1970), pp. 59–60.

2. Walter Gropius, *Scope of Total Architecture* (New York: Collier Books, 1962), pp. 15, 67.

27

¡No pasarán! ("They shall not pass")
Defending the republic during the Spanish civil war. (Biblioteca Nacional, Madrid)

The Tortured Decade, 1930–1939

"They shall not pass," proclaimed the charismatic Spanish communist Dolores Ibarruri (ee-bah-RUHR-ee) (1895–1989), whose impassioned speeches and radio broadcasts helped inspire the heroic defense of Madrid during the civil war that gripped Spain, and captured the attention of the world, during the later 1930s. Known as *La Pasionaria*—the passion flower—Ibarruri became a living legend for her role in defending the Spanish republic against the antidemocratic Nationalists seeking to overthrow it. But the Republican side lost, and she spent thirty-eight years in exile before returning to Spain in 1977, after the end of the dictatorship that resulted from the Spanish civil war.

In her effort to rally the Republican side, Ibarruri stressed the political power of women, and women were prominent in the citizen militias defending Madrid and other Spanish cities. Women fought for the republic partly because it seemed to open new opportunities for them, especially as it became more radical by 1936. But just as some women welcomed the new direction, others became politically active on the opposing Nationalist side—to support the church, to combat divorce, and to defend a separate sphere for women as the guardians of private life and family values.

The ideological polarization that characterized the Spanish civil war reflected the expanding reach of politics in the 1930s, when economic depression and the challenge from new, antidemocratic governments immeasurably complicated the European situation. The measures used to realign the international economy after World War I had seemed effective for most of the 1920s, but by 1929, they were beginning to backfire, helping to trigger the Great Depression. During the early 1930s, the economic crisis intensified socio-political strains all over the Western world—and beyond, heightening anti-Western feeling. In Germany, the Depression helped undermine the Weimar Republic and opened the way for the new Nazi regime under Adolf Hitler, whose policies led through a series of diplomatic crises to a new European war.

German Nazism paralleled Italian fascism in its reliance on a single charismatic leader, its willingness to use violence, and its hostility to both parliamentary democracy and Marxist socialism. But Nazism emphasized racism and anti-Semitism in a way that Italian fascism did not, and it more radically transformed its society.

At the same time, Stalin's communist regime in the Soviet Union seemed to converge, in some ways, with these new fascist regimes—especially with German Nazism. So, though they expressed widely different aims, Stalinism and Nazism are sometimes lumped together as instances of "totalitarianism." Both apparently sought control over all aspects of society, partly through the use of secret police agencies. But on closer inspection, the forms of coercion and violence in the Soviet and German regimes by the later 1930s were quite

FOCUS QUESTIONS

- With what array of measures did governments respond to the Great Depression?

- Why did the Stalinist attempt to build "socialism in one country" lead to the "terror-famine" of 1932–1933 and the "great terror" of 1937–1938?

- Through what measures did the Nazi regime claim to be improving the quality of the German population?

- Why did the "popular front" strategy prove counterproductive in both France and Spain?

- Why did the other countries not stop Hitler's Germany before it was strong enough to start a new European war in 1939?

This icon will direct you to additional materials on the website: www .cengage.com/history/ noble/westciv6e.

See our interactive eBook for map and primary source activities.

different, and the extent to which each can be understood as an instance of totalitarianism remains controversial.

Fascism, Nazism, and communism seemed able to sidestep—or surmount—the ills of the Depression, yet they stood opposed to the parliamentary democracy that had long seemed the direction of progressive political change. So the democratic movement appeared to lose its momentum in the face of the political and economic challenges of the 1930s. The defeat, by early 1939, of the democratic republic in Spain by the authoritarian Nationalists seemed to exemplify the political direction of the decade.

THE GREAT DEPRESSION

With what array of measures did governments respond to the Great Depression?

If any single event can be said to have triggered the world economic crisis of the early 1930s, it was the stock market crash of October 1929 in the United States. But that crash had such an impact only because the new international economic order after World War I was extremely fragile. By October 1929, in fact, production was already declining in all the major Western countries except France.

The economies of Germany and the states of east-central Europe remained particularly vulnerable after the war, and in the increasingly interdependent economic world, their weaknesses magnified problems that started elsewhere. The crash of the U.S. stock market led to a restriction of credit in central Europe, which triggered a more general contraction in production and trade. Facing cruel dilemmas, policymakers proved unable to master the situation for the first few years of the crisis.

Causes of the Depression

Certain economic sectors, especially coal mining and agriculture, were already suffering severe problems by the mid-1920s, well before the stock market crash. British coal exports fell partly because oil and hydroelectricity were rapidly developing as alternatives. Unemployment in Britain was never less than 10 percent, even in the best of times between the wars. In agriculture, high prices worldwide during the war produced oversupply, which, in turn, led to a sharp drop in prices once the war was over. During the later 1920s, bumper harvests of grain and rice in many parts of the world renewed the downward pressure on prices. The result of low agricultural prices was a diminished demand for industrial goods, which impeded growth in the world economy.

Throughout the 1920s, finance ministers and central bankers had difficulty juggling the economic imbalances created by the war, centering on war debts to the United States and German reparations obligations to France, Britain, and Belgium. The strains in the system finally caught up with policymakers by 1929, when an international restriction of credit forced an end to the international economic cooperation that had been attempted throughout the decade.

The shaky postwar economic system depended on U.S. bank loans to Germany, funneled partly by international agreements, but also drawn by high interest rates. By 1928, however, U.S. investors were rapidly withdrawing their capital from Germany in search of the higher returns to be made in the booming U.S. stock market. This shift tightened credit in Germany. Then, the crash of the overpriced U.S. market in October 1929 deepened the problem by forcing suddenly strapped American investors to pull still more of their funds out of Germany. This process continued over the next two years, weakening the major banks in Germany and the other countries of central Europe, which were closely tied to the German economy. In May 1931, the bankruptcy of Vienna's most powerful bank, the Credit-Anstalt, made it clear that a crisis of potentially catastrophic proportions was in progress.

Despite attempts at adjustment on the international level, fears of bank failure or currency devaluation led to runs on the banks and currencies of Germany and central Europe. To maintain the value of the domestic currency, and thereby to resist the withdrawal of capital, government policymakers raised interest rates. This measure was not sufficient to stem the capital hemorrhage, but by restricting credit still more, it further dampened domestic economic activity.

Finally, the Germans seemed to have no choice but to freeze foreign assets—that is, to cease allowing conversion of assets held in German marks to other currencies. In this atmosphere, investors seeking the safest place for their capital tried to cash in currency for gold—or for British pounds, which could then be converted to gold. Europe's flight to gold, however, soon put such pressure on the British currency that Britain was forced to devalue the pound and sever it from the gold standard in September 1931. This proved the definitive end of the worldwide system of economic exchange based on the gold standard that had gradually crystallized during the nineteenth century.

The absence of a single standard of exchange, combined with various currency restrictions, made foreign trade more difficult, thereby diminishing it further. So did the scramble for tariff protection that proved a widespread response to the developing crisis. Crucial was the U.S. Smoot-Hawley Tariff Act of June 1930, which raised taxes on imports by 50 to 100 percent, forcing other nations to take comparable steps. Even Britain, long a bastion of free trade, adopted a peacetime tariff for the first time in nearly a century with the Import Duties Act of 1932, which imposed a 10 percent tax on most imports.

The decline of trade spread depression throughout the world economic system. By 1933, most major European countries were able to export no more than two-thirds, and in some cases as little as one-third, of the amount they had sold in 1929. At the same time, losses from international bank failures contracted credit and purchasing power and furthered the downward spiral, until by 1932 the European economies had shrunk to a little over half their 1929 size. This was the astonishing outcome of the short-lived prosperity of the 1920s.

Consequences and Responses

The Depression was essentially a radical contraction in economic activity; with less being produced and sold, demand for labor declined sharply. In Germany, industrial production by early 1933 was only half what it had been in 1929, and roughly six million Germans, or one-third of the labor force, were unemployed. In Germany, as elsewhere, the decline in employment opportunities helped produce a backlash against the ideal of the "new woman," working outside the home, which had been a prominent aspect of the new freedom of the 1920s. Even those men and women who hung on to jobs suffered from growing insecurity.

During the first years of the Depression, central bankers everywhere sought to balance budgets in order to reassure investors and stabilize currencies. With economies contracting and tax revenues declining, the only way to balance the budget was to sharply reduce government spending. In addition, governments responded to the decline in exports by forcing wages down, seeking to enhance competitiveness abroad. But by cutting purchasing power at home, both these measures reinforced the slowdown in economic activity.

CHRONOLOGY

October 1929	U.S. stock market crash helps trigger Great Depression
December 1929	Forced collectivization in Soviet agriculture begins
June 1930	Smoot-Hawley Tariff Act (U.S.)
May 1931	Bankruptcy of Vienna's Credit-Anstalt
January 1933	Hitler becomes German chancellor
December 1934	Assassination of Kirov
March 1935	Hitler announces rearmament
October 1935	Italy invades Ethiopia
March 1936	Germany remilitarizes the Rhineland
May 1936	Blum becomes French popular front prime minister
July 1936	Spanish civil war begins
March 1938	Third Moscow show trial; Bukharin and others convicted and executed
	Anschluss: Germany absorbs Austria
September 1938	"Appeasement": Munich conference ends Sudetenland crisis
November 1938	Crystal Night pogrom
March 1939	Dismemberment of Czechoslovakia
May 1939	Pact of Steel binds fascist Italy and Nazi Germany
August 23, 1939	Nazi-Soviet Pact
September 1, 1939	Germany invades Poland
September 3, 1939	Britain and France declare war on Germany

Unemployment in Britain
The Depression hit Britain hard—and its effects continued to be felt throughout the 1930s. These unemployed shipyard workers from Jarrow, in northeastern England, are marching to London in 1936 to present a protest petition. (Hulton Archive/Getty Images)

Economic policymakers based their responses on the "classical" economic model that had developed from the ideas of Adam Smith in the eighteenth century (see page 598). According to this model, a benign "invisible hand" ensured that a free-market price for labor, for capital, and for goods and services would produce an ongoing tendency toward economic equilibrium. A downturn in the business cycle was a normal and necessary adjustment; government interference would only upset this self-adjusting mechanism.

By 1932, however, it was clear that the conventional response was not working, and governments began seeking more actively to stimulate the economy. Although the British economist John Maynard Keynes would outline the rationale for governmental intervention in technical economic terms in 1936, governments could only experiment, and strategies varied widely. (See the feature, "The Written Record: The Government's Role in Managing a Free-Market Economy.") In the United States, Franklin D. Roosevelt (1882–1945) defeated the incumbent president, Herbert Hoover, in 1932 with the promise of a New Deal—a commitment to increase government spending to restore purchasing power. In fascist Italy, a state agency created to infuse capital into failing companies proved a reasonably effective basis for collaboration between government and business. In Germany, economics minister Hjalmar Schacht mounted an energetic assault on the economic problem after Hitler came to power in 1933. Government measures sealed off the German mark from international fluctuations, stimulated public spending—partly on rearmament—and kept wages low. By 1935, Germany was back to full employment. This success added tremendously to Hitler's popularity.

High unemployment in Norway, Sweden, and Denmark helped Social Democrats win power in all three of these Scandinavian countries by the mid-1930s. The new left-leaning governments responded to the economic crisis not by a frontal assault on capitalism, but by pioneering the "welfare state," providing such benefits as health care, unemployment insurance, and family allowances. To pay for the new welfare safety net, the Scandinavian countries adopted a high level of progressive taxation and pared military expenditures to a minimum. The turn to a welfare state eased the immediate human costs of the Depression and helped restore production by stimulating demand. At the same time, the Scandinavian model attracted much admiration as a "third way" between free-market capitalism and the various dictatorial extremes.

In the other European democracies, the Depression proved more intractable. Although Britain saw some recovery by the mid-1930s, it was especially the rearmament of the later 1930s,

The Government's Role in Managing a Free-Market Economy

In 1936, at the height of the Depression, the British economist John Maynard Keynes published The General Theory of Employment, Interest and Money, which proved the most influential work in economics of the twentieth century. While recognizing the advantages of a free-market economy, Keynes noted that capitalism seemed to entail a built-in tendency toward unemployment, dramatically evident in the Depression. Thus some people were attracted to socialist or statist alternatives, which might include, for example, the wholesale nationalization of industry. But Keynes insisted that a more active role for government in managing the capitalist economy could overcome the tendency toward unemployment while preserving a democratic framework and the advantages of a market economy. Government could manage the economy especially through the "socialization of investment"—absorbing money through taxation and spending it to stimulate the economy toward full employment.

The outstanding faults of the economic society in which we live are its failure to provide for full employment and its arbitrary and inequitable distribution of wealth and incomes....

...I conceive, therefore, that a somewhat comprehensive socialisation of investment will prove the only means of securing an approximation to full employment; though this need not exclude all manner of compromises and of devices by which public authority will co-operate with private initiative. But beyond this no obvious case is made out for a system of State Socialism which would embrace most of the economic life of the community. It is not the ownership of the instruments of production which it is important for the State to assume. If the State is able to determine the aggregate amount of resources devoted to augmenting the instruments and the basic rate of reward to those who own them, it will have accomplished all that is necessary. Moreover, the necessary measures of socialisation can be introduced gradually and without a break in the general traditions of society....

...The central controls necessary to ensure full employment will, of course, involve a large extension of the traditional functions of government. Furthermore, the modern classical theory has itself called attention to various conditions in which the free play of economic forces may need to be curbed or guided. But there will still remain a wide field for the exercise of private initiative and responsibility. Within this field the traditional advantages of individualism will still hold good.

Let us stop for a moment to remind ourselves what these advantages are. They are partly advantages of efficiency—the advantages of decentralisation and of the play of self-interest....

Whilst, therefore, the enlargement of the functions of government, involved in the task of adjusting to one another the propensity to consume and inducement to invest, would seem to a nineteenth-century publicist or to a contemporary American financier to be a terrific encroachment on individualism, I defend it, on the contrary, both as the only practicable means of avoiding the destruction of existing economic forms in their entirety and as the condition of the successful functioning of individual initiative....

The authoritarian state systems of today seem to solve the problem of unemployment at the expense of efficiency and of freedom. It is certain that the world will not much longer tolerate the unemployment which, apart from brief intervals of excitement, is associated—and, in my opinion, inevitably associated—with present-day capitalistic individualism. But it may be possible by a right analysis of the problem to cure the disease whilst preserving efficiency and freedom.

QUESTIONS

1. Why does Keynes argue for a considerably expanded role for government in coordinating the capitalist economy?

2. In what sense is Keynes trying to save free-market capitalism in light of the Depression and the appeal of the alternatives emerging in Italy, Germany, and the Soviet Union?

Source: From John Maynard Keynes, The General Theory of Employment, Interest and Money, pp. 372, 378–381. Reprinted by permission of J. S. Dring.

financed by borrowing, or deficit spending, that got the British economy growing again. France, less dependent on international trade, experienced the consequences of the world crisis only gradually. But by the early 1930s, France, too, was suffering its effects, which lingered to the end of the decade, helping to poison the political atmosphere.

The Impact Beyond the West

The radical restriction of international trade meant a sharp decline in demand for the basic commodities that colonial and other regions exported to the industrialized West. Economic strains fed nationalist, anti-Western sentiments in colonial nations. The increase in misery among rural

Gandhi Advocates Nonviolence

Mohandas Gandhi, a successful English-educated lawyer, emerged as a major force in the movement for Indian independence just after World War I. Calling first for a strategy of noncooperation with the British colonial overlords, Gandhi gradually developed a philosophy of nonviolent civil disobedience, which won widespread sympathy for the cause of Indian independence. The following excerpts from articles published in 1935 and 1939—years notable for outbreaks of violence elsewhere—explain the significance of nonviolence to Gandhi's overall strategy.

Non-violence to be a creed has to be all-pervasive. I cannot be non-violent about one activity of mine and violent about others. That would be a policy, not a life force. That being so, I cannot be indifferent about the war that Italy is now waging against Abyssinia.... India has an unbroken tradition of non-violence from times immemorial. But at no time in her ancient history, as far as I know it, has it had complete nonviolence in action pervading the whole land. Nevertheless, it is my unshakeable belief that her destiny is to deliver the message of non-violence to mankind....

...India as a nation is not non-violent in the full sense of the term.... Her non-violence is that of the weak.... She lacks the ability to offer physical resistance. She has no consciousness of strength. She is conscious only of her weakness. If she were otherwise, there would be no communal problems, nor political. If she were non-violent in the consciousness of her strength, Englishmen would lose their role of distrustful conquerors. We may talk politically as we like and often legitimately blame the English rulers. But if we, as Indians, could but for a moment visualize ourselves as a strong people disdaining to strike, we should cease to fear Englishmen whether as soldiers, traders or administrators, and they to distrust us. Therefore if we became truly non-violent we should carry Englishmen with us in all we might do. In other words, we being millions would be the greatest moral force in the world, and Italy would listen to our friendly word....

... [W]hen society is deliberately constructed in accordance with the law of non-violence, its structure will be different in material particulars from what it is today. But I cannot say in advance what the government based wholly on non-violence will be like.

What is happening today is disregard of the law of non-violence and enthronement of violence as if it were an eternal law. The democracies, therefore, that we see at work in England, America and France are only so called, because they are no less based on violence than Nazi Germany, Fascist Italy or even Soviet Russia. The only difference is that the violence of the last three is much better organized than that of the three democratic powers. Nevertheless we see today a mad race for outdoing one another in the matter of armaments. And if and when the clash comes, as it is bound to come one day, the democracies win, they will do so only because they will have the backing of their peoples who imagine that they have a voice in their own government whereas in the other three cases the peoples might rebel against their own dictatorships.

Holding the view that without the recognition of non-violence on a national scale there is no such thing as a constitutional or democratic government, I devote my energy to the propagation of nonviolence as the law of our life—individual, social, political, national and international. I fancy that I have seen the light, though dimly. I write cautiously, for I do not profess to know the whole of the Law. If I know the successes of my experiments, I know also my failures. But the successes are enough to fill me with undying hope. I have often said that if one takes care of the means, the end will take care of itself. Non-violence is the means, the end for every nation is complete independence.

QUESTIONS

1. What is the difference between "strong" and "weak" nonviolence in Gandhi's thinking?

2. Why does Gandhi play down the difference between the democracies and the dictatorships of the West?

Source: From Raghavan Iyer, ed., *The Essential Writings of Mahatma Gandhi,* 1991, pp. 245–247, 262–263. Reprinted by permission of the Navajivan Trust.

villagers in India, for example, spread the movement for national independence from urban elites to the rural masses. In this context, Mohandas Gandhi, who had become known by 1920 for advocating noncooperation with the British, became the first leader to win a mass following throughout the Indian subcontinent (see pages 717 and 729). Encouraging villagers to boycott British goods, Gandhi accented simplicity, self-reliance, and an overall strategy of nonviolent civil disobedience based on Indian traditions. (See the feature, "The Global Record: Gandhi Advocates Nonviolence.")

In Japan, the strains of the Great Depression helped produce precisely the turn to imperialist violence that Gandhi sought to counter. Densely populated, yet lacking raw materials, Japan was particularly dependent on international trade and reacted strongly as increasing tariffs elsewhere cut sharply into Japanese exports. Led by young army officers who were already eager for a less subservient form of Westernization, Japan turned to aggressive imperialism. As justification, the Japanese began arguing that they were spearheading a wider struggle to free East Asia from Western imperialism. (See the feature, "The Global Record: Japan's 'Pan-Asian' Mission" on page 802 in Chapter 28.) Attacking in 1931, Japanese forces quickly reduced Manchuria to a puppet state, but the Japanese met stubborn resistance when they began seeking to extend this conquest to the rest of China in 1937.

Japanese pressure indirectly advanced the rise of the Chinese communist movement, led by Mao Zedong (Mao Tse-tung, 1893–1976). Securing a base in the Yanan district in 1936, Mao began seeking to apply Marxism-Leninism to China through land reform and other measures to link the Communist Party elite to the Chinese peasantry. Mao was notable among those adapting Western ideas to build an indigenous movement that would at once overcome Western imperialism and create an alternative to Western liberal capitalism.

SECTION SUMMARY

- The new international economic interdependence after World War I entailed strains that were difficult to understand at the time—and that eventually helped produce the Great Depression.

- The effort to respond to the economic downturn through the principles of classical economics only deepened the crisis.

- The new regimes of the extreme left and right won greater prestige in some circles because they seemed to be surviving the global economic crisis more successfully than the capitalist democracies.

- Gradually, the democratic governments began trying out more innovative, interventionist responses to the Depression.

- By restricting imports into the industrialized West, the Depression hurt the non-Western world and helped fuel anticolonialist sentiment.

THE STALINIST REVOLUTION IN THE SOVIET UNION

Why did the Stalinist attempt to build "socialism in one country" lead to the "terror-famine" of 1932–1933 and the "great terror" of 1937–1938?

Seeking to build "socialism in one country," Joseph Stalin led the Soviet Union during the 1930s through an astounding transformation that mixed achievement with brutality and terror in often tragic ways. The resulting governmental system, which gave Stalin unprecedented power, proved crucial to the outcome of the experiment that had begun with the Russian Revolution of 1917. But whether the fateful turn of the 1930s had been implicit in the Leninist revolutionary model, or whether it stemmed mostly from unforeseen circumstances and Stalin's idiosyncratic personality, has long been controversial.

Crash Industrialization and Forced Collectivization

Stalin's program of rapid industrialization based on forced **collectivization** in agriculture began in earnest at the beginning of 1930. It entailed an assault on the better-off peasants, or *kulaks*, who were often sent to labor camps in Siberia while their lands were taken over by the government. The remaining peasants were herded into new government-controlled collective farms. So unpopular was this measure that many peasants simply killed their livestock or smashed their farm implements rather than have them collectivized. By 1934, the number of cattle in the Soviet Union was barely half what it had been in 1928.

Collectivization served, as intended, to squeeze from the peasantry the resources needed to finance industrialization, but it was carried out with extreme brutality. What was being squeezed was not merely a surplus—the state's extractions cut into subsistence. So while Soviet agricultural exports increased after 1930, large numbers of peasants starved to death. The great famine that developed during 1932–1933 resulted in between five million and six million deaths, over half of them in Ukraine. This "terror-famine" went unrecorded in the Soviet press, and the Soviets refused help from international relief agencies.

By 1937, almost all Soviet agriculture took place on collective farms—or on state farms set up in areas not previously under agriculture. However, restrictions on private plots and livestock ownership were eased slightly after 1933, and partly as a result, agriculture rebounded and living standards began to rise. By the late 1930s, moreover, significant increases in industrial output had established solid foundations in heavy industry, including the bases for military production.

collectivization Soviet program under Stalin that reshaped agriculture by forcing peasants into government-controlled collective farms in order to better finance rapid industrialization.

Collectivization in Soviet Agriculture At the "New Life" collective farm, not far from Moscow, women stand for the morning roll call. The Soviet collectivization effort of the 1930s rested in important measure on the forced mobilization of peasant women. (Russian State Film & Photo Archive at Krasnogorsk (RGAKFD))

Soviet propaganda, including art in the official socialist realist style, glorified the achievements of the new Soviet industrial and agricultural workers. "Stakhanovism" (stah-KAH-nov-izm), named for a coal miner who had heroically exceeded his production quota in 1935, became the term for the prodigious economic achievements that the regime valued as it proclaimed the superiority of the communist system.

But whatever its successes, this forced development program created many inefficiencies and entailed tremendous human costs. The Soviet Union could probably have done at least as well, with much less suffering, through other strategies of industrial development. Moreover, Stalin's program departed from certain socialist principles—egalitarianism in wages, for example—that the regime had taken very seriously during the late 1920s. By 1931, bureaucratic managers, concerned simply with maximizing output, were openly favoring workers in certain industries. Collective bargaining and the right to strike had vanished from the workers' arsenal.

From Opposition to Terror, 1932–1938

Stalin's radical course, with its brutality and uncertain economic justification, quickly provoked opposition. During the summer of 1932, a group centered on M. N. Ryutin (ree-YOU-tin) circulated among party leaders a two-hundred-page tract calling for a retreat from Stalin's economic program and a return to democracy within the party. It advocated readmitting those who had been expelled—including Stalin's archenemy, Leon Trotsky. Moreover, the document strongly condemned Stalin personally, describing him as "the evil genius of the Russian Revolution, who, motivated by a personal desire for power and revenge, brought the Revolution to the verge of ruin."[1]

Stalin promptly had Ryutin and his associates ousted from the party, then arrested and imprisoned. But especially as the international situation grew menacing during the 1930s, Stalin became ever more preoccupied with the scope for further opposition. Both Germany and Japan exhibited expansionist aims that might threaten Soviet territories. Trotsky from exile might work with foreign agents and Soviet dissidents to sabotage the Soviet development effort.

In December 1934, the assassination of Sergei Kirov (KIH-roff), party leader of Leningrad (the former Petrograd), indicated the potential for violence. But whether Stalin was actually responsible for the assassination, or simply felt vulnerable because of it, has long been in dispute. In any case, the determination to root out "wreckers," those assumed to be sabotaging the grandiose Soviet experiment, led gradually to purges, **show trials**, and even a kind of terror, with several categories of citizens vulnerable to arrest by the secret police. By the time it wound down, early in 1939, this "great terror" had significantly changed the communist regime—and Soviet society. But though the bare facts are clear, what to make of them is not.

In the three Moscow show trials, held during a twenty-month period from 1936 to 1938, noted Bolsheviks, including Nikolai Bukharin and major functionaries such as Genrikh Yagoda, recently removed as chief of the secret police, confessed to a series of sensational trumped-up charges: that they had been behind the assassination of Kirov, that they would like to have killed Stalin, that they constituted an "anti-Soviet, Trotskyite center," spying for Germany and Japan and preparing to sabotage Soviet industry in the event of war. Almost all the accused, including Bukharin and others who had been central to the 1917 revolution, were convicted and executed. Soviet authorities did not dare risk public trial for the few who refused, even in the face of torture, to play their assigned roles and confess. Among them was Ryutin, who was shot in secret early in 1937.

During 1937, a purge wiped out much of the top ranks of the army, with half the entire officer corps shot or imprisoned in response to unfounded charges of spying and treason. The Communist Party underwent several purges, culminating in the great purge of 1937 and 1938. Of the roughly two thousand delegates to the 1934 congress of the Communist Party, over half were shot during the next few years.

Although heated controversy remains over the number of victims of the Stalinist revolution, the totals are staggering. According to one influential high-end estimate, 8.5 million of the approximately 160 million people in the Soviet Union were arrested during 1937 and 1938, and of these, perhaps 1 million were executed by shooting. Half of those belonging to the Communist Party—1.2 million people—were arrested; of these, 600,000 were executed, and most of the rest died in **gulag** labor camps. Altogether, the terror surrounding the several purges resulted in as many as 8 million deaths. Estimates of the death toll from all of Stalin's policies of the 1930s, including forced collectivization, range as high as 20 million.

Communism and Stalinism

What was going on in this bizarre and lethal combination of episodes? Obviously, Stalinism was one possible outcome of Leninist communism, but was it the logical, even the inevitable, outcome? Leninism had accented centralized authority and the scope for human will to force events, so it may have created a framework in which Stalinism was likely to emerge. Yet Stalin's personal idiosyncrasies and growing paranoia seem to have been crucial for the Soviet system to develop as it did. But though he ended up the regime's undisputed leader, Stalin was part of a wider dynamic.

It was long assumed that Stalin was pursuing a coordinated policy of terror to create a system of total control. Yet recent research has shown that he was often merely improvising, responding to a situation that had become chaotic, out of control, as the Communists tried to carry through a revolution in a backward country. No one had ever attempted this sort of forced industrialization based on a centrally planned economy. At once idealistic, inexperienced, and suspicious, the regime's leaders really believed that failures must be due to sabotage—that "wreckers" were seeking to undermine the heroic Soviet experiment. Moreover, though Stalin tended to blow them out of proportion, there were genuine threats to the Soviet regime and his own leadership by the mid-1930s.

Whereas the terror was long viewed as almost random, it is now clearer that those in the upper and middle reaches of the Soviet system were the most vulnerable. Top officials encouraged ordinary workers to provide information about plant managers and local party officials who seemed incompetent or corrupt. And whether to serve the revolution or to vent personal resentments, such workers often took the initiative in denouncing their superiors, thereby playing important roles in the dynamic that developed.

But what explains the "confessions" that invariably resulted from the bizarre show trials? The accused sometimes succumbed to torture, and to threats to their families. But some, at least, offered false confessions because they believed that in doing so, they were still serving the communist cause. All along, the revolution had required a willingness to compromise personal

show trials Trials staged for ideological and propaganda reasons in the USSR.

gulag Originally an acronym for "main camp administration," it refers to the network of forced labor camps for political prisoners in the Soviet Union. There were at least 476 camps in all.

- Forced collectivization was a way—ultimately a brutal way—of extracting the agricultural surplus from the peasantry to finance rapid industrialization in the Soviet Union.

- The *gulag*, the network of forced labor camps, expanded dramatically with the Stalinist revolution of the 1930s—and especially with the "great terror" of 1937–1938.

- Soviet leaders really believed that failures must be due to sabotage—that "wreckers" were seeking to undermine the heroic communist experiment.

- Although Stalin's ultimate responsibility is clear, the great terror of 1937–1938 grew not from some conscious design, but from a momentum that spun out of control.

- Stemming from an effort to root out "wreckers," the terror especially affected those in the upper and middle reaches of the Soviet system.

scruples, including "bourgeois" concerns about personal honor and dignity. Even though false, these confessions could help the communist regime ward off the genuine dangers it faced. So in confessing, the accused would be serving the long-term cause, which they believed to be bigger than Stalin and the issues of the moment. What some could not see—or admit—was that the triumph of Stalinism was fatally compromising the original revolutionary vision.

Although much was unplanned and even out of control, Stalin's ultimate responsibility for the lethal dynamic of the later 1930s is undeniable. At the height of the terror, he personally approved lists for execution, and he took advantage of the chain of events to crush all actual or imagined opposition. By 1939, Stalin loyalists constituted the entire party leadership.

Even as some turned away in disillusionment or despair, others found the regime's ruthlessness in rooting out its apparent enemies evidence of its ongoing revolutionary purpose. And whereas Stalin was not a charismatic leader like Hitler or Mussolini, he was coming for many to embody the ongoing promise of the communist experiment.

HITLER AND NAZISM IN GERMANY

Through what measures did the Nazi regime claim to be improving the quality of the German population?

Adolf Hitler German dictator whose aggressive foreign policy led to World War II and whose policies of anti-Semitism and racial purity led to the murder of millions.

Beset with problems from the start, the Weimar Republic lay gravely wounded by 1932. Various antidemocratic groups competed to replace it. The winner was the Nazi movement, led by **Adolf Hitler**, who became chancellor in January 1933. It was especially Hitler's new regime in Germany that made the 1930s so tortured, for Hitler not only radically transformed German society, but fundamentally altered the power balance in Europe.

Nazism took inspiration from Italian fascism, but Hitler's regime proved more dynamic—and more troubling—than Mussolini's. Nazism was not conventionally revolutionary, in the sense of mounting a frontal challenge to the existing socioeconomic order. Some of its themes were traditionalist and even anti-modernizing. But in the final analysis, Nazism was anything but conservative. Indeed, it constituted a direct assault on what had long been held as the best of Western civilization.

The Emergence of Nazism and the Crisis of the Weimar Republic

National Socialist German Workers' (Nazi) Party (NSDAP) The political party that grew from the movement that German dictator Adolf Hitler made his vehicle to power.

The **National Socialist German Workers' (Nazi) Party (NSDAP)** emerged from the turbulent situation in Munich just after the war. A center of leftist agitation, the city also became a hotbed of the radical right, nurturing a number of new nationalist, militantly anticommunist political groups. One of them, a workers' party founded under the aegis of the right-wing Thule Society early in 1919, attracted the attention of Adolf Hitler, who soon gave it his personal stamp.

Adolf Hitler (1889–1945) had been born not German but Austrian, the son of a middling government official. By 1913, he had become a German nationalist hostile to the multinational Habsburg empire, and he emigrated to Germany to escape service in the Austrian army. He was not opposed to military service per se, however, and when war broke out in 1914, he immediately volunteered to serve in the German army.

Corporal Hitler experienced firsthand the fighting at the front and, as a courier, performed bravely and effectively. Indeed, he was in a field hospital being treated for gas poisoning when the war ended. Although his fellow soldiers considered him quirky and introverted, Hitler found the war experience crucial; it was during the war, he said later, that he "found himself."

Following his release from the hospital, Hitler worked for the army in routine surveillance of extremist groups in Munich. In this role, he joined the infant German Workers' Party late in 1919. When his first political speech at a rally in February 1920 proved a resounding success, Hitler began to believe he could play a special political role. From this point, he gradually developed the confidence to lead a new nationalist, anticommunist, and anti-Weimar movement.

But Hitler jumped the gun in November 1923 when, with Erich Ludendorff at his side, he led the Beer Hall Putsch in Munich, an abortive attempt to launch a march on Berlin to overthrow the republic. On trial after this effort failed, Hitler gained greater national visibility as he denounced the Versailles treaty and the Weimar government. Still, *Mein Kampf* (*My Battle*), the political tract that he wrote while in prison during 1924, sold poorly. To most, Hitler was simply a right-wing rabble-rouser whose views were not worth taking seriously.

His failure in 1923 convinced Hitler that he should exploit the existing political system, but not challenge it directly, in his quest for power on the national level. Yet Hitler did not view the NSDAP as just another political party, playing by the same rules as the others. Thus, most notably, the Nazi Party maintained a paramilitary arm, the *Sturmabteilung* (SA), which provoked a good deal of antileftist street violence. Still, the Nazis remained confined to the margins of national politics, even as late as 1928, when they attracted only 2.6 percent of the vote in elections to the Reichstag.

The onset of the economic depression by the end of 1929 produced problems that the Weimar democracy could not handle—and that radically changed the German political framework. The pivotal issue was unemployment insurance, which became a tremendous financial burden for the government as unemployment grew. The governing coalition fell apart over the issue in March 1930, and this proved to be the end of normal parliamentary government in Weimar Germany.

President Paul von Hindenburg called on Heinrich Brüning (1885–1970), an expert on economics from the Catholic Center Party, to become chancellor. Brüning was to spearhead a hard-nosed, deflationary economic program intended to stimulate exports by lowering prices. Like most middle-class Germans, Brüning feared inflation, disliked unemployment insurance, and believed that Germany could not afford public works projects to pump up demand—the obvious alternative to his deflationary policy. But when he presented his program to the Reichstag, he encountered opposition not only from those on the left, but also from conservatives, eager to undermine the republic altogether. As a result, Brüning could get no parliamentary majority. Rather than resigning or seeking a compromise, he invoked Article 48, the emergency provision of the Weimar constitution, which enabled him to govern under presidential decree.

When this expedient provoked strenuous protests, Brüning dissolved the Reichstag and scheduled new elections for September 1930. A more conciliatory tack might have enabled the chancellor to build a new parliamentary majority—and save parliamentary government. In any case, the outcome of the elections was disastrous—for Brüning, and ultimately for Germany as well. While two of the democratic, pro-Weimar parties lost heavily, the two extremes, the Communists and the Nazis, improved their totals considerably. Indeed, this was a major breakthrough for the Nazis, whose share of the vote jumped from 2.6 percent to 18.3 percent of the total.

Brüning continued to govern, still relying on President Hindenburg and Article 48 rather than majority support in the Reichstag. But his program of raising taxes and decreasing government spending failed to revive the economy. Meanwhile, the growth of the political extremes helped fuel an intensification of the political violence and street fighting that had bedeviled the Weimar Republic from the beginning.

By this point, conservatives close to Hindenburg sensed the chance to replace the fragmented parliamentary system with some form of authoritarian government. A new, tougher regime would not only attack the economic crisis, but also stiffen governmental resistance against the apparent threat from the left. In May 1932, those advisers finally persuaded Hindenburg to dump Brüning, and two of them, Franz von Papen (PAH-pin) (1878–1969) and General Kurt von Schleicher (SHLY-shur) (1882–1934), each got a chance to govern in the months that followed. But neither succeeded, partly because of the daring strategy Hitler adopted.

When, following the ouster of Brüning, new elections were held in July 1932, the Nazis won 37.3 percent of the vote and the Communists 14.3 percent. Together, the two extremes controlled a majority of the seats in the Reichstag. Hitler, as the leader of what was now the Reichstag's largest party, refused to join any coalition—unless he could lead it as chancellor. Meanwhile, the authoritarian conservatives around President Hindenburg wanted to take advantage of the Nazis' mass support for antidemocratic purposes.

Finally, in January 1933, with government at an impasse, Papen lined up a new coalition that he proposed to Hindenburg to replace Schleicher's government. Hitler would be chancellor, Papen himself vice chancellor, and Alfred Hugenberg (1865–1951), the leader of the Nationalist Party, finance minister. For months, Hindenburg had resisted giving Hitler a chance to govern, but he felt this combination might work to establish a parliamentary majority, to box out the left, and to contain Nazism. So Hindenburg named Hitler Germany's chancellor on January 30, 1933.

It became clear virtually at once that the outcome of the crisis was a dramatic change of regime, the triumph of Hitler and Nazism. But though the Nazis had always wanted to destroy the Weimar Republic, they were not directly responsible for overthrowing it. The rise of Nazism was more a symptom than a cause of the crisis of Weimar democracy.

In one sense, the Weimar Republic collapsed from within, largely because the German people disagreed fundamentally about priorities after the war—and then again with the onset of the Depression. Thus, the new democracy produced unstable government based on multiparty coalitions, and it fell into virtual paralysis when faced with the economic crisis by 1930. At the same time, however, those around Hindenburg were particularly quick to begin undercutting democratic government in 1930, as the economic crisis seemed to intensify the threat from the extreme left.

With unemployment growing during the first years of the 1930s, both the Nazis and the Communists gained electoral support, but the Germans voting for the Nazis were not simply those most threatened economically. Nor did the Nazi Party appeal primarily to the uneducated or socially marginal. Rather, the party served as a focus of opposition for those alienated from the Weimar Republic itself. Although the Nazis did relatively poorly among Catholics and industrial workers, they put together a broad, fairly diverse base of electoral support, ranging from artisans and small shopkeepers to university students and civil servants. But though Hitler was clearly anti-Weimar, anticommunist, and anti-Versailles, his positive program remained vague; those who voted for the Nazis were not clear what they might be getting. In light of economic depression and political impasse, however, it seemed time to try something new.

The Consolidation of Hitler's Power, 1933–1934

When Hitler became chancellor, it was not obvious that a change of regime was beginning. Like his predecessors, he could govern only with the president's approval, and governmental institutions like the army, the judiciary, and the diplomatic corps, though hardly bastions of democracy, were not in the hands of committed Nazis. But even though an element of caution and cultivated ambiguity remained, a revolution quickly began, creating a new regime, the Third Reich.

On February 23, just weeks after Hitler became chancellor, a fire engulfed the Reichstag building in Berlin. It was set by a young Dutch communist acting on his own, but it seemed to suggest that a communist uprising was imminent. This sense of emergency gave Hitler an excuse to restrict civil liberties and imprison leftist leaders, including the entire Communist parliamentary delegation. Even in this atmosphere of crisis, the Nazis could not win a majority in the Reichstag elections of March 5. But support from the Nationalists and the Catholic Center Party enabled the Nazis to win Reichstag approval for an enabling act granting Hitler the power to make laws on his own for the next four years, bypassing both the Reichstag and the president.

Although the Weimar Republic was never formally abolished, the laws that followed fundamentally altered government, politics, and public life in Germany. The other parties were either outlawed or persuaded to dissolve, so that in July 1933, the Nazi Party was declared the only legal party. When President Hindenburg died in August 1934, the offices of chancellor and president were merged, and Germany had just one leader, Adolf Hitler, holding unprecedented power. Members of the German armed forces now swore loyalty to him personally.

During this period of power consolidation, Hitler acted decisively but carefully, generally accenting normalization. To be sure, his methods occasionally gave conservatives pause, most notably when he had several hundred people murdered in the "blood purge" of June 30, 1934. But this purge was directed especially against the SA, led by Ernst Röhm (1887–1934), who had had pretensions of controlling the army. His removal seemed evidence that Hitler was taming the radical elements in his own movement. In fact, however, this purge led to the ascendancy of the *Schutzstaffel* (SS), the select Nazi elite, directed by Heinrich Himmler (1900–1945). Linked to the Gestapo, the secret political police, the SS became the institutional basis for the most troubling aspects of Nazism.

Schutzstaffel (SS)
Specially selected Nazi elite, entrusted with the most sensitive ideological tasks of the Nazi regime—and responsible for many of its worst atrocities.

Hitler and Children Adolf Hitler was often portrayed as the friend of children. This photograph accompanied a story for an elementary school reader that described how Hitler, told it was this young girl's birthday, picked her from a crowd of well-wishers to treat her "to cake and strawberries with thick, sweet cream." (Bayerische Staatsbibliothek Munchen/Fotoarchiv Hoffmann)

Hitler's Worldview and the Dynamics of Nazi Practice

In achieving the chancellorship and in expanding his power thereafter, Hitler proved an adept politician, but he was hardly a mere opportunist, seeking to amass power for its own sake. The central components of Hitler's thinking—geopolitics, biological racism, anti-Semitism, and Social Darwinism—were by no means specifically German. They could be found all over the Western world by the early twentieth century.

Geopolitics claimed to offer a scientific understanding of world power relationships based on geographical determinism. In his writings of the 1920s, Hitler warned that Germany faced imminent decline unless it confronted its geopolitical limitations. To remain fully sovereign in the emerging new era of global superpowers like the United States, Germany would have to act quickly to expand its territory. Otherwise, it would end up like Switzerland or the Netherlands.

For decades, German imperialists had argued about whether Germany was better advised to seek overseas colonies or to expand its reach in Europe. As Hitler saw it, Germany's failure to make a clear choice had led to its defeat in World War I. Now choice was imperative, and current geopolitical thinking suggested the direction for expansion. Far-flung empires relying on naval support were said to be in decline. The future lay with land-based states—unified, geographically contiguous, with the space necessary for self-sufficiency. By expanding eastward into Poland

and the Soviet Union, Germany could conquer the living space, or *Lebensraum*, necessary for agricultural-industrial balance—and ultimately for self-sufficiency.

Though limited and mechanistic, this geopolitical way of thinking is at least comprehensible, in light of the German vulnerabilities that had become evident during World War I. The other three strands of Hitler's worldview were much less plausible, though each had become prominent during the second half of the nineteenth century. Biological racism insisted that built-in racial characteristics determine what is most important about any individual. Anti-Semitism went beyond racism in claiming that Jews had played, and continued to play, a special and negative role in history. The fact that the Jews were dispersed and often landless indicated that they were different—and parasitical. Finally, Social Darwinism, especially in its German incarnation, accented the positive role of struggle—not among individuals, as in a prominent American strand, but among racial groups.

The dominant current of racist thinking found the "Aryans" to be healthy, creative, and superior. Originally the Sanskrit term for "noble," *Aryan* gradually came to indicate the ancient language assumed to have been the common source of the modern Indo-European languages. An Aryan was simply a speaker of one of those languages. By the late nineteenth century, however, the term had become supremely ill defined. In much racist thinking, Germanic peoples were somehow especially Aryan, but race mixing had produced impurity—and thus degeneration. Success in struggle with the other races was the ultimate measure of vitality, the only proof of racial superiority for the future.

Hitler brought these themes together by emphasizing that humanity is not special, but simply part of nature, subject to the same laws of struggle and selection as the other animal species. Humanitarian ideals were thus dangerous illusions. As he put it to a group of officer cadets in 1944:

> Nature is always teaching us…that she is governed by the principle of selection: that victory is to the strong and that the weak must go to the wall. She teaches us that what may seem cruel to us, because it affects us personally or because we have been brought up in ignorance of her laws, is nevertheless often essential if a higher way of life is to be attained. Nature…knows nothing of the notion of humanitarianism, which signifies that the weak must at all costs be protected and preserved even at the expense of the strong.
>
> Nature does not see in weakness any extenuating reasons…on the contrary, weakness calls for condemnation.[2]

To Hitler, the Jews were not simply another of the races involved in this endless struggle. Rather, as landless parasites, they embodied the principles—from humanitarianism to class struggle—that were antithetical to the healthy natural struggle among racial groups. "Jewishness" was bound up with the negative, critical intellect that dared suggest things ought to be not natural but just, even that it was up to human beings to change the world, to make it just. The Jews were the virus keeping the community from a healthy natural footing. Marxist communism, embodying divisive class struggle as well as utopian humanitarian ideals, was fundamentally Jewish.

The central features of Nazism in practice, from personal dictatorship to the extermination of the Jews, followed from Hitler's view of the world. First, the racial community must organize itself politically for this ceaseless struggle. Individuals are but instruments for the success of the racial community. Parliamentary democracy, reflecting short-term individual interests, fosters selfish materialism and division, thereby weakening that community. The political order must rest instead on a charismatic leader, united with the whole people through bonds of common blood.

Nazi Aims and German Society

To create a genuine racial community, or *Volksgemeinschaft*, it was necessary to unify society and instill Nazi values, thereby making the individual feel part of the whole—and ultimately an instrument to serve the whole. This entailed more or less forced participation in an array of Nazi groupings, from the Women's Organization to the Hitler Youth, from the Labor Front to the "Strength Through Joy" leisure-time organization. Common participation meant shared experiences, such as weekend hikes and a weekly one-dish meal. Even the most ordinary, once-private activities took on a public or political dimension. Moreover, the Nazis devised unprecedented ways to stage-manage public life, using rituals like the Hitler salute, symbols like the swastika, new media like radio and film, and carefully orchestrated party rallies—all in an effort to foster this sense of belonging. (See the feature, "The Visual Record: Film as Propaganda.")

The Nazi regime enjoyed considerable popular support, but even after Hitler was well entrenched in power, most Germans did not grasp the regime's deeper dynamic. Some welcomed the sense of unity, the feeling of belonging and participation, especially after what had seemed the alienation and divisiveness of the Weimar years. Moreover, Hitler himself was immensely popular, partly because of his personal charisma, partly because his apparently decisive leadership was a welcome departure from the near paralysis of the Weimar parliamentary system. But most important, before the coming of war in 1939, he seemed to go from success to success, surmounting the Depression and repudiating the major terms of the hated Versailles treaty.

Hitler's propaganda minister, Joseph Goebbels (1897–1945), played on these successes to create a "Hitler myth," which made Hitler seem at once a hero and a man of the people, even the embodiment of healthy German ideals against the excesses and corruption that could be attributed to the Nazi Party. This myth became central to the Nazi regime, but it merely provided a façade behind which the real Hitler could pursue partially hidden, longer-term aims. These aims were not publicized directly because the German people did not seem ready for them. In this sense, then, support for Hitler and his regime was broad but shallow during the 1930s.

Moreover, resistance increased as the regime became more intrusive. Youth gangs actively opposed the official Hitler Youth organization as it grew increasingly overbearing and militaristic by the late 1930s. But people resisted especially by minimizing their involvement with the regime, retreating into the private realm, in response to the Nazi attempt to make everything public.

Did such people feel constantly under threat of the Gestapo, the secret police? In principle, the Gestapo could interpret the will of the *Führer*, or leader, and decide whether any individual citizen was "guilty" or not. And the Gestapo was not concerned about due process; on occasion, it simply bypassed the regular court system. But the Gestapo did not terrorize Germans at random. Its victims were generally members of specific groups, people suspected of active opposition, or people who protected those the Gestapo had targeted.

Moreover, changes and contradictions in Nazi goals allowed considerable space for personal choice. During the struggle for power, the Nazis had emphasized the woman's role as wife and mother and deplored the ongoing emancipation of women. Once Hitler came to power, concerns about unemployment reinforced these views. Almost immediately, Hitler's government began offering interest-free loans to help couples set up housekeeping if the woman agreed to leave the labor force. Such efforts to increase the German birthrate reinforced the emphasis on child rearing in Nazi women's organizations. Nonetheless, the size of the family continued to decrease in Germany, as elsewhere in the industrialized world during the 1930s.

Beginning in 1936, when rapid rearmament began to produce labor shortages, the regime did an about-face and began seeking to attract women back to the workplace, especially into jobs central to military preparation. These efforts were not notably successful, and by 1940, the military was calling for the conscription of women into war industries.

Further, the Nazis valued the family only insofar as it was congruent with the "health" of the racial community. They were determined to promote that health by actually implementing radical eugenics measures that had been discussed, but not seriously implemented, during the Weimar years. The Nazi regime encouraged childbearing and large families on the part of those considered fit, while simultaneously discouraging those considered unfit from having children. In pursuit of these goals, the regime regulated marriage, essentially politicized the family, and compromised traditional family values again and again.

Just months after coming to power in 1933, Hitler brushed aside the objections of Vice Chancellor Franz von Papen, a Catholic, and engineered a law mandating the compulsory sterilization of persons suffering from certain allegedly hereditary diseases. Medical personnel sterilized some 400,000 people, the vast majority of them "Aryan" Germans, during the Nazi years.

Eugenics was essentially one of two prongs of the Nazis' radical population policy. The other sought ethnic homogeneity, especially through measures directed against Germany's small Jewish minority. Although the regime began immediately to single out the Jews, Nazi Jewish policy remained an improvised hodgepodge prior to World War II. Within weeks after Hitler became chancellor in 1933, new restrictions limited Jewish participation in the civil service, in the professions, and in German cultural life—and quickly drew censure from the League of Nations. The Nuremberg Laws, announced at a party rally in 1935, included prohibition of sexual relations and marriage between Jewish and non-Jewish Germans. Beginning in 1938, the Jews had to carry special identification cards and to add "Sarah" or "Israel" to their given names.

THE RESPONSE OF THE GERMAN PEOPLE

WOMEN, FAMILY, AND REPRODUCTION

NAZI POLICY TOWARD GERMAN JEWS

Film as Propaganda

One of the extraordinary pieces of evidence from the Nazi period is *Triumph of the Will,* a documentary film on the sixth Nazi Party rally, which took place from September 4 to 10, 1934, in the historic city of Nuremberg, by this time the official site for such party rallies. Directed by a talented young woman named Leni Riefenstahl (1902–2003), *Triumph of the Will* has long been recognized as one of the most compelling propaganda films ever made. What can we learn from this film about how the Nazis understood and used propaganda? What was the Nazi regime trying to convey in sponsoring the film, with the particular images it contained?

A sense of the scope for political propaganda was one of the defining features of the Nazi movement virtually from its inception. In his quest for power, Hitler allotted an especially significant role to his future propaganda minister, Joseph Goebbels. Both Hitler and Goebbels saw that new media and carefully orchestrated events might be used to shape the political views of masses of people.

The Nazi Party held the first of what would become annual conventions in Nuremberg in 1927. From the start, these meetings were rallies of the faithful, intended to give the Nazi movement a sense of cohesion and common purpose; but they increasingly became carefully staged propaganda spectacles, with banners and searchlights, parades and speeches. When, by 1934, the regime had completed the task of immediate power consolidation, it seemed time to seize the potential of the film medium to carry the spectacle beyond those present in Nuremberg. The intention to make a film thus influenced the staging of the 1934 rally. Film would transform the six-day event into a single potent work of art.

When Hitler came to power, Goebbels, as propaganda minister, assumed control of the German film industry, and he was particularly jealous of his prerogatives in this sphere. If there was to be a film of one of the Nuremberg rallies, he assumed that he would be in charge. So he objected strenuously when Hitler decided that Riefenstahl, who was not even a party member, should film the 1934 rally.

Already popular as an actress, Riefenstahl had established her own filmmaking company in 1931, before she turned 30. Her first film won the admiration of Hitler, who sought her out and eventually proposed that she direct the film of the party rally. Although she was an artist with no special interest in politics, Riefenstahl, like many Germans, believed at this point that Hitler might be able to revive Germany's fortunes. So despite considerable reluctance, she bowed to Hitler's persistence and agreed to do the film—though only after she was guaranteed final control over editing. Her relations with Goebbels remained strained, but Hitler continued to support her as she made *Triumph of the Will.*

Riefenstahl developed the 107-minute film by editing 61 hours of footage that covered everything from Hitler's arrival and motorcade to the closing parades and speeches. As depicted on film, the party rally does not convey an overt ideological message. We hear Hitler simply trumpeting German renewal, not attacking Jews or glorifying conquest. Most striking in Riefenstahl's portrayal are the unity and epic monumentality that Nazism had apparently brought to Germany thanks to Hitler's leadership.

The film opens as Hitler emerges from dramatic cloud formations to arrive by airplane, descending from the sky like a god. He appears throughout the film as an almost superhuman figure, even, as in the shot shown here, as inspired, possessed, uncanny. Above all, he is a creator who shapes reality by blending will and art, forging masses of anonymous individuals into one people, one racial community, ready for anything. Those individuals seem, from one perspective, to lose their individuality in a monolithic mass, as in the shot of the parade grounds. But their sense of involvement in grandiose purposes charges them emotionally, even gives them a kind of ecstasy. The symbols, the massed banners, the ritualistic show of conformity, all strengthened this sense of participation in the new people's community. But unity and community were not ends in themselves; the film exalted military values and depicted a disciplined society organized for war.

Triumph of the Will extended participation in the spectacle to those who were not actually present in Nuremberg. Because the film chiseled the sprawling event into a work of art, seeing the film was in some ways more effective than being there. The Nazis looked for every means possible to involve the whole society in ritualistic spectacles that could promote a sense of belonging and unity. In addition to film, they made effective use of radio, even subsidizing the purchase of radio sets, or "people's receivers." Such new media were to help ordinary Germans feel a more meaningful kind of belonging than Weimar democracy made possible. But this was only an emotional involvement, not the active participation of free citizens invited to make rational choices.

But though Hitler and other Nazi leaders claimed periodically to be seeking a definitive solution to Germany's "Jewish problem," the dominant objective during the 1930s was to force German Jews to emigrate. About 60,000 of Germany's 550,000 Jews left the country during 1933 and 1934, and perhaps 25 percent had gotten out by 1938. The fact that the regime stripped emigrating Jews of their assets made emigration more difficult. Potential host countries, concerned about unemployment during the Depression, were especially unwilling to take in substantial numbers of Jews if they were penniless.

Triumph of the Will had its premiere in March 1935, with Hitler in the audience. It won several prizes in Germany and abroad but enjoyed only mixed success with the German public, especially outside the large cities. For some, it was altogether too artistic, and the Nazi regime did not use it widely for overt propaganda purposes. Still, the Nazis commissioned no other film about Hitler, for *Triumph of the Will* captured the way he wanted to be seen. Indeed, Hitler praised the film as an "incomparable glorification of the power and beauty of our Movement."

As seen in *Triumph of the Will*, the Leader ...

QUESTIONS

1. Why did Hitler feel it so important to film a Nazi party rally—and even to plan the rally with the filming in mind?

2. What relationship between Hitler and the Nazi movement does *Triumph of the Will* convey?

...and the Disciplined, Tightly Knit Community of Followers (Both photos from the Museum of Modern Art/Film Stills Archive)

On November 9, 1938, using the assassination of a German diplomat in Paris as a pretext, the Nazis staged the *Kristallnacht* **(Crystal Night)** pogrom, during which almost all the synagogues in Germany and about seven thousand Jewish-owned stores were destroyed. Between 30,000 and 50,000 relatively prosperous Jews were arrested and forced to emigrate after their property was confiscated. Although the German public had generally acquiesced in the earlier restrictions on Jews, this pogrom, with its wanton violation of private property, shocked many Germans.

Kristallnacht **(Crystal Night)** Organized Nazi assault on Jewish businesses and synagogues during the night of November 9–10, 1938, following the assassination of a German diplomat in Paris.

Concentration camps—supplementary detention centers—had become a feature of the Nazi regime virtually at once, but prior to 1938, they were used primarily to hold political prisoners. As part of the Crystal Night pogrom, about 35,000 Jews were rounded up and sent to the camps, but most were soon released as long as they could document their intention to emigrate. When World War II began in 1939, the total camp population was about 25,000. The systematic physical extermination of the Jews began only during World War II.

EUTHANASIA AND NAZI PREPARATION FOR WAR

euthanasia program
The Nazi program of systematically killing people deemed superfluous or threatening to Germany's racial health because of their physical or mental disabilities.

However, the killing of others deemed superfluous or threatening to the racial community began earlier, with the so-called **euthanasia program** initiated under volunteer medical teams in 1939. Its aim was to eliminate chronic mental patients, the incurably ill, and people with severe physical handicaps. Those subject to such treatment were overwhelmingly ethnic Germans, not Jews or foreigners. Although the regime did all it could to make it appear the victims had died naturally, a public outcry developed, especially among relatives and church leaders, by 1941, when the program was largely discontinued. But by then, it had claimed 100,000 lives and seems essentially to have achieved its initial objectives.

This "euthanasia" program was based on the sense, fundamental to radical Nazism, that war was the norm and readiness for war the essential societal imperative. In war, societies send individuals to their deaths and, on the battlefield, make difficult distinctions among the wounded, letting some die in order to save those most likely to survive and return to battle. Struggle necessitates selection, which requires overcoming humanitarian scruples—especially the notion that "weakness" calls for special protection. Thus, it was desirable to kill even ethnic Germans who were deemed unfit, as "life unworthy of life."

Preparation for war was the core of Nazism in practice. The conquest of living space in the east would make possible a more advantageous agricultural-industrial balance. The result would be not only the self-sufficiency necessary for sovereignty, but also the land-rootedness necessary for racial health. Such a war of conquest would strike not only the allegedly inferior Slavic peoples of the region, but also detested communism, centered in the Soviet Union.

The point of domestic reorganization was to marshal the community's energies and resources for war. Because German business interests generally seemed congruent with Nazi purposes, Nazi aims did not appear to require some revolutionary assault on business elites or the capitalist economy. But the Nazis had their own road to travel, and beginning in 1936, they proved quite prepared to bend the economy, and to coordinate big business, to serve their longer-term aims of war-making.

The Nazi drive toward war during the 1930s transformed international relations in Europe. The responses of the other European powers, as they sought to deal with Hitler, reflected the increasingly polarized political context of the period. Before considering the fortunes of Hitler's foreign policy, we must consider fascism as a wider phenomenon—and the efforts of the democracies, on the one hand, and the Soviet Union, on the other, to come to terms with it.

SECTION SUMMARY

- The Nazis did not directly overthrow the Weimar Republic but ended up the beneficiaries when it reached an impasse during 1930–1933.

- The central components of Hitler's thinking—geopolitics, biological racism, anti-Semitism, and Social Darwinism—were neither original with Hitler nor specifically German.

- Among ordinary Germans, support for Hitler and his regime was broad but shallow during the 1930s.

- A radical eugenics program, entailing forced sterilization and eventually the actual killing of those deemed unfit, was central to Nazi action on the domestic level during the 1930s.

- During the 1930s, the Nazis began stripping German Jews of citizenship rights as part of a haphazard effort to encourage—or force—Jews to emigrate.

FASCIST CHALLENGE AND ANTIFASCIST RESPONSE, 1934–1939

Why did the "popular front" strategy prove counterproductive in both France and Spain?

Communism, fascism, and Nazism all repudiated the parliamentary democracy that had been the West's political norm. Each seemed subject to violence and excess, yet each had features that some found attractive, especially in light of the difficult socioeconomic circumstances of the 1930s. But communists and adherents of the various forms of fascism were bitterly hostile to each other, and the very presence of these new political systems caused polarization all over Europe.

Beginning in 1934, communists sought to join with anyone who would work with them to defend the democratic framework against further fascist assaults. Without democracy, the very survival of communist parties was in doubt. This effort led to new antifascist coalition governments in Spain and France. In each case, however, the Depression restricted maneuvering room, and these governments ended up furthering the polarization they were seeking to avoid. By mid-1940, democracy had fallen in Spain, after a brutal civil war, and even in France, in the wake of military defeat.

European Fascism and the Popular Front Response

Although some across Europe who were disaffected with democracy and hostile to communism found genuine fascism attractive, the line between fascism and conservative authoritarianism blurred in the volatile political climate of the 1930s. To many, any retreat from democracy appeared a step toward fascism.

In east-central Europe, political distinctions became especially problematic. Movements like the Arrow Cross in Hungary and the Legion of the Archangel Michael in Romania modeled themselves on the Italian and German prototypes, but they never achieved political power. Those who controlled the antidemocratic governments in Hungary and Romania, as in Poland, Bulgaria, and Yugoslavia, were authoritarian traditionalists, not fascists. Still, many government leaders in the region welcomed the closer economic ties with Germany that Hitler's economics minister, Hjalmar Schacht, engineered. The difference between authoritarianism and fascism remained clearest in Austria, where Catholic conservatives undermined democracy during 1933 and 1934. They were actively hostile to the growing pro-Nazi agitation in Austria, partly because they wanted to keep Austria independent.

In France, various nationalist, anticommunist, and anti-Semitic leagues gathered momentum during the early 1930s. They covered a spectrum from monarchism to outspoken profascism, but together they constituted at least a potential threat to French democracy. In February 1934, right-wing demonstrations against the Chamber of Deputies provoked a bloody clash with police and forced a change of ministry. As it began to seem that even France might be vulnerable, those from the center and left of the political spectrum began to consider collaborating to resist fascism. The communists, especially, took the initiative by promoting **popular fronts** of all those seeking to preserve democracy.

This was a dramatic change in strategy for international communism. Even as Hitler was closing in on the German chancellorship in the early 1930s, German Communists, following Comintern policy, continued to attack their socialist rivals rather than seek a unified response to Nazism. But by 1934, the threat of fascism seemed so pressing that Communists began actively promoting electoral alliances and governing coalitions with socialists and even liberal democrats to resist its further spread. From 1934 until 1939, Communists everywhere consistently pursued this "popular front" strategy.

By the 1930s, however, it was becoming ever harder to know what was fascist, what was dangerous, and what might lead where. As fears intensified, perceptions became as important as realities. Popular front governments, intended to preserve democracy against what appeared to be fascism, could seem to conservatives to be leaning too far to the left. Ideological polarization made democracy extraordinarily difficult. The archetypal example proved to be Spain, where a tragedy of classical proportions was played out.

popular fronts   A term for antifascist electoral alliances and governing coalitions that communists promoted from 1934 until 1939 to resist the further spread of fascism.

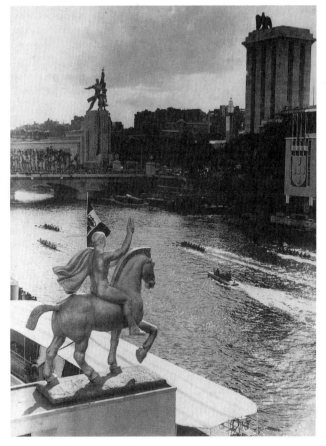

Ideological Confrontation   At a major international exhibition in Paris in 1937, the new antidemocratic political regimes made bold propaganda statements. With a sculpture from fascist Italy's pavilion in the foreground, we look across the Seine River to a classic representation of the ideological warfare of the 1930s: the Soviet Pavilion, on the left, facing the German Pavilion, on the right. Crowning the Soviet building is the noted sculpture by Vera Muchina, *Worker and Collective Farmer*.   (AP Photos)

From Democracy to Civil War in Spain, 1931–1939

Spain became a center of attention in the 1930s, when its promising new parliamentary democracy, launched in 1931, led to civil war in 1936 and the triumph of a repressive authoritarian regime in 1939. An earlier effort at constitutional monarchy had fizzled by 1923, when King Alfonso XIII (1886–1941) supported a new military dictatorship. But growing opposition led first to the resignation of the dictator in 1930 and then, in April 1931, to the end of the monarchy and the proclamation of a republic. The elections for a constituent assembly that followed in June produced a solid victory for a coalition of liberal democrats and Socialists, as well as much hope for substantial reform.

A significant agrarian reform law was passed in 1932, but partly because of the difficult economic context, the new government was slow to implement it. Feeling betrayed, Socialists and agricultural workers became increasingly radical, producing growing upheaval in the countryside. Radicalism on the left made it harder for the moderates to govern and, at the same time, stimulated conservatives to become more politically active.

A right-wing coalition known as the CEDA, led by José Maria Gil Robles (heel ROH-blayce) (1898–1980), grew in strength, becoming the largest party in parliament with the elections of November 1933. In light of its parliamentary strength, the CEDA had a plausible claim to a government role, but it was kept from participation in government until October 1934. It seemed to the left, in the ideologically charged atmosphere of the time, that the growing role of the CEDA was a prelude to fascism.

A strong Catholic from the traditional Spanish right, Gil Robles refused to endorse the democratic republic as a form of government, but he and the CEDA were willing to work within it. So the Spanish left may have been too quick to see the CEDA as fascist—and to react when the CEDA finally got its government role. However, Mussolini and Hitler had each come to power more or less legally, from within parliamentary institutions. The German left had been criticized for its passive response to the advent of Hitler; the Spanish left wanted to avoid the same mistake.

Thus, when the CEDA finally got a role in the government, the left responded during the fall of 1934 with quasi-revolutionary uprisings in Catalonia and Asturias, where a miners' commune was put down only after two weeks of heavy fighting. In the aftermath, the right-leaning government of 1935 began undoing some of the reforms of the left-leaning government of 1931–1933, though still legally, within the framework of the parliamentary republic.

In February 1936, a popular front coalition to ward off fascism won a narrow electoral victory, sufficient for an absolute majority in parliament. As would be true in France a few months later, electoral victory produced popular expectations that went well beyond the essentially defensive purposes of the popular front. Hoping to win back the leftist rank and file and head off what seemed a dangerous attempt at revolution, the new popular front government began to implement a progressive program, now including the land reform that had been promised but not implemented earlier. It was too late, however, to undercut the growing radicalization of the masses. A wave of land seizures began in March 1936, followed by the most extensive strike movement in Spanish history, which by June was becoming clearly revolutionary in character.

Finally, in mid-July, several army officers initiated a military uprising against the government. Soon led by General Francisco Franco (1892–1975), these Nationalist insurgents took control of substantial parts of Spain. But elsewhere they failed to overcome the resistance of the republican Loyalists, those determined to defend the republic. So the result was not the intended military takeover but a brutal civil war, with numerous atrocities committed by both sides (see **MAP 27.1**).

Foreign intervention by the end of 1936 intensified the war's ideological ramifications. Both Fascist Italy and Nazi Germany actively supported the Nationalist insurgency. On the Republican side, the Communists, initially a distinct minority on the Spanish left, gradually gained the ascendancy, partly because they were disciplined and effective, partly because Soviet assistance enhanced their prestige.

Republican Loyalists assumed that Franco and the Nationalists represented another instance of fascism. But though he used the trappings of fascism in seeking to gain popular support, Franco was a traditional military man whose leadership role did not rest on personal charisma. He was not a fascist, but an authoritarian emphasizing order and Spain's Catholic traditions.

Meanwhile, the republic's leaders had to fight a civil war while dealing with continuing revolution in their own ranks. Developing especially in Catalonia from the uprisings of 1936,

🌐 MAP 27.1—The Spanish Civil War, 1936–1939

The Nationalist insurgents quickly took over most of northern and eastern Spain in 1936 and then gradually expanded their territory. The fall of Madrid early in 1939 marked the end of the fighting. The revolutionary effort of 1936 and 1937 within the Republican zone was centered in Barcelona.

(Source: Adapted from *The Times Atlas of World History*, 3d ed. Reprinted by permission of HarperCollins Publishers Ltd. © HarperCollins Publishers Ltd.)

that revolution was not communist but anarcho-syndicalist in orientation. The Communists, true to popular front principles, insisted that this was no time for such "infantile leftist" revolutionary experiments. What mattered, throughout the Republican zone, was the factory discipline necessary to produce essential war materiel. As a consequence, the Communists, under Stalin's orders, were instrumental in putting down the anarchist revolution in Catalonia in June 1937.

Despite considerable heroism on the Loyalist side, however, this single-minded prosecution of the civil war did not prove enough to defeat the military insurgency. The war ended with the fall of Madrid to the Nationalists in March 1939. General Franco's authoritarian regime governed Spain until his death in 1975.

In Spain, as in Weimar Germany, the lack of consensus in a new republic made parliamentary democracy difficult, and the wider ideological framework magnified the difficulties. With the political boiling point so low, the left and the right each saw the other in extreme terms and assumed that extraordinary response to the other was necessary. Thus, the left tended to view even conservatives operating within a parliamentary framework as "fascist," and both sides were relatively quick to give up on a democratic republic that seemed to be tilting too far in the wrong direction.

Picasso: *Guernica* Created for the Spanish Pavilion at the 1937 Paris Exhibition, Pablo Picasso's painting conveys horror and outrage—his response to the German bombing of the Basque town of Guernica (gair-NEE-kah, in Spanish; GWAIR-nee-kah, as customarily rendered in English) on a crowded market day in 1937, during the Spanish civil war. Picasso's stark, elemental imagery came to symbolize the violence and suffering of the whole era. (Pablo Picasso, *Guernica* [1937, May–early June]. Oil on canvas. Art Resource, NY. © 2002 Artists Rights Society [ARS], New York/ADAGP, Paris)

France in the Era of the Popular Front

In France, as in Spain, concern to arrest the spread of fascism led to a popular front coalition that governed the country from 1936 to 1938. Although it did not lead to civil war, the popular front was central to the French experience of the 1930s, producing polarization and resignation and undermining confidence in the Third Republic.

Beginning in 1934, the French Communists took the initiative in approaching first the Socialists, then the Radicals, to develop a popular front coalition. In reaching out to the Radicals, the Communists stressed French patriotism and made no demand for significant economic reforms. Stalin gave this effort a major push in 1935 when, in a stunning change in the communist line, he stressed the legitimacy of national defense and explicitly endorsed French rearmament.

In the elections of April and May 1936, the popular front won a sizable majority in the Chamber of Deputies, putting the Socialists' leader, Léon Blum (1872–1950), in line to become France's first Socialist prime minister. The Communists pledged full support of the new Blum government, but to avoid fanning fears, they did not participate directly. However, despite the popular front's moderate and essentially defensive aims, the situation quickly began to polarize after the elections.

Fearing that the new Blum government would be forced to devalue the French currency, and thereby diminish the value of assets denominated in francs, French investors immediately began moving their capital abroad. At the same time, the popular front victory produced a wave of enthusiasm among workers that escaped the control of popular front leaders and culminated in a spontaneous strike movement, the largest France had ever seen. By early June, it had spread to all major industries nationwide. Although the workers' demands—for collective bargaining, a forty-hour workweek, and paid vacations—were not extraordinary, the movement involved sit-down strikes as well as the normal walkouts, and thus seemed quasi-revolutionary in character. The major trade union confederation, the Communists, and most Socialists, including Blum himself, saw the strikes as a danger to the popular front, with its more modest aims of defending the republic, and eagerly pursued a settlement.

That settlement, the Matignon (mah-tin-YON) Agreement of June 8, 1936, was a major victory for the French working class. Having been genuinely frightened by the strikes and now reassured that the popular front government would at least uphold the law, French industrialists were willing to make significant concessions. So the workers got collective bargaining, elected shop stewards, and wage increases as a direct result of Matignon, then a forty-hour week and paid vacations in a reform package promptly passed by parliament.

In the enthusiasm of the summer of 1936, other reforms were enacted as well, but after that, the popular front was forced onto the defensive. Two problems undermined its energy and cohesion: the noncooperation of French business and the Spanish civil war. The cautious response of Blum, the Socialist prime minister, is striking in each case, but he faced a situation with little maneuvering room.

From the outset, Blum stressed that he had no mandate for revolution, and as France's first Socialist prime minister, he felt it essential to prove that a Socialist could govern responsibly. Thus, he did not respond energetically to the capital flight, even though it produced serious currency and budgetary difficulties.

In responding to the Spanish civil war, Blum had to decide whether the French government should help the beleaguered Spanish republic, at least by sending supplies. Although he initially favored such help, Blum changed his mind under pressure from three sides. The Conservative government of Stanley Baldwin in Britain was against it. So was the French right; some even suggested that French intervention would provoke a comparable civil war in France. Moreover, the Radicals in his own coalition were generally opposed to helping the Spanish republic, so intervention would jeopardize the cohesion of the popular front itself.

Rather than help supply the Spanish republic, Blum promoted a nonintervention agreement among the major powers, including Italy and Germany. Many Socialists and Communists disliked Blum's cautious policy, especially as it became clear that Mussolini and Hitler were violating their hands-off pledges. As Blum stuck to nonintervention, the moral force of the popular front dissolved.

In 1938, a new government under the Radical Edouard Daladier (dah-lah-dee-YAY) (1884–1970), still nominally a creature of the popular front, began dismantling some of the key gains of 1936, even attacking the forty-hour week. Citing productivity and national security concerns, Daladier adopted pro-business policies and succeeded in attracting capital back to France. But workers, watching the gains they had won in 1936 slip away, felt betrayed. At the same time, businessmen and conservatives began blaming the workers' gains—such as the five-day week—for slowing French rearmament. Although such charges were not entirely fair, they indicated how poisoned the atmosphere in France had become in the wake of the popular front.

As France began to face the possibility of a new war, the popular front was widely blamed for French weakness. When war came at last, resignation and division were prevalent, in contrast with the patriotic unity and high spirits of 1914. It was partly for that reason that France was so easily defeated by Germany in 1940. And when France fell, the democratic Third Republic fell with it.

SECTION SUMMARY

- In light of the ideological polarization of the 1930s, many people found it difficult to distinguish between conservative authoritarianism and fascism.

- In a dramatic change in their international strategy, the Communists in 1934 began promoting "popular fronts," which were to bring together all those seeking to preserve democracy against fascism.

- The wider ideological framework magnified the difficulties of parliamentary democracy in Spain, contributing to the polarization that led to civil war.

- Although he sometimes exploited the trappings of fascism, General Franco was not a fascist but an authoritarian Catholic traditionalist.

- Though intended simply to preserve democracy, the popular front experiment in France produced a backlash and was widely blamed for French weakness as war loomed by the end of the 1930s.

THE COMING OF WORLD WAR II, 1935–1939

Why did the other countries not stop Hitler's Germany before it was strong enough to start a new European war in 1939?

Despite the promising adjustments of the 1920s, many of the problems that accompanied the World War I peace settlement were still in place when Hitler came to power. And Hitler had consistently trumpeted his intention to overturn that settlement. What scope was there for peaceful revision? Could the threat of war stop Hitler? By the last years of the 1930s, these questions tortured the Western world as Hitler went from one success to another, raising the possibility of a new and more destructive war. The power balance rested on the responses not only of the Western democracies, but of fascist Italy and the Soviet Union as well.

The Reorientation of Fascist Italy

During its first decade in power, Benito Mussolini's fascist regime in Italy concentrated on domestic reconstruction, especially the effort to mobilize people through their roles as producers within a new corporative state (see pages 738–739). But though corporativist institutions were gradually constructed, with great rhetorical fanfare, they bogged down in bureaucratic meddling. Corporativism proved more the vehicle for regimentation than for a more direct kind of participation. Fascism seemed to have stalled, partly because of compromise with prefascist elites and institutions, and partly because of its own internal contradictions. But the change in the international situation after Hitler came to power offered Mussolini some welcome space for maneuver.

Though Italy, like Germany, remained dissatisfied with the territorial status quo, it was not obvious that fascist Italy and Nazi Germany had to end up in the same camp. For one thing, Italy was anxious to preserve an independent Austria as a buffer with Germany, whereas many Germans and Austrians favored the unification of the two countries. Such a greater Germany might then threaten the gains Italy had won at the peace conference at Austria's expense. When, in 1934, Germany seemed poised to absorb Austria, Mussolini helped force Hitler to back down. He even warned that Nazism, with its racist orientation, threatened the best of European civilization.

As it began to appear that France and Britain might have to work with the Soviet Union to check Hitler's Germany, French and British conservatives pushed for good relations with Mussolini's Italy to provide ideological balance. So Italy was well positioned to play off both sides as Hitler began shaking things up on the international level. In 1935, just after Hitler announced significant rearmament measures, unilaterally repudiating provisions of the Versailles treaty for the first time, Mussolini hosted a meeting with the French and British prime ministers at Stresa, in northern Italy. In an overt warning to Hitler's Germany, the three powers agreed to resist "any unilateral repudiation of treaties which may endanger the peace of Europe."

However, Mussolini was already preparing to extend Italy's possessions in East Africa to encompass Ethiopia (also called Abyssinia). He assumed that the French and British, who needed his support against Hitler, would not offer significant opposition. Ethiopia had become a League of Nations member in 1923—sponsored by Italy, but opposed by Britain and France because it still practiced slavery. After a border incident, Italian troops invaded in October 1935, prompting the League to announce sanctions against Italy.

These sanctions were applied haphazardly, largely because France and Britain wanted to avoid damaging their longer-term relations with Italy. In any case, the sanctions did not deter Mussolini, whose forces prevailed through the use of aircraft and poison gas by May 1936. But they did make Italy receptive to German overtures in the aftermath of its victory. And the victory made Mussolini more restless. Rather than seeking to play again the role of European balancer, he sent Italian troops and materiel to aid the Nationalists in the Spanish civil war, thereby further alienating democratic opinion elsewhere.

Conservatives in Britain and France continued to push for accommodation with Italy, hoping to revive the "Stresa front" against Hitler. Some even defended Italian imperialism in East Africa. But Italy continued its drift toward Germany. Late in 1936, Mussolini spoke of a new **Rome-Berlin Axis** for the first time. During 1937 and 1938, he and Hitler exchanged visits. Finally, in May 1939, Italy joined Germany in an open-ended military alliance, the Pact of Steel, but Mussolini made it clear that Italy could not be ready for a major European war before 1943.

Partly to strengthen this developing relationship, fascist Italy adopted anti-Semitic racial laws, even though Italian fascism had not originally been anti-Semitic. Indeed, the party had attracted Jewish Italians to its membership in about the same proportion as non-Jews. Although the imperial venture in Ethiopia had been popular among the Italian people, the seeming subservience to Nazi Germany displeased even many fascists. Such opposition helped keep Mussolini from intervention when war broke out in September 1939.

Rome-Berlin Axis
Alliance between Hitler's Nazi Germany and Mussolini's fascist Italy, which began informally in 1936, then was cemented by an open-ended military alliance, the Pact of Steel, in 1939.

Restoring German Sovereignty, 1935–1936

During his first years in power, through 1936, Hitler could be understood as merely restoring German sovereignty, revising a postwar settlement that had been misconceived in the first place. However uncouth and abrasive he might seem, it was hard to find a basis for opposing him. Yet with the beginning of rearmament in 1935, and especially with the **remilitarization of the Rhineland** in March 1936, Hitler fundamentally reversed the power balance established in France's favor at the peace conference.

France's special advantage had been the demilitarization of the entire German territory west of the Rhine River and a 50-kilometer strip on the east bank. The measure had been reaffirmed at Locarno in 1925, now with Germany's free agreement, and it was guaranteed by Britain and Italy. Yet, on a Saturday morning in March 1936, that advantage disappeared as German troops moved into the forbidden area. The French and British acquiesced, uncertain of what else to do. After all, Hitler was only restoring Germany to full sovereignty.

But Hitler was not likely to stop there. As a result of the war and the peace, three new countries—Austria, Czechoslovakia, and Poland—bordered Germany (see **MAP 27.2**). In each, the peace settlement had left trouble spots involving the status of ethnic Germans; in each, the status quo was open to question.

remilitarization of the Rhineland The reoccupation of Germany's Rhineland territory by German troops in March 1936, in clear violation of the Treaty of Versailles.

🌐 **MAP 27.2—The Expansion of Nazi Germany, 1936–1939**

Especially with the remilitarization of the Rhineland in 1936, Hitler's Germany began moving, step by step, to alter the European power balance. In September 1939, the Soviet Union also began annexing territory, capitalizing on its agreement with Germany the month before.

Austria, Czechoslovakia, and Appeasement

As early as 1934, Hitler had moved to encompass his homeland, Austria, but strenuous opposition from Italy led him to back down. The developing understanding with Mussolini by 1936 enabled Hitler to focus again on Austria—initiating the second, more radical phase of his prewar foreign policy. On a pretext in March 1938, German troops moved into Austria, which was promptly incorporated into Germany. This time, Mussolini was willing to acquiesce, and Hitler was genuinely grateful.

The Treaty of Versailles had explicitly prohibited this *Anschluss*, or unity of Austria with Germany, though that prohibition violated the principle of self-determination. It was widely believed in the West, no doubt correctly, that most Austrians favored unity with Germany now that the Habsburg Empire had broken up. The *Anschluss* could thus be justified as revising a misconceived aspect of the peace settlement.

Czechoslovakia presented quite a different situation. Although it had preserved democratic institutions, the country included restive minorities of Magyars, Ruthenians, Poles, and—concentrated especially in the Sudetenland, along the German and Austrian borders—about 3.25 million Germans. After having been part of the dominant nationality in the old Habsburg Empire, those Germans were frustrated with their minority status in the new Czechoslovakia. Worse, they seemed to suffer disproportionately from the Depression. Hitler's agents actively stirred up their resentments.

Leading the West's response, when Hitler began making an issue of Czechoslovakia, was Neville Chamberlain (1869–1940), who followed Stanley Baldwin as Britain's prime minister in May 1937. An intelligent, vigorous, and public-spirited man from the progressive wing of the Conservative Party, Chamberlain has long been derided as the architect of the **"appeasement"** of Hitler at the Munich conference of 1938, which settled the crisis over Czechoslovakia. Trumpeted as the key to peace, the Munich agreement proved but a step to the war that broke out less than a year later. Yet, though it failed, Chamberlain's policy of appeasement stemmed not from cowardice or mere drift, and certainly not from some unspoken pro-Nazi sentiment.

Rather than let events spin out of control, as seemed to have happened in 1914, Chamberlain sought to master the difficult international situation through creative bargaining. Surely, he felt, the excesses of Hitler's policy resulted from the mistakes of Versailles; redo the settlement on a more realistic basis, and Germany would behave responsibly. The key was to pinpoint the sources of Germany's frustrations and, as Chamberlain put it, "to remove the danger spots one by one."

Moreover, in Britain as elsewhere, there were some who saw Hitler's resurgent Germany as a bulwark against communism, which might spread into east-central Europe—especially in the event of another war. Indeed, the victor in another war might well be the revolutionary left. To prevent such an outcome was worth a few concessions to Hitler.

The Czechs, led by Eduard Beneš (BAY-naish) (1884–1948), made some attempt to liberalize their nationality policy. But by April 1938, they were becoming ever less sympathetic to Sudeten German demands for autonomy, especially as German bullying came to accompany them. Tensions between Czechoslovakia and Germany mounted, and by late September 1938, war appeared imminent, despite Chamberlain's efforts to mediate. Both the French and the British began mobilizing, with French troops manning the Maginot Line for the first time.

A 1924 treaty bound France to come to the aid of Czechoslovakia in the event of aggression. Moreover, the Soviet Union, according to a treaty of 1935, was bound to assist Czechoslovakia if the French did so. And throughout the crisis, the Soviets pushed for a strong stand in defense of Czechoslovakia against German aggression. For both ideological and military reasons, however, the British and French were reluctant to line up for

appeasement   The policy employed by Britain's prime minister, Neville Chamberlain, to defuse the 1938 crisis with Germany's Adolf Hitler. Chamberlain acquiesced to Hitler's demands to annex the Sudetenland portion of Czechoslovakia, but this proved merely a step toward the war that broke out less than a year later.

The Illusion of Peace   Neville Chamberlain, returning home to Britain from Munich to a hero's welcome, waves the peace declaration that was supposed to have brought "peace in our time." This was late September 1938. Less than a year later, Europe was again at war.   (Central Press/Hulton Archive/Getty Images)

war on the side of the Soviet Union. The value of the Soviet military was uncertain, at best, at a time when the Soviet officer corps had just been purged.

By September, Hitler seemed eager to smash the Czechs by force, but when Mussolini proposed a four-power conference, he was persuaded to talk again. At Munich late in September, Britain, France, Italy, and Germany settled the matter, with Czechoslovakia and the Soviet Union excluded. Determined not to risk war over what seemed Czech intransigence, the British ended up agreeing to what Hitler had wanted all along—not merely autonomy for the Sudeten Germans, but German annexation of the Sudetenland.

The Munich agreement specified that all Sudeten areas with German majorities be transferred to Germany. Plebiscites were to be held in areas with large German minorities, and Hitler pledged to respect the sovereignty of the now diminished Czechoslovak state. Chamberlain and his French counterpart, Edouard Daladier, each returned home to a hero's welcome, having transformed what had seemed certain war to, in Chamberlain's soon-to-be-notorious phrase, "peace in our time."

Rather than settle the nationality questions bedeviling Czechoslovakia, the Munich agreement only provoked further unrest. Poland and Hungary, eager to exploit the new weakness of Czechoslovakia, agitated successfully to annex disputed areas with large numbers of their respective nationalities. Then unrest stemming from Slovak separatism afforded a pretext for Germany to send troops into Prague in March 1939. The Slovak areas were spun off as a separate nation, while the Czech areas became the Protectorate of Bohemia and Moravia. Less than six months after the Munich conference, most of what had been Czechoslovakia had landed firmly within the Nazi orbit (see **MAP 27.2**). It was no longer possible to justify Hitler's actions as an effort to unite all Germans in one state.

Poland, the Nazi-Soviet Pact, and the Coming of War

With Poland, the German grievance was still more serious, for the new Polish state had been created partly at German expense. Especially galling to Germans was the Polish corridor, which cut off East Prussia from the bulk of Germany in order to give Poland access to the sea. The city of Danzig (now Gdansk, Poland), historically Polish, but part of Germany before World War I, was left a "free city," supervised by the League of Nations.

Disillusioned by Hitler's dismemberment of Czechoslovakia and angered by the Germans' menacing rhetoric regarding Poland, Chamberlain announced on March 31, 1939, that Britain and France would intervene militarily should Poland's independence be threatened. Chamberlain was not only abandoning the policy of appeasement; he was making a clear commitment to the Continent, of the sort that British governments had resisted since 1919. He could do so partly because Britain was rapidly rearming. By early 1940, in fact, Britain was spending nearly as large a share of its national income on the military as Germany was. But Chamberlain's assertive statement was not enough to deter Hitler, who seems to have been determined to settle the Polish question by force. In an effort to localize the conflict, however, Hitler continued to insist that German aims were limited and reasonable. Germany simply wanted Danzig and German transit across the corridor; it was the Polish stance that was rigid and unreasonable. Hitler apparently believed that Polish stubbornness would alienate the British and French, undercutting their support. And as the crisis developed by mid-1939, doubts were increasingly expressed, on all sides, that the British and French were really prepared to aid Poland militarily—that they had the will "to die for Danzig."

Although they had been lukewarm to Soviet proposals for a military alliance, Britain and France began to negotiate with the Soviet Union more seriously during the spring and summer of 1939. But reservations about the value of a Soviet alliance continued to gnaw at Western leaders. For one thing, Soviet troops could gain access to Germany only by moving through Poland or Romania. But each had territory gained at the expense of Russia in the postwar settlement, so the British and French, suspicious of Soviet designs, were reluctant to insist that Soviet troops be allowed to pass through either country.

Even as negotiations between the Soviet Union and the democracies continued, the Soviets came to their own agreement with Nazi Germany on August 23, 1939, in a pact that astonished the world. Each side had been denouncing the other, and although Hitler had explored the possibility of Soviet neutrality in May, serious negotiations began only that August, when the Soviets got the clear signal that a German invasion of Poland was inevitable. It now appeared that no Soviet

Nazi-Soviet Pact Surprise agreement between the Soviet Union and Nazi Germany in August 1939 that each would remain neutral if the other went to war against some other nation.

alliance with Britain and France could prevent war. Under these circumstances, a nonaggression pact with Germany seemed better to serve Soviet interests than a problematic war on the side of Britain and France. So the Soviets agreed with the Germans that each would remain neutral in the event that either became involved in a war with some other nation.

The Soviet flip-flop stemmed partly from disillusionment with the British and French response to the accelerating threat of Nazism. The democracies seemed no more trustworthy, and potentially no less hostile, than Nazi Germany. But the Soviets were playing their own double game. A secret protocol to the **Nazi-Soviet Pact** apportioned major areas of east-central Europe between the Soviet Union and Germany. As a result, the Soviets soon regained much of what they had lost after World War I, when Poland, Finland, and other states had been created or aggrandized with territories that had been part of the tsarist empire.

The Nazi-Soviet Pact seemed to give Hitler the free hand he wanted in Poland. With the dramatic change in alignment, the democracies were surely much less likely to intervene. But Chamberlain, again determined to avoid the hesitations of 1914, publicly reaffirmed the British guarantee to Poland on August 25. Britain would indeed intervene if Germany attacked. And after the German invasion of Poland on September 1, the British and French responded with declarations of war on September 3.

With each step on the path to war, Hitler had vacillated between apparent reasonableness and wanton aggressiveness. Even in invading Poland, he apparently still hoped to localize hostilities. But he was certainly willing to risk a more general European war, and the deepest thrust of his policy was toward an all-out war of conquest—first against Poland, but ultimately against the Soviet Union. War was essential to the Nazi vision, and only when the assault on Poland became a full-scale war did the underlying purposes of Nazism become clear.

SECTION SUMMARY

- In light of the ideological polarization of the period, even the efforts to check Hitler by Britain and France, the major European democracies, depended partly on their relations with fascist Italy and the Soviet Union.

- Germany's remilitarization of the Rhineland in March 1936 prompted no military response by France and Britain, even though Germany's move removed the trump card that France had won with the Versailles treaty.

- In "appeasing" Hitler, Neville Chamberlain was not simply caving in but was seeking, through creative diplomacy, to remove the present sources of international hostility.

- Disillusioned by Hitler's course after the Munich agreement of September 1938, Chamberlain announced in March 1939 that Britain and France would intervene militarily should Germany threaten Poland's independence.

- Although they came to terms with Hitler's Germany in 1939, partly from mistrust of Britain and France, the Soviets quickly pursued their own aggressive aims in north-central Europe.

CHAPTER SUMMARY

The Great Depression caught decision makers in the democracies unprepared. Reflecting conventional economic thinking, their initial response was to keep government budgets balanced. But this required cutting government spending on such measures as unemployment benefits, which not only added to the human misery, but also intensified the economic contraction. The further effort to protect domestic economies through higher tariffs also worsened the downturn by restricting global trade. Only after several years, and for quite disparate reasons, did governments begin increasing spending and thereby stimulating renewed economic growth.

Stalin sought to rekindle the Russian revolutionary experiment by attempting to build "socialism in one country." The essential prerequisite was rapid industrialization, to be financed by squeezing the peasantry through forced collectivization in agriculture. Both the collectivization itself and the ensuing extractions of agricultural produce were extremely brutal, culminating in the "terror-famine" of 1932–1933. Partly because of its brutality, and partly because its economic results were mixed at best, the Stalinist departure produced opposition even from within the Communist Party. Seeking to root out those who might be sabotaging the Soviet experiment, Communist leaders embarked on a series of purges and show trials, but their effort gradually spun out of control, producing the "great terror" of 1937–1938.

FOCUS QUESTIONS

- With what array of measures did governments respond to the Great Depression?

- Why did the Stalinist attempt to build "socialism in one country" lead to the "terror-famine" of 1932–1933 and the "great terror" of 1937–1938?

- Through what measures did the Nazi regime claim to be improving the quality of the German population?

- Why did the "popular front" strategy prove counterproductive in both France and Spain?

- Why did the other countries not stop Hitler's Germany before it was strong enough to start a new European war in 1939?

Population engineering, based on eugenics on the one hand, racism and anti-Semitism on the other, was central to the Nazis' domestic program. Determined to implement radical eugenics measures that had been discussed but not implemented under the Weimar Republic, the regime launched a program of forced sterilization in 1933. By the eve of World War II, German medical personnel were actually killing mental patients, the terminally ill, and others deemed unfit. Even as they sought to "improve" the "Aryan" population through such eugenics measures, the Nazis also sought ethnic homogeneity, especially by stripping German Jews of citizenship rights in an effort to force emigration.

Hitler's consolidation of power in Germany and the apparent threat of fascism in France in 1934 prompted leaders of the Comintern to make resistance to the spread of fascism their top priority. To that end, communists spearheaded the formation of "popular fronts" with socialists and others concerned to preserve democratic institutions. But though it produced electoral successes in 1936 in Spain and France, the strategy proved polarizing. Popular front victories produced radical pressures that popular front governments had trouble containing. Those pressures eventually produced a backlash from the right. Partly as a result, democracy was defeated in both Spain and France by 1940.

Hitler's aggressive foreign policy provided an unprecedented challenge to the European order, but the leading democracies, Britain and France, were slow to respond. Eagerness to avoid another war affected their reactions, as did the ideological polarization of the decade. Up to a point, Hitler's steps could seem legitimate, in terms of principles of national sovereignty and ethnic self-determination that had been compromised to Germany's disadvantage at the Paris Peace Conference. In 1939, when Hitler's further steps could no longer be justified in such terms, the democracies, led by Britain, at last began to stiffen. However, Hitler was determined to crush Poland. Although the Nazi-Soviet Pact seemed to make the intervention of Britain and France less likely, the Nazi leader was more than willing to risk another European war.

KEY TERMS

collectivization (p. 761)

show trials (p. 763)

gulag (p. 763)

Adolf Hitler (p. 764)

National Socialist German Workers' (Nazi) Party (NSDAP) (p. 764)

Schutzstaffel **(SS)** (p. 766)

Kristallnacht **(Crystal Night)** (p. 771)

"euthanasia" program (p. 772)

popular fronts (p. 773)

Rome-Berlin Axis (p. 778)

remilitarization of the Rhineland (p. 779)

appeasement (p. 780)

Nazi-Soviet Pact (p. 782)

This icon will direct you to additional materials on the website: www .cengage.com/history/ noble/westciv6e

NOTES

1. Quoted in Robert Conquest, *The Great Terror: A Reassessment* (New York: Oxford University Press, 1990), p. 24.

2. Quoted in Helmut Krausnick et al., *Anatomy of the SS State* (New York: Walker, 1968), p. 13.

e See our interactive eBook for map and primary source activities.

28

Atomic Bombing of Nagasaki, August 9, 1945
When this photo was taken, from an observation plane 6 miles up, thirty-five thousand people on the ground had already died. (akg-images)

The Era of the Second World War, 1939–1949

"The effects could well be called unprecedented, magnificent, beautiful, stupendous and terrifying. No man-made phenomenon of such tremendous power had ever occurred before.....Thirty seconds after the explosion came first, the air blast pressing hard against the people and things, to be followed almost immediately by the strong, sustained, awesome roar which warned of doomsday and made us feel that we puny things were blasphemous to dare tamper with the forces heretofore reserved to The Almighty."[1]

So wrote Brigadier General Thomas F. Farrell, who had just witnessed the birth of the atomic age. On July 16, 1945, watching from a shelter 10,000 yards away, Farrell had seen the first explosion of an atomic bomb at a remote, top-secret U.S. government testing ground near Alamogordo, New Mexico. Such a weapon had been little more than a theoretical possibility when World War II began, and it required a remarkable concentration of effort, centered first in Britain, then in the United States, to make possible the awesome spectacle that confronted General Farrell. Exceeding most expectations, the test revealed a weapon of unprecedented power and destructiveness.

Within weeks, the United States dropped two other atomic bombs—first on Hiroshima, then on Nagasaki—to force the surrender of Japan in August 1945. Thus ended the Second World War, the conflict that had begun six long years earlier with the German invasion of Poland. At first, Germany enjoyed remarkable success, prompting Italy to intervene and encouraging Japanese aggressiveness as well. But Britain held on even after its ally, France, fell to Germany in 1940. Then the war changed character in 1941 when Germany attacked the Soviet Union and Japan attacked the United States.

Britain, the United States, and the Soviet Union quickly came together in a "Grand Alliance," which spearheaded the victorious struggle against the Axis powers—Germany, Italy, and Japan. In Europe, the Soviet victory in a brutal land war with Germany proved decisive. In East Asia and the Pacific, the Americans gradually prevailed against Japan. The American use of the atomic bomb to end the war was the final stage in an escalation of violence that made World War II the most destructive war in history.

The ironic outcome of the Second World War was a new cold war between two of the victors, the United States and the Soviet Union. Emerging from the war with far greater power and prestige, each assumed a world role that would have been hard to imagine just a few years earlier. By the end of the 1940s, these two superpowers had divided Europe into

FOCUS QUESTIONS

- What were the outcomes of the war as of late spring 1941, before the German invasion of the Soviet Union and the intervention of the United States?

- What was the place of the Holocaust in the Nazi effort to begin constructing a "new order" in eastern Europe?

- How did the Grand Alliance of Britain, the United States, and the Soviet Union come together against the Axis powers?

- How did the Allies manage to defeat Nazi Germany in World War II, after Germany's remarkable initial successes?

- What was the relationship between the Allied victory in World War II and the coming of the cold war?

This icon will direct you to additional materials on the website: www .cengage.com/history/ noble/westciv6e.

See our interactive eBook for map and primary source activities.

competing spheres of influence. Indeed, the competition between the United States and the Soviet Union almost immediately became global in scope, creating a bipolar world. And the cold war between them was especially terrifying because, seeking military advantage, they raced to stockpile ever more destructive nuclear weapons. Thus, the threat of nuclear annihilation helped define the cold war era.

World War II led to the defeat of Italy, Germany, and Japan and, in this sense, resolved the conflicts that had caused it. But the experience of this particular war changed the world forever. Before finally meeting defeat, the Nazis were sufficiently successful to begin implementing their "new order" in Europe, especially in the territories they conquered to the east. As part of this effort, in what has become known as the Holocaust, they began systematically murdering Jews in extermination camps, eventually killing as many as 6 million. The most destructive of the camps was at Auschwitz (OWSH-vits), in what had been Poland. Often paired after the war, Auschwitz and Hiroshima came to stand for the incredible new forms of death and destruction that the war had spawned—and that continued to haunt the world long after it had ended, posing new questions about the meaning of Western civilization.

GERMAN MILITARY SUCCESSES, 1939–1941

What were the outcomes of the war as of late spring 1941, before the German invasion of the Soviet Union and the intervention of the United States?

Instead of the enthusiasm evident in 1914, the German invasion of Poland on September 1, 1939, produced a grim sense of foreboding, even in Germany. Well-publicized incidents, such as the German bombing of civilians during the Spanish civil war and the Italian use of poison gas in Ethiopia, suggested that the frightening new technologies introduced in World War I would now be used on a far greater scale. This would be a much uglier war, more directly involving civilians.

Still, as in 1914, there were hopes at first that this new war could be localized and brief. Poland fell quickly, and Hitler publicly offered peace to Britain and France, seriously thinking that might be the end of it. The British and French refused to call off the war, but from 1939 through 1941, the Nazis won victory after victory, establishing the foundation for their new order in Europe.

Initial Conquests and "Phony War"

The Polish army was large enough to have given the Germans a serious battle. But in adapting the technological innovations of World War I, Germany had developed a new military strategy based on rapid mobility. Soon popularly known as *Blitzkrieg*, or lightning war, this strategy employed swift, highly concentrated offensives based on mobile tanks covered with concentrated air support, including dive-bombers that struck just ahead of the tanks. In Poland, this strategy proved decisive. The French could offer only token help, and the last Polish unit surrendered on October 2, barely a month after the fighting had begun. The speed of the German victory stunned the world.

Meanwhile, the Soviets began cashing in on the pact they had made with Nazi Germany a few weeks before. It offered a precious opportunity to undo provisions of the World War I settlement that had significantly diminished the western territories of the former Russian Empire. On September 17, with the German victory in Poland assured, Stalin sent Soviet forces westward to share in the spoils. Soon, Poland was again divided between Germany and Russia, just as most of it had been before 1914. The Baltic states of Estonia, Latvia, and Lithuania soon fell as well.

When Finland proved less pliable, the Soviets invaded in November 1939. In the ensuing "Winter War," the Finns held out bravely, and the Soviets managed to prevail by March 1940 only by taking heavy casualties. The difficult course of the war in Finland seemed to confirm suspicions that Stalin's purge during the mid-1930s had substantially weakened the Soviet army. Still, by midsummer 1940, the Soviet Union had regained much of the territory lost to Russia during the upheavals that followed the revolution of 1917.

In the west, little happened during the strained winter of 1939–1940, known as the "Phony War." Then, on April 9, 1940, the Germans attacked Norway and Denmark in a surprise move to preempt a British and French scheme to cut off the shipment of Swedish iron ore to Germany. Denmark fell almost at once, while the staunch resistance in Norway was effectively broken by the end of April. The stage was set for the German assault on France.

The Fall of France, 1940

On May 10, 1940, Germany attacked France and the Low Countries. The Germans invaded France through the Ardennes Forest, above the northern end of the Maginot Line—terrain so difficult the French had discounted the possibility of an enemy strike there (see pages 730–731). As in 1914, northern France quickly became the focus of a major war, pitting French forces and their British allies against invading Germans. But this time, in startling contrast to World War I, the Battle of France was over in less than six weeks, a humiliating defeat for the French.

The problem for France was not lack of men and materiel, but strategy. Germany had only a slight numerical advantage in tanks but used mobile tanks and dive-bombers to mount rapid, highly concentrated offensives. Anticipating another long, defensive war, France had dispersed its tanks among infantry units along a broad front. Once the German tank column broke through the French lines, it quickly cut through northern France and moved toward the North Sea. France's poor showing convinced the British that rather than commit troops and planes to a hopeless battle in France, they should get out and regroup for a longer global war. Early in June, 200,000 British troops—as well as 130,000 French—escaped German encirclement and capture through a difficult evacuation at Dunkirk (see **MAP 28.1**).

By mid-June, Germany had won a decisive victory. As the French military collapsed, the French cabinet resigned, to be replaced by a new government under Marshal Philippe Pétain, who had led the successful French defense of Verdun during World War I. Pétain's government first asked for an armistice and then engineered a change of regime. The French parliament voted by an overwhelming majority to give Pétain exceptional powers, including the power to draw up a new constitution. So ended the parliamentary democracy of the Third Republic, which seemed responsible for France's weakness. The republic gave way to the more authoritarian **Vichy** (VEE-shee) regime, named after the resort city to which the government retreated as the Germans moved into Paris. The end of the fighting in France

CHRONOLOGY

September 1, 1939	Germany invades Poland
November 1939– March 1940	Soviets wage "Winter War" against Finland
April 9, 1940	Germany attacks Denmark and Norway
May 10	Germany attacks the Netherlands, Belgium, and France
June 22, 1941	Germany attacks the Soviet Union
August	Churchill and Roosevelt agree to the Atlantic Charter
December 7, 1941	Japan attacks Pearl Harbor
August 1942– February 1943	Battle of Stalingrad
November 1942	Allied landings in North Africa
April–May 1943	Warsaw ghetto revolt
July	Soviet victory in Battle of Kursk-Orel
July	Allied landings in Sicily; fall of Mussolini; Italy asks for an armistice
November	Teheran conference
June 6, 1944	D-Day: Allied landings in Normandy
February 1945	Yalta conference
May 7–8, 1945	Germany surrenders
June 1945	Founding of the United Nations
July–August 1945	Potsdam conference
August 6, 1945	U.S. atomic bombing of Hiroshima
August 15, 1945	Japan announces surrender
March 1947	Truman Doctrine
August 1947	India and Pakistan achieve independence
May 1948	Foundation of the state of Israel
1949	Communist takeover in China
June 1948–May 1949	Berlin blockade and airlift
August 1949	First Soviet atomic bomb
September 1949	Founding of the Federal Republic in West Germany

🌐 MAP 28.1—World War II: European Theaters

Much of Europe saw fighting during World War II, although different fronts were important at different times. What proved decisive was the fighting that ensued in the vast expanse of the Soviet Union after the Germans invaded in June 1941.

Vichy France Authoritarian French government, headquartered in the town of Vichy, that followed the Third Republic after France's defeat by Nazi Germany in 1940. The government collaborated with the victorious Germans, who occupied Paris.

Charles de Gaulle The youngest general in the French army, he called on French forces to follow his lead and continue the fight against Nazi Germany after the fall of France in June 1940.

resulted in a kind of antidemocratic revolution, but one in which the French people, stunned by military defeat, at first acquiesced.

According to the armistice agreement, the French government was not only to cease hostilities, but also to collaborate with the victorious Germans. French resistance began immediately, however. In a radio broadcast from London on June 18, **Charles de Gaulle** (1890–1970), the youngest general in the French army, called on French forces to rally to him to continue the fight against Nazi Germany. The military forces stationed in the French colonies, as well as the French troops that had been evacuated at Dunkirk, could form the nucleus of a new French army. Under the present circumstances of military defeat and political change, de Gaulle's appeal seemed quixotic at best. Most French colonies went along with what seemed the legitimate French government at Vichy—to which de Gaulle was a traitor. Yet a new Free French force grew from de Gaulle's remarkable appeal, and its subsequent role in the war compensated, in some measure, for France's humiliating defeat in 1940.

Winston Churchill and the Battle of Britain

With the defeat of France, Hitler seems to have expected that Britain, now apparently vulnerable to German invasion, would come to terms. And certainly some prominent Britons questioned the wisdom of remaining at war. But the British war effort found a new and effective champion in **Winston Churchill** (1874–1965), who replaced Neville Chamberlain as prime minister on May 10, when the German invasion of western Europe began. Although Churchill had been prominent in British public life for years, his career to this point had not been noteworthy for either judgment or success. He was obstinate, difficult, something of a curmudgeon. Yet he rose to the wartime challenge, becoming one of the notable leaders of the modern era. In speeches to the House of Commons during the remainder of 1940, he inspired his nation with perhaps the most memorable words of the war. Though some found a negotiated settlement with Germany even more sensible in light of the outcome in France, Churchill's dogged promise of "blood, toil, tears, and sweat" helped rally the British people, so that later he could say, without exaggeration, that "this was their finest hour."

Winston Churchill
British prime minister during World War II, his courage and decisiveness made him widely seen as one of modern Britain's greatest leaders.

After the fall of France, Churchill's Britain promptly moved to full mobilization for a protracted war. Indeed, Britain developed the most thoroughly coordinated war economy of all the belligerents, producing more tanks, aircraft, and machine guns than Germany did between 1940 and 1942. The National Service Act of 1941 subjected men ages 18 to 50 and women ages 20 to 30 to military or civilian war service. The upper age limits were subsequently raised to meet the demand for labor. Almost 70 percent of the 3 million people added to the British workforce during the war were women.

Britain, then, intended to continue the fight even after France fell. Hitler weighed his options and decided to attack. In light of British naval superiority, he hoped to rely on aerial bombardment to knock the British out of the war without an actual invasion. The ensuing Battle of Britain culminated in the nightly bombing of London from September 7 through November 2, 1940, killing fifteen thousand people and destroying thousands of buildings. But the British held. Ordinary people holed up in cellars and subway stations, while the fighter planes of the Royal Air Force fought back effectively, inflicting heavy losses against German aircraft over Britain.

Although the bombing continued into 1941, the British had withstood the worst the Germans could deliver, and Hitler began looking to the east, his ultimate objective all along. In December 1940, he ordered preparations for Operation Barbarossa, the assault on the Soviet Union. Rather than continuing the attack on Britain directly, Germany would use submarines to cut off shipping—and thus the supplies the British needed for a long war. Once Germany had defeated the Soviet Union, it would enjoy the geopolitical basis for world power, while Britain, as an island nation relying on a dispersed empire, would eventually be forced to come to terms.

Italian Intervention and the Spread of the War

Lacking sufficient domestic support, and unready for a major war, Mussolini could only look on as the war began in 1939. But as the Battle of France neared its end, it seemed safe for Italy to intervene, sharing in the spoils of what appeared certain victory. Thus, in June 1940, Italy declared war, expecting to secure territorial advantages in the Mediterranean, starting with Corsica, Nice, and Tunisia, at the expense of France. Italy also hoped eventually to supplant Britain in the region—and even to take the Suez Canal.

Although Hitler and Mussolini got along reasonably well, their relationship was sensitive. When Hitler seemed to be proceeding without Italy during the first year of the war, Mussolini grew determined to show his independence. Finally, in October 1940, he ordered Italian forces to attack Greece. But the Greeks mounted a strong resistance, thanks partly to the help of British forces from North Africa.

Meanwhile, Germany had established its hegemony in much of east-central Europe without military force, often by exploiting grievances over the outcome of the Paris Peace Conference in 1919. In November 1940, Romania and Hungary joined the Axis camp, and Bulgaria followed a few months later. But in March 1941, just after Yugoslavia had similarly committed to the Axis, a coup overthrew the pro-Axis government in Yugoslavia, and the new Yugoslav government prepared to aid the Allies.

British Resistance   At the height of the German bombing of Britain in 1940, Winston Churchill and his wife, Clementine, survey the damage in London.   (J. A. Hampton/Topical Hulton Archive/Getty Images)

SECTION SUMMARY

- In implementing its innovative *Blitzkrieg* strategy, Germany employed rapid, highly concentrated offensives that combined tanks and airpower to great effect.

- After Poland fell quickly, Hitler offered peace to Britain and France, seriously thinking that this particular war might be over.

- Once German victory in Poland was assured, the Soviet Union began sharing the spoils and, by midsummer 1940, had regained much of the territory lost during the upheavals that followed the Russian Revolution.

- In dramatic contrast with World War I, France in 1940 fell to German invasion in less than six weeks.

- The defeat of France led to the end of the Third Republic and the advent of the authoritarian Vichy regime, which was obliged by the armistice agreement to collaborate with Nazi Germany.

- Inspired by Churchill's determined leadership, the British withstood the sustained German air assault during the second half of 1940 and finally forced Hitler to alter his overall strategy.

By this point, Hitler had decided it was expedient to push into the Balkans with German troops, both to reinforce the Italians and to consolidate Axis control of the area. As the war's geographic extent expanded, its stakes increased, yet the Germans continued to meet every challenge. By the end of May 1941, they had taken Yugoslavia and Greece (see **MAP 28.1**).

At the same time, the war was spreading to North Africa and the Middle East because of European colonial ties. The native peoples of the area sought to take advantage of the conflict to pursue their own independence. Iraq and Syria became involved, as the Germans, operating from Syria, administered by Vichy France, aided anti-British Arab nationalists in Iraq. But most important proved to be North Africa, where Libya, an Italian colony since 1912, lay adjacent to Egypt, with its strong British presence.

Under General Erwin Rommel, the famous "Desert Fox," Axis forces won remarkable victories in North Africa from February to May 1941. But successful though they had been, the German forays into North Africa and the Balkans had delayed the crucial attack on the Soviet Union.

THE ASSAULT ON THE SOVIET UNION AND THE NAZI NEW ORDER

What was the place of the Holocaust in the Nazi effort to begin constructing a "new order" in eastern Europe?

German troops invaded the Soviet Union on June 22, 1941. Although the Germans enjoyed the expected successes for a while, the Soviets eventually prevailed, spearheading the Allied victory in Europe. Supplies from their new Allies—Britain and eventually the United States—aided the Soviet cause, but the surprising strength of the Soviet military effort proved the most important factor. In winning the war, the Soviets suffered incredible casualties, and after they gained the initiative, they proceeded with particular brutality as they forced the invading Germans back into Germany.

In part, at least, the Soviets were responding to the unprecedented form of warfare unleashed by the Nazis. While preparing for the attack on the Soviet Union, Hitler had made it clear to the Nazi leadership that this was to be no ordinary military engagement but a war of racial-ideological extermination. The Germans penetrated well into the Soviet Union, reaching the apex of their power late in 1942. German conquests by that point enabled Hitler to begin constructing the new, race-based European order he had dreamed of. As part of this process, the Nazis began systematically killing Jews, first by shooting, then by mass-gassing them in specially constructed death camps.

An Ambiguous Outcome, 1941–1942

In ordering preparations for Operation Barbarossa in December 1940, Hitler decided to risk attacking the Soviet Union before knocking Britain out of the war. Then he invaded the Balkans and North Africa in what may have been an unnecessary diversion. In retrospect, it is easy to pinpoint that combination as his fatal mistake. But in light of the Soviet purges of the 1930s and what seemed the poor performance of the Soviet army against Finland, Hitler had reason to believe the Soviet Union would crack relatively easily. Western military experts had come to similar conclusions, estimating that German forces would need but six weeks to take Moscow. And if Germany were to defeat the Soviet Union with another *Blitzkrieg*, it could gain control of the oil and other resources required for a longer war against Britain and, if necessary, the United States.

Attacking the Soviet Union on June 22, 1941, German forces achieved notable successes during the first month of fighting, partly because Stalin was so unprepared for this German betrayal. Ignoring warnings of an impending German assault, he had continued to live up to his end of the 1939 bargain with Hitler, even supplying the Germans with oil and grain. After the attack, Russia's defenses were at first totally disorganized, and by late November, German forces were within 20 miles of Moscow.

But the Germans were ill-equipped for Russian weather, and as an early and severe winter descended, the German offensive bogged down. In December, the Soviets mounted a formidable surprise counterattack near Moscow. The German *Blitzkrieg*, which had seemed a sure thing in July, had failed. Germany might still prevail, but a different strategy would be required.

The Germans, however, still had the advantage. Although German forces failed to take the key city of Leningrad in 1941, they cut it off by blockade and, until early 1944, kept it under siege with relentless bombing and shelling. During the summer

—by Illingworth.

Forgive me, comrade . . . On June 23, 1941, the day after Nazi Germany attacked the Soviet Union, the *London Daily Mail* published this cartoon depicting Hitler's betrayal of his 1939 pact with Stalin. (Solo Syndication/Associated Newspapers)

of 1942, they mounted another offensive, moving more deeply into the Soviet Union than before, reaching Stalingrad in November. But this proved the deepest penetration of German forces—and the zenith of Nazi power in Europe.

Hitler's New Order

By the summer of 1942, Nazi Germany dominated the European continent as no power had before (see **Map 28.2**). German military successes allowed the Nazi regime to begin building a new order in the territories under German domination. Satellite states in Slovakia and Croatia, and client governments in Romania and Hungary, owed their existence to Nazi Germany and readily adapted to the Nazi system. Elsewhere in the Nazi orbit, some countries proved eager collaborators; others did their best to resist; still others were given no opportunity to collaborate but were ruthlessly subjugated instead.

The Nazis' immediate aim was simply to exploit the conquered territories to serve the continuing war effort. Precisely as envisioned, access to the resources of so much of Europe made Germany considerably less vulnerable to naval blockade than during World War I. France proved a particularly valuable source of raw materials; by 1943, for example, 75 percent of French iron ore went to German factories.

But the deeper purposes of the war were also clear in the way the Nazis treated the territories under their control, especially in the difference between east and west. Western Europe experienced plenty of atrocities, but Nazi victory there still led to something like conventional military occupation. The Germans tried to enlist the cooperation of local authorities in countries like Denmark, the Netherlands, and France, though with mixed results. And whereas the Nazis exploited the economy of France, for example, it never became clear what role France might play in Europe after a Nazi victory. However, in Poland, and later in the conquered parts of the Soviet Union, there was no pretense of cooperation, and it was immediately clear what the Nazi order would entail.

After the conquest of Poland, the Germans annexed the western part of the country outright and promptly executed, jailed, or expelled members of the Polish elite—professionals, journalists, business leaders, and priests. The Nazis prohibited the Poles from entering the professions and restricted even their right to marry. All the Polish schools and most of the churches were simply closed.

In the rest of Poland, known as the General Government, Nazi policy was slightly less brutal at first. Most churches remained open, and Poles were allowed to practice the professions, but the Nazis closed most schools above the fourth grade, as well as libraries, theaters, and museums, as they sought to root out every expression of Polish culture. Some Poles in this area were forced into slave labor, but a final decision as to whether the Polish population was to be exterminated, enslaved, or shipped off to Siberia was postponed—to be made after the wider war had been won.

With the conquest of Poland, Nazi leaders proclaimed that a new era of monumental resettlement in eastern Europe had begun. Germans selected for their racial characteristics were now resettled in the part of Poland annexed to Germany. Most were ethnic Germans who had been living outside Germany. During the fall of 1942, Heinrich Himmler's *Schutzstaffel* (SS), the select Nazi elite, began to arrest and expel peasants from the rest of Poland to make way for further German resettlement. By 1943, perhaps 1 million Germans had been moved into what had been Poland.

After the assault on the Soviet Union, Hitler made it clear that eastern Europe as far as the Ural Mountains was to be opened for German settlement. War veterans were to be given priority, partly because the German settlers would have to be tough to resist the Slavs, who would be concentrated east of the Urals. Himmler told SS leaders that to prepare for German colonization, Germany would have to exterminate 30 million Slavs in the Soviet Union. After the invasion, the SS promptly began executing prisoners of war, as well as any Soviet leaders they could find. However, the Nazis expected that several generations would be required for the resettlement of European Russia.

The Holocaust

Conquest of the east also opened the way to a more radical solution to the "Jewish problem" than the Nazis had contemplated before. Under the cover of war, they began actually killing the Jews within their orbit. Thus began the process, and the experience, that has come to be known as the Holocaust.

When and why this radical policy was chosen remains controversial. Although prewar Nazi rhetoric occasionally suggested the possibility of such physical extermination, talk of a "final solution to the Jewish problem" seemed to mean forced emigration. Although the precise chain

MAP 28.2—The Nazi New Order in Europe, 1942

At the zenith of its power in 1942, Nazi Germany controlled much of Europe. Concerned most immediately with winning the war, the Nazis sought to coordinate the economies of their satellite states and conquered territories. But they also began establishing what was supposed to be an enduring new order in eastern Europe. The inset shows the locations of the major Nazi concentration camps and the six extermination camps the Nazis constructed in what had been Poland.

of events that led to a more radical approach will no doubt remain uncertain, it was surely bound up with the fortunes of the war.

THE GHETTOS

The conquest of Poland, with a Jewish population of 3.3 million, gave the Nazis control over a far greater number of Jews than ever before. In 1940, as part of their effort to create a new order, the Nazis began confining Polish Jews to ghettos set up in Warsaw and five other cities. Although much brutality and many deaths accompanied this process, the Nazis had not yet adopted a policy of systematic killing. Indeed, at first, no one knew what the ultimate fate of these Jews was to be. At this point, Nazi authorities were concentrating on removing, or even killing, non-Jewish Poles to make way for German resettlement. The fate of the Jews would be decided later. However, as the Polish ghettos grew more crowded and difficult to manage, Nazi officials in Poland began pressing for a more immediate solution.

THE SS PLAN FOR ANNIHILATION

Accompanying the military forces invading the Soviet Union were specially trained SS units assigned to kill Communist Party officials and adult male Jews. But soon some began murdering Jewish women and children as well. By late November 1941, the Nazis had killed 136,000 Jews, most by shooting, in the invaded Soviet territories. But this mode of killing proved both inefficient and psychologically burdensome—even for these specially trained killers. By late summer 1941, their experience in the Soviet Union, combined with the problems in the Polish ghettos, led Nazi leaders to begin seeking a more systematic and impersonal method of mass extermination.

The most likely scenario is that Hitler settled on physical extermination of the Jews in the thrill of what seemed impending victory over the Soviet Union. At the end of July 1941, Reinhard Heydrich of the SS began developing a detailed plan, and by the fall, the Nazis were sending German and Austrian Jews to the ghettos in Poland and actively impeding further Jewish emigration from Europe.

Systematic killing of Jews began later that fall. The Nazis took advantage of the personnel and the methods—especially the use of poison gas—that had proven effective during the "euthanasia" campaign of 1939 through 1941 in Germany (see page 772). By March 1942, they had constructed several extermination camps with gas chambers and crematoria, intended to kill large numbers of Jews and dispose of their bodies as efficiently as possible. The first victims were the Polish Jews who had already been confined to ghettos. The Nazis brutally suppressed attempts at resistance, like the Warsaw ghetto uprising of April and May 1943.

NAZI DEATH CAMPS

During the war, the Nazis constructed six death camps, although not all were operating at peak capacity at the same time. All six were located in what had been Poland (see inset, **MAP 28.2**). Horrifying though they were, the concentration camps in Germany, such as Dachau, Buchenwald, and Bergen-Belsen, were not extermination camps, although many Jews died in them late in the war.

Auschwitz-Birkenau
The largest of Nazi Germany's six extermination camps, all of which were located in what had been Poland.

The largest of the six death camps was the **Auschwitz-Birkenau** complex, which became the principal extermination center in 1943. The Nazis shipped Jews from all over Europe to Auschwitz, which was killing about twelve thousand people a day at the height of its operation in 1944. Auschwitz was one of two extermination camps that included affiliated slave-labor factories, in which Jews considered most able to work were often literally worked to death. Among the companies profiting from the arrangement were two of Germany's best known, Krupp and IG Farben.

The Jews typically arrived at one of the camps crammed into cattle cars on special trains. SS medical doctors subjected new arrivals to "selection," picking some for labor assignments and sending the others, including most women and children, to the gas chambers. Camp personnel made every effort to deceive Jews who were about to be killed, to lead them to believe they were to be showered and deloused. Even in camps without forced-labor factories, Jews were compelled to do much of the dirty work of the extermination operation. But under the brutal conditions of the camps, those initially assigned to work inevitably weakened; most were then deemed unfit and put to death.

SECRECY SURROUNDING THE CAMPS

The Nazis took every precaution to hide what was going on in the death camps. The SS personnel involved were sworn to silence. Himmler insisted that if secrecy was to be maintained, the operation would have to be quick—and total, to include women and children, "so that no Jews will remain to take revenge on our sons and grandsons." Indeed, he constantly sought to accelerate the process, even though it required labor and transport facilities needed for the war effort.

Himmler and the other major SS officials, such as Rudolf Höss (HOESS), the commandant at Auschwitz, or Adolf Eichmann (IKE-mahn), who organized the transport of the Jews to the camps,

The End of the Warsaw Ghetto   In April 1943, the sixty thousand Jews remaining in the Warsaw ghetto revolted rather than face shipment to the extermination camps. Many died in the ensuing fighting; others perished as the Germans set fire to the ghetto. Almost all the rest were captured and sent to their deaths at Treblinka. Before it was put down in May, the uprising killed at least three hundred Germans.   (AP Photos)

were not simply sadists who enjoyed humiliating their victims. Rather, they took satisfaction in doing what they believed was their duty without flinching, without signs of weakness. Addressing a group of SS members in 1943, Himmler portrayed the extermination of the Jews as a difficult "historical task" that they, the Nazi elite, must do for their racial community: "Most of you know what it means to see a hundred corpses piled up, or five hundred, or a thousand. To have gone through this and—except for cases of human weakness—to have remained decent, that has made us tough. This is an unwritten, never to be written, page of glory in our history."[2]

However, as Himmler's casual reference to "cases of human weakness" suggests, a minority of camp guards and others failed to live up to this image and indulged in wanton cruelty toward their helpless victims. For some, the extermination process became the occasion to act out sadistic fantasies. But though this dimension is surely horrifying, the bureaucratic, factory-like nature of the extermination process has seemed still more troubling in some respects, for it raises questions about the nature of modern rationality itself. The mass killing of Jews required the expertise of scientists, doctors, and lawyers; it required the bureaucratic organization of the modern state—all to provide the most efficient means to a monstrous end.

Despite the overriding emphasis on secrecy, reports of the genocide reached the West almost immediately in 1942. At first, however, most tended to discount them as wartime propaganda of the sort that had circulated during World War I, when stories about Germans eating Belgian babies whipped up war fever. Skepticism about extermination reports was easier because there were a few concentration camps, like Theresienstadt (teh-REZ-eh-en-shtat) in the former Czechoslovakia, that housed Jews who had been selected for special treatment. These camps were not used for extermination and were not secret; the Red Cross was even allowed to inspect

Theresienstadt several times. Those outside, and the German people as well, were led to believe that all the Jews were being interned, for the duration of the war, in camps like these, much as Japanese Americans were being interned in camps in the western United States at the same time. But even as the evidence grew, President Roosevelt, citing military priorities, refused pleas from Jewish leaders in 1944 to bomb the rail line into Auschwitz. As he saw it, the way to save as many Jews as possible was to win the war as quickly as possible.

AN ARRAY OF VICTIMS

The Nazis' policy of actually murdering persons deemed undesirable or superfluous did not start with, and was not limited to, the Jews. First came the "euthanasia" program in Germany, and the war afforded the Nazis the chance to do away with an array of other "undesirables," including Poles, Sinti and Roma ("Gypsies"), communists, homosexuals, and vagrants. The Nazis also systematically killed perhaps 2 million Soviet prisoners of war. So the most radical and appalling aspect of Nazism did not stem from anti-Semitism alone. This must not be forgotten, but neither must the fact that the Jews constituted by far the largest group of victims—perhaps 5.7 to 6 million, almost two-thirds of the Jews in Europe. (See the feature, "The Visual Record: Holocaust Snapshots.")

Collaboration in Nazi Europe

In rounding up Jews for extermination, and in establishing their new order in Europe, the Nazis found willing collaborators among several of the countries within their orbit. Collaboration with the victorious Nazi regime seemed to some the best way to pursue their own nationalist agendas. Croatia, earlier part of Yugoslavia, was eager to round up Jews and Gypsies, as well as to attack Serbs, as part of its effort to establish itself as a nation-state. But national circumstances varied across Europe, and so did degrees of collaboration. In Denmark, Norway, and the Netherlands, the Nazis thought racial kinship would matter, but they never found sufficient support to make possible genuinely independent collaborationist governments. Denmark did especially well at resisting the German effort to round up Jews, as did Italy and Bulgaria.

Vichy France was somewhere in the middle, and thus, it has remained particularly controversial. When the Vichy regime was launched during the summer of 1940, Marshal Pétain, its 84-year-old chief of state, enjoyed widespread support. Pétain promised to maximize French sovereignty and shield his people from the worst aspects of Nazi occupation. At the same time, the Vichy government claimed to be implementing its own "national revolution," returning France to authority, discipline, and tradition after the shambles of the Third Republic. Vichy's revolution was anti-Semitic and hostile to the left, so it seemed compatible, up to a point, with Nazism. And at first, Germany seemed likely to win the war. Thus, Pétain's second-in-command, Pierre Laval (la-VAHL), was willing to collaborate actively with the Nazis. The Vichy regime ended up doing much of the Nazis' dirty work for them—rounding up workers for forced shipment to German factories, hunting down members of the anti-German resistance, and picking up Jews to be sent to the Nazi extermination camps.

After the war, Pétain, Laval, and others were found guilty of treason by the new French government. Because of his advanced age, Pétain was merely imprisoned, while Laval and others were executed. Despite the contributions of de Gaulle's Free French and the French resistance, the shame of Vichy collaboration continued to haunt France, deepening the humiliation of the defeat in 1940.

Toward the Soviet Triumph

The import of what happened elsewhere in Europe depended on the outcome of the main event, the German invasion of the Soviet Union. Although the German Sixth Army, numbering almost 300,000 men, reached Stalingrad by late 1942, the Germans could not achieve a knockout. The Soviets managed to defend the city in what was arguably the pivotal military engagement of World War II. While some Soviet troops fought street by street, house by house, others counterattacked, encircling the German force. Hitler refused a strategic retreat, but his doggedness backfired. By the end of January 1943, the Soviets had captured the remaining German troops, very few of whom survived to return to Germany. Perhaps 240,000 German soldiers died in the Battle of **Stalingrad** or as prisoners afterward. But the price to the Soviets for their victory was far greater: A million Soviet soldiers and civilians died at Stalingrad.

Although the Germans resumed the offensive on several fronts during the summer of 1943, the Soviets won the tank battle of Kursk-Orel in July, and from then on, Stalin's Red Army moved relentlessly westward, forcing the Germans to retreat. By February 1944, Soviet troops had pushed the Germans back to the Polish border, and the outcome of the war was no longer in doubt.

Stalingrad Decisive World War II battle in which Soviet forces launched repeated counterattacks on Germany's Sixth Army, stopping it from advancing farther and finally forcing it to surrender.

The Soviet victory was incredible, in light of the upheavals of the 1930s and the low esteem in which most held the Soviet military in 1941. Portraying the struggle as "**the Great Patriotic War**" for national defense, Stalin managed to rally the Soviet people against the Germans. Rather than emphasize communist themes, he recalled the heroic defenses mounted against invaders in tsarist times, including the resistance to Napoleon in 1812. But though the Soviets ultimately prevailed, the cost in death, destruction, and suffering was almost unimaginable. For example, by the time Soviet forces finally broke the siege of Leningrad in January 1944, a million people in the city had died, most from starvation, freezing, or disease. And the Soviets won on the battlefield partly by taking incredible numbers of casualties.

The invading Germans gained access to major areas of Soviet industry and oil supply, and by the end of 1941 the country's industrial output had been cut in half. Yet the Soviet Union was able to weather this blow and go on to triumph. Outside help contributed, but only 5 to 15 percent of Soviet supplies came from the West. Between 1939 and 1941, Soviet leaders had begun building a new industrial base east of the Urals. And when the Germans invaded in 1941, the plant and equipment of 1,500 enterprises were dismantled and shipped by rail for reassembly farther east, out of reach of German attack. Then, beginning in 1942, thousands of brand-new factories were constructed in eastern regions as well.

Moreover, the earlier purges of the armed forces proved to have done less long-term damage than outside observers had expected. If anything, the removal of so many in the top ranks made it easier for talented young officers like Georgi Zhukov (1896–1974), who would become the country's top military commander, to rise quickly into major leadership positions.

When the United States entered the war in December 1941, the Soviets were fighting for survival. They immediately began pressuring the United States and Britain to open another front in Europe, preferably by landing in northern France, where an Allied assault could be expected to have the greatest impact. But the Allies did not invade northern France and open a major second front until June 1944. By then, the Soviets had turned the tide in Europe on their own.

"the Great Patriotic War" Term for World War II devised by Joseph Stalin to rally Soviet citizens against the German invasion.

SECTION SUMMARY

- Although the German invasion of the Soviet Union in 1941 failed to bring the expected quick victory, the Germans drove still further into the country in 1942—but then met defeat at the Battle of Stalingrad.

- Brutal though it was, Nazi policy in northern and western Europe approached something like conventional military occupation, whereas in the conquered territories of the east, first and most dramatically in the former Poland, the Nazis engaged in radical population engineering as they began constructing a race-based "new order."

- By the end of 1941, the Holocaust became a systematic program as the Nazis decided to kill Jews and others by adapting the methods developed through the "euthanasia" program.

- Although the Jews constituted by far the largest group of victims, the Nazis also killed an array of others, from homosexuals to Soviet prisoners of war.

- After defeating the Germans at Kursk-Orel in July 1943, the Soviets began steadily advancing toward Germany, thereby turning the tide in Europe well before the U.S.-British landing in northern France opened a major second front in June 1944.

Stalingrad, November 1942 From September 1942 until the German surrender early in February 1943, this city on the Volga River saw some of the heaviest fighting of World War II. The Soviet victory, in the face of incredible casualties, was arguably the turning point of the war in Europe. (Sovfoto/Eastfoto)

Holocaust Snapshots

What are we to make of these pictures? In one sense, they appear to be ordinary snapshots of the sort that became popular between the wars, as inexpensive cameras became common consumer items for the first time. But these photographs are hardly ordinary; they depict disturbing aspects of the Nazi effort to exterminate the Jews between 1941 and 1945. So we wonder, who took these pictures—and why? Why did these particular images seem worth preserving? What do such photographs tell us about the mentality that made possible the monstrous process that we have come to know as the Holocaust?

More than 50 percent of the victims of the Holocaust died in the six extermination camps, the camps with systematic gassing facilities. Almost a quarter died from such factors as malnutrition, disease, or exhaustion while in transit, in the ghettos, or in the labor or concentration camps. The rest—more than one quarter of the victims— were killed individually, mostly by shooting, up close.

These photos, and many others like them, were taken by members of Hamburg-based Reserve Battalion 101 of the "order police," made famous through the somewhat conflicting accounts of Christopher R. Browning and Daniel Jonah Goldhagen.[3] This local branch of the complex German police system was sent to assist in the removal of Jews from a remote section of Poland in July 1942. Only upon arriving in the village of Józefów did these ordinary policemen find that their first task was to shoot large numbers of defenseless Jews one by one. When given their collective charge, these men were offered a chance to pull back from the actual murder of Jews. But the vast majority did what they were told—why?

We know that the men of Battalion 101 had not been specially selected and trained for such a task. Indeed, they were unprepared and surprised when, upon arriving in Józefów, they learned what they were there to do. Browning suggests that many of the men felt that they had to be tough, following orders based on government policy, whatever it entailed. Moreover, they did not want to appear weak or leave the dirty work to their comrades. Others tried not to think about what they were doing or masked it through heavy drinking.

But photographs like these suggest a further step. Ordinary Germans took them not so that they could forget, obviously, but precisely to remember and commemorate their participation. Indeed, the very act of taking the photographs was essential to their dehumanization and humiliation of the Jews. Notice the photo on the left, taken during the liquidation of the ghetto at Lukow, Poland, probably in the fall of 1942. Three of the four police officers are looking directly at the camera. Some of the officers have stern facial expressions, as if they are trying to convey their toughness and power. Others, such as the officer at far left, smile broadly for the camera. The Jews, meanwhile, are humiliated by being forced to kneel and raise their hands above their heads.

In the other photograph, Jews are shown digging their own graves. Unlike the one taken at Lukow, no officers appear in this photo and no one is posing for the camera. Yet somehow even this image seemed worth preserving in a snapshot.

What did these Germans find so memorable about what they were doing? We may first assume that sheer anti-Semitism was the key, a notion that Goldhagen wholeheartedly supports. He argues that these photographs manifest a virulent anti-Semitism endemic in German society even before the rise of Nazism. But most experts deny that German anti-Semitism had been especially pronounced before Hitler came to power, so something more complex was surely at work in the minds of these policemen. Especially as the Nazi revolution yielded an apocalyptic war of race, ideology, and annihilation, the Nazi regime's ongoing campaign to demonize the Jews affected the responses to the Jews by ordinary Germans. The Jews came to seem not merely superfluous, but alien and threatening.

Thus, the key variable was not anti-Semitism but the momentum of the Nazi revolution itself. By 1942, a sense of the extraordinariness of the overall Nazi enterprise had produced an altered frame of mind in many reaches of German society. For example, a doctor involved in the earlier "euthanasia" program, Friedrich Mennecke, sought, in his letters to his wife, to chronicle for posterity this, "the greatest of times" in which he was privileged to participate.[4] In the same vein, historians Michael Burleigh and Wolfgang Wippermann found, as central to the Holocaust, "the group intoxication with violence and the prospect of going outside the limits of received moral norms."[5]

The ongoing Nazi revolution caught up even the members of Reserve Battalion 101 in essential roles. So those who took, and kept, and perhaps showed off these photographs were not merely ordinary human beings, or even ordinary Germans, but ordinary *Nazified* Germans. To some extent they, too, believed themselves to be involved in an enterprise that was grandiose, unprecedented, and of world-historical import. They did not merely follow orders, but came to experience the "extraordinary exhilaration" that Saul Friedländer found central to the overall extermination process.[6] Partly as a result, they sometimes fell into the gratuitous cruelty evident in many of the photographs they took. Most of these men would not have been capable of such cruelty under ordinary circumstances.

When the veterans of police Battalion 101 were put on trial in the 1960s, one of them, Erwin Graffman, noted that only after the fact had it occurred to him that the killing had been wrong.[7] When acting, he had believed in the essential rightness of the wider Nazi revolution. The participation of such people is not to be explained simply through

Lukow, Poland, July 1942 (Yad Vashem Film and Photo Archive)

Lomazy, Poland, August 1942 (Courtesy, ZstL, Ludwigsburg, Germany)

universal, ahistorical mechanisms, as if "we all could have done it." Those operating from within the framework of the Nazi revolution were especially likely to have treated the Jews as they did, not just killing them, but often humiliating them—and finding something memorable in the process.

Thus, for these perpetrators, the import of capturing the extraordinary enterprise through snapshots. But twenty years later, those who took them found it almost impossible to explain what had been their mindset at the time. As Browning noted, "it was a different time and place, as if they had been on another political planet, and the political values and vocabulary of the 1960s were useless in explaining the situation in which they had found themselves in 1942."[8] Yet these haunting images remain.

QUESTIONS

1. What, beyond sheer anti-Semitism, seems to have stimulated the policemen of Battalion 101 to preserve these scenes for posterity?

2. Does Erwin Graffman seem credible, or merely self-serving, when he says that, at the time these photographs were taken, he genuinely believed what he was doing was right?

A GLOBAL WAR, 1941–1944

How did the Grand Alliance of Britain, the United States, and the Soviet Union come together against the Axis powers?

Franklin Delano Roosevelt U.S. president who served from 1933 to 1945, through the Great Depression of the 1930s and most of World War II.

World War II proved unprecedented in its level of violence, partly because it eclipsed even World War I in its geographical reach. The European colonial presence quickly drew the war to North Africa and the Middle East. But the war's early results in Europe also altered the power balance in East Asia and the Pacific, where the Russians and the Japanese had long been antagonists. During the 1930s, the United States had also become involved in friction with Japan. By 1941, President **Franklin Delano Roosevelt** was openly favoring the anti-Axis cause, though it took a surprise attack by the Japanese in December 1941 to bring the United States into the war.

Japan and the Origins of the Pacific War

Lacking the raw materials essential for industry, Japan had been especially concerned about foreign trade and spheres of economic influence as it modernized after 1868. By the interwar period, the Japanese had become unusually reliant on exports of textiles and other products. During the Depression of the 1930s, when countries all over the world adopted protectionist policies, Japan suffered from increasing tariffs against its exports. This situation tilted the balance in Japanese ruling circles from free-trade proponents to those who favored a military-imperialist solution.

To gain economic hegemony by force, Japan could choose either of two directions. The northern strategy, concentrating on China, would risk Soviet opposition as well as strong local resistance. The southern strategy, focusing on southeast Asia and the East Indies, would encounter the imperial presence of Britain, France, the Netherlands, and the United States.

Japan opted for the northern strategy in 1931, when it took control of Manchuria, in northeastern China. But the Japanese attempt to conquer the rest of China, beginning in 1937, led only to an impasse by 1940. Japanese aggression in China drew the increasing hostility of the United States, a strong supporter of the Chinese nationalist leader Jiang Jieshi (Chiang Kaishek) (1887–1975), as well as the active opposition of the Soviet Union. Clashes with Soviet troops along the border between Mongolia and Manchuria led to significant defeats for the Japanese in 1938 and 1939.

By 1941, Germany's victories in Europe had seriously weakened Britain, France, and the Netherlands, the major European colonial powers in southeast Asia and the East Indies. The time seemed right for Japan to shift to a southern strategy. Rather than focus on China, the Japanese would seek control of southeast Asia, a region rich in such raw materials as oil, rubber, and tin—precisely what Japan lacked. To keep the Soviets at bay, Japan agreed to a neutrality pact with the Soviet Union in April 1941.

Japan had already joined with Nazi Germany and fascist Italy in an anticommunist agreement in 1936. In September 1940, the three agreed to a formal military alliance. For the Germans, alliance with Japan was useful to help discourage U.S. intervention in the European war. Japan, for its part, could expect the major share of the spoils of the European empires in Asia. However, diplomatic and military coordination between Germany and Japan remained minimal.

The United States began imposing embargoes on certain exports to Japan in 1938, in response to the Japanese aggression in China. After Japan had assumed control of Indochina, nominally held by Vichy France, by the summer of 1941, the United States imposed total sanctions, and the British and Dutch followed, forcing Japan to begin rapidly drawing down its oil reserves. Conquest of the oil fields of the Dutch East Indies now seemed a matter of life and death to the Japanese.

These economic sanctions heightened the determination of Japanese leaders to press forward aggressively now, when the country's likely enemies were weakened or distracted. But the Japanese did not expect a definitive victory over the United States in a long, drawn-out war. Rather, they anticipated, first, that their initial successes would enable them to grab the resources to sustain a longer war if necessary, and, second, that Germany would defeat Britain, leading the United States to accept a compromise peace allowing the Japanese what they wanted—a secure sphere of economic hegemony in southeast Asia.

🌐 MAP 28.3—The War in East Asia and the Pacific

After a series of conquests in 1941 and 1942, the Japanese were forced gradually to fall back before advancing U.S. forces. When the war abruptly ended in August 1945, however, the Japanese still controlled much of the territory they had conquered.

The Japanese finally provoked a showdown on December 7, 1941, with a surprise attack on Pearl Harbor, a U.S. naval base in Hawaii. The next day, Japanese forces seized Hong Kong and Malaya, both British colonies, and attacked Wake Island and the Philippines, both under U.S. control. The United States promptly declared war; in response, Hitler kept an earlier promise to Japan and declared war on the United States. World War II was now unprecedented in its geographic scope (see **MAP 28.3**).

Much like their German counterparts, Japanese forces got off to a remarkably good start. By the summer of 1942, Japan had taken Thailand, the Dutch East Indies, the Philippines, and the Malay Peninsula. Having won much of what they had been seeking, the Japanese began devising the Greater East Asia Co-Prosperity Sphere, their own "new order" in the conquered territories. (See the feature, "The Global Record: Japan's 'Pan-Asian' Mission.")

The United States in Europe and the Pacific

During the first years of the war in Europe, the United States did not have armed forces commensurate with its economic strength; in 1940, in fact, its army was smaller than Belgium's. But the United States could be a supplier in the short term and, if it chose to intervene, a major player

Japan's "Pan-Asian" Mission

With the coming of war against the Western powers in 1941, the Japanese could claim to be freeing Asians from Western imperialism and establishing a new economic order in East Asia and the Pacific. This selection from an essay titled "Our Present War and Its Cultural Significance," written just after the bombing of Pearl Harbor by the well-known author Nagayo Yoshio (1888–1961), accents Japan's anti-Western mission in the region. Yoshio understood, especially from his country's recent experience in China, that Asians might find Japanese hegemony just as oppressive as Western domination. Although it served Japan's own economic interests and was often applied brutally, Japanese "pan-Asianism" helped fuel the reaction against Western imperialism in Asia and the Pacific, with lasting results after the war.

Whenever Japan has faced a powerful enemy it has been the *yamato damashii* [Japanese national spirit] which provided the basis of our courage. Now that we can talk in retrospect of the Sino-Japanese War, I am afraid our national spirit has not been given a proper chance to be aroused, due to the deplorable fact that we had to fight with China, our sister nation, with no foreseeable conclusion to look forward to. ... While desperately fighting with a country which we made our enemy only reluctantly we were trying to find out a principle, an ethic based upon a new view of the world, which would justify our course of action. ... The China incident was not only insufficient to fulfill this goal but also met with insurmountable obstacles. Consequently, time and opportunity ripened to declare war against the United States and England....

...We would have nothing to say for ourselves if we were merely to follow the examples of the imperialistic and capitalistic exploitation of Greater East-Asia by Europe and the United States....

...It is true that the science of war is one manifestation of a nation's culture. But from this time on we have to realize the increasing responsibility on our part if we are to deserve the respect of the people of East-Asian countries as their leaders, in the sphere of culture in general (not only the mere fusion and continuance of Western and Oriental cultures but something surpassing and elevating them while making the most out of them) such as the formation of national character, refinement, intellect, training to become a world citizen, etc....

The sense of awe and respect with which the Orientals have held the white race, especially the Anglo-Saxons, for three hundred years is deep-rooted almost beyond our imagination. It is our task to realize this fact and deal with this servility at its root, find out why the white people became the objects of such reverence. It goes without saying that we cannot conclude simplemindedly that their shrewdness is the cause. Also we have to be very careful not to impose the *hakko ichiu* [the gathering of the whole world under one roof] spirit arbitrarily upon the Asians. If we make this kind of mistake we might antagonize those who could have become our compatriots and thus might also blaspheme our Imperial rule....

To sum up, we have finally witnessed the dawn of a new principle which we had been searching for over ten years.... The phrase "Greater East-Asian Co-prosperity Sphere" is no longer a mere abstract idea.

QUESTIONS

1. Why, according to the author, did the Japanese effort in China sow confusion about Japan's wider aims?

2. What role was Japan to play in Southeast Asia if it was *not* merely to replace Western imperialistic exploitation with another form?

Source: From "Our Present War and Its Cultural Significance" by Nagayo Yashio, translated by Mitsuko Iriye, in *Modern Asia and Africa*, edited by William H. McNeill and Mitsuko Iriye (Oxford University Press, 1971).

Lend-Lease Act Act by the U.S. Congress authorizing President Franklin Roosevelt to lend or lease weapons or other aid to countries the president designated.

over the longer term. With the **Lend-Lease Act** of March 1941, intended to provide war materiel without the economic dislocations of World War I, the United States lined up on the side of Britain against the Axis powers. In August 1941, a meeting between Churchill and Roosevelt off the coast of Newfoundland produced the Atlantic Charter, the first tentative agreement about the aims of the anti-Axis war effort. The Americans extended lend-lease to the Soviet Union the next month.

But though Roosevelt was committed to the anti-Axis cause, isolationist sentiment remained strong in the United States. The Japanese attack on Pearl Harbor inflamed American opinion and enabled Roosevelt at last to bring his country into the war as an active belligerent. By May 1942, the United States had joined with Britain and the Soviet Union in a formal military alliance against the Axis powers.

From the start, mutual suspicions marked the relationship between the two democracies and the Soviet Union. Initially, Britain and the United States feared that the Soviets might even seek a separate peace, as Russia had in World War I. The Soviets, for their part, worried that these newfound allies, with their long-standing anticommunism, might hold back from full commitment or even seek to undermine the Soviet Union.

In response to pressure from Stalin, Britain and the United States agreed to open a second front in Europe as soon as possible. But the Nazis dominated the Continent, so opening such a front required landing troops from the outside. It proved far more difficult to mount an effective assault on Europe than either Churchill or Roosevelt anticipated in 1942. The resulting delays furthered Stalin's suspicions that his allies were only too eager to have the Soviets do the bulk of the fighting against Nazi Germany—and weaken themselves in the process.

The United States agreed with its new allies to give priority to the war in Europe. But because it had to respond to the direct Japanese assault in the Pacific, the United States was not prepared to act militarily in Europe right away. What it could do, however, was supply the British with the ships needed to overcome German submarines, which seriously threatened shipping to Britain by 1942.

In the Pacific theater, in contrast, it was immediately clear that the United States would bear the brunt of the fighting against Japan. Although the Japanese went from one success to another during the first months of the war, they lacked the long-term resources to exploit their initial victories. In May 1942, the Battle of Coral Sea—off New Guinea, north of Australia—ended in a stalemate, stopping the string of Japanese successes. Then in June, the United States defeated the Japanese navy for the first time in the Battle of Midway, northwest of Hawaii. After the United States stopped attempted Japanese advances in the Solomon Islands and New Guinea early in 1943, U.S. forces began steadily advancing across the islands of the Pacific toward Japan (see **Map 28.3**).

The Search for a Second Front in Europe

As the Soviet army fought the Germans in the Soviet Union, the United States and Britain tried to determine how they could help tip the scales in Europe, now an almost impregnable German fortress. Stalin kept urging a direct assault across the English Channel, which, if successful, would have the greatest immediate impact. Churchill, however, advocated attacking the underbelly of the Axis empire by way of the Mediterranean, which would first require winning control of North Africa. And it was that strategy the Allies tried first, starting in 1942.

By May 1943, step one of Churchill's plan had succeeded, but North Africa was valuable primarily as a staging ground for an Allied attempt to penetrate Europe from the south (see **Map 28.1**). Meeting at the Moroccan city of Casablanca in January 1943, Churchill and Roosevelt agreed that British and American forces would proceed from North Africa to Sicily and up through mainland Italy from there. The Soviets, still pushing for an invasion across the English Channel into France, objected that the Germans could easily block an Allied advance through the long, mountainous Italian peninsula.

Crossing from North Africa, Allied troops landed in Sicily in July 1943, prompting the arrest of Mussolini and the collapse of the fascist regime. Supported by King Victor Emmanuel III, the Italian military commander, Pietro Badoglio (bah-DOHL-yo), formed a new government to seek an armistice. Meanwhile, Allied forces moved on to the Italian mainland, but the Germans quickly occupied much of Italy in response. They even managed a daring rescue of Mussolini and promptly reestablished him as puppet leader of a new rump republic in northern Italy, now under German control. Just as the Soviets had warned, the Germans sought to block the Italian peninsula, and it was not until nine months later, in June 1944, that the Allies reached Rome. So Churchill's strategy of assaulting Europe from the south proved less than decisive.

Only when Churchill, Roosevelt, and Stalin met for the first time, at Teheran, Iran, in November 1943, did they agree that the next step would be to invade western Europe from Britain. Preparations had been underway since early 1942, but the operation was complex and hazardous. Finally, Allied troops crossed the English Channel to make an amphibious landing on the beaches of Normandy, in northern France, on June 6, 1944, known to history as **D-Day**. Partly by deceiving the Germans seeking to defend the area, they were quickly able to consolidate their positions.

The success of the D-Day invasion opened a major second front in Europe at last. Now, American-led forces from the west and Soviet forces from the east worked systematically toward Germany. The one substantial German counterattack in the west, the Battle of the Bulge in December 1944, slowed the Allies' advance, but on March 7, 1945, Allied troops crossed the Rhine River (see **Map 28.1**).

By June 1944, when Allied forces landed at Normandy, Soviet forces had already crossed the 1939 border with Poland as they moved steadily westward. But in August, the Soviets stopped before reaching Warsaw, allowing the Nazis to crush a notable uprising by the Polish resistance that took place from August to October. The Polish Home Army, as it was called, was seeking to liberate Warsaw on its own, without waiting for the Soviets, who seemed likely to impose communism on Poland. In putting down the uprising, the German occupying forces suffered

D-Day The complex Allied amphibious landings in Normandy, France, on June 6, 1944, that opened a second major European front in World War II.

SECTION SUMMARY

- Japan turned to a more aggressive, expansionist foreign policy during the 1930s, largely because its economy, heavily dependent on exports, proved especially vulnerable during the Great Depression.

- Although Japan and Nazi Germany joined in a military alliance, diplomatic and military coordination between them was minimal during World War II.

- Delays in opening a major second front in Europe furthered Stalin's suspicions that Britain and the United States were happy to let the Soviets bear the brunt of the burden in the fight against Nazi Germany.

- After the Allied invasion of Italy failed to make a conclusive difference on the continental level, Churchill, Roosevelt, and Stalin agreed in November 1943 that, as the next step, the democracies would invade western Europe from Britain.

- In making their continental landings in Italy and France, the Western democracies left it to the Soviets to drive the German forces from east-central Europe.

ten thousand casualties, and then destroyed much of the city in retaliation. Meanwhile, the major Soviet thrust began cutting south, through Romania, which surrendered in August, and on into the Danube Valley in Hungary and Yugoslavia during the fall. Only in January 1945, did the Soviets resume their advance, taking Warsaw and moving westward toward Germany.

Now, with the defeat of Germany simply a matter of time, Allied concern shifted to the postwar order. Churchill, especially, worried about the implications of the Soviet advances in east-central Europe and the Balkans. As a supplement to the D-Day landings, he wanted to strike from Italy through Yugoslavia into east-central Europe. But the Americans resisted; Churchill's priorities, they felt, reflected outmoded concerns over spheres of influence. So the Allies concentrated instead on a secondary landing in southern France in August 1944. This assault, in which Free French forces were prominent, led quickly to the liberation of Paris. But because the Allies made both their landings in France, and not in southeastern Europe, the Western democracies were involved only in the liberation of western Europe. It was the Soviets who drove the Germans from east-central Europe. This fact, and the resulting geographic distribution of military strength, fundamentally affected the postwar order.

D-Day, 1944   Allied forces land at Normandy, early in the morning of June 6, 1944, at last opening a major second front in Europe.   (National Archives, Washington)

THE SHAPE OF THE ALLIED VICTORY, 1944–1945

How did the Allies manage to defeat Nazi Germany in World War II, after Germany's remarkable initial successes?

The leaders of the Soviet Union, Britain, and the United States sought to mold the postwar order at two notable conferences in 1945. Even as they brought different aspirations to the table, they had to deal together with the legacy of a war of unprecedented destructiveness. At the same time, they also had to face the hard military realities that had resulted from the fighting so far: Each country had forces in certain places but not in others. The result was an informal division of Europe into spheres of influence among the victors.

The most serious question the Allies faced concerned Germany, which was widely held responsible for the two world wars, as well as for Nazism with all its atrocities—including the concentration and extermination camps, discovered with shock and horror by the advancing Allied armies in 1945. Germany was to be forced to surrender unconditionally; there would be no negotiation or armistice. But what should be done with the country over the longer term?

In the Pacific theater, as in Europe, the way the war ended had major implications for the postwar world. The United States decided to use the atomic bomb, a weapon so destructive that it forced a quick Japanese surrender. The suddenness of the ending helped determine the fate of the European empires in Asia.

The Yalta Conference: Shaping the Postwar World

When Stalin, Roosevelt, and Churchill met at Yalta, a Soviet Black Sea resort, in February 1945, Allied victory was assured, and the three leaders accomplished a great deal. Yet controversy has long surrounded the **Yalta conference**. Western critics have charged that the concessions made to Stalin consigned east-central Europe to communist domination and opened the way to the dangerous cold war of the next forty years. At the time, however, the anticipation of victory produced a relatively cooperative spirit among the Allies. Thus, they firmed up plans for military occupation of Germany in separate zones, for joint occupation of Berlin, and for an Allied Control Council, composed of the military commanders-in-chief, which would make policy for all of Germany by unanimous agreement.

Yalta conference
1945 meeting between Stalin, Roosevelt, and Churchill in which they began outlining plans for the postwar order, including the military occupation of Germany.

Each of the Allies had special concerns, but each got much of what it was seeking at Yalta. Roosevelt was eager for Soviet help against Japan as soon as possible. In exchange for territorial concessions in Asia and the Pacific, Stalin agreed to declare war on Japan within three months of the German surrender.

Churchill, meanwhile, worried about the future of Europe in light of the American intention, which Roosevelt announced at Yalta, to maintain occupation troops in Europe for only two years after the war. To help balance Soviet power on the Continent, Churchill felt it essential to restore France as a great power. To this end, he urged that France be granted a share in the occupation of Germany and a permanent seat on the Security Council of the proposed new international organization, the **United Nations** (see page 812). Roosevelt agreed, even though he had little use for Charles de Gaulle or what he viewed as the pretensions of the French.

United Nations
International organization of nations founded in 1945 to encourage peace, cooperation, and recognition of human rights.

It seemed to the Americans that both Britain and the Soviet Union remained too wedded to traditional conceptions of national interest as they sought to shape the postwar world. Hence, one of Roosevelt's major priorities was to secure British and Soviet commitment to the United Nations before the three allies began to disagree over particular issues. He won that commitment at Yalta, but only by giving in to Churchill on the sensitive matter of British colonies.

Because anti-imperial sentiment worked to Japan's advantage in Asia, the United States had pestered Britain on the colonial issue since early in the war. Roosevelt even asked Churchill in 1941 about British intentions in India. So prickly was Churchill that he proclaimed in 1942, "I have not become the King's First Minister in order to preside over the liquidation of the British Empire." The parties agreed at Yalta that the British Empire would be exempt from an anticipated measure to bring former colonies under United Nations trusteeship after the war.

Although it was not the only question on the table, the future of the former Axis territories was central to the seaside deliberations. By the time of the conference, those territories were already being divided into spheres of influence among the Allies, and in light of troop locations, the eventual alignment was probably inevitable. In Italy, where U.S. and British forces held sway, the two democracies had successfully resisted Stalin's claim for a share in the administration. In east-central Europe, however, the Soviet army was in control. Still, the United States, with its vision of a new world order, objected to spheres of influence and insisted that democratic principles be applied everywhere. At Yalta, this American priority led to an awkward compromise over east-central Europe: The new governments in the area were to be both democratic and friendly to the Soviet Union.

Most important to the Soviets was Poland, with its crucial location between the Soviet Union and Germany. Although they insisted that communists lead the new Polish government at the outset, the Soviets compromised by allowing a role for the noncommunist Polish government-in-exile in London and by promising free elections down the road. The Allies agreed that Poland would gain substantial German territory to its west to make up for the eastern territory it had already lost to the USSR (see **MAP 28.4**).

In addition, the United States and Britain were to have a role in committees set up to engineer the transition to democracy in the rest of east-central Europe. However, only the Soviets had troops in the area, and those committees proved essentially powerless. The sources of future tension were already at work at Yalta, but they generally remained hidden by the high spirits of approaching victory.

Victory in Europe

Although the tide had turned in 1943, Germany managed to continue the war by exploiting its conquered territories and by more effectively allocating its domestic resources for war production. Thanks partly to the efforts of armaments minister Albert Speer, war production grew

🌐 MAP 28.4—The Impact of World War II in Europe

As a result of World War II, the Soviet Union expanded its western borders and Poland shifted westward at the expense of Germany. Territorial changes added to the wartime disruption and produced a flood of refugees. The cold war division of Europe did not depend on immediate territorial changes, but soon Germany itself came to be divided on east-west lines.

sharply between 1941 and 1944, so Germany had plenty of weapons even as the war was ending. The Germans even proved able to withstand the systematic bombing of cities that the British, especially, had thought might prove decisive.

Beginning in 1942, British-led bombing attacks destroyed an average of half the built-up area of seventy German cities, sometimes producing huge firestorms. The bombing of the historic city of Dresden in February 1945 killed at least sixty thousand civilians in the most destructive air assault of the war in Europe. But despite this widespread destruction, such bombing did not undermine morale or disrupt production to the extent expected. Even in the face of steady Allied bombing, the Germans managed to increase their war production during 1943 and 1944.

But Germany encountered two crucial bottlenecks that finally crippled its military effort: It was running out of both oil and military personnel. Despite making effective use of synthetics, the Nazi war machine depended heavily on oil from Romania. And although the terror bombing of cities did not have the anticipated impact, the more precisely targeted bombing favored by U.S. strategists significantly affected the outcome. In May 1944, the United States began bombing oil fields in Romania and refineries and synthetic oil plants in Germany. Then, late in August 1944, Soviet troops crossed into Romania, taking control of the oil fields. Soon Germany lacked enough fuel even to train pilots. So serious were the bottlenecks by 1945 that the German air force could not use all the aircraft that German industry was producing.

Soviet troops moving westward finally met U.S. troops moving eastward at the Elbe River in Germany on April 26, 1945. With his regime now thoroughly defeated and much of his country in ruins, Hitler committed suicide in his underground military headquarters in Berlin on April 30. The war in Europe finally ended with the German surrender to General Dwight D. Eisenhower at Reims, France, on May 7 and to Marshal Zhukov at Berlin on May 8. The world celebrated the end of the fighting in Europe, but an element of uncertainty surrounded the Allied victory. East-West differences were increasingly coming to the fore within the anti-German alliance.

The Potsdam Conference and the Question of Germany

The immediate question for the victorious Allies was the fate of Germany, which they confronted at the last of their notable wartime conferences, at **Potsdam**, just outside Berlin, from July 17 to August 2, 1945. The circumstances were dramatically different from those at Yalta just months before. With Hitler dead and Germany defeated, no common military aim provided unity. And of the three Allied leaders who had been at Yalta, only Stalin remained. President Roosevelt had

Potsdam conference
A July–August 1945 meeting held at Potsdam, Germany, between the USSR, the United States, and Great Britain to implement their earlier agreements concerning the treatment of defeated Germany.

The Soviet Victory in Europe   After forcing the Germans back for almost two years, Soviet troops reached Berlin in April 1945. After a day of heavy fighting and bombardment, the Soviets took the Reichstag building, in the heart of the devastated German capital, on April 30. Here two Soviet sergeants, Yegorov and Kantariya, plant the Soviet flag atop the Reichstag, symbolizing the Soviet victory in the decisive encounter of World War II in Europe.   (ITAR-TASS/Sovfoto)

died in April, so his successor, Harry Truman (1884–1972), represented the United States. In Britain, Churchill's Conservatives lost the general election during the first days of the conference, so Clement Attlee (1883–1967), the new Labour prime minister, assumed the leadership of the British delegation.

At Potsdam, the Allies had to determine how to implement their earlier agreements about Germany, which, devastated by bombing and devoid of a government, depended on the Allied occupying forces even for day-to-day survival. For a time, U.S. policymakers had even considered destroying Germany's industrial capacity in perpetuity. However, cooler heads understood that the deindustrialization, or "pastoralization," of Germany would not be in anyone's economic interests. Moreover, as the democracies grew increasingly suspicious about Soviet intentions, an economically healthy Germany seemed necessary to help in the balance against the Soviet Union.

For their part, the Soviets had reason to take a much harder line against Germany. Having been ravaged by invading German forces twice within living memory, the Soviet Union wanted to weaken Germany both territorially and economically. And of the three victors, the Soviets had suffered a greatly disproportionate share of the wartime destruction and economic loss, so they also sought to exploit the remaining resources of Germany by exacting heavy reparations. Moreover, the British and the Americans accepted the Soviet proposal that Germany's eastern border with Poland be shifted substantially westward, to the line formed by the Oder and Neisse (NYE-suh) Rivers. But just as Poland gained at the expense of Germany, the Soviet Union kept a substantial slice of what had been eastern Poland (see **MAP 28.4**).

Each of the three Allies had responsibility for administering a particular zone of occupation, but they were supposed to coordinate their activities in a common policy toward Germany. This effort was to include de-Nazification, demilitarization, and an assault on concentrations of economic power—to root out what seemed to have been the sources of Germany's antidemocratic and aggressive tendencies. But East-West disagreements over economic policy soon undermined the pretense of joint government.

The Atomic Bomb and the Capitulation of Japan

In the Pacific, Japan had been forced onto the defensive by September 1943, and though it mounted two major counterattacks during 1944, the Japanese navy was crippled by shortages of ships and fuel by the end of the year. However, as the situation grew more desperate for Japan, Japanese ground soldiers battled ever more fiercely, often fighting to the death or taking their own lives rather than surrendering. Beginning late in 1944, aircraft pilots practiced *kamikaze* (kah-mih-KAH-zee), suicidally crashing planes filled with explosives into U.S. targets. The Japanese used this tactic especially as the Americans sought to take Okinawa in the spring of 1945. The U.S. forces finally prevailed in June, but only after the most bitter combat of the Pacific war (see **MAP 28.3**).

In conquering Okinawa, American forces got close enough for air raids on the Japanese home islands. But though the United States was now clearly in control, it seemed likely that an actual invasion of Japan would be necessary to force a Japanese surrender. Some estimated that, because the Japanese could be expected to fight even more desperately to defend their own soil, invasion might well cost the United States 1 million additional casualties. It was especially for this reason that the Americans decided to try to end the war in an altogether different way—by using an atomic bomb.

In 1939, scientists in several countries, including Germany, had started to advise their governments that new, immensely destructive weapons based on thermonuclear fission were theoretically possible. The German economics ministry began seeking uranium as early as 1939, but Hitler promoted jet- and rocket-propelled terror weaponry instead, especially the V-2 rocket bombs that the Germans began showering on England in the fall of 1944. Still, fear that the Nazis were developing atomic weapons lurked behind the Allied effort to produce the ultra-lethal bomb as quickly as possible.

Although the British were the first to initiate an atomic weapons program, by late 1941 the Americans were building on what they knew of British findings to develop their own crash program, known as the Manhattan Project. Constructing an atomic bomb proved far more difficult and costly than most had expected in 1941, and it took a concerted effort by the United States to have atomic weapons ready for use by mid-1945.

The U.S. decision to use the atomic bomb on Japanese civilians has been one of the most controversial of modern history. The decision fell to the new president, Harry Truman, who had known nothing of the bomb project when Roosevelt died in April 1945. During the next few months, Truman listened to spirited disagreement among American policymakers. Was it necessary actually to drop the bomb to force the Japanese to surrender? Since the ultimate victory of the United States was not in doubt, some argued that it would be enough simply to demonstrate the new weapon to the Japanese in a test firing.

By July, when the Allies met at Potsdam, the United States was prepared to use the bomb. But President Truman first warned Japan that if it did not surrender at once, it would be subjected to destruction immeasurably greater than Germany had just suffered. The Japanese ignored the warning, although the United States had begun area-bombing Japanese cities a few months before. The bombing of Tokyo in March produced a firestorm that gutted one-fourth of the city and killed over 80,000 people. In light of the Japanese refusal to surrender, the use of the atomic bomb seemed to Truman the logical next step.

At 8:15 on the morning of August 6, 1945, from a height of 32,000 feet above the Japanese city of Hiroshima, an American pilot released the first atomic bomb to be used against an enemy target. The bomb exploded after 45 seconds, 2,000 feet above the ground, killing 80,000 people outright and leaving tens of thousands more to die in the aftermath. Three days later, on August 9, the Americans exploded a second atomic bomb over Nagasaki, killing perhaps 50,000 people. Although sectors of the Japanese military held out for continued resistance, Emperor Hirohito (hee-roh-HEE-toh) (1901–1989) finally announced Japan's surrender on August 15. The bombing of civilians had discredited the Japanese military, which not only had proved unable to defend the country but had systematically misled the Japanese people about their country's prospects.

The war in the Pacific ended more suddenly than had seemed possible just a few months earlier (see **MAP 28.3**). This worked in favor of the various national liberation or decolonization movements that had developed in Asia during the war, for the Europeans had little opportunity to reestablish their dominance in the colonial territories they had earlier lost to the Japanese. In the Dutch East Indies, the Japanese had encouraged anticolonial sentiment, even helping local nationalists create patriotic militias. After the war, the Dutch were never able to reassert their control against this Indonesian nationalist movement. But though the war had severely weakened the old Western imperialism in Asia and the Pacific, what would replace it remained unclear.

Death, Disruption, and the Question of Guilt

World War II left as many as 60 million people dead—three times as many as World War I. The Soviet Union, Poland, and Germany suffered by far the highest casualty figures; for each, the figure was considerably higher than in World War I. An appalling 23 million Soviet citizens died, over half of them civilians. Poland lost over 6 million, the vast majority civilians, including 3 million Jews. Germany lost 5 million to 6 million, including perhaps 2 million civilians.

In contrast, casualty rates for Italy, Britain, and France were lower than in World War I. Italy suffered 200,000 military and 200,000 civilian deaths. Total British losses, including civilians, numbered 450,000, to which must be added 120,000 from the British Empire. Despite its quick defeat, France lost more lives than Britain because of the ravages of German occupation: the 350,000 deaths among French civilians considerably exceeded the British figure, closer to 100,000.

The United States lost 300,000 servicemen and 5,000 civilians. Figures for Japan are problematic, partly because the Japanese claim that 300,000 of those who surrendered to the Soviets in 1945 have remained unaccounted for. Apart from this number, 1.74 million Japanese servicemen died from 1941 to 1945, more from hunger and disease than from combat, and 300,000 civilians died in Japan, most from U.S. bombing.

During the war, Jews, Poles, and others deemed undesirable by the Nazis had been rounded up and shipped to ghettos or camps, where the great majority had died. Of those Jews who were still alive when the Nazi camps were liberated, almost half died within a few weeks. Even those who managed to return home sometimes faced pogroms during the difficult months that followed; forty Jews were killed in the worst of them, at Kielce (KYEL-tsuh), Poland, in 1946.

Late in the war, as German forces in the east retreated, ethnic Germans living in Poland, Czechoslovakia, Hungary, and elsewhere in east-central Europe began seeking refuge in Germany. They were fleeing the Soviet advance but also seeking to escape the growing wave of anti-German resentment in those countries. Once the war was over, the Poles began expelling ethnic Germans from the historically German areas that were now to become Polish. These Germans were sometimes sent to detention camps, and when they were shipped out, it was often in cattle cars. According to some estimates, as many as 2 million died in the process. At the same time, the uprooting of Poles that had begun during the war continued as Poles were systematically forced from the Polish territories incorporated into the Soviet Union.

In Czechoslovakia, the government expelled 3.5 million Germans from the Sudetenland area by 1947. All told, at least 7 million German refugees moved west into the shrunken territory of the new Germany by that year. They were among the 16 million Europeans who were permanently uprooted and transplanted during the war and its immediate wake. And the process continued at a diminished rate thereafter. By 1958, perhaps 10 million Germans had either left or been forced out of the new Poland, leaving only about 1 million Germans still living there.

Nuremberg trials The war crimes trials conducted in Nuremberg, Germany. Most of the twenty-four defendants were convicted of war crimes and "crimes against humanity."

As the end of the war approached, Europeans began attempting to assess guilt and to punish those responsible for the disasters of the era. In the climate of violence, resistance forces in France, Italy, and elsewhere often subjected fascists and collaborators to summary justice, sometimes through quick trials in ad hoc courts. In Italy, this process led to 15,000 executions, in France 10,000. French women accused of sleeping with German soldiers were shamed by having their heads shaved.

The most sensitive confrontation with the recent past took place in Germany, where the occupying powers imposed a systematic program of de-Nazification. In the western zones, German citizens were required to attend lectures on the virtues of democracy and to view the corpses of the victims of Nazism. In this context, the Allies determined to identify and bring to justice those responsible for the crimes of Hitler's regime. This effort led to the **Nuremberg trials** of 1945 and 1946, the most famous of a number of war crimes trials held in Germany and the occupied countries after the war.

Although Hitler, Himmler, and Goebbels had committed suicide, the occupying authorities apprehended for trial twenty-four individuals who had played important but very different roles in Hitler's Third Reich. All but three were convicted of war crimes and crimes against humanity. Twelve were sentenced to death; of those, two committed suicide, and the other ten were executed.

Questions about their legitimacy dogged the Nuremberg trials from the start. To a considerable extent, the accused were being judged according to law made after the fact. The notion of "crimes against humanity" remained vague. Moreover, even insofar as a measure of international law was in force, it was arguably binding only on states, not individuals. But in light of the unprecedented atrocities of the Nazi regime, there was widespread agreement among the victors that the Nazi leaders could not be treated simply as defeated adversaries.

SECTION SUMMARY

- The future of east-central Europe was but one of the items on the agenda at Yalta, where each of the Big Three achieved some of its major aims concerning the shape of the postwar world.

- As a result of the agreements at Yalta and Potsdam, the reconstituted Poland was shifted substantially westward at the expense of Germany.

- Although the terror bombing of cities did not undermine the German war effort, the more precisely targeted bombing of industrial and military targets hastened Germany's defeat, especially by cutting off oil supplies.

- Because the war in the Pacific ended so suddenly, as the result of the atomic bombing of Japan by the United States, the Europeans had little opportunity to reestablish their dominance in the colonial territories they had earlier lost to the Japanese.

- Of the twenty-four Germans charged with war crimes and crimes against humanity in the Nuremberg trials of 1945 and 1946, twenty-one were convicted, of whom twelve were sentenced to death.

INTO THE POSTWAR WORLD

What was the relationship between the Allied victory in World War II and the coming of the cold war?

Even after the fighting stopped in 1945, remarkable changes continued as the forces unleashed by the war played themselves out. In a number of war-torn countries, the legacies of wartime resistance movements helped shape the political order and priorities for beginning anew. At the same time, differences between the Soviets and the Western democracies began to undermine the wartime alliance, soon producing the division of Germany and a bipolar Europe. Thus, the conclusion of World War II led directly to the danger of a third world war, which might involve nuclear weapons and thus prove immeasurably more destructive than the last.

In addition to the dramatic changes in Europe, the wider effects of the war brought to the forefront a whole new set of issues, from anticolonialism to the Arab-Israeli conflict to the spread of communism in the non-Western world. These issues would remain central for decades. By 1949, however, it was already possible to discern the contours of the new postwar world, a world with new sources of hope, but also with conflicts and dangers hardly imaginable ten years earlier.

Resistance and Renewal

Though the Nazis had found some willing collaborators, the great majority of those living under German occupation came to despise the Nazis as their brutality became ever clearer. Nazi rule meant pillage, forced labor in Germany, and the random killing of hostages in reprisal for resistance activity. In one extreme case, the Germans destroyed the Czech village of Lidice (LIH-dyit-seh), killing all its inhabitants, in retaliation for the assassination of SS security chief Reinhard Heydrich in 1942.

Clandestine movements of resistance to the occupying Nazi forces gradually developed all over Europe. In western Europe, resistance was especially prominent in France and, beginning in 1943, northern Italy, which was subjected to German occupation after the Allies defeated Mussolini's regime. But the anti-German resistance was strongest in Yugoslavia, Poland, and the occupied portions of the Soviet Union, where full-scale guerrilla war against the Germans and their collaborators produced the highest civilian casualties of World War II.

The role of the resistance proved most significant in Yugoslavia, where the Croatian Marxist Josip Broz, taking the pseudonym Tito (1892–1980), forged the opponents of the Axis powers into a broadly based guerrilla army. Its initial foe was the inflated Croatian state that the Germans, early in 1941, carved from Yugoslavia and entrusted to the pro-Axis Croatian separatist movement, the Ustashe (oo-STAH-zhee). But Tito's forces soon came up against a rival resistance movement, led by Serb officers, that tended to be pro-Serb, monarchist, and anticommunist. By 1943, Tito led 250,000 men and women in what had become a vicious civil war, one that deepened ethnic divisions and left a legacy of bitterness. Tito's forces prevailed, enabling him to create a communist-led government in Yugoslavia late in the war.

In France and Italy as well, communists played leading roles in the wartime resistance movements. As a result, the Communist Party in each country overcame the disarray that followed from the Nazi-Soviet Pact of 1939, and after the war, each enjoyed a level of prestige that would have been unthinkable earlier.

In the French case, the indigenous resistance, with its significant communist component, generally worked well with de Gaulle and the Free French, operating outside France until August 1944. Still, de Gaulle took pains to cement his own leadership in the overall struggle. Among the measures to this end, he decreed women's suffrage for France, partly because women were playing a major role in the resistance. After the liberation of France in 1944, he sought to control a potentially volatile situation by disarming the resistance as quickly as possible.

The western European resistance movements are easily romanticized, their extent and importance overstated. Compared with regular troops, resistance forces were poorly trained, equipped, and disciplined. In France, fewer than 30 percent of the nearly 400,000 active resisters had firearms in 1944. But though the Allies never tried to use them in a systematic way, the resistance movements made at least some military contribution, especially through sabotage. And they boosted national self-esteem for the longer term, helping countries humiliated by defeat and occupation make a fresh start after the war.

But had governments and institutions outside Germany done all they could—especially as the dimensions of the Nazi exterminations began to come into focus? Especially controversial has been the response of Pope Pius XII (r. 1939–1958), who declined to take the moral high ground and denounce Nazi atrocities explicitly. He felt that he could not censure the Nazis without also censuring the Soviets, at that point allies in the anti-Nazi cause. He also feared for the fortunes of the Catholic Church as an institution in areas under German control, including Rome itself during the pivotal nine months from September 1943 to June 1944. The mission of the church was not merely to save lives, but above all to save souls—and for that, the institution was essential. Many felt, however, that stronger moral leadership by the Catholic Church would have stiffened resistance to the Nazis, stimulated aid to individual Jews, and enhanced the overall self-confidence of the West as it faced the post-Holocaust future.

Conflicting Visions and the Coming of the Cold War

Starting with the Atlantic Charter of 1941, Roosevelt had sought to ensure that the common effort against the Axis powers would lead to a firmer basis for peace, to be framed through a new international organization after the war. At a conference at Dumbarton Oaks in Washington, D.C., in September 1944, the United States proposed the structure for a new "United Nations." Meeting in San Francisco from April to June 1945, delegates from almost fifty anti-Axis countries translated that proposal into a charter for the new organization. As Roosevelt had envisioned, the major powers were given a privileged position as permanent members of the Security Council, each with veto power. To dramatize its departure from the Geneva-based League of Nations, which the United States had refused to join, the United Nations was headquartered in New York. In July 1945, the U.S. Senate approved U.S. membership in the international body almost unanimously.

By the end of the war, several international meetings had used the United Nations title. In July 1944, the United Nations Monetary and Financial Conference at Bretton Woods, New Hampshire, brought together delegates from forty-four nations to deal with problems of currency and exchange rates. The outcome of the conference, the Bretton Woods Agreement, laid the foundation for international economic exchange in the noncommunist world for the crucial quarter century of economic recovery after the war. In addition, the conference gave birth to the International Monetary Fund and the International Bank for Reconstruction and Development, which played major roles even into the twenty-first century.

Whereas the United States envisioned a world order based on the ongoing cooperation of the three victors, the Soviet Union had a different agenda. Its top priority was to create a buffer zone of friendly states in east-central Europe, especially as a bulwark against Germany. While seeking this sphere of influence, Stalin gave the British a free hand to settle the civil war between communists and anticommunists in Greece, and he did not push for revolution in western Europe. The strong communist parties that had emerged from the resistance movements in Italy and France were directed to work within broad-based democratic fronts rather than try to take power.

The Division of Germany

It was especially conflict over Germany that cemented the developing division of Europe. Neither the democracies nor the Soviets lived up to all their agreements concerning Germany, but in light of the fundamental differences in priorities, cooperation between the two sides was bound to be difficult at best.

At Potsdam, the West had accepted Soviet demands for German reparations, but the Soviets, rather than wait for payment, began removing German factories and equipment for reassembly in the Soviet Union. To ensure that they got their due, the Soviets wanted access to the economic resources not simply of the Russian occupation zone, but of the whole of Germany. The United States and Britain, in contrast, gave priority to economic reconstruction and quickly began integrating the economies of the Western zones for that purpose.

Finally, as part of their effort to spur economic recovery, the United States and Britain violated Allied agreements by introducing a new currency without Soviet consent. Stalin answered in June 1948 by blockading the city of Berlin, cutting its western sectors off from the main Western occupation zones, almost 200 miles west (see **Map 28.4**). The Western Allies responded with a massive airlift that kept their sectors of Berlin supplied for almost a year, until May 1949, when the Soviets finally backed down.

By 1948, two separate German states began emerging from the Allied occupation zones. With Allied support, a "parliamentary council" of West German leaders met during 1948 and 1949 and produced a document that, when ratified in September 1949, became the "Basic Law" of a new Federal Republic of Germany, with its capital at Bonn. This founding document was termed simply the Basic Law, as opposed to the constitution, to emphasize the provisional character of the new West German state. To create a state limited to the west was not to foreclose the future reunification of Germany. But as it became clear that a new state was being created in the Western zones, the Soviets settled for a new state in their zone, in eastern Germany. Thus, the Communist-led German Democratic Republic, with its capital in East Berlin, was born in October 1949.

The "Iron Curtain" and the Emergence of a Bipolar World

In east-central Europe, only Yugoslavia and Albania had achieved liberation on their own, and the communist leaders of their resistance movements had a plausible claim to political power. Elsewhere, the Soviet army had provided liberation, and the Soviet military presence remained the decisive political fact as the war ended. Under these circumstances, the Soviets were able to work with local communists to install new regimes, led by communists and friendly to the Soviet Union, in most of east-central Europe. But though Churchill warned as early as 1946 that an **"iron curtain"** was descending from the Baltic to the Adriatic, the process of Soviet power consolidation was not easy, and it took place gradually, in discrete steps over several years. By 1949, communist governments, relying on Soviet support, controlled Poland, Czechoslovakia, East Germany, Hungary, Romania, and Bulgaria, with Yugoslavia and Albania also communist but capable of a more independent line.

Communism might have spread still farther in Europe, and perhaps beyond, but the West drew the line at Greece. There, as in Yugoslavia, an indigenous, communist-led resistance movement had become strong enough to contend for political power by late 1944. But when it sought to oust the monarchical government that had just returned to Greece from exile, the British intervened, helping the monarchy put down the leftist uprising. Although Stalin gave the Greek communists little help, communist guerrilla activity continued, thanks partly to support from Tito's Yugoslavia. In 1946, a renewed communist insurgency escalated into civil war.

As U.S.-Soviet friction turned into a **cold war**, both countries began taking a more active interest in the Greek conflict, though Soviet intentions remained uncertain. After the financially strapped Labour government in Britain reduced its involvement early in 1947, the United States stepped in to support the Greek monarchy against the communists. American policymakers feared that communism would progress from the Balkans through Greece to the Middle East. Thus, in March 1947, President Truman announced the **Truman Doctrine**, which committed the United States to the "containment" of communism throughout the world. (See the feature, "The Written Record: 'Containment' as a Cold War Strategy.") American advisers now began reequipping the anticommunist forces in Greece. Faced with this determined opposition from the West, Stalin again pulled back, but the Greek communists, with their strong indigenous support, were not defeated until 1949.

Thus, the wartime marriage of expediency between the Soviet Union and the Western democracies gradually fell apart in the war's aftermath. Only in Austria, jointly occupied by the Soviets and the Western democracies, were the former Allies able to arrange the postwar transition in a

"iron curtain" Term used by Winston Churchill in a speech on March 5, 1946, to warn that, thanks to Soviet policy, a formidable de facto barrier was emerging in Europe, cutting the Soviet sphere off from the West and threatening the long-term division of the Continent.

cold war The hostile standoff between the Soviet Union and the United States that began after World War II, as Europe was divided into spheres of influence between the two superpowers and the United States vowed to resist the further spread of communism.

Truman Doctrine The U.S. policy of containment, or limiting communist expansion, as outlined by President Harry Truman in 1947.

Gandhi and Anticolonialism   An apostle of nonviolence, Mohandas Gandhi became one of the most admired individuals of the century as he spearheaded the movement for Indian independence. He is pictured (*center*) in December 1942 with the British statesman Sir Stafford Cripps (*left*), who had come to India to offer a plan for Indian self-government. Despite the good spirit evident here, Cripps's mission failed; Gandhi and his movement held out for full independence.   (Bettmann/Corbis)

"Containment" as a Cold War Strategy

As a foreign service officer, George F. Kennan (1904–2005) emerged as the U.S. government's leading authority on the dynamics of Soviet foreign policy by the later 1940s. After analyzing Soviet postwar objectives in his now-famous "long telegram" from Moscow to the U.S. State Department in 1946, Kennan returned to the United States to become director of the State Department's Policy Planning Staff from 1947 to 1949. With hawks pondering a preemptive strike on the Soviet Union and doves stressing mutual accommodation, Kennan forcefully advocated a middle position, a strategy of "containment," in an article published anonymously in the journal Foreign Affairs *in 1947. And his views prevailed. An uncertain experiment when it began in 1947, containment proved successful—arguably for the reasons Kennan anticipated.*

[The Soviet Union] is under no ideological compulsion to accomplish its purposes in a hurry. ... Thus the Kremlin has no compunction about retreating in the face of superior force. And being under the compulsion of no timetable, it does not get panicky under the necessity for such retreat. Its political action is a fluid stream which moves constantly, wherever it is permitted to move, toward a given goal....

...The patient persistence by which it is animated means that it can be effectively countered not by sporadic acts which represent the momentary whims of democratic opinion but only by intelligent long-range policies on the part of Russia's adversaries—policies no less steady in their purpose, and no less variegated and resourceful in their application, than those of the Soviet Union itself.

In these circumstances it is clear that the main element of any United States policy toward the Soviet Union must be that of a long-term, patient but firm and vigilant containment of Russian expansive tendencies. It is important to note, however, that such a policy has nothing to do with outward histrionics: with threats or blustering or superfluous gestures of outward "toughness." While the Kremlin is basically flexible in its reaction to political realities, it is by no means unamenable to considerations of prestige. ... It is a *sine qua non* of successful dealing with Russia that the foreign government in question should remain at all times cool and collected and that its demands on Russian policy should be put forward in such a manner as to leave the way open for a compliance not too detrimental to Russian prestige.

In the light of the above, it will be clearly seen that the Soviet pressure against the free institutions of the western world is something that can be contained by the adroit and vigilant application of counter-force at a series of constantly shifting geographical and political points, corresponding to the shifts and manoeuvres of Soviet policy, but which cannot be charmed or talked out of existence....

... Soviet power is only a crust concealing an amorphous mass of human beings among whom no independent organizational structure is tolerated. ... If, consequently, anything were ever to occur to disrupt the unity and efficacy of the Party as a political instrument, Soviet Russia might be changed overnight from one of the strongest to one of the weakest and most pitiable of national societies....

...It is...a question of the degree to which the United States can create among the peoples of the world generally the impression of a country which knows what it wants, which is coping successfully with the problems of its internal life and with the responsibilities of a World Power, and which has a spiritual vitality capable of holding its own among the major ideological currents of the time. To the extent that such an impression can be created and maintained, the aims of Russian Communism must appear sterile and quixotic, the hopes and enthusiasm of Moscow's supporters must wane, and added strain must be imposed on the Kremlin's foreign policies. For the palsied decrepitude of the capitalist world is the keystone of Communist philosophy....

...The United States has it in its power to increase enormously the strains under which Soviet policy must operate, to force upon the Kremlin a far greater degree of moderation and circumspection than it has had to observe in recent years, and in this way to promote tendencies which must eventually find their outlet in either the break-up or the gradual mellowing of Soviet power.

QUESTIONS

1. What conception of the Soviet Union and its aims led Kennan to propose a policy of containment?

2. What would containment actually entail on a practical level as a response to Soviet moves?

3. Why did Kennan believe that the United States had to be unified, consistent, and principled in everything it did if it was eventually to prevail in the cold war?

reasonably amicable way. The Soviets accepted the neutralization of a democratic Austria as the occupying powers left in 1955. Elsewhere, Europe was divided into two antagonistic power blocs.

The antagonism between the two superpowers became more menacing when the Soviets exploded their first atomic bomb in August 1949, intensifying the postwar arms race. By then, in fact, the United States was on its way to the more destructive hydrogen bomb. The split between these two nations, unmistakable by 1949, established the framework for world affairs for the next forty years.

The West and the New World Agenda

At the same time, other dramatic changes around the world suggested that, with or without the cold war, the postwar political scene would be hard to manage. Events in India in 1947, in Israel in 1948, and in China in 1949 epitomized the wider new hopes and uncertainties spawned by World War II.

Although the British, under U.S. pressure, had reluctantly promised independence for India in order to elicit Indian support during the war, British authorities and Indian leaders had continued to skirmish. Mohandas Gandhi (see pages 729 and 760) was twice jailed for resisting British demands and threatening a massive program of nonviolent resistance to British rule. But by 1946, the British lacked the will and the financial resources to maintain their control on the subcontinent. Thus, Britain acquiesced as the new independent states of India and Pakistan emerged on August 15, 1947. Allowing independence to India, long the jewel of the British Empire, raised questions about Britain's role in the postwar world and portended a wider disintegration of the European colonial system.

INDEPENDENCE IN INDIA

Questions about the fate of the Jews, who had suffered so grievously during World War II, were inevitable as well. Almost two-thirds of the Jews of Europe had been killed, and many of the survivors either had no place to go or had decided that they could never again live as a minority in Europe. Many concluded that the Jews must have a homeland of their own. For decades, such Zionist sentiment (see page 714) had centered on the biblical area of Israel, in what had become, after World War I, the British mandate of Palestine. Jewish immigration to the area accelerated during the interwar period, causing friction with the Palestinian Arabs.

THE CREATION OF ISRAEL

Concerned about access to Middle Eastern oil, the British sought to cultivate good relations with the Arab world after World War II. Thus, they opposed further immigration of Jews to Palestine, as well as proposals to carve an independent Jewish state from the area. The United States, however, was considerably more sympathetic to the Zionist cause. As tensions grew, Jewish terrorists blew up the British headquarters in Jerusalem, and the British decided to abandon what seemed a no-win situation. In September 1947, they announced their intention to withdraw from Palestine, leaving its future to the United Nations. In November, the UN voted to partition Palestine, creating both a Jewish and a new Arab Palestinian state (see **MAP 28.5**).

Skirmishing between Jews and Arabs became full-scale war in December 1947, and in that context, the Jews declared their independence as the new state of Israel on May 14, 1948. When the fighting ended in 1949, the Israelis had conquered more territory than had been envisioned in the original partition plan, and the remaining Arab territories fell to Egypt and Jordan, rather than forming an independent Palestinian

🌐 **MAP 28.5—The Proposed Partition of Palestine and the Birth of the State of Israel**

In November 1947, the United Nations offered a plan to partition the British mandate of Palestine, but complications immediately arose. The Jews of the area won their own state, Israel, but the Palestinian Arabs were left stateless. Thus, tensions continued in the area.

SECTION SUMMARY

- Although it had spurned the League of Nations after World War I, the U.S. Senate approved U.S. membership in the United Nations almost unanimously in July 1945.

- Concerned primarily to win a secure sphere of influence in east-central Europe, especially as a bulwark against Germany, Stalin took a moderate position with regard to western Europe and did not seek to foment communist revolution.

- Disagreements over economic policy, especially, fed the split that led to the creation of two separate German states, one oriented toward the West, the other oriented toward the Soviet Union, in 1949.

- The communist challenge in Greece by 1947 prompted the Truman Doctrine, which committed the United States to the "containment" of communism throughout the world.

- The granting of independence to India in 1947, the creation of the state of Israel in 1948, and the communist takeover in China in 1949 indicated the new world agenda emerging after World War II.

state. Thus was born the new state of Israel, partly a product of the assault on the Jews during World War II. Yet it was born amid Arab hostility and Western concerns about oil, so its long-term prospects remained uncertain.

COMMUNISM IN CHINA

In 1949, the communist insurgency in China under Mao Zedong (Mao Tsetung) (see page 761) finally triumphed over the Chinese Nationalists under Jiang Jieshi (Chiang Kai-shek), who fled to the island of Taiwan. During the war, the Communists had done better than the Nationalists at identifying themselves with the Chinese cause against both Japanese and Western imperialism. After their victory, the Chinese Communists enjoyed great prestige among other "national liberation" movements struggling against Western colonialists. To many in the West, however, the outcome in China by 1949 simply intensified fears that communism was poised to infect the unsettled postwar world.

CHAPTER SUMMARY

Using an effective new offensive strategy, Germany quickly defeated Poland in 1939, but Britain and France refused Hitler's peace overtures in the aftermath. After France fell to German invasion eight months later, the Third Republic gave way to the authoritarian Vichy regime, which was obliged to collaborate with Nazi Germany. When the British again refused to come to terms, Hitler launched a sustained air assault on Britain. The British withstood it, but Hitler remained confident of containing Britain over the longer term. Even when the reckless intervention of Italy forced Hitler's attention to North Africa and the Balkans, the Germans won further successes, which suggested that the Soviet Union would fall in a matter of weeks in the wake of Germany's invasion of June 1941.

FOCUS QUESTIONS

- What were the outcomes of the war as of late spring 1941, before the German invasion of the Soviet Union and the intervention of the United States?

- What was the place of the Holocaust in the Nazi effort to begin constructing a "new order" in eastern Europe?

- How did the Grand Alliance of Britain, the United States, and the Soviet Union come together against the Axis powers?

- How did the Allies manage to defeat Nazi Germany in World War II, after Germany's remarkable initial successes?

- What was the relationship between the Allied victory in World War II and the coming of the cold war?

In dealing with their conquered territories first in Poland, then in the Soviet Union, the Nazis were concerned with population engineering and ideology; Jewish policy was distinctly secondary. Even when Jews were confined to ghettos in Poland, there was no plan to kill them. But ghettoization produced problems of its own, so Nazi forces were instructed to shoot Soviet Jews once the invasion of the Soviet Union began. Such shooting also proved to be problematic, so gradually the Nazi leadership decided on a more systematic method—mass extermination by gassing, to start with the Jews in the ghettos in Poland. Such a program could be envisioned, and implemented, especially because of the precedent of the "euthanasia" program in Germany. Once it began, the process of mass killing developed a momentum of its own, especially as it became clear that Germany was likely to lose the war.

After a disastrous start in the face of German invasion, Soviet forces stiffened in the fall of 1941, then, in December, mounted a formidable counterattack. That same month, the United States declared war on Germany in the aftermath of the bombing of Pearl Harbor by the Japanese. Meanwhile, the British, having withstood the German air assault, were regrouping for a protracted war. Common hostility to the Axis powers brought Britain, the Soviet Union, and the United States together in a "Grand Alliance" early in 1942, but mutual suspicions between the democracies, on the one hand, and the Soviet Union, on the other, marked the relationship. Above all, Stalin worried that Britain and the United States were dragging their feet in opening a major second front on the European continent. By the time of the D-Day landings in France in June 1944, the Soviets were steadily forcing the Germans back on the eastern front.

Even after all the upheavals of the 1930s, the Soviets proved able to spearhead the Allied victory in Europe, though they suffered incredibly heavy casualties in the process. Stalin managed to rally the Soviet people, and the Soviet military and industrial effort proved more effective than outside observers had thought possible. But the efforts of the democracies in North Africa, Italy, and France contributed to the final victory as well. And American-led bombing of military and industrial targets, especially oil refining facilities, seriously compromised Germany's capacity to wage war by the end.

The Grand Alliance began unraveling soon after the war was over, especially because the priorities of the Soviets differed considerably from those of the two democracies. Having been invaded, and devastated, by German forces twice in a generation, the Soviets were determined to have friendly states on their borders, especially in Poland. And having suffered from direct German military invasion as the other two victors had not, the Soviets were also determined to extract reparations from Germany, even including plant and equipment to be dismantled and carried back to the Soviet Union. By 1949, two competing German states had emerged, and Europe was clearly divided between East and West.

KEY TERMS

Vichy France   (p. 788)

Charles de Gaulle   (p. 788)

Winston Churchill   (p. 789)

Auschwitz-Birkenau   (p. 794)

Stalingrad   (p. 796)

"the Great Patriotic War"
   (p. 797)

**Franklin Delano
   Roosevelt**   (p. 800)

Lend-Lease Act   (p. 802)

D-Day   (p. 803)

Yalta conference
   (p. 805)

United Nations   (p. 805)

Potsdam conference
   (p. 807)

Nuremberg trials
   (p. 810)

"iron curtain"   (p. 813)

cold war   (p. 813)

Truman Doctrine   (p. 813)

 This icon will direct you to additional materials on the website: www .cengage.com/history/ noble/westciv6e.

NOTES

1. From Farrell's full account as related by General Leslie Groves in his "Memorandum to the Secretary of War," dated July 18, 1945, in *The American Atom: A Documentary History of Nuclear Policies from the Discovery of Fission to the Present*, ed. Philip L. Cantelon, Richard G. Hewlett, and Robert C. Williams, 2d ed. (Philadelphia: University of Pennsylvania Press, 1991), pp. 56–57.

2. Quoted in Karl Dietrich Bracher, *The German Dictatorship: The Origins, Structure, and Effects of National Socialism*, trans. Jean Steinberg (New York: Praeger, 1970), p. 423.

3. Christopher R. Browning, *Ordinary Men: Reserve Police Battalion 101 and the Final Solution in Poland*, with a new afterward (New York: HarperCollins, 1998); Daniel Jonah Goldhagen, *Hitler's Willing Executioners: Ordinary Germans and the Holocaust* (New York: Random House [Vintage], 1997).

4. Michael Burleigh, *Death and Deliverance: "Euthanasia" in Germany, c. 1900–1945* (Cambridge: Cambridge University Press, 1994), p. 221.

5. Michael Burleigh and Wolfgang Wippermann, *The Racial State: Germany, 1933–1945* (Cambridge: Cambridge University Press, 1991), p. 98.

6. Martin Broszat and Saul Friedländer, "A Controversy About the Historicization of National Socialism," in Peter Baldwin, ed., *Reworking the Past: Hitler, the Holocaust, and the Historians' Debate* (Boston: Beacon Press, 1990), pp. 120–121.

7. Goldhagen, *Hitler's Willing Executioners*, pp. 279–280.

8. Browning, *Ordinary Men*, p. 72.

e **See our interactive eBook for map and primary source activities.**

29

CHAPTER OUTLINE

The Search for Cultural Bearings

Prosperity and Democracy in Western Europe

The Communist Bloc: From Consolidation to Stagnation

Europe, the West, and the World

The Collapse of the Soviet System, 1975–1991

Berlin Wall, November 1989
East Germans stream through the dismantled Berlin Wall into West Berlin. (AP Photo/Lionel Cironneau)

An Anxious Stability: The Age of the Cold War, 1949–1989

The atmosphere was festive, euphoric. Those who came to celebrate could hardly believe it was happening, for it had been unthinkable just a few months before. Yet happening it was, one of the defining events of the twentieth century, live on television. This was November 1989, and the Berlin Wall was coming down.

Erected to stop emigration from communist East Germany to the West in 1961, the wall had become an all-too-tangible symbol of the division of Europe, and much of the world, after World War II. As a physical barrier of concrete and barbed wire, the Berlin Wall had divided families and caused much human suffering. Indeed, 191 people died and 5,000 were arrested trying to cross it. But the East German government, desperate by 1989 to preserve its legitimacy, opened the wall on November 9 and began dismantling it within days. However, it proved too late. The communist regime in East Germany collapsed as part of a wider anticommunist revolution that finally enveloped even the Soviet Union itself in 1991. The anxious cold war era was suddenly over; virtually no one had foreseen its abrupt ending.

Although Berlin had been a particular hot spot, the cold war was global in scope. It seemed that confrontation between the Soviet Union and the United States might take place almost anywhere, sparking the cold war into a hot war threatening nuclear annihilation. And indeed confrontation came closest not over Berlin, but over Soviet missiles in Cuba in 1962. That crisis was surmounted, and East-West relations alternately warmed and cooled during the quarter century that followed.

Both halves of Europe had to operate within the bipolar framework, but the Western and Soviet blocs confronted different challenges and evolved in different ways. The countries of western Europe adjusted to a diminished international role as they recognized their dependence on U.S. leadership and gradually lost their overseas colonies. The change in scale led many politicians and intellectuals to advocate some form of European union, which might eventually enable the western Europeans to deal with the superpowers on a more equal basis. On the domestic level, the immediate postwar situation was so unsettled that few western European countries could simply return to the prewar norm. Postwar reconstruction rested on a new consensus that government must play a more active role in promoting economic growth and social welfare. By the 1960s, the promise of shared prosperity was realized to a remarkable extent. But changing circumstances by the early 1970s threatened the consensus that postwar prosperity had made possible.

FOCUS QUESTIONS

- What seemed the most likely overall cultural directions as western Europeans pondered priorities in light of all the disasters surrounding the era of the two world wars?

- What factors led to the surprisingly rapid restoration of democracy in much of continental western Europe after World War II?

- How did Soviet policy evolve after the death of Stalin in 1953?

- How did the place of western Europe in world affairs change during the cold war era?

- What led to the collapse of the communist system in the Soviet Union and its satellite states?

 This icon will direct you to additional materials on the website: www .cengage.com/history/ noble/westciv6e.

 See our interactive eBook for map and primary source activities.

Although the Soviet Union had suffered immensely in winning World War II, the communist regime emerged from the war with renewed legitimacy. During the 1950s and 1960s, the Soviet system achieved some significant successes, but its efforts to outgrow its Stalinist framework were halting. By 1980, the system was becoming rigid and stagnant. Thus, the dramatic changes in the Soviet bloc that came to a head in 1989, leading to the opening of the Berlin Wall and, by 1991, to the end of communism in Europe. Only as it was ending, more than four decades after World War II, was it possible to recognize that the anxious cold war era had been one of relative stability and peace.

THE SEARCH FOR CULTURAL BEARINGS

What seemed the most likely overall cultural directions as western Europeans pondered priorities in light of all the disasters surrounding the era of the two world wars?

The events from World War I to the cold war added up to an unprecedented period of disaster for Europe. Europeans were bound to ask what had gone wrong and what could be salvaged from the ruins of a culture that had made possible the most destructive wars in history, as well as fascism, totalitarianism, and the Holocaust.

The cold war framework crucially shaped responses all over the Western world. Some embraced the Soviet Union or sought a renewed Marxism. Opposition to communism helped stimulate others to return to religious or classical traditions or to embrace what seemed the American model. But the anxieties stemming from superpower rivalry, and especially the nuclear arms race, were bound to temper any renewed optimism.

Absurdity and Commitment in Existentialism

The postwar mood of exhaustion and despair found classic expression in the work of the Irish-born writer Samuel Beckett (1906–1989), especially in his plays *Waiting for Godot* (1952) and *Endgame* (1957). Through Beckett's characters, we see ourselves going through the motions, with nothing worth saying or doing. The only redeeming element is the comic pathos we feel as we watch ourselves ludicrously manipulating the husks of a worn-out culture.

existentialism A philosophical and cultural movement, often associated with Jean-Paul Sartre and Albert Camus, for whom an authentic human response to an apparently meaningless universe entailed commitment and responsibility.

The same sense of anxiety and despair led to the vogue of **existentialism**, a movement that marked philosophy, the arts, and popular culture from the later 1940s until well into the 1950s. The existentialists explored what it means to be human in a world cast adrift from its cultural moorings, with no mutually accepted guideposts, standards, or values. Although it developed from ideas that the German thinker Martin Heidegger (1889–1976) had developed in his *Being and Time* (1927), existentialism became influential especially through the works of two Frenchmen, Jean-Paul Sartre (SAH-truh) (1905–1980) and Albert Camus (ka-MOO) (1913–1960). Each had been involved in the French resistance, Camus in a particularly central role as editor of an underground newspaper. For both, an authentic human response to a world spinning out of control entails engagement, commitment, and responsibility—even though every action is fraught with risk.

Rather than accept the bleak, ludicrously comic vision of Beckett's plays, Camus sought to show how we might go on living in a positive, affirmative spirit, even in a world that seemed simply absurd in one sense, especially after the recent disasters in Europe. Conventional values like friendship and tolerance could be made usable again, based on the simple fact that we human beings are all caught up in this unmasterable situation together. People suffer and die, but as we come together to help as best we can, we might at least learn to stop killing one another.

Camus split from Sartre in a disagreement over the ongoing value of Marxism and the communist experiment in the Soviet Union. Though never an orthodox communist, Sartre found potential for human liberation in the working class, in communist political parties, even in the Soviet Union itself, which he saw as the strongest alternative to U.S. imperialism. By the 1950s, he was portraying existentialism as fundamentally a way to revitalize Marxism.

By contrast, Camus, who had started as a communist in the 1930s, had grown disillusioned with communism even before the war, and his major political tract, *The Rebel* (1951), was partly an attack on Marxism and communism. Establishing new bases for human happiness and solidarity meant recognizing limits to what human beings could accomplish, limits even to our demands for freedom and justice. These were precisely the limits that the new political movements of the century had so disastrously overstepped. Communism, like fascism, was part of the problem, not the solution.

Marxists and Traditionalists

Sartre was among the many European intellectuals who believed that Marxism had won a new lease on life from the wartime resistance. As they saw it, Marxism could be revamped for the West, without the Stalinist excesses of the Soviet Union. Marxism remained a significant strand in Western political culture throughout the cold war era, but it also attracted periodic waves of denunciation.

In Italy, as in France, the communists' major role in the resistance enhanced their prestige, preparing the way for the extraordinary posthumous influence of Antonio Gramsci (GRAHM-she) (1891–1937), a founder of the Italian Communist Party who had spent most of the fascist period in prison. His *Prison Notebooks*, published during the late 1940s, became influential throughout the world and helped make Marxism a powerful force in postwar Italian culture. Seeking to learn the lessons of the fascist triumph in Italy, Gramsci pointed Marxists toward a flexible political strategy, attuned to the special historical circumstances of each country. Thanks partly to Gramsci's legacy, Italy had the most innovative and important communist party outside the communist world for several decades after the war.

Loosely Marxist ideas were central to the renewal of political activism in the West by the late 1960s, although Marxism proved more effective as a critique of capitalism than as a blueprint for change. The best-known spokesman for that renewed radicalism was the German-born social thinker Herbert Marcuse (mar-KOO-zuh) (1898–1979), who explored the cultural mechanisms through which capitalism perpetuates itself in *One-Dimensional Man* (1964).

Even during the late 1940s, however, others, like Camus, denied that any recasting could overcome the inherent flaws in Marxism. Damaging revelations about the excesses of Stalinism during the 1930s seemed to confirm the view that communism was "the God that failed." By the mid-1970s, the disturbing portrait of the Soviet gulag, or forced-labor-camp system, by the exiled Soviet writer Alexander Solzhenitsyn (soul-zhen-EET-sin) (1918–2008) stimulated another wave of anticommunist thinking. And whether or not Marxism was necessarily Stalinist and repressive in implication, its relevance to the increasingly prosperous industrial democracies of western Europe seemed increasingly open to question.

Those hostile to Marxism often insisted that the West had to reconnect with older traditions if it were to

CHRONOLOGY

June 1947	Marshall Plan announced
April 1949	Formation of NATO
1951	Formation of the European Coal and Steel Community
March 5, 1953	Death of Stalin
June	Workers' revolt in East Germany
1955	West Germany joins NATO
	Warsaw Pact
February 1956	Khrushchev de-Stalinization speech
October–November 1956	Suez crisis
November 1956	Hungarian reform movement crushed
October 4, 1957	*Sputnik I* launched
January 1, 1958	Common Market launched
1958	Beginning of Fifth Republic in France
November 1959	Bad Godesberg congress: reorientation of German socialism
August 1961	Berlin Wall erected
March 1962	Algerian independence from France
October 1962	Cuban missile crisis
October 1964	Ouster of Khrushchev
May 1968	Days of May uprising in France
August 1968	"Prague Spring" reform movement crushed
October 1969	Brandt becomes West German chancellor
1973	First OPEC oil crisis
1975	Communist victory in Vietnam
October 1978	Election of Pope John Paul II
May 1979	Thatcher becomes prime minister of Britain
September 1980	Formation of Solidarity in Poland
April 1980	Formation of independent Zimbabwe from Southern Rhodesia
May 1981	Mitterrand becomes president of France
November 10, 1982	Death of Brezhnev
March 1985	Gorbachev comes to power in the Soviet Union
April 1986	Chernobyl disaster
1989	Collapse of communism in east-central Europe
1991	Collapse of communism in the Soviet Union
	Dissolution of the Soviet Union

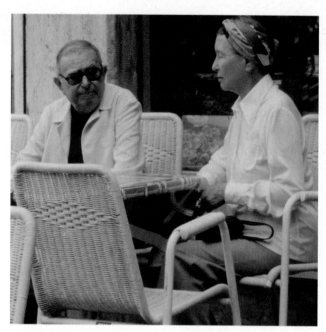

Sartre and de Beauvoir   Among the most influential intellectual couples of the century, Jean-Paul Sartre and Simone de Beauvoir emerged as leaders of French existentialism by the later 1940s.   (Gianni Giansanti/Sygma/Corbis)

avoid further horrors. Especially in the first years after the war, many, like the French Catholic thinker Jacques Maritain (mar-eh-TAN) (1882–1973), held that only a return to religious traditions would suffice. For the American-born British writer T. S. Eliot (1888–1965), the essential return to tradition had to embrace family and locality, as well as religion. Without a return to tradition, Eliot warned, the West could expect more excesses such as fascism and totalitarianism in the future.

The Intellectual Migration and Americanism

The extraordinary migration of European artists and intellectuals to the United States to escape persecution during the 1930s and 1940s profoundly affected the cultural life of the postwar period. An array of luminaries arrived on American shores, from the composer Igor Stravinsky to the physicist Albert Einstein, from the architect Walter Gropius to the radical social theorist Herbert Marcuse.

Before this cross-fertilization, American culture had remained somewhat provincial, sometimes proudly and self-consciously so. All the direct contact with these Europeans by the 1940s helped propel the United States into the Western cultural mainstream. No longer could "Western" culture be identified primarily with Europe. In some spheres—painting, for example—Americans were now confident enough to claim the leadership for the first time.

But the American abstract expressionism emerging by the later 1940s owed something to European existentialism, and it became possible only because so many of the most innovative European painters had come to New York, where the Americans had been able to learn their lessons firsthand. At the same time, European painters, such as Jean Dubuffet (doo-boo-FAY) (1901–1985) in France and Francis Bacon (1910–1992) in Britain, created new forms of their own—sometimes playful, sometimes brutal—as they sought the new visual imagery that seemed appropriate to Western culture after decades of upheaval.

Even in the United States, artists began reacting against the deep seriousness of abstract expressionism during the mid-1950s. One new direction led by the early 1960s to "pop art," which was "American" in a different sense, featuring the ordinary objects and mass-produced images of modern consumerist culture. (See the feature, "The Visual Record: Pop Art.")

Some Europeans were eager to embrace what seemed distinctively American because America had remained relatively free of the political ideologies that seemed to have led Europe to totalitarianism and ruin. By the 1950s, there was much talk of "the end of ideology," with America offering a healthier alternative, combining technology, value-free social science, and scientific management. Whereas the old European way led either to mere theorizing, to political extremism, or to polarization and impasse, the American approach got results by tackling problems one at a time, so that they could be solved by experts.

Such Americanism fed the notion that Europe needed a clean break based on technological values. If such a break was necessary, however, what was to become of the European tradition, for centuries, the center of gravity of the West and until recently dominant in the world? Did anything distinctively European remain, or was Europe doomed to lick its wounds in the shadow of America? These questions lurked in the background as Europeans faced the difficult task of economic and political restoration.

SECTION SUMMARY

- Existentialism and the plays of Samuel Beckett expressed the sense of exhaustion and lack of bearings in Western culture after World War II.

- Cold war concerns helped fuel an often bitter debate between Marxists and anti-Marxists that continued, off and on, from the later 1940s well into the 1970s.

- Some held that a return to religious and other traditions offered the only antidote in light of the disasters surrounding the era of the two world wars.

- The migration of European artists and intellectuals to America profoundly affected cultural relations between America and western Europe, especially during the early years of the cold war era.

- As they sought a fresh start for Europe, many western Europeans sought to adapt what they took to be American practicality.

Dubuffet: *Spinning Round* Seeking to depart from the European tradition of sophisticated, well-made art, Jean Dubuffet developed imagery that was at once crude and primitive, playful and whimsical. (Tate, London/Art Resource, NY)

PROSPERITY AND DEMOCRACY IN WESTERN EUROPE

What factors led to the surprisingly rapid restoration of democracy in much of continental western Europe after World War II?

By 1941, democracy seemed to be dying on the European continent, yet it quickly revived in western Europe after World War II, taking root more easily than most had thought possible. The bipolar international framework helped. The United States actively encouraged democracy, and Europeans, fearing the spread of communism, were happy to follow the American lead. Success at economic reconstruction was important as well. Not only was there greater prosperity, but governments could afford to deliver on promises of enhanced security, social welfare, and equal opportunity. It also mattered that western Europeans learned from past mistakes.

Economic Reconstruction and the Atlantic Orientation

It is hard to imagine how desperate the situation in much of western Europe had become by 1945. Major cities, like Rotterdam, Hamburg, and Le Havre, lay largely in ruins. Production had declined to perhaps 25 percent of the prewar level in Italy, to 20 percent in France, and to a mere 5 percent in southern Germany. Cigarettes, often gained through barter from American soldiers, served widely as a medium of exchange.

Although the U.S. commitment to assist European economic reconstruction was not originally a cold war measure, the developing cold war context added urgency to the American effort. The key was the Marshall Plan, which U.S. secretary of state General George Marshall outlined in 1947 and which channeled $13.5 billion in aid to western Europe by 1951.

Cold war concerns deepened the partnership in April 1949, when the United States spearheaded a military alliance, the **North Atlantic Treaty Organization (NATO)**, that included much of western Europe. The Soviets were tightening their grip on their satellite states in east-central Europe, and the NATO alliance was intended to check any further Soviet expansion. The Soviets

North Atlantic Treaty Organization (NATO) An alliance for regional defense, created in 1949 by the United States, Canada, and western European nations, whose members agree to defend one another from attack by nonmember countries.

Pop Art

Hamburgers, comic strips, soup-can labels, familiar images of entertainment icons—such was the stuff of "pop art," which burst onto the New York art scene in the early 1960s and came to exert a widespread cultural influence. Indeed, with their imaginative renderings of familiar images and whimsical sculptures of everyday objects, artists like Andy Warhol (1928–1987), Roy Lichtenstein (1923–1997), and Claes Oldenburg (b. 1929) helped shape the experience of the later twentieth century. But was this serious art or simply a joke, a parody, a put-on? Were the pop artists poking fun at the triviality of modern society, or were they deepening our encounter with defining aspects of contemporary culture? Whatever their intent, what does this striking new art form tell us about the direction of Western culture in the decades after World War II?

The term *pop art* was coined in England in the 1950s, when a group of artists and critics became interested in bridging the cultural gap between "fine art" and the emerging popular culture of mass media and machine-produced images, of advertising and automobiles. Like everyone else, they associated that consumerist mass culture with America—the America of Hollywood, Detroit, and Madison Avenue. And they found it more vital than the conventional fine art of the period. The American pop artists were similarly fascinated by the impersonal, mass-produced, often expendable quality of the objects and images that have come to surround us.

Pop art was part of a wider reaction against the deeply serious abstract expressionist painting that emerged in New York just after the Second World War. By the early 1950s, abstract expressionists like Jackson Pollock (1912–1956) and Mark Rothko (1903–1970) had created images of unprecedented power, whether seeking to forge an artistic identity in the face of nothingness or to transcend selfhood in a cosmic wholeness. In the mid-1950s, however, younger artists, "tired of the stink of artists' egos," began reacting against the self-importance of abstract expressionism. For these younger artists, art did not have to be a vehicle for the psychological expression of the artist or a quest for "the tragic and timeless." Although the reaction took several forms, pop art proved the most influential. The pop movement emerged especially in the United States, and it interested Europeans as typically American—fresh and fascinating or garish and vulgar, depending on one's point of view.

Oldenburg: *Floor Burger*, 1962 (Claes Oldenburg [American, b. 1929], *Floor Burger*, 1962. Canvas filled with foam rubber and cardboard boxes, painted with acrylic paint, 132.1 x 213.4 cm. Art Gallery of Ontario, Toronto. Reproduced with permission of Claes Oldenburg.)

Whereas the abstract expressionists had sought to rise above the everyday world, Claes Oldenburg's sculptures played with the scale and context of the most ordinary objects—a mixer, a three-pronged plug, a lipstick, a hamburger—to deepen our involvement with the everyday things that surround us. In this sense, the aim of pop art was not simply to parody or satirize, but to affirm our relationship with the trappings of ordinary life. Hollywood, Detroit, and Madison Avenue were all right after all; indeed, they had become the centers of Western culture by the later twentieth century.

Though anonymous and impersonal, the modern world of mass production, mass consumption, and mass media is "popular" because its images and objects are accessible to us all. In fact, they bombard us from all directions, giving shared shape and definition to our everyday lives. This is our world, the pop artists were saying, and they were creating the art appropriate to our time. They invite us to relax and enjoy that world, but they also enhance our experience by making art from it, thereby awakening us to its novelty and vitality.

But some viewers have found an element of melancholy, nostalgia, even tragedy just beneath pop art's eye-catching

had considerable superiority in conventional forces, which had ready access to western Europe, but U.S. nuclear superiority provided a balance. Indeed, the American nuclear guarantee to western Europe was the cornerstone of the NATO alliance.

By the 1950s, economic recovery was so impressive in continental western Europe that many were referring to an "economic miracle." Western Europeans took advantage of the need to rebuild by adopting up-to-date methods and technologies, though economic strategies differed from one country to the next. The new German government intervened in the economy only to ensure free competition. In France, by contrast, many were determined to use government

Warhol: *Marilyn Diptych*, 1962 (Tate Gallery, London/Art Resource, NY. © Artists Rights Society [ARS], New York/ADAGP, Paris)

surface. In a world of mass media and reproduced images, more of our experience becomes secondhand and literally superficial. Likewise, pop subjects, from fast food to billboards, have no deeper meaning, no expressive personal agenda. With his multiplied image of Marilyn Monroe, Andy Warhol dealt not with the actress herself but with the obsessive familiarity of her image. He cultivated a deadpan, detached style that reflected the machine-made quality of his subject matter—the quality that made the images he started with so familiar in the first place. But even as, on one level, he embraced aspects of the new mass culture, Warhol was exploring precisely the emotional detachment—and the accompanying trivialization of emotion—at work in the culture that had produced the images he adapted. Especially in his paintings treating impersonal newspaper images of disaster and death, Warhol bore witness to our indifference—and perhaps to a cosmic meaninglessness as well. One expert has noted that "in Warhol's pictures of the material objects and other false idols that most of us worship, the pain lies just below the bright surfaces of the images and waits passively to engage us."*

The advent of pop art provoked a series of questions that remain unanswered: Is the embrace of the mass-produced and commercial, at the expense of traditional "fine art" values, a symptom of exhaustion or a healthy affirmation of contemporary popular culture, so bound up with the commercial world? Or is pop art perhaps a valuable comment on the emptiness of that culture, with its impersonal conformity, garish commercialism, and mechanical repetition? In the final analysis, were the pop artists abandoning the artist's lofty mission and giving in to the ordinary? Or were they the first to show us what "Western civilization" had come to mean by the late twentieth century?

QUESTIONS

1. Does pop art seem to be embracing, or poking fun at, the modern world of consumerism and advertising?

2. What is "popular" about pop art?

---

* Eric Shanes, *Warhol* (New York: Portland House, 1991), p. 41.

to modernize the country, thereby overcoming the weakness that had led to defeat. So France adopted a flexible, pragmatic form of government-led economic planning, spearheaded by the technocrat Jean Monnet (moh-NAY) (1888–1979). By 1951, French industrial production had returned to its prewar peak, and by 1957, it had risen to twice the level of 1938. Indeed, strong and sustained rates of economic growth were achieved throughout much of western Europe until the late 1960s, although Britain lagged considerably.

As part of the new postwar consensus, labor was supposed to be brought more fully into economic decision making. Thus, for example, the trade unions participated in the planning

Ban the Bomb　As nuclear tension escalated during the 1950s, some people built air-raid shelters; others took to the streets in antinuclear protests. The protest movement was especially prominent in Britain, where the noted philosopher Bertrand Russell (1872–1970) played a central role. Here, at the right of those seated, he awaits arrest during a sit-in demonstration outside the British Defense Ministry.　(Jimmy Sime/Hulton Archive/Getty Images)

process in France. In Germany, the codetermination law of 1951 provided for labor participation in management decisions in heavy industry, and labor representatives were given access to company books and full voting memberships on boards of directors. This measure ultimately made little difference in the functioning of the affected firms, but it helped head off any return to trade-union radicalism.

Wages stayed relatively low at first. By the 1960s, however, labor began demanding—generally with success—to share more fully in the new prosperity. Now, rather abruptly, much of western Europe took on the look of a consumer society, with widespread ownership of automobiles, televisions, and other household appliances.

Social Welfare and the Issue of Gender

welfare state　The concept, especially prevalent in Western countries after World War II, that government should adopt large-scale social welfare measures, while maintaining a primarily capitalistic economy.

Western governments began to adopt social welfare measures late in the nineteenth century (see page 648–649), and by the 1940s, a degree of governmental responsibility for unemployment insurance, workplace safety, and old-age pensions was widely accepted. Some Europeans, seeking renewal after the war, found attractive models in Sweden and Denmark, where the outlines of a **welfare state** had emerged by the 1930s (see page 758).

SWEDEN　Sweden's economy remained fundamentally capitalist, based on private ownership; even after World War II, its nationalized, or government-run, sector was not large by European standards. But the system of social insurance in Sweden was the most extensive in Europe, and the government worked actively with business to promote full employment and to steer the economy in directions deemed socially desirable. Moreover, the welfare state came to mean a major role for the Swedish trade unions, which won relatively high wages for workers and even enjoyed a quasi-veto power over legislation.

At the same time, the Swedish government began playing a more active role in spheres of life that had formerly been private, from sexuality to child rearing. Thus, for example, drugstores were required to carry contraceptives beginning in 1946. Sweden was the first country to provide sex education in the public schools; optional beginning in 1942, it became compulsory in 1955. By 1979, the Swedes were limiting corporal punishment—the right to spank—and prohibiting the sale of war toys. This deprivatization of the family stemmed from a sense, especially pronounced in Sweden, that society is collectively responsible for the well-being of its children.

Social Welfare in Sweden
With the state playing a major role, Sweden proved a pioneer in responding to the family and children's issues that became increasingly prominent after World War II. Here children play at a day-care center in Stockholm in 1953. (Pressens Bild/Scanpix/Sipa Press)

Although the Swedish model was extreme in certain respects, most of western Europe moved in the same direction in an effort to establish the foundations for democratic renewal after the war. In Britain, for example, it was widely assumed that greater collective responsibility for the well-being of all British citizens was appropriate, in light of the shared hardships the war had imposed. Moreover, the successes of government planning and control during the war suggested that once it was over, government could assume responsibility for the basic needs of the British people, guaranteeing full employment and providing a national health service. But the Labour Party, led by Clement Attlee, seemed better equipped to deliver on that promise than the Conservatives, whose leader, Winston Churchill, was hostile to welfare state notions.

When Britain held its first postwar elections, in July 1945, Churchill's Conservatives suffered a crushing loss to Labour, which promptly began creating the British welfare state. Although some expected, and others feared, that the result would be a form of socialism, the new direction did not undermine the capitalist economic system. The Labour government nationalized some key industries, but 80 percent of the British workforce remained employed in private firms in 1948. Moreover, even under Labour, the British government did not seek the kind of economic planning role that government was playing in France.

The core of the British departure was a set of government-sponsored social welfare measures that significantly affected the lives of ordinary people. These included old-age pensions; insurance against unemployment, sickness, and disability; and allowances for pregnancy, child rearing, widowhood, and burial. The heart of the system was free medical care, to be provided by the National Health Service, created in November 1946 and operating by 1948.

In Britain, as elsewhere, gender roles were inevitably at issue as government welfare measures were debated and adopted. Were married women to have access to the welfare system as individual citizens or as members of a family unit, responsible for child rearing and dependent on their husbands as breadwinners? Should government seek to enable women to be both mothers and workers, or should government help make it possible for mothers not to have to work outside the home?

As during the First World War, the percentage of women in the workforce had increased significantly during World War II, but both women and men proved eager to embrace the security of traditional domestic patterns once the war was over. So the war did not change gender patterns of work even to the extent that World War I had done. In Britain, women made up about 30 percent of the labor force in 1931, 31 percent in 1951. Thus, the embrace of welfare measures took place at a time of renewed conservatism in conceptions of gender roles.

BRITAIN

British feminists initially welcomed provisions of the British welfare state that recognized the special role of women as mothers. The government was to ease burdens by providing family allowances, to be paid directly to mothers of more than one child to enable them to stay home with their children. This seemed a more progressive step than the long-standing British trade-union demand for a "family wage," sufficient to enable the male breadwinner to support a family. But though women were now to be compensated directly for their role as mothers, the assumptions about gender roles remained much the same.

FRANCE

In France, which had refused even to grant women the vote after World War I, the very different situation after 1945 stimulated an especially innovative response to gender and family issues. After the experience of defeat, collaboration, and resistance, the French were determined to pursue both economic dynamism and individual justice. But they also remained concerned with population growth, so they combined incentives to encourage large families with measures to promote equal opportunity and economic independence for women.

As they expanded the role of government after the war, the French tended, more than the British, to assume that paid employment for women was healthy and desirable. New laws gave French women equal access to civil service jobs and guaranteed equal pay for equal work. At the same time, the French recognized that women had special needs as mothers, but also that husbands shared the responsibility for parenting. So the French system provided benefits for women during and after pregnancy and then family allowances that treated the two parents as equally essential. At the same time, the system viewed women as individual citizens, regardless of marital or economic status. Thus, all were equally entitled to pensions, health services, and job-related benefits.

Although female participation in the paid labor force declined after the war, it began rising throughout the West during the 1950s, and then accelerated during the 1960s, reaching new highs in the 1970s and 1980s. Thanks partly to the expansion of government, the greatest job growth was in the service sector—in social work, health care, and education, for example—and many of these new jobs went to women. From about 1960 to 1988, the percentage of women aged 25 to 34 in the labor force rose from 38 to 67 in Britain, from 42 to 75 in France, and from 49 to 87 in Germany.

These statistics reflect significant changes in women's lives, but even as their choices expanded in some respects, women became more deeply aware of enduring limits to their opportunities. Thus, a new feminist movement emerged by the early 1970s, drawing intellectual inspiration from *The Second Sex*, a pioneering work published in 1949 by the French existentialist Simone de Beauvoir (1908–1986).

The Restoration of Democracy

Much of continental western Europe faced the challenge of rebuilding democracy after defeat and humiliation. With the developing cold war complicating the situation, the prospects for democracy were by no means certain in the late 1940s. Although the division of Germany weakened communism in the new Federal Republic, in France and Italy strong communist parties had emerged from the wartime resistance and claimed to point the way beyond conventional democracy altogether.

GERMANY

The new Federal Republic of Germany held its first election under the Basic Law in August 1949, launching what proved to be a stable and successful democracy. Partly to counter the Soviet Union, but also to avoid what seemed the disastrous mistake of the harsh peace settlement after World War I, the victors sought to help get West Germany back on its feet as quickly as possible. At the same time, West German political leaders, determined to avoid the mistakes of the Weimar years, now better understood the need to compromise, to take responsibility for governing the whole nation.

To prevent the instability that had plagued the Weimar Republic, the creators of the new government strengthened the chancellor in relation to the Bundestag, the lower house of parliament. In the same way, the Basic Law helped establish a stable party system by discouraging splinter parties and by empowering the courts to outlaw extremist parties. And the courts found reason to outlaw both the Communist Party and a Neo-Nazi Party during the formative years of the new German democracy.

The West German republic proved more stable than the earlier Weimar Republic, partly because the political party system was now considerably simpler. Two mass parties, the Christian Democratic Union (CDU) and the Social Democratic Party (SPD), were immediately predominant, although a third, the much smaller Free Democratic Party (FDP), proved important for coalition purposes.

Konrad Adenauer (1876–1967), head of the CDU, the largest party in 1949, immediately emerged as West Germany's leading statesman. A Catholic who had been mayor of Cologne under Weimar, he had withdrawn from active politics during the Nazi period, but he reemerged after the war to lead the council that drafted the Basic Law. As chancellor from 1949 to 1963, he oriented the new German democracy toward western Europe and the Atlantic bloc, led by the United States.

The new bipolar world confronted West Germany with a cruel choice. By accepting the bipolar framework, the country could become a full partner within the Atlantic bloc. But by straddling the fence instead, it could keep open the possibility that Germany could be reunified as a neutral and disarmed state. When the outbreak of war in Korea in 1950 intensified the cold war, the United States pressured West Germany to rearm and join the Western bloc. Although some West Germans resisted, Adenauer prevailed, committing the Federal Republic to NATO in 1955. Adenauer was eager to anchor the new Federal Republic to the West, partly to buttress the new democracy in West Germany, but also to cement U.S. support in the face of what seemed an ongoing Soviet threat to German security.

By the late 1950s, the West German economy was recovering nicely, and the country was a valued member of the Western alliance. Adenauer's CDU seemed so potent that the other major party, the SPD, appeared to be consigned to permanent—and sterile—opposition. Frustrated with its outsider status, the SPD began to shed its Marxist trappings in an effort to widen its appeal. Prominent among those pushing in this direction was **Willy Brandt** (1913–1992), who became mayor of West Berlin in 1957, and who would become the party's leader in 1963. At its watershed national congress at Bad Godesberg in 1959, the party officially gave up talk of the class struggle and adopted a more moderate program.

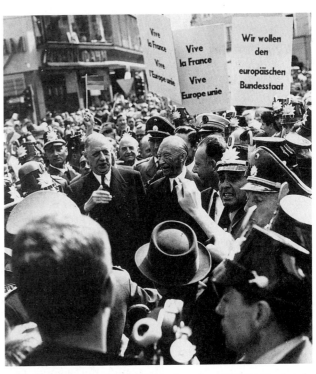

Franco-German Cooperation French president Charles de Gaulle (*left*) and West German chancellor Konrad Adenauer (*right*) draw an enthusiastic crowd in Bonn in September 1963. De Gaulle was in the West German capital for the first formal meeting after France and West Germany had signed a friendship treaty in January. Each of the two leaders strongly advocated the new cooperation between their countries, and that cooperation proved a cornerstone of the unprecedented peace and prosperity in western Europe after World War II. (akg-images)

Adenauer stepped down in 1963 at the age of 87, after fourteen years as chancellor. The contrast with Weimar, which had known twenty-one different cabinets in a comparable fourteen-year period, could not be more striking. The Adenauer years proved to Germans that democracy could mean effective government, economic prosperity, and foreign policy success. Still, Adenauer had become somewhat authoritarian by his later years, and it was arguable that West Germany had become overly reliant on him and his party.

During the years from 1963 to 1969, the CDU proved it could govern without Adenauer, and the SPD came to seem ever more respectable, even joining as the junior partner in a government coalition with the CDU in 1966. Finally, in October 1969, new parliamentary elections brought Brandt to the chancellorship, and the SPD became responsible for governing West Germany for the first time since the war.

Brandt sought to provide a genuine alternative to the CDU without undermining the consensus that had developed around the new regime since 1949. He wanted especially to improve relations between West Germany and the Soviet bloc, but this required a more independent foreign policy than Adenauer and his successors had followed. Under Adenauer, the Federal Republic had refused to deal with East Germany at all. So Brandt's opening to the East, or *Ostpolitik* (OST-po-luh-teek), was risky for a socialist chancellor seeking to prove his respectability. But he pursued it with skill and success.

In treaties with the Soviet Union, Czechoslovakia, and Poland during the early 1970s, West Germany accepted the main lines of the postwar settlement. This was to abandon any claim to the former German territory east of the Oder-Neisse line, now in Poland. Brandt also managed to improve relations with East Germany. After the two countries finally agreed to mutual diplomatic recognition, each was admitted to the United Nations in 1973. Brandt's overtures made possible closer economic ties between them, and even broader opportunities for ordinary

Konrad Adenauer
Leading statesman of post–World War II Germany, who oriented the country toward western Europe and the United States and proved to Germans that democracy could mean effective government, economic prosperity, and foreign policy success.

Willy Brandt Social Democratic West German chancellor whose policy of opening to the East, or *Ostpolitik*, made possible closer economic ties between West and East Germany and helped ordinary citizens interact across the east-west border.

citizens to interact across the east-west border. His *Ostpolitik* was widely popular and helped deepen the postwar consensus in West Germany.

FRANCE, ITALY, AND SOUTHERN EUROPE

In France and Italy, unlike West Germany, the communists constituted a potent force in light of their major roles in wartime resistance movements. The presence of Western troops in France and Italy gave the leverage to noncommunists, however, and Moscow directed the communists in both countries to settle for the moderate course of participation in broad political coalitions. Still, the United States intervened persistently in each nation to minimize the communists' role. Though support for the communists in France continued to grow until 1949, the French Communist Party settled into a particularly doctrinaire position, maintaining strict subservience to the Soviet Union, and found itself increasingly marginalized thereafter.

As the leader of the French resistance effort, Charles de Gaulle immediately assumed the dominant political role after the liberation of France in August 1944. But he withdrew, disillusioned, from active politics early in 1946, as the new Fourth Republic returned to the unstable multiparty coalitions that had marked the later years of the Third Republic. Still, governmental decision making changed significantly as the nonpolitical, technocratic side of the French state gained power in areas such as economic planning. And government technocrats survived the fall of the Fourth Republic in 1958, when de Gaulle returned to politics in a situation of crisis stemming from France's war to maintain control of Algeria (see page 839).

It was clear that de Gaulle's return signified a change of regime. After the French legislature gave him full powers for six months, his government drafted a new constitution, which was then approved by referendum in the fall of 1958. The result was the new Fifth Republic, which featured a stronger executive—and soon a president elected directly by the people and not dependent on the Chamber of Deputies. Only with the advent of de Gaulle's Fifth Republic did government in postwar France begin to assume definitive contours.

Italy's political challenge, after more than twenty years of fascism, was even more dramatic than France's. Shortly after the war, the Italians adopted a new democratic constitution and voted to end the monarchy, thereby making modern Italy a republic for the first time. But much depended on the balance of political forces, which quickly crystallized around the Christian Democratic Party (DC), oriented toward the Catholic Church, and the strong Communist Party. Many Italian moderates with little attachment to the church supported the Christian Democrats as the chief bulwark against communism. And though they consistently had to work with smaller parties to attain a parliamentary majority, the Christian Democrats promptly assumed the dominant role, which they maintained until the early 1990s.

The Communists continued to offer the major opposition, typically winning 25 to 35 percent of the vote in national elections. Taking their cue from Gramsci's writings, they adopted a proactive strategy to make their presence felt in Italian life and to demonstrate the superiority of their diagnoses and prescriptions. They found considerable success as they organized profit-making cooperatives for sharecroppers, ran local and regional governments, and garnered the support of intellectuals, journalists, and publishers. But though the Communists proved they could operate constructively within a democratic framework, their longer-term objective remained unclear into the 1970s. Could they function as part of a majority governing coalition within a democratic political system?

By the 1960s, the new democracies in Germany, France, and Italy seemed firmly rooted, and during the 1970s, Greece, Spain, and Portugal also established workable democracies after periods of dictatorial rule. Following the death of Francisco Franco in 1975, almost forty years after his triumph in the Spanish civil war, democracy returned to Spain more smoothly than most had dared hope. Franco ordained that a restoration of the monarchy would follow his death, and King Juan Carlos (b. 1938; r. 1975–) served as an effective catalyst in the transition to democracy. The new constitution of 1978 dismantled what was left of the Franco system so that, for example, Catholicism was no longer recognized as the official religion of the Spanish state.

New Discontents and New Directions

Even as democracy seemed to be thriving in western Europe, political disaffection began to threaten the consensus by the late 1960s. At that point, western Europe was at the height of the new prosperity, so the discontent did not stem from immediate economic circumstances. A new radicalism similarly emerged in the United States during the 1960s. Although this American radicalism developed especially from the civil rights movement and from opposition to the U.S. war in Vietnam, a sense that ordinary people were not truly empowered by contemporary democratic institutions fed the new radicalism on both sides of the Atlantic.

The most dramatic instance of radical protest in western Europe was the "Days of May" uprising of students and workers that shook France during May and June of 1968. The movement's aims were amorphous or utopian, and cooperation between students and workers proved sporadic. But the episode gave vent to growing discontent with the aloofness of the technocratic leaders and the unevenness of the modernization effort in de Gaulle's France. Despite impressive economic growth, many ordinary people were coming to feel left out as public services were neglected and problems worsened in such areas as housing and education.

In Italy, frustration with the stagnation of the political system bred radical labor unrest by 1969 and then a major wave of terrorism during the 1970s. By this time, many radical young people found the Communists too caught up in the system to be genuinely innovative, yet still too weak to break the Christian Democrats' lock on power. Because the Italian Communists, unlike the German Social Democrats, never established their credibility as a national governing party, the Christian Democrats grew ever more entrenched, becoming increasingly arrogant and corrupt.

In Germany, the Green movement, formed by peace and environmental activists during the late 1970s, took pains to avoid acting like a conventional party. Concerned that Germany, with its central location, would end up the devastated battleground in any superpower confrontation, the Greens opposed deployment of additional U.S. missiles on German soil and called for an alternative to the endless arms race. The SPD, as the governing party in an important NATO state, seemed unable to confront this issue and lost members as a result.

Prominent among the new political currents emerging by the early 1970s was the renewed feminist movement, which recalled the earlier movement for women's suffrage. This drive for "women's liberation" sought equal opportunities for women in education and employment. It was striking, for example, that despite major steps toward equal educational opportunity in postwar France, the country's prestigious engineering schools did not begin admitting women until the 1980s. But feminists also forced new issues onto the political stage as they worked, for example, to liberalize divorce and abortion laws.

The Energy Crisis and the Changing Economic Framework

As the political situation in western Europe became more volatile by the early 1970s, events outside Europe made it clear how interdependent the world had become—and that the West did not hold all the trump cards. In the fall of 1973, Egypt and Syria attacked Israel, seeking to recover the losses they had suffered in a brief war in 1967. Although the assault failed, the Arab nations of the oil-rich Middle East came together in the aftermath to retaliate against the Western bloc for supporting Israel. By restricting the output and distribution of oil, the Arab-led Organization of Petroleum Exporting Countries (OPEC) produced a sharp increase in oil prices and a severe economic disruption all over the industrialized world.

The 1970s proved to be an unprecedented period of "stagflation"—sharply reduced rates of growth, combined with inflation and rising unemployment. The economic miracle was over, partly because the process soon to be known as globalization was now taking off. The European economies were subject to growing competition from non-Western countries, most notably Japan. In light of increasing global competition and rising unemployment, the labor movement was suddenly on the defensive throughout the industrialized West. And the changing circumstances inevitably strained the social compact that had enabled western Europe to make a fresh start after the war.

Rethinking the Welfare State

In much of western Europe, the reach of government continued to expand into the 1970s, when reforms in Italy, for example, made available a wider range of state services—from kindergarten and medical care to sports and recreational facilities—than ever before. But during the 1970s, some began to question both the monetary costs of such measures and their implications for European competitiveness in the global economy.

Although much publicity surrounded the postwar British welfare state, by the early 1970s the percentage of the British economy devoted to public expenditure for welfare, housing, and education—18.2 percent—was about average for the industrialized nations of the West. Sweden had the highest figure at 23.7 percent, and by that point, 40 percent of Sweden's national income was devoted to taxes to finance the system—the highest rate of taxation in the world. But pressures on

Thatcher's Conservative Revolution As British prime minister from 1979 to 1990, Margaret Thatcher led an assault on the welfare state and a renewed embrace of free-market economics in Britain. Together with U.S. president Ronald Reagan, who greatly admired her, she came to symbolize the retreat from government that marked the 1980s. Thatcher is shown at a political rally in London in 1987. (D. Hudson/Sygma/Corbis)

Margaret Thatcher
Conservative prime minister of Britain from 1979 to 1990, she promoted privatization and free enterprise at the expense of the welfare state and the British labor unions.

the welfare state were especially striking in Sweden at the same time. Swedish opinion-makers grew increasingly doubtful that a welfare state could nurture the initiative and productivity needed for success in international economic competition. Sweden found itself less competitive, both because its wages were high and because it was not keeping abreast of technological developments.

In Britain, a dramatic assault on the welfare state began developing at the same time, especially because the postwar British economy, having lagged behind the others of the industrialized West, suffered especially with the more difficult economic circumstances of the 1970s. Between 1968 and 1976, the country lost one million manufacturing jobs.

During the 1970s, each of Britain's two major political parties made a serious effort to come to grips with the situation, but neither succeeded, especially because neither could deal effectively with Britain's strong trade unions. But when the militantly conservative **Margaret Thatcher** (b. 1925) became prime minister in 1979, it was clear that Britain was embarking on a radically different course.

Thatcher insisted that Britain could reverse its economic decline only by fostering a new "enterprise culture," restoring the individual initiative that had been sapped, as she saw it, by decades of dependence on government. So her government made substantial cuts in taxes and corresponding cuts in spending for education, national health, and public housing. It also fostered privatization, selling off an array of state-owned firms from Rolls-Royce to British Airways. The government even sold public housing to tenants, at as much as 50 percent below market value, a measure that helped win considerable working-class support.

At the same time, several new laws curtailed trade union power, and Thatcher refused to consult with union leaders as her predecessors had done since the war. A showdown was reached with the yearlong coal miners' strike of 1984–1985, one of the most bitter and violent European strikes of the century. Its failure in the face of government intransigence further discredited the labor movement and enhanced Thatcher's prestige.

Even critics admitted that Thatcher's policies had produced a significant change in British attitudes in favor of enterprise and competition. And Britain's economic performance certainly improved in the wake of the Thatcher revolution. But the gap between rich and poor widened, and the old industrial regions of the north were left further behind.

SECTION SUMMARY

- The continuing American commitment to western Europe, on both the economic and military diplomatic levels, helped provide a framework for democratic restoration.

- Government promises of enhanced social welfare and equality of opportunity were essential to a new social compact in the years of democratic reconstruction in western Europe.

- Konrad Adenauer led West Germany into the American-led Atlantic bloc as part of his effort to cement democratic institutions in the new West Germany.

- Discontent with the quality of democracy surfaced on both sides of the Atlantic by the 1960s, even before the economic downturn of the 1970s.

- The traditional socialist left, and even the welfare state, were on the defensive in many parts of western Europe by the 1980s.

THE COMMUNIST BLOC: FROM CONSOLIDATION TO STAGNATION

How did Soviet policy evolve after the death of Stalin in 1953?

By the late 1950s, policymakers in the West were increasingly concerned that the Soviet Union, though rigid and inhumane in important respects, might have significant advantages in the race with the capitalist democracies. Westerners worried especially about producing enough scientists and engineers to match the Soviets. With the Great Depression still in memory, some economists held that central planning might prove more efficient, and more likely to serve social justice, than capitalism. The sense that the communist system offered formidable competition added to the anxieties in the U.S.-led Atlantic bloc.

Nonetheless, the flawed political and economic order that had emerged under Stalin continued in the Soviet Union. And when it was imposed on the countries within the Soviet orbit after the war, it produced widespread resentment—and new dilemmas for Soviet leaders. Efforts to make communism more flexible after Stalin's death in 1953 proved sporadic. The Soviet suppression of the reform movement in Czechoslovakia during the "Prague Spring" of 1968 seemed to indicate the inherent rigidity of the Soviet system.

Dilemmas of the Soviet System in Postwar Europe, 1949–1955

Even in victory, the Soviet Union had suffered enormously in the war with Nazi Germany. Especially in the more developed western part of the country, thousands of factories, and even whole towns, lay destroyed, and there were severe shortages of everything from labor to housing. Yet the developing cold war seemed to require that military spending remain high.

At the same time, the Soviet Union faced the challenge of solidifying the new system of satellite states it had put together in east-central Europe. Partly in response to U.S. initiatives in western Europe, the Soviets sought to mold the new communist states into a secure, coordinated bloc of allies. In the economic sphere, the Soviets founded a new organization, COMECON, as part of their effort to lead the economies of the satellite states away from their earlier ties to the West and toward the Soviet Union (see **MAP 29.1**). In the military-diplomatic sphere, the Soviets countered NATO in 1955 by bringing the Soviet bloc countries together in a formal alliance, the **Warsaw Pact**, which provided for a joint military command and mutual military assistance.

Warsaw Pact Military-diplomatic alliance of Soviet bloc countries, created to counter NATO.

From the start, Yugoslavia had been a point of vulnerability for the Soviet system. Communist-led partisans under Josip Tito had liberated Yugoslavia from the Axis on their own, and they had not needed the Red Army to begin constructing a new communist regime (see page 811). Tito was willing to work with the Soviets, but because he had his own legitimacy, he could be considerably more independent than those elsewhere whose power rested on Soviet support. Thus, the Soviets deemed it essential to bring Tito to heel, lest his example encourage too much independence in the other communist states.

But Tito broke with the Soviet Union in 1948, and Stalin responded by cracking down on potential opponents throughout the Soviet bloc. Though the terror did not approach the massive scale of 1937-1938 (see page 763), the secret police again executed those suspected of deviation, inspiring fear even among the top leadership. As such repression proceeded in the satellite states, opposition strikes and demonstrations developed as well, finally reaching a crisis point in East Germany in 1953.

In East Berlin, a workers' protest against a provision to increase output or face wage cuts promptly led to political demands, including free elections and the withdrawal of Soviet troops. Disturbances soon spread to the other East German cities. Though this spontaneous uprising was not well coordinated, Soviet military forces had to intervene to save the East German communist regime. But the East German protest helped stimulate strikes and antigovernment demonstrations elsewhere in the Soviet bloc as well, convincing Soviet leaders that adjustments were necessary. However, at this point, the leadership of the Soviet Union was again being sorted out, for Stalin had died early in 1953, a few months before the crisis in East Germany came to a head.

🌐 **MAP 29.1—Military Alliances and Multinational Economic Groupings, 1949–1989**
The cold war split was reflected especially in the two military alliances: NATO, formed in 1949, and the Warsaw Pact, formed in 1955. Each side also had its own multinational economic organization, but the membership of the EEC, or Common Market, was not identical to that of NATO. Although communist, Yugoslavia remained outside Soviet-led organizations, as did Albania for part of the period.

De-Stalinization Under Khrushchev, 1955–1964

Although a struggle for succession followed Stalin's death, the political infighting involved a reasonable degree of give-and-take, as opposed to terror and violence. The winner, Nikita Khrushchev (KROOSH-choff) (1894–1971), was slightly crude, even something of a buffoon, but he outmaneuvered his rivals by 1955, partly because they repeatedly underestimated him. Although his period of leadership was brief, it was eventful indeed—and in some ways, the Soviet system's best chance for renewal.

At a closed session of the Soviet Communist Party's twentieth national congress in February 1956, Khrushchev made a dramatic late-night speech denouncing the criminal excesses of the Stalinist system and the "cult of personality" that had developed around Stalin himself. Khrushchev's immediate aim was to undercut his hard-line rivals, but he also insisted that key features of Stalinism had amounted to an unnecessary deviation from Marxism-Leninism. So the advent of Khrushchev suggested the possibility of liberalization and reform.

But could liberalization be contained within the framework of Soviet leadership, or was it likely to threaten the system itself? The test case proved to be Hungary, where reformers led by the moderate communist Imre Nagy had taken advantage of the liberalizing atmosphere by mid-1956 to begin dismantling collective farms and moving toward a multiparty political system. They even called for Soviet troops to withdraw, to enable Hungary to leave the Warsaw Pact and become neutral. These were not changes within the system, but challenges to the system itself. When a democratic coalition government was set up by November, the Soviets used tanks to crush the Hungarian reform movement. Thousands were killed during the fighting or subsequently executed, and 200,000 Hungarians fled to the West.

Yet even the crackdown in Hungary did not mean a return to the old days of Stalinist rigidity in the Soviet bloc. The Soviets understood that the system had to become more palatable, but liberalization was to be contained within certain limits. Above all, it could not challenge communist monopoly rule and the Warsaw Pact. After 1956, the satellites were granted greater leeway, and showed greater diversity, than had previously seemed possible. Hungary's new leader, János Kádár (1912–1989), collectivized agriculture more fully than before, but he also engineered a measure of economic decentralization, allowing scope for local initiatives and market mechanisms.

In East Germany, in contrast, Walter Ulbricht (1893–1973) concentrated on central planning and heavy industry in orthodox fashion. The East German economy became the most successful in the Soviet bloc, primarily because here the new communist regime fell heir to a skilled industrial labor force. Still, that economic growth was built on low wages, so East German workers were tempted to emigrate to West Germany as the West German economic miracle gleamed ever brighter during the 1950s. The special position of Berlin, in the heart of East Germany yet still divided among the occupying powers, made such emigration relatively easy, and 2.6 million East Germans left for the West between 1950 and 1962. With a population of only 17.1 million, East Germany could not afford to let this hemorrhaging continue. Thus, in August 1961, the Ulbricht regime erected the Berlin Wall, an ugly symbol of the cold war division of Europe.

From Liberalization to Stagnation

As a domestic leader, Khrushchev proved erratic, but he was an energetic innovator, willing to experiment. He jettisoned the worst features of the police state apparatus, including some of the infamous forced-labor camps, and offered several amnesties for prisoners. He also liberalized cultural life and gave workers greater freedom to move from one job to another. The economic planning apparatus was decentralized somewhat, affording more scope for local initiatives and placing greater emphasis on consumer goods. The government expanded medical and educational facilities and, between 1955 and 1964, doubled the nation's housing stock, substantially alleviating a severe housing shortage.

In 1957, the Soviets launched the first artificial satellite, *Sputnik I*, assuming the lead in the ensuing space race, and they sent the first human into space in 1961. Such achievements suggested that even ordinary Soviet citizens had reason for optimism. More generally, the communist regimes throughout the Soviet bloc entered the 1960s with confidence after achieving excellent rates of economic growth during the 1950s.

Yet Khrushchev had made enemies with his erratic reform effort, and this led to his forced retirement in October 1964. After the unending experiment in the economy, his opponents wanted to consolidate, to return to stability and predictability. But not until 1968 did it become clear that the liberalization and innovation of the Khrushchev era were over.

By early 1968, a significant reform movement had developed within the Communist Party in Prague, the capital of Czechoslovakia. Determined to avoid the fate of the Hungarian effort in 1956, the reformers emphasized that Czechoslovakia was to remain a communist state and a full member of the Warsaw Pact. But within that framework, they felt, it should be possible to invite freer cultural expression, to democratize the Communist Party's procedures, and to broaden participation in public life.

However, efforts to reassure the Soviets alienated some of the movement's supporters, who stepped up their demands. As earlier in Hungary, the desire for change seemed to outstrip the intentions of the movement's organizers. Finally, in August 1968, Soviet leaders sent tanks into Prague to crush the reform movement. This end of the **Prague Spring** closed the era of relative flexibility and cautious innovation in the Soviet bloc that had begun in 1953.

A period of relative stagnation followed under Leonid Brezhnev (BREZH-nef) (1906–1982), a careful, consensus-seeking bureaucrat. In dealing with the United States, Brezhnev helped engineer significant moves toward arms control and an easing of tensions. But despite this *détente*, the "Brezhnev Doctrine" made it clear that the Soviet Union would intervene as necessary to help established communist regimes remain in power. For the Soviet satellite states, there seemed no further hope of reform from within. But even as resignation marked the first years after 1968, forces soon emerged that undermined the whole communist system.

Prague Spring The attempt by Czechoslovakian reformers in 1968 to gain freer cultural expression, democratization of Communist Party procedures, and broader participation in public life within the framework of a communist state.

SECTION SUMMARY

- The imposition of Stalinist forms of governing in the new Soviet satellite states produced tensions that led the whole satellite system to a breaking point by 1953.

- Nikita Khrushchev's speech of February 1956, denouncing the excesses of Stalinism, opened the way to a measure of liberalization and reform in the Soviet Union.

- The Soviet suppression of the Hungarian revolution in the fall of 1956 indicated a strict set of limits, but the Soviet satellite states had some freedom to set their own course thereafter.

- The East German government erected the Berlin Wall in August 1961 to stop people from moving to West Berlin—and from there to other parts of West Germany.

- In light of the Soviet suppression of the Prague Spring reform movement in 1968, there seemed little scope for reforming the communist systems from within.

The End of the Prague Spring Moving tanks into Prague in August 1968, Soviet leaders ended the widely admired reform movement in Czechoslovakia. Though there were protests, as shown here on August 20, the outcome was a foregone conclusion once the Soviets decided to intervene. The ending of the Prague Spring proved a watershed for the fate of communism in Europe. (Josef Kondelka/Magnum Photos)

EUROPE, THE WEST, AND THE WORLD

How did the place of western Europe in world affairs change during the cold war era?

By the early 1950s, Europe seemed dwarfed by the two superpowers and, for the foreseeable future, divided by the conflict between them. The colonial networks that had manifested European predominance unraveled rapidly at the same time. One obvious response was some form of European integration. A unified Europe might eventually become a global superpower in its own right. Although the first steps toward European unity did not go as far as visionaries had hoped, a new group of leaders established lasting foundations by the late 1950s. Still, the cold war framework limited the new union's geographical extent and the scope of its activity for decades.

The Cold War Framework

That cold war tensions could produce dangerous military conflict quickly became clear as superpower divisions over Korea, which had been jointly liberated from the Japanese by the Americans and the Soviets, led to the complex Korean War (1950–1953). Although the United States had previously declared Korea outside the U.S. defense perimeter, it intervened in support of noncommunist South Korea in the face of an attempt by communist North Korea, encouraged by Stalin, to unify Korea as a communist state. The war was inconclusive, leaving the Korean peninsula divided more or less as before, but it prompted the United States to extend containment to the global level and to step up military production.

In retrospect, however, it is clear that the most intense phase of the cold war ended with Stalin's death in 1953. In his speech to the twentieth party congress in 1956, Khrushchev repudiated the previous Soviet tenet that a military showdown between the communist world and Western capitalist imperialism was inevitable. During a visit to the United States in 1959, he stressed that the ongoing competition between the two sides could be peaceful. However, despite summit conferences and sporadic efforts at better relations, friction between the Soviet Union and the United States continued to define the era.

Indeed, a new peak of tension was reached in October 1962, when the Soviets began placing missiles in Cuba, just 90 miles from the United States. Cuba had developed close ties with the Soviet Union after a 1959 revolution led by Fidel Castro (b. 1926). With Castro beginning to develop a communist system, a U.S.-supported force of Cuban exiles sought to invade Cuba and foment insurrection against the new regime in April 1961. This effort proved a fiasco, but it indicated to the Soviets that the new Cuban regime was vulnerable to overthrow from the United States.

Although the United States had placed offensive missiles in NATO member Turkey, adjacent to the Soviet Union, the Soviet attempt to base missiles in Cuba seemed an intolerable challenge to the U.S. administration. President John F. Kennedy (1917–1963) responded with a naval blockade of Cuba, and for several days, the superpowers seemed on the verge of military confrontation. Finally, the Soviets agreed to withdraw their missiles in exchange for a U.S. promise not to seek to overthrow the communist government of Cuba. The Americans also agreed informally to remove their offensive missiles from Turkey. Khrushchev's willingness to retreat antagonized hard-liners in the Soviet military and contributed to his ouster from power two years later. Yet Khrushchev himself viewed the outcome in Cuba as a victory. By challenging the United States with missiles, the Soviets had helped secure the survival of the Cuban communist regime, which was now less vulnerable to overthrow by the United States. The Cuban missile crisis was the closest the superpowers came to direct, armed confrontation during the cold war period.

At the same time, it became increasingly clear that international communism was not the monolithic force it had once seemed. The most dramatic indication was the Sino-Soviet split, which developed during the 1950s as the Chinese Communist Party, under Mao Zedong, solidified its power. In the long struggle that led to their victory in 1949, the Chinese Communists had often had no choice but to go their own way, and during the 1940s especially, Stalin had been willing to subordinate any concern for their cause to Soviet national interests. After taking power in 1949, the Chinese Communists pursued their own path to development without worrying about the Soviet model. Not without reason, the Soviets feared that the independent, innovative Chinese might be prepared to challenge Soviet leadership in international communism. By the early 1960s, the Chinese Communists' path had become appealing to many in the non-Western world, though it attracted dissident communists in the West as well.

The Varieties of Decolonization

The advent of a new world configuration, with a circumscribed place for Europe, found dramatic expression in the rapid disintegration of the European colonial empires after World War II (see **Map 29.2**). The war itself had been a major catalyst for independence movements throughout the world. In southeast Asia and the Pacific, quick Japanese conquests revealed the tenuous hold of France, the Netherlands, and Britain on their domains. And it was not colonial reconquest that marked the end of the war, but the atomic bomb and the victory of the United States, which took a dim view of conventional European colonialism.

The effort of the Netherlands to regain control of the Dutch East Indies led to four years of military struggle against the Indonesian nationalist insurgency. Especially after the humiliations of defeat and occupation during World War II, many of the Dutch took pride in their imperial role. The struggle lasted from 1945 to 1949, when the Dutch finally had to yield as their former colony became independent Indonesia.

Britain was the most realistic of the European colonial powers, grasping the need to compromise and work with emerging national leaders in light of decolonization pressures. Nevertheless, British resistance in 1956 provoked an international crisis over the status of the Suez Canal in Egypt (see **Map 28.1** on page 788). Once a British protectorate, Egypt had remained under British

THE SUEZ CRISIS

🌐 MAP 29.2—Decolonization, 1945–1980

During a thirty-five-year period after World War II, the European empires in Africa, Asia, and the Pacific gradually came apart as the former colonies became independent nations.

influence after nominally becoming sovereign in 1922. But a revolution in 1952 produced a new government of Arab nationalists, led by the charismatic Colonel Gamal Abdel Nasser (1918–1970). In 1954, Britain agreed with Egypt to leave the Suez Canal zone within twenty months, though the zone was to be international, not Egyptian, and Britain was to retain special rights there in the event of war. In 1956, however, Nasser announced the nationalization of the canal, partly so that Egypt could use its revenues to finance public works projects.

Suez crisis Crisis prompted by Egypt's nationalization of the British-owned Suez Canal. The effort of Britain, France, and Israel to seize the canal prompted a strong negative reaction in world opinion, forcing them to withdraw.

Determined to resist, the British won the support of Israel and France, each of which had reason to fear the pan-Arab nationalism that Nasser's Egypt was now spearheading. Late in 1956, Britain, Israel, and France orchestrated a surprise attack on Egypt. But their troops met stubborn Egyptian resistance, and the British and French encountered decisive defeat in the diplomatic maneuvering that accompanied the fighting. Both the United States and the Soviet Union opposed the attack, as did world opinion. The old European powers had sought to act on their own, by the old rules, but the outcome of this **Suez crisis** demonstrated how limited their reach had become.

THE FRENCH IN VIETNAM

Still, the 1956 debacle did not convince France to abandon its struggle to retain Algeria. And that struggle proved the most wrenching experience that any European country was to have with decolonization. For the French, the process started not in North Africa, but in Indochina, in southeast Asia, during World War II.

Led by the communist Ho Chi Minh (1890–1969), the Indochinese anticolonialist movement gained strength resisting the Japanese during the war. Then, before the French could return, Ho established a political base in northern Vietnam in 1945. But in 1946, French authorities in Indochina deliberately provoked an incident to undercut negotiations and start hostilities. Eight years of difficult guerrilla war followed, creating a major drain on the French economy.

With its strongly anticolonialist posture, the United States was unsympathetic to the French cause at first. But the communist takeover in China in 1949 and the outbreak of war in Korea in 1950 made the French struggle in Indochina seem a battle in a larger war against communism in Asia. By 1954, the United States was covering 75 percent of the cost of the French effort. Nonetheless, when the fall of the fortified area at Dien Bien Phu in May 1954 signaled a decisive French defeat, the United States decided to pull back and accept a negotiated settlement. Partly at the urging of its European allies, the United States had concluded that the Soviet threat in Europe must remain its principal concern.

France worked out the terms of independence for Vietnam in 1955. The solution, however, entailed a North-South partition to separate the communist and anticommunist forces, pending elections to unify the country. The anticommunist regime the United States sponsored in the South resisted holding the elections, so the country remained divided (see **MAP 29.2**). With the Americans providing first advisers, then, beginning in 1964, active military support, South Vietnam sought unsuccessfully to defeat a guerrilla insurgency supported by the communist North. After defeating the United States and South Vietnam, the communist heirs of those who had fought the French assumed the leadership of a reunified Vietnam in 1975.

In France, the defeat in Indochina in 1954 left a legacy of bitterness, especially among army officers, many of whom felt that French forces could have won had they not been undercut by politicians at home. When the outcome in Indochina emboldened Arab nationalists in North Africa to take up arms against the French colonial power, the French army was anxious for a second chance—and the French government was willing to give it to them. Algeria had been under French control since 1830, and it had a substantial minority of ethnic Europeans, totaling over a million, or 10 percent of the population.

THE WAR IN ALGERIA

Although France gradually committed 500,000 troops to Algeria, the war bogged down into what threatened to become a lengthy stalemate, with increasing brutality on both sides. As it drained French lives and resources, the war became a highly contentious political issue in France. The situation came to a head during the spring of 1958, when the advent of a new ministry, rumored to favor a compromise settlement, led to violent demonstrations, engineered by the sectors of the French army in Algeria. Military intervention in France itself seemed likely to follow—and with it, the danger of civil war.

It was at this moment of genuine emergency that Charles de Gaulle returned to lead the change to the Fifth Republic. Those determined to hold Algeria welcomed him as their savior. But de Gaulle fooled them, working out a compromise with the Algerian rebels that ended the war and made Algeria independent in 1962. Only de Gaulle could have engineered this outcome without provoking still deeper political division in France.

INDEPENDENCE IN SUB-SAHARAN AFRICA

The outcomes of decolonization in sub-Saharan Africa depended on several factors: the number and intransigence of European settlers, the extent to which local elites had emerged, and the confidence of the Europeans that they could retain their influence if they agreed to independence. The transition was smoothest in British West Africa, where the Gold Coast achieved independence as Ghana, first as a dominion of the British Commonwealth in 1957, and then as a fully independent republic in 1960. Few British settlers lived in that part of Africa, and the small, relatively cohesive African elite favored a moderate transition, not revolution.

Where British settlers were relatively numerous, however, the transition to independence was much more difficult. The very presence of Europeans had impeded the development of cohesive local elites, so movements for independence in those areas tended to become more radical, threatening the expropriation of European-held property. In Southern Rhodesia, unyielding European settlers resisted the British government's efforts to promote a compromise. A white supremacist government declared its independence from Britain in 1965, fueling a guerrilla war. The Africans won independence as Zimbabwe only in 1980.

The reaction against Eurocentrism that accompanied the turn from colonialism was not confined to those who had been subjected to European imperialism. There was much interest among Westerners in the work of Frantz Fanon (1925–1961), a black intellectual from Martinique who became identified especially with the cause of the Algerian rebels. In *The Wretched of the Earth* (1961), Fanon found the West spiritually exhausted and called on the peoples of the non-Western world to go their own way, based on their own values and traditions. (See the feature, "The Global Record: The Legacy of European Colonialism.")

The process of decolonization led to a remarkable transformation in the thirty-five years after World War II. Forms of colonial rule that had been taken for granted before World War I stood discredited, virtually without defenders, by the late twentieth century. Europeans were

The Legacy of European Colonialism

In the following passages from The Wretched of the Earth *(1961), Frantz Fanon probes the negative consequences of colonialism—for both colonizers and colonized—and tries to show why a radical, even violent break from colonialism was necessary. In his conclusion, he offers a stirring call to the colonized world to repudiate the West, whose claims to offer universal values he finds hypocritical in the extreme.*

The violence which has ruled over the ordering of the colonial world, which has ceaselessly drummed the rhythm for the destruction of native social forms and broken up without reserve the systems of reference of the economy, the customs of dress and external life, that same violence will be claimed and taken over by the native at the moment when, deciding to embody history in his own person, he surges into the forbidden quarters....

...In the colonial context the settler only ends his work of breaking in the native when the latter admits loudly and intelligibly the supremacy of the white man's values. In the period of decolonization, the colonized masses mock at these very values, insult them, and vomit them up.

...All that the native has seen in his country is that they can freely arrest him, beat him, starve him: and no professor of ethics, no priest has ever come to be beaten in his place, nor to share their bread with him. As far as the native is concerned, morality is very concrete; it is to silence the settler's defiance, to break his flaunting violence—in a word, to put him out of the picture....

...The colonialist bourgeoisie, in its narcissistic dialogue, expounded by the members of its universities, had in fact deeply implanted in the minds of the colonized intellectual that the essential qualities remain eternal in spite of all the blunders men may make: the essential qualities of the West, of course....Now it so happens that during the struggle for liberation, at the moment that the native intellectual comes into touch again with his people,...[a]ll the Mediterranean values—the triumph of the human individual, of clarity, and of beauty...are revealed as worthless, simply because they have nothing to do with the concrete conflict in which the people is engaged.

Individualism is the first to disappear....The colonialist bourgeoisie had hammered into the native's mind the idea of a society of individuals where each person shuts himself up in his own subjectivity, and whose only wealth is individual thought. Now the native who has the opportunity to return to the people during the struggle for freedom will discover the falseness of this theory. The very forms of organization of the struggle will suggest to him a different vocabulary. Brother, sister, friend—these are words outlawed by the colonialist bourgeoisie, because for them my brother is my purse, my friend is part of my scheme for getting on. The native intellectual...will...discover the substance of village assemblies, the cohesion of people's committees, and the extraordinary fruitfulness of local meetings and groupments. Henceforward, the interests of one will be the interests of all, for in concrete fact *everyone* will be discovered by the troops, *everyone* will be massacred—or *everyone* will be saved....

Leave this Europe where they are never done talking of Man yet murder men everywhere they find them....For centuries they have stifled almost the whole of humanity in the name of a so-called spiritual experience. Look at them today swaying between atomic and spiritual disintegration....

Come then, comrades, the European game has finally ended; we must find something different. We today can do everything, so long as we do not imitate Europe, so long as we are not obsessed by the desire to catch up with Europe.

QUESTIONS

1. On what basis does Fanon believe that even native intellectuals who have embraced Western values can be won back for the anticolonialist cause?

2. What Western value does Fanon claim is the first to be repudiated—and why?

Source: Excerpts from *The Wretched of the Earth* by Frantz Fanon, copyright © 1963 by Presence Africaine. Used by permission of Grove/Atlantic, Inc.

now accepting the principle of national self-determination for non-Europeans. But decolonization hardly offered a neat and definitive solution. In formerly colonial territories, new political boundaries often stemmed from the ways Europeans had carved things up, rather than from indigenous ethnic or national patterns. Moreover, questions remained about the longer-term economic relationships between the Europeans and their former colonies.

Economic Integration and the Origins of the European Union

As the old colonialism increasingly fell into disrepute, many found in European unity the best prospect for the future. Although hopes for full-scale political unification were soon frustrated, the movement for European integration achieved significant successes in the economic sphere, especially through the European Economic Community, or Common Market, established in 1957.

The impetus for economic integration came especially from a new breed of "Eurocrats"—technocrats with a supranational, or pan-European, outlook. A notable example was Robert Schuman (1886–1963), a native of Lorraine, which had passed between France and Germany four times between 1870 and 1945. After serving as a German officer in World War I, he was elected to the French Chamber of Deputies in 1919 just after Lorraine was returned to France. As French foreign minister after World War II, Schuman was responsible for a 1950 plan to coordinate French and German production of coal and steel. The Schuman Plan quickly encompassed Italy, Belgium, the Netherlands, and Luxembourg to become the European Coal and Steel Community (ECSC) in 1951. Working closely with Schuman was Jean Monnet, who served as the ECSC's first president. From this position, he pushed for more thoroughgoing economic integration. The successes of the ECSC led the same six countries to agree to a wider "Common Market," officially known as the **European Economic Community (EEC),** in 1957.

European Economic Community (EEC)
Common market formed by Belgium, France, West Germany, Italy, Luxembourg, and the Netherlands to promote free trade.

After the merger of the governing institutions of the several European supranational organizations in 1967, the term *European Community* (EC) and later *European Union* (EU) came to indicate the institutional web that had emerged since the launching of the European Coal and Steel Community in 1951. Meanwhile, its membership gradually expanded, encompassing, during the cold war era, Denmark, Ireland, and Britain in 1973, Greece in 1981, and Spain and Portugal in 1986 (see **MAP 29.1**). For newly democratic countries like Spain, Portugal, and Greece, Common Market membership became a pillar of the solidifying democratic consensus.

The immediate aim of the original EEC was to facilitate trade by eliminating customs duties between its member countries and by establishing common tariffs on imports from the rest of the world. For each member of the EEC, tariff reduction meant access to wider markets abroad, but also the risks of new competition in its own domestic market. However, the EEC proved advantageous to so many that tariff reduction proceeded well ahead of schedule. By 1968, the last internal tariffs had been eliminated.

With tariffs dropping, trade among the member countries nearly doubled between 1958 and 1962. For example, French exports of automobiles and chemicals to Germany increased more than eightfold. Partly because the increasing competition stimulated initiative and productivity, industrial production within the EEC increased at a robust annual rate of 7.6 percent during those years.

Despite these successes, vigorous debate accompanied the development of the EEC during the 1960s. To enable goods, capital, and labor to move freely among the member countries, some coordination of social and economic policy was required. But were the member states prepared to give up some of their own sovereignty to the Common Market to make that coordination possible?

In the mid-1960s, French president de Gaulle forced some of the underlying uncertainties to the fore. Though he had willingly turned from the old colonialism, de Gaulle was not prepared to compromise French sovereignty, and he was not persuaded that supranational integration offered the best course for postwar Europe. With the end of the Algerian war in 1962, France began playing an assertively independent role in international affairs. Thus, for example, de Gaulle developed an independent French nuclear force, curtailed the French role in NATO, and recognized the communist People's Republic of China.

This determination to assert France's sovereignty led to friction between de Gaulle and the supranational Eurocrats of the Common Market. A dispute over agricultural policy brought matters to a head in 1965. The immediate result was a compromise, but de Gaulle's tough stance served to check the increasing supranationalism evident in the EEC until then. As the economic context became more difficult during the 1970s, it became still harder to maintain the EEC's cohesion. So, although the Common Market was an important departure, it did not overcome traditional national sovereignty or give western Europe a more muscular world role during the first decades after World War II.

SECTION SUMMARY

- Dependent on the United States for their security, the western European countries had limited freedom of action in world affairs during the cold war era.

- Though the decolonization process varied considerably from case to case, the long-standing European colonial networks gradually dissolved after World War II.

- Desires to remove the sources of war and to enhance Europe's economic competitiveness fueled the movement toward European integration, including the formation of the European Economic Community (Common Market) in 1957.

- French president Charles de Gaulle envisioned a more independent role for Europe from within the cold war framework, but that role was to be based on French leadership, not European integration.

THE COLLAPSE OF THE SOVIET SYSTEM, 1975–1991

What led to the collapse of the communist system in the Soviet Union and its satellite states?

Though the reasons were different, the Soviet bloc, like the West, encountered economic stagnation during the 1970s. The deteriorating situation finally produced a major Soviet reform effort by the mid-1980s. At the same time, new forms of opposition developed in the satellite states after the crushing of the Prague reform movement in 1968. The intersection of these forces led to the unraveling of the satellite system in 1989, and then to the collapse of the Soviet communist regime in 1991. This outcome stunned Western observers, who had come to take the anxious stability of the cold war framework for granted.

Economic Stagnation in the Soviet Bloc

The impressive rates of economic growth achieved in much of the Soviet bloc continued into the 1960s. However, such success came especially from adding labor—women and underemployed peasants—to the industrial workforce. By the end of the 1960s, that process was reaching its limits, so increasingly, the challenge for the Soviet bloc was to boost productivity through technological innovation.

By the late 1970s, however, the Soviets were falling seriously behind the West as a new technological revolution gathered force. Continuing development in high technology demanded the freedom to experiment and exchange ideas and the flexibility to anticipate innovation and shift resources. The Soviet system, with its direction from the top, proved too rigid. Moreover, as that system bogged down, the expense of the arms race with the United States dragged ever more seriously on the Soviet economy. Ordinary Soviet citizens grew increasingly frustrated as the communist economy proved erratic in providing even basic consumer goods. Yet major functionaries enjoyed access to special shops and other privileges.

In satellite countries, such as Poland and Hungary, the communist governments managed for a while to win mass support by borrowing from foreign banks to provide meat and other consumer goods at artificially low prices—"sausage-stuffing," some called it. But as the lending banks came to realize, by the end of the 1970s, that such loans were not being used to enhance productivity, these governments found it much harder to borrow. Thus, they began having to impose greater austerity.

Throughout the Soviet bloc, frustration grew, especially among women, who seemed to bear a disproportionate share of the burdens. Women were more likely to be employed outside the home in the communist countries than in the West. About 90 percent of adult women in the Soviet Union and East Germany had paid jobs by 1980. Yet, not only were these women concentrated in jobs with low pay and prestige, but they also still bore the major responsibility for child-care, housework, and shopping. They had few of the labor-saving devices available in the West, and they often had to spend hours in line to buy ordinary consumer items. Dissatisfaction among women fed an underground protest movement that began developing in the Soviet bloc in the mid-1970s—an indication of the growing strains in the overall system.

The Crisis of Communism in the Satellite States

For many intellectuals in the Soviet bloc, the Soviet suppression of the Prague Spring in 1968 ended any hope that communism could be made to work. The immediate outcome was a sense of hopelessness, but by the mid-1970s, a new opposition movement had begun to take shape, especially in Hungary, Poland, and Czechoslovakia. It centered initially on underground (or *samizdat*) publications, privately circulated writings that enabled dissidents to share ideas critical of the regime.

In one sense, these dissidents realized, intellectuals and ordinary people alike were powerless in the face of heavy-handed communist government. But they came to believe they could make a difference simply by "living the truth," ceasing to participate in the empty rituals of communist rule. And mere individual honesty could have political potential, especially because of the Helsinki Accords on human rights that the Soviet bloc countries had accepted in 1975.

The meeting of thirty-five countries in Helsinki, Finland, in 1975 was one of the most important fruits of the *Ostpolitik*, or opening to the East, that Willy Brandt began pursuing after becoming West Germany's chancellor in 1969 (see page 829). Eager to grasp Brandt's offer to regularize the status of East Germany and to confirm the western border of Poland, the Soviet bloc found it expedient to accept the detailed agreement on human rights included in the resulting **Helsinki Accords**.

Though merely symbolic, in one sense, the human rights agreement proved a touchstone for initiatives that would help bring the whole Soviet system crashing down. Through various "Helsinki Watch" groups monitoring civil liberties, anticommunists in the satellite states managed to assume moral leadership. By demanding that the communist governments live up to their agreements, and by noting the gap between idealistic pretense and grim reality, opposition intellectuals began to cast doubts on the very legitimacy of the communist regimes.

The most significant such group was Charter 77, which emerged in Czechoslovakia in response to the arrest of a rock group, "The Plastic People of the Universe." Long-haired and antiestablishment like their counterparts in the West, the Plastic People were deemed filthy, obscene, and disrespectful of society by the repressive Czechoslovak regime. In 1977, protesting the crackdown on the group, 243 individuals signed "Charter 77"—using their own names and addresses, living the truth, acting as if they were free to register such an opinion.

A leader in Charter 77 was the writer Václav Havel (HAH-vul) (b. 1936), who noted that, after 1968, the hope for change depended on people organizing themselves, outside the structures of the party-state, in diverse, independent social groupings. (See the feature, "The Written Record: Power from Below: Living the Truth.") Havel and a number of his associates were in and out of jail as the government sought to stave off this protest movement. Despite the efforts of Havel and his colleagues, however, government remained particularly repressive, and ordinary people relatively passive, in Czechoslovakia until the late 1980s. For quite different reasons, Hungary and Poland offered greater scope for change.

Even after the failed reform effort of 1956, Hungary proved the most innovative of the European communist countries. Partly because its government allowed small-scale initiatives outside the central planning apparatus, Hungary was able to respond more flexibly to the growing economic stagnation. This openness to economic experimentation enabled reformers within the Hungarian Communist Party to gain the upper hand. Amid growing talk of "socialist pluralism," the Hungarian elections of 1985 introduced an element of genuine democracy. Increasingly open to a variety of viewpoints, the Hungarian Communists gradually pulled back from their long-standing claim to a monopoly of power.

The reform effort that built gradually in Hungary stemmed especially from aspirations within the governing elite. More dramatic was the course of change in Poland, where workers and intellectuals, at odds even as recently as 1968, managed to come together during the 1970s. When Polish workers struck in 1976, in response to a cut in food subsidies, intellectuals formed a committee to defend them. This alliance had become possible because dissident intellectuals

Women's Work in the Soviet Union   This cartoon adapts the caryatid form from ancient sculpture to depict the special burdens that were coming to wear more heavily on women as the Soviet economy bogged down. Intended to commemorate International Women's Day, the image appeared in the Soviet magazine *Krokodil* in 1984.   (*Krokodil Magazine*, March 1984)

Helsinki Accords
Agreements signed by thirty-five countries in Helsinki, Finland, that committed the signatories to recognize existing borders, to increase economic and environmental cooperation, and to promote freedom of expression, religion, and travel.

were coming to emphasize the importance of grassroots efforts that challenged the logic of the communist system without attacking it directly.

An extra ingredient from an unexpected quarter also affected the situation in Poland, perhaps in a decisive way. In 1978, the College of Cardinals of the Roman Catholic Church departed from long tradition and, for the first time since 1522, elected a non-Italian pope. Even more startling was the fact that the new pope was from Poland, behind the iron curtain. He was Karol Cardinal Wojtyla (voy-TILL-ah) (1920–2005), the archbishop of Cracow, who took the name John Paul II.

After World War II, the Polish Catholic Church had been unique among the major churches of east-central Europe in maintaining and even enhancing its position. It worked just enough with the ruling Communists to be allowed to carve out a measure of autonomy. For many Poles, the church remained a tangible institutional alternative to communism and the focus of national consciousness in the face of Soviet domination. Thus, the new pope's visit to Poland in 1979 had an electrifying effect on ordinary Poles, who took to the streets by the millions to greet him—and found they were not alone. This boost in self-confidence provided the catalyst for the founding of a new trade union, **Solidarity**, in August 1980.

> **Solidarity** A trade union formed in communist Poland, it became the nucleus of widespread demands for change—including independent labor organizations, the right to strike, and freedom of expression.

Led by a shipyard electrician, Lech Walesa (va-WEN-sah) (b. 1943), Solidarity emerged from labor discontent in the vast Lenin shipyard in Gdansk, on the Baltic Sea (see **MAP 29.1**). Demanding the right to form their own independent unions, seventy thousand workers took over the shipyard, winning support both from their intellectual allies and from the Catholic Church. Support for Solidarity grew partly because the government, facing the crisis of its "sausage stuffing" strategy, was cutting subsidies and raising food prices. But the new union developed such force because it placed moral demands first—independent labor organizations, the right to strike, and freedom of expression. Reflecting the wider opposition thinking in east-central Europe, Solidarity was not to be bought off with lower meat prices, even had the government been able to deliver them.

After over a year of negotiation, compromise, and broken promises, the tense situation came to a head in December 1981, when the government under General Wojciech Jaruzelski (yah-roo-ZELL-skee) (b. 1923) declared martial law and outlawed Solidarity, imprisoning its leaders. Strikes in protest were crushed by military force. So much for that, it seemed: another lost cause, another reform effort colliding with inflexible communist power, as in 1953, 1956, and 1968. But this time, it was different, thanks especially to developments in the Soviet Union.

The Quest for Reform in the Soviet Union

The death of Leonid Brezhnev in 1982 paved the way for a reform effort that began in earnest when **Mikhail Gorbachev** (GOR-ba-choff) (b. 1931) became Soviet Communist Party secretary in 1985. Gorbachev's effort encompassed four intersecting initiatives: arms reduction; liberalization in the satellite states; *glasnost* (GLAHZ-nost), or "openness" to discussion and criticism; and *perestroika* (pair-es-TROY-kah), or economic "restructuring." This was to be a reform within the Soviet system. There was no thought of giving up the Communist Party's monopoly on power or embracing a free-market economy. The reformers still took it for granted that communism could point the way beyond Western capitalism, with its shallow consumerism. But they had to make communism work.

> **Mikhail Gorbachev** Soviet Communist Party secretary who attempted to reform the Soviet communist system through arms reduction; liberalization in the satellite states; *glasnost;* and *perestroika.*

Gorbachev understood that "openness" was a prerequisite for "restructuring." The freedom to criticize was essential to check abuses of power, which, in turn, was necessary to overcome the cynicism of the workers and improve productivity. Openness was also imperative to gain the full participation of the country's most creative people, whose contributions were critical if the Soviet Union was to become competitive in advanced technology.

The main thrust of *perestroika* was to depart from the rigid economic planning mechanism by giving local managers more autonomy. But any restructuring was bound to encounter resistance, especially from those with careers tied to the central planning apparatus. And Gorbachev's program made only partial headway in this crucial sector.

The Anticommunist Revolution in East-Central Europe

Meanwhile, in Poland, repression continued, but Walesa, from prison, managed to keep his movement together, as the ideas of Solidarity continued to spread underground. Then the advent of Gorbachev in 1985 changed the overall framework, in light of his belief that reform

Power from Below: Living the Truth

Considering the scope for change in the communist world by the late 1970s, Václav Havel imagines a conformist grocer who routinely puts a sign in his window with the slogan "Workers of the world, unite!" simply because it is expected. That same grocer, says Havel, has the power to break the system, which rests on innumerable acts of everyday compliance. Havel finds this system "post-totalitarian" because it rests on neither the coercion nor the fanatical belief that, in some combination, had sustained the earlier totalitarian systems. At the same time, he senses that aspects of the "post-totalitarian" order reveal, in stark and garish terms, more general modern tendencies that are merely masked in the Western democracies. So the West did not offer an easy model; in fact, it might actually have something to learn from the forms of opposition that Havel saw emerging in the communist bloc.

The real meaning of the greengrocer's slogan has nothing to do with what the text of the slogan actually says. Even so, this real meaning is quite clear and generally comprehensible because the code is so familiar: the greengrocer declares his loyalty ... in the only way the regime is capable of hearing; that is, by accepting the prescribed *ritual*, by accepting appearances as reality, by accepting the given rules of the game. In doing so, however, he has himself become a player in the game, thus making it possible for the game to go on, for it to exist in the first place. ...

In the end, is not the greyness and emptiness of life in the post-totalitarian system only an inflated caricature of modern life in general? And do we not stand (although in the external measures of civilization, we are far behind) as a kind of warning to the West, revealing its own latent tendencies?

Let us now imagine that one day something in our greengrocer snaps and he stops putting up the slogans merely to ingratiate himself. He stops voting in elections he knows are a farce. He begins to say what he really thinks at political meetings. ... He rejects the ritual and breaks the rules of the game. He discovers once more his suppressed identity and dignity. ...

... By breaking the rules of the game, he has disrupted the game as such. He has exposed it as a mere game. He has shattered the world of appearance, the fundamental pillar of the system. ... He has shown everyone that it *is* possible to live within the truth. Living within the lie can constitute the system only if it is universal. The principle must embrace and permeate everything. There are no terms whatsoever on which it can coexist with living within the truth, and therefore everyone who steps out of line *denies it in principle and threatens it in its entirety.* ...

And since all genuine problems and matters of critical importance are hidden beneath a thick crust of lies, it is never quite clear when the proverbial last straw will fall, or what that straw will be. This ... is why the regime prosecutes, almost as a reflex action preventively, even the most modest attempts to live within the truth.

... The crust presented by the life of lies is made of strange stuff. As long as it seals off hermetically the entire society, it appears to be made of stone. But the moment someone breaks through in one place, when one person cries out, "The emperor is naked!"—when a single person breaks the rules of the game, thus exposing it as a game—everything suddenly appears in another light and the whole crust seems then to be made of a tissue on the point of tearing and disintegrating uncontrollably. ...

The post-totalitarian system is only one aspect ... of this general inability of modern humanity to be the master of its own situation. The automatism of the post-totalitarian system is merely an extreme version of the global automatism of technological civilization. The human failure that it mirrors is only one variant of the general failure of modern humanity. ...

It would appear that the traditional parliamentary democracies can offer no fundamental opposition to the automatism of technological civilization and the industrial-consumer society, for they, too, are being dragged helplessly along by it. People are manipulated in ways that are infinitely more subtle and refined than the brutal methods used in the post-totalitarian societies.

QUESTIONS

1. Why does Havel believe that small, everyday acts of conformity actually constitute the post-totalitarian system?

2. What relationship between the communist bloc and the Western democracies is Havel positing?

in the satellites was necessary to complement restructuring in the Soviet system. As the Polish economy, already in difficulty by 1980, reached a crisis in 1987, Solidarity began stepping up its efforts.

When proposed price increases were rejected in a referendum, the Polish government imposed them by fiat. Strikes demanding the relegalization of Solidarity followed during the spring of 1988. The government again responded with military force, but Solidarity-led strikes in August forced

Lech Walesa and Solidarity A shipyard electrician, Walesa spearheaded the dissident Polish trade union, Solidarity, formed in 1980, and then emerged from prison to lead the movement that eventually undercut the communist regime in Poland in 1989. Here he addresses a rally during a strike at the Lenin shipyard in Gdansk in August 1988. (Corbis Sygma)

government leaders to send signals that they might be prepared to negotiate. With the economy nearing collapse, the government recognized that it could no longer govern on its own.

The "Round Table" negotiations that followed early in 1989 proved pivotal. Not only did the government consent to legalize Solidarity, but it agreed to make the forthcoming elections free enough for the opposition genuinely to participate. The elections of June 1989 produced an overwhelming repudiation of Poland's communist government, forcing President Jaruzelski to give Solidarity a chance to lead. Not all members of the opposition felt it wise to accept government responsibility under such difficult economic circumstances, but finally Tadeusz Mazowiecki (mah-zo-VYETS-kee), Walesa's choice and one of the movement's most distinguished intellectuals, agreed to form a government.

The chain of events in Poland culminated in one of the extraordinary events of modern history—the negotiated end of communist rule. That a communist government might give up power voluntarily had been utterly unforeseen. It happened partly because the Soviet Union under Gorbachev was seeking reform and thus had become much less likely to intervene militarily. It also helped that the Polish Catholic Church was available to act as mediator, hosting meetings, reminding both sides of their shared responsibilities in the difficult situation facing their country. By some accounts, General Jaruzelski, who seemed for most of the 1980s to be just another military strongman and Soviet lackey, had proved to be a national hero for his grace, perhaps even ingenuity, in yielding power to the opposition. But most important was the courage, the persistence, and the vision of Solidarity itself.

Although the Hungarians were already breaking out of the communist mold, it was especially the Polish example that suggested to others in the Soviet bloc that the whole system was open to challenge. During 1989, demands for reform and, increasingly, for an end to communist rule spread through east-central Europe by means of the domino effect that had preoccupied the Soviets from the start. By the end of that year, the Soviet satellite system was in ruins (see **Map 30.1** on page 854).

A marked increase in illegal emigration from East Germany to the West had been one manifestation that the system was starting to unravel. During 1989, the reform-minded Hungarian Communists decided to stop impeding East Germans, many of whom vacationed in Hungary, from emigrating to the West at the Hungarian border with Austria. If the communist reformers in East Germany were to have any chance of turning the situation around, they had to relax restrictions on travel and even grant the right to emigrate. They began preparing to do both as part of a host of reforms intended to save the system. On November 9, 1989, the East German communist regime did the unthinkable and opened the Berlin Wall, which was promptly dismantled altogether. Germans now traveled freely back and forth between East and West. Although the fate of the Soviet Union itself remained uncertain, the opening of the wall signaled the end of the cold war. It was no longer a bipolar world.

By this point, discontented East Germans envisioned not simply reforming the communist system, but ending it altogether. Within weeks, it was clear that the rhythm of events was beyond the control of East Germany's reform communists, who opened the way for German reunification in 1990. Despite some nervousness, the four postwar occupying powers—the United States, Britain, France, and the Soviet Union—gave their blessing as the Federal Republic incorporated the five East German states. The communist system in East Germany simply dissolved.

Although some in West Germany were hesitant about immediate reunification, especially because of the economic costs that seemed likely, West German chancellor Helmut Kohl (KOLE) (b. 1930) sought to complete the process as quickly as possible. By early 1990, the emigration of East Germans to the West had become a flood. West German law treated these Germans as citizens, entitled to social benefits, so their arrival in such numbers presented a considerable financial burden. It seemed imperative for West Germany to regularize the situation as quickly as possible, assuming responsibility for the East and restoring its economy.

The division of Germany, symbolized by the Berlin Wall, had been central to the bipolar cold war world. Now Germany was a unified country for the first time since the Nazi era. What role would the new Germany play?

The End of the Soviet Union

Meanwhile, in the Soviet Union, what began as a restructuring of the communist system became a struggle for survival of the system itself. The much-trumpeted *glasnost* produced greater freedom in culture and politics, but Gorbachev sought to avoid alienating hard-line Communists, so he compromised, watering down the economic reforms essential to *perestroika*. The result proved a set of half measures that only made things worse. Because so little was done to force the entrenched Soviet bureaucracy to go along, the pace of economic reform was lethargic. The essential structures of the command economy weakened, but free-market forms of exchange among producers, distributors, and consumers did not emerge to replace them.

In 1986, an accidental explosion at the Soviet nuclear power plant at Chernobyl, in Ukraine (see **MAP 29.3**), released two hundred times as much radiation as the atomic bombs dropped on Hiroshima and Nagasaki combined. The accident contaminated food supplies and forced the abandonment of villages and thousands of square miles of formerly productive land. The radioactivity released would eventually hasten the deaths of at least 100,000 Soviet citizens. Despite his commitment to openness, Gorbachev reverted to old-fashioned Soviet secrecy for several weeks after the accident, in an effort to minimize what had happened. As a result, the eventual toll was far greater than it need have been. The accident and its aftermath seemed stark manifestation of all that was wrong with the Soviet system—its arrogance and secrecy, its premium on cutting corners to achieve targets imposed from above.

By the end of the 1980s, Soviet citizens felt betrayed by their earlier faith that Soviet communism was leading to a better future. A popular slogan spoke sarcastically of "seventy years on the road to nowhere." The economic situation was deteriorating, yet people were free to discuss alternatives as never before. As the discussion came to include once-unthinkable possibilities, such as privatization and a market economy, it became clear that the whole communist system was in jeopardy.

By mid-1990, moreover, the union of Soviet republics itself tottered on the verge of collapse. Lithuania led the way in calling for outright independence. But the stakes were raised enormously when the Russian republic, the most important in the USSR, followed Lithuania's lead. In June 1990, the newly elected chairman of Russia's parliament, Boris Yeltsin (1931–2007), persuaded the Russian republic to declare its sovereignty. Yeltsin had grown impatient with the slow pace of economic and political change. As a further challenge to Gorbachev, he dramatically resigned from the Communist Party during its televised national congress in July 1990. When, in June 1991, free elections in the Russian republic offered the first clear contest between communists determined to preserve the system and those seeking to replace it, the anticommunist Yeltsin was elected the republic's president by a surprising margin.

After tilting toward the hard-liners late in 1990, Gorbachev sought a return to reform after Yeltsin's election as Russia's president. He even engineered a new party charter that jettisoned much

⊕ Map 29.3—The Dissolution of the Soviet Union

As crisis gripped the Soviet system by the late 1980s, the republics of the Soviet Union began declaring first their sovereignty, and then their independence. Most of the fifteen republics that had made up the Soviet Union became part of a much looser confederation, the Commonwealth of Independent States, in 1991 and 1992.

SECTION SUMMARY

- The economies of the Soviet bloc were encountering stagnation by the 1970s, especially because they proved less adept than the capitalist economies at technological innovation.

- Disparate factors converged in Poland to yield the trade union Solidarity, which proved decisive in undermining the communist system in Poland.

- Seeking to overcome Soviet stagnation, Mikhail Gorbachev spearheaded a reform effort around *glasnost*, or "openness," and *perestroika*, or economic "restructuring," beginning in 1985.

- Changes in government policy in Poland and Hungary during 1989 produced a domino effect that led to the opening of the Berlin Wall and the fall of the communist regimes in east-central Europe.

- As Gorbachev's reform effort proved insufficient, the republics of the Soviet Union began pulling away, leading, by 1991, to the disintegration of the communist system and the breakup of the Soviet Union itself.

of the Marxist-Leninist doctrine that had guided communist practice since the revolution. In August, the hard-liners struck back with a coup that forced Gorbachev from power—but only for a few days. Yeltsin, supported by ordinary people in Moscow, stood up to the conspirators, while the secret police refused to follow orders to arrest Yeltsin and other opposition leaders. The coup quickly fizzled, but the episode galvanized the anticommunist movement and radically accelerated the pace of change.

Although Gorbachev was restored as head of the Soviet Union, the winner was Yeltsin, who quickly mounted an effort to dismantle the party apparatus before it could regroup. Anticommunist demonstrations across much of the Soviet Union toppled statues of Lenin and dissolved local party networks. In a referendum in December 1991, Ukraine, the second most populous Soviet republic, overwhelmingly voted for independence. Not only the communist system, but the Soviet Union itself was simply disintegrating. Late in December, Gorbachev finally resigned, paving the way for the official dissolution of the Soviet Union on January 1, 1992 (see **Map 29.3**). The European map again included Russia, as well as, in a matter of months, fourteen other sovereign states from what had been the Soviet Union.

CHAPTER SUMMARY

Western Europeans faced a situation of unprecedented cultural uncertainty as they pondered priorities in the wake of all that had befallen Europe from 1914 to 1949. Whereas some explored the loss of bearings, others called for a return to tradition, and still others found renewed possibilities in the Marxist tradition. At the same time, deeper interaction with the United States during and immediately after World War II led many to look to America for a more successful model, free of the ideological extremes that, it seemed, had helped lead Europe to disaster.

The United States sought to assist the rebuilding of western Europe, and partly because of American help, the western Europeans were able to restore their economies—and even surpass prewar production levels—with remarkable speed. And economic success greatly facilitated the restoration of democracy. At the same time, the shared experience of wartime led to a new social compact based on greater government responsibility for economic well-being and social welfare. By 1968, however, the Western democracies were beginning to experience unforeseen strains, some of which then deepened with the slowdown in economic growth during the 1970s.

In the Soviet bloc, Stalin's death in 1953 brought an end to the most repressive features of the communist system. Under his successor, Nikita Khrushchev, the Soviet Union seemed able to compete with the United States in areas from education to space travel. But the experiment with various forms of central planning in the Soviet bloc proved ever less successful. At the same time, the crushing of opposition and reform efforts, from East Berlin in 1953 to Prague in 1968, suggested that the Soviets were prepared to intervene as necessary to keep their satellites on a communist path.

The bipolar cold war framework meant a diminished influence in world affairs for the states of western Europe. Even their own security, in the face of the potential Soviet threat, seemed to depend on the United States. At the same time, the western Europeans gradually gave up control of their remaining colonial possessions, though not without instances of fighting and bitterness, evident most notably in the French effort to retain Algeria. However, France joined with Germany in the first key steps toward European integration, and such leaders as Charles de Gaulle and Willy Brandt showed the scope for European initiatives from within the limiting cold war framework.

Even as they faced new economic and political strains by the 1970s, the nations of western Europe could take for granted a substantial measure of prosperity and political legitimacy. In the communist part of Europe, in contrast, growing economic stagnation fueled a much deeper form of political disaffection during the 1970s and 1980s. New modes of opposition arose in Poland and Czechoslovakia, while in Hungary and eventually in the Soviet Union itself, communist leaders sought to renew the system from within. But the crisis of Soviet-style communism proved too deep, and by the end of 1991, discontent had produced forces for change that led to the breakup of the Soviet Union and the unraveling of the communist system in Europe.

FOCUS QUESTIONS

- What seemed the most likely overall cultural directions as western Europeans pondered priorities in light of all the disasters surrounding the era of the two world wars?

- What factors led to the surprisingly rapid restoration of democracy in much of continental western Europe after World War II?

- How did Soviet policy evolve after the death of Stalin in 1953?

- How did the place of western Europe in world affairs change during the cold war era?

- What led to the collapse of the communist system in the Soviet Union and its satellite states?

This icon will direct you to additional materials on the website: www.cengage.com/history/noble/westciv6e.

See our interactive eBook for map and primary source activities.

KEY TERMS

existentialism (p. 820)

North Atlantic Treaty Organization (NATO) (p. 823)

welfare state (p. 826)

Konrad Adenauer (p. 829)

Willy Brandt (p. 829)

Margaret Thatcher (p. 832)

Warsaw Pact (p. 833)

Prague Spring (p. 835)

Suez crisis (p. 838)

European Economic Community (EEC) (p. 841)

Helsinki Accords (p. 843)

Solidarity (p. 844)

Mikhail Gorbachev (p. 844)

CHAPTER OUTLINE

The Changing International Framework after the Cold War

Globalization and the Uncertainties of Democratic Capitalism

Lifestyles and Identities

The West in a Global Age

STABILITY | GROWTH | JOBS

A New World Order?

Meeting in London early in April 2009, leaders from around the world sought to coordinate responses to the most severe global economic crisis since the Great Depression of the 1930s. Despite the common aim, this meeting of leading economic powers and major multi-national financial organizations was notable for the range and diversity of the interests represented. Among the twenty-nine leaders who gathered for this photo are (first row, third through seventh from the left) French President Nicolas Sarkozy, Saudi Foreign Minister Prince Saud al-Faisal, Chinese President Hu Jintao, British Prime Minister Gordon Brown, and Brazilian President Lula Ignacio de Silva; (second row, second through fifth from the left) Indian Prime Minister Manmohan Singh, Turkish President Recep Tayyip Erdogan, U.S. President Barack Obama, and Russian President Dmitry Medvedev; (second row, second from the right) German Chancellor Angela Merkel; and (third row, fourth from the right) Japanese Prime Minister Taro Aso. (ERIC FEFERBERG/AFP/Getty Images)

A Continuing Experiment: The West and the World Since 1989

In April 2009 an entity known as the **Group of 20 (G-20)**, representing nineteen nations and the European Union (EU), met in London in its second attempt to deal with what was becoming the worst global economic crisis since the Great Depression of the 1930s. The group had met first in Washington the previous November, although signs of a financial and banking crisis had become evident by August 2007. That crisis stemmed most basically from a collapse in housing prices in a number of countries, including, most prominently, the United States, Britain, Ireland, Spain, and Iceland. But by April 2009 the financial crisis had led to a full-blown economic crisis: production and international trade were shrinking and unemployment was rapidly rising throughout the world.

Those involved in the G-20 represented almost 90 percent of the world's economy. In light of the magnitude of the crisis, a meeting of leaders of the world's largest economies was obviously essential. But these meetings marked a turning point in including such a wide array of countries, including several rapidly developing non-Western nations that had recently become major global economic players.

When, in the wake of depression and war, the Bretton Woods agreements of 1944 reworked the world's financial system (see page 812), it was largely the United States and Great Britain who called the shots. The economic problems of the 1970s, caused especially by rapid increases in oil prices (see page 831), led the world's seven largest economic powers (the United States, Japan, Germany, France, Britain, Italy, and Canada) to begin meeting regularly in an effort to coordinate economic policies. Seeking to avoid the isolation of Russia after the fall of communism, this **Group of Seven (G-7)** invited Russia to join, even though the size of the Russian economy did not warrant inclusion. So the G-7 became the G-8 (Group of 8).

By 2008, with such countries as China, India, and Brazil increasingly central to the world economy, the G-8 appeared anachronistic. The world's economies were so interconnected that response to the crisis clearly had to involve a much wider array of countries. The G-20 included, in addition to those in the G-8, Argentina, Australia, Brazil, China, India, Indonesia, Mexico, Saudi Arabia, South Africa, South Korea, and Turkey. The EU was also a member, even though four of its member nations were members of the G-20 as well. The emergence of the G-20 pointed to reform of the key institutions established at Bretton Woods—the World Bank and the International Monetary Fund—to give more say to the increasingly important economies outside the West.

FOCUS QUESTIONS

- Why and how did the relationship between western Europe and the United States change after the end of the cold war?

- What forces raised new questions about the effectiveness of Western-style democracy by the early years of the twenty-first century?

- How did the changes bound up with globalization affect identities in the West?

- What questions emerged as the West faced new crises all over the globe after the end of the cold war?

This icon will direct you to additional materials on the website: www .cengage.com/history/ noble/westciv6e.

See our interactive eBook for map and primary source activities.

Group of 20 (G-20) Informal grouping of twenty major economies, including a number from outside the West.

Group of Seven (G-7) This informal association of the world's seven largest economic powers (the United States, Japan, Germany, France, Britain, Italy, and Canada) began meeting during the 1970s in an effort to coordinate economic policies.

The turn to a new international economic order reflected the impact of the globalization process that, through the free flow of goods, credit, and currency, was drawing ever more of the world into a single competitive market economy. At the same time, however, a backlash against globalization had been growing since the later 1990s. Because the economic crisis seemed to demonstrate globalization's risks and dangers, it led to more insistent calls for financial controls and trade barriers to insulate national economies. So even as the G-20 summit meetings seemed to constitute a coordinated global response to the crisis, they also provoked fears and protests around the world.

At its two meetings, the G-20 sought to resist antiglobalization pressures by agreeing to promote still freer international trade. It also called for greater global uniformity in financial regulation and accounting standards. But even as national leaders sought to act in concert at these international meetings, they tended to go their own way on the national level, partly because the countries of the world found themselves caught up in the crisis in quite different ways. Some, like the United States, were net debtors, owing more to others than others owed to them. Others, like China, were net creditors. Some, like Germany, were more dependent on exports than were others, like France. Some were better able—or more willing—to stimulate their economies through deficit spending, itself a form of borrowing, and one that might threaten inflation down the road. Especially in light of such differences, the question was whether so large and heterogeneous a grouping as the G-20 could act effectively to coordinate responses to the economic crisis.

The economic crisis developed from within the wider new international framework that had emerged after the end of the cold war. That framework had quickly come to entail ethnic conflict in parts of Europe and tensions within the Western alliance. The former communist countries scrambled to institute Western-style democratic capitalism, and many of them were accepted into the European Union (EU) during the first decade of the twenty-first century. But even in the established Western democracies, unprecedented economic, technological, and demographic change raised new questions, some of which threatened the political consensus that had crystallized since World War II.

Quite apart from its economic effects, globalization seemed to make the world more unified and homogeneous, yet the backlash against it included the embrace of traditional cultural expressions, such as the headscarf worn by many Muslim women in Europe. But that backlash also included violence and terrorism. And it raised new questions about cultural pluralism, assimilation, and the meaning of citizenship all over the Western world.

THE CHANGING INTERNATIONAL FRAMEWORK AFTER THE COLD WAR

Why and how did the relationship between western Europe and the United States change after the end of the cold war?

The disintegration of the Soviet system by 1991 meant the swift, unexpected end of the bipolar cold war framework that had defined the era since World War II (see **MAP 30.1**). An immediate and troubling outcome was renewed ethnic conflict in parts of Europe. Although Czechoslovakia divided peacefully into two nations, the Czech and Slovak Republics, on January 1, 1993, ethnic concerns elsewhere produced violence and massive human rights violations. Violence also found expression in increased international terrorism by the early twenty-first century. Efforts to address the unforeseen problems of the post–cold war world raised questions about the respective roles of multinational entities, such as NATO, the EU, and the UN.

New Power Relationships in the West

Although its role was less clear with the end of the Soviet threat, NATO began expanding in 1999 to encompass most of the former communist states of eastern Europe, from Poland to Bulgaria. To those countries, NATO membership meant the definitive repudiation of the cold war division of Europe.

Whereas the collapse of communism meant renewed pride and independence for the former satellite states, Russia initially felt humiliated as a onetime superpower that was now diminished in size, struggling economically, and was far less influential in world affairs. Russian leaders disliked the expansion of NATO, and they grew belligerent when, by 2008, NATO seemed poised to admit countries like Georgia and Ukraine, which had been part of the Soviet Union itself. As the Russians saw it, NATO had always been directed at Russia, and its expansion towards Russia could only threaten Russian security.

Germany, which promptly reunified as communism collapsed, seemed a major beneficiary of the end of the cold war. Whereas some worried that the new Germany might return to bullying and aggressiveness, others were eager to have Germany assume a stronger diplomatic and even military role, and thus, the responsibilities commensurate with its population and economic strength.

The Federal Republic officially moved its capital from provincial Bonn to Berlin in 1999, when a costly makeover of the old parliament (Reichstag) building had been completed. As it happened, precisely as the refurbished building was opened, German forces were involved in their first combat roles since World War II, participating in NATO air strikes in response to what seemed genocidal aggression in Yugoslavia. Still, though Germany contributed significantly to international peacekeeping efforts, many Germans remained reluctant to support an expanded international military role. German military spending remained low compared with that of the United States, Britain, and France.

The European Union

As the **European Union (EU)** continued to expand by the early twenty-first century, it became clear that it constituted one of the notable experiments in Western history. Though still very much in progress, that experiment had produced a complex web of institutional arrangements that was bizarre and complex in one sense, bold and innovative in another.

RENEWING THE UNION

After the oil crises of the 1970s, and amid concern over economic stagnation, the twelve members of the European Community committed themselves in 1985 to creating a true single market with genuinely free competition by the end of 1992. Meeting at Maastricht, in the Netherlands, in 1991, leaders of the member countries agreed to a new "Treaty on European Union," which,

CHRONOLOGY

October 3, 1990	Reunification of Germany
1991	Beginning of fighting in Yugoslavia
February 1992	Maastricht agreements signed, expanding scope of European Union
December 14, 1996	Bosnian peace accords signed
May 1997	Blair becomes prime minister of Britain
1998	UN establishes international criminal court in The Hague
1999	Euro launched as currency of European Union
	NATO bombing of Serbia in response to Serb policies in Kosovo
	Renewal of Russia's war with Chechnya
May 2000	Putin becomes president of Russia
2001	Milosevic put on trial for war crimes at The Hague
September 11, 2001	Terrorist attacks on United States
March–April 2003	U.S.- and British-led forces overthrow Saddam Hussein's regime in Iraq
September 2003	WTO meeting in Cancún, Mexico, breaks up amid protests
2004	EU adds ten new member countries, for a total of twenty-five
March 11, 2004	Terrorist bombings on commuter trains in Madrid
May–June 2005	EU draft constitution rejected in referenda in France and the Netherlands
July 7, 2005	Terrorist attack on the London public transportation system
October–November 2005	Riots by Muslim youth in Paris and other French cities
November 2005	Angela Merkel becomes German chancellor
2007	Beginnings of global finacial crisis
May 2007	Sarkozy becomes president of France
August 2008	Russia defeats Georgia in conflict over breakaway border regions
January 2009	Obama becomes U.S. president

● Map 30.1—Europe in the Early Twenty-First Century

The reunification of Germany and the breakup of the Soviet Union, Yugoslavia, and Czechoslovakia fundamentally altered the map of Europe during the 1990s.

European Union (EU)
New name for the European Community after the Maastricht agreements of 1991. As of 2008, it consisted of twenty-seven member countries.

Maastricht agreements
1991 agreements among member states of the European Union. They agreed to expand cooperation on social, foreign, judicial, and security matters and adopted a timetable for common economic policies.

STRUCTURE AND ORGANIZATION

euro The common currency launched by the European Union in 1999 and 2002 to eliminate the cost of currency exchange and boost trade and economic interaction.

among other things, provided for a common policy on workers' rights and a common currency and central banking structure by 1999. Although the EU's members eventually ratified most of the **Maastricht agreements**, member countries could opt out of certain provisions. Even as the new common currency, the **euro**, was introduced in two major steps, in 1999 and 2002, four of the now-fifteen EU members, including Britain, remained outside the common currency mechanism. Still, the common currency facilitated a notable increase in supranational mergers and takeovers—a trend that threatened some, but promised greater international competitiveness for European firms.

So successful was the EU that others clamored to join. The EU added ten new member countries in 2004, and then two more in 2007, increasing the membership to twenty-seven. Ten of these twelve new members were formerly communist countries, where the lure of membership had significantly strengthened democracy. The EU had insisted on democratic institutions and alignment with EU procedures as a condition of membership. And just as EU membership had helped transform the economies of once-poor countries like Greece, Ireland, Spain, and Portugal, the new members from east-central Europe seemed poised to profit economically as well.

By the early twenty-first century, the EU included a network of five interlocking institutions, seated in Brussels, Strasbourg, Luxembourg, and Frankfurt. Much of its power was wielded by an unelected elite of technical experts in the EU's core body, the Commission in Brussels. Thus, critics charged that the EU suffered from a "democratic deficit," but defenders countered that only insofar as it was apolitical could the Commission pursue the wider interests of the community, rather than merely representing national interests.

By the early twenty-first century, "Europe" had become a kind of hybrid, at once a collection of sovereign states and a genuinely supranational entity, thanks to the gradual, incremental emergence

The Democratic Reichstag, Berlin The centerpiece of the renovation of the German parliament building, completed in 1999, was the addition of a glass dome, intended to manifest the openness of Germany's democracy as its capital moved from Bonn to Berlin. (Reimer Wulf/akg-images)

of the EU over more than fifty years. In spheres such as trade, agriculture, and the environment, the EU was dominant; national governments had little freedom of action. But other spheres, such as defense, taxation, and criminal justice, remained mostly national prerogatives. The question was whether the EU would continue to expand its sphere of competence—and in what directions.

The creation of an internal customs union, benign though it seemed, had never committed the EU to freer trade with nonmember countries—the United States, for example, or the developing nations of the non-Western world. Indeed, 40 percent of EU spending by 2008 went to the widely criticized **Common Agricultural Policy (CAP)**, entailing subsidies to protect farmers from outside competition. Political opposition to change remained strong, especially in France, which, by 2008, was receiving twice as much from these subsidies as any other EU member.

Common Agricultural Policy (CAP) A major pillar of the European Union, it entailed subsidies to protect farmers from outside competition. The CAP was widely criticized by advocates of freer world trade.

Especially with expansion coming in 2004, it seemed essential that the EU clarify and streamline its procedures through a formal constitution. But the EU's momentum was unexpectedly halted when, in May 2005, French voters rejected the EU's new draft constitution in a referendum. Voters in the Netherlands followed suit shortly thereafter. Most of the EU's member states required approval only by their elected parliaments, and such approval had, for the most part, been readily forthcoming. But the setbacks in France and the Netherlands indicated doubts and frustrations that could be found throughout Europe. Some felt that the recent expansion had itself been too radical a step, especially as discussion continued over further expansion to include, for example, Turkey, Albania, and Ukraine. Concerns about economic well-being were also at work; some worried that the recent eastward expansion of the EU had intensified competition from lower-wage countries, leading to downward pressures on living standards at home.

With the Lisbon Treaty of December 2007, the EU made a second try at systematic reorganization. If ratified, the treaty would, among other things, provide for a president and a foreign minister to represent the EU in world affairs. Although the vast majority of the members approved the Lisbon Treaty, Irish voters rejected it in June 2008. Efforts to reach a compromise followed, but the future of the Lisbon Treaty remained uncertain.

THE CONSTITUTION AND NEW MEMBER STATES

Ethnic Conflict and Peacekeeping Roles

As the members of the European Union struggled to create a supranational entity, forces in the opposite direction—subnational, religious, ethnic, tribal—grew more powerful in parts of the West, sometimes producing violent conflict. The most dramatic instance was in postcommunist

🌐 **MAP 30.2—Ethnic Conflict in the Balkans and East-Central Europe**

Much of east-central Europe, and particularly the Balkans, has long been an area of complex ethnic mixture. The end of communist rule opened the way to ethnic conflict, most tragically in what had been Yugoslavia. This map shows ethnic distribution in the region in the mid-1990s.

Yugoslavia, where ethnic and religious conflict led to the disintegration of the country in a series of brutal wars among Serbs, Croats, Bosnian Muslims, and ethnically Albanian Kosovars (see **MAP 30.2**). Defining events of the 1990s, these wars proved a major challenge for the new international order after the cold war.

THE WAR IN BOSNIA Although much was made of ancient ethnic and religious differences once Yugoslavia began falling apart, the area had long traditions of pluralism and tolerance. Ethnic relations had been poisoned, however, by recent events, especially the civil war during World War II (see page 811). The situation had remained reasonably stable under Josip Tito's independent communist regime, which insisted on Yugoslav unity while affording some measure of regional autonomy. But within a few years of Tito's death in 1980, intellectuals concerned about cultural distinctiveness began undermining the wider Yugoslav identity that Tito had sought to foster.

After the fall of communism, Slovenia and Croatia declared themselves independent of Yugoslavia in May 1991. At the same time, the Serb leader of the remaining Yugoslavia, Slobodan Milosevic (mih-LOH-suh-vitch) (1941–2006), a former communist, embraced Serb nationalism at least partly to maintain his own power. His aim was to unite all the Serbs, two million of whom lived outside Serbia, mostly in Croatia and Bosnia-Herzegovina.

Starting in 1991, Milosevic proceeded with extreme brutality, fostering **ethnic cleansing**—forced relocation or mass killing to rid the territory in question of non-Serb inhabitants. In the Bosnian capital, Sarajevo, a culturally diverse city known for its tolerant, cosmopolitan atmosphere, more than 10,000 civilians, including 1,500 children, were killed by shelling and sniper fire during a Serb siege from 1992 to early 1996.

When a Serb mortar killed thirty-seven civilians in a marketplace in Sarajevo in August 1995, NATO forces responded with air strikes that led to peace accords and the end of fighting by early 1996. Although the peace agreement envisioned a unified Bosnian state, the contending Serbs, Croats, and Bosnian Muslims quickly began carving out separate spheres, violating agreements about repatriation and the rights of minorities. Even over a decade later, Bosnia remained ethnically divided and dependent on the international peacekeeping force stationed there.

ethnic cleansing An effort, through forced relocation or even mass killing, to remove an unwanted ethnic group from a particular geographical area. This tactic was implemented by Yugoslavian ruler Slobodan Milosevic to unite all Serbs.

THE WAR IN KOSOVO

The next phase of the Yugoslav tragedy centered on the province of Kosovo (KOH-suh-voh), which Serbs viewed as the cradle of their nationhood (see **MAP 30.2**). For complex historical reasons, however, Serbs had long constituted only a minority of its population. The majority were ethnic Albanians. The fissuring of Yugoslavia emboldened the Kosovars, who had come to envision full independence, as opposed to mere autonomy within the Serbian part of what remained of Yugoslavia.

When Milosevic struck against the Kosovars in the spring of 1999, ruthlessly pursuing ethnic cleansing, the Western powers again intervened, first convening a meeting with Serb and Kosovar leaders on Kosovo's future. When the Serb-led remnant of Yugoslavia refused to sign, NATO made good on its threats to bomb Serbia in retaliation. The bombing, concentrated on such economic targets as bridges and power stations, continued for eleven weeks in late 1999.

Critics argued that it set a dubious precedent to attack Serbia for refusing a settlement that would have ceded territory and opened the rest of the country to quasi-occupation by NATO. No one denied that Kosovo was part of Serbia, so the NATO action was an overt interference in the internal affairs of a sovereign state. Even the notion that the operation was a humanitarian response to genocide seemed hypocritical to some, who asked why the international community had done nothing in response to the far more systematic genocide in the African nation of Rwanda in 1994, when 800,000 people had been killed in a hundred days. Defenders countered that it was partly because of the soul-searching in the aftermath of Rwanda that the Western countries were now changing the rules and taking responsibility for concerted action.

Once the NATO bombing began, the Serbs intensified their ethnic cleansing of Kosovo, burning homes, forcing 800,000 refugees to flee into neighboring countries. But the bombing finally led both the Serbs and the Kosovars to pull back from their more extreme demands, and Russia joined in the multinational peacekeeping force in Kosovo in the aftermath. Still, the outcome bore little relationship to the multiethnic pluralism NATO had been seeking. As Kosovars came to dominate the now-ravaged territory, still nominally part of Serbia, they carried out ethnic cleansing of their own. Ethnic Albanians came to constitute over 90 percent of Kosovo's 2 million people, and ethnic separation became the rule. Finally, in February 2008, Kosovo declared its independence. Most of the world quickly recognized the new state, even in the face of fierce opposition from Serbia and Russia.

WAR CRIMES TRIALS

Although Milosevic was the first sitting head of state to be indicted for war crimes, he proved resilient, initially surviving his defeat in Kosovo in 1999. He lost the presidential election in September 2000, however, and the following year, under pressure from the international community, the Serbian government within the rump Yugoslav confederation turned him over to a UN war crimes tribunal in The Hague. There, as his trial dragged on, he died in prison in 2006.

Others accused of war crimes were the Bosnian Serb leader Radovan Karadžić (KA-rahd-zich) and his top general, Ratko Mladic (MLAH-ditch), who was charged with the slaughter of as many as 8,000 Bosnian Muslim men when his forces took the town of Srebrenica (shreb-reh-NEET-sah) in 1995. Even after their indictments, each long evaded capture, partly because they were deemed heroes by many Serbs. Finally, however, Karadžić was apprehended and went on trial in The Hague in 2008. Like Milosevic, he denied the legitimacy of the court and refused to cooperate in its proceedings.

Mourning in Bosnia On July 11, 2009, a Muslim woman mourns by the grave of a relative during the reburial of 534 newly identified victims of the massacre of up to 8,000 Muslim men by Bosnian Serb forces at Srebrenica in 1995. Each year on July 11, the anniversary of the massacre, bones excavated from mass graves are matched to a name and reburied at the nearby Memorial Center of Potocari. As of the 2009 ceremony, over 4,000 of the victims had been reburied at the Memorial Center. (Damir Sagolj/Reuters/Landov)

Responding to Global Terrorism

Also complicating international relations was an increase in the scale and extent of terrorism, sometimes pitting non-Westerners against the West. European venues ranged from Northern Ireland to the Basque region of northern Spain to the rebellious Russian republic of Chechnya to the subways of London.

With this new terror already erupting, a terrorist attack of unprecedented proportions shook the United States on September 11, 2001. Suicide hijackers seized four large airliners, crashing one into each of the towers of the World Trade Center in New York City and another into the Pentagon, just outside Washington, D.C. Passengers on the fourth plane, apparently also headed for Washington, forced it to crash in Pennsylvania. The World Trade Center crashes collapsed both towers, which had been among the world's most visible landmarks. The coordinated attacks claimed the lives of over three thousand people from eighty-two countries.

The United States proclaimed this assault an act of war, and the NATO alliance invoked Article 5 for the first time: The attack on one of its members was to be treated as an attack against all. U.S. leaders promptly assigned responsibility to al Qaeda, an international terrorist network led by the wealthy Saudi Arabian Osama bin Laden, who was living in exile in Afghanistan. There, he and others of his network were protected by the Taliban regime, whose extreme, radically fundamentalist version of Islam they shared in certain respects.

Led by President George W. Bush, the United States initiated military action against the Taliban regime later in 2001. Several

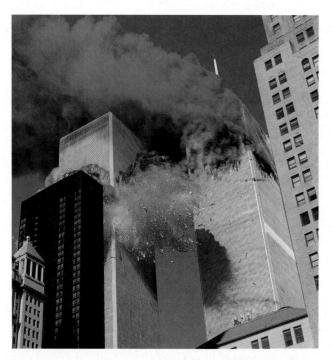

Terror in New York City, September 11, 2001 With one of the twin towers of the World Trade Center burning from an attack at 8:45 A.M., a second hijacked plane crashed into the second tower less than an hour later. By the end of the morning, both towers had collapsed. (Chao Soi Cheong/AP/Wide World Photos)

weeks of U.S. bombing enabled Afghan opposition forces to oust the Taliban government and force al Qaeda onto the defensive. But both bin Laden and the Taliban survived, and the outcome in Afghanistan remained uncertain as of 2009. Al Qaeda regrouped sufficiently to launch terrorist attacks against Western interests in Morocco in 2002 and Saudi Arabia in 2003. Then, in March 2004, the network struck in Europe for the first time with a series of terrorist bombings on commuter trains in Madrid, killing over 200 people.

But terror could be bred in Western countries as well. The four terrorists who blew themselves up on the London public transportation system in July 2005, killing 52 others, were British citizens, Muslims of Pakistani descent, acting on their own. Whatever its sources, such terrorism posed an ongoing threat to Western security and complicated the West's relations with the non-Western world.

Divisions Over the Invasion of Iraq

The United States won widespread support for its effort to combat international terrorism. But the Americans encountered formidable opposition in 2002 when the Bush administration began to call for the overthrow of Saddam Hussein's regime in Iraq. The Iraqi dictator was charged with stockpiling chemical and biological weapons of mass destruction in violation of a UN agreement. Iraq was also accused of developing a nuclear weapons program and supporting terrorist networks like al Qaeda. Moreover, Saddam had long tyrannized the Iraqi people.

As it began to appear that the United States might be prepared to act unilaterally, the Iraq issue became one of the most divisive in recent history, seriously straining Western relations. An array of countries, with France, Germany, and Russia in the forefront, insisted that UN weapons inspectors be given more time to assess Iraqi compliance. Yet the American call for military action won a good deal of international support. Most notably, British prime minister Tony Blair made Britain a full partner of the United States. But even in countries like Britain, whose governments supported U.S. policy, the public tended to be strongly opposed to a military showdown in Iraq.

When it became clear they could not win UN endorsement, the United States and Britain sent military forces into Iraq in March 2003 and toppled Saddam Hussein's regime within six weeks. In the aftermath of the invasion, it had gradually become clear that Iraq had not been actively developing weapons of mass destruction. In addition, evidence suggested that both the U.S. and British governments had relied to some extent on faulty intelligence or had used intelligence selectively to justify the invasion.

The military success proved easier than most people had expected, but the tasks of reconstruction proved far more difficult than U.S. officials had envisioned, especially because an anti-occupation insurgency developed after the United States declared active hostilities ended on May 1, 2003. Sectarian and ethnic violence seriously complicated the effort of Iraqi leaders to develop a workable new government.

A "surge" in U.S. troop strength in 2007 helped reduce the violence, and in November 2008, the Iraqi parliament approved a troop withdrawal agreement with the United States. American forces were to withdraw to bases by the middle of 2009 and to leave Iraq altogether by the end of 2011. Whereas some found this outcome a vindication of the invasion, critics argued that America was being forced to leave, and that the outcome was not likely to be the unified, democratic, and stable Iraq that President Bush had said was the American aim. One possibility was a return to sectarian violence, which might spill over, inflaming religious and ethnic divisions in much of the Middle East. At the same time, the war had been hugely costly to all parties. As one measure, two million Iraqis had fled their country as refugees since 2003.

U.S. Unilateralism

A major source of friction between the United States and Europe was growing U.S. **unilateralism**—the country's willingness to go its own way in the world on the basis of what seemed its own interests. As the world's superpower, the United States was increasingly prone to such unilateralism during the 1990s, and then moved more decisively in that direction after the terrorist attacks of September 2001.

While an overwhelming majority of nations—120, to be exact—supported the establishment of the UN's International Criminal Court in The Hague in 1998, the United States was among only seven that opposed it. Then, as the court was being established, the United States sought an exemption for itself because it worried that American peacekeepers might be especially tempting targets of false accusations of war crimes. Such concerns were not groundless, and

unilateralism Term describing the increasing willingness of the United States to go its own way in world affairs after the end of the cold war, and especially after the terrorist attacks on the United States in September 2001.

they indicated the unique problems the United States faced as the world's undisputed, and often resented, superpower. But many found it disturbing that the United States did not want to play by the same rules as the vast majority.

Some Europeans continued to look to the UN to check American hegemony, but others, including many non-Europeans, found a stronger European military and diplomatic presence the best potential balance to the United States. EU forces were prominent in peacekeeping missions in Macedonia, Bosnia, Kosovo, Afghanistan, and Congo. Yet the Europeans were much less willing than Americans to use force in the first place. As of early 2006, the United States was spending 3.4 percent of its gross domestic product (GDP) on defense, Europe 1.9 percent.

Still, some observers noted the scope for the United States and Europe to play complementary roles in world affairs. Americans were better at fighting wars, but Europeans might be better at preventing them. Precisely because they were not prone to threaten force, Europeans could play a constructive role of moral suasion, even if it was up to the Americans to provide the muscle.

Many Europeans welcomed the election of Barack Obama to the U.S. presidency in November 2008 because he seemed likely to adopt a more conciliatory and less unilateralist stance. But how, more specifically, Obama might renew or deepen the partnership between the United States and Europe remained to be seen.

SECTION SUMMARY

- The end of the cold war opened the way to a series of new issues that the West had to confront, even as it also changed power relationships within the West itself.

- The European Union expanded and gathered strength, but also encountered unforeseen setbacks.

- Ethnic conflict contributed to the breakup of Yugoslavia in a series of wars that included major human rights violations and significant dilemmas for peacekeepers.

- International terrorism, often reflecting tensions between the West and the Islamic world, became a major concern throughout the West.

- Increasing U.S. unilateralism, evident most dramatically in the U.S.-led invasion of Iraq, alienated many Europeans.

GLOBALIZATION AND THE UNCERTAINTIES OF DEMOCRATIC CAPITALISM

What forces raised new questions about the effectiveness of Western style democracy by the early years of the twenty-first century?

Democracy had become the unchallenged norm in western Europe by the 1980s, and after the fall of communism, the former Soviet bloc countries seemed eager to adopt the western European model. But though patterns in several of the former communist countries came to approximate those of the mature democracies, the transition proved problematic in others, most dramatically in Russia. Even in the established democracies, globalization combined with technological and demographic changes to alter the socioeconomic framework, producing new challenges for governments and even threatening the socioeconomic compact that had emerged after World War II.

The Postcommunist Experiment

The former communist countries had little experience with the give-and-take of democratic politics, and their fragile new political systems had to engineer the difficult transition to a free-market economy. With their economies close to chaos as the transition began, the effort led to unemployment, inflation, and widespread corruption. No longer could ordinary people count on the subsidized consumer goods or the welfare safety net the communist regimes had provided. While many suffered great hardship, some former communist functionaries quickly got rich by taking over state-owned companies.

The case of Poland showed that strains and risks remained, even within the new framework of democratic governance and market economy. Although GDP grew by 50 percent from 1990 to 2005, as Poland attracted considerable foreign investment, the costs were high for those left out. In 2006, unemployment stood at 18 percent, ever more people were falling into poverty, and the gap between rich and poor was widening. The state was widely seen as weak, bloated, inefficient, and highly corrupt. Services were poor, and the tax system was full of loopholes. Low electoral turnouts manifested widespread disillusionment with the new political class—and even doubts about democracy itself.

MAP 30.3—GDP per Capita in Europe, 2008

Gross domestic product (GDP) per capita is a widely recognized measure of national economic success. By the early twenty first century, this measure varied dramatically among the European countries, revealing the wide disparity in economic well-being across the Continent. The former communist countries continued to lag, even as some were growing at impressive rates. The U.S. figure was $42,000, and Canada's was $32,900. (Figures are from 2008, before the worst of the economic crisis.)

In Russia, where communism had far deeper roots than elsewhere in the former Soviet bloc, the transition from communism proved even more difficult. Although privatization proceeded rapidly, it mostly benefited former Communist Party functionaries, some of whom became instant multimillionaires. By the mid-1990s, Russia had evolved a kind of "crony capitalism," with a small group of economic oligarchs manipulating much of the economy through dubious banking practices and outright extortion—and paying no taxes. After ten years, the postcommunist Russian economy had shrunk to perhaps half its former size. Especially sobering were the demographic effects: Russians were dying young and having few children. By 2001, the population had dropped to 143 million—a decline of 6 million people in ten years.

The combination of economic stringency and governmental weakness produced a chilling increase in street crime, from muggings to auto theft. Moreover, dozens of journalists, politicians, and business leaders were murdered gangland style, with the killers never apprehended. Particularly appalling was the 2006 assassination of the highly respected journalist Anna Politkovskaya (po-lit-koff-SKY-ah), who was killed in broad daylight, with her body left in the elevator of her apartment. In November 2008, the trial of three men suspected of involvement in her murder was suspended amid deepening controversy.

As Russia's president during the first postcommunist years, Boris Yeltsin seemed a committed reformer—surely the best hope for an orderly transition to democracy and a market economy. He enjoyed widespread support from the Western democracies, but among Russians, the difficult circumstances produced disenchantment with reform, nostalgia for the stability of communism, and much resentment of the West.

Vladimir Putin Emerged in 1999 to become Russia's dominant political leader.

As it sought to engineer the transition to democratic capitalism, the Yeltsin government had to deal with the attempted defection of Chechnya (CHECH-nyah), a small, largely Muslim republic located in the Caucasus (see **Map 29.3** on page 848). Long restive under Russian control, the Chechens began demanding independence after the collapse of the Soviet Union in 1991, finally provoking war with Russia in 1994. In the aftermath of a compromise in 1996, Chechen hard-liners oppressed the Russian minority, kidnapping and enslaving some, and even killed journalists and international aid workers. When Chechnyan Islamic militants began spreading the anti-Russian message to adjacent Dagestan, Russia renewed full-scale war with Chechnya in 1999.

This renewed confrontation made possible the rise of **Vladimir Putin** (POO-tin), who had been director of Russia's secret police. Calling for a tough stance on Chechnya, Putin was Yeltsin's choice for prime minister in 1999, and he immediately delivered on his promise to clear Dagestan of Chechen terrorists. Whereas most Russians had disliked the earlier confrontation with Chechnya, by now they had had enough—not only of Chechen defiance, but also of Russian weakness. Putin's popularity soared as he talked tough and acted tougher. A brutal Russian assault late in 1999 left much of Chechnya, especially the capital, Grozny, in ruins.

Under Vladimir Putin, Russia was sometimes aggressive in seeking to establish a leading role in a number of the states that were formerly part of the Soviet Union. Russian relations with Ukraine were particularly rocky as Ukraine angled for membership in NATO and even, eventually, the European Union. Putin is shown here speaking informally with Ukrainian prime minister Yulia Tymoshenko at a meeting of many of the former Soviet republics at Chisinau, the capital of Moldova, on November 14, 2008. (Alexei Nikolsky/RIA Novosti/Reuters/Landov)

In poor health and increasingly erratic, Yeltsin resigned at the end of 1999, essentially to make way for Putin, who was elected president in 2000, and then reelected in 2004. Although Putin was prohibited by law from running again in 2008, his hand-picked successor, Dmitry Medvedev (med-VYEH-dev), was elected easily, and Putin continued to wield power from his new post as prime minister.

As Russia's leader, Putin strengthened the Russian state against the forces of disintegration that emerged after communism, and he remained quite popular among Russians. Still, outside observers tended to give his performance decidedly mixed marks. In the economic sphere, the post-Soviet decline seemed at last to have been reversed by 2006, thanks in part to high prices for Russia's abundant oil and gas. Tax collection had improved, some well-run companies had emerged, and the Russian middle class was clearly expanding. But the political order suffered from secrecy and governmental inaccessibility. The media were increasingly concentrated and subject to restrictions and controls.

To counter demographic decline, Putin's government sought to promote a baby boom. A 2007 law expanded maternity leave benefits and granted mothers educational and other vouchers for a second child and for any children thereafter. Putin also increased spending on health and social programs. But more important, the economic upturn made child rearing a more plausible option for Russian couples. Still, though births began rising after 2006, deaths continued to outpace births, and Russian life expectancy was the lowest in Europe. Some demographic experts warned that because the number of women of childbearing age was still to decline, Russia was caught in a "demographic pit" that would be hard to escape.

Stinging from Russia's post-Soviet weakness, a considerable majority of Russians supported Putin as he sought to establish a Russian sphere of influence and to win international acceptance as a major international player. In the summer of 2008, a showdown between Russia and Georgia, a small, former Soviet republic (see **Map 30.1**), over two breakaway Georgian provinces produced controversy over Russia's place in the new international order.

After becoming independent with the breakup of the Soviet Union, Georgia developed close ties with the United States, especially after U.S.-educated Mikheil Saakashvili (sah-kahsh-VEE-lee) was elected president in 2004. As of August 2008, Georgia had 2,000 troops in Iraq, making it the third largest contributor to the coalition, after the United States and Britain. Georgia aspired to NATO membership, as did the much larger former Soviet republic of Ukraine, yet Russian authorities repeatedly asserted that they would not accept NATO membership for either. Still, Georgia and Ukraine were now sovereign states, in principle, free to make their own decisions about international alignments and foreign policy.

Dispute over NATO membership lay in the background as a confrontation between Russia and Georgia developed over the status of Abkhazia and South Ossetia, provinces that, though nominally part of Georgia, had never effectively been incorporated into the country after it became independent. Populated largely by ethnic groups that were neither Georgian nor Russian, both provinces sought to break definitively from Georgia. They looked for support to Russia, which warned repeatedly that it would send troops to block any Georgian effort to encompass the two provinces.

When Saakashvili used force against South Ossetia in July 2008, the Russians intervened as promised, quickly routing Georgia's troops early in August. Saakashvili seemed to have anticipated active support from the West, especially the United States, but the Americans were already involved in difficult wars in Afghanistan and Iraq, and it was not clear what more forceful response would have been possible in any case. So Georgia had to settle for strong protests against Russian belligerence from the United States and its NATO allies.

Other countries that had been part of the Soviet empire, especially Ukraine, but also the Baltic states and Poland, watched nervously, asking themselves what support they could expect from the West in the event of some comparable Russian threat. To be sure, those like Poland and the Baltic states that were now NATO members faced what seemed a very different situation. Still, the Poles and even the Czechs were eager to accept a U.S. missile shield, even in the face of Russian opposition, because of nervousness about the scope for renewed Russian expansionism.

Russia had clearly drawn a line over Georgia, but how far might its ambitions go? For some, Russia's belligerence suggested a return to cold war aspirations, but now with naked national self-interest replacing even the pretense of ideological aims. Especially at a time of record oil prices and growing concerns in the West over long-term sources of energy, Russia seemed to be returning to the struggle for spheres of influence and control of resources that had characterized the nineteenth century.

But others accented Russia's defensiveness. It was not unreasonable, they insisted, for Russia to worry that NATO expansion threatened Russian security, even that the presence of NATO on Russia's borders could destabilize the Russian Confederation itself. Moreover, the Russians had a plausible case in arguing that if the West was to allow Kosovo to break way from Serbia, it should also be prepared to allow the dissident provinces to break away from Georgia.

Two Models of Democratic Capitalism

By the 1980s, much of western Europe had caught up with the United States in standard of living, and it was increasingly clear that two models of democratic capitalism were at work—and to some extent in competition. The U.S. model, largely shared by Britain since the Thatcher period (see page 832), stressed free enterprise and the market, whereas continental western Europe had evolved a **social market economy,** with greater commitment to security, consensus, and communitarian values. The European model provided a more substantial safety net—in health care, for example—as well as a stronger commitment to subsidized transportation and day care.

In some respects, it was almost as if the Americans and Europeans had passed in the night in the decades since World War II. In the United States, which had long prided itself on its egalitarianism vis-à-vis class-bound Europe, disparities between rich and poor had become greater than anywhere in the developed world by the early twenty-first century. In business firms, the ratio of executive compensation to worker salaries was dramatically higher in the United States than in Europe.

Perhaps still more significant was the difference in attitudes toward such disparities. Wary of extreme inequalities of income, Europeans tended to view unrestricted competition more as a threat than an opportunity. Whereas most Europeans found the inequalities and insecurities of American life unacceptable, Americans accented the scope for upward mobility that their

social market economy A model of democratic capitalism, practiced in much of continental Europe, that seeks to temper free-market principles with communitarian values and a substantial social safety net.

system offered. As long as anyone could get rich, it did not matter that some were much richer than others. Americans were far more likely than Europeans to see themselves as moving up. In France, 75 percent of young people aspired to a civil service job, primarily because of the security such a job seemed to entail.

Americans had grown more skeptical than Europeans about government and its capacity to provide social services. Accustomed to a strong government role in society, Europeans had difficulty understanding how such measures as government-sponsored health care could cause waves of controversy among Americans.

New Economic Competitors

Just as the West became concerned with economic challenges from the Soviet Union in the 1950s, Japan by the later 1970s, and a wider array of East Asian "tigers" by the 1980s, it came to view China, and to a lesser extent India, as potential economic superpowers by the early twenty-first century. Although still nominally communist, China was increasingly willing to compete in the global economic marketplace and did well at manufacturing, thanks especially to a cheap, disciplined labor force. With its favorable trade balance, China came to hold such a large share of the U.S. national debt that it seemed capable, at least potentially, of compromising the independence of American foreign policy.

The former communist countries of east-central Europe proved tremendously appealing to manufacturing companies in the West, especially automakers. Although the communist system had not proved competitive over the long term, it had left a reasonably good infrastructure, as well as a skilled and disciplined labor force costing only about 20 percent as much as elsewhere in the EU. By 2006, major carmakers in France, Germany, and Italy were being forced to cut jobs and benefits at home in order to remain competitive. But it was not only the new EU members that were attracting such investment. Volkswagen was building new plants in Russia and China. Some were predicting that auto manufacture in western Europe would cease altogether in ten to fifteen years.

Responding to New Economic Challenges

As global economic competition intensified, governments throughout western Europe found it more difficult to pay for all the benefits they had gradually come to promise. By the early 1990s, some found the social compact all too generous—and unsustainable. Falling birthrates and aging populations meant that relatively fewer workers would have to foot the pension and health care bills for increasing numbers of older people. Although most agreed that reform was necessary, reform proposals led to protests, and governments found it difficult to address the problem.

European Leaders French President Nicolas Sarkozy and German Chancellor Angela Merkel, both conservatives, proved popular, pragmatic, and highly visible leaders. Here Sarkozy welcomes Merkel as she arrives at the Elysée Palace in Paris, June 11, 2009. (Philippe Wojazer/Reuters/Landov)

Even with the renewed prosperity of the 1980s, unemployment in western Europe reached levels not seen since the Great Depression. During the 1990s, high unemployment persisted in much of Europe, even as it declined to postwar lows in the United States. The difference reflected differences in the structure of labor markets, which gave the U.S. economy greater flexibility. As a result of laws, labor agreements, and the postwar consensus now in place, European workers who had jobs were more secure than their American counterparts. But European employers were less able to adapt to changing conditions by laying off workers or hiring new ones with different skills. In this area, too, government reform efforts provoked strenuous protests in Europe.

Upon becoming Germany's first female chancellor in November 2005, the conservative Angela Merkel sought the measures necessary to streamline the German economy. But in light of the near dead heat in the national elections that September, she had to rely on an unstable "grand coalition" of the two largest parties—her own conservatives and the socialists. Though Merkel proved an effective international leader on several issues, her continued dependence on this coalition hampered her efforts at structural reform.

Even as western Europe was finding it difficult to sustain its social market model in the face of increasing global competition, the financial crisis of 2008 led many Europeans to reaffirm the superiority of the European system. Critics charged that it was reckless borrowing and lax oversight in America that had brought the global financial system to the verge of collapse. They also noted the much higher savings rates in Europe. Whereas U.S. consumers had saved 9 percent of their disposable income from 1950 to 1985, the rate steadily declined thereafter to around zero by 2008.

As American leaders, responding to the crisis, appeared to vacillate on priorities, both French president **Nicolas Sarkozy** and British prime minister Gordon Brown sought to take the lead, especially in engineering state intervention to rescue faltering banks. Brown's strategy, especially, prompted the U.S. government to change course and follow his lead.

Nicolas Sarkozy Activist French president, from the political right, elected in 2007.

The Europeans could credibly lead in this direction because, despite a recent tendency toward privatization, they had a much stronger tradition of state intervention and ownership. At the same time, the more substantial safety net in Europe was likely to cushion the economic fall, at least up to a point. Moreover, both Sarkozy and Brown insisted that stronger and more uniform international standards of disclosure, accounting, transparency, and regulation would need to follow the present emergency measures. But it was not clear that European leadership in response to the crisis portended superior economic performance for the European system over the longer term.

Immigration, Assimilation, and Citizenship

By the first years of the new millennium, as globalization proceeded and immigration increased, concerns about national community, cultural diversity, and the meaning of citizenship were becoming central all over Europe. Although anti-immigrant politicians like Jean-Marie Le Pen in France and Jörg Haider (HY-dur) in Austria typically won only 15 to 20 percent of the vote, they articulated a wider sense among the public that immigrant communities were responsible not only for increasing crime, but also for a weakening of the common values necessary to sustain society.

The place of Muslims became especially controversial, partly because there were so many of them. Some countries did not count religion in the national census, so the number in western Europe was uncertain. Estimates ranged from 15 to 20 million, and the number was projected to grow to 15 percent of the population by 2050, because of both continued immigration and higher birthrates. But the place of Muslims caused controversy also because so many were religiously observant even as Europe, though Christian in its dominant tradition, was evidently becoming ever more secular; thus, especially, the scope for a clash of cultures.

It was striking that the Netherlands and Denmark, two small countries widely known for openness and tolerance, became flash points as controversy over the place of Muslims grew. In the Netherlands in 2004, a Dutch national of Moroccan descent brutally assassinated Theo Van Gogh for having made a film denouncing the treatment of women in Islamic societies. The screenplay was by Ayaan Hirsi Ali, a woman raised as a Muslim in Somalia, and by this point, an outspoken critic of the treatment of women by Muslim men. She was a member of the Dutch parliament, where she served from 2003 to 2006. And she herself remained under threat of death after the murder of Van Gogh.

Claiming that fears of violence against anyone perceived to be denigrating Islam were leading to self-censorship, the editor of a Danish newspaper, *Jyllands-Posten*, published twelve cartoons depicting the Islamic prophet Muhammad, one wearing a turban in the shape of a bomb, in September 2005. News of the cartoons gradually spread, provoking outrage across the Muslim world early in 2006. Scores of people were killed, and the cartoonists themselves received death threats and had to go into hiding. Any depiction of the prophet Muhammad would have offended Muslims, who traditionally have been particularly concerned to ward off idolatry, the worship of images. But Muslims found the Danish cartoons gratuitously offensive.

The largest Muslim population in western Europe was in France—by 2008 roughly 6 million, or 10 percent of the population. Many were French citizens, the second- or third-generation

Cartoon Protest On February 18, 2006, Muslims march through central London in an angry but peaceful protest against the publication in the Western press of cartoons seeming to caricature the prophet Muhammad. (AP Photos/Peter Willows)

descendants of immigrants who had begun coming to France from Algeria and other former French African colonies in the 1950s when, as the postwar economic miracle gathered force, France needed workers. But beginning in the early 1970s, jobs had become increasingly scarce.

With open citizenship central to the French self-understanding, French law accorded citizenship automatically to second-generation immigrants, on the assumption that these offspring would be readily assimilated. However, the Muslim community in France had not been well assimilated, and by the end of the 1980s, finger-pointing on all sides had begun. Whereas the French left defended cultural diversity and its compatibility with citizenship, the right complained that citizenship was being devalued as a mere convenience, requiring no real commitment to the national community. Critics, such as Le Pen, charged that many from recent immigrant families did not want to assimilate.

An especially symptomatic episode in 1989—the "affair of the scarves"—made it clear that the place of Muslims in France had become a central and volatile issue. Three teenaged Muslim girls were suspended from school on the grounds that, in wearing the traditional Muslim headscarf, they were violating a long-standing law banning religious displays in public schools. The girls insisted they were not seeking to flaunt their religion or to convert others; the point was simply that Islamic teaching required women to cover their heads in public as a sign of modesty. Yet in the eyes of some Westerners, that practice reflected the second-class status of women in Islamic civilization. To defend the right to wear the scarves was thus to condone the oppression of women.

An uncertain compromise resulted from this episode, and the issue continued to smolder as the Muslim presence in France increased. In 2004, the French National Assembly passed, by an overwhelming margin, a new law to ban conspicuous religious displays in French public schools, hospitals, and other government buildings. Although large Christian crosses and Jewish yarmulkes, or skullcaps, were also at issue, the law seemed especially to target the Muslim headscarf. The law was passed despite massive protest marches in cities throughout France and elsewhere.

Many non-Muslims supported the right of women to wear the scarf precisely on the grounds of pluralism, tolerance, and freedom of expression. Yet some of those opposing the new law sought not to preserve diversity, but to keep Muslim girls in the public schools to expose them to secular influence and to promote long-term assimilation. In the short term, they argued, any law restricting religious expression would spawn separate Islamic schools, thereby deepening the divisions already evident in France.

By the first decade of the new century, French Muslims were clustered in deteriorating high-rise ghetto suburbs ringing Paris and other cities. Whereas young Muslims were widely blamed for criminality, they themselves complained of police harassment and job discrimination. Certainly they experienced very high rates of unemployment, well over 40 percent in many areas. And thus, it was feared, they were increasingly prone to militancy or Islamic fundamentalism.

As the police sought to crack down on crime, an incident late in October 2005 provoked a riot among Muslim youth in the ghetto suburb of Clichy-sous-Bois. During the next few days, waves of looting and car-burning spread to cities throughout France. The rioting continued well into November, until the government declared a state of emergency and deployed sharply increased security forces. It was France's worst civil unrest since the Days of May in 1968 (see page 831). President Jacques Chirac admitted that the riots had dramatized problems that had to be addressed promptly. Some observers called for a form of affirmative action to bring French Muslims, or French citizens of North African descent, into positions of greater prominence in business, politics, and the media, spheres in which they were virtually absent.

In winning the French presidency in 2007, Nicolas Sarkozy promised a tough stance against illegal immigration and immigrant crime. Thus, he attracted some of the vote that had been going to Le Pen, reducing Le Pen's share to 11 percent, the lowest in twenty-five years. But once in office, Sarkozy proved pragmatic and practiced affirmative action for those with immigrant backgrounds. And though controversy had surrounded the ban on religious dress in public buildings when it went into effect in 2004, by 2008, it was widely accepted by all faiths. More generally, Muslims seemed increasingly prepared to say that they felt welcome in France, and many non-Muslims grew accustomed to having large mosques in their midst.

By the early twenty-first century, the tendency all over Europe was to push assimilation—the formation of citizens sharing the mainstream values of the national community. This meant a retreat from the multiculturalism that had been prevalent on the European left, and that had made the persistence of immigrant subcultures seem a virtue. Whereas some conflated the assimilationist impulse with racism, others insisted that, on the contrary, anyone could belong, regardless of race or ethnicity, but that belonging required adopting the dominant culture, not holding to cultural differences.

In the Netherlands, Muslims had often used the Internet to equate the country's pluralistic tolerance with mere decadence. In 2006, the Netherlands adopted a law, the first of its kind anywhere, requiring that prospective immigrants take a "civic integration examination" testing their willingness to accept the tolerant openness of Dutch culture. The chairman of a leading Dutch Muslim organization defended the measure, suggesting that all immigrants needed to be prepared to embrace modernity. It seemed significant evidence of a turning point in the Netherlands when a Moroccan-born immigrant, Ahmed Aboutaleb, was installed as mayor of Rotterdam early in 2009. He, too, insisted that immigrants must be prepared to adopt Dutch values.

SECTION SUMMARY

- Although the transition from communism to some variety of capitalism proved difficult throughout the former Soviet bloc, it proved especially problematic in Russia.

- From within the wider democratic concensus, there was a split between much of continental western Europe, with its "social market economy," and the United States, which had greater confidence in free-market capitalism and less confidence in government.

- Especially in continental western Europe, the challenges of globalization suggested the need for reforms—reforms that proved difficult to engineer through the democratic process.

- Concerns about the assimilation of immigrant communities in much of Europe raised new and volatile political issues.

LIFESTYLES AND IDENTITIES

How did the changes bound up with globalization affect identities in the West?

Even as matters of diversity and citizenship were becoming mainstream political concerns, they were very much bound up with wider issues of personal identity. And in that respect, they intersected in complex ways with other potential influences on identity, from consumerism to religion to gender.

By the mid-1960s, the remarkable postwar economic growth had created a secular, consumerist society throughout much of the West, establishing patterns of life that continued into the twenty-first century, when cell phones and personal computers were commonplace. But changing lifestyles dictated new choices, and the new affluence challenged traditional sources of personal identity in unexpected ways, producing new concerns—and sometimes conflict. Important groups of non-Westerners rejected Western secular consumerism altogether.

Supranational, National, and Subnational Identities

By the late 1980s, consumerism and the widening impact of American popular culture—from blue jeans and American TV to shopping malls and theme parks—suggested a growing homogenization in the capitalist democracies. But Americanization threatened long-standing European identities, and Europeans sometimes adopted special measures to preserve distinctiveness. The EU specified that EU television programming had to be at least 40 percent EU-made, while the French mandated that at least every third popular song played on the radio had to be French.

But were quotas and mandates really necessary to preserve distinctiveness? The American chain Starbucks, which had revolutionized the serving of coffee in the United States, found it hard to penetrate continental Europe, which had its own long traditions of coffee-making. Even as many were coming to assume that American pop culture was irresistible, it became clear that European viewers were increasingly picking local TV programming on their own, quite apart from quotas. By 2003, every EU country was well above the 40 percent minimum for local programming, with the average at 62 percent.

Meanwhile, the growing prominence of the supranational EU, and doubts about the significance of national politics, nourished a renewed premium on subnational identities in such European regions as Flanders, Corsica, Scotland, and Catalonia. Flemings and Corsicans, Scots and Catalans, actively sought to preserve some measure of their distinct cultures and languages in the face of contemporary pressures toward standardization. In Britain, Tony Blair fostered the "devolution" of powers from the central government in London to Scottish and Welsh assemblies in 1999. Those powers were limited, but a decade later, many Scots, especially, were calling for an enhanced role for their regional parliament.

National sentiment grew especially uncertain in Italy, which had had a relatively brief and problematic history as a unified nation. Although its movement for national unification had drawn widespread enthusiasm throughout the Western world in the nineteenth century (see pages 618–622), by the 1990s, disillusionment with national politics made many Italians particularly eager to embrace the EU. At the same time, some renewed their identification with region or locality. Resentful of the national government's ties to the less prosperous south, a new political movement, the Northern League, emerged during the 1990s to push for the north to become an independent nation. Whatever the seriousness of such literal separatism, the Northern League's persistent strength suggested that "Italian" had become less important as a basis of individual identity in Italy's relatively prosperous north.

Class Identities and Trade Unions

The advent of a media-driven consumerist society produced greater homogeneity of experience and taste and a corresponding de-emphasis on class as a basis of identity. One symptom was the decline of the trade-union movement, long central to working-class identity and advancement.

Changing labor patterns reinforced the decline of organized labor, which was decidedly on the defensive throughout western Europe and the United States by the 1980s. The increasing danger of unemployment undercut the leverage of the unions. And as the economy grew more complex, workers were less likely to think of themselves as members of a single, unified working class.

Still, union membership varied considerably from country to country, and some unions found new ways of exerting influence. In a survey of union membership as a percentage of the work force in twelve industrialized countries in 2001, Denmark and Sweden had the highest figures—around 80 percent. The figures for Italy, Germany, and Britain were all around 30 percent. The lowest figures were in France (10 percent) and the United States (14 percent). Despite some much publicized militancy in resisting government efforts at pension reform, the unions generally had moved beyond their earlier confrontational posture to an increasing pragmatism.

In Germany, local union councils made informal agreements with big companies that, while technically violating Germany's restrictive labor regulations, helped keep jobs in Germany. At the same time, some German-based multinational companies, such as Volkswagen, actively sought to head off trouble with German unions by agreeing to guidelines specifying how they would operate worldwide. By committing itself to giving its workers elsewhere proper pay and working conditions, as well as the right to unionize, Volkswagen was agreeing not merely to seek the lowest bidder, as globalization sometimes seemed to demand. In this respect, too, the unions were still making a difference.

Economic Growth and Environmental Concerns

The impact of rapid economic growth on the European landscape and cityscape provoked ever greater concern by the last third of the twentieth century. The number of automobiles in western Europe increased from 6 million in 1939 to 16 million by 1959 to 42 million by 1969. Almost overnight, traffic and air pollution fundamentally changed the face of Europe's old cities. In 1976, five statues that had supported the Eastern Portico of the Erectheum Temple on the Acropolis in Athens since the fifth century B.C. were replaced by replicas and put in a museum to save them from the rapid decay that air pollution was causing.

With the end of communist rule, it became obvious that the years of communism had produced environmental degradation on an appalling scale in the Soviet bloc. But even with the fall of communism, it was hard to break from the old, often polluting patterns because jobs and energy sources often depended on them. For years, Ukraine could not afford to replace the remaining nuclear reactors at Chernobyl, despite safety and environmental risks that the 1986 accident had only worsened (see page 847). International aid finally enabled Ukraine to close the plant in 2000.

The greater affluence in western Europe made possible, and sometimes dictated, more creative responses to pollution and other environmental side effects of economic growth. Many cities adopted pedestrian-only zones to restrict automobile traffic, and some experimented with road-pricing measures in an effort to reduce traffic in central cities.

The United States had joined the other industrialized nations in signing the Kyoto agreement of 1997, designed to limit emissions of the "greenhouse gases," widely held by scientists to be causing global warming, with potentially catastrophic consequences. But questioning the scientific evidence and citing concerns about economic growth, the United States pulled out of the agreement in 2001, causing much resentment in Europe and elsewhere. With 5 percent of the world's population, the United States was responsible for 25 percent of the world's greenhouse gas emissions per year.

Still, global warming was increasingly recognized, in the United States as elsewhere, as a serious issue. The question was what needed to be done, and how to muster the political will to do it. One possibility was the further use of nuclear power, long controversial because of safety, waste disposal, and other environmental concerns. Even as such countries as Germany and the United States pulled back during the 1970s, France continued to develop nuclear power until, by 2008, 77 percent of French electricity was nuclear-generated, as compared, for example, with 19 percent in the United States. The French took pride in their technical expertise in the nuclear area. By this point, however, support for nuclear power was increasing all over the Western world, in light of concern about global warming and high oil prices.

Religious Identities

Whereas religious affiliation and church or synagogue attendance remained relatively stable in the United States, Europeans abandoned churches in droves after the mid-1950s. As church attendance dropped, popular culture revolved less around religious festivals and holy days. Moreover, in assuming responsibility for social welfare, European governments had gradually taken over much of the charitable role that the churches had long played.

Seeking to change with the times, the Catholic Church undertook a notable modernization effort under the popular Pope John XXIII (r. 1958–1963). But under his more conservative successors, the church became caught up in controversy, especially over issues, such as abortion, that women had brought to the fore. By the 1990s, its conservative social policy had put the Catholic Church on the defensive. Still, the active, highly visible role of Pope John Paul II (r. 1978–2005) (see page 844) in a variety of spheres attracted widespread admiration. His death in 2005 led to an enormous outpouring of affection.

In such traditionally Catholic countries as France, Italy, and Spain, many people considered themselves "cultural Catholics" and ignored church rulings they found inappropriate, especially those concerning sexuality, marriage, and gender roles. In referenda in 1974 and 1981, two-thirds of Italians defied the Vatican by voting to legalize divorce and approve abortion rights. Even in heavily Catholic Ireland, the electorate approved, though narrowly, the legalization of divorce in 1995, after having defeated it overwhelmingly in a referendum just nine years before.

When surveys showed that 80 percent of Spaniards considered themselves Catholic by the twenty-first century, even the cardinal-bishop of Madrid admitted that for many, "Catholic" was not a way of life but merely a label, perhaps linked to national identity. Other surveys showed that whereas in 1975, the year of the dictator Francisco Franco's death, 61 percent of Spaniards reported regular church attendance, that figure had dropped to 19 percent by the early twenty-first century. Even 46 percent of those calling themselves Catholic admitted that they almost never went to church. By 2008, Christian Church attendance in many western European countries, including Britain, hovered at 5 percent. But while religious affiliations weakened in western Europe, the Russian Orthodox Church experienced a notable revival after the collapse of communism.

In parts of the West, religious and ethnic identities blurred, sometimes enhancing the potential for conflict. Even after the breakup of the wider Soviet Union gave independence to the predominantly Muslim central Asian republics, the remaining Russian Federation included more than twenty million Muslims, or about 15 percent of the overall population. In both absolute numbers and percentage terms, this was the largest Muslim population in Europe. Included were those who identified themselves as Muslims in cultural terms, even if they did not practice the Islamic religion.

A significant Islamic revival among Russian Muslims followed the collapse of communism, producing increasing friction with the central authorities. In 2002, the interior ministry banned women from wearing headscarves in photos for official documents. The Russian supreme court upheld the ban in response to an appeal by Islamic women that it violated Russia's constitutionally guaranteed freedom of religion. At the same time, the Russian army refused to allow Muslim services on military bases.

Family Life and Gender Roles

The new affluence significantly affected demographic patterns, partly because contraception became more readily available. Indeed, the advent of the birth control pill, widely obtainable by the late 1960s, fostered a secular lifestyle. At the same time, falling birthrates meant an aging population, and thus all the concerns about paying for the pensions and other welfare measures central to the postwar social compact.

In western Europe, as in the United States, a remarkable baby boom had followed the end of World War II and carried into the early 1960s. But the birthrate declined rapidly thereafter, so family size had diminished markedly by 1990. In Italy, the number of births in 1987 was barely half the number in 1964, when the postwar baby boom reached its peak. By 1995, the population was not sustaining itself in a number of European countries, including Italy (see **Map 30.4**). Thus, though some were reluctant to admit it, immigration was essential to sustain the working-age population. By 2008, Italy had the oldest population in Europe, with 20 percent of the population 65 or older. Germany was a close second. The figure for the United States was 12 percent, though the Americans, too, were aging rapidly.

The feminist movement that had reemerged in the late 1960s gradually expanded its focus beyond the quest for formal equality of opportunity. Examining subtle cultural obstacles to equality led feminists to the more general issue of gender—the way societies make sense of sexual difference and allocate social roles on that basis. By the late twentieth century, gender was central not only to public policy, but also to private relationships and life choices in much of the Western world.

By the 1970s, women sought measures, such as government-subsidized day care, that would enable them to combine paid employment with raising a family. At the same time, governments increasingly understood the value of policies to encourage both productive working parents and effective childhood development. Setting the pace was France, where the government began making quality day care available to all during the 1980s. Government subsidies kept costs within reach for ordinary working families. In addition, 95 percent of French children ages 3 to 6 were enrolled in the free public nursery schools available by the early 1990s.

The French model seemed to work well in combining child support with equal opportunity for paid employment. In simultaneously offering day care and allowances to concentrate on parenting, French government programs seemed to give French mothers a genuine choice as to whether to work outside the home. And French policy was sufficiently pro-baby to help give France Europe's highest birthrate. Overall, French family policy was widely popular; the key question was whether France could afford it.

Also much at issue by the early twenty-first century were the rights of homosexual couples—to adopt children, for example, or to have their partnerships legally recognized as marriage. Whether married or not, were homosexual partners entitled to job benefits, such as health care, which often were available to heterosexual couples?

The interrelationship of family, gender, sexuality, and personal self-realization, never static, was evolving in new ways—a crucial aspect of the ongoing experiment in the West.

SECTION SUMMARY

- The advent of a consumer society, increasingly on a global level, affected supranational, national, and subnational identities in complex, often unforeseen ways.

- The de-emphasis on class as a basis of identity contributed to the decline of the trade-union movement.

- Economic growth seemed to have adverse effects on the environment, though there was disagreement over how best to respond.

- The strength of religious identities diminished in much of Europe, though there was considerable variation from country to country.

- Affluence led to new ways of conceiving gender roles and family life.

Nelson Mandela and the Universality of Human Values

For all the admiration that continued to surround those who had helped undermine Soviet-style communism, the most revered person in the West and the world at the beginning of the twenty-first century was surely the black South African Nelson Mandela (b. 1918). As a militant in the African National Congress, which was seeking to overcome the brutally segregationist apartheid system in South Africa, he spent twenty-seven years in prison. He was released in 1990 as part of a wider amnesty granted by South Africa's new president, F. W. De Klerk (b. 1936). Responding to international pressures, including effective trade sanctions, De Klerk wanted Mandela's help in restructuring the South African system. The two were central to the ensuing negotiations that repealed apartheid and began the transition to a nonracial democracy in South Africa. When the first elections were held under the new system in 1994, Mandela was elected president of South Africa. In this passage from the conclusion to his autobiography, he articulates the idealism that inspired his remarkable achievement and made him a symbol of shared human values to Westerners and non-Westerners alike.

On the day of the inauguration, I was overwhelmed with a sense of history. In the first decade of the twentieth century, a few years after the bitter Anglo-Boer War and before my own birth, the white skinned peoples of South Africa patched up their differences and erected a system of racial domination against the dark-skinned peoples of their own land. The structure they created formed the basis of one of the harshest, most inhumane societies the world has ever known. Now, in the last decade of the twentieth century, and my own eighth decade as a man, that system had been overturned forever and replaced by one that recognized the rights and freedoms of all peoples regardless of the color of their skin.

That day had come about through the unimaginable sacrifices of thousands of my people, people whose suffering and courage can never be counted or repaid. I felt that day, as I have on so many other days, that I was simply the sum of all those African patriots who had gone before me. That long and noble line ended and now began again with me. I was pained that I was not able to thank them and that they were not able to see what their sacrifices had wrought....

I never lost hope that this great transformation would occur. Not only because of the great heroes I have already cited, but because of the courage of the ordinary men and women of my country. I always knew that deep down in every human heart, there is mercy and generosity. No one is born hating another person because of the color of his skin, or his background, or his religion. People must learn to hate, and if they can learn to hate, they can be taught to love, for love comes more naturally to the human heart than its opposite. Even in the grimmest times in prison, when my comrades and I were pushed to our limits, I would see a glimmer of humanity in one of the guards, perhaps just for a second, but it was enough to reassure me and keep me going....

I was not born with a hunger to be free. I was born free—free in every way that I could know....

But then I slowly saw that not only was I not free, but my brothers and sisters were not free. I saw that it was not just my freedom that was curtailed, but the freedom of everyone who looked like I did. That is when I joined the African National Congress, and that is when the hunger for my own freedom became the greater hunger for the freedom of my people. It was this desire for the freedom of my people to live their lives with dignity and self-respect that animated my life, that transformed a frightened young man into a bold one, that drove a law-abiding attorney to become a criminal, that turned a family-loving husband into a man without a home, that forced a life loving man to live like a monk. I am no more virtuous or self-sacrificing than the next man, but I found that I could not even enjoy the poor and limited freedoms I was allowed when I knew my people were not free. Freedom is indivisible; the chains on any one of my people were the chains on all of them, the chains on all of my people were the chains on me.

It was during those long and lonely years that my hunger for the freedom of my own people became a hunger for the freedom of all people, white and black. I knew as well as I knew anything that the oppressor must be liberated just as surely as the oppressed. A man who takes away another man's freedom is a prisoner of hatred, he is locked behind the bars of prejudice and narrow-mindedness. I am not truly free if I am taking away someone else's freedom, just as surely as I am not free when my freedom is taken from me. The oppressed and the oppressor alike are robbed of their humanity.

When I walked out of prison, that was my mission, to liberate the oppressed and the oppressor both. Some say that has now been achieved. But I know that that is not the case. The truth is that we are not yet free; we have merely achieved the freedom to be free, the right not to be oppressed. We have not taken the final step of our journey, but the first step on a longer and even more difficult road. For to be free is not merely to cast off one's chains, but to live in a way that respects and enhances the freedom of others. The true test of our devotion to freedom is just beginning.

...After climbing a great hill, one only finds that there are many more hills to climb. I have taken a moment here to rest, to steal a view of the glorious vista that surrounds me, to look back on the distance I have come. But I can rest only for a moment, for with freedom comes responsibilities, and I dare not linger, for my long walk is not yet ended.

QUESTIONS

1. In what sense is Mandela appealing to human values, as opposed to the values or special circumstances of a particular group?

2. Why does Mandela suggest that the struggle for freedom is essentially endless?

THE WEST IN A GLOBAL AGE

What questions emerged as the West faced new crises all over the globe after the end of the cold war?

By the early twenty-first century, the West was part of a world that was, in one sense, dramatically less Eurocentric than it had been a century before, when European imperialism was at its peak. Events in the West competed for attention with OPEC oil prices, Chinese trade practices, and Iran's nuclear program. Decisions vitally affecting the industrialized West might be made anywhere. Just as capital and information flowed more quickly across national borders, so could epidemic diseases emerging in some distant jungle. This was the reverse side of the new interconnectedness of a global world. A planetary culture, a threatened environment, an interdependent economy, and an increasing sense of international responsibility required people to think in global terms as never before. (See the feature, "The Global Record: Nelson Mandela and the Universality of Human Values.")

Uniformity and Diversity in the "Global Village"

By the last decades of the twentieth century, a kind of global culture began to emerge for the first time. Indeed, talk of a single "global village" became commonplace. But just as "Americanization" produced concerns about preserving distinctiveness elsewhere in the West, "globalization" led to comparable concerns on a global level. Although the process promised a better life for many people in less developed countries, valuable diversity was seemingly being lost in an ever more uniform world. For instance, half the world's 6,500 languages were expected to disappear during the twenty-first century.

Skyscrapers in booming Asian cities looked much like skyscrapers in the West. Indeed, they were often designed by the same architects. Businessmen in conservative Western dress made postwar Japan the world's second-largest economy. American firms transferred billing and even customer service operations to lower-cost India, even as India was becoming a major player in computer technology. "Americanization" made such products as Coca-Cola and McDonald's burgers familiar not just in Europe, but worldwide. Especially among urban youth, a common style emerged that owed much to American popular culture. Meanwhile, for everyone from scientists to business leaders to airline pilots, English became the common language.

At work, however, was not simply Western or American cultural imperialism. What resulted in many spheres, from food to popular music, was a complex fusion, as elements from diverse cultures enriched one another even as distinctive features remained. The British tourist board declared Indian curry to be the official British dish, testimony to the number of Indian restaurants in Britain—itself testimony to the enduring impact of the Indian heritage on Britain.

Even multinational media conglomerates increasingly accented local content. When Viacom launched MTV in the 1980s, the producers assumed that since the pop music culture was universal, a single channel would succeed everywhere. But it quickly became evident that success required local variation. Between 2001 and 2003, MTV launched fourteen new channels, for a total of thirty-eight around the world. Each was tailored to local tastes, with no emphasis on an American link. One MTV executive observed, "we don't even call it an adaptation of American content: it's local content creation.... The American thing is irrelevant."[1] So whereas the advent of MTV had initially seemed an instance of cultural imperialism, the program's evolution manifested—and contributed to—the more complex global cross-fertilization in process.

Mutual Interdependence and Patterns of Development

The world's population had reached 1 billion in 1800, 2 billion in 1930. In 1999, it reached 6 billion, having doubled since 1960. This was the fastest rate of world population growth ever, and by the 1990s, virtually all of that growth was in the developing countries of Africa, Asia, and Latin America (see **Map 30.4**). As of mid-2008, world population stood at 6.7 billion and was projected to reach nearly 10 billion by 2050. But growth was expected to slow with the cultural

🌐 Map 30.4—World Population Trends, 2002–2015

This map shows populations in 2002, as well as projected average annual growth rates from 2002 to 2015, in countries throughout the world. In the developed countries of the West, populations are relatively high but growing slowly, if at all. Most of the world's population growth is occurring in the less-developed countries outside the West.

(Source: Data from www.worldbank.org)

changes accompanying development, including the integration of more women into the workforce. Whereas world population was growing 1.2 percent a year as of 2008, growth was projected to decline to 0.5 percent by 2050.

Growing concern about the environment intensified the sense of global interdependence and pointed to the need for international cooperation. Such problems as global warming, the loss of biodiversity, and the deterioration of the ozone layer were inherently supranational in scope. Yet environmental concerns also complicated relations between the industrialized nations and the rest of the world. Countries seeking to industrialize encountered environmental constraints that had not been at issue when the West industrialized. The challenge for the West was to foster protection of the environment in poorer regions of the globe without imposing unfair limitations on economic growth.

Also bringing home mutual interdependence was the rapid spread of contagious, sometimes fatal diseases with the intensification of contacts around the world. Some of those diseases were apparently new, or at least previously unknown. As the world grew more crowded, humans intruded into previously untouched jungles and forests, intensifying interaction among species that had formerly remained largely separated. The crowding of animals for food production also fed the genesis and spread of new diseases. Officials of the UN's **World Health Organization (WHO)** stressed in 2005 that they lacked the global infrastructure to head off the sort of pandemic that might result, for example, from a further mutation in the "bird flu" virus.

AIDS (acquired immune deficiency syndrome), a sexually transmitted disease caused by the HIV virus, had apparently spread from chimpanzees to humans in Africa earlier in the twentieth century, although it began to be recognized only in the late 1970s. It then expanded throughout the world beginning in the 1980s. Particularly devastating in Africa, AIDS remained a major concern in the early twenty-first century.

World Health Organization (WHO) Established as a specialized agency of the United Nations in 1948, it serves as the coordinating authority on international public health. It is headquartered in Geneva, Switzerland.

Controversy Over Economic Globalization

Although many forces fed globalization, the most potent was international capitalism itself. The capitalist ideal of free and open markets sounded appealing, and economic models, based on comparative advantage, could explain how everybody wins through expanded economic exchange. The world economy was not a zero-sum game. But whatever the virtues of free markets in principle, experience showed globalization to be a multi-edged sword, producing complex, often-contradictory results.

The network of supranational agencies, starting with the World Bank and the International Monetary Fund, that had developed from the Bretton Woods Agreement of 1944 had long drawn praise for helping to keep the world economy stable and growing. Also central, especially in promoting free trade, was the **World Trade Organization (WTO)**, which grew from a 1947 multilateral trade agreement. By the late 1990s, however, these organizations, together with the G-8, had become focal points for the increasing concerns about globalization. Beginning with a meeting of the WTO in Seattle in 1999, large demonstrations, or even riots, routinely surrounded the meetings of these organizations.

Those protesting were often naive about economics and the benefits of free trade. But their protests raised significant questions about wages, working conditions, environmental impact, and international financial arrangements that were not always adequately addressed in the prevailing economic models. Most fundamentally at issue was whether it made sense to foster free trade and globalization without greater consistency in social and environmental policy. In the absence of common standards, free trade was not likely to be fair trade. Under present circumstances, trade agreements seemed to threaten a loss of jobs in the developed world and the exploitation of less-developed countries at the same time. Critics charged that globalization was not helping the poorer nations to catch up, as theory would have it, but leaving them ever further behind. The challenge was to find some balance between free trade and regulation within an increasingly global economy.

The Question of Global Responsibility

If people were forced to think in global terms as never before, how far did global responsibility extend in a world that remained divided into sovereign nation-states? The series of brutal, sometimes genocidal conflicts from Yugoslavia to Rwanda to Liberia that marked the post–cold war period fostered a growing sense of collective responsibility on the part of what was increasingly called "the international community." Amorphous though it was, that entity seemed to take on real existence by the end of the 1990s. But who or what constituted "the international community" and the conditions under which it should act remained uncertain.

Of course, a prominent international organization was already in place—the United Nations, the fruit of the hopes for a better world in light of World War II. By the 1990s, no one denied that it had achieved significant successes in areas such as nutrition, health, and education. But UN forces were often overburdened as they took on the often-incompatible objectives of peacekeeping and humanitarian relief—sometimes in areas where there was no real peace to keep. The need to seem impartial sometimes paralyzed UN peacekeepers. And the UN's members, especially its leaders on the Security Council, frequently disagreed over what should be done.

Still, the UN was a visible presence, even as concerns for national sovereignty compromised its ability to act. After ad hoc UN war crimes tribunals began dealing with the atrocities that had taken place in the Balkans and Rwanda, the UN established its permanent International Criminal Court in The Hague in 1998. Its charge was to bring to justice those responsible for war crimes or crimes against humanity. Supporters also cited the UN's successes in organizing relief in the wake of disasters, such as a devastating 2005 earthquake in Pakistan, and its at least partial successes in the war-torn Democratic Republic of Congo, where it disarmed militias, organized elections, and helped millions of people return to their homes.

Supplementing the efforts of governments and the supranational UN was a network of **nongovernmental organizations (NGOs)**, such as the Red Cross, Amnesty International, and Doctors Without Borders, that had emerged over the years to deal with humanitarian relief or human rights issues. Collectively, they were a major presence on the international scene by the early twenty-first century and central to the international community.

But those seeking to provide aid or maintain peace were often forced to deal with semi-criminal elements who diverted humanitarian aid to buy weapons or who took peacekeepers

World Trade Organization (WTO) Growing from a multilateral trade agreement in 1947, it sought, with mixed success, to promote freer trade throughout the world. By the early twenty-first century, WTO meetings tended to draw demonstrations by antiglobalization activists.

nongovernmental organizations (NGOs) Private, independent organizations designed to deal with humanitarian relief and human rights issues. Though unaffiliated with governments or the United Nations, they became central to the international community.

The Question of Western Responsibility

The end of the cold war helped open the way to ethnic conflict, terrorism, and, in some areas, the breakdown of government as violent warlords fought for control. With the world more interconnected than ever before, it was increasingly assumed that "the international community," spearheaded by the rich countries of the West, ought to respond to tragedy anywhere. But quite apart from the difficult questions of leadership and coordination, it was not clear what level of risk, and expense, the West was prepared to assume. In the following excerpt, Brian Urquhart, born in Britain in 1919 and long a senior official of the United Nations, offers a pointed analysis of the issues that came to the fore as the West experimented with a more active response to tragedies around the world.

What is to be done when hundreds of thousands of people in a hitherto little-known region of the world are hounded from their homes, massacred, or starved to death in a brutal civil war, or even in a deliberate act of genocide? To our credit, we no longer turn away from the face of evil, but we still don't know how to control it. As the new century dawns, one of the biggest problems for international organizations and their member governments is to learn how to react to the great human emergencies that still seem to occur regularly in many parts of the world. . . .

The so-called "international community" is anything but a constitutional system. As far as it is organized at all, it is an institutional arrangement, unpredictable and slow to act. It usually responds only when disaster has already struck and when its members, usually in the UN Security Council, can agree to take action. Even then, since the UN has no standing forces or substantial resources of its own, its action, if it can be agreed upon, is likely to be too little and too late.

In his opening address to the General Assembly on September 20, 1999, Secretary-General Kofi Annan made an impassioned plea for UN intervention in cases of gross violations of human rights. The reactions of governments to Annan's remarks showed very clearly how far the world still has to go before evil can be systematically dealt with internationally. Most comments on Annan's speech were critical and stressed the paramount importance of national sovereignty; some even saw humanitarian intervention as a cloak for American or Western hegemony or neocolonialism. Only a small minority of Western countries supported Sweden's position that the collective conscience of mankind demands action.

A new idea of "human security" has now taken its place alongside the much older concept of "international peace and security." It has emerged as the result of a vaguely defined and fitful international conscience on the part of the liberal democracies, and it has been encouraged both by the prodigious growth of nongovernmental organizations and by the communications revolution. However, the rules and the means for protecting human security are still tentative and controversial, not least because virtually any situation threatening human security is likely to raise questions of national sovereignty. No government wants to set up a system which may, at some point in the future, be invoked against itself.

. . . Humanitarian action as it emerged in the aftermath of World War II was principally concerned with refugee resettlement and the reconstruction of war-shattered countries. In those innocent days, humanitarian relief was seen as a nonpolitical activity, dictated by the needs of the afflicted and by the resources and expertise available to meet them . . . . That relatively nonpolitical concept of humanitarianism has come to a brutal end with the rising importance of warlords and the conflicts within states of the post–cold war world. The international sponsors of humanitarian aid are no longer dealing with more or less responsible governments. . . .

. . . "The whole aid community has been overtaken by a new reality," the IRC [International Rescue Committee] stated. "Humanitarianism has become a resource . . . and people are manipulating it as never before. Sometimes we just shouldn't show up for a disaster." . . .

QUESTIONS

1. Why did the West find it so difficult to respond to the sorts of disasters that came to the fore after the cold war?

2. Why did even humanitarian aid come to seem increasingly ineffective under certain circumstances?

Source: "The Question of Western Responsibility" from Brian Urquhart, "In the Name of Humanity," *The New York Review of Books*, April 27, 2000, pp. 19–21.

and aid workers hostage—or even killed them. In 1994, for the first time, more UN civilian aid workers (twenty-four) than peacekeeping soldiers were killed in the line of duty. And the death toll for aid workers rose rapidly during the decade.

The conflicts that developed in hot spots around the world after the cold war spawned an increasing sense that it was up to the Western-led international community to "do something." But do what—and at what cost? What aims were realistic? During the first decade of the new century, the international community was widely called upon to end the apparent ongoing genocide in the Darfur region of Sudan. But there was no consensus on what degree of response was appropriate or on how it should be coordinated. (See the feature, "The Written Record: The Question of Western Responsibility.")

Questioning the Meaning of the West

Although in one sense "globalization" meant "Westernization" to advocates and critics alike, its accelerating pace bred deeper uncertainty about what was specifically Western—about the meaning and value of the Western tradition. Indeed, the need to respond both to the challenges of the competitive global economy and to the increasingly volatile international environment occasioned friction and fragmentation within the West.

Cultural differences between Europeans and Americans seemed to be deepening by the early twenty-first century. As a corollary of religious differences between the two, the United States experienced periodic controversy over the teaching of Darwinian evolution in the public schools—controversy that would have been unthinkable in Europe. In the same way, homosexuality and abortion tended to stir greater controversy in America than they did among Europeans.

In light of the disruptions of the twentieth century, the place of history became especially problematic in Europe. At the same time, the radical transformation in the half century since World War II in some ways cut Europeans off from their own traditions. The uneasy contemporary relationship with the past, especially the traumatic past of the earlier twentieth century, took especially pointed form in the neo-expressionist painting prominent in Germany and Italy by the late twentieth century.

For a generation after World War II, European artists, unsure of their direction, had tended to follow the lead of New York. But by the late 1960s, the new generation that included such painters as the German Anselm Kiefer (b. 1945) and the Italian Sandro Chia (KEE-ah) (b. 1946) sought to confront the recent past—and thus, the meaning of a tradition that now included fascism, total war, and the Holocaust. What did it mean to be German, Italian, or even European in light of this difficult past and the globalizing present and future? Wrestling with the interface of recent history and national identity, Kiefer and Chia conveyed the paradox and ambiguity that many felt as the rapidly changing West encountered the layers of its own cultural tradition.

The ongoing effort to come to terms with the recent past produced controversy and sometimes seemed to open old wounds, as earlier fascist or communist sympathies came under scrutiny. In Italy and France, questions about collaboration and resistance during World War II produced periodic waves of bitterness. Even how to remember and commemorate the Holocaust produced much dispute, although Berlin's Holocaust memorial, opened in 2005, indicated the widespread agreement that commemoration of some sort was essential.

By the early twenty-first century, bitter debate had raged for several decades over the legitimacy of "Western civilization" as a concept. Some critics highlighted the geographical imprecision of "the West" and claimed that the words *Western* and *civilization* had been juxtaposed simply to justify conquest and domination. Even among those who recognized a distinctive Western cultural tradition, some found it elitist and limiting. In their view, Western culture had defined itself around a group of artifacts—writings, paintings, monuments—that reflected the experience of a very restricted circle.

Others countered that imperialism and assumptions of superiority had not been confined to the West. Moreover, they continued, the West had been the source of ideas—the "rights of man," the scope for eliminating exploitation—that were now being eagerly embraced in the non-Western world. Even the charges of cultural elitism directed against the Western tradition stemmed from a democratic impulse that had itself grown from within that tradition. And by the last decades of the twentieth century, that impulse had prompted historians to focus on ordinary people and a far wider circle of cultural interpreters, thereby dramatically expanding the "canon"—the body of works considered worthy of attention.

Questions about the Western tradition and its contemporary relevance were bound up with the advent of *postmodernism*, a term widely used by the early 1990s for a cultural orientation that had been gathering force for decades. (See the feature, "The Visual Record: Postmodern Architecture.") Postmodernism reflected a certain conception of what *modernism* had meant, even a sense that modernism had defined an era that was ending. But what was ending—and how it was bound up with the debate over Western civilization—was not so clear.

Postmodernism emerged partly as confidence in the scope for a neutral, objective social science began to decline during the 1960s. That confidence had reflected the belief in reason that

Kiefer: Osiris and Isis   The German artist Anselm Kiefer combined unusual materials to create haunting images that often suggested the horrors of recent history. In this work, dated 1985–1987, the interpenetrating layers of human culture include images of ruin and death, hope and resurrection.   (Anselm Kiefer Osiris und Isis (Osiris and Isis), 1985–1987; painting; oil and acrylic emulsion with additional three-dimensional media, 150 in. × 220 $\frac{1}{2}$ in. × 6 $\frac{1}{2}$ in. (381 cm × 560.07 cm × 16.51 cm); Collection SFMOMA, Purchased through a gift of Jean Stein by exchange, the Mrs. Paul L. Wattis Fund, and the Doris and Donald Fisher Fund; © Anselm Kiefer)

had emerged from the Scientific Revolution and the Enlightenment. Reason had seemed universal, not limited to any particular culture, and it was assumed to be applicable to the human as well as the natural world.

To apply reason seemed "modern," and the West, apparently having progressed by applying reason, had long understood itself to be in the forefront of modernity. Everyone else was scrambling to catch up through the universal process of modernization. Such was the "master narrative" through which the West had understood its place in the world during the modern era.

But even as globalization proceeded during the late twentieth century, Western thinkers retreated from this long-standing master narrative. There was no question that capitalism had spread from Europe, but the West was not necessarily the model, the standard of development. Thus the growing interest in the non-Western world, and the increasing respect for its diverse traditions, that came to mark Western culture by the last decades of the twentieth century.

Postmodernists questioned claims of certainty, objective truth, and intrinsic meaning in language, in works of art, and ultimately in all cultural expressions. Some held that such claims were assertions of privilege in what was essentially a political struggle for power—the power to set the wider social agenda. Especially in the United States, the postmodernist reaction led by the 1980s to the vogue of the French philosopher and historian Michel Foucault (foo-KOH) (1926–1984), who had sought to show that the power to specify what counts as knowledge was the key to social or political power. Since, from this perspective, all knowledge was suspect, Foucault's accents invited mistrust and disruption.

Postmodern Architecture

Three building complexes, one by an Italian working in Japan, another by an American working in Germany, and a third by a Spaniard working in Spain: They look dramatically different, yet they were built at roughly the same time. Do they have anything in common? In fact, each was rejecting earlier "modern" architecture, and each expressed what came to be known as "postmodernism" by the last two decades of the twentieth century.

Modernism in architecture, design, and urban planning had emerged especially during the 1920s from sources like the German Bauhaus, which turned resolutely from tradition to embrace the modern industrial age (see page 751). During the first two decades after World War II, this modernist approach triumphed at last, transforming cities throughout the world. Now known as "the international style," it reflected the wider self-understanding of the modern world, centered in the West. "Modern" meant rationality and efficiency, clarity and regularity, machine precision and mass culture. Ornament, decoration, symbolism, and historical reference had little or no place.

At issue, in fact, was not just a particular style of building but a new relationship with history. As modern, we seemed to be living on the cutting edge of history, in the eternal present, endlessly being cut off from our past. Henry Ford, widely taken as the personification of modernity in his time, put the matter directly: "History is bunk."

But by the 1960s, a reaction began to develop in architecture and urban planning, reflecting deeper thinking about history, about what it meant to be modern, and about the contemporary relationship with cultural traditions, including older buildings. In 1977, the architectural critic Charles Jencks, in his book, *The Language of Post-Modern Architecture,* used the term *postmodernism* to characterize what now seemed to be a new movement or direction.

The earlier notion of modernity was coming to seem dubious in an emerging world of global interchange and plural perspectives. Memory, history, and the presence of the past were more, not less, important as accelerating technological change made possible instant communication and constant access to information across the globe. Yet, there was sometimes irony, uncertainty, or paradox in the coexistence of old and new.

Postmodernist architects did not merely reject the earlier modernism, and certainly their aim was not simply to revive previous styles, such as classical or Gothic, though elements of them, as embodiments of our living history, might be incorporated in postmodern buildings. For example, look at the photo above of the Palazzo Hotel, designed by the Italian Aldo Rossi (1931–1997). Set in a Japanese city, the hotel clearly recalls Italian buildings, even those of the fascist period, themselves ambiguously modern, with references to the classical tradition and especially ancient Rome. For the façade, constructed of red marble and brick crossed with green steel moldings, Rossi combined contrasting materials, uncertain scale, and historical reference in a striking, even uncanny way.

Aldo Rossi: Il Palazzo Hotel, Fukuoka, Japan (Courtesy, Nacasa & Partners, Inc.)

Moreover, postmodernist architects were just as committed to modern techniques and materials as the modernists. They reacted, however, against the modernist pretense of a single right way, the rejection of ornament and history, and the reduction of architecture to function and the logic of machines. Postmodernists did not simply accept but actively celebrated messiness, variety, mixture, and complexity. The American Frank Gehry (b. 1929) suggested impermanence as well as postmodern pluralism in his complex of three office buildings in Düsseldorf, Germany (opposite page, top). Notice how the project incorporates modernist elements—flat roofs, identical prefabricated windows—but provides remarkable variety and contrast by cladding one of the units in red brick, one in mirror-polished stainless steel, and the third in white plaster. At the same time, the uniform, angled windows contrast with the curved surfaces. None of the three is the right way; rather, they play evocatively against one another.

Santiago Calatrava (b. 1951) drew on an even wider frame of reference to create shapes that were never before part of our built environment. Calatrava used highly sculptured forms for the building shown here (opposite page, bottom)—the centerpiece of a science museum complex built in the bed of a diverted river in his native Valencia, Spain. Taking advantage of his engineering background,

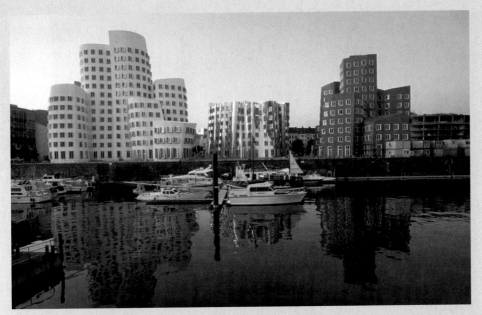

Frank Gehry: Der Neue Zollhof (The New Customs House), Düsseldorf, Germany (Thomas Mayer, photographer)

he created unexpected spaces and sculptural surfaces that went beyond tradition altogether. With structures suggesting bones and tendons, he conveyed the dynamics of movement, of folding, opening, and closing—even the opening and closing of an eye.

Dramatically different though they appear, these three architectural statements share the wider postmodern framework. Rossi invokes the past to resist change; Gehry plays with the past, even the recent modernist past, while suggesting impermanence; Calatrava transcends the present outcome of the past, but without the limitations, the particular discipline, that modernism imposed. Rather than submit to the logic of the machine, he felt free to experiment more boldly, devising radically new forms. Each of the three architects represents a strand in the wider, complex, and contradictory postmodernist approach to history and tradition, including the tradition of modernism itself.

QUESTIONS

1. In what sense are the buildings we see here recognizably *post*modern, in the sense of consciously rejecting earlier modernist tenets?

2. How do Rossi, Gehry, and Calatrava differ in their approach to change and history?

Santiago Calatrava: City of Arts and Sciences, Valencia, Spain (Oliver Schuh, Palladium Photodesign)

Old and New in Contemporary Europe   Especially with the transformation of Europe since World War II, new styles intersect with living artifacts from the past to form sometimes ironic combinations. Here, in a neighborhood in Milan, Italy, teenagers wearing blue jeans and backpacks seem oblivious to the legacies of Roman antiquity and Christianity that are prominent around them. (© 1999, George Steinmetz)

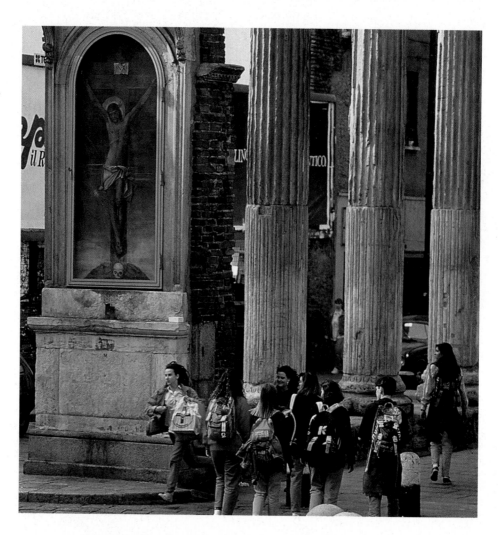

SECTION SUMMARY

- Although globalization meant cultural homogeneity in one sense, it also produced unforeseen forms of cultural fusion and a deeper appreciation of cultural diversity.

- Economic globalization produced a backlash, often targeting multinational entities like the World Trade Organization, on the grounds that free trade was too often exploitative and unfair.

- Even as it increasingly felt responsible for dealing with disasters around the world, the West, leading "the international community," was often unsure how best to respond.

- Cultural differences between Europeans and Americans, as reflected, for example, in attitudes toward religion or the role of government, seemed to be deepening by the early twenty-first century.

- Even as the concept of "Western civilization" was debated in the West, intellectual leaders sought to show how Western notions of reason and democracy could be given renewed relevance.

At the same time, however, an array of equally innovative thinkers, from the German Jürgen Habermas (b. 1929) to the American Richard Rorty (1931–2007), sought a more constructive orientation based on a renewed, no longer arrogant understanding of Western traditions, including the place of reason and democracy.

For those embracing this more constructive approach, the point was not to celebrate Western civilization but simply to understand it—as the framework that continued to shape the West and, less directly, the world. That tradition included much that might be criticized, and its present outcome entailed much that might be changed. Habermas, in particular, was a persistent and often radical critic of what he saw as the disparity between Western democratic ideals and contemporary social and political practices. But effective criticism had to rest on free inquiry and rational understanding, as opposed to prejudice or wishful thinking. The invitation to think freely about the Western tradition, to criticize and change it, rested on precisely that tradition; indeed, the scope for such criticism and change had been central to the Western belief in reason. That openness remained perhaps the West's most fundamental legacy.

CHAPTER SUMMARY

With the end of the cold war, the United States and the nations of western Europe no longer faced a common communist adversary, so close collaboration seemed less pressing to both sides. Greater freedom for Europe to set its own course stimulated the expansion and deepening of the European Union. And whereas the West was mostly united in response to increasing terrorism, Western nations split over the wisdom of the U.S.-led invasion of Iraq, which, to many Europeans, seemed to indicate an unwelcome unilateralism on the part of the United States.

Although democracy was the unquestioned norm, a variety of changes posed new challenges for governments and the political order more generally. In light of aging populations and increasing global competition, western European countries found it ever harder to pay for the benefits promised as part of the postwar social compact. Yet reform efforts provoked protests that led governments to back down. Adding to political volatility was growing concern over the assimilation of immigrants.

Increasing economic globalization expanded horizons, but also affected the self-understanding of individuals in complex ways. Skeptical Europeans often equated globalization with Americanization and promoted various measures to preserve distinctiveness. However, people disagreed over whether what was to be preserved was "European," national, or local. Ways of understanding class, gender, and the place of religion also changed, though in some countries more than others.

An array of challenges, from new diseases to genocidal aggression, called for coordinated multinational responses. Although the UN played more visible roles after the cold war, it was an unwieldy organization whose effectiveness was sometimes limited. Even its specialized entities, such as the World Health Organization, sometimes lacked the resources and the clout to coordinate multinational responses. In dealing with politically inspired humanitarian crises in the non-Western world, the West found it difficult to develop a consistent and workable policy of intervention.

Changing relationships between the West and the non-Western world prompted new questions about the meaning and ongoing relevance of "Western civilization" as a concept. Some suggested that the whole "modern" conception of history, which had assumed a privileged leadership role for the West, had fallen away. But wider cultural encounters helped bring home the centrality of Western notions of openness and pluralism.

FOCUS QUESTIONS

- Why and how did the relationship between western Europe and the United States change after the end of the cold war?

- What forces raised new questions about the effectiveness of Western-style democracy by the early years of the twenty-first century?

- How did the changes bound up with globalization affect identities in the West?

- What questions emerged as the West faced new crises all over the globe after the end of the cold war?

KEY TERMS

Group of 20 (G-20) (p. 851)

Group of Seven (G-7) (p. 851)

European Union (EU) (p. 854)

Maastricht agreements (p. 854)

euro (p. 854)

Common Agricultural Policy (CAP) (p. 855)

ethnic cleansing (p. 857)

unilateralism (p. 859)

Vladimir Putin (p. 862)

social market economy (p. 863)

Nicolas Sarkozy (p. 865)

World Health Organization (WHO) (p. 873)

World Trade Organization (WTO) (p. 874)

nongovernmental organizations (NGOs) (p. 874)

 This icon will direct you to additional materials on the website: www .cengage.com/history/ noble/westciv6e.

NOTES

1. Quoted in *The Economist*, April 5, 2003, p. 59.

See our interactive eBook for map and primary source activities.

INDEX